myexcel online.com
Stand out from the crowd

COPYRIGHT

SPECIAL SALES

For more information about buying this book in bulk quantities, or for special sales opportunities (which may include custom cover designs, and content particular to your business or training goals), please send us an email to support@myexcelonline.com

CONNECT WITH US

Website, blog & podcast: https://www.myexcelonline.com

iPhone App: https://www.myexcelonline.com/iphone

Android App: https://www.myexcelonline.com/android

Email Support: support@myexcelonline.com

AUTHOR BIOGRAPHY

 John Michaloudis is the Founder of <u>MyExcelOnline.com</u>. John is currently living in the North of Spain, is married and has two beautiful kids. John holds a Bachelor's Degree in Commerce (Major in Accounting) and speaks English/Australian, Greek and Spanish.

 Bryan Hong is a contributor at <u>MyExcelOnline.com</u>. He is currently living in the Philippines and is married to his wonderful wife Esther. Bryan is also a Microsoft Certified Systems Engineer with over 10 years of IT and teaching experience!

FREE MICROSOFT EXCEL ONLINE COURSE

As a thank you for your support, we would want to give you a **free Microsoft Excel Online Course** that has 77 video tutorials, 20+ Hours and 10 Modules of different Excel topics such as Excel Functions, Formatting, Tables, Charts, Pivot Tables, Macros, Power Query, Power BI and so much more!

For the **private access link and the password** to this 20+ Hour Excel Course, please go to the **last page of the book**.

TABLE OF CONTENTS

DOWNLOADABLE EXCEL PRACTICE WORKBOOKS

Excel as a tool gets better everyday with new features being released. That means many more tips to unearth and learn! Adding these top Excel tips to your Excel toolbox will make you stand out from your peers and help you accomplish more in a shorter time. It will also turn you into an Excel guru, so watch out!

To get the most value out of this book, **please download the workbooks** and practice the 101 Excel Tips in this book. Then follow our step by step guide.

Make mistakes! That is fine. You may not get it the first time around (we certainly didn't) but when you do, you will be a step closer to Excel stardom!

For the **download link** that has all the workbooks covered in this book, please go to the **last page of the book**. We are using **Microsoft Office 365** for the majority of this book as this has all the latest features.

Read on and enjoy what the world of Excel has to offer.

EXCEL TIPS

Why Excel?

Microsoft Excel is a very powerful software application which was developed by Microsoft in 1985 and is used by over 800 million users worldwide and more than 95% of users don't know its full capabilities and true power.

An Excel Spreadsheet is the go-to software to analyze, sort, or create financial presentations with key business insights.

It is widely used by organizations for calculating, accounting, preparing charts, budgeting, project management, and various other tasks. The different uses of an Excel spreadsheet are in fact limitless!

Let us quickly go over the basics of using Excel.

Opening an Excel Spreadsheet

To open an Excel Spreadsheet, follow the steps below:

STEP 1: Click on the Window icon on the left side of the Taskbar and then scroll below to find "Excel".

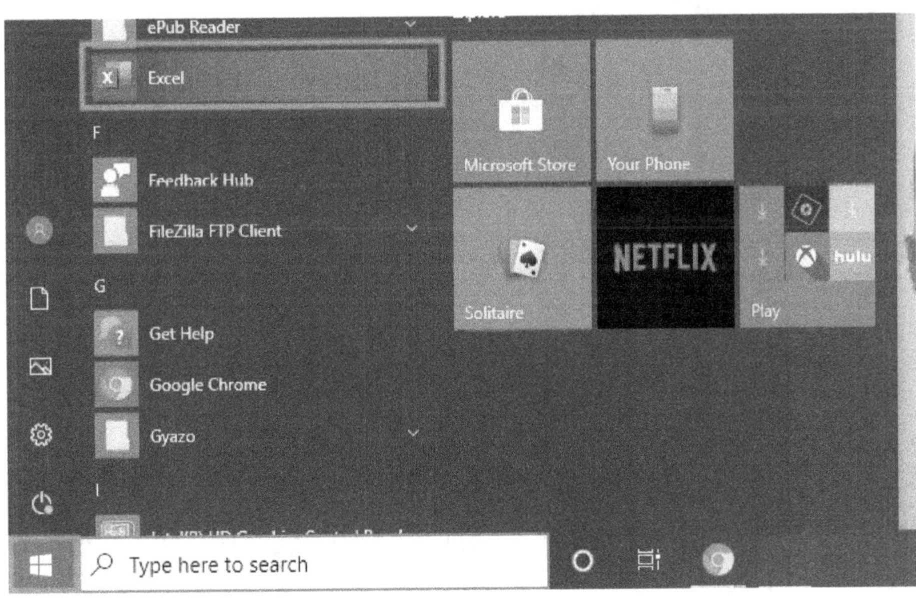

STEP 2: You can either click on the "**Blank Workbook**" button to open a blank Excel spreadsheet or select from the list of pre-existing templates provided by Excel.

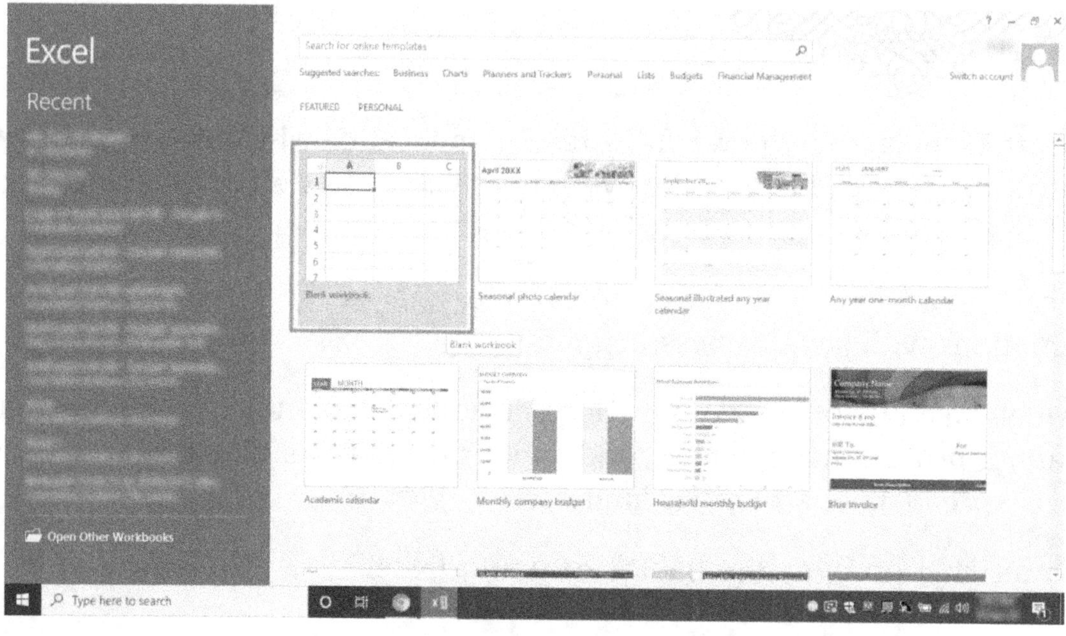

To open an existing Excel spreadsheet, click on the "*Open Other Workbooks*" and select the Excel sheet you want to work on.

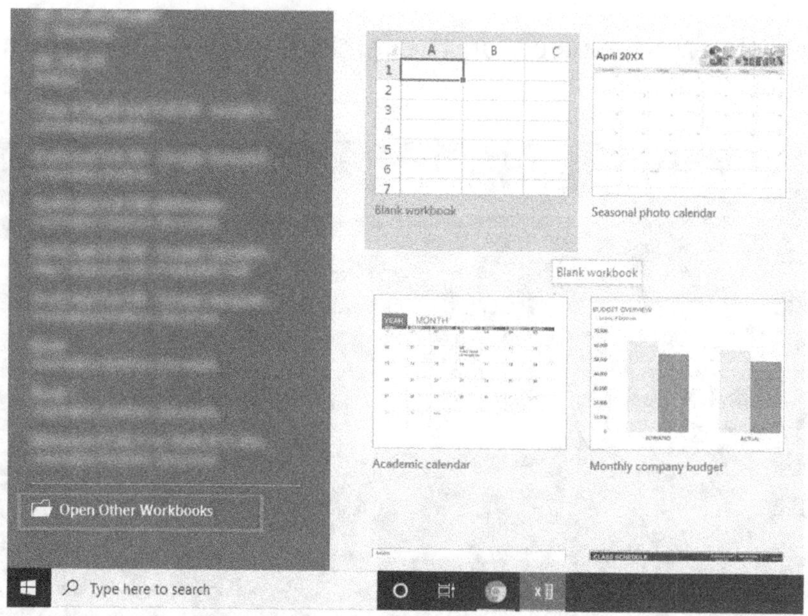

STEP 3: An Excel spreadsheet is now opened and you are ready to explore the wonderful world of Excel.

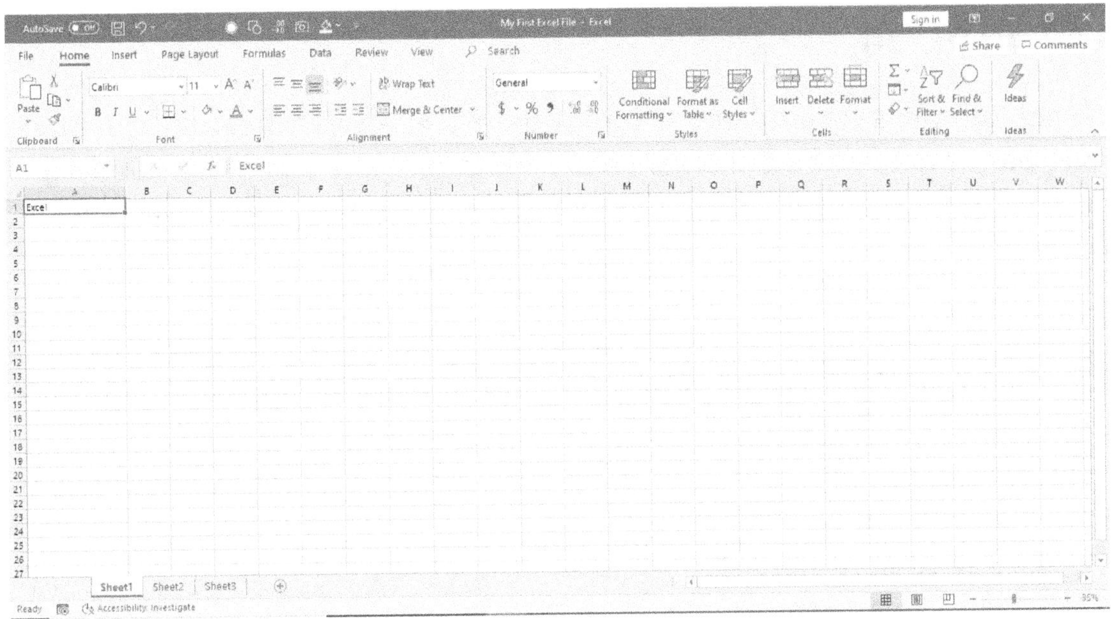

Understanding the Different Elements of an Excel Spreadsheet

To explore the different ways on using Excel you should be familiar with the different elements of Excel first.

Excel Workbook and **Excel Worksheet** are often used interchangeably, but they do have different meanings. An Excel Workbook is an Excel file with the extension ".xlsx" or ".xls" whereas an Excel Worksheet is a single sheet inside the Workbook. Worksheets appear as tabs along the bottom of the screen.

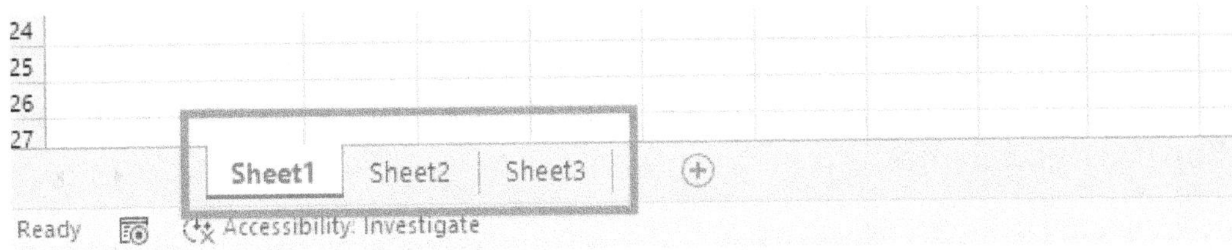

Now that you are clear about these two terms, let's move forward and understand the layout of an Excel Spreadsheet. It is a crucial step if you want to know how to use Excel efficiently.

Excel Ribbon

The Excel Ribbon is located at the top of the Excel Spreadsheet and just below the title bar or name of the worksheet. It comprises various tabs including Home, Insert, Page Layout, Formulas, Data, etc. Each tab contains a specific set of commands.

We are using Microsoft 365 for the majority of this book.

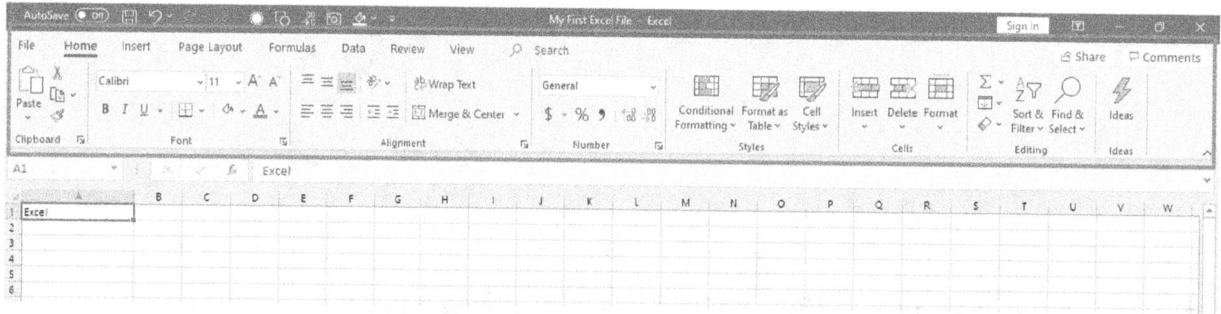

By default, each Excel spreadsheet contains the following Tabs - *File, Home, Insert, Page Layout, Formulas, Data, Review,* and *View.*

- **File Tab** can be used to Open a new or existing file, Save, Print, Share/Export/Publish a file, see your Account details, give Feedback and customize Excel with its various Options

- **Home Tab** can be used to copy, cut, or paste cells, format data with Fonts, Alignment, Number, Styles, Conditional Formatting, Excel Tables, Cells, Sort & Filter, Find & Select and Analyze Data with Ideas.

- **Insert Tab** can be used to insert Pivot Tables, Tables, Pictures, Illustrations, Charts, Maps, Pivot Charts, Sparklines, Links, Text Boxes, Word Art and Symbols.

- **Page Layout Tab** can be used to prepare the Excel spreadsheet for printing and exporting data. You can change the Theme, Margin, Orientation, Size, Print Area, and the Background.

- **Formula Tab** in Excel can be used to insert a Function, define Names, and has tools to audit Formulas.

- **Data Tab** can be used to Get Data from different sources, Manage Queries, Sort & Filter, Remove Duplicates, Data Validation, Convert Text to Columns, and perform Forecasting.

- **Review Tab** can be used to Insert Comments, Protect the Workbook, Check Spelling, Track Changes, and perform Translations.

- **View Tab** can be used to change the view of the Excel Sheets and make it easy to view the data. You can also Zoom In, Out and Freeze Panes.

You should be familiar with these tabs so you can understand how to use Excel efficiently. You can even customize these Tabs using the following steps:

STEP 1: Right-click on the ribbon and click on "**Customize the Ribbon**"

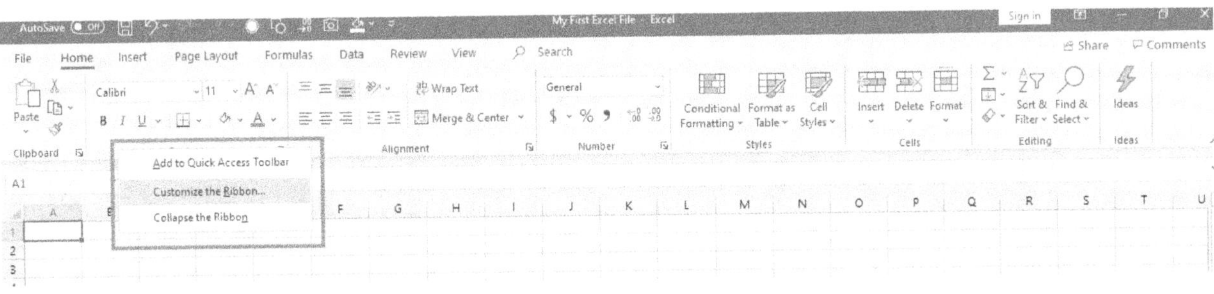

STEP 2: An Excel Options dialog box will open, click on the **New Tab**.

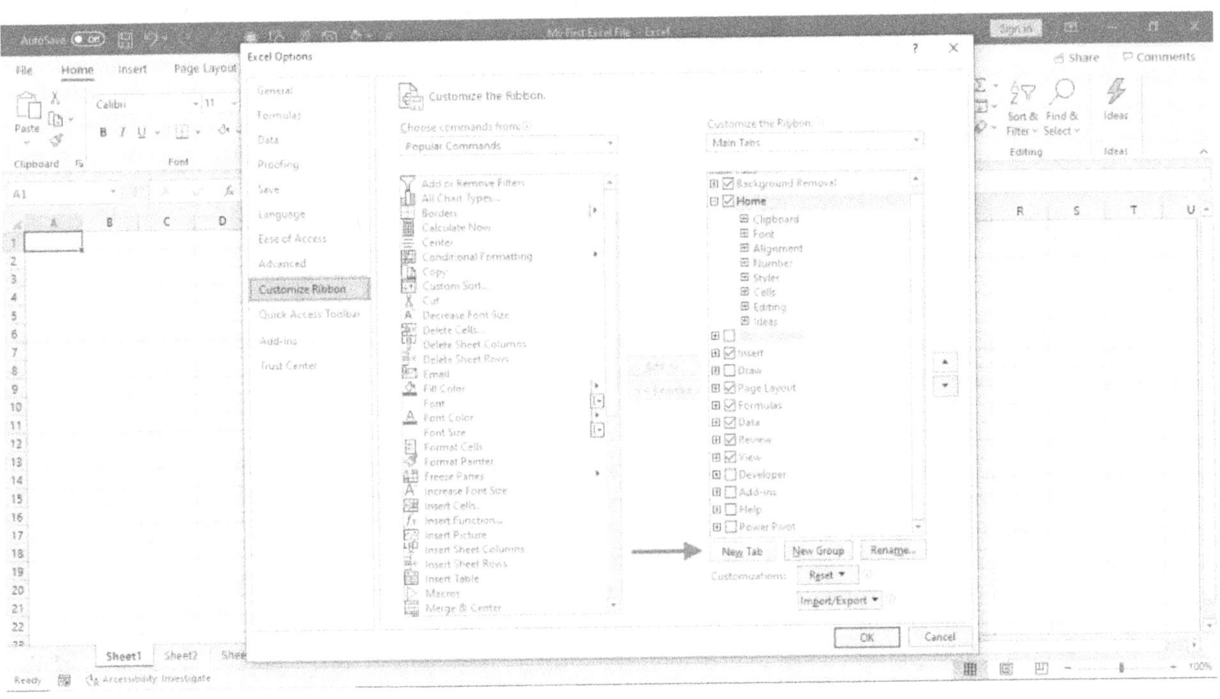

STEP 3: Select that newly created tab and click on **Rename** and give it a name e.g. *Custom* and then press **OK**

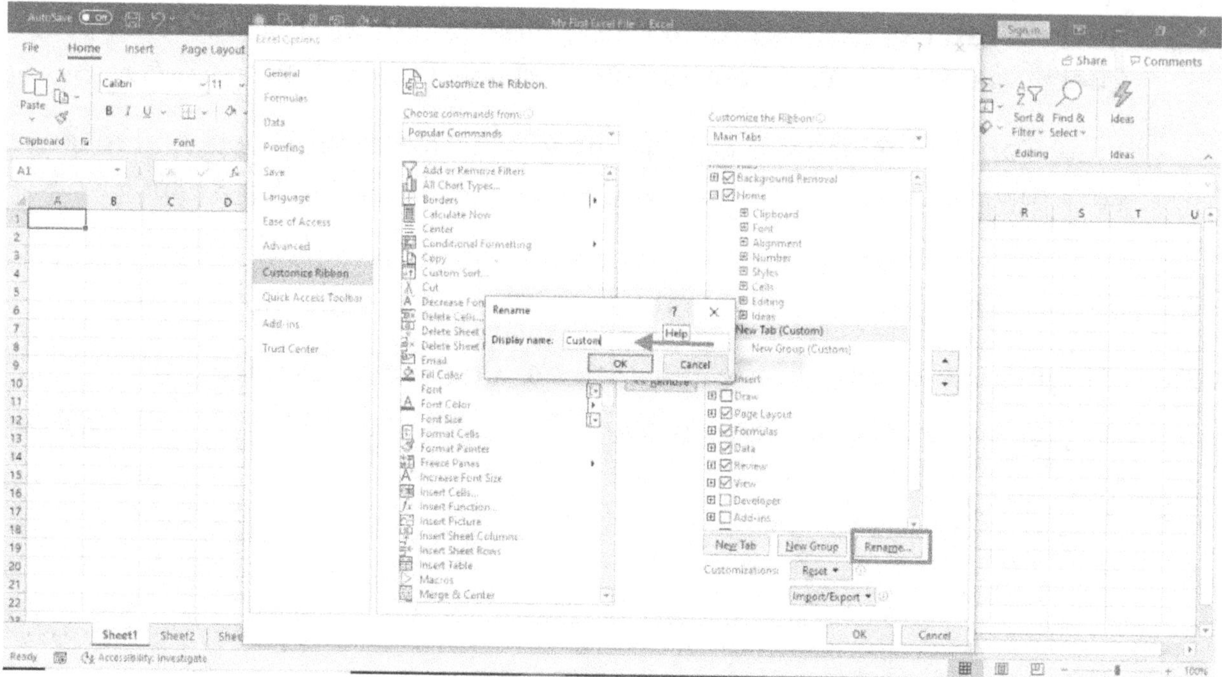

STEP 4: Now you can add the command(s) that you want to this newly created Tab by simply clicking on a command from the **Popular Commands** drop down and click on **Add >>** and then press **OK**

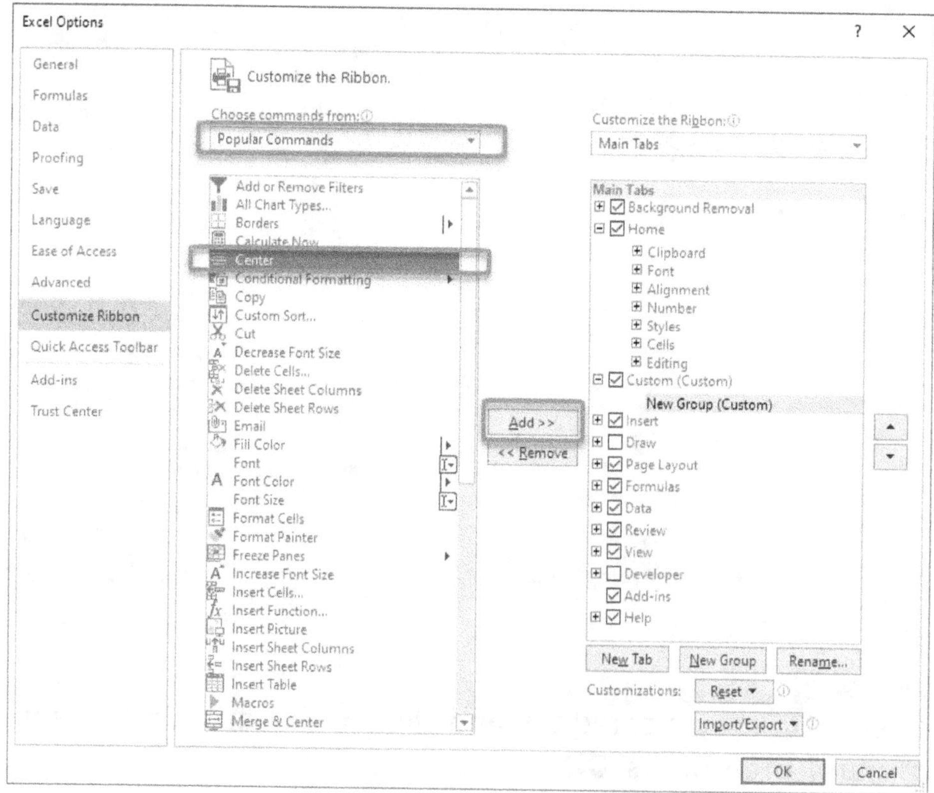

This will create a New Tab called "**Custom**" with a popular command "**Center**".

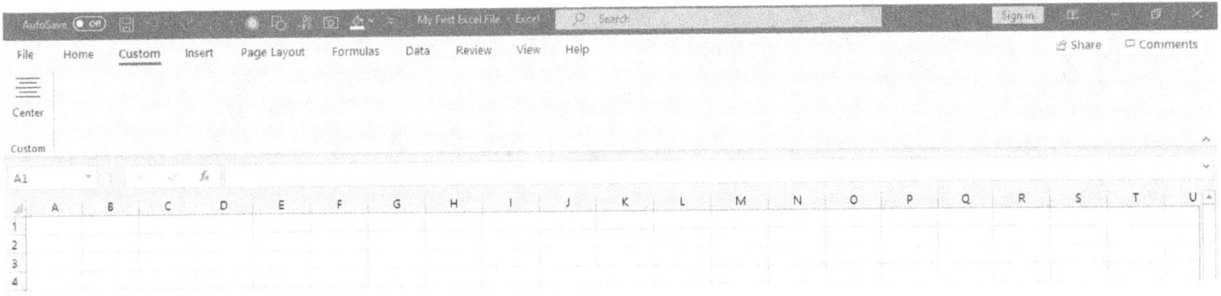

Under each Tab, there are various buttons grouped together. For Example - Under the **Home** Tab, all font-related buttons are bundled together under the **Group** name "*Font*".

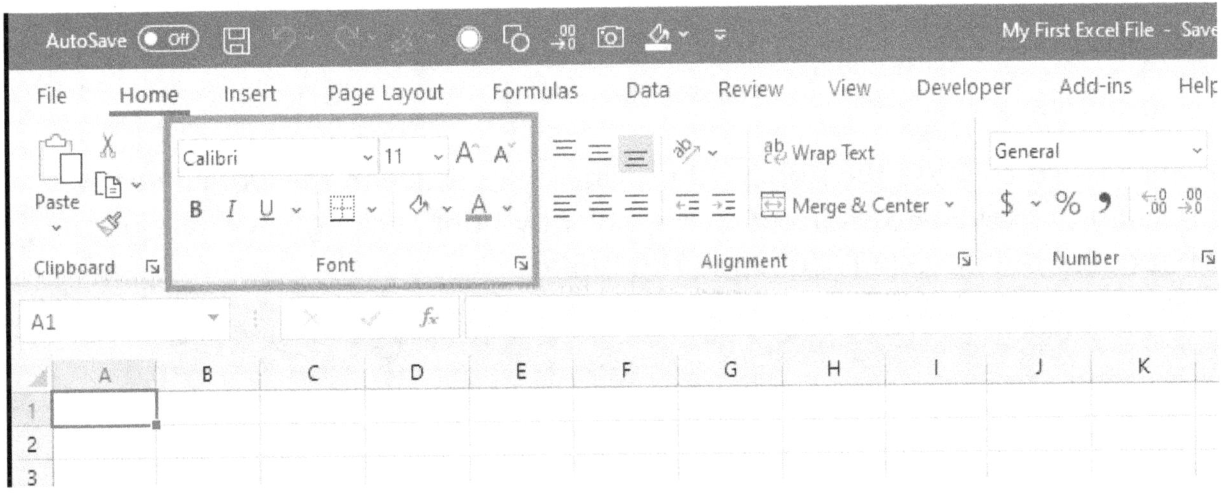

You can access other features related to that group by clicking on the small arrow at the bottom right hand corner of each Group. Once you click on that arrow, a dialog box will open up and you can make further edits.

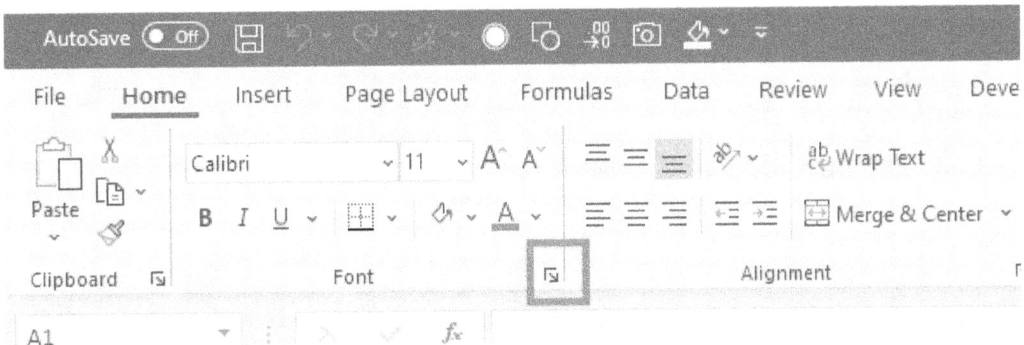

There is also a **search bar** available next to the tabs which was introduced in Excel 2019 and Office 365. You can type the feature that you are after and Excel will find it for you.

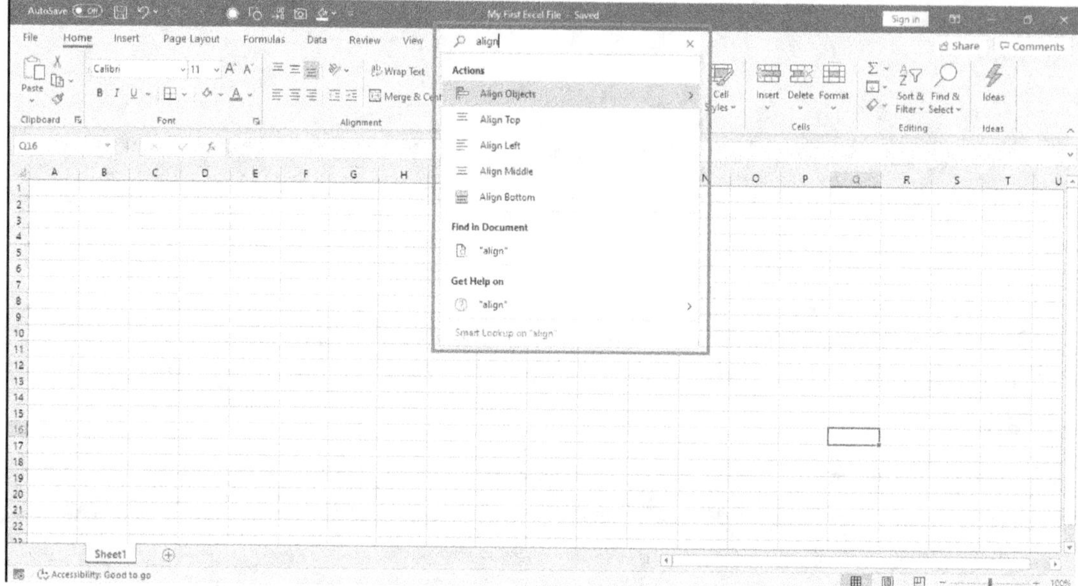

You can also collapse the ribbon to provide extra space in the worksheet by pressing the keyboard shortcut **Ctrl + F1** or by right-clicking anywhere on the ribbon and then clicking "**Collapse the Ribbon**".

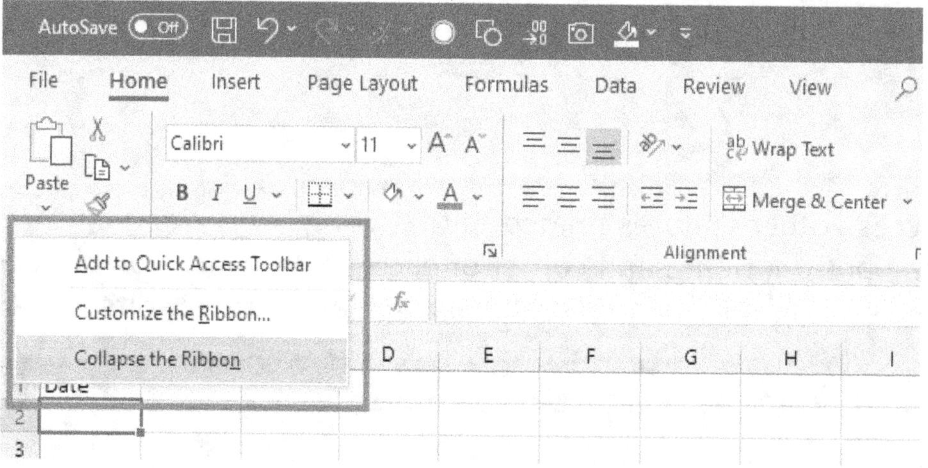

This will collapse and hide the Ribbon! Press **Ctrl + F1** to show the ribbon again.

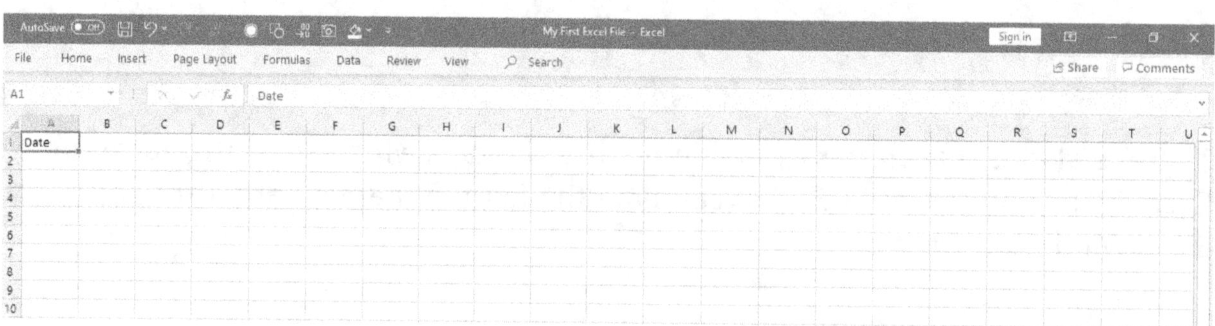

Formula Bar

Excel's Formula bar is the area just below the Excel Ribbon. It contains two parts - on the left is the name box (it stores the cell address) and on the right is the contents of the currently selected cell. It is used to type values, text or an Excel formula or function.

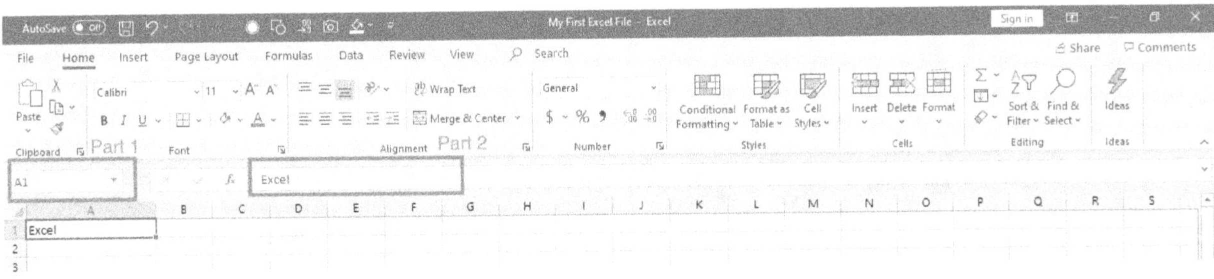

You can hide or unhide the formula bar by checking/unchecking "Formula Bar" under the **View** Tab.

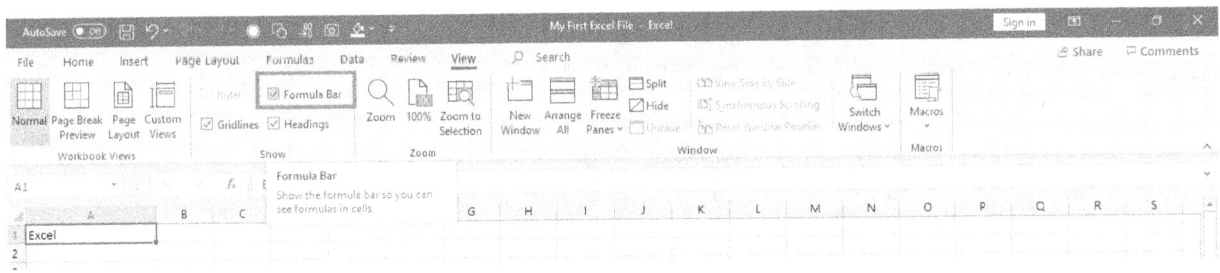

You can also expand the formula bar if you have a large formula and its contents are not entirely visible. Click on the small arrow at the end of the formula bar and it will be expanded.

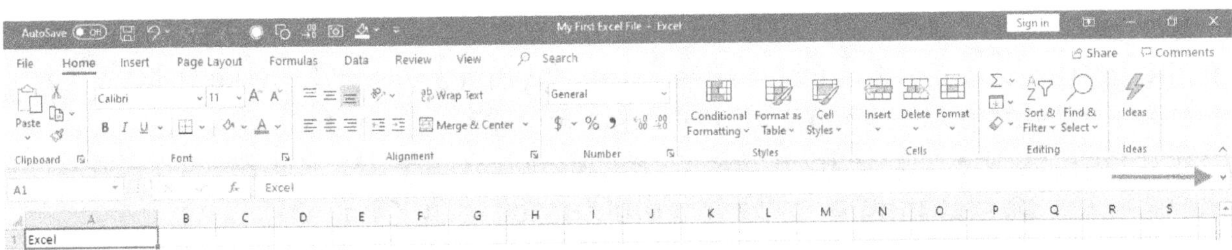

The expanded formula bar:

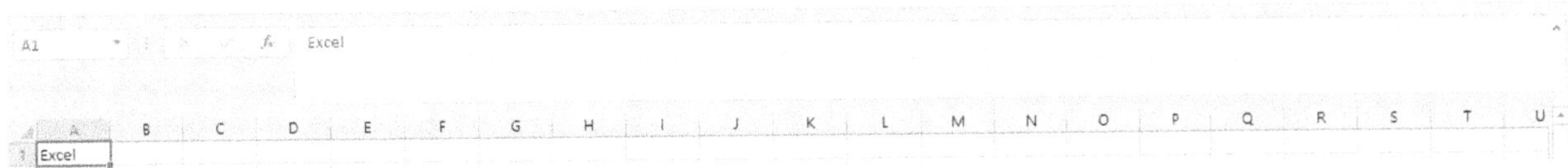

Working with Worksheets

At the bottom left hand corner of the worksheet, all the Excel worksheets are shown. You can access an Excel sheet by simply clicking on it.

To add more Excel sheets, click on the "+" sign next to a Sheet which will add a new blank Excel Sheet.

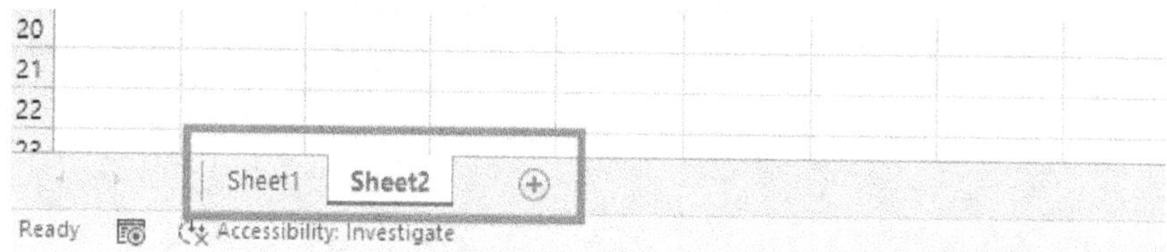

You can reorder the Excel sheets in your workbook by dragging them to a new location with your left mouse button.

You can also rename each Excel sheet by **Right Clicking on a Sheet Name > Click on Rename > Type the Name > Press Enter**.

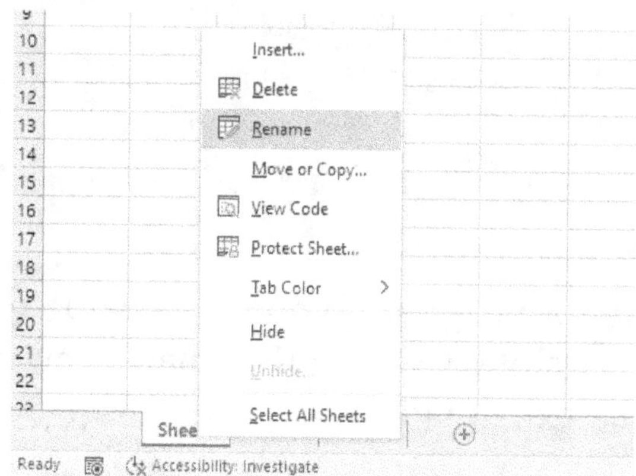

At the bottom right of the Excel spreadsheet, you can quickly zoom the document by using the minus and plus symbols. To zoom to a specific percentage, in the ribbon menu go to the **View tab > Click Zoom > Click on the specific percentage or type in your custom % > Click OK**.

There are different Excel workbook views available at the left of the zoom control: *Normal View, Page Break View,* and *Page Layout View.* You can select the view as per your choice.

Cell & Excel Spreadsheet Basics

Any information including text, number, or an Excel formula can be inserted within a **Cell**. Letters are used to label Columns and numbers are used to label Rows.

An intersection of a Row and Column is called a **Cell**. In the image below, cell **C4** is the intersection of **Row 4** and **Column C.**

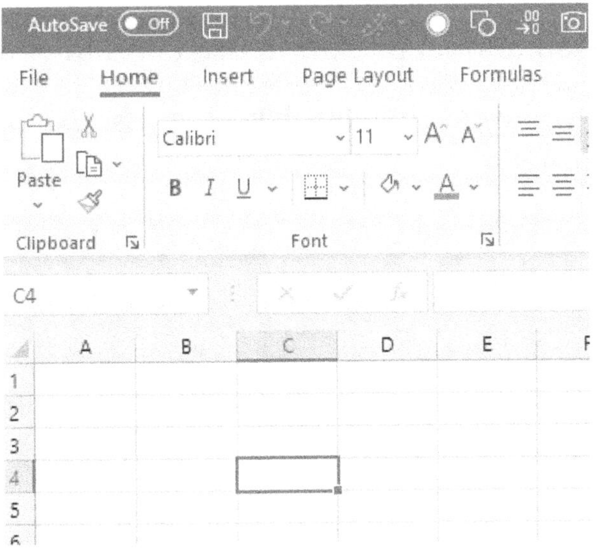

You can refer to a series of cells as a range by putting a colon between the first and last cells within the range. For example, the reference to the range starting from A1 to C10 will be **A1: C10.** This is great when you are using an Excel formula.

You can also select a range of cells by left clicking on the mouse and scrolling down/up/left/right.

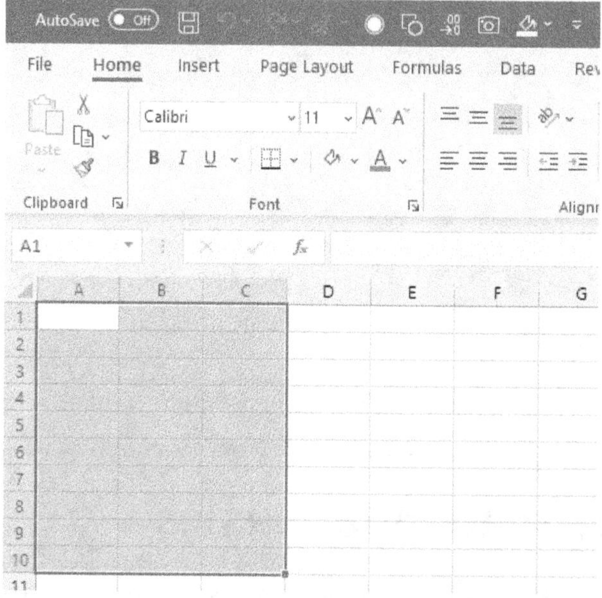

Now that you are familiar with the different elements in an Excel Spreadsheet, let's show you how to use Excel to enter data and do some calculations!

Entering Data in an Excel Spreadsheet

Follow this step -by-step tutorial on how to use excel to enter data below:

STEP 1: Click the cell you want to enter data into. For Example, lets enter some sales data, so click on **A1**

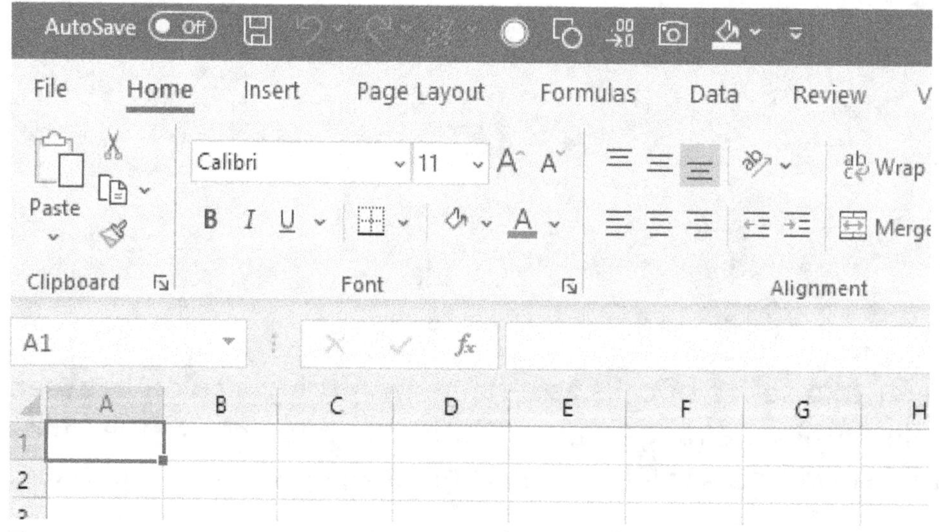

 Type what you want to add, say, *Date*. You will see that the same data will be visible on the Formula Bar as well.

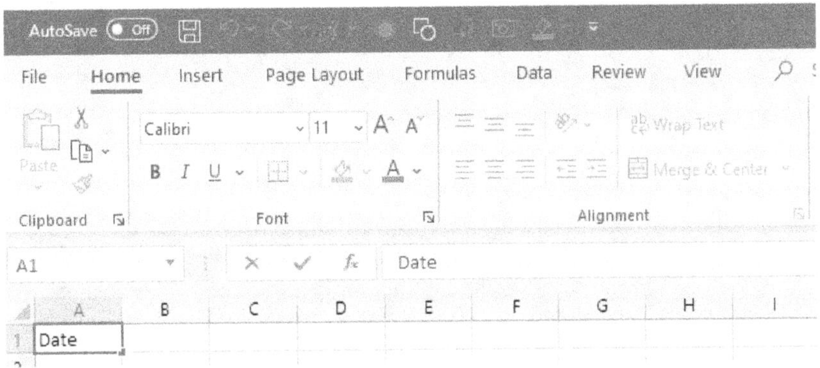

STEP 3: Press Enter. This will store the written data on the selected cell and move the selection to the next available cell, which is **A2** in this example

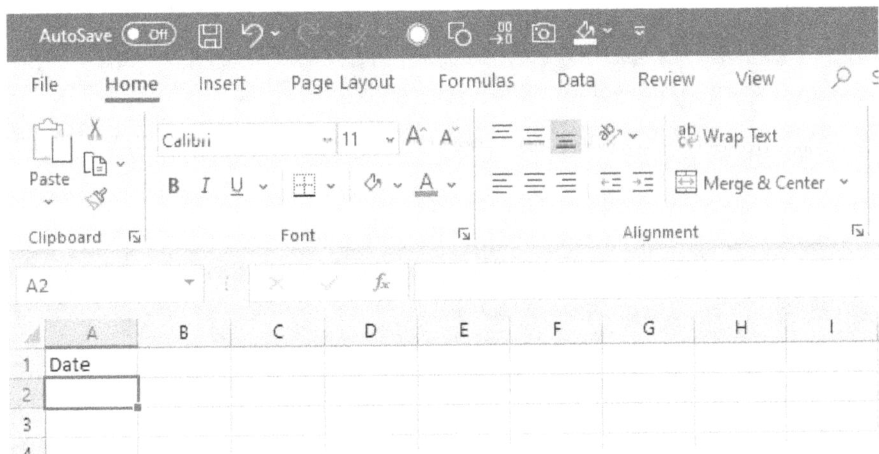

To make any changes in the cell, simply click on it and make the changes.

You can copy (**Ctrl + C**), Cut (**Ctrl + X**) any data from one Excel worksheet and paste it (**Ctrl + V**) to the same or another Excel worksheet.

Basic Calculations in an Excel Spreadsheet

Now that you have understood how to use Excel to enter data, let's do some calculations on the data. Let's say you want to add two numbers: *4* and *5 in the Excel spreadsheet.*

Follow the steps below on how to use Excel to add two numbers:

STEP 1: Start with the = sign to tell Excel that you are ready to enter a calculation.

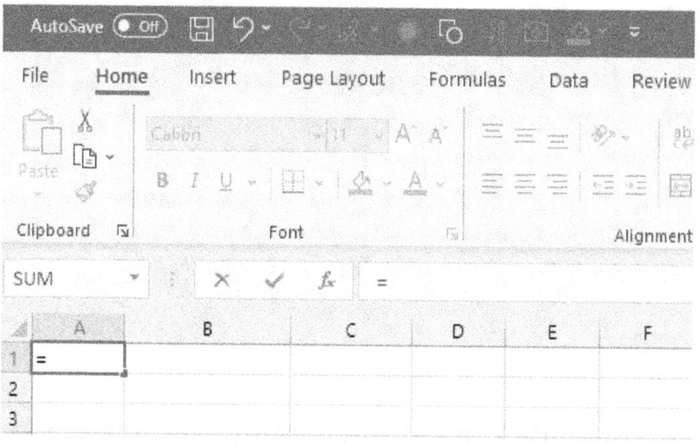

STEP 2: Type number 4.

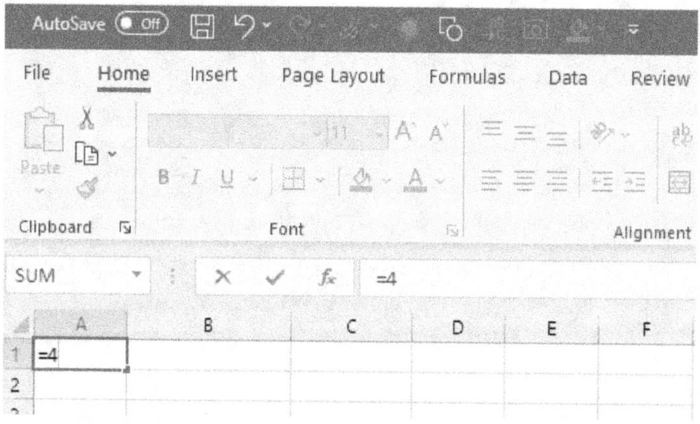

STEP 3: Type the + symbol to add

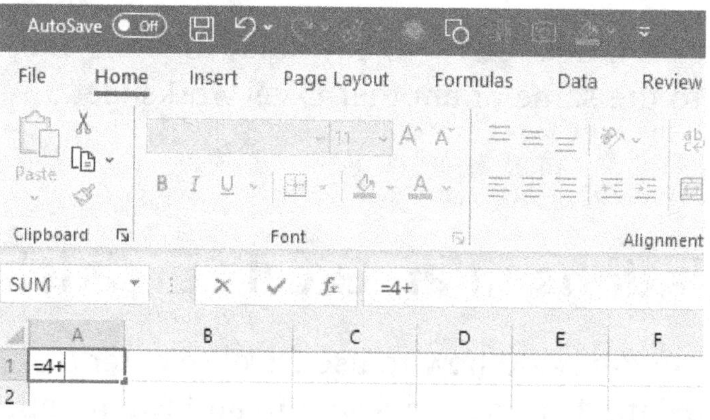

STEP 4: Type the number **5**

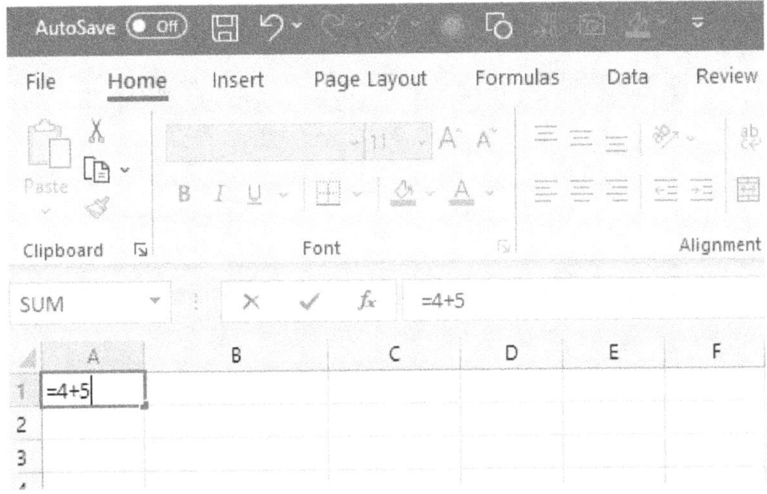

STEP 5: Press Enter.

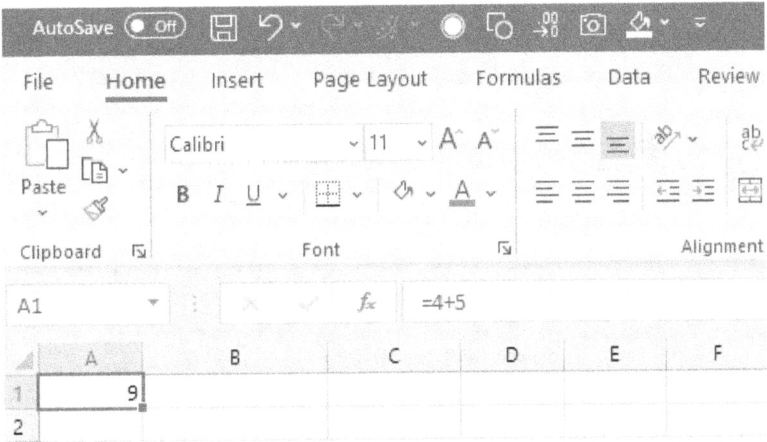

You will see the result **9** is displayed in the cell A1 and the formula is still displayed in the formula bar.

Let's try to use a cell reference to make calculations.

In the example below, you have **Column A** that contains the number of products sold and **Column B** that contains the price per product and you need to calculate the total amount in **Column C**.

To calculate the total amount, follow the steps below:

STEP 1: Select cell C2

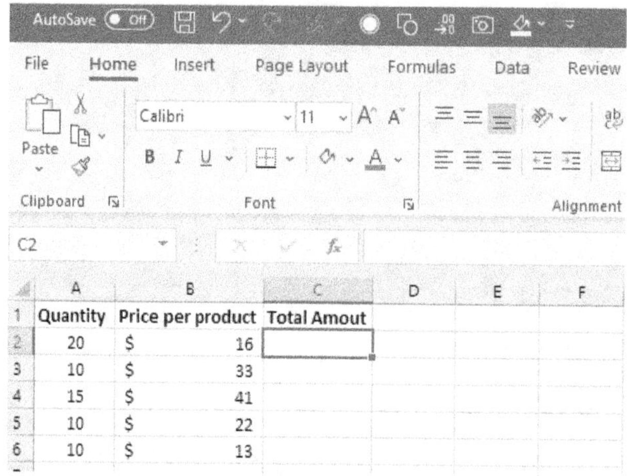

STEP 2: Type = to start the formula

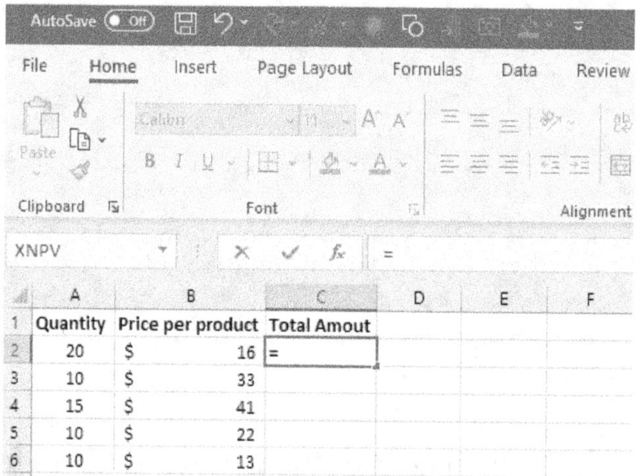

STEP 3: Select cell A2 with your mouse cursor or by using the left arrow key to go left 2 cells.

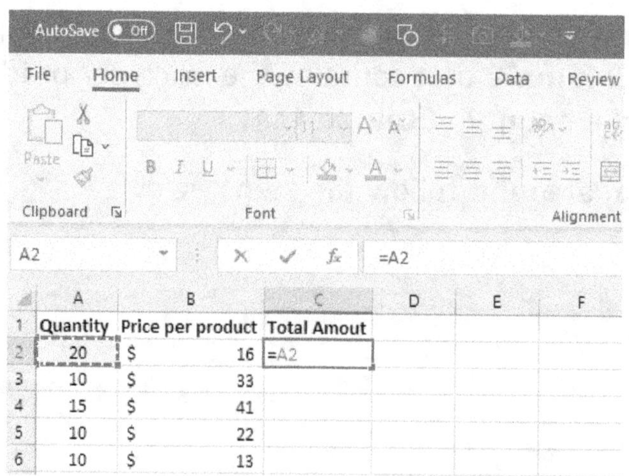

STEP 4: Type the multiplication sign *

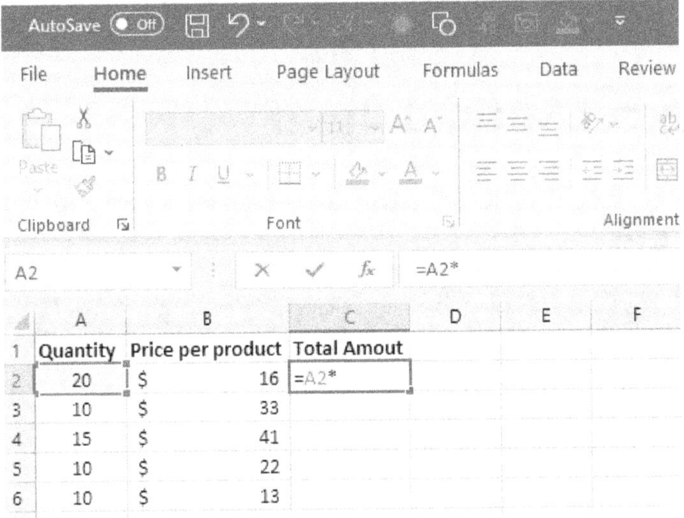

STEP 5: Select cell B2 with your mouse or using the left keyboard arrow

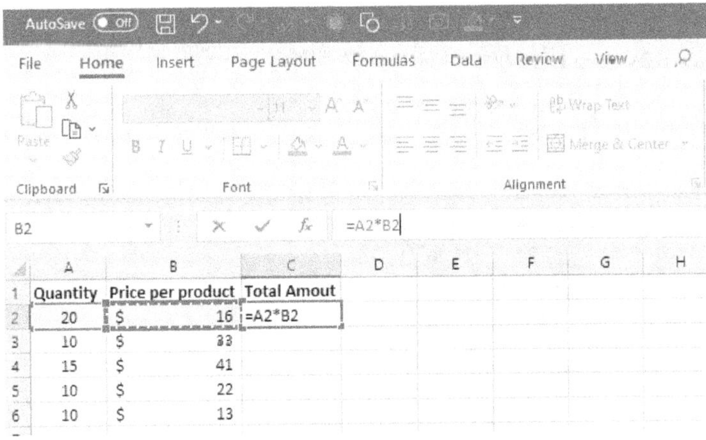

STEP 6: Press **Enter** and you will see the result

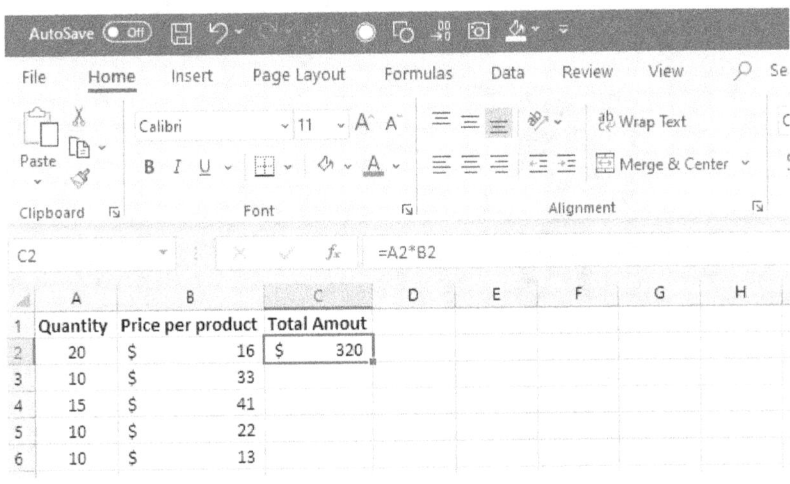

You can use various calculation operators, such as Arithmetic, Comparison, Text Concatenation and Reference operators that will be useful for you to have a clear and complete idea on how to use Excel.

Saving an Excel Spreadsheet

To save your work in Excel, click on the **Save** button on the *Quick Access Toolbar* or press **Ctrl + S**.

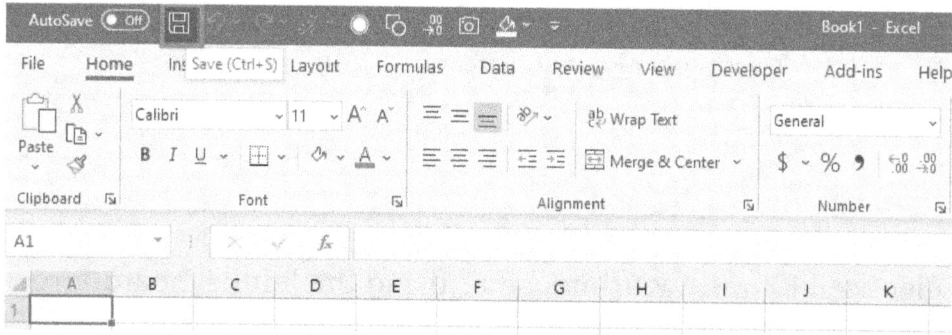

If you are trying to save a file for the first time, then follow these steps:

STEP 1: Press **Ctrl + Shift +S** or Click on the "**Save As**" button under the **File** tab.

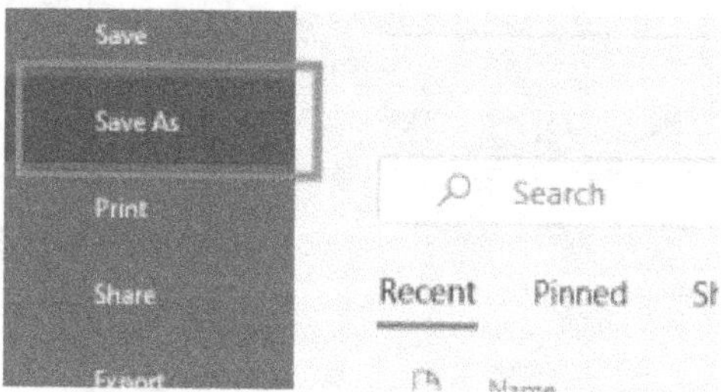

STEP 2: Click on "**Browse**" and choose the location on your desktop where you want to save the file. You can also save it on the cloud using OneDrive.

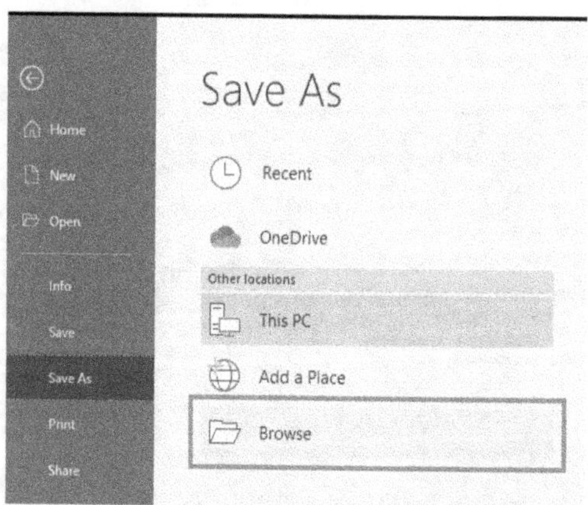

STEP 3: In the **File name** box, enter a name for your new Excel workbook.

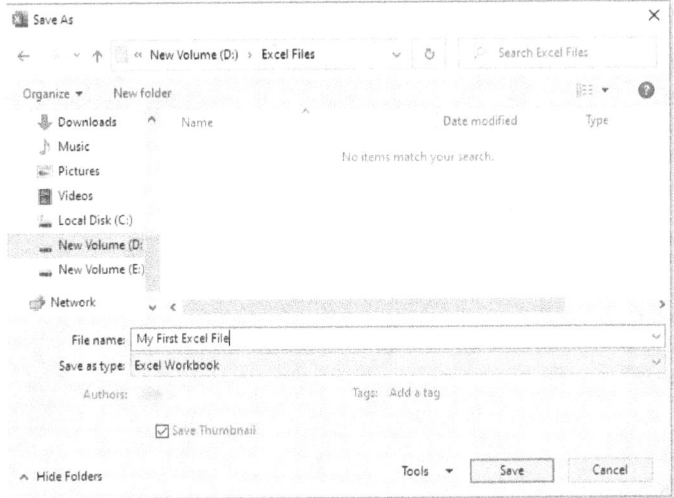

STEP 4: Click **Save**

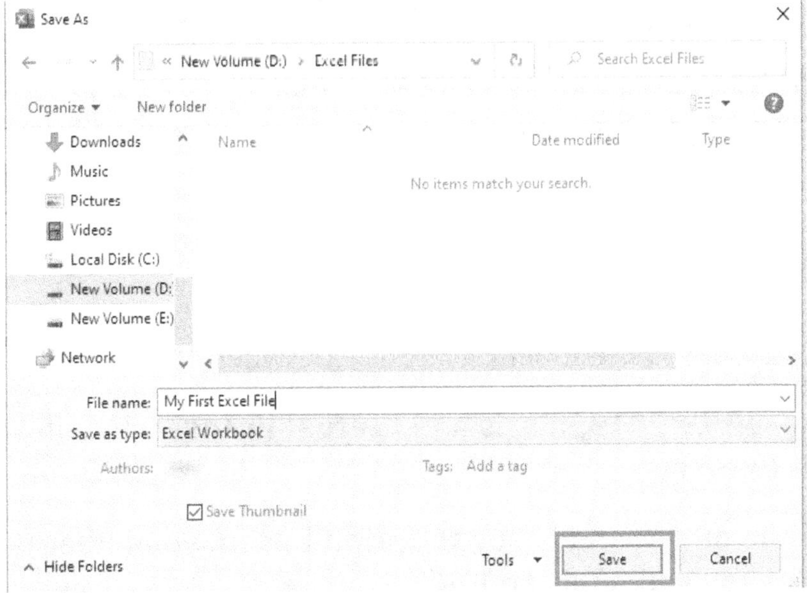

Excel is a completely unexplored & exciting world for you right now and you are going to learn so much along your journey.

My advice is to take baby steps, learn how to use one Excel feature, apply it to your data, make mistakes and keep on practicing!

Follow through with the Excel Tips in this book and your Excel confidence will skyrocket!

Now it's time to explore the various Excel tips...

Excel 2019 VS Office 365

Ever wondered what is the difference between **Excel 2019 and Office 365**? Look no further as we will give you a detailed comparison on **Excel 2019 VS Office 365**!

We will be using Excel 2019 and Office 2019 interchangeably as they pertain to the entire package.

First things first, what is the main difference between the two?

If you purchase **Office 2019**, this is a **perpetual license** wherein you pay once and you own it forever.

Office 365 on the other hand is **subscription-based**, you either pay a monthly fee or annual fee to keep on using it.

On paper, the own-it-forever sounds better right? But there is more than meets the eye, keep on reading!

Cost Comparison

Let us have a look first from a cost standpoint, here's a table that compares the subscription based Office 365 versus the perpetual Office 2019:

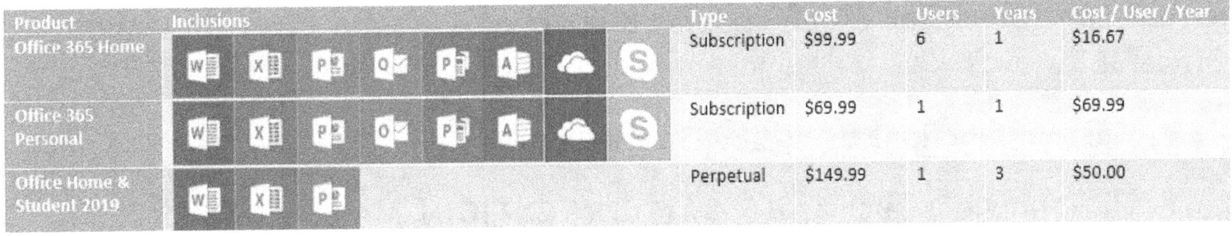

Product	Inclusions		Type	Cost	Users	Years	Cost / User / Year
Office 365 Home			Subscription	$99.99	6	1	$16.67
Office 365 Personal			Subscription	$69.99	1	1	$69.99
Office Home & Student 2019			Perpetual	$149.99	1	3	$50.00

Office 365 has two offerings:

Office 365 Home allows you to have 6 users maximum just for $99.99 a year

Office 365 Personal allows for 1 user for $69.99 a year

Which means if you have at least 2 users, then **Office 365 Home** becomes a better deal instantly as compared to **Office 365 Personal**.

For **Office 2019**, we are making the **assumption that the software has 3 years of ownership**, before you upgrade your software to the newer version. This allows us to compute to a cost of $50.00 a year.

And if you see the inclusions, there are more Office Applications included in the Office 365 package. (e.g., Outlook, Publisher, Access, OneDrive, Skype).

So from a cost perspective, **Office 365 Home is the better deal**, assuming you have at least 2 users (up to a maximum of 6!).

Value Comparison

From a feature's perspective are they exactly the same?

Office 365 has one major advantage over Office 2019: **Office 365 constantly gets updated with new features every couple of months!**

Office 2019 and Office 365 right now are almost at par in terms of features at the time of this writing. However, give it some time, and Office 365 will be ahead in terms of the features race.

Another good thing, is the changes are gradual in Office 365 and you get them right away. Compared to the perpetual Office 2019, the changes are more drastic when you upgrade from one perpetual Office version to another (e.g. Office 2016 to Office 2019).

Here is an example list of the updates that are new in both Excel 2019 and Office 365:

- Custom functions using **JavaScript**

- New functions such as **IFS, SWITCH, TEXTJOIN, MAXIFS, MINIFS**

- **Co-authoring** for multiple users

- Assigning **default behavior for Pivot Tables**

- **3D Models**

- **Custom visuals** such as bullet charts, speedometers and even word clouds!

The list will grow longer for Office 365 each year but in Office 2019, there will not be any new updates.

Do I need to be online to use Microsoft Office 365? One common misconception is that with Office 365 is you have to be connected to the internet to use it.

It's not true! **Office 365 is installed locally** on your computer, similar to how Office 2019 is installed. We suggest moving over to the subscription model, as it keeps your Office applications up to date and you will reap the benefits sooner too!

Imagine seeing a sparkling new feature, then only to discover that your perpetual Office installation does not support it! Office 365 removes this issue outright, as you get it right away as included in your subscription.

And remember, this does not only apply to Excel, but also to all your Office applications as well! (e.g. Word, PowerPoint)

I hope this has been helpful for you in terms of comparing Office 365 and Office 2019. **If you can get Office 365, I highly suggest to go for it!**

(Disclaimer: We do not make any money or are affiliated with Office 365; we just want you to have the best solution at the most affordable price!)

What Excel Version Do I Have?

We know that Microsoft Excel has different features across different versions and there are several Excel versions as the time of writing, like Excel 2003, 2007, 2010, 2013, 2016 and 2019!

So whenever I use Microsoft Excel, I want to know right away which **Excel Version** I am using. And boy, do I get confused to tell what Excel Version I am using!

Not to worry, as I will show you a few cool ways where you can determine the **Excel Version** right away!

P.S. *If you want to upgrade to the latest & greatest version of Microsoft Excel, you can by choosing the Office 365 Business Plans*

Office 365

You can see search icon **(magnifying glass)** at the top.

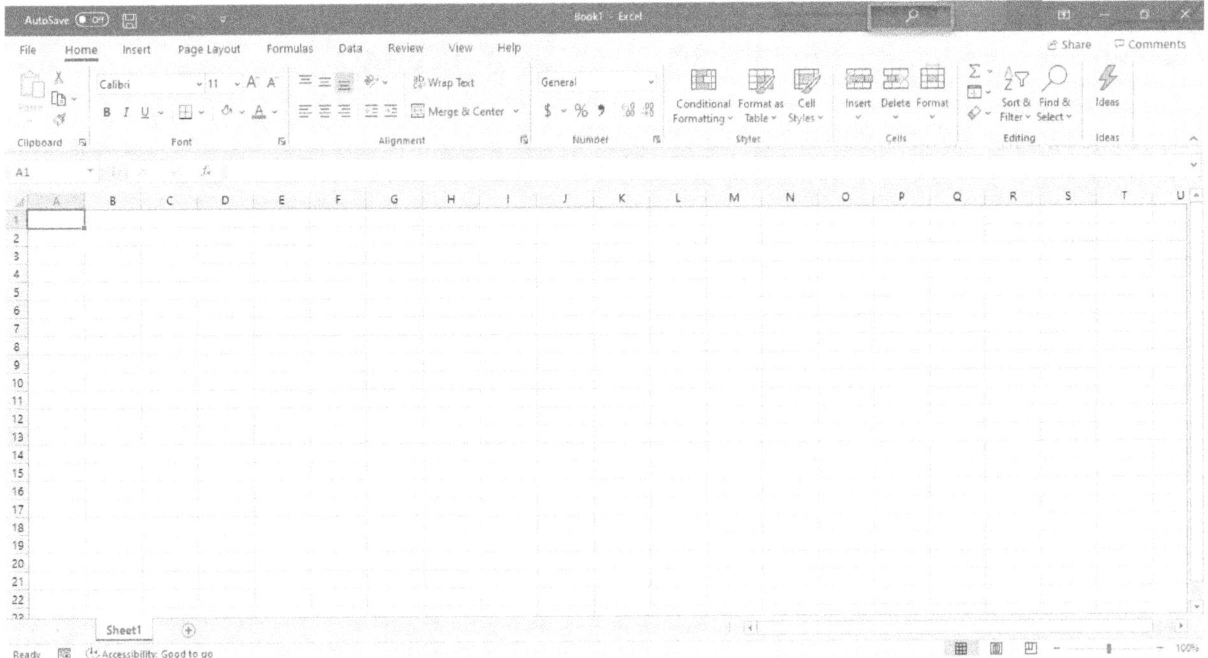

Microsoft Excel 2019 and 2016

You can see **"Tell me what you want to do"** text at the top.

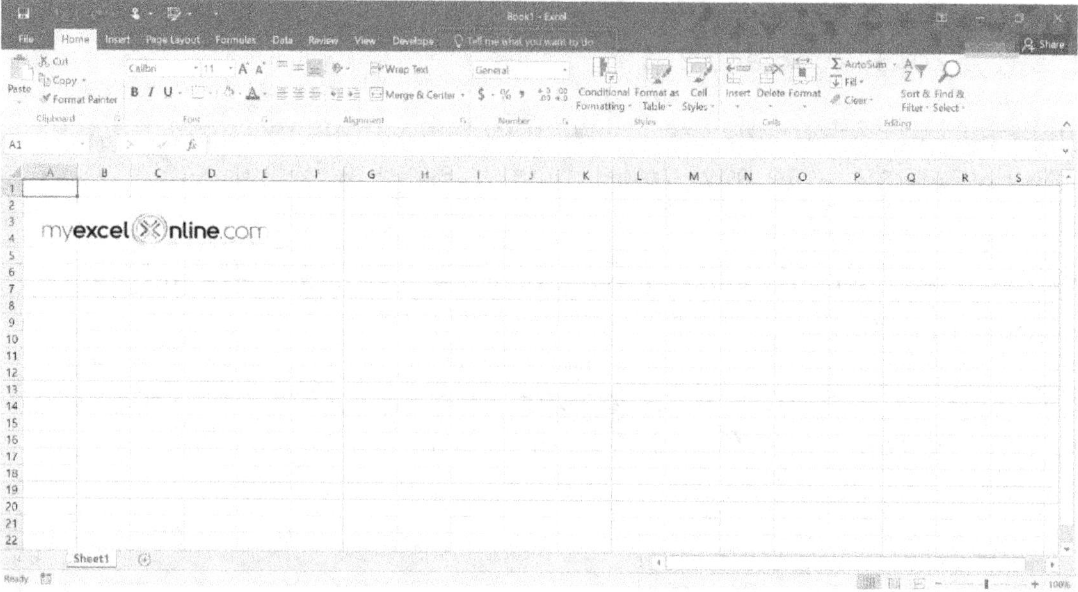

Microsoft Excel 2013

WHAT? Are you still using this version?

You can see that the Ribbon tabs are all in **Capital Letters!**

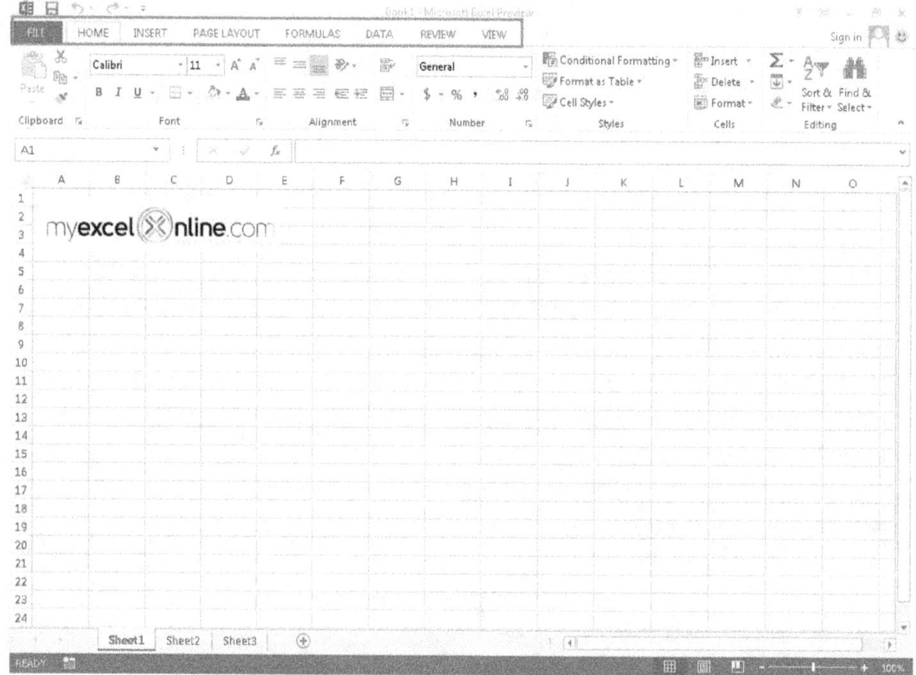

Microsoft Excel 2010

You can see the **Rounded File Menu Button** at the top left-hand corner...

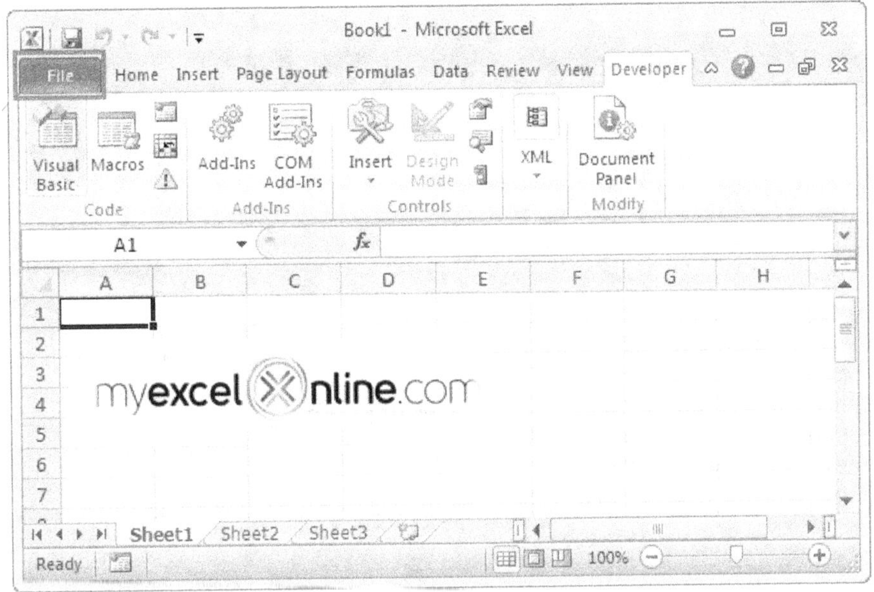

Microsoft Excel 2007

You can see the **Rounded Microsoft Office Icon** at the top left-hand corner...

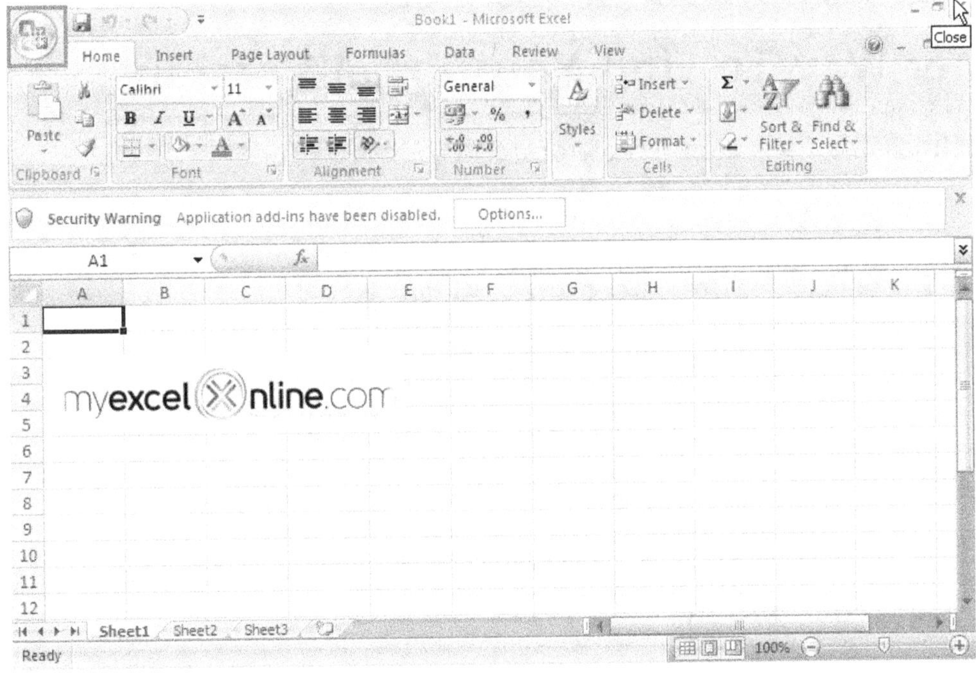

Microsoft Excel 2003

The giveaway here is it looks like **Windows XP,** and this means you already need an upgrade!

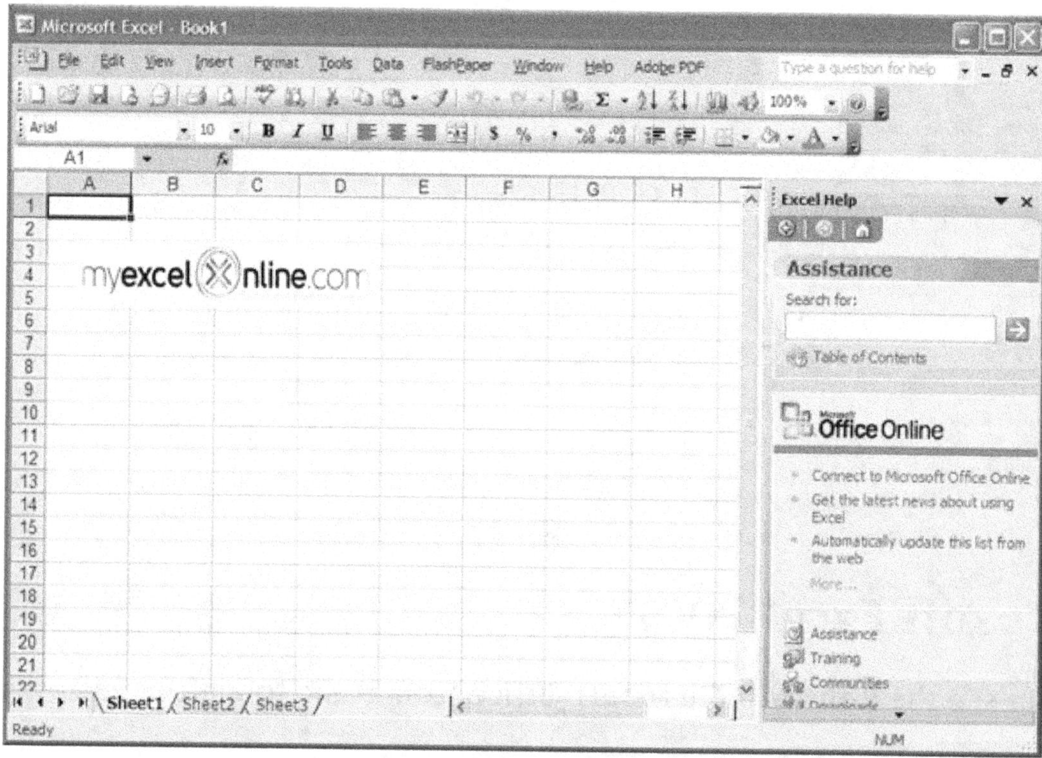

Another Way To Find Your Excel Version...

You can check for the exact Excel version by going to:

Office 365: **File > Account > About Excel**

Microsoft Excel 2019: **File > Account > About Excel**

Microsoft Excel 2016: **File > Account > About Excel**

Microsoft Excel 2013: **File > Account > About Excel**

Microsoft Excel 2010: **File > Help > About Microsoft Excel**

Microsoft Excel 2007: **Rounded Microsoft Office Icon > Excel options > Resources > About button.**

Microsoft Excel 2003: In the menu go to the **Help** tab and then click on **About Microsoft Excel** (If you do not see this option in the menu you are probably using Excel 2007 or higher!).

Here is what it looks like in Excel 2016:

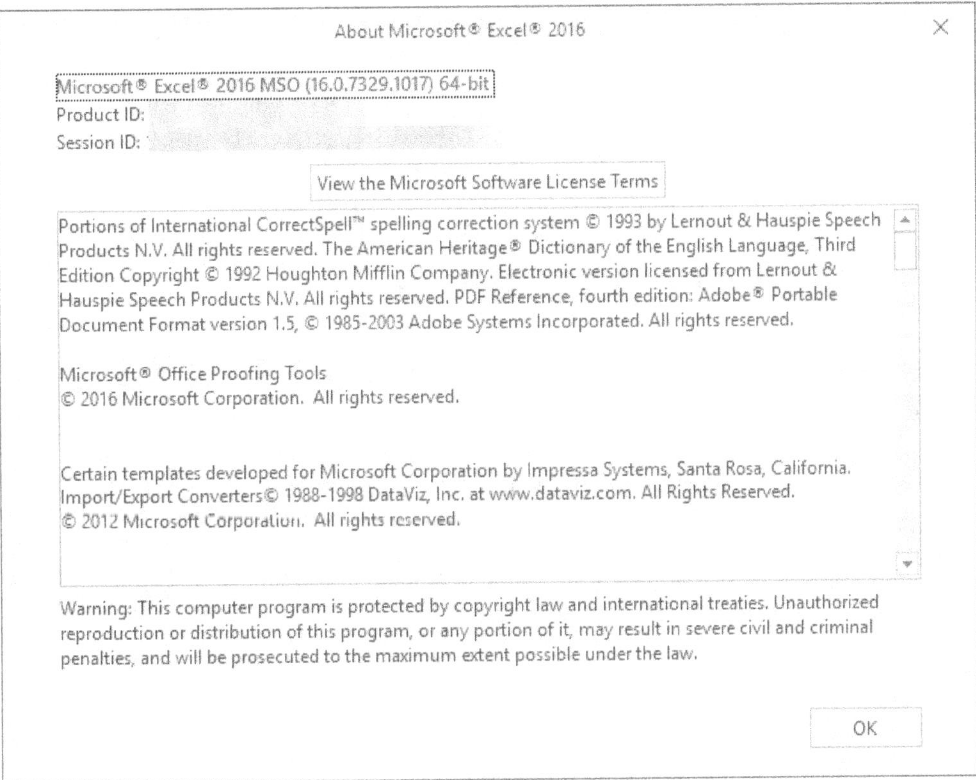

10 Excel Double Click Mouse Tricks

There are a lot of times when the mouse beats the keyboard in terms of efficiency in Excel.

Here are **Top 10 Excel Double Click Mouse Tricks** for **Excel Power Users** like you!

You will have a fun time increasing your productivity with these tricks!

#1: Show or Hide the Excel Ribbon

There are times where we just want more space in our Excel Window and it is very easy to hide the Ribbon.

Double click on the **active tab** in your Excel Ribbon to **hide it**.

Then you can double click again to **show the Excel Ribbon**.

#2: Use Format Painter as Many Times as You Want

This is one very cool trick that saved me a lot of time! I wanted to copy the formatting, and I had to click the Format Painter multiple times.

It was cumbersome! Turns out there's an option to **lock in your Format Painter**, so that you can reuse it again and again!

Pick the cells you want to copy the format from.

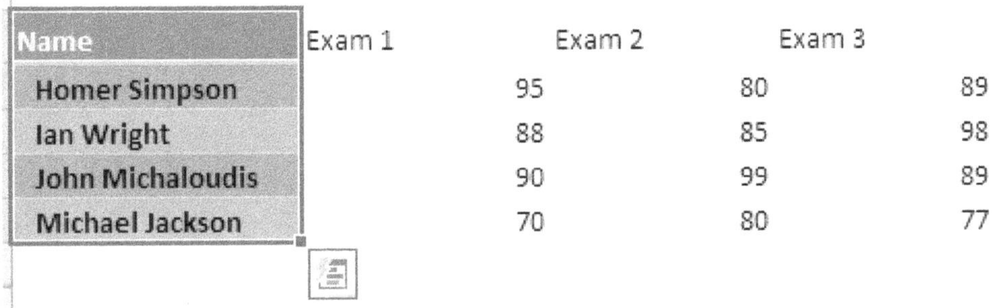

Double-click the **Format Painter button**.

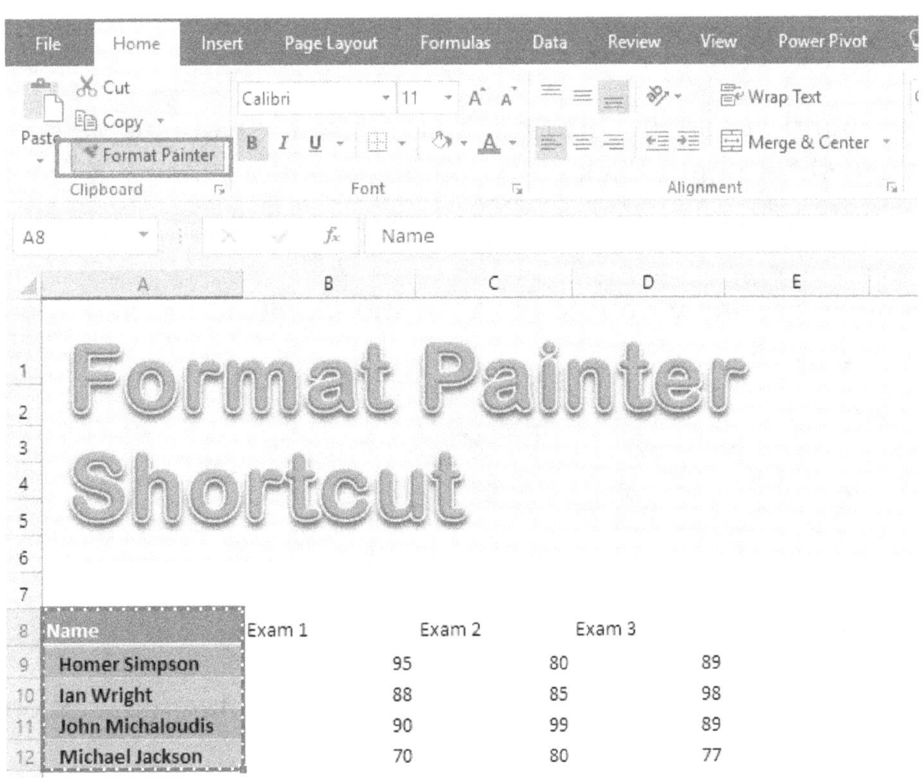

You can now apply it again and again without pressing the Format Painter button!

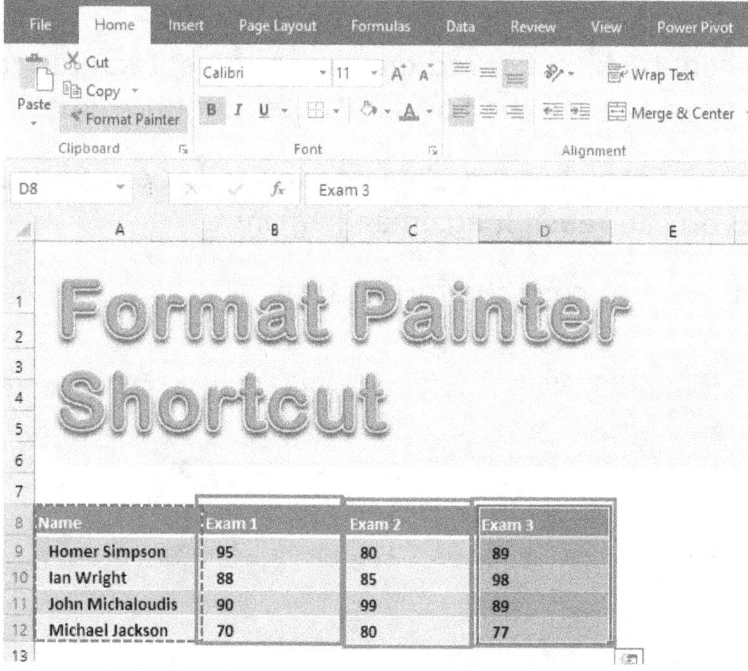

#3: Rename Worksheets

Way before I found out about this tip, I had to rename worksheets by right-clicking on the sheet name, click on the Rename option, then type my name.

That's a lot of steps!

An easier way, is to simply **double click on the sheet name** and you can rename it right away!

#4: Fill Formulas Down Vertically

Imagine you had a Table, and you are creating a new column based on a formula's output.

You can apply the same formula to the rest of the column with just a double-click.

Pick the cell that **contains your formula.**

Product	Price	Quantity	Total
Apple	15	10	$150.00
Orange	22	5	
Grapes	12	6	
Mango	15	3	

Double-click the lower right corner of the cell to copy the formula to the rest of the column.

Product	Price	Quantity	Total
Apple	15	10	$150.00
Orange	22	5	
Grapes	12	6	
Mango	15	3	

You now have your formula applied to the whole column!

Product	Price	Quantity	Total
Apple	15	10	$150.00
Orange	22	5	$110.00
Grapes	12	6	$72.00
Mango	15	3	$45.00

#5: Edit a Shape's Text Quickly

If you have shapes, you can quickly edit shapes with just a double-click.

Double-click on your shape and you can edit the text of the shape quickly.

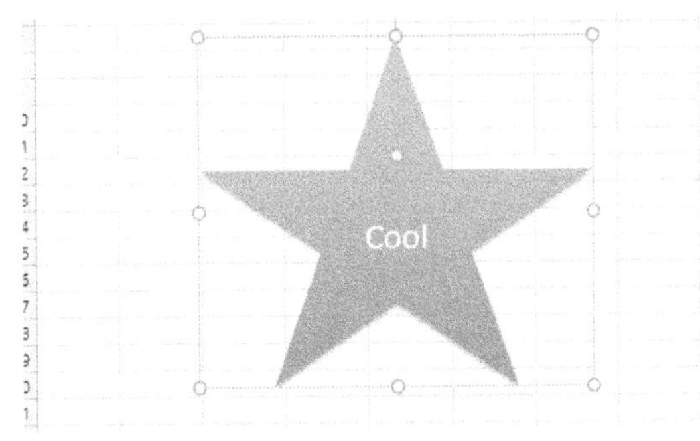

#6:   Auto Adjust Column Widths

There are a lot of times when I had data in a column but I could not see all of my data because the columns were too cramped!

Instead of adjusting the columns manually, there is a great double-click tip.

Double-click on the right edge of the column header you wish to resize and it will resize the column automatically for you!

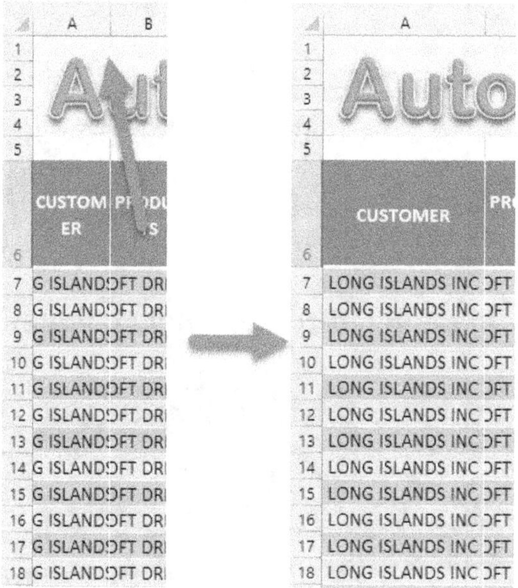

#7: Moving Across Cells of Your Data

Whenever I had a large set of data, I had to painstakingly scroll up & down, left to right, to move across the data...and boy, does it take a long time to scroll to the end of the data!

Turns out, there is a trick to quickly move across your data through double clicks!

Pick a cell you want to start on with.

CUSTOMER	PRODUCTS	ORDER DATE	SALES	FINANCIAL YEAR	SALES MONTH	SALES QTR	CHANNEL PARTNERS
LONG ISLANDS INC	SOFT DRINKS	2012-04-13	24,640	2012	January	Q1	Acme, inc.
LONG ISLANDS INC	SOFT DRINKS	2012-12-21	24,640	2012	February	Q1	Widget Corp
LONG ISLANDS INC	SOFT DRINKS	2012-12-24	29,923	2012	March	Q1	123 Warehousing
LONG ISLANDS INC	SOFT DRINKS	2012-12-24	66,901	2012	April	Q2	Demo Company
LONG ISLANDS INC	SOFT DRINKS	2012-12-29	63,116	2012	May	Q2	Smith and Co.
LONG ISLANDS INC	SOFT DRINKS	2012-06-28	38,281	2012	June	Q2	Foo Bars
LONG ISLANDS INC	SOFT DRINKS	2012-06-28	57,650	2012	July	Q3	ABC Telecom

Double click on the edge of where you want to go to.

For example, if we double click on the **bottom edge of the cell**, that means we will go **downwards** to the end of the data.

CUSTOMER	PRODUCTS	ORDER DATE	SALES	FINANCIAL YEAR	SALES MONTH	SALES QTR	CHANNEL PARTNERS
LONG ISLANDS INC	SOFT DRINKS	2012-04-13	24,640	2012	January	Q1	Acme, Inc.
LONG ISLANDS INC	SOFT DRINKS	2012-12-21	24,640	2012	February	Q1	Widget Corp
LONG ISLANDS INC	SOFT DRINKS	2012-12-24	29,923	2012	March	Q1	123 Warehousing
LONG ISLANDS INC	SOFT DRINKS	2012-12-24	66,901	2012	April	Q2	Demo Company
LONG ISLANDS INC	SOFT DRINKS	2012-12-29	63,116	2012	May	Q2	Smith and Co.
LONG ISLANDS INC	SOFT DRINKS	2012-06-28	38,281	2012	June	Q2	Foo Bars
LONG ISLANDS INC	SOFT DRINKS	2012-06-28	57,650	2012	July	Q3	ABC Telecom

We have been quickly transported to our end of the data, without scrolling at all!

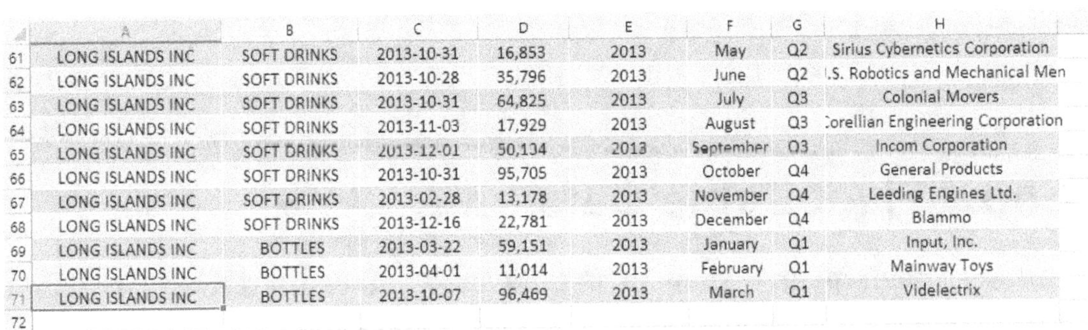

	A	B	C	D	E	F	G	H
61	LONG ISLANDS INC	SOFT DRINKS	2013-10-31	16,853	2013	May	Q2	Sirius Cybernetics Corporation
62	LONG ISLANDS INC	SOFT DRINKS	2013-10-28	35,796	2013	June	Q2	I.S. Robotics and Mechanical Men
63	LONG ISLANDS INC	SOFT DRINKS	2013-10-31	64,825	2013	July	Q3	Colonial Movers
64	LONG ISLANDS INC	SOFT DRINKS	2013-11-03	17,929	2013	August	Q3	Corellian Engineering Corporation
65	LONG ISLANDS INC	SOFT DRINKS	2013-12-01	50,134	2013	September	Q3	Incom Corporation
66	LONG ISLANDS INC	SOFT DRINKS	2013-10-31	95,705	2013	October	Q4	General Products
67	LONG ISLANDS INC	SOFT DRINKS	2013-02-28	13,178	2013	November	Q4	Leeding Engines Ltd.
68	LONG ISLANDS INC	SOFT DRINKS	2013-12-16	22,781	2013	December	Q4	Blammo
69	LONG ISLANDS INC	BOTTLES	2013-03-22	59,151	2013	January	Q1	Input, Inc.
70	LONG ISLANDS INC	BOTTLES	2013-04-01	11,014	2013	February	Q1	Mainway Toys
71	LONG ISLANDS INC	BOTTLES	2013-10-07	96,469	2013	March	Q1	Videlectrix
72								

#8: Access Chart Formatting Options Quickly

Whenever I had a chart and wanted to format it, I had to right-click the chart to select the formatting options. Turns out it is easily accessible through double clicking!

Double click on the border of your chart to access the formatting options.

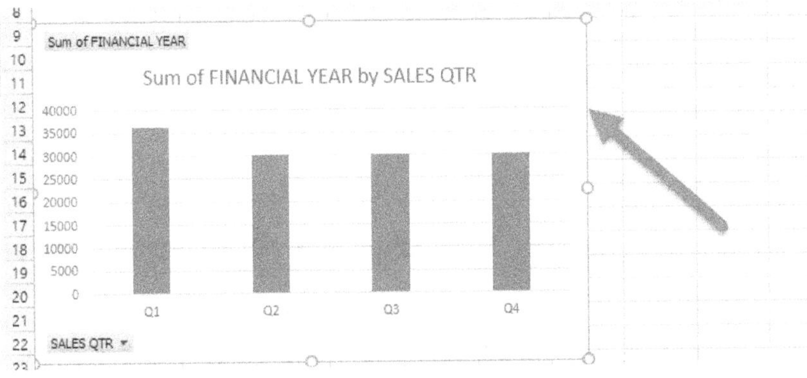

The Format Panel is shown right away.

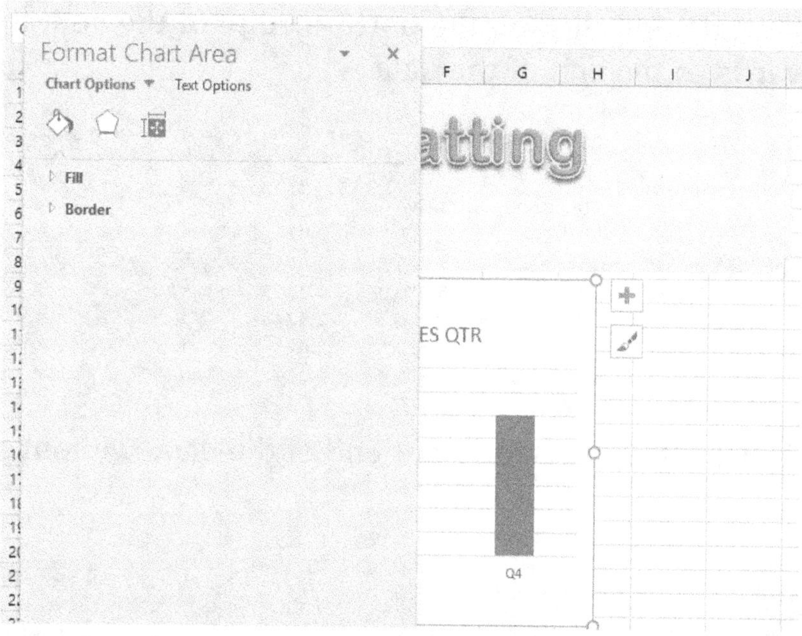

#9: Show Pivot Table Data

Have you ever been given a Pivot Table, however you wanted to investigate the source data behind it to gain a better understanding?

Double click will help you with this too!

Have your **Pivot Table** ready.

Pick a cell that you wanted to drill down on. In our example, **Q1 Sum of FINANCIAL YEAR**

SALES QTR ▾	Sum of FINANCIAL YEAR
Q1	36222
Q2	30183
Q3	30183
Q4	30183

Double click on that cell.

Excel will open a **new worksheet with the data relating to that cell**.

(This data is for show only and any changes made here will not be reflected in the Pivot Table. You can press CTRL + Z to delete this new Sheet).

#10: Close Workbook

You can also use the double click to close your Excel Workbook!

Go to the **upper left corner** of your Excel Application.

Double click on it and your **Excel Workbook will close.**

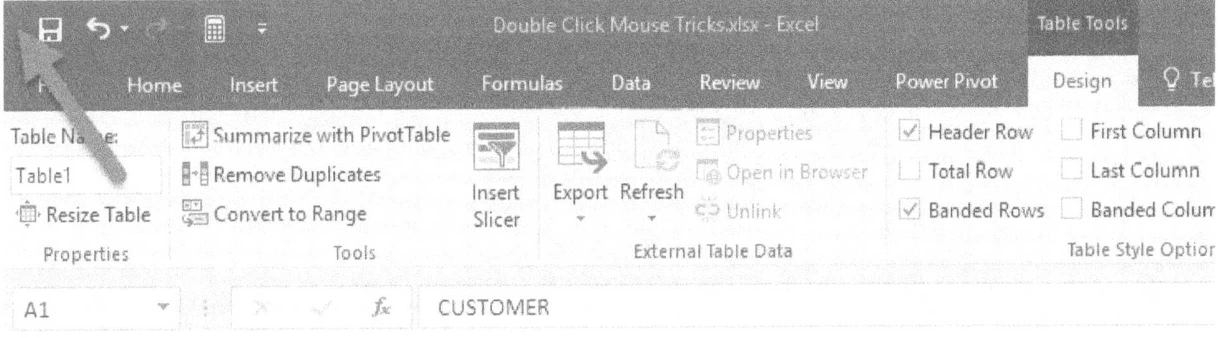

3 Excel Keyboard Tips for Power Users

There are a lot of hidden keyboard tricks to increase your efficiency in Excel. I am surprised myself with these hidden gems!

Here are **Top 3 Excel Keyboard Tips** for **Excel Power Users** like you!

You will have a fun time increasing your productivity with these tricks!

POWER TRICK #1: Display the Format Cells Dialog [CTRL + 1]

I used to have workbooks full of unformatted text and I want to check how to format them quickly and see the list of possible options.

Thankfully, here's a quick tip that will speed up this process **by using a keyboard shortcut to display the Format Cells Dialog**!

Let us use an existing workbook with unformatted phone numbers, and let us fix the format of this!

PHONE NUMBER
18171234567
18171234568
18171234569
18171234575
18171234579

STEP 1: To quickly change the formatting, select all the cells.

PHONE NUMBER
18171234567
18171234568
18171234569
18171234575
18171234579

Press on your keyboard:

CTRL + 1

 Select the Format that best applies to what you need. Go to **_Special >_** **_Phone Number > English (United States)_**

Click OK.

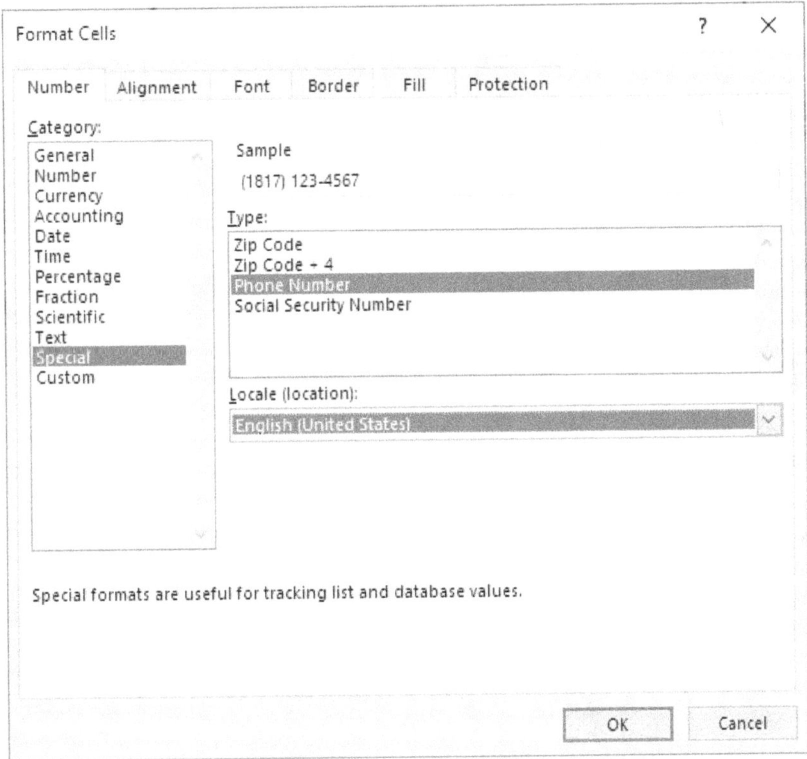

Your Phone Numbers are now formatted.

PHONE NUMBER
(1817) 123-4567
(1817) 123-4568
(1817) 123-4569
(1817) 123-4575
(1817) 123-4579

POWER TRICK #2: Changing Enter Key Behavior in Excel [ENTER]

Data Entry in Excel is a tedious process if Excel does not play its part. The great thing with Excel is it is very customizable. One of the common scenarios is when I want Excel to move in a different direction when I press the **ENTER** key.

The normal behavior for the **ENTER** key is to move downwards.

However, in our scenario, I'm trying to list down the **exam scores for each student**, so it would make sense every time I press the **ENTER** key, we would move from **left to right**:

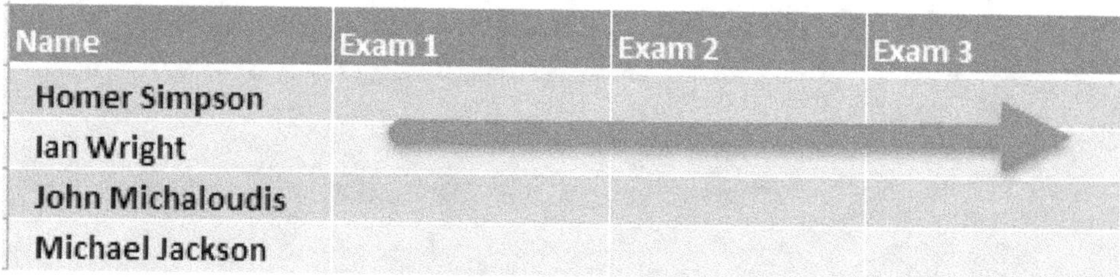

STEP 1: Go to **File.**

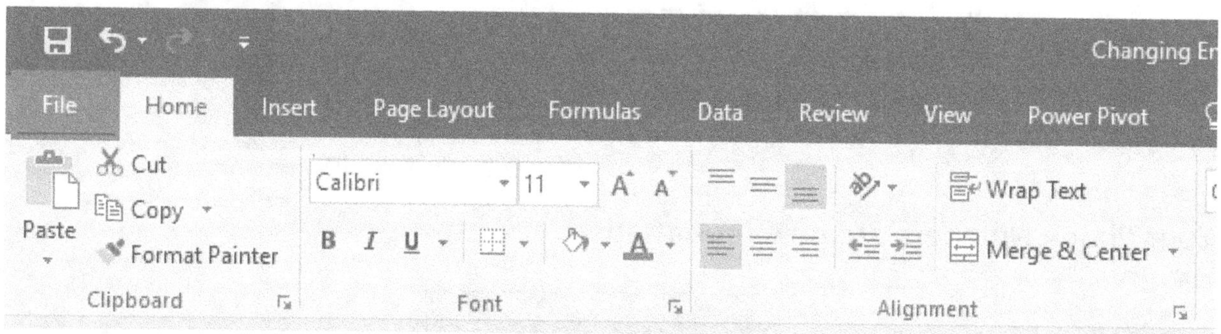

STEP 2: Go to **Options.**

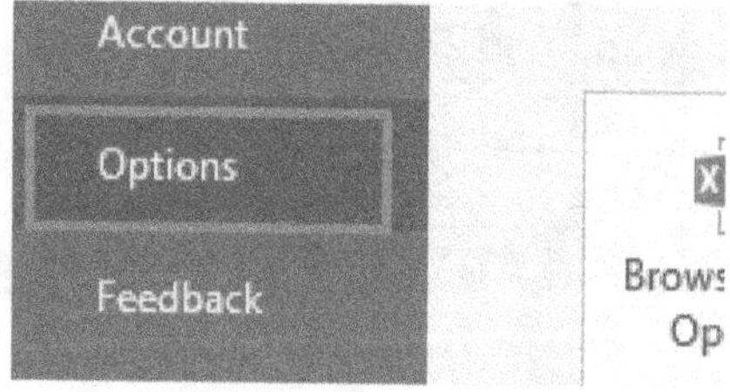

STEP 3: Go to **Advanced > After pressing Enter, move selection > Direction: Right.**

This will change our **ENTER** direction from Up to Down, into **Left to Right**.

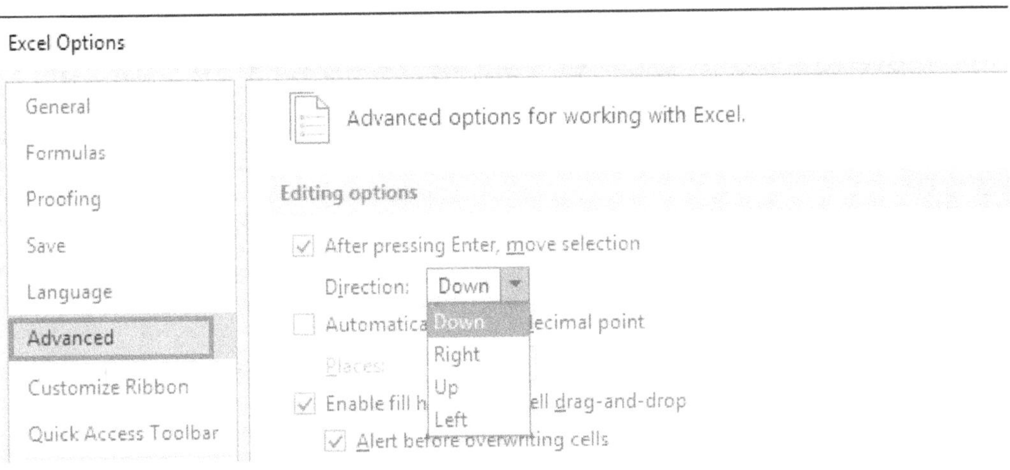

STEP 4: Try it out! Enter a couple of scores and press **ENTER**. It will now move to the **right,** now data entry just got a lot more fun!

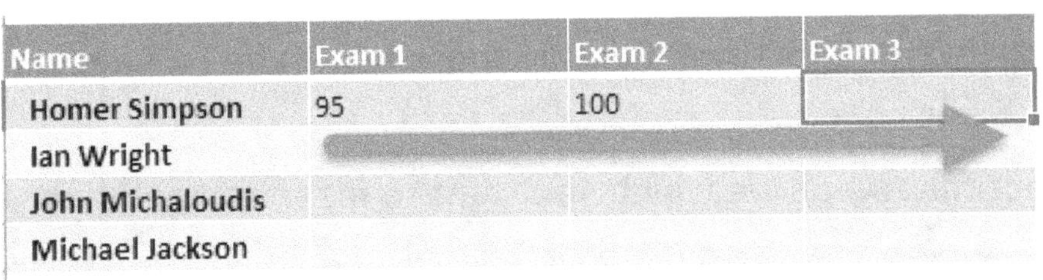

POWER TRICK #3: Move Over Multiple Worksheets [CTRL + PAGE UP / PAGE DOWN]

There are a lot of times when I had workbooks with **a lot of worksheets** inside. Whenever I had to check each sheet one by one, it was a tedious process as I had no choice but to click the sheets one by one!

Thankfully, here's a quick tip that will speed up **by using a keyboard shortcut to move over multiple worksheets**!

Let us use an existing workbook with multiple worksheets to demonstrate this.

Our workbook has multiple sheets inside:

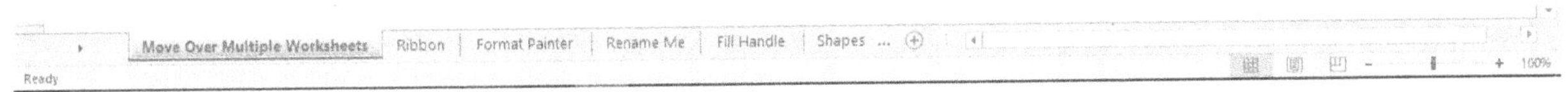

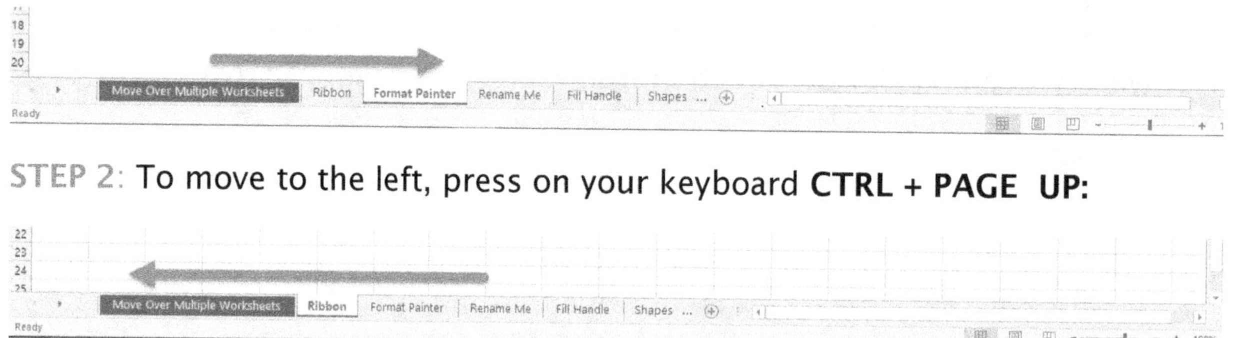

STEP 2: To move to the left, press on your keyboard **CTRL + PAGE UP:**

BONUS TRICK: Repeat Last Action in Excel [F4]

Many times, you might have faced a situation where you **need to do a bunch of tasks repeatedly** while working on an Excel worksheet.

You may need to **insert a blank row or column, add a black border, red fill to a cell**, and repeating the same task again and again can be quite time-consuming.

If you want to insert blank rows multiple times using the F4 keyboard shortcut, follow the steps below:

STEP 1: **Select** the row above which you want to insert a blank row.

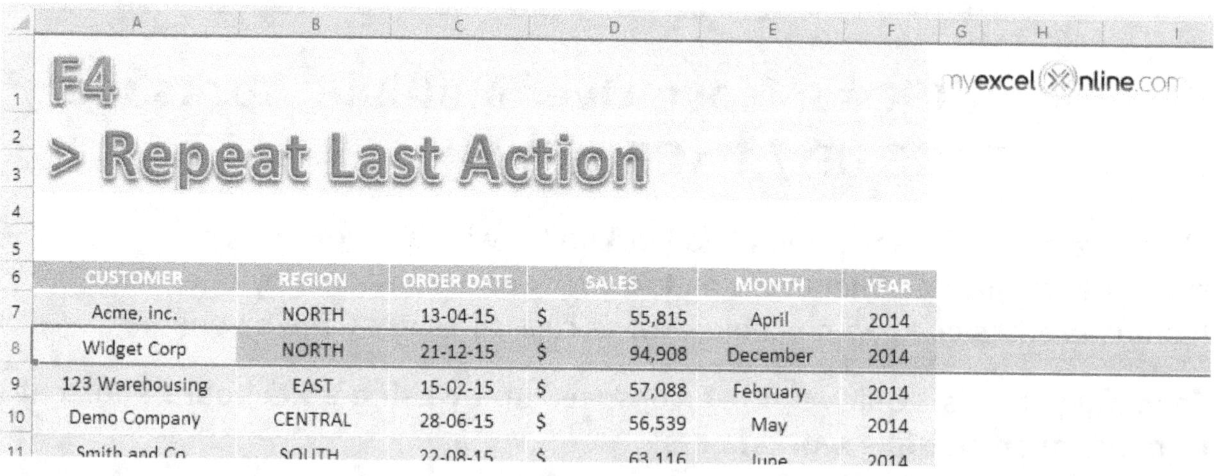

CUSTOMER	REGION	ORDER DATE	SALES	MONTH	YEAR
Acme, inc.	NORTH	13-04-15	$ 55,815	April	2014
Widget Corp	NORTH	21-12-15	$ 94,908	December	2014
123 Warehousing	EAST	15-02-15	$ 57,088	February	2014
Demo Company	CENTRAL	28-06-15	$ 56,539	May	2014
Smith and Co	SOUTH	22-08-15	$ 63,116	June	2014

STEP 2: Right-Click and select **Insert.**

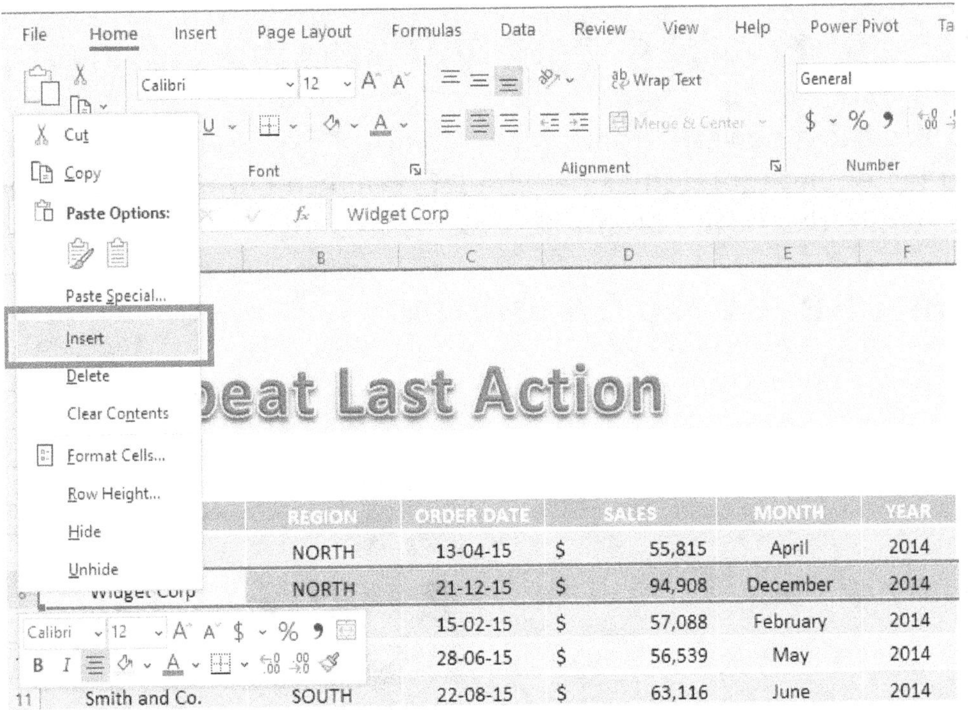

A new row is added!

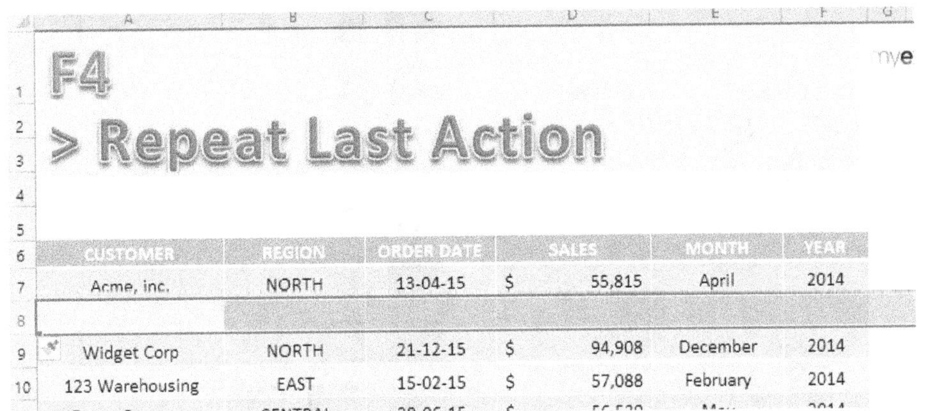

STEP 3: To repeat this action, simply press **F4**. A new row is added!

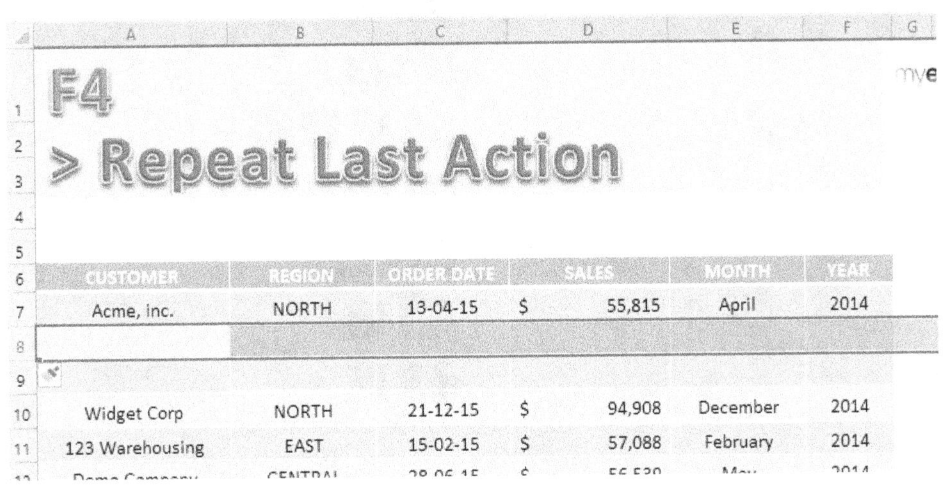

333 Shortcuts for Windows and Mac

Microsoft Excel is a powerful tool which has many Excel keyboard shortcuts to make you faster and more efficient. **The left column contains shortcuts for Windows, while the right column has Mac shortcuts.**

Frequent Keyboard Shortcuts

Action	Windows	Mac
Add borders	Ctrl Shift &	⌘ ⌥ 0
Add or remove filter	Ctrl Shift L	⌘ ⇧ F
Bold	Ctrl B	⌘ B
Center align cell contents	Alt H A C	⌘ E
Choose a fill color	Alt H H	
Close workbook	Ctrl W	⌘ W
Copy	Ctrl C	⌘ C
Cut	Ctrl X	⌘ X
Delete column	Ctrl -	⌘ -
Display find and replace (find)	Ctrl F	⌘ F
Display find and replace (replace)	Ctrl H	^ H
Find next match	Shift F4	⌘ G
Find previous match	Ctrl Shift F4	⌘ ⇧ G
Hide selected columns	Ctrl 0	^ 0
Hide selected rows	Ctrl 9	^ 9
Left align cell contents	Alt H A L	⌘ L
New workbook	Ctrl N	⌘ N
Open context menu	Shift F10	Fn ⇧ F10
Open workbook	Ctrl O	⌘ O
Paste	Ctrl V	⌘ V

Print	Ctrl P	⌘ P
Remove cell contents	Delete	Fn Delete
Right align cell contents	Alt H A R	⌘ R
Save workbook	Ctrl S	⌘ S
Undo	Ctrl Z	⌘ Z
Unhide columns	Ctrl Shift 0	^ ⇧ 0
Unhide rows	Ctrl Shift 9	^ ⇧ 9
Zoom in	Ctrl Alt +	⌥ ⌘ +
Zoom out	Ctrl Alt -	⌥ ⌘ -

Inside the Ribbon Shortcuts

Activate selected button	Space	Space
Expand / collapse the ribbon	Ctrl F1	⌘ ⌥ R
Move to left command	Shift Tab	⇧ Tab
Move to right command	Tab	Tab
Move to submenu when a main menu is open	←	←
Move to the next command in open menu	↓	↓
Open a context menu	Shift F10	Fn ⇧ F10
Open the list for selected command	↓	↓
Open the menu for selected button	Alt ↓	⌥ ↓
Select active tab and activate access keys	Alt	
Select active tab and activate access keys	F10	

Cell Navigation Shortcuts

Action	Windows	Mac
Cycle through text boxes / Images	Ctrl Alt 5	
Enter the End mode	End	Fn →
Exit navigation of text boxes / Images	Esc	Esc
Extend selection of cells to last used cell	Ctrl Shift End	Fn ^ ⇧ →
Move one cell down	↓	↓
Move one cell left	←	←
Move one cell right	→	→
Move one cell up	↑	↑
Move one screen down in worksheet	PgDn	Fn ↓
Move one screen left in worksheet	Alt PgUp	Fn ⌥ ↑
Move one screen right in worksheet	Alt PgDn	Fn ⌥ ↓
Move one screen up in a worksheet	PgUp	Fn ↑
Move to beginning of a worksheet	Ctrl Home	Fn ^ ←
Move to bottom edge of data region	Ctrl ↓	^ ↓
Move to cell in the upper left corner	Home ScrLk	Fn ^ ←
Move to last cell on a worksheet	Ctrl End	Fn ^ →
Move to left edge of data region	Ctrl ←	^ ←
Move to next cell to the right	Tab	Tab
Move to next sheet in workbook	Ctrl PgDn	Fn ^ ↓
Move to previous sheet in workbook	Ctrl PgUp	Fn ^ ↑
Move to right edge of data region	Ctrl →	^ →
Move to the previous cell	Shift Tab	⇧ Tab
Move to top edge of data region	Ctrl ↑	^ ↑
Open list of choices on a cell	Alt ↓	⌥ ↓
Show Go To Dialog	Ctrl G	^ G

Formatting Cell Shortcuts

Action	Windows	Mac
Apply Currency format	Ctrl Shift $	^ ⇧ $
Apply Date format	Ctrl Shift #	^ ⇧ #
Apply General format	Ctrl Shift ~	^ ⇧ ~
Apply Number format	Ctrl Shift !	^ ⇧ !
Apply or remove bold formatting	Ctrl B	⌘ B
Apply or remove italic formatting	Ctrl I	⌘ I
Apply or remove strikethrough formatting	Ctrl 5	⌘ ⇧ X
Apply or remove underline	Ctrl U	⌘ U
Apply outline border to cells	Ctrl Shift &	⌘ ⌥ 0
Apply Percentage format	Ctrl Shift %	^ ⇧ %
Apply Scientific format	Ctrl Shift ^	^ ⇧ ^
Apply Time format	Ctrl Shift @	^ ⇧ @
Check spelling	F7	Fn F7
Copy formula from above cell	Ctrl '	^ '
Copy selected cells	Ctrl C	⌘ C
Cut selected cells	Ctrl X	⌘ X
Display the Quick Analysis options	Ctrl Q	
Edit active cell	F2	^ U
Enter current date	Ctrl ;	^ ;
Enter current time	Ctrl Shift ;	⌘ ;
Fill down from cell above	Ctrl D	^ D
Fill right from cell left	Ctrl R	^ R

Action	Windows	Mac
Format fonts in Format Cells dialog	Ctrl Shift F	^ ⇧ F
Insert a note	Shift F2	Fn ⇧ F2
Insert Table	Ctrl T	^ T
Insert threaded comment	Ctrl Shift F2	
Open and edit a note	Shift F2	Fn ⇧ F2
Open and reply to threaded comment	Ctrl Shift F2	
Open Delete dialog to delete cells	Ctrl -	⌘ -
Open Format Cells dialog	Ctrl 1	⌘ 1
Open Insert dialog to insert cells	Ctrl Shift +	⌘ ⇧ +
Open Paste Special dialog	Ctrl Alt V	^ ⌘ V
Open the Insert hyperlink dialog	Ctrl K	⌘ K
Paste selected cells	Ctrl V	⌘ V
Remove outline border to selected cells	Ctrl Shift _	⌘ ⌥ _
Show or hide objects	Ctrl 6	^ 6
Show or hide outline symbols	Ctrl 8	^ 8
Toggle formulas on and off	Ctrl `	^ `

Making Selection Shortcuts

	Windows	Mac
Complete cell entry and select above cell	**Shift** **Enter**	⇧ Return
Extend cell selection downwards	**Shift** **↓**	⇧ ↓
Extend cell selection to the left	**Shift** **←**	⇧ ←
Extend cell selection to the right	**Shift** **→**	⇧ →
Extend cell selection to top	**Ctrl** **Shift** **Home**	Fn ^ ⇧ ←
Extend cell selection upwards	**Shift** **↑**	⇧ ↑
Extend selection to last bottom cell	**Ctrl** **Shift** **↓**	^ ⇧ ↓
Extend selection to last left cell	**Ctrl** **Shift** **←**	^ ⇧ ←
Extend selection to last right cell	**Ctrl** **Shift** **→**	^ ⇧ →
Extend selection to last top cell	**Ctrl** **Shift** **↑**	^ ⇧ ↑
Fill selected cell range with the current entry	**Ctrl** **Enter**	^ Return
Repeat last action	**Ctrl** **Y**	⌘ Y
Select all objects when an object is selected	**Ctrl** **Shift** **Space**	
Select current and next worksheet	**Ctrl** **Shift** **PgDn**	
Select current and previous worksheet	**Ctrl** **Shift** **PgUp**	
Select current array	**Ctrl** **/**	^ /
Select current region around the cell	**Ctrl** **Shift** *****	⇧ ^ Space
Select differences in column	**Ctrl** **Shift** **|**	^ ⇧	
Select differences in row	**Ctrl** ****	^ \\
Select entire column	**Ctrl** **Space**	^ Space
Select entire row	**Shift** **Space**	⇧ Space

Select entire worksheet	Ctrl A	⌘ A
Select first command on menu	Home	Fn ←
Select only visible cells	Alt ;	⌘ ⇧ Z
Start a new line	Alt Enter	^ ⌥ Return
Toggle add to selection mode	Shift F8	Fn ⇧ F8
Toggle extend mode	F8	Fn F8
Undo last action	Ctrl Z	⌘ Z

Ribbon Tab Shortcuts

Go to Search field	Alt Q
Open Data tab	Alt A
Open File page	Alt F
Open Formulas tab	Alt M
Open Home tab	Alt H
Open Insert tab	Alt N
Open Page Layout tab	Alt P
Open Review tab	Alt R
Open View tab	Alt W

Working with Formula Shortcuts

Action	Windows	Mac
Autosum selection of cells	Alt =	⌘ ⇧ T
Calculate active worksheet	Shift F9	Fn ⇧ F9
Calculate all worksheets	F9	Fn F9
Cancel entry in formula bar	Esc	Esc
Complete entry in formula bar	Enter	Return
Copy the value from the cell above	Ctrl Shift "	^ ⇧ "
Create chart in a new sheet	F11	Fn F11
Create embedded chart	Alt F1	Fn ⌥ F1
Define name for references	Ctrl F3	Fn ^ F3
Display function arguments dialog	Ctrl A	^ A
Display message for error checking button	Alt Shift F10	
Edit active cell	F2	^ U
Expand or collapse formula bar	Ctrl Shift U	^ ⇧ U
Force Calculate all worksheets	Ctrl Alt F9	
Input array formula	Ctrl Shift Enter	^ ⇧ Return
Insert a function	Shift F3	Fn ⇧ F3
Insert function arguments	Ctrl Shift A	^ ⇧ A
Invoke Flash Fill	Ctrl E	
Move to end of text when in the formula bar	Ctrl End	Fn ^ →
Move to next record of data form	Enter	Return
Open macro dialog	Alt F8	Fn ⌥ F8
Open Visual Basic For Applications (VBA) Editor	Alt F11	Fn ⌥ F11
Paste a name	F3	
Select text in formula bar to end	Ctrl Shift End	Fn ^ ⇧ →
Toggle absolute or relative references	F4	⌘ T

Power Pivot Shortcuts

Action	Windows	Mac
Cancel process or close dialog	Ctrl + Esc	
Copy selected data	Ctrl + C	⌘ + C
Delete table	Ctrl + D	^ + D
Move table	Ctrl + M	
Move to first cell in table	Ctrl + Home	Fn + ^ + ←
Move to first cell of row	Ctrl + ←	^ + ←
Move to last cell in table	Ctrl + End	Fn + ^ + →
Move to last cell of row	Ctrl + →	^ + →
Move to next table	Ctrl + PgDn	Fn + ^ + ↓
Move to previous table	Ctrl + PgUp	Fn + ^ + ↑
Move to the first cell of column	Ctrl + ↑	^ + ↑
Move to the last cell of column	Ctrl + ↓	^ + ↓
Open AutoFilter Menu dialog	Alt + ↓	⌥ + ↓
Open Go To dialog	F5	Fn + F5
Recalculate all formulas	F9	Fn + F9
Redo last action	Ctrl + Y	⌘ + Y
Rename table	Ctrl + R	^ + R
Save file	Ctrl + S	⌘ + S
Select cells to first column cell	Shift + PgDn	Fn + ⇧ + ↓
Select cells to first row cell	Shift + Home	Fn + ⇧ + ←
Select cells to last column cell	Shift + PgUp	Fn + ⇧ + ↑
Select cells to last row cell	Shift + End	Fn + ⇧ + →
Select current column	Ctrl + Space	^ + Space
Select current row	Shift + Space	⇧ + Space
Select entire table	Ctrl + A	⌘ + A
Undo last action	Ctrl + Z	⌘ + Z

Function Key Shortcuts

Action	Windows	Mac
Add non-adjacent cell to a selection	Shift F8	Fn ⇧ F8
Add or update cell note	Shift F2	Fn ⇧ F2
Calculate all worksheets	F9	Fn F9
Calculates active worksheet	Shift F9	Fn ⇧ F9
Close Excel	Alt F4	⌘ Q
Close workbook window	Ctrl F4	⌘ W
Create chart of the selected range	F11	Fn F11
Display message for error checking button	Alt Shift F10	
Display shortcut menu	Shift F10	Fn ⇧ F10
Edit the active cell	F2	^ U
Force calculate all worksheets	Ctrl Alt F9	
Insert new worksheet	Alt Shift F1	Fn ⇧ F11
Insert new worksheet	Shift F11	Fn ⇧ F11
Maximize workbook	Ctrl F10	Fn ^ F10
Minimize workbook	Ctrl F9	⌘ M
Open Excel Help	F1	⌘ /
Open Go To dialog	F5	Fn F5
Open Insert Function dialog	Shift F3	Fn ⇧ F3
Open Macro dialog	Alt F8	Fn ⌥ F8
Open Paste Name dialog	F3	
Open print preview	Ctrl F2	⌘ P

Action	Windows	Mac
Open Save As dialog	F12	⌘ ⇧ S
Open Spelling dialog	F7	Fn F7
Open Thesaurus	Shift F7	Fn ⇧ F7
Open VBA Editor	Alt F11	Fn ⌥ F11
Perform moving of window	Ctrl F7	
Perform resizing of window	Ctrl F8	
Repeat last action	F4	⌘ Y
Restore window size of workbook	Ctrl F5	
Show or hide ribbon	Ctrl F1	⌘ ⌥ R
Switch panes	F6	Fn F6
Switch panes in reverse	Shift F6	Fn ⇧ F6
Switch to next workbook	Ctrl F6	^ Tab
Toggle extend mode	F8	Fn F8
Toggle key tips	F10	

Drag and Drop Shortcuts

Action	Windows	Mac
Drag and copy	Ctrl Drag	⌥ Drag
Drag and cut	Drag	Drag
Drag and insert	Shift Drag	⇧ Drag
Drag and insert copy	Ctrl Shift Drag	⌥ ⇧ Drag
Drag selection to worksheet	Alt Drag	⌘ Drag
Drag to duplicate the worksheet	Ctrl Drag	⌥ Drag

Macros and VBA Shortcuts

Autocomplete code	Ctrl Space
Delete line of code	Ctrl Y
Open Intellisense Dropdown	Ctrl J
Open Visual Basic For Applications (VBA) Editor	Alt F11 — Fn ⌥ F11
Redo last action	Alt E R
Show quick info	Ctrl I
Step through code	F8 — ⌘ ⇧ I

Pivot Table Shortcuts

Group selected items	Alt Shift →
Hide selected item or field	Ctrl -
Open Calculated Field dialog	Shift Ctrl =
Open field list for cell	Alt ↓
Select entire table	Ctrl Shift *
Select first item in Field List	Home
Select last item in Field List	End
Select next item in Field List	↓
Select or clear a check box	Space
Select previous item in Field List	↑
Ungroup selected items	Alt Shift ←

Power BI Shortcuts

Activate Selection pane	`F6`
Collapse a table	`←`
Comment lines in DAX	`Ctrl` `/`
Comment multiple lines in DAX	`Ctrl` `K` `C`
Copy	`Ctrl` `C`
Copy line down in DAX	`Alt` `Shift` `↓`
Copy line up in DAX	`Alt` `Shift` `↑`
Create line break with auto-indent	`Shift` `Enter`
Delete a word in DAX	`Ctrl` `Delete`
Delete multiple lines in DAX	`Ctrl` `Shift` `K`
Enter lines of code in DAX	`Ctrl` `Alt` `↓`
Enter lines of code in DAX	`Ctrl` `Alt` `↑`
Expand a table	`→`
Find the highlighted word	`Ctrl` `D`
Go to line number in DAX	`Ctrl` `G`
Indent line in DAX	`Ctrl` `]`
Insert cursor in DAX	`Alt` `Click`
Insert line above in DAX	`Ctrl` `Shift` `Enter`
Insert line below in DAX	`Ctrl` `Enter`
Interact with a Slicer	`Ctrl` `→`

Jump to matching bracket in DAX	Ctrl	Shift	\
Move an object down in layering	Ctrl	Shift	B
Move an object up in layering	Ctrl	Shift	F
Move focus backward in section	Shift	Tab	
Move focus between sections	Ctrl	F6	
Move focus forward in section	Tab		
Move focus to Visual menu	Alt	Shift	F10
Move line down in DAX	Alt	↓	
Move line up in DAX	Alt	↑	
Multi-select	Ctrl	Shift	
Multi-select objects	Ctrl	Space	
New line in DAX	Alt	Enter	
Open context menu	Shift	F10	
Outdent line in DAX	Ctrl	[	
Paste	Ctrl	V	
Restart Intellisense	Alt	I	
Select all occurrences of current selection	Ctrl	Shift	L
Select all occurrences of current word	Ctrl	F2	
Select an object	Space		
Select current line in DAX	Ctrl	I	
Select nearest word in DAX	Alt	Shift	→
Select object	Enter		
Show data	Alt	Shift	F11
Show keyboard shortcuts	Shift	?	
Toggle commenting of code	Alt	Shift	A
Toggle commenting of lines that has a word	Ctrl	+	
Toggle object visibility	Ctrl	Shift	S
Uncomment lines in DAX	Ctrl	\	
Uncomment multiple lines in DAX	Ctrl	K	U

Other Shortcuts

Action	Windows	Mac
Add border bottom in Format Cells	Alt B	⌘ ⌥ ↓
Add border donward diagonal in Format Cells	Alt D	
Add border horizontal interior in Format Cells	Alt H	
Add border left in Format Cells	Alt L	⌘ ⌥ ←
Add border right in Format Cells	Alt R	⌘ ⌥ →
Add border top in Format Cells	Alt T	⌘ ⌥ ↑
Add border upward diagonal in Format Cells	Alt U	
Add border vertical interior in Format Cells	Alt V	
Clear cell content	Backspace	Delete
Clear cell content while keeping cell format	Delete	Fn Delete
Clear slicer filter	Alt C	⌥ C
Close an open menu or dialog	Esc	Esc
Delete one character to the left	Backspace	Delete
Delete one character to the right	Delete	Fn Delete
Delete to the end of line	Ctrl Delete	^ Delete
Display control menu for Excel window	Alt Space	?
In End Mode, move to bottom cell in column	End ↓	↓
In End Mode, move to left cell in row	End ←	←
In End Mode, move to right cell in row	End →	→
In End Mode, move to top cell in column	End ↑	↑
Insert new line in cell	Alt Enter	^ ⌥ Return
Move to start of row	Home	Fn ←

Action	Windows	Mac
Move to unlocked cells in protected worksheet	Tab	Tab
Open dropdown list	Alt ↓	⌥ ↓
Select or clear a check box	Space	Space
Selects the entire worksheet	Ctrl Shift Space	⌘ A
Switch to next tab in dialog	Ctrl Tab	^ Tab
Switch to Normal view	Alt W L	
Switch to Page Break Preview view	Alt W I	
Switch to Page Layout view	Alt W P	
Switch to previous tab in dialog	Ctrl Shift Tab	^ ⇧ Tab
Toggle End mode	End	Fn →
Toggle full screen	Ctrl Shift F1	^ ⌘ F
Toggle total row of table	Ctrl Shift T	⌘ ⇧ T

AutoRecover in Excel

AutoRecover in Excel is a lifesaver feature! Imagine if you have an unsaved workbook, then you closed it by accident after working on it for hours. As long as you have it opened for at least 10 minutes, Excel is smart enough to keep a copy of this for you!

First things first, let us have a quick look at the AutoRecover settings in Excel so that we can have a better understanding of how it works.

STEP 1: Go to *File > More > Options*

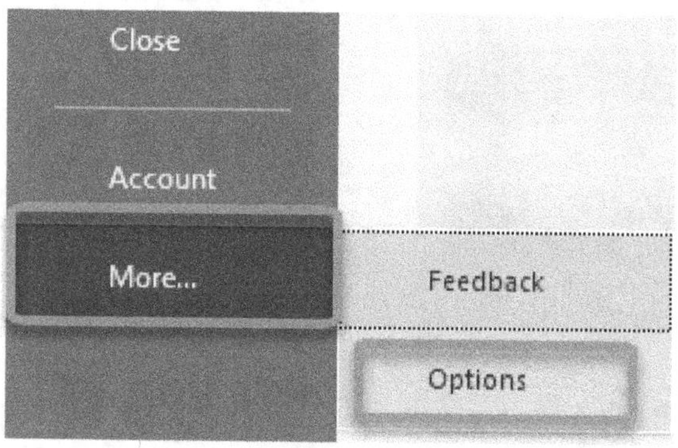

STEP 2: Go to **Save**. This is where our crucial settings lie. You will see the following:

- Saves every 10 minutes

- Your AutoRecover file location

So you know AutoRecover has your back if you have your unsaved workbook opened for at least 10 minutes.

The next question is, how do we get our unsaved workbooks?

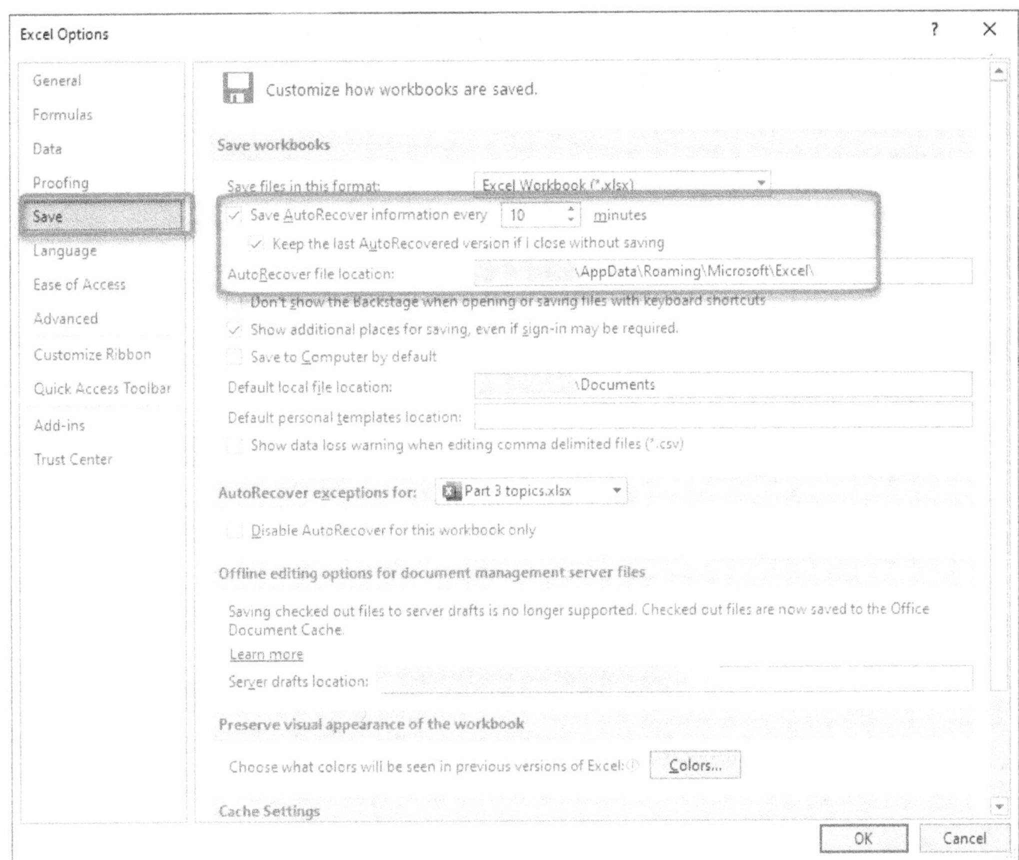

STEP 3: Close the window. Go to **File > Open > Recover Unsaved Workbooks**.

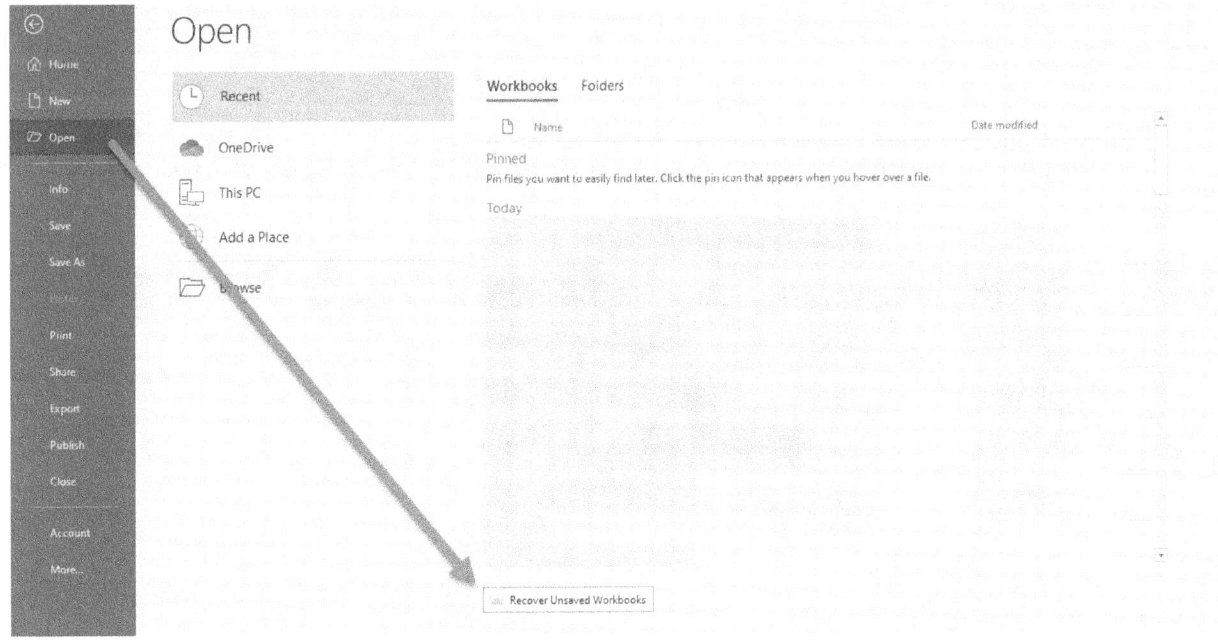

You now have your unsaved workbooks! Now you have to open them one by one, until you find the workbook you are looking for.

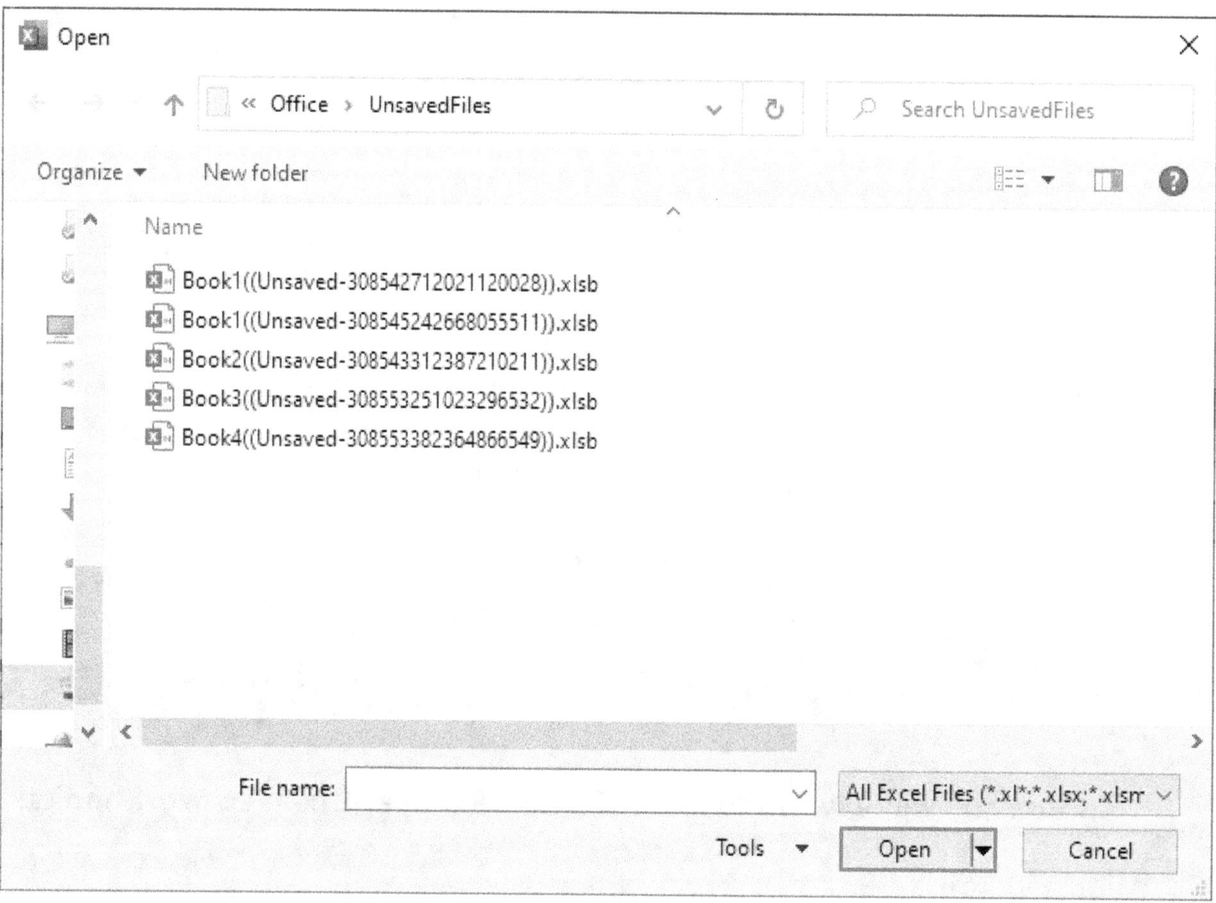

STEP 4: Once you found the right one and opened it, click **Save As** to save a copy.

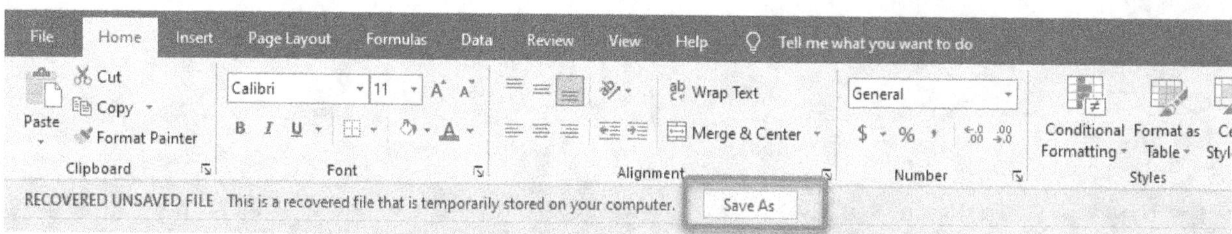

Convert Excel to PDF & PDF to Excel

Excel and PDF are the **two most popular file types** and you might need to **convert from one format to another** time to time.

PDF files are a widely used format for electronic documents. They are used when you need to save a file without modification so that it can be easily shared and printed. By default, an Excel Workbook is **saved as a .xlsx** file type.

But how do you save it as a PDF format? Read on to see how it's done both ways!

Convert Excel to PDF

PDFs can be easily shared and can be viewed on any platform without a change in format. So, learning how to convert Excel to PDF is extremely essential!

There are **5 different methods** in which you can convert from Excel to PDF:

#1: Using Save As Option

STEP 1: Select the Excel table that you want in the PDF Format.

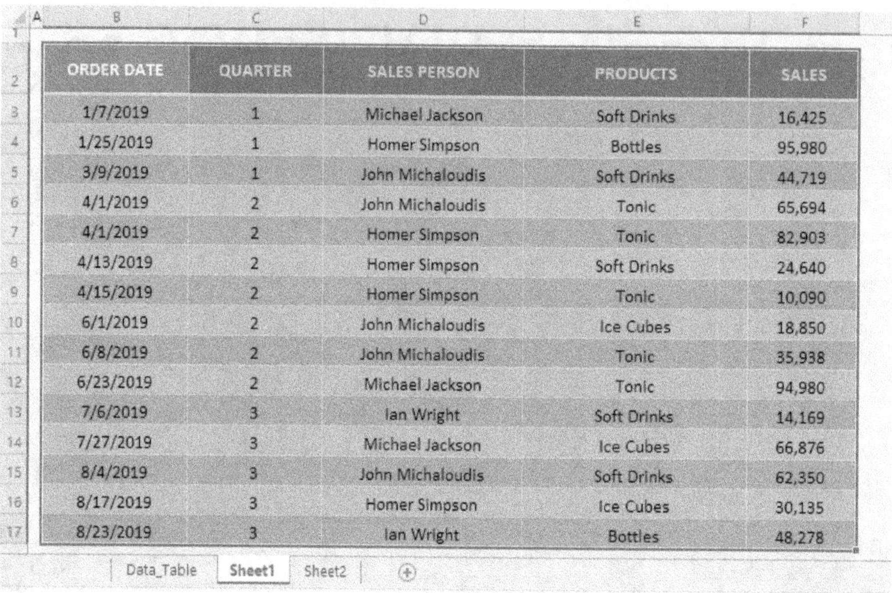

ORDER DATE	QUARTER	SALES PERSON	PRODUCTS	SALES
1/7/2019	1	Michael Jackson	Soft Drinks	16,425
1/25/2019	1	Homer Simpson	Bottles	95,980
3/9/2019	1	John Michaloudis	Soft Drinks	44,719
4/1/2019	2	John Michaloudis	Tonic	65,694
4/1/2019	2	Homer Simpson	Tonic	82,903
4/13/2019	2	Homer Simpson	Soft Drinks	24,640
4/15/2019	2	Homer Simpson	Tonic	10,090
6/1/2019	2	John Michaloudis	Ice Cubes	18,850
6/8/2019	2	John Michaloudis	Tonic	35,938
6/23/2019	2	Michael Jackson	Tonic	94,980
7/6/2019	3	Ian Wright	Soft Drinks	14,169
7/27/2019	3	Michael Jackson	Ice Cubes	66,876
8/4/2019	3	John Michaloudis	Soft Drinks	62,350
8/17/2019	3	Homer Simpson	Ice Cubes	30,135
8/23/2019	3	Ian Wright	Bottles	48,278

Data_Table **Sheet1** Sheet2 ⊕

STEP 2: Click on **File** Tab.

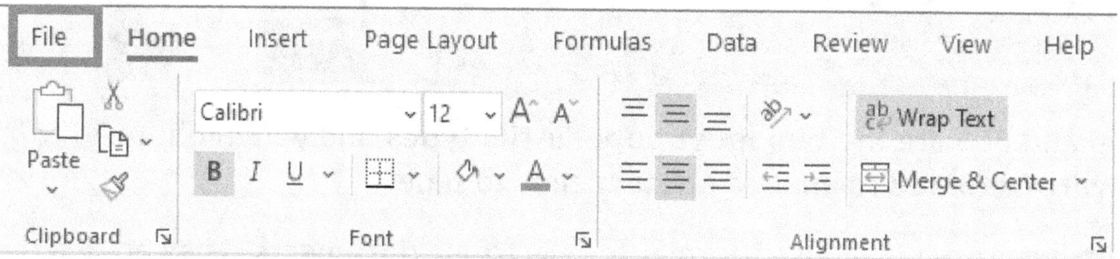

STEP 3: Select **Save As** > **Browse**.

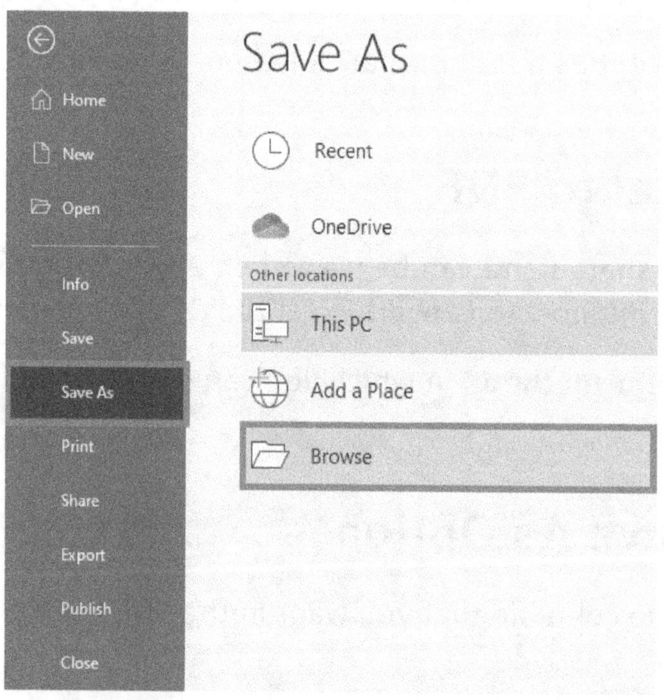

STEP 4: In the **Save As** dialog box, **select the location** where you want to save the PDF file.

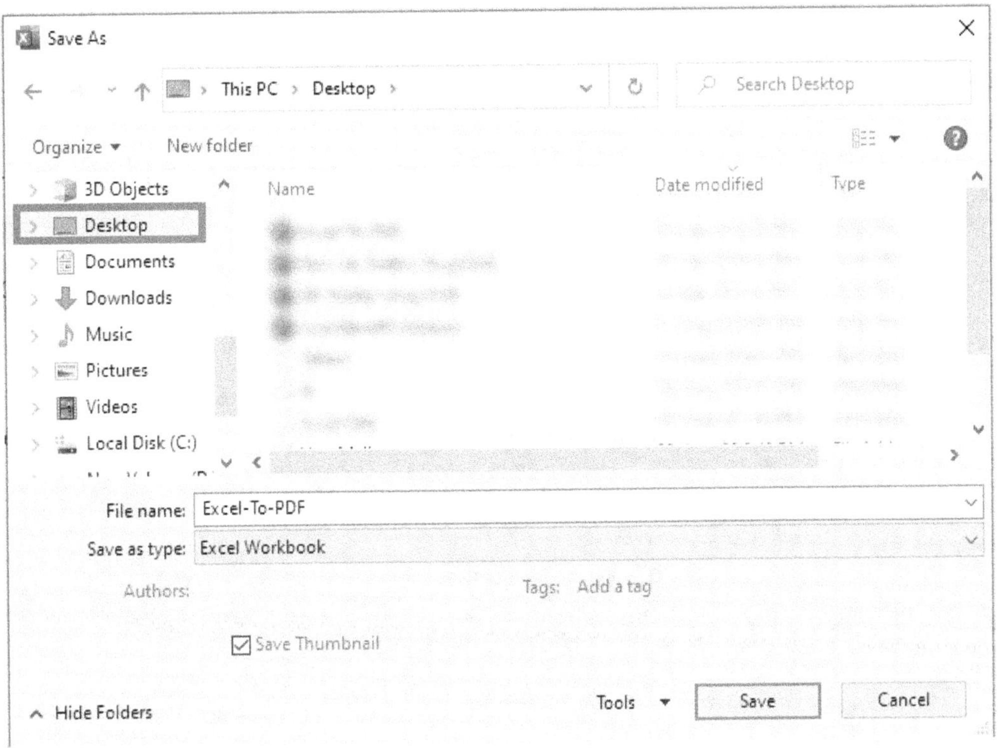

STEP 5: Under Save as type dropdown, select **PDF**.

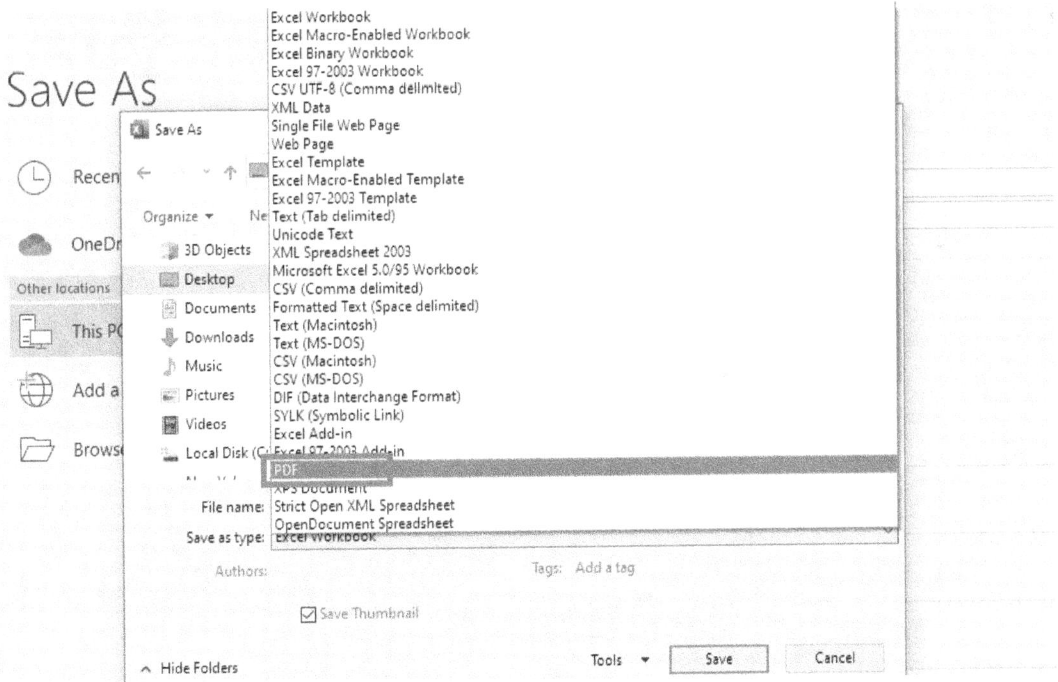

STEP 6: Click in the **Options** button to customize the PDF file you want to create.

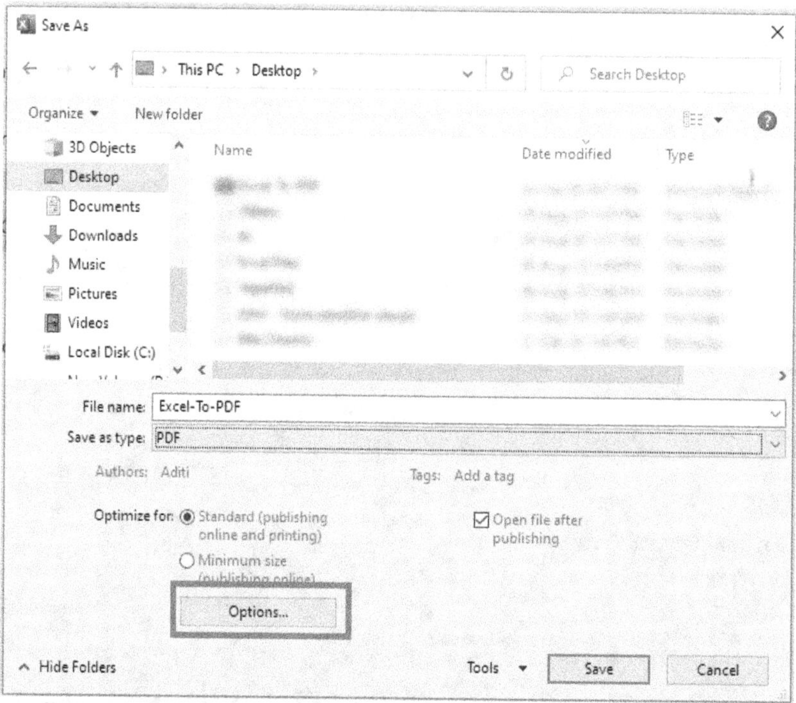

STEP 7: In the **Options** dialog box, Go to **Publish what** section and click on **Selection**. Then, Click **OK**.

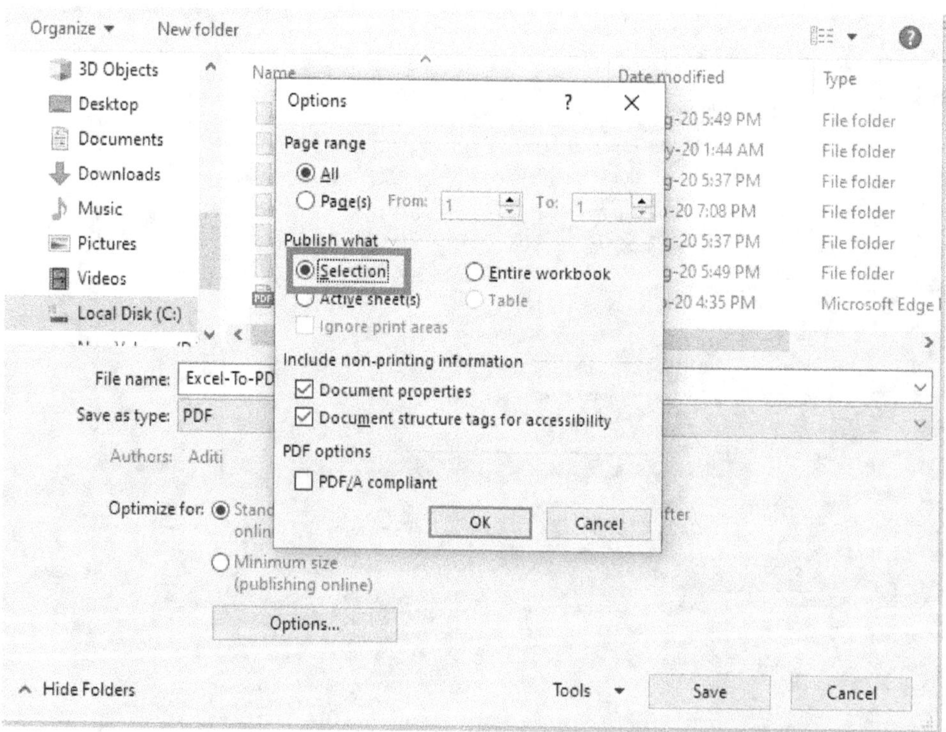

This will help you to publish only what you have selected on the sheet. To publish the entire sheet, click on *Active Sheet(s)*, and to publish the workbook click on the *Entire Workbook*.

STEP 8: Click **Save**.

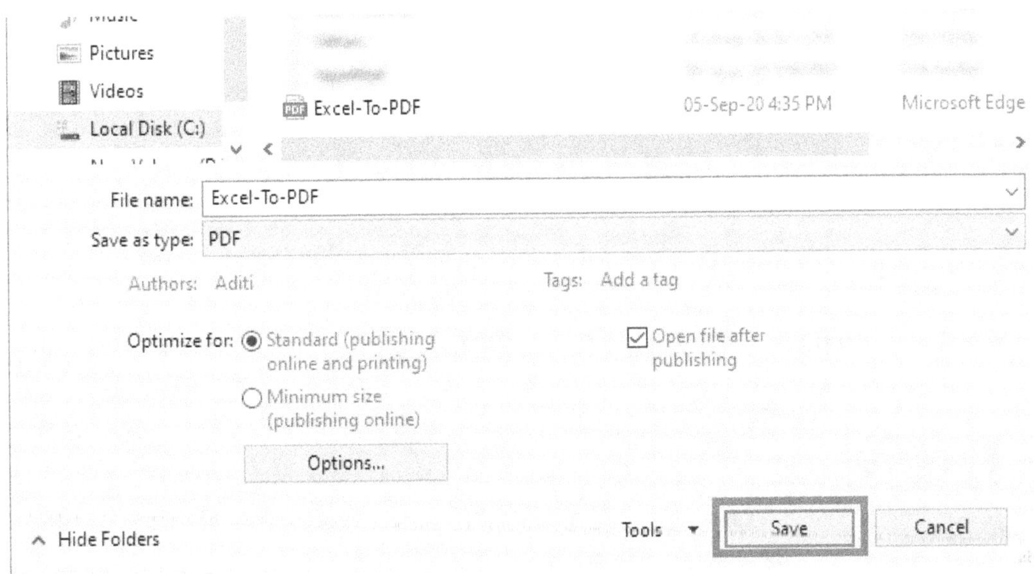

This will save your Excel Table in the PDF format.

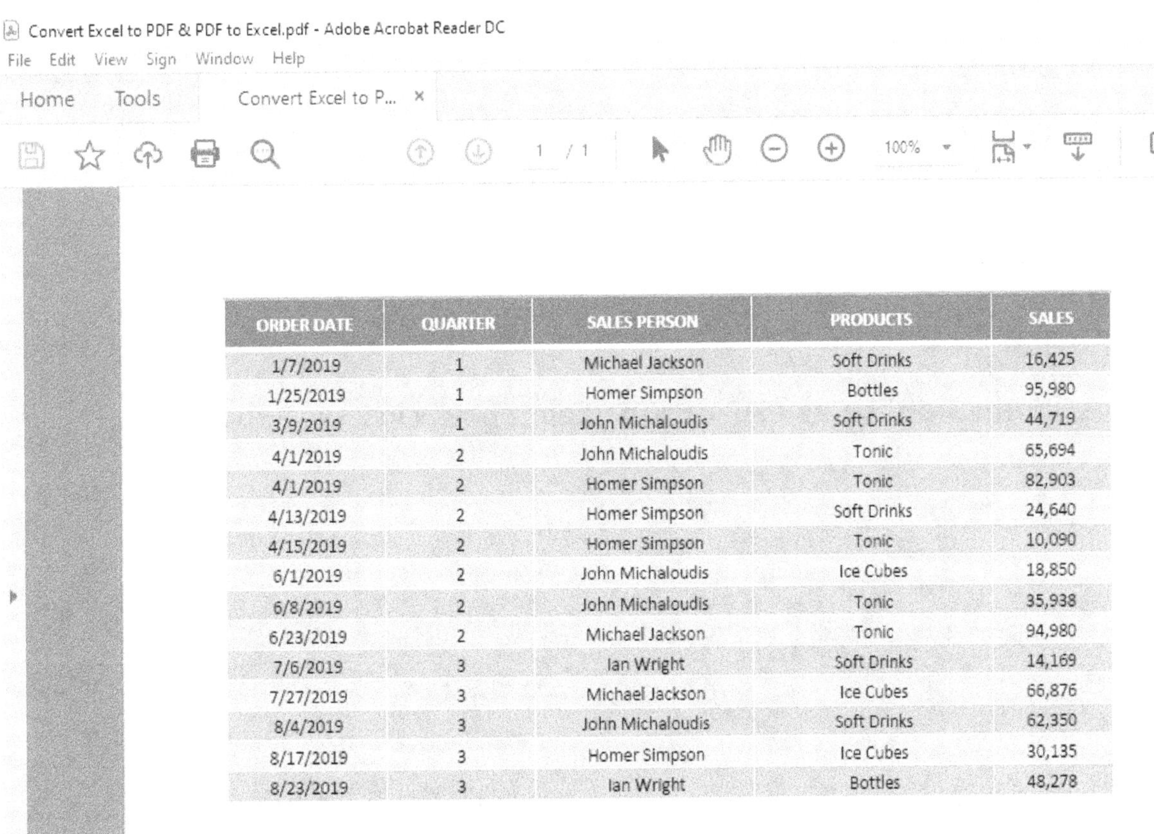

ORDER DATE	QUARTER	SALES PERSON	PRODUCTS	SALES
1/7/2019	1	Michael Jackson	Soft Drinks	16,425
1/25/2019	1	Homer Simpson	Bottles	95,980
3/9/2019	1	John Michaloudis	Soft Drinks	44,719
4/1/2019	2	John Michaloudis	Tonic	65,694
4/1/2019	2	Homer Simpson	Tonic	82,903
4/13/2019	2	Homer Simpson	Soft Drinks	24,640
4/15/2019	2	Homer Simpson	Tonic	10,090
6/1/2019	2	John Michaloudis	Ice Cubes	18,850
6/8/2019	2	John Michaloudis	Tonic	35,938
6/23/2019	2	Michael Jackson	Tonic	94,980
7/6/2019	3	Ian Wright	Soft Drinks	14,169
7/27/2019	3	Michael Jackson	Ice Cubes	66,876
8/4/2019	3	John Michaloudis	Soft Drinks	62,350
8/17/2019	3	Homer Simpson	Ice Cubes	30,135
8/23/2019	3	Ian Wright	Bottles	48,278

#2: Using Export Option

The Export option in Excel will provide you with a **quicker way** to save your file as PDF.

STEP 1: Go to the **File** Tab.

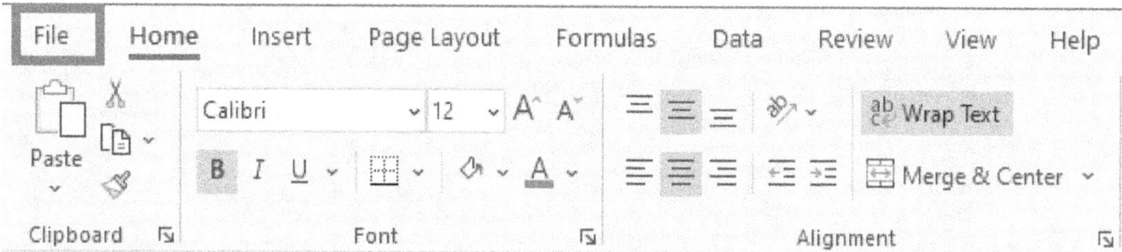

STEP 2: Click on **Export** > **Create PDF/XPS Document** > **Create PDF/XPS** button.

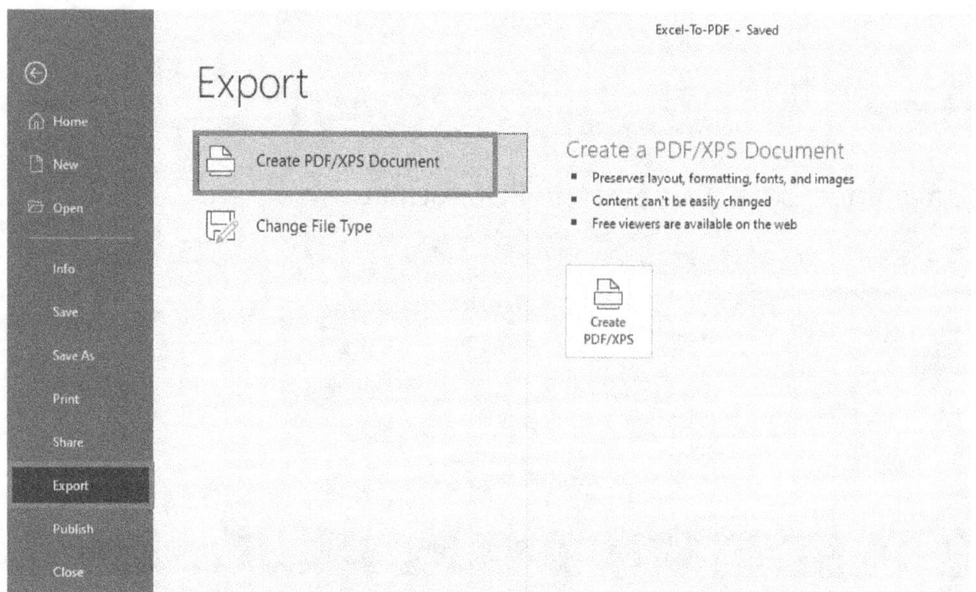

STEP 3: In the **Publish as PDF or XPS** dialog box, click on **Publish**.

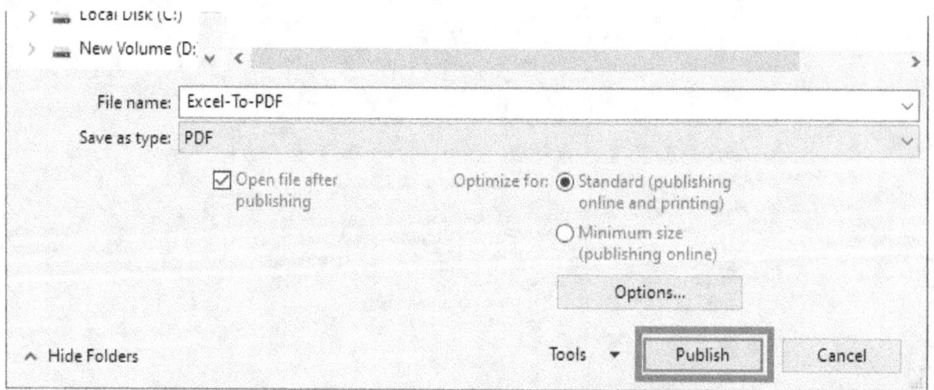

#3: Export using Quick Access Toolbar

If converting Excel to PDF is a regular task for you, you can add it to the Quick Access Toolbar (QAT). Follow the steps below to add the **Publish as PDF** option to the QAT:

STEP 1: **Right Click** on the QAT to customize it.

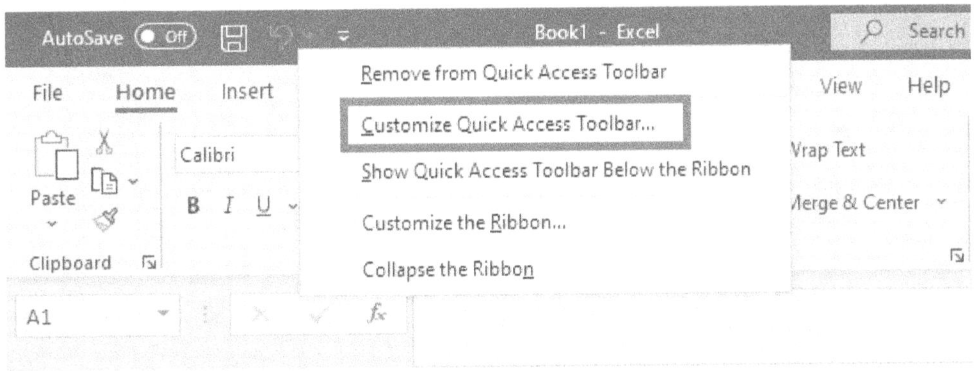

STEP 2: In the Excel Options dialog box, select **Quick Access Toolbar** > **Publish as PDF or XPS** > **Add**.

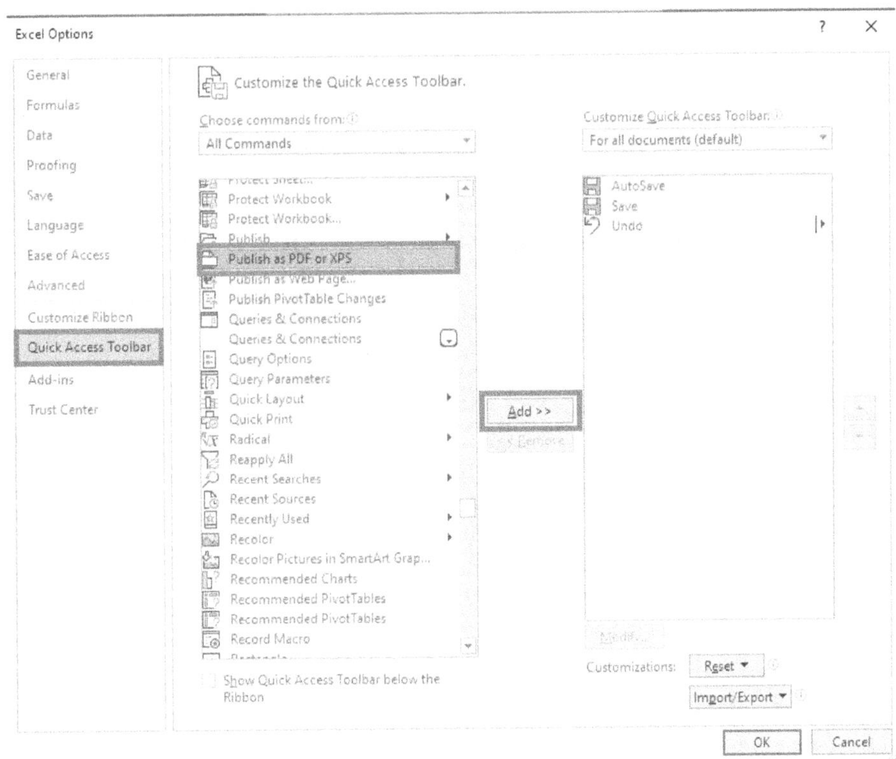

STEP 3: This will add **Publish as PDF** under Customize Quick Access Toolbar. Now, **Click OK**.

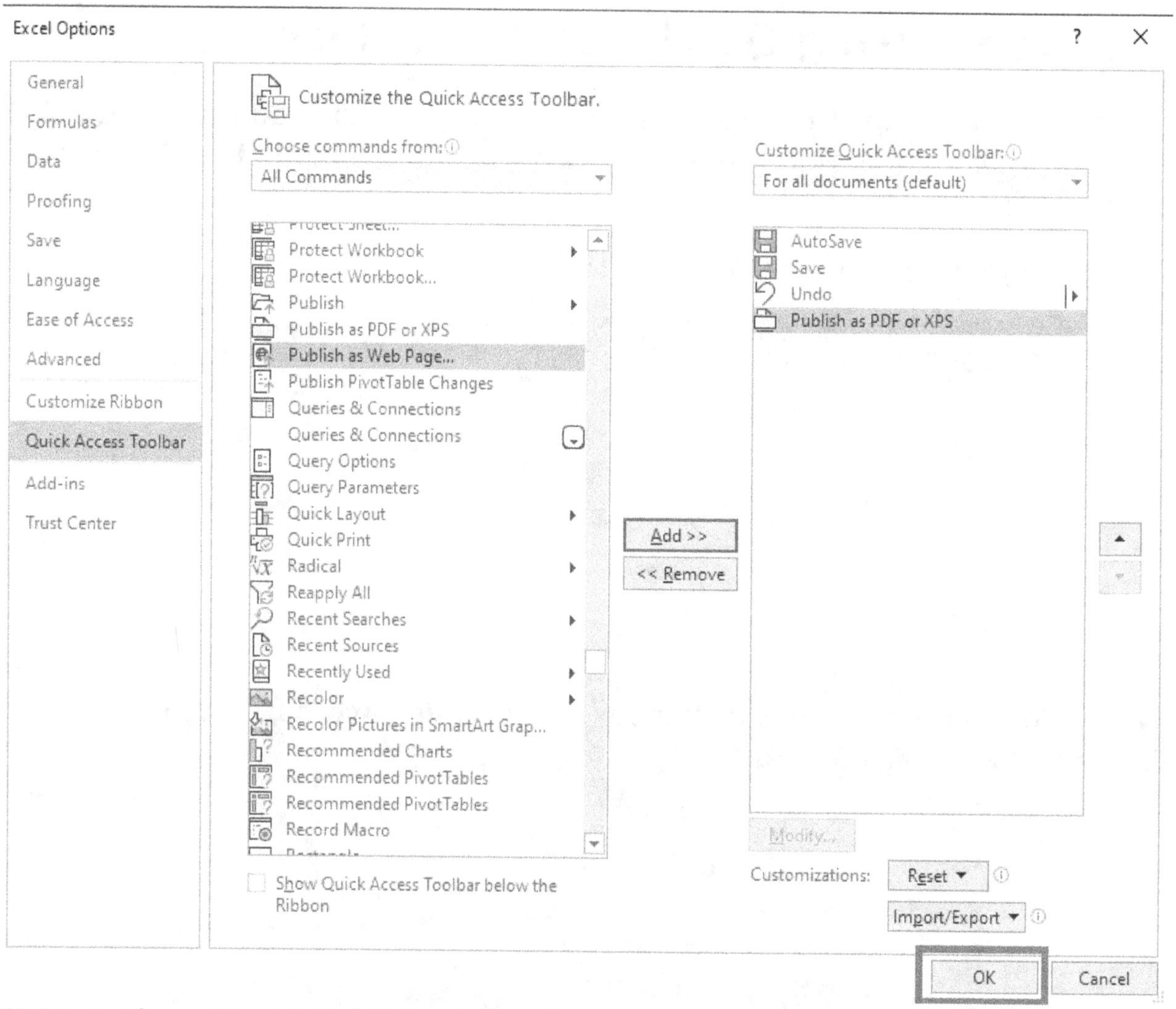

STEP 4: This will add **Publish as PDF/XPS** to the **Quick Access Toolbar**.

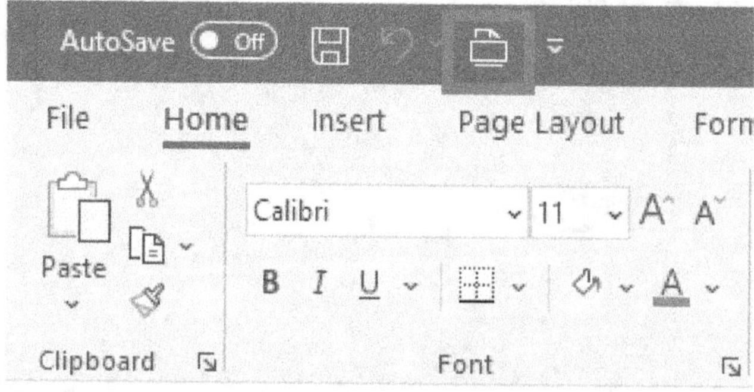

STEP 5: Simply click on the icon, select the file location you want to save it at and click on Publish.

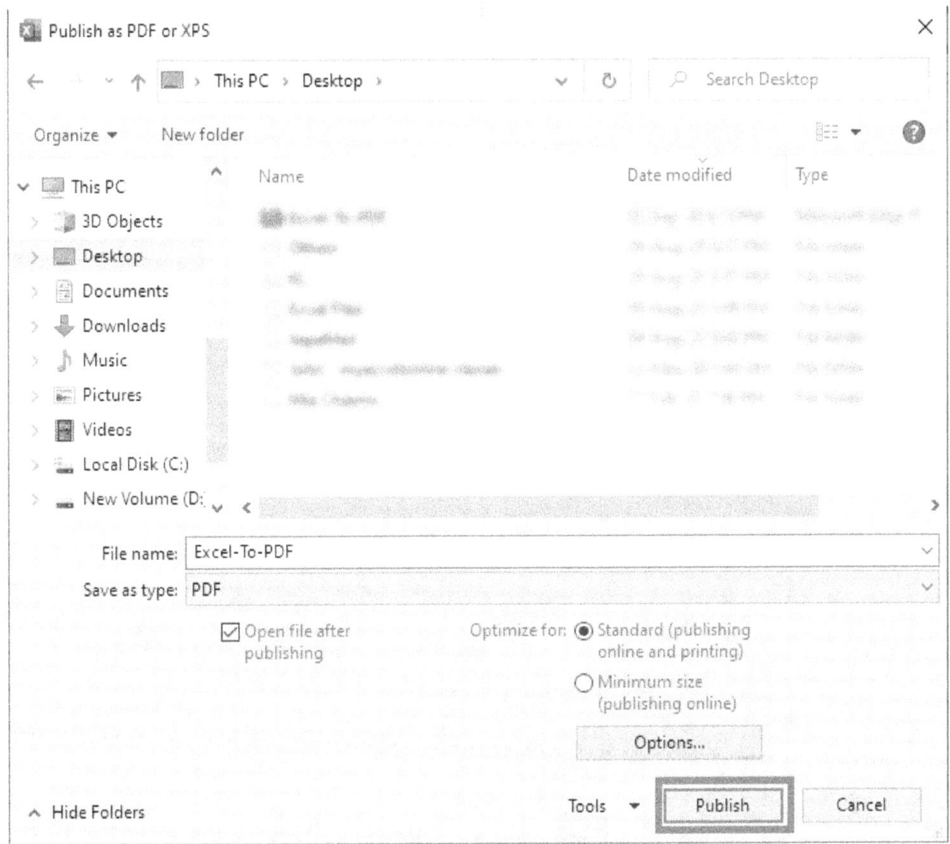

#4: Email PDF using Quick Access Toolbar

If you want to attach an Excel file as PDF in an email, you can add it to the Quick Access Toolbar (QAT).

Follow the steps below to add email PDF inside the QAT:

STEP 1: **Right Click** on the QAT to customize it.

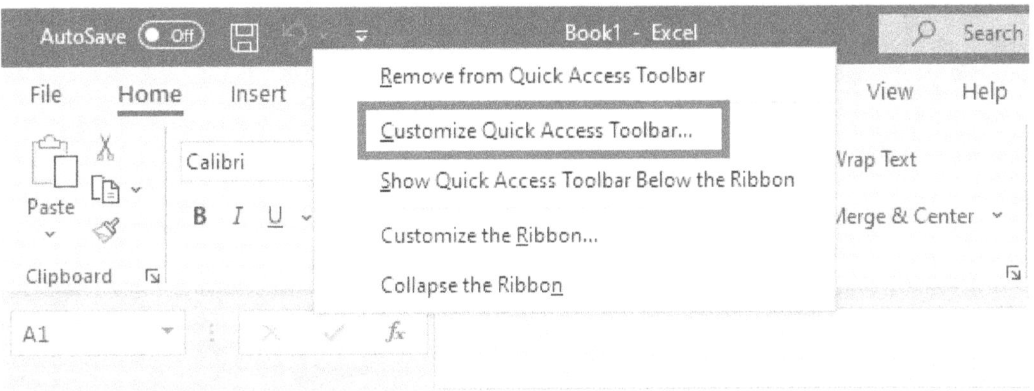

STEP 2: In the Excel Options dialog box, select **Quick Access Toolbar** > **E-mail as PDF Attachment** > **Add**.

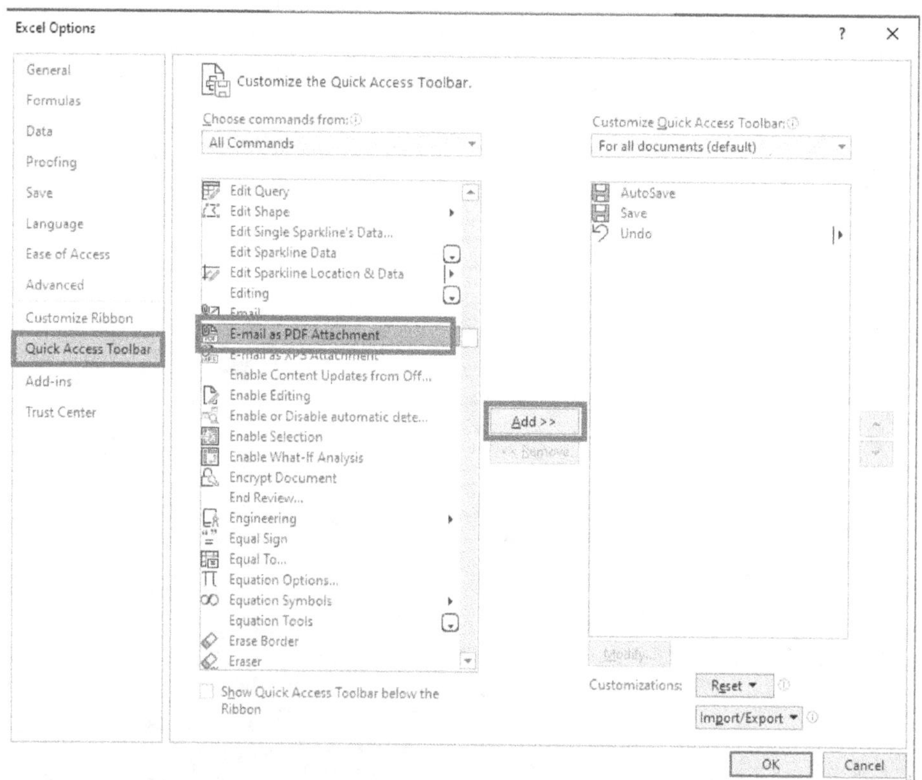

STEP 3: This will add **E-mail as PDF Attachment** under Customize Quick Access Toolbar. Now, **Click OK**.

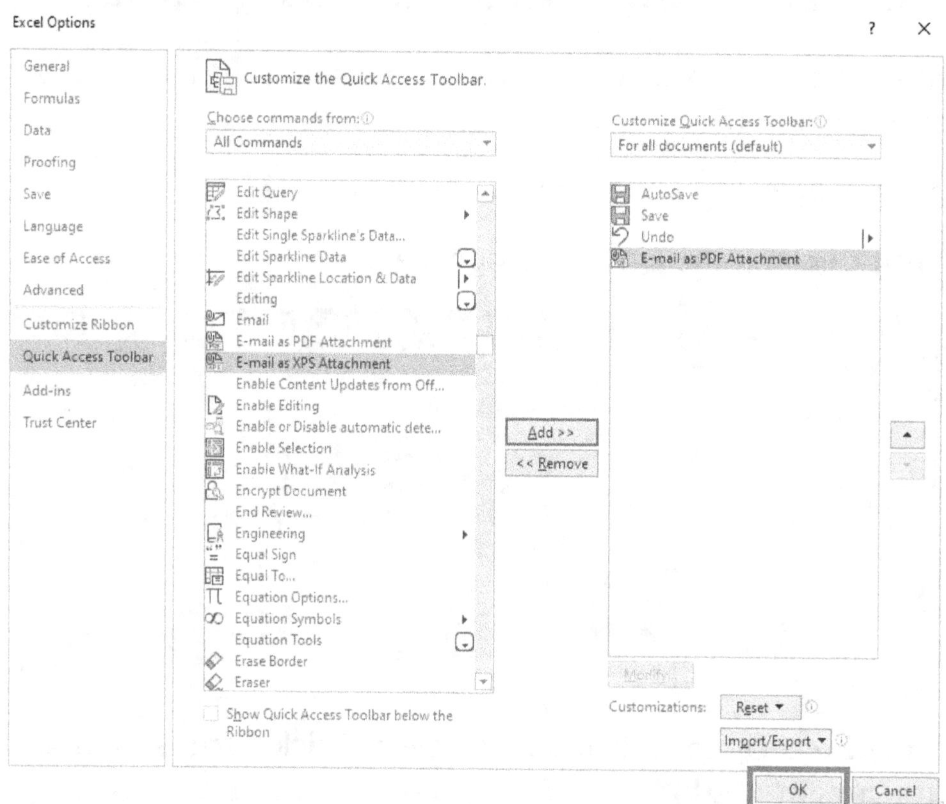

 Click on this newly created icon to send your Excel workbook as a PDF attachment in an email.

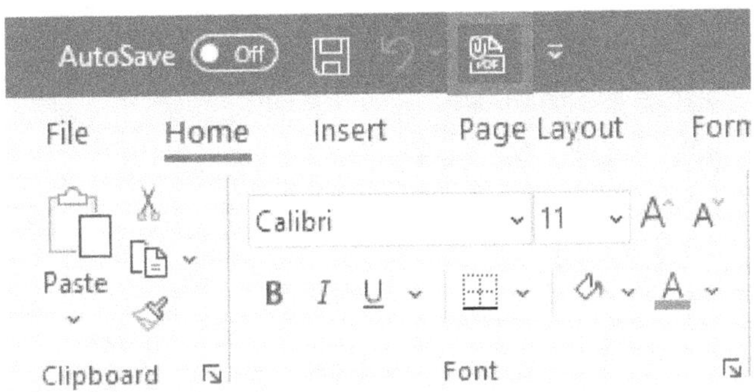

And now you have your pdf inside a new email message.

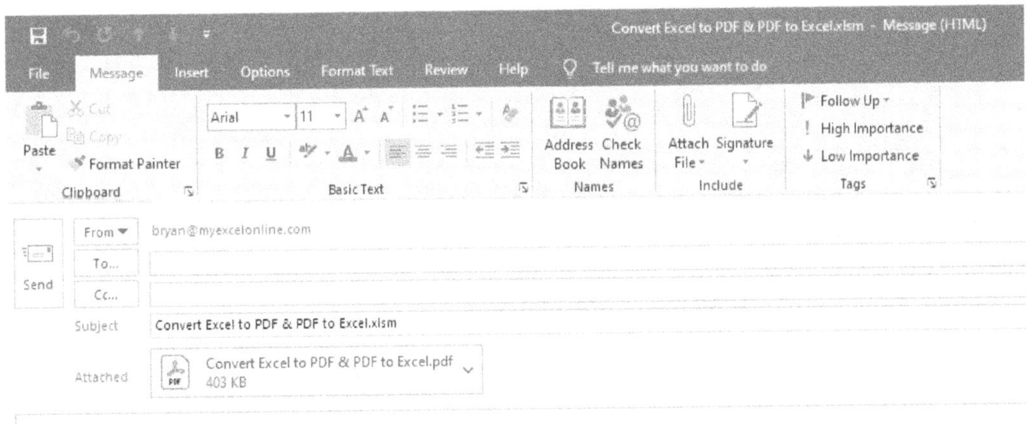

#5: Using VBA Macro

You can also **use VBA code to publish a range in Excel into PDF**. This VBA Macro will prompt you to provide the range you wish to export and then select the location, to automatically export Excel to PDF.

```
Sub PrintSelectionToPDF()
'Declaration of Variables
Dim rng As Range
Dim strFilePath As String
Dim strFile As String
Dim file As Variant

'Check first if a range has been selected
If Selection.Count = 1 Then
Set rng = Application.InputBox("Please select a range", "Get Range", Type:=8)
Else
Set rng = Selection
End If
```

```vba
'Create the filename with the path - the default filename is
ExceltoPdf.pdf
strFile = "ExceltoPdf.pdf"
strFile = ThisWorkbook.Path & "\" & strFile
'We open a save prompt for the username to select the location and
filename
file = Application.GetSaveAsFilename(InitialFileName:=strFile,
FileFilter:="PDF Files (*.pdf), *.pdf", Title:="Select location for
the PDF file")

'Start the export process of the selected range
If file <> "False" Then
rng.ExportAsFixedFormat Type:=xlTypePDF, Filename:=file,
Quality:=xlQualityStandard, IncludeDocProperties:=True,
IgnorePrintAreas:=False, OpenAfterPublish:=False
MsgBox "PDF file has been successfully created: " & strFile
Else
MsgBox "Unable to create PDF file", vbOKOnly, "No File Selected"
End If
End Sub
```

Follow the steps below to use this code to Export selection to PDF:

STEP 1: Press **Alt + F11** to open VBA Editor.

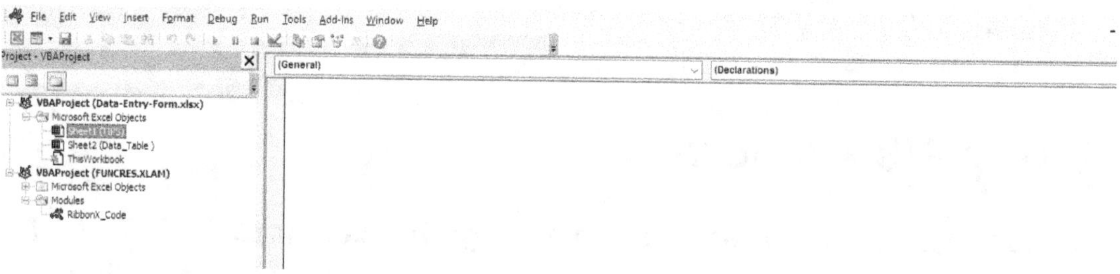

STEP 2: Right Click on the sheet name and then select **Insert > Module**.

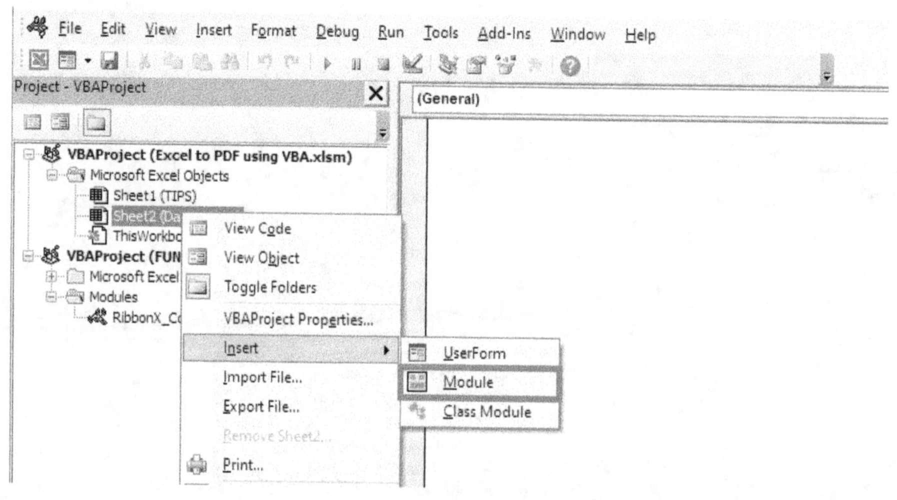

STEP 3: **Copy-paste** the VBA code from above into here.

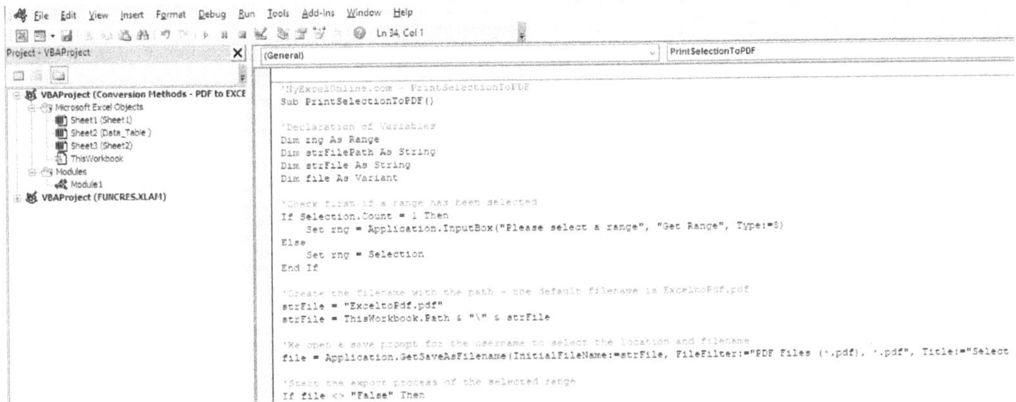

STEP 4: Press **Ctrl + S** to save the file and then click **No**.

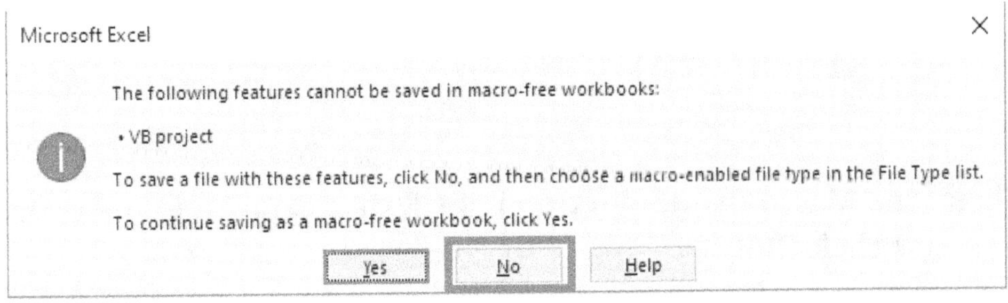

STEP 5: In the Save as dialog box, choose **Excel macro-enabled workbook** from the drop down list and click the **Save** button.

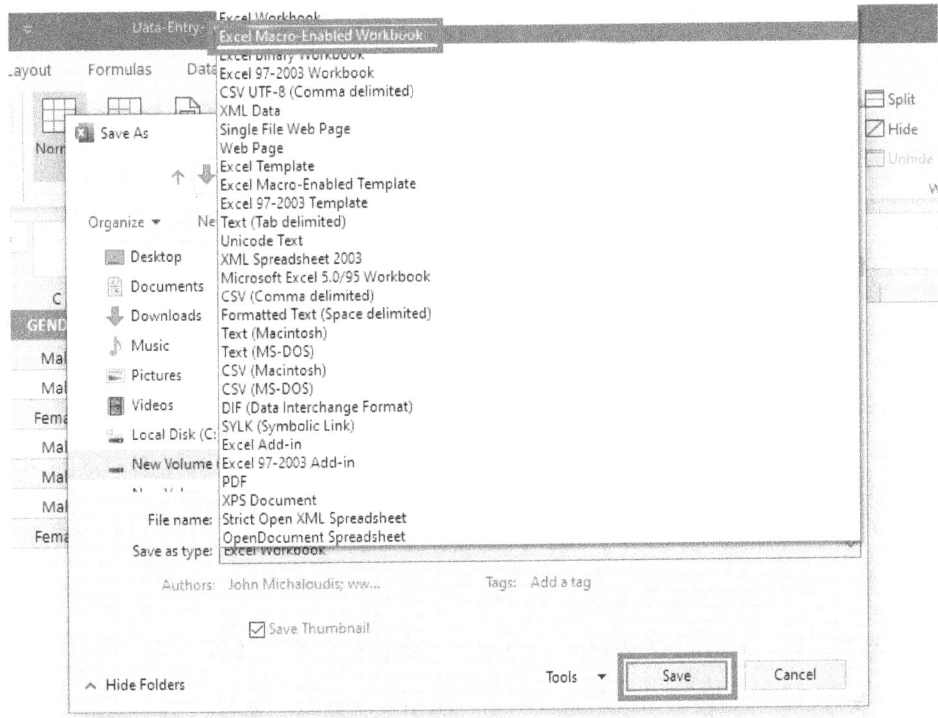

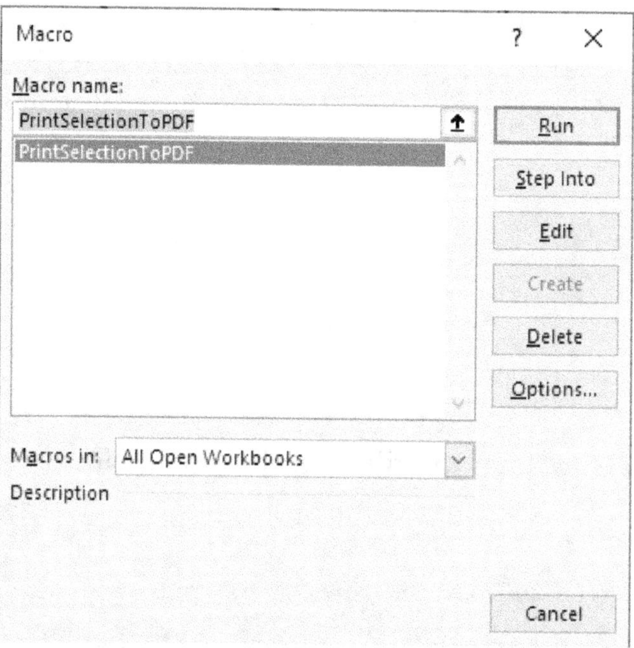

STEP 7: Select the Macro **PrintSelectionToPDF** that is located in **All Open Workbooks** and click **Run**.

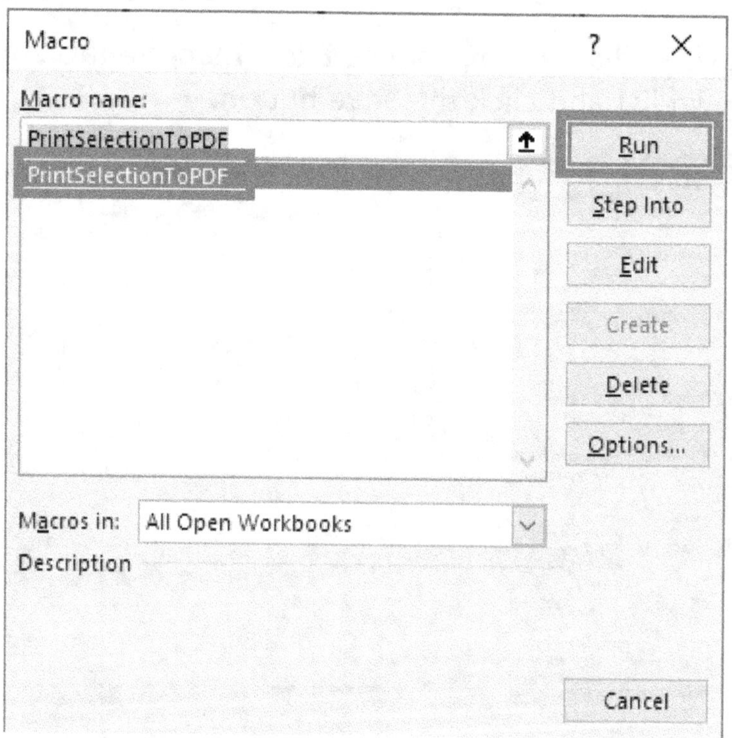

STEP 8: In the dialog box, type the required range **A1: F8.**

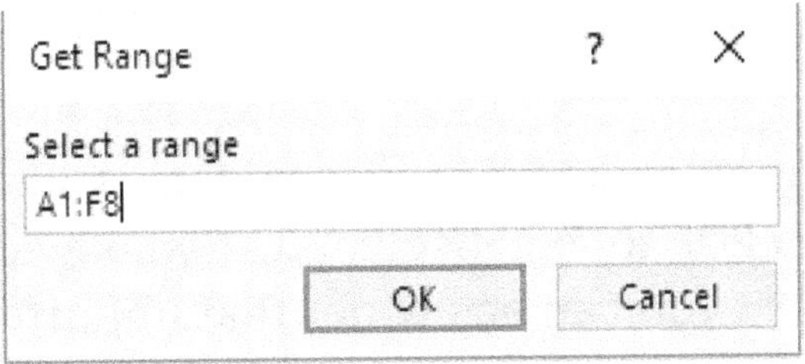

STEP 9: Select the location and press **Save**.

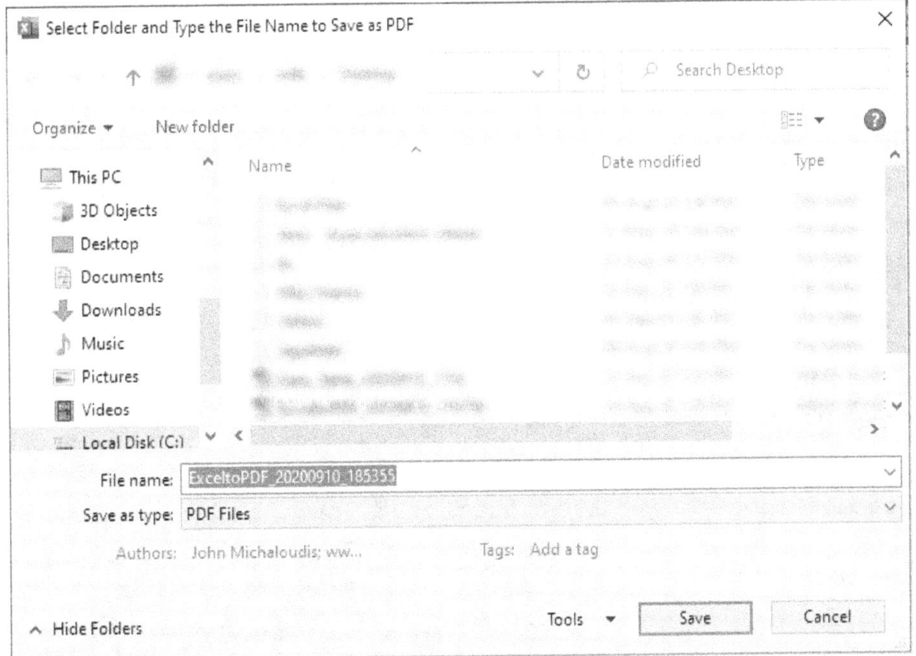

This is how you can convert the range **A1: F8** in excel to PDF.

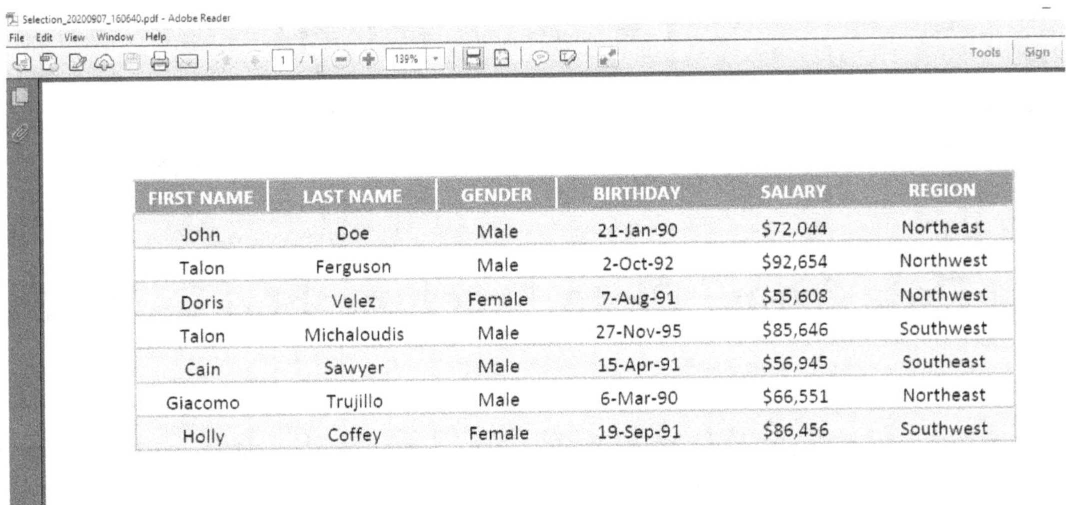

FIRST NAME	LAST NAME	GENDER	BIRTHDAY	SALARY	REGION
John	Doe	Male	21-Jan-90	$72,044	Northeast
Talon	Ferguson	Male	2-Oct-92	$92,654	Northwest
Doris	Velez	Female	7-Aug-91	$55,608	Northwest
Talon	Michaloudis	Male	27-Nov-95	$85,646	Southwest
Cain	Sawyer	Male	15-Apr-91	$56,945	Southeast
Giacomo	Trujillo	Male	6-Mar-90	$66,551	Northeast
Holly	Coffey	Female	19-Sep-91	$86,456	Southwest

Convert PDF to Excel

PDF does not allow users to make edits on the data, so it's useful to learn how to convert the data from PDF to Excel so you can make edits inside Excel. If you have a table saved in PDF, you can easily get that imported into Excel and work on it easily.

	A	B	C	D	E	F
1	ORDER DATE	QUARTER	SALES PERSON	PRODUCTS	SALES	
2	07-01-19	1	Michael Jackson	Soft Drinks	16425	
3	25-01-19	1	Homer Simpson	Bottles	95980	
4	09-03-19	1	John Michaloudis	Soft Drinks	44719	
5	01-04-19	2	John Michaloudis	Tonic	65694	
6	01-04-19	2	Homer Simpson	Tonic	82903	
7	13-04-19	2	Homer Simpson	Soft Drinks	24640	
8	15-04-19	2	Homer Simpson	Tonic	10090	
9	01-06-19	2	John Michaloudis	Ice Cubes	18850	
10	08-06-19	2	John Michaloudis	Tonic	35938	
11	23-06-19	2	Michael Jackson	Tonic	94980	
12	06-07-19	3	Ian Wright	Soft Drinks	14169	
13	27-07-19	3	Michael Jackson	Ice Cubes	66876	
14	04-08-19	3	John Michaloudis	Soft Drinks	62350	
15	17-08-19	3	Homer Simpson	Ice Cubes	30135	
16	23-08-19	3	Ian Wright	Bottles	48278	
17	13-09-19	3	John Michaloudis	Soft Drinks	65422	
18	14-09-19	3	Michael Jackson	Ice Cubes	23979	
19	21-10-19	4	Ian Wright	Soft Drinks	26687	
20	03-11-19	4	Ian Wright	Tonic	68789	
21	28-11-19	4	John Michaloudis	Tonic	87184	
22	02-12-19	4	Michael Jackson	Soft Drinks	71262	

Import Data from PDF to Excel method using Excel 365

In most cases, you will be able to simply copy & paste the data and format it to get the desired result. But if that is not working for you, use the **Import Data method** in Excel.

Follow the steps to import data from PDF to Excel (Excel 365 only):

STEP 1: Go to **Data** Tab > **Get Data** > **From File** > **From PDF**.

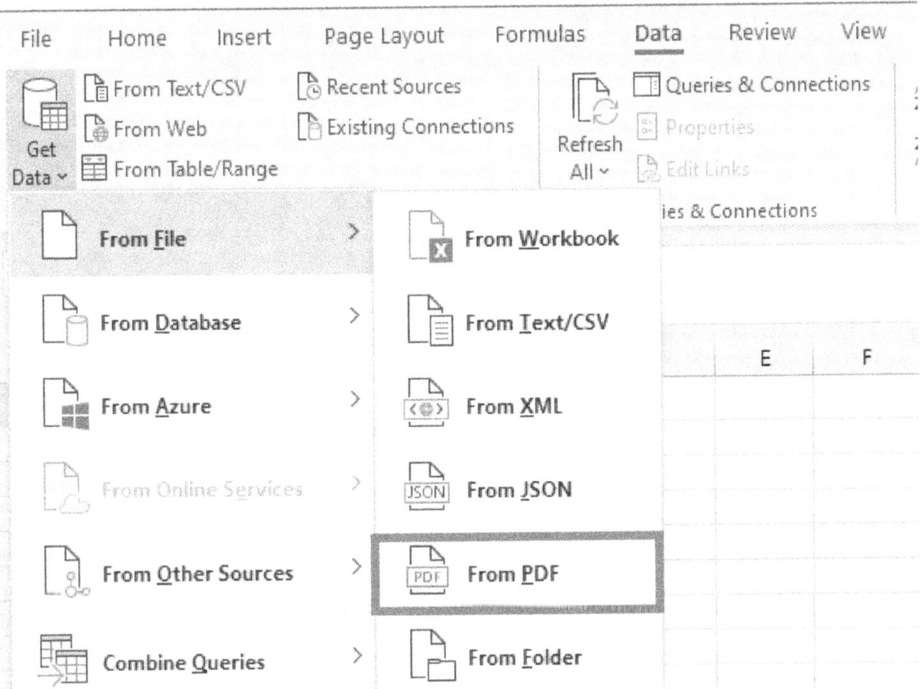

STEP 2: In the **Import Data** dialog box, select the location of the PDF file, and click on **Import**.

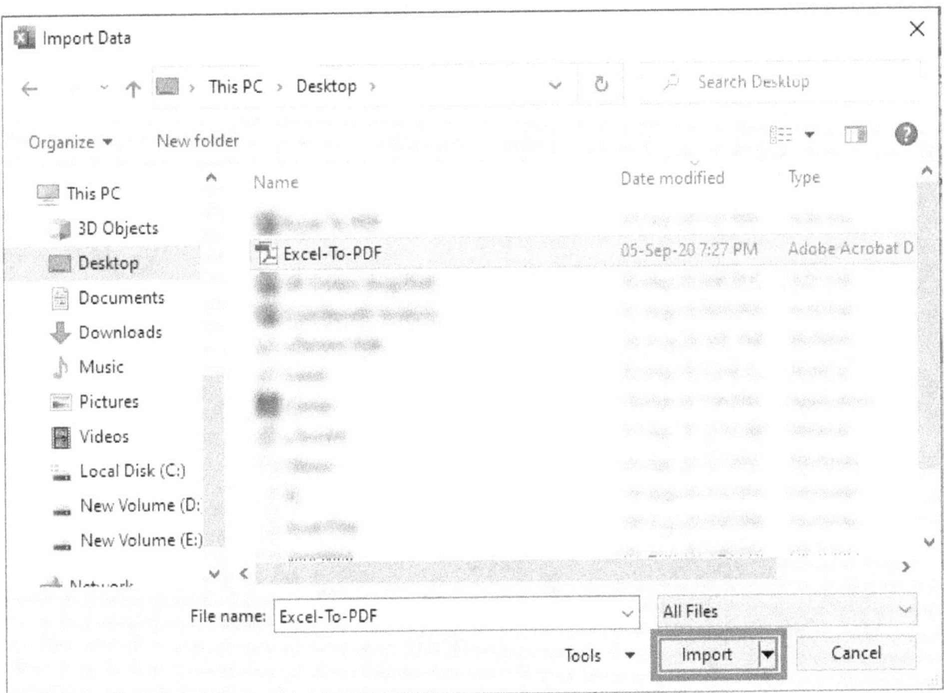

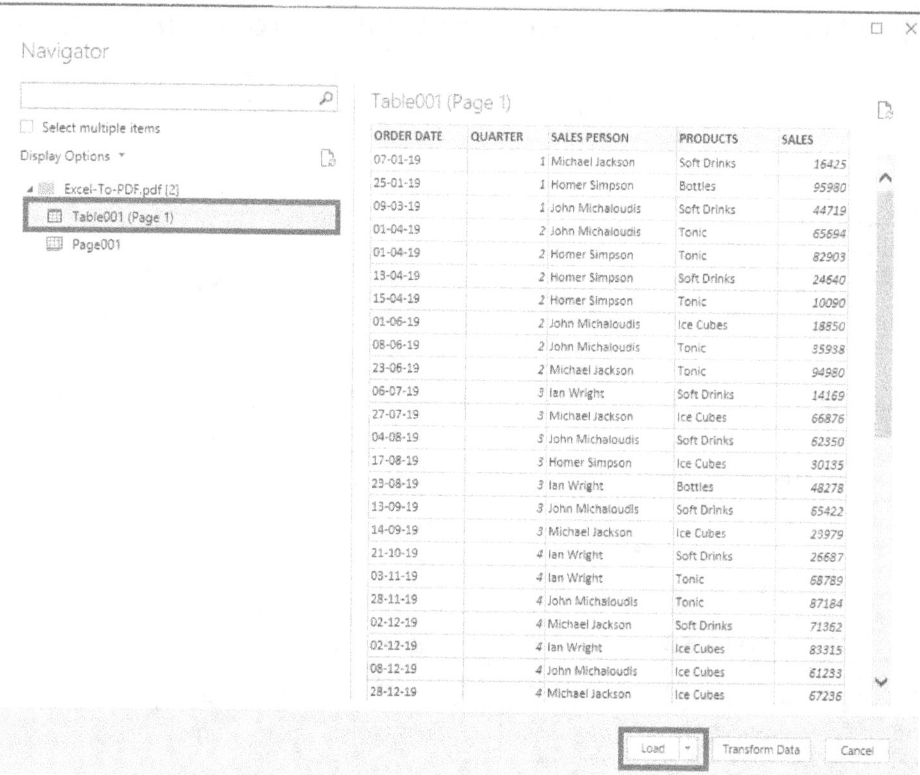

This will convert the table from PDF to Excel!

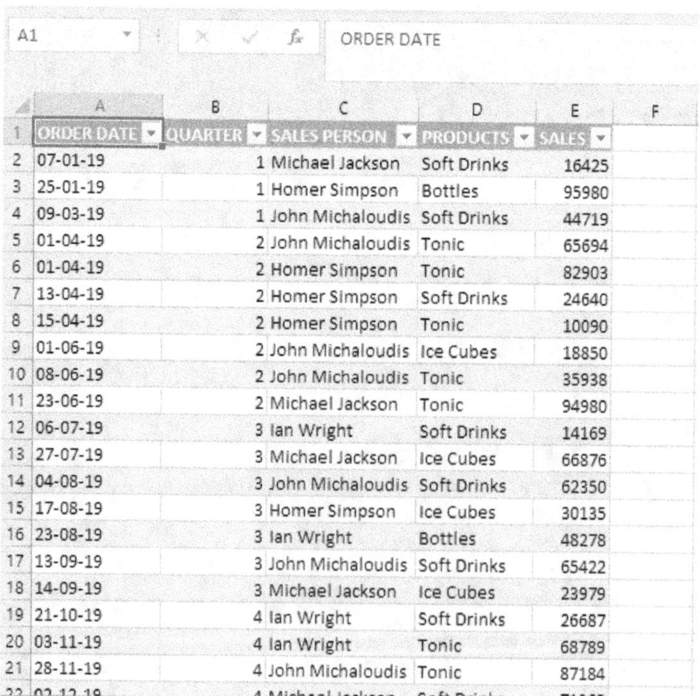

Distribute and Align Shapes in Excel

Imagine you have a lot of shapes in your Excel file and the shapes are all over the place!

You want to organize the shapes but it seems a pain to move them one by one!

What would you do? Thankfully, Excel allows you to **distribute and align shapes**!

STEP 1: Hold the **CTRL** key and select all of the shapes you want to move:

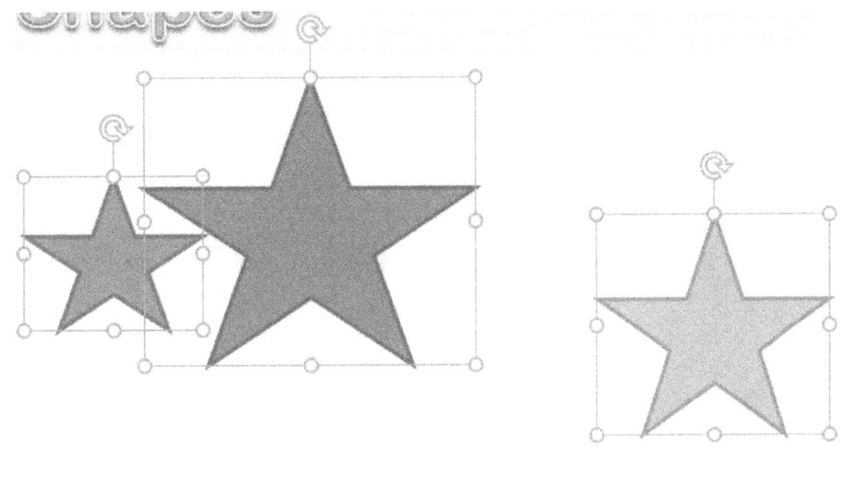

STEP 2: Go to **Format > Arrange > Align > Align Bottom**

You can Align the shapes to the direction that you want (Left, Center, Right, Top, Middle, Bottom)

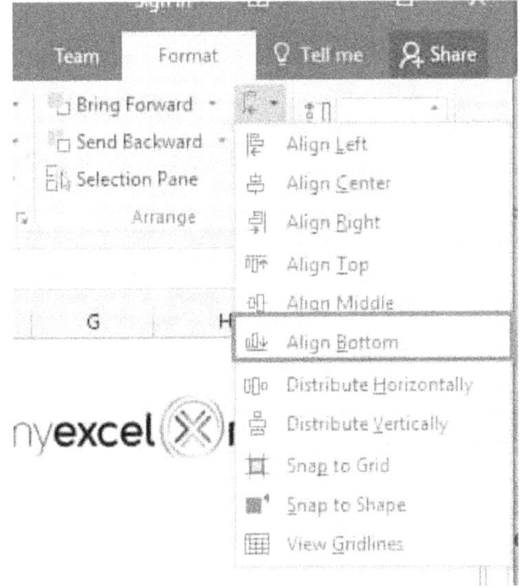

 Go to **Format > Arrange > Align > Distribute Horizontally**

You can Distribute the shapes either Horizontally or Vertically.

This will ensure the distance between the shapes are equally distributed.

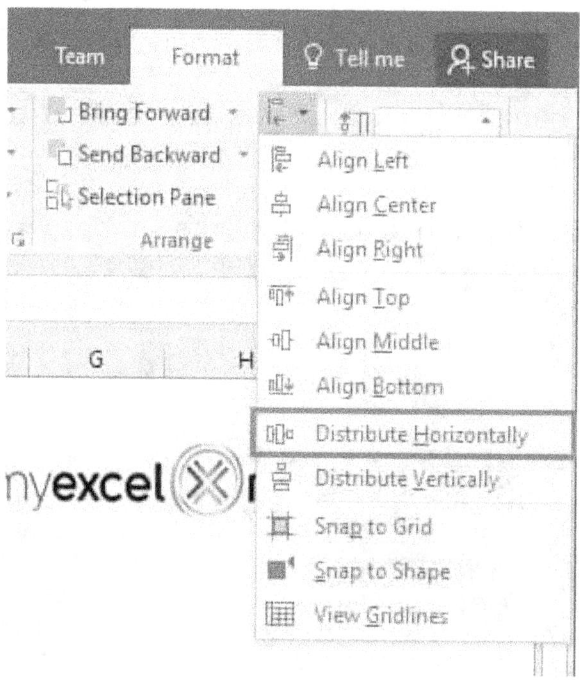

Your shapes are now in good shape! (Pun intended)

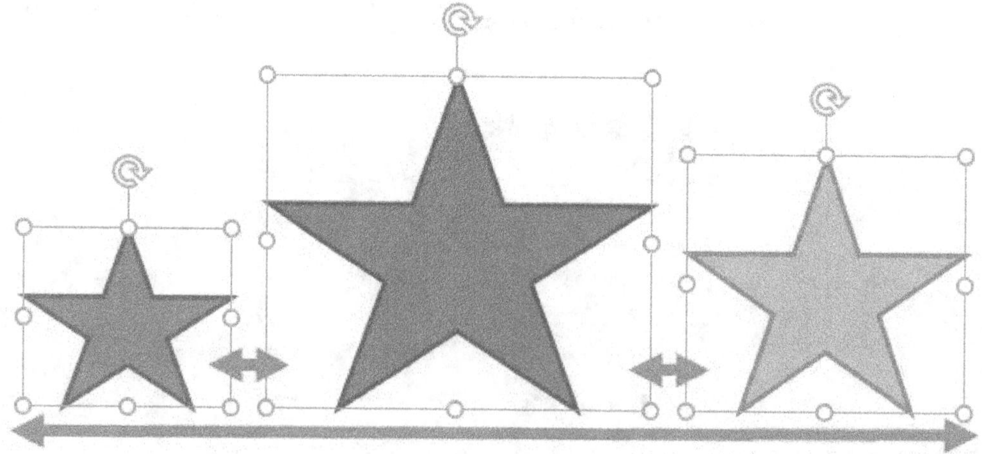

Fill From 1 to 10,000

Ever tried filling down a column with incremental numbers from 1 to 10,000? There are multiple ways to achieve this using formulas, fill handles and so forth.

That could involve a lot of steps. However, Excel has a hidden tip that can do this for you quickly!

STEP 1: Type in your first number.

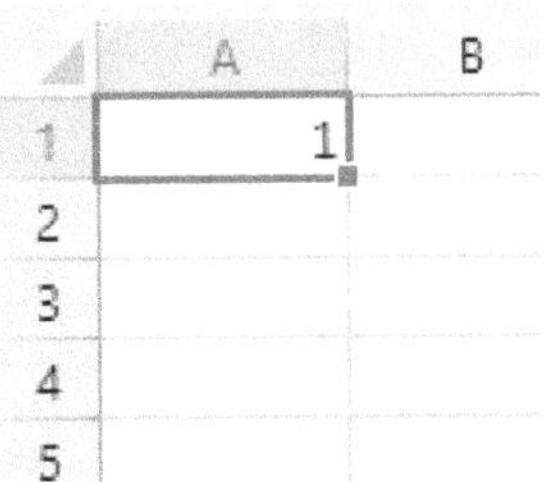

STEP 2: Go to **Home > Editing > Fill > Series**

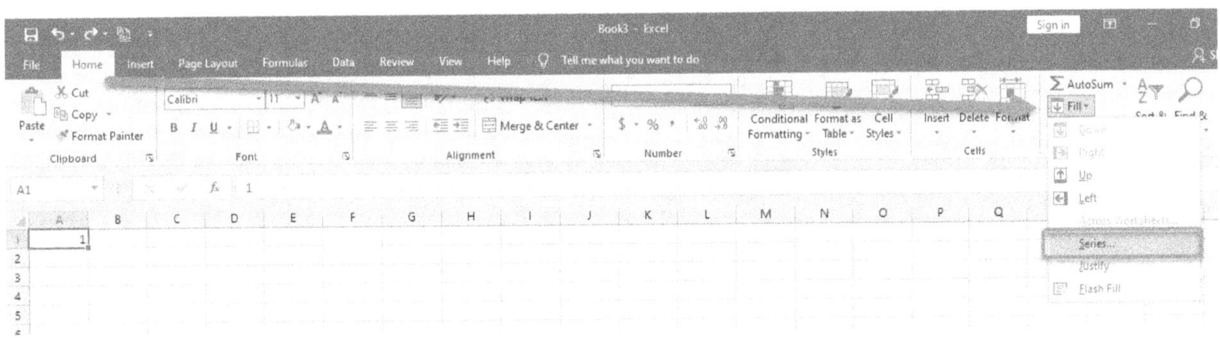

STEP 3: Select **Columns** and set the **Stop Value** to 10000. This will populate your column from 1 to 10,000.

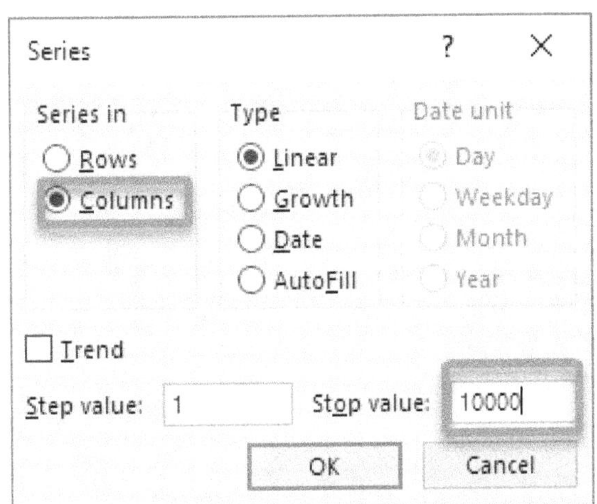

And you have it now in a flash!

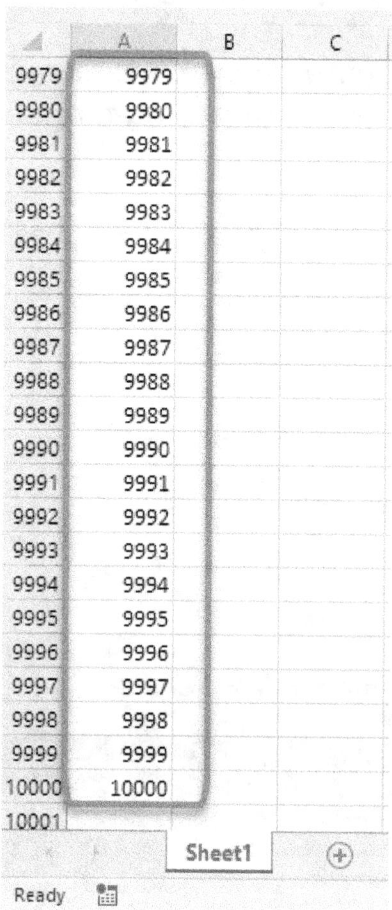

Fill Handle Tips

Excel knows to fill down/right when you are working with dates, days, months, years and even quarters. That is very helpful and quick.

When you fill any values, an *Auto Fill Options* box pops up which you can click and select the different options available.

If you are filling dates, then you have the option to auto fill by Weekdays, Months and Years. How cool is that!

Another trick is if you want to fill down an incremental number, say from 1 to 2,3,4,5,6.....

To do this you need to enter the number 1 in a cell, hold down the **CTRL** key and then fill down that cell which will increment the numbers.

Try these tricks for yourself by practicing below:

STEP 1: **Drag down on the lower right corner** to populate the dates.

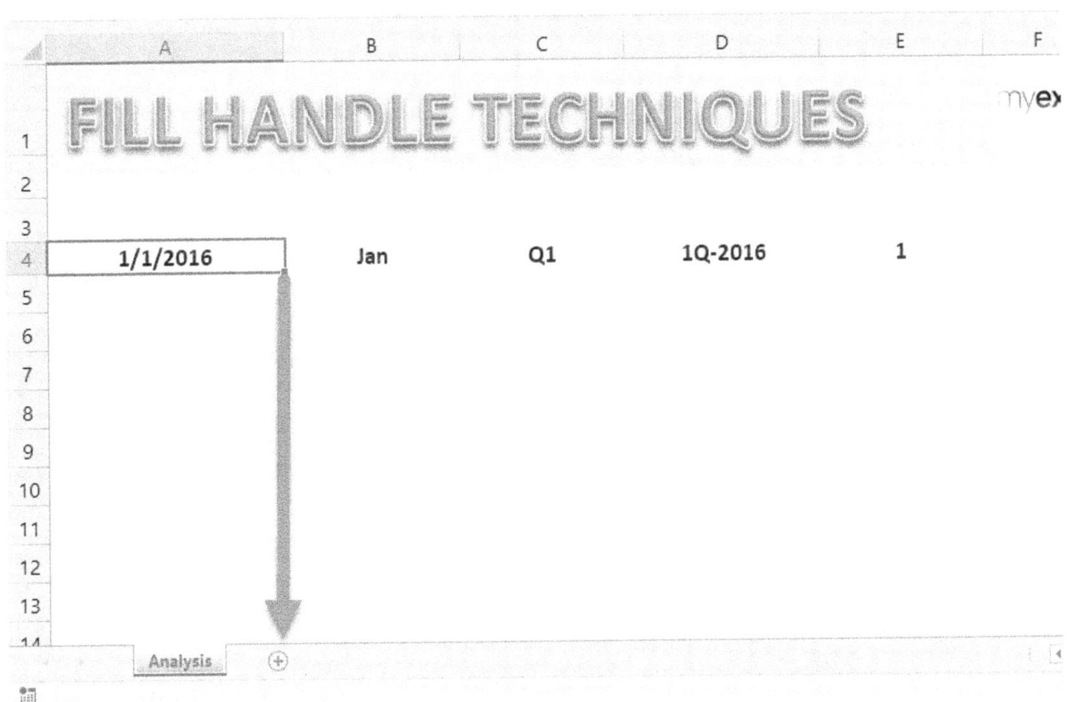

Now we have the dates in incremental order populated!

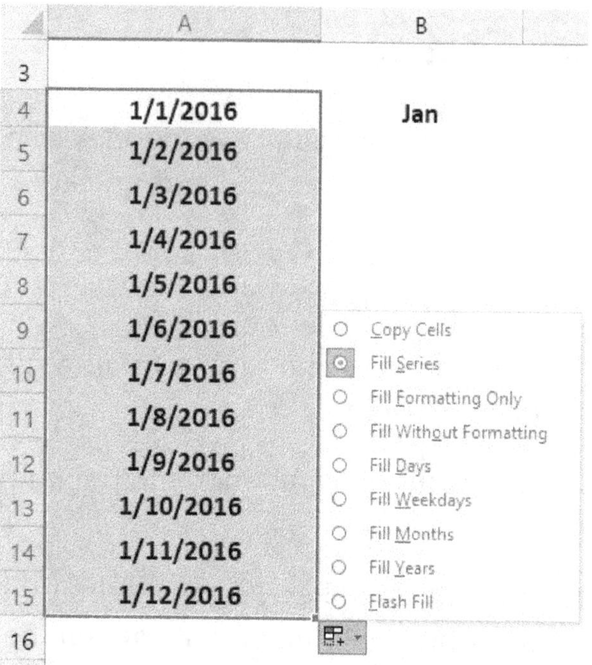

Click on the **Auto Fill Options** to try out different options. Select *Fill Weekdays* and see how the weekdays get populated.

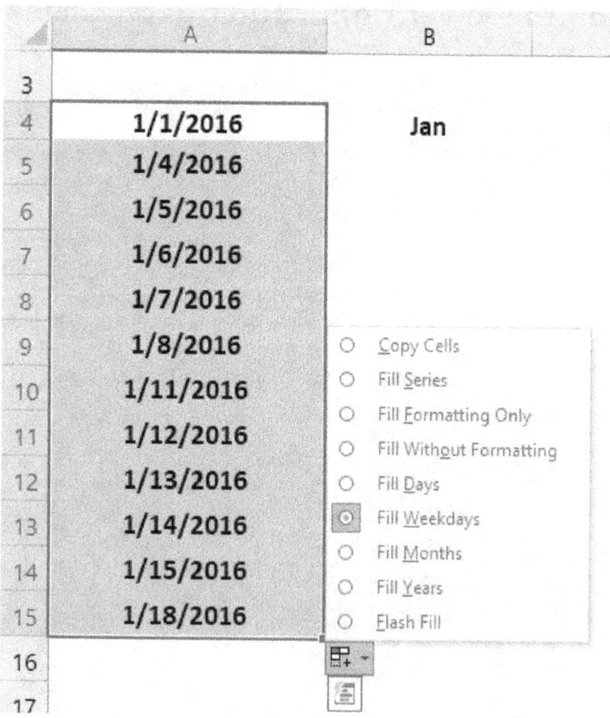

Now select *Fill Months* and see every month getting populated.

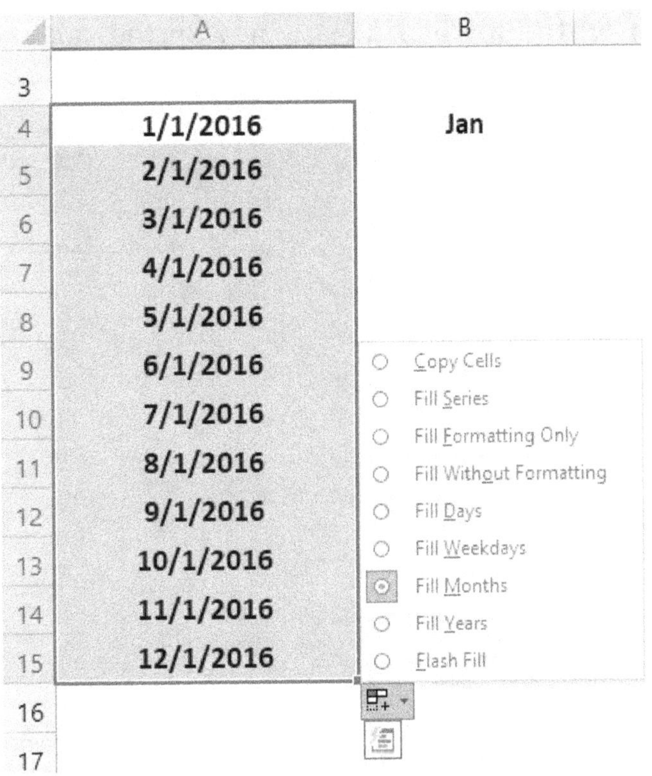

Now select *Fill Years* and see every year getting populated.

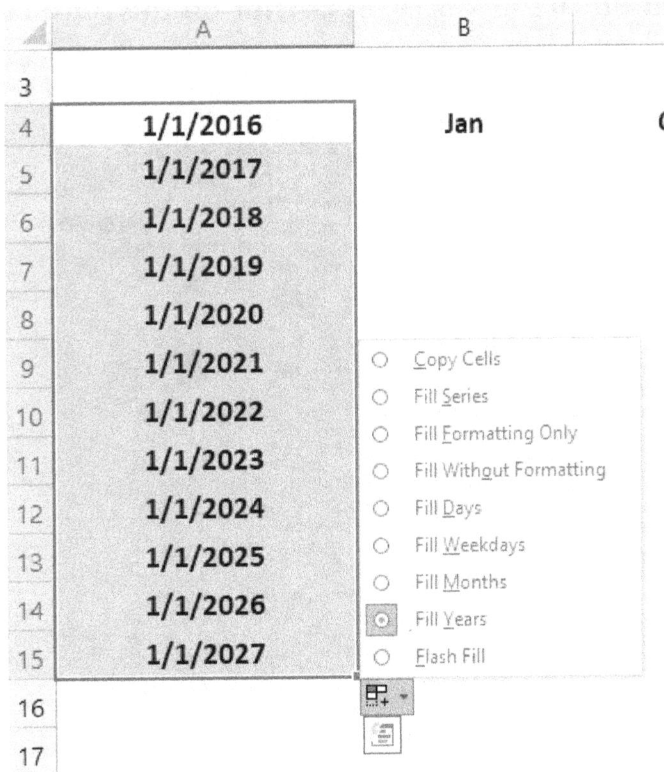

STEP 2: **Drag down on the lower right corner** on the second column to populate the months.

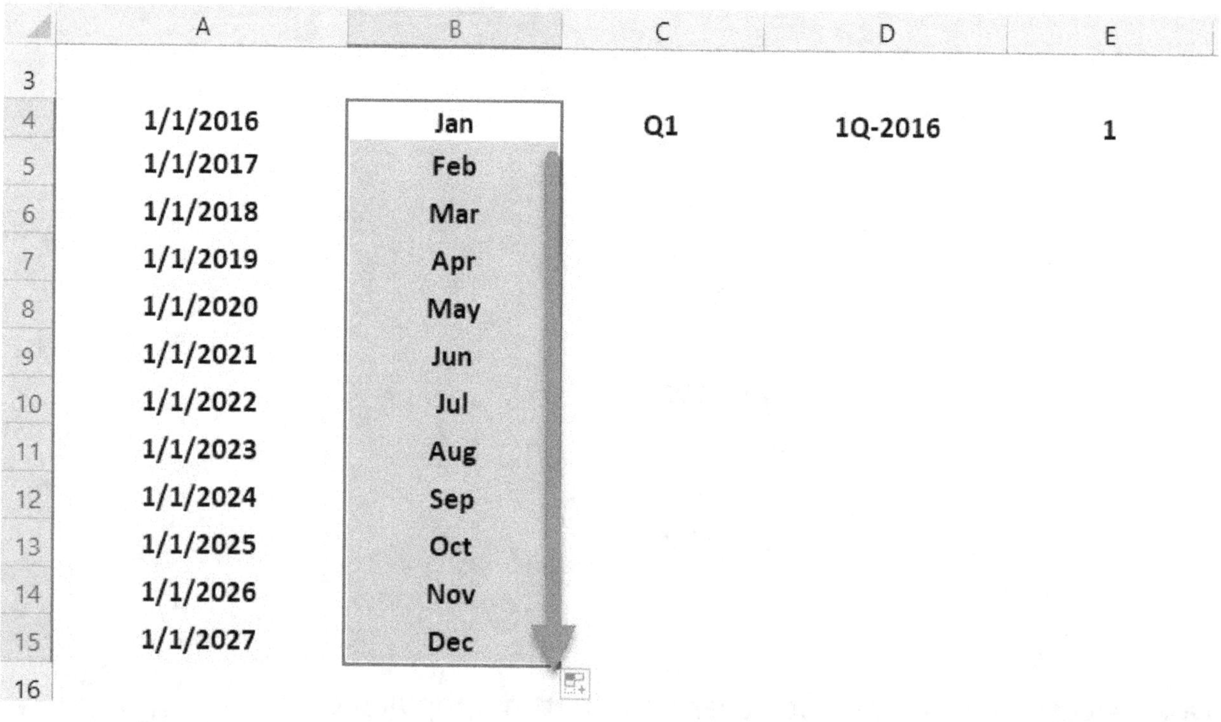

STEP 3: **Drag down on the lower right corner** on the third column to populate the quarters.

 Drag down on the lower right corner on the fourth column to populate the quarters with years.

	A	B	C	D	E
3					
4	1/1/2016	Jan	Q1	1Q-2016	1
5	1/1/2017	Feb	Q2	2Q-2016	
6	1/1/2018	Mar	Q3	3Q-2016	
7	1/1/2019	Apr	Q4	4Q-2016	
8	1/1/2020	May		1Q-2017	
9	1/1/2021	Jun		2Q-2017	
10	1/1/2022	Jul		3Q-2017	
11	1/1/2023	Aug		4Q-2017	
12	1/1/2024	Sep		1Q-2018	
13	1/1/2025	Oct		2Q-2018	
14	1/1/2026	Nov		3Q-2018	
15	1/1/2027	Dec		4Q-2018	
16					
17					

STEP 5: **Hold the CTRL key and drag down on the lower right corner** on the last column to populate the number incrementally.

	A	B	C	D	E	F
3						
4	1/1/2016	Jan	Q1	1Q-2016	1	
5	1/1/2017	Feb	Q2	2Q-2016	2	
6	1/1/2018	Mar	Q3	3Q-2016	3	
7	1/1/2019	Apr	Q4	4Q-2016	4	
8	1/1/2020	May		1Q-2017	5	
9	1/1/2021	Jun		2Q-2017	6	
10	1/1/2022	Jul		3Q-2017	7	
11	1/1/2023	Aug		4Q-2017	8	
12	1/1/2024	Sep		1Q-2018	9	
13	1/1/2025	Oct		2Q-2018	10	
14	1/1/2026	Nov		3Q-2018	11	
15	1/1/2027	Dec		4Q-2018	12	
16						
17						

Insert a Watermark

Ever wanted to insert watermark in Excel? You could show this to mark that your workbook is in draft mode with the word DRAFT behind it, or add your logo in the background so as to make your workbook stand out in a professional way.

But Excel does not have this functionality ready for you, so what now?

I will show you how to insert watermark in Excel Workbooks with this quick workaround!

Here is our starting workbook:

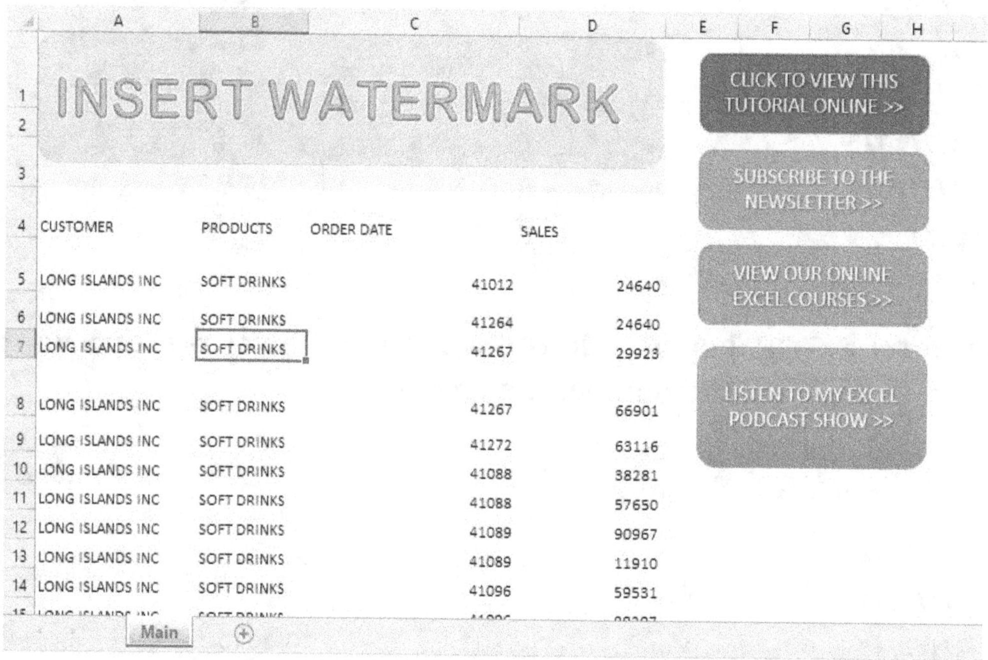

STEP 1: Go to *Insert > Text > Header & Footer*

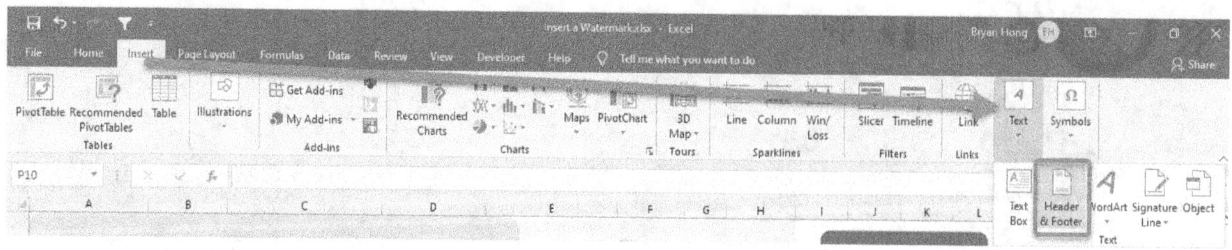

STEP 2: You will see that the header has been added. Go to *Header & Footer Tools > Design > Picture*

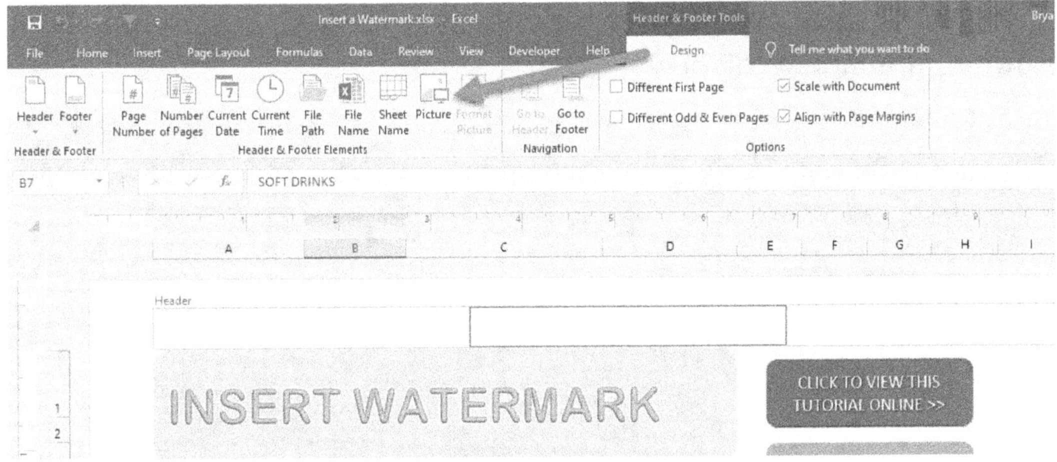

STEP 3: Select **Browse** if you want to insert a picture that you already have

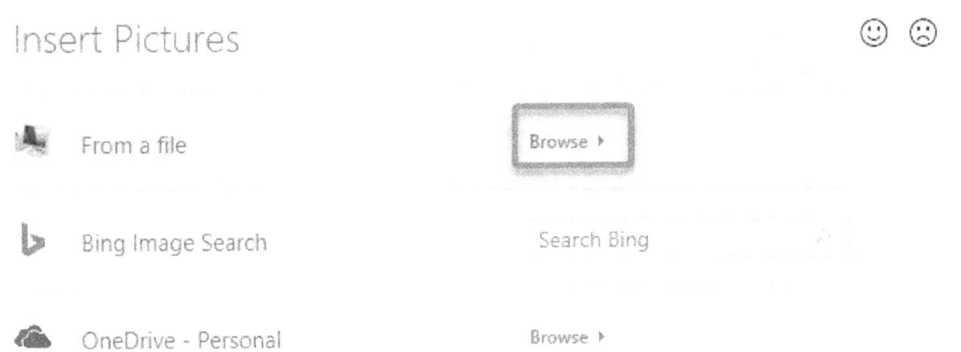

STEP 4: Select the image that you want to use as a watermark. Click **Insert**

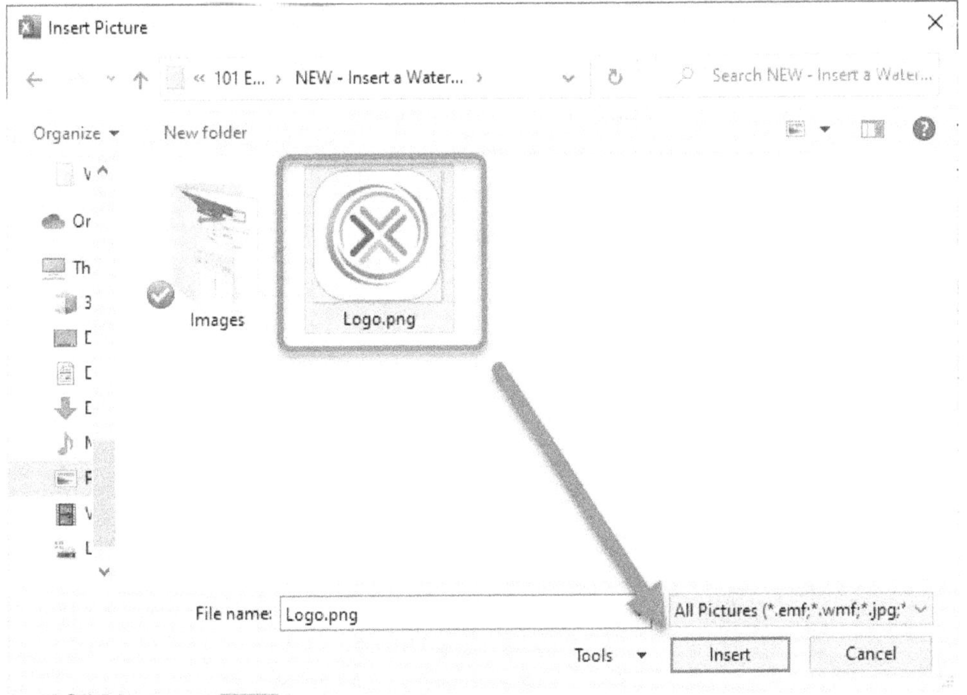

You can see **&[Picture]** displayed in your header. Click anywhere outside the header for your image to display

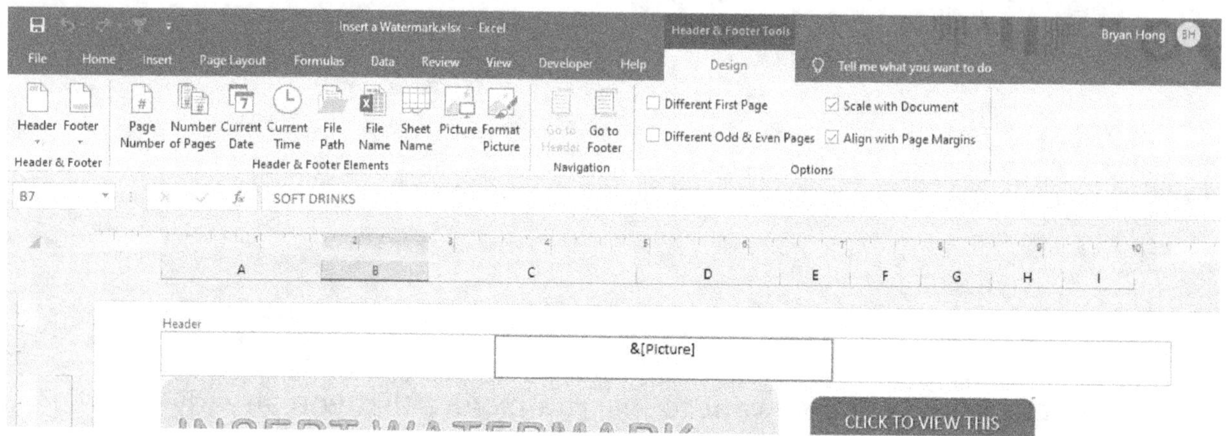

STEP 5: Let us make some tweaks to our watermark. Go to ***Header & Footer Tools > Design > Format Picture***

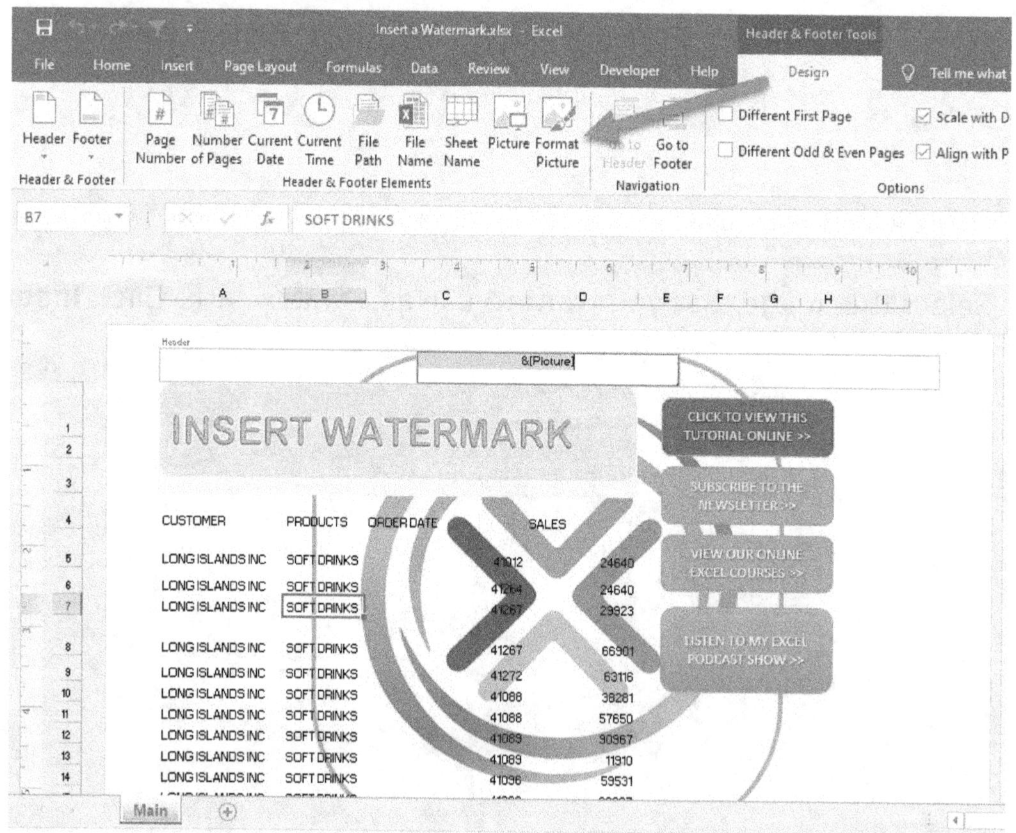

Go to ***Picture > Color*** and select **Washout**. You can make additional changes. Click **OK**

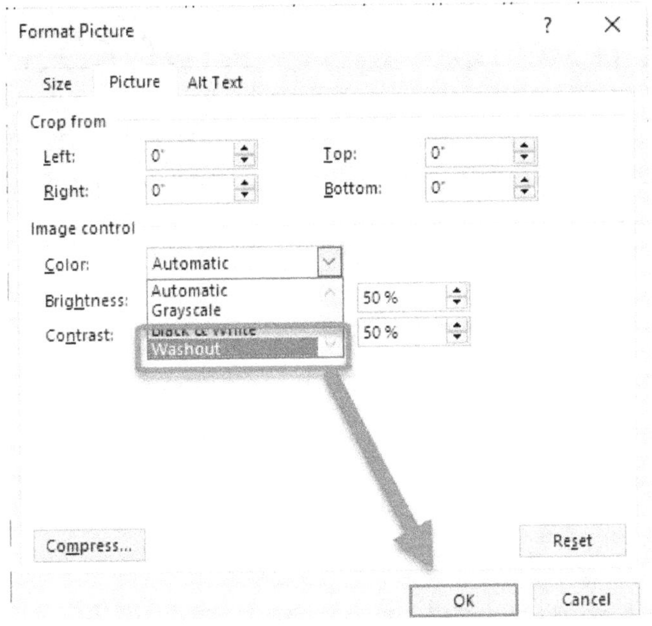

Now you have your watermark ready!

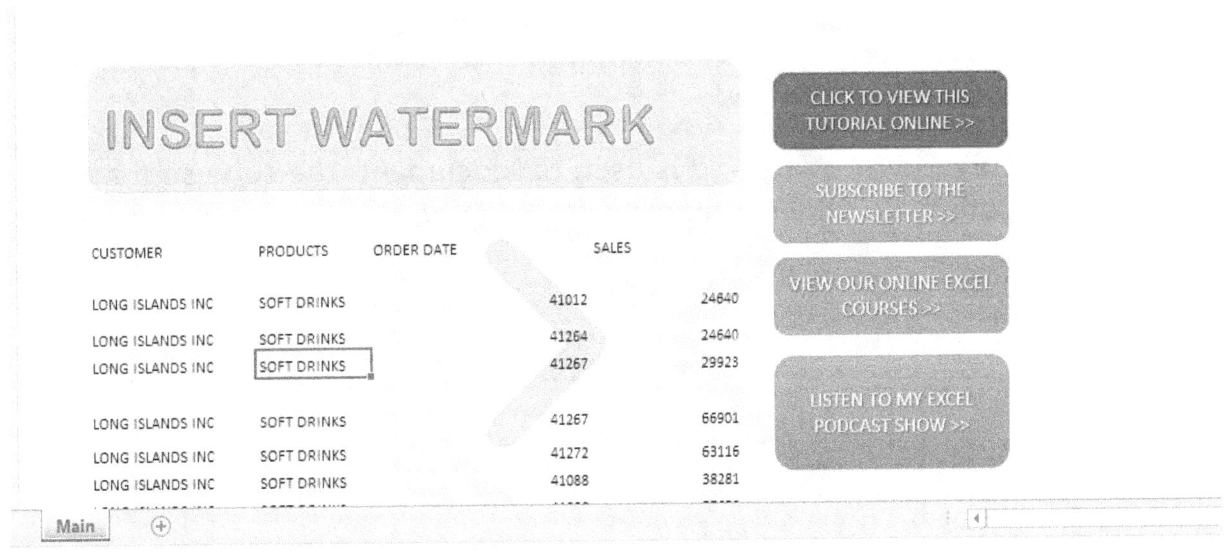

Macros: How to Use Macros

If this is your first time using a Macro, read the introductory section here so that you will be more comfortable with the various Macro lingo.

Here are a few of the most common Macro concepts:

Variables:

We use variables a lot in our code. Variables are containers of your data that is represented by a name you specify. In other words, they are a great way to store and manipulate data.

Loops:

Looping is one of the most crucial programming techniques. It allows us to repetitively do something with just a few lines of code.

Code Comments:

Any line that is **preceded by an apostrophe '** - turns into a green line of code in the Visual Basic Editor window.

This line is ignored in the code and is used to "document" the code so that it is easier for you/others to understand what the code does.

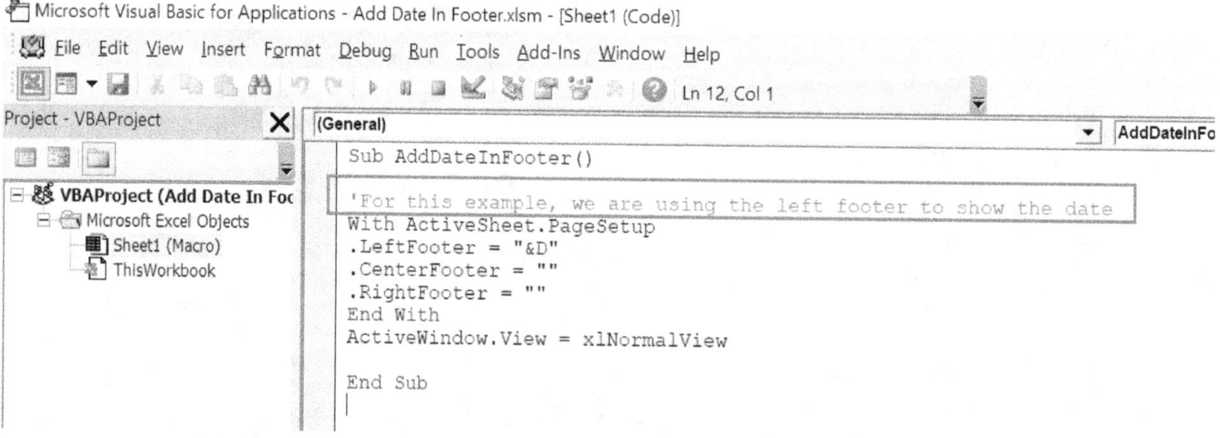

Backup your files!

Before using any of the Macros in your Excel files, a best practice is to back up the Excel file first. This is to provide a safety net if data gets modified in a different way than you expect. You can safely test the Macro this way with your current data and load the previous file if unintended changes take place.

- **Code** – this is the VBA text

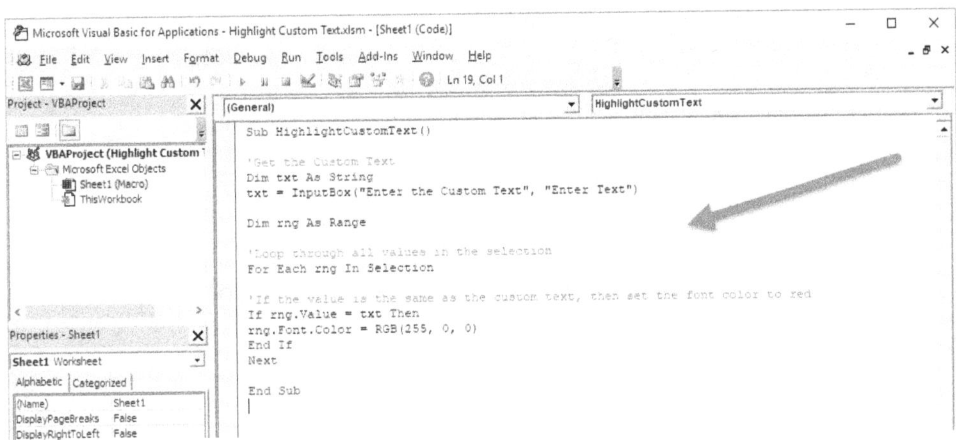

- **Visual Basic Editor** – this is the window where we write/paste our VBA code in. You can get to this window by going to ***Developer > Code > Visual Basic*** or shortcut ***ALT+F11***

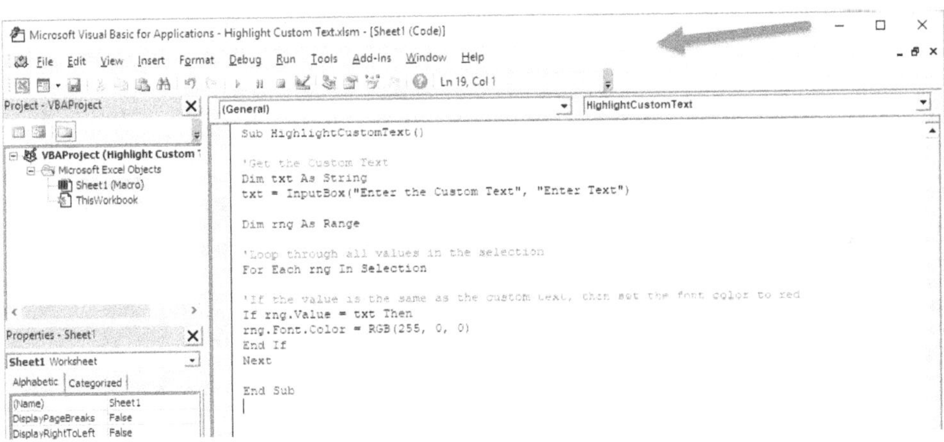

- **Procedures** – these are also called Macros and serve as the containers of our code. Notice that there are no spaces in the procedure name: ***AddDateInFooter()***

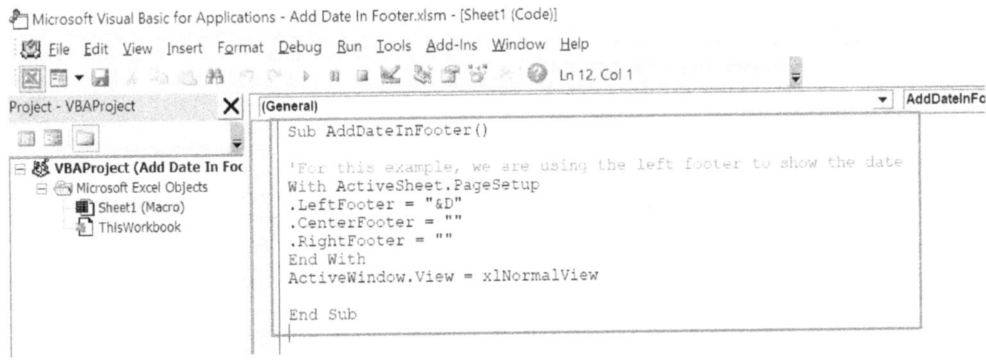

- **Modules** – these are containers of the Procedures

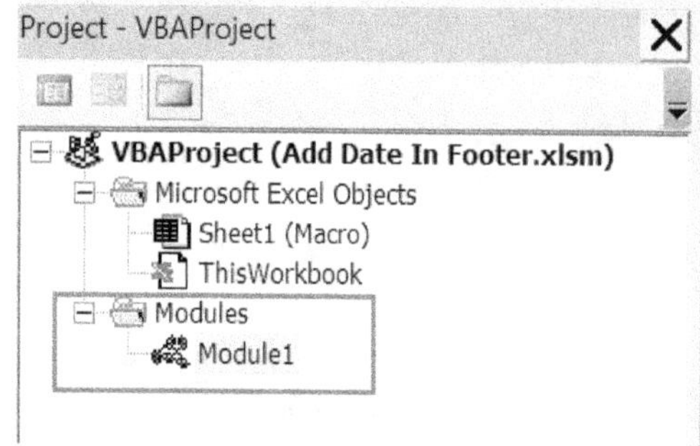

Project – this is a container of Modules. A single Excel workbook is a project of VBA code

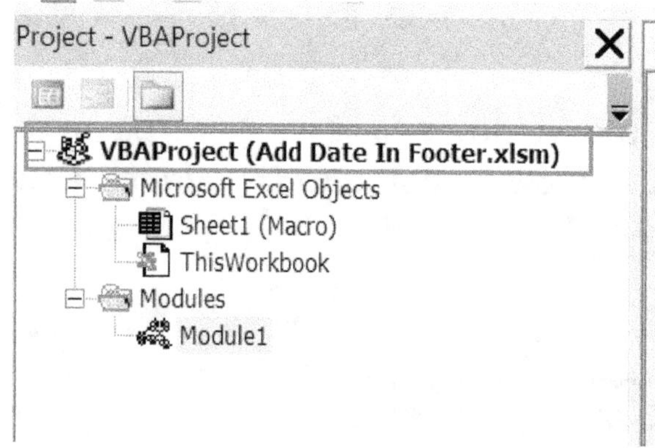

Here is a list of common keywords you will see in Macros. You can always refer back to this list as you go through the examples in the book:

Keyword	Definition
as	Used when defining the data type of a variable
dim	Used for declaring variables
each	Combined with the For keyword (e.g. "for each…") to access the individual components in a collection
else	Combined with the then keyword for alternate scenarios
end	Used to end a procedure
exit	Used to leave a procedure prior to the end statement
for	Used to iterate one or more actions a specific number of times
function	Defines a block of code that can return a value
if	Used for specifying conditions
integer	Used to define a number between -32,768 and 32,767
is	Compares two object references
long	Used to define a number between -2,147,483,648 and 2,147,486,647
next	Used with the For keyword to create set of repetitive instructions
on error	Used to capture and handle errors properly
resume	Used with the On Error keyword to handle errors properly

string	Used to define text variables
sub	Defines a block of code that does not return a value
then	Combined with the If keyword for alternate scenarios
to	Used with the For keyword when repeating
with	Used to perform multiple operations on a single object

Running a Macro

Running a Macro is very straightforward:

Go to **_Developer > Code > Macros_**

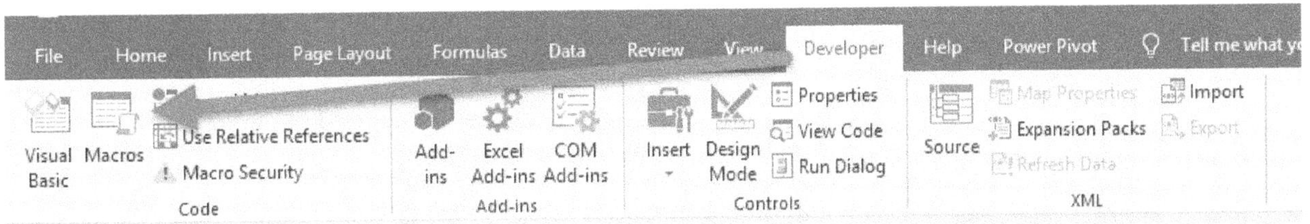

Macros can be located in:

- This Workbook; or
- All Open Workbooks

Make sure your Macro name is selected from the list.

Click **Run**.

Then your code will execute from there.

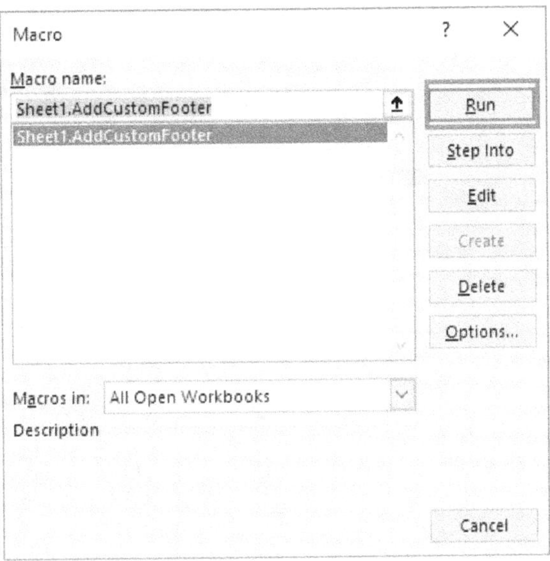

Using the Quick Access Toolbar to run a Macro

If you use a specific Macro frequently, then it is a good idea to add it to the *Quick Access Toolbar* in Excel for easy access.

Go to ***Customize Quick Access Toolbar Dropdown > More Commands***

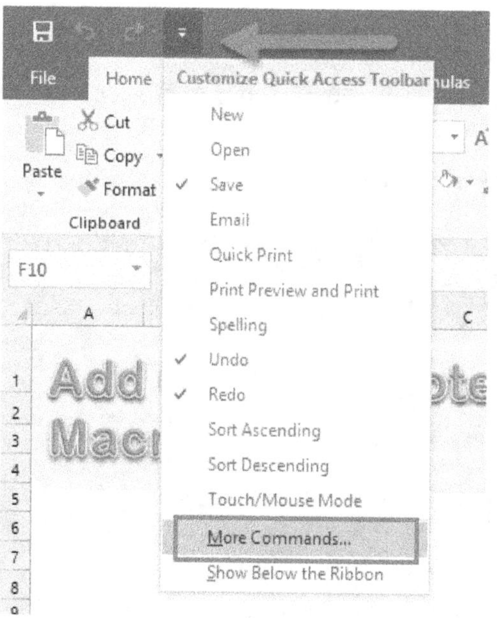

Under the ***Choose commands from*** drop down, make sure to select ***Macros.***

Pick your Macro and click ***Add.***

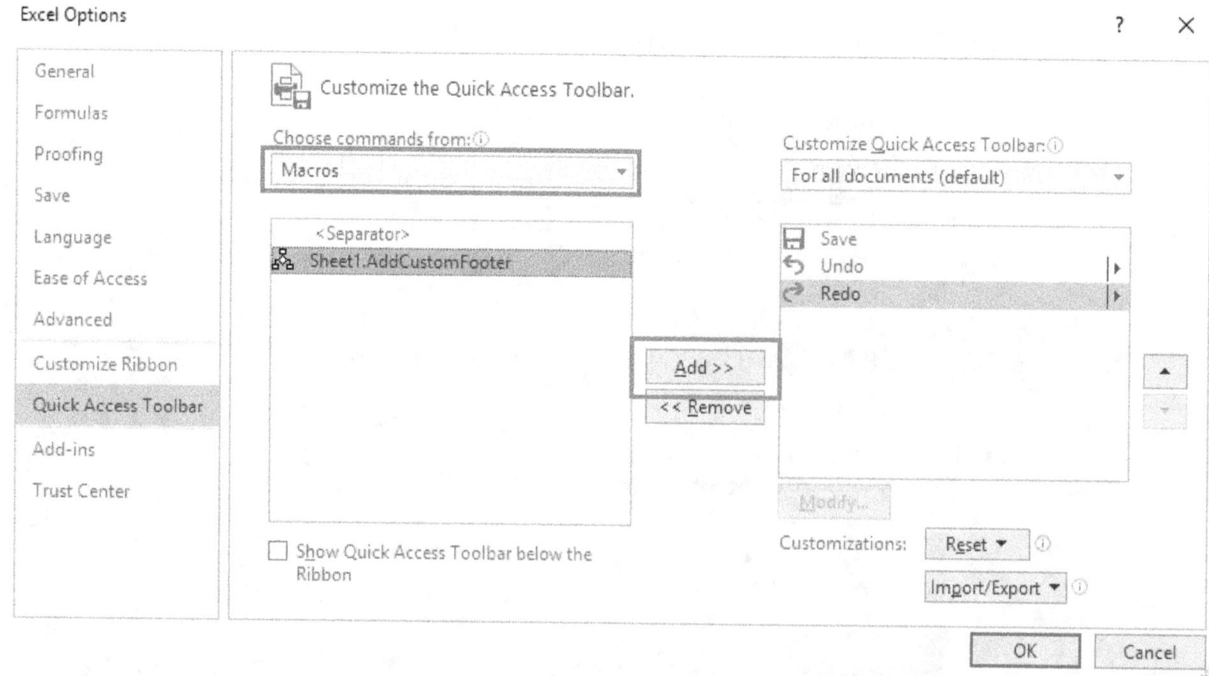

Your Macro should now be added to the Toolbar. Click **OK.**

Click on the Macro icon that is now located on the top or bottom of your Ribbon and it will now run this Macro!

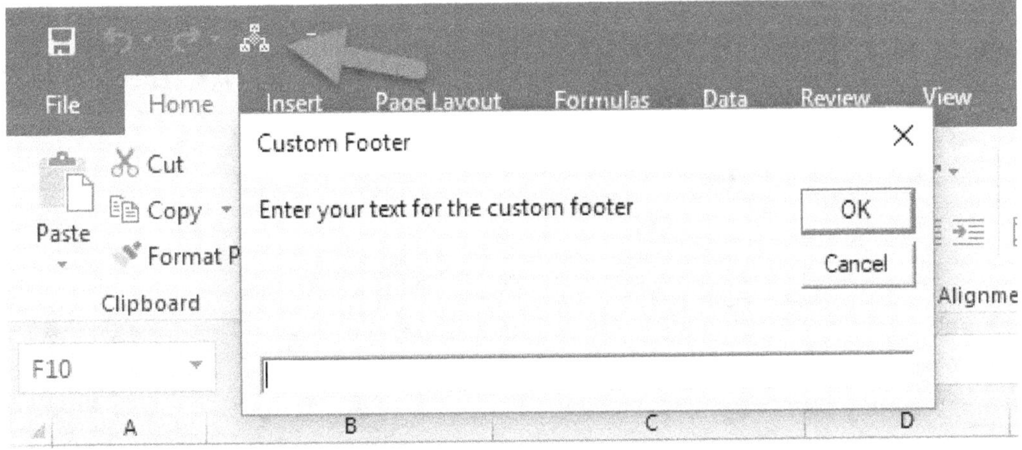

Macros: Enabling VBA in Excel

Most Excel workbooks do not have the ***Developer*** tab activated.

This is needed in order to execute & create Macros. We can easily enable it in a few steps! Make sure you have Excel open...

STEP 1: Right click anywhere on your Ribbon and select ***Customize the Ribbon***:

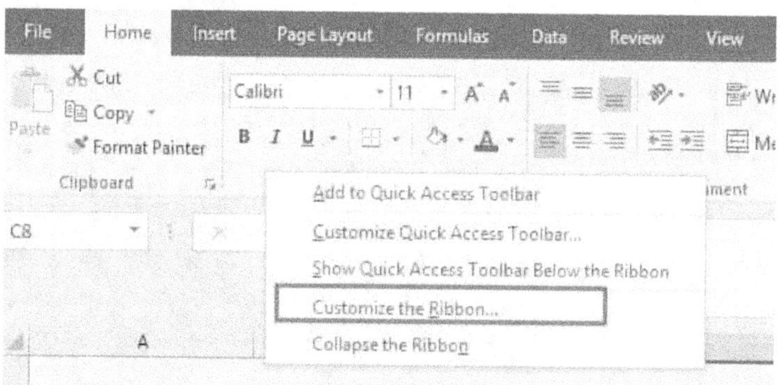

STEP 2: Make sure the **Customize Ribbon** is selected. Then select the **Developer** option under **Main Tabs**. Click **OK**.

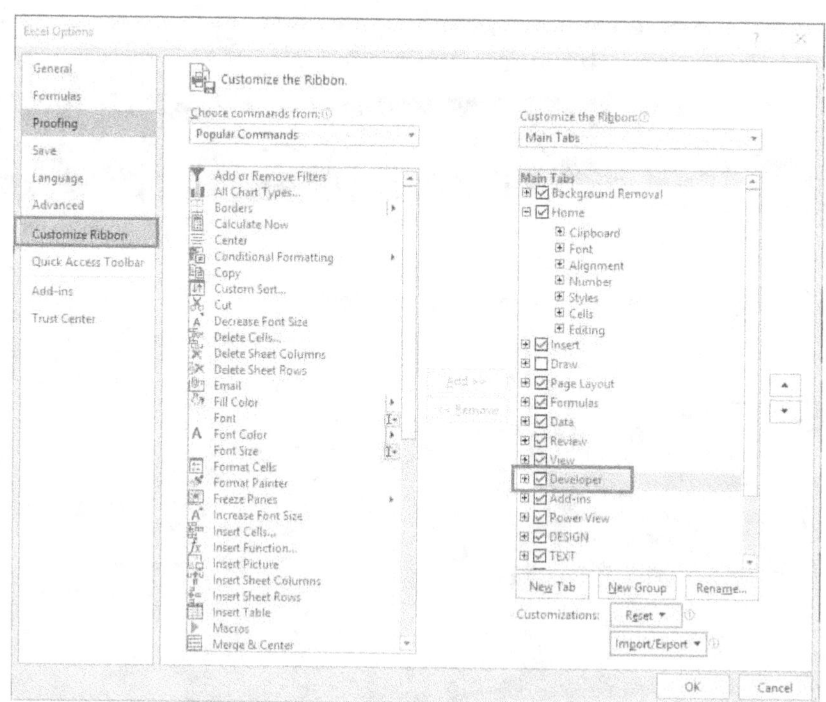

After that you should be able to see the **Developer** tab enabled:

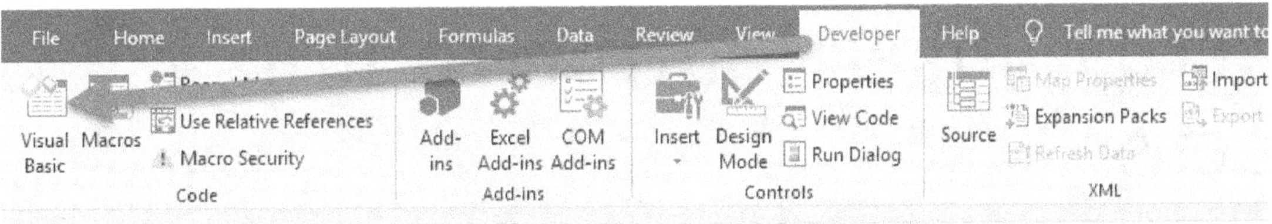

.XLSX vs .XLSM

For a Macro to run, the Workbook's file extension should be in a **.xlsm** format – which is a Macro enabled format.

You can change this under:

File > Save As > Save As Type > Excel Macro-Enabled Workbook(*.xlsm)

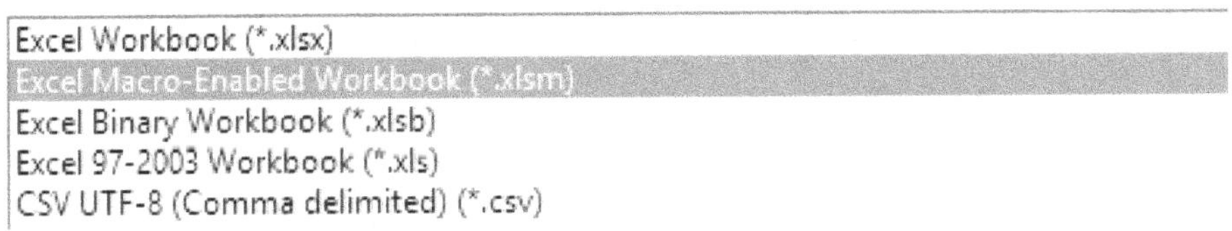

Enabling All Macros

To ensure all Macros in this book will run without any issues, go to *File > Options > Trust Center > Trust Center Settings > Macro Settings*

Ensure **Enable all macros** is selected. Click **OK.**

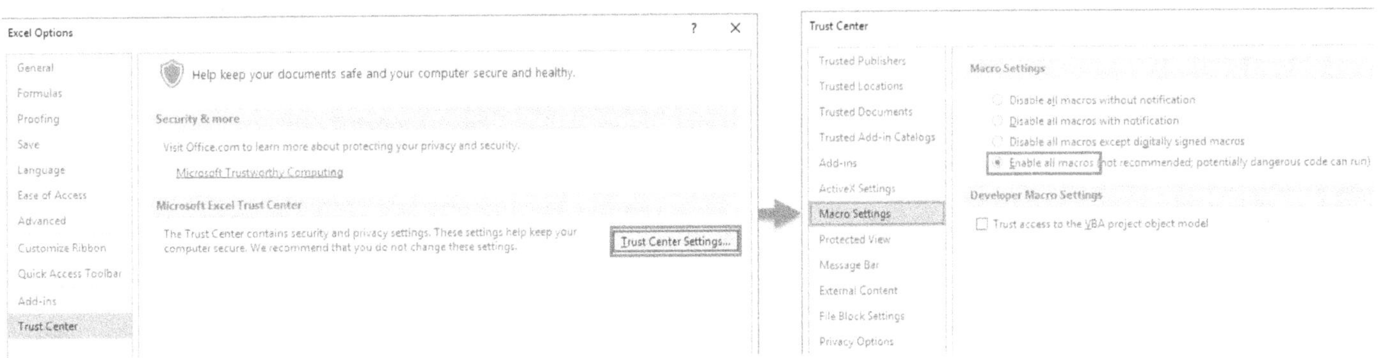

Macros: Insert Button to Run a Macro

What does it do?

We can insert a button and configure it to run a specific Macro. It makes things simpler and the user only needs to click this button every time they want to execute the Macro.

We will be using the **Autofit Columns** Macro Workbook to demonstrate how to create our own button.

The Macro will autofit all of the columns to fit to its contents.

You can use this technique to create buttons to run any Macro.

Final Result:

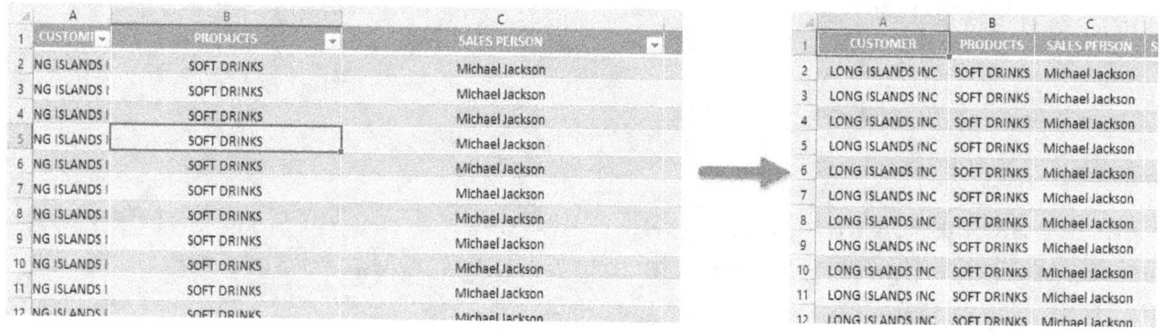

STEP 1: Let us select a shape you prefer. Go to *Insert > Illustrations > Shapes > Rounded Rectangle*:

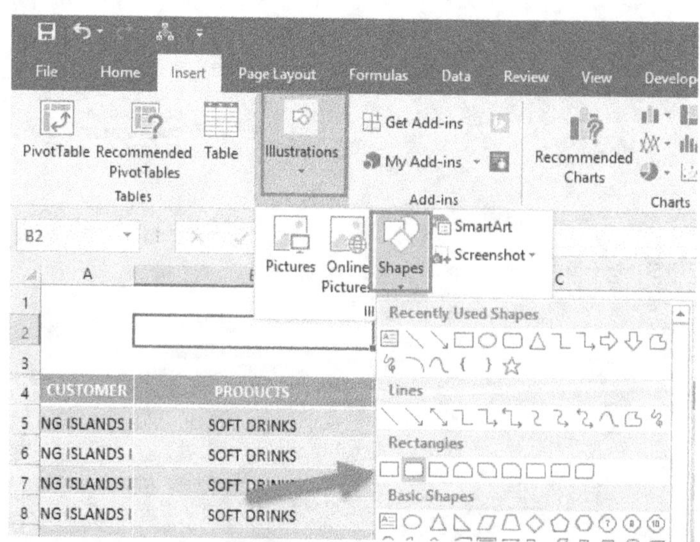

STEP 2: Place the shape anywhere on the sheet that you want.

Double click on the shape to type the text: **Autofit All Columns**.

You can change the font, font size, and center the text as well.

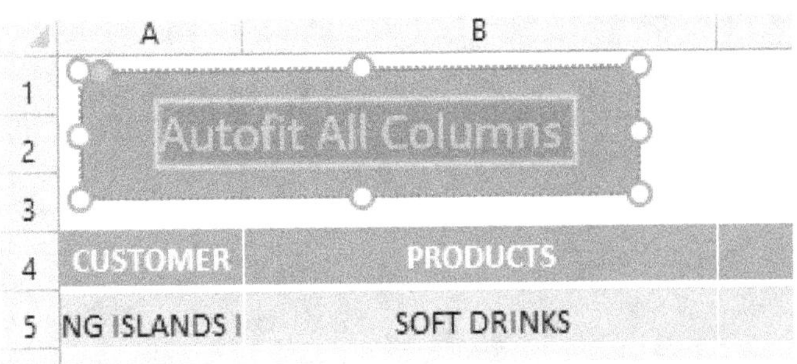

STEP 3: Right click on your shape and select **Assign Macro**

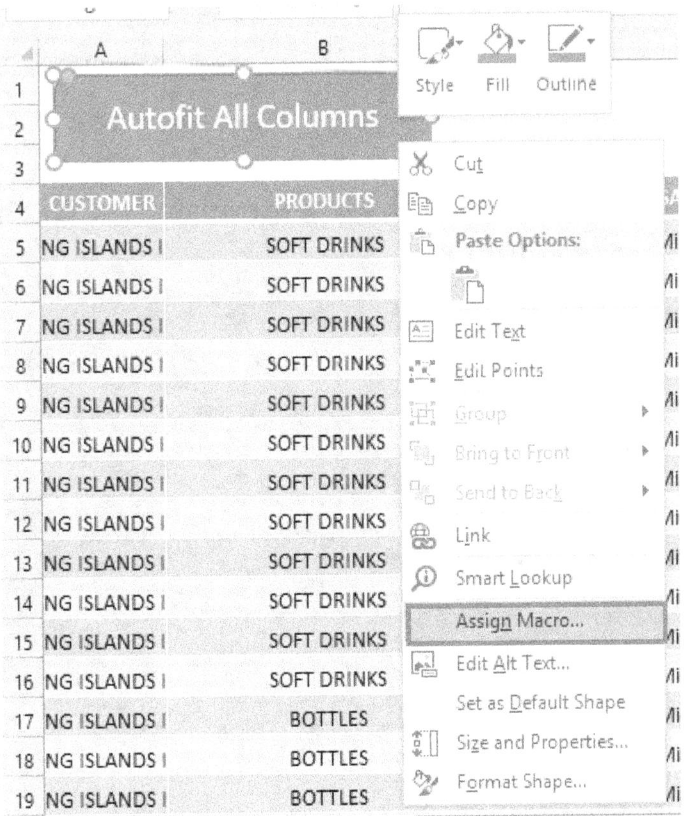

STEP 4: We have one Macro that is already created for you.

Select **This Workbook** from the dropdown, then select the **AutoFitAllColumns** Macro. Click **OK.**

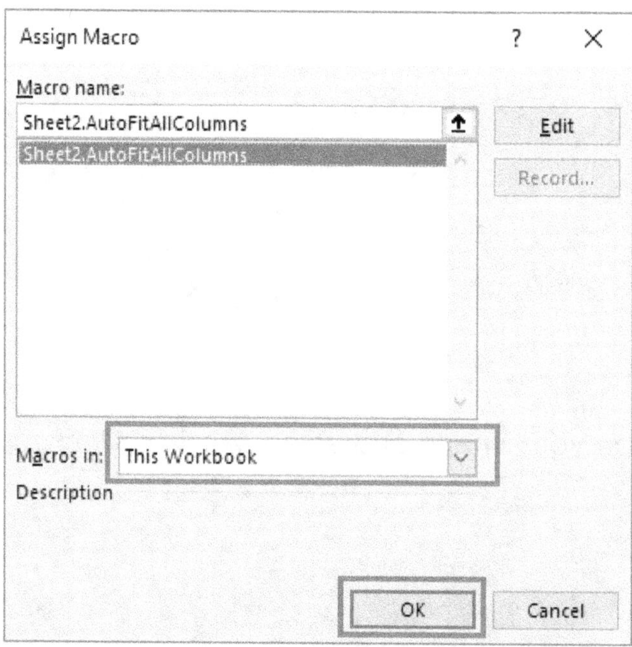

Let us try it out now! Click on your shape/button and see the magic happen! All of your columns are now autofitted!

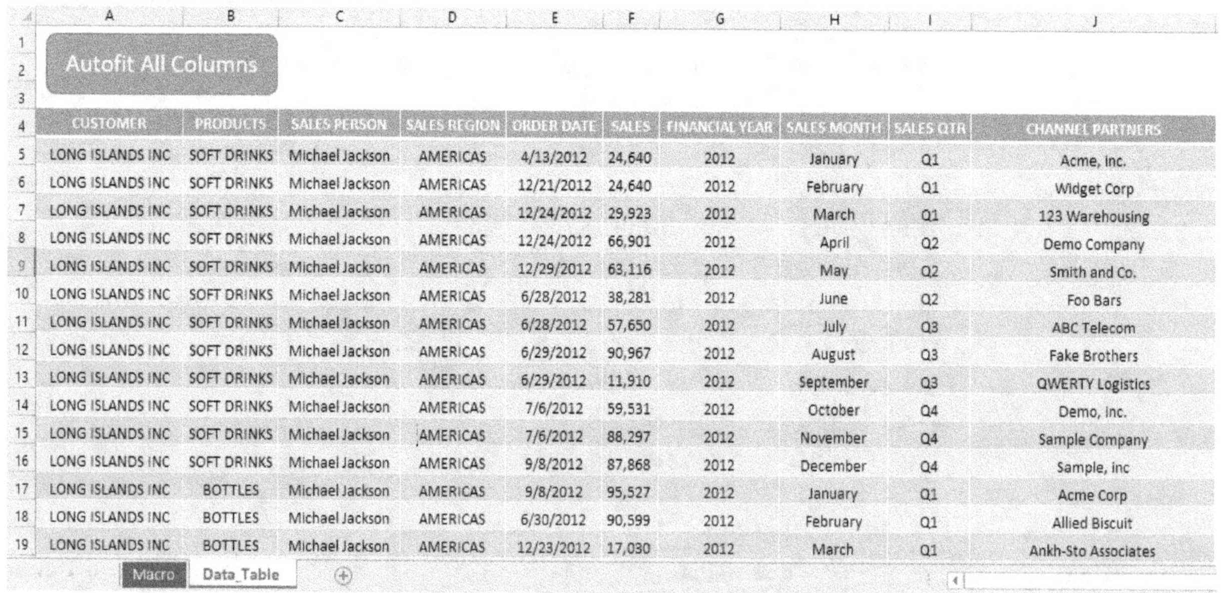

	CUSTOMER	PRODUCTS	SALES PERSON	SALES REGION	ORDER DATE	SALES	FINANCIAL YEAR	SALES MONTH	SALES QTR	CHANNEL PARTNERS
5	LONG ISLANDS INC	SOFT DRINKS	Michael Jackson	AMERICAS	4/13/2012	24,640	2012	January	Q1	Acme, Inc.
6	LONG ISLANDS INC	SOFT DRINKS	Michael Jackson	AMERICAS	12/21/2012	24,640	2012	February	Q1	Widget Corp
7	LONG ISLANDS INC	SOFT DRINKS	Michael Jackson	AMERICAS	12/24/2012	29,923	2012	March	Q1	123 Warehousing
8	LONG ISLANDS INC	SOFT DRINKS	Michael Jackson	AMERICAS	12/24/2012	66,901	2012	April	Q2	Demo Company
9	LONG ISLANDS INC	SOFT DRINKS	Michael Jackson	AMERICAS	12/29/2012	63,116	2012	May	Q2	Smith and Co.
10	LONG ISLANDS INC	SOFT DRINKS	Michael Jackson	AMERICAS	6/28/2012	38,281	2012	June	Q2	Foo Bars
11	LONG ISLANDS INC	SOFT DRINKS	Michael Jackson	AMERICAS	6/28/2012	57,650	2012	July	Q3	ABC Telecom
12	LONG ISLANDS INC	SOFT DRINKS	Michael Jackson	AMERICAS	6/29/2012	90,967	2012	August	Q3	Fake Brothers
13	LONG ISLANDS INC	SOFT DRINKS	Michael Jackson	AMERICAS	6/29/2012	11,910	2012	September	Q3	QWERTY Logistics
14	LONG ISLANDS INC	SOFT DRINKS	Michael Jackson	AMERICAS	7/6/2012	59,531	2012	October	Q4	Demo, Inc.
15	LONG ISLANDS INC	SOFT DRINKS	Michael Jackson	AMERICAS	7/6/2012	88,297	2012	November	Q4	Sample Company
16	LONG ISLANDS INC	SOFT DRINKS	Michael Jackson	AMERICAS	9/8/2012	87,868	2012	December	Q4	Sample, inc
17	LONG ISLANDS INC	BOTTLES	Michael Jackson	AMERICAS	9/8/2012	95,527	2012	January	Q1	Acme Corp
18	LONG ISLANDS INC	BOTTLES	Michael Jackson	AMERICAS	6/30/2012	90,599	2012	February	Q1	Allied Biscuit
19	LONG ISLANDS INC	BOTTLES	Michael Jackson	AMERICAS	12/23/2012	17,030	2012	March	Q1	Ankh-Sto Associates

Macros: Add Macro to Quick Access Toolbar

What if there's a Macro that you're using all of the time, day in, day out? We can **add a Macro to the Quick Access Toolbar** in Excel for easy access!

Download the file which has our sample macro inside the Excel Workbook.

The sample macro (*Macro2*) will set your selected text to **yellow, bold and italic**:

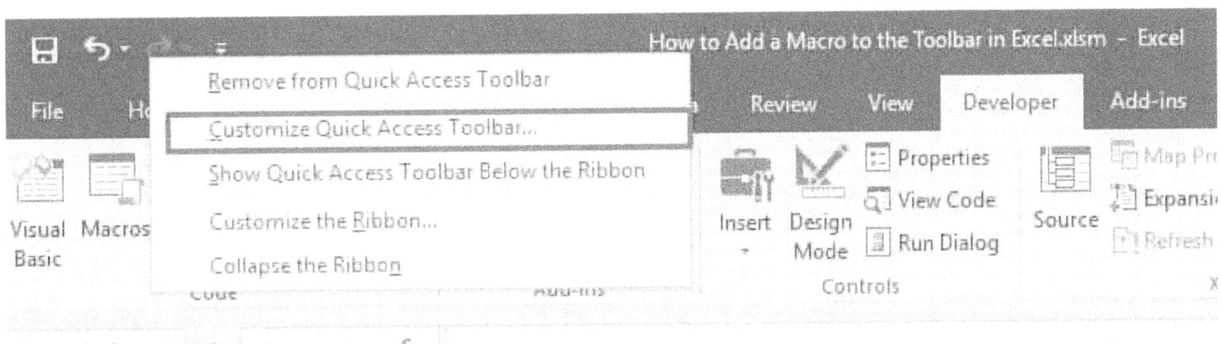

STEP 1: Right click on the top Ribbon and select **Customize Quick Access Toolbar.**

STEP 2: On **Choose commands from**, select **Macros** from the drop down.

Select **Macro2** and click **Add >>**

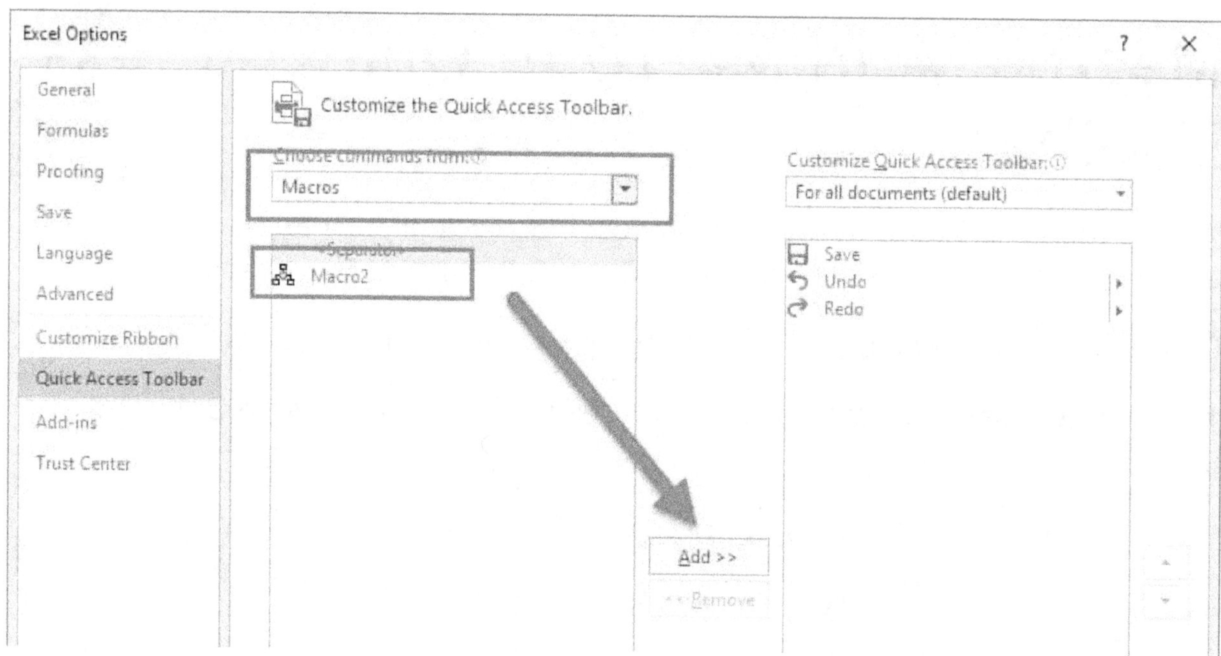

On the right side, make sure **Macro2** is selected and click on **Modify**.

Select any Symbol that you like to represent this macro and click **OK**.

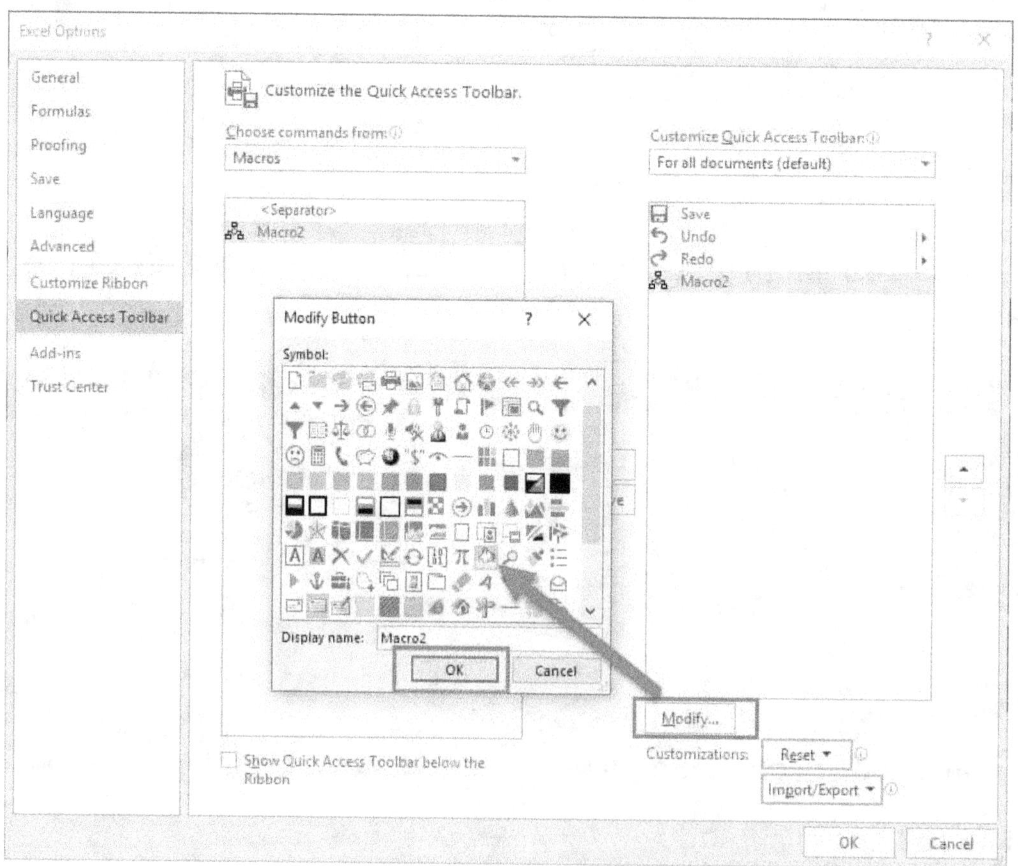

Click **OK** to finish the setup.

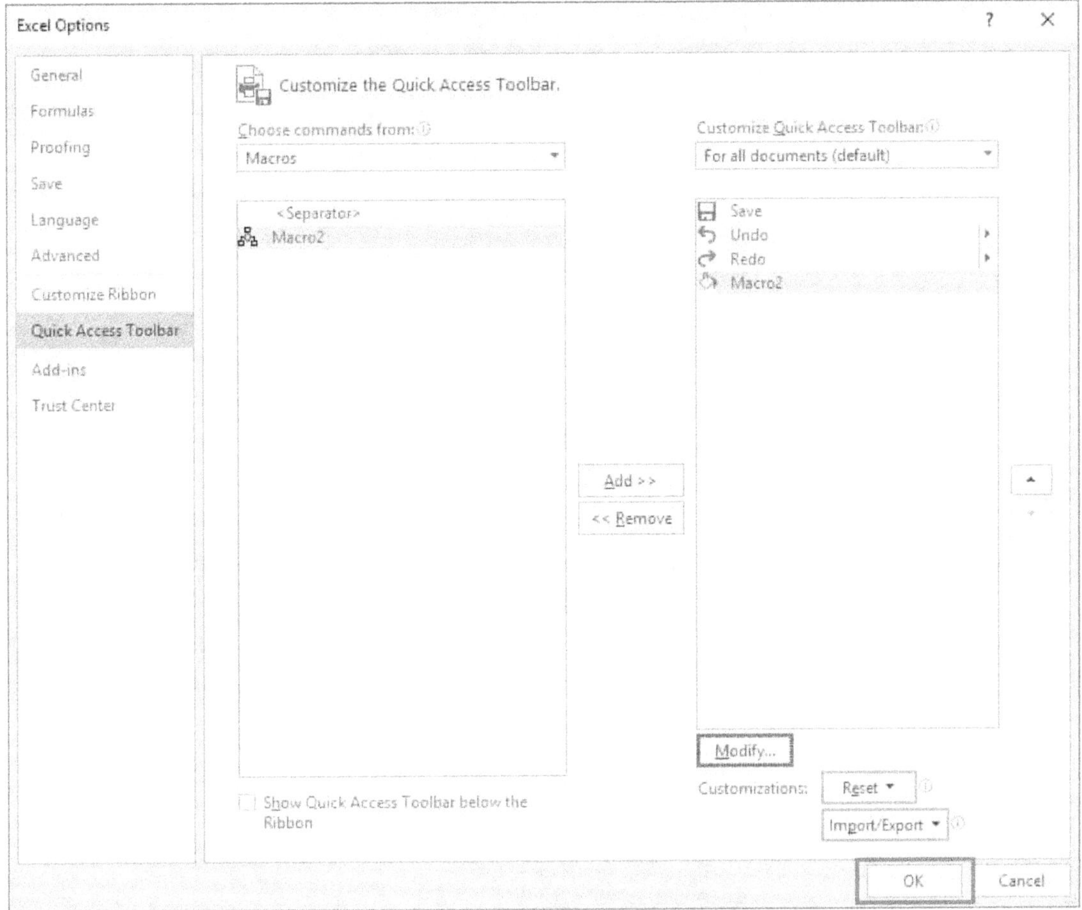

STEP 3: Now let us try out the macro in action!

Select a range of cells and try out your new **Quick Access Toolbar button!**

That was easy! Now you can access your macro with just one click!

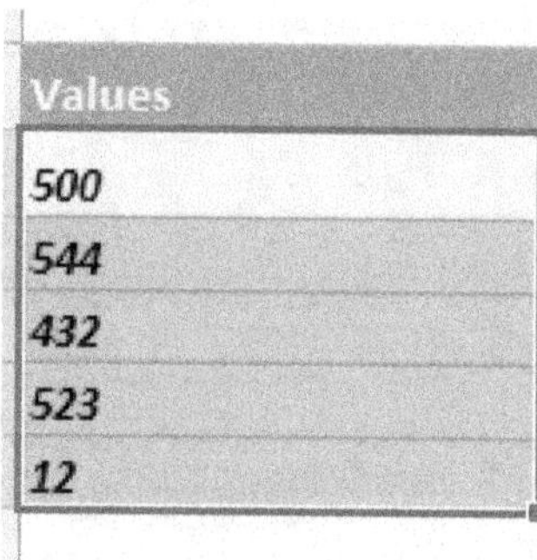

Microsoft Office 365 Tips: Ideas, Stocks & Stock Images

If you have an **Office 365 subscription** it is a whole lot of fun as Microsoft constantly adds new features and you get to explore them right away.

I have 3 cool features to share so check out these hidden gems with your Office 365 subscription!

FEATURE #1: Ideas in Excel

Ideas (also called **Analyze Data**) is a cool feature that allows you to ask questions about your data in plain English. Excel will then provide a quick visual summary or discover trends in your data.

To get the most of Ideas, you need an **Excel Table** with data.

STEP 1: Go to **Home > Ideas**

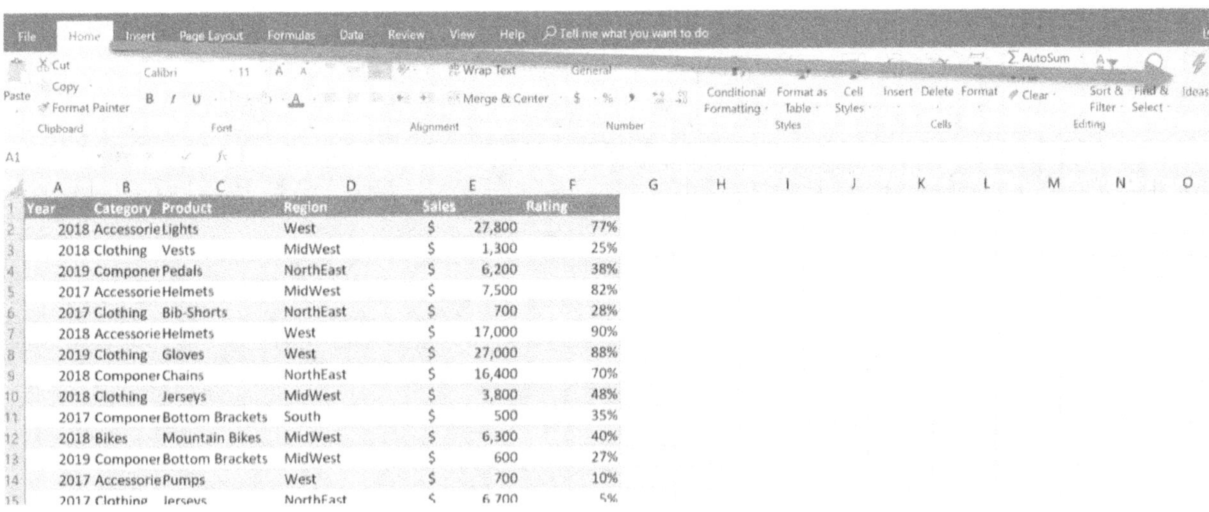

STEP 2: Excel will immediately offer you a couple of ideas on how to represent your data to perform analysis. If you are happy with one of them, click the **Insert** button.

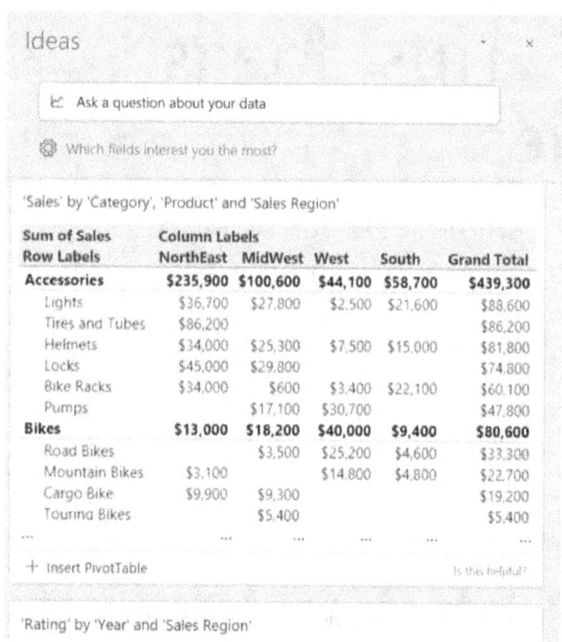

Sum of Sales	Column Labels				
Row Labels	NorthEast	MidWest	West	South	Grand Total
Accessories	**$235,900**	**$100,600**	**$44,100**	**$58,700**	**$439,300**
Lights	$36,700	$27,800	$2,500	$21,600	$88,600
Tires and Tubes	$86,200				$86,200
Helmets	$34,000	$25,300	$7,500	$15,000	$81,800
Locks	$45,000	$29,800			$74,800
Bike Racks	$34,000	$600	$3,400	$22,100	$60,100
Pumps		$17,100	$30,700		$47,800
Bikes	**$13,000**	**$18,200**	**$40,000**	**$9,400**	**$80,600**
Road Bikes		$3,500	$25,200	$4,600	$33,300
Mountain Bikes	$3,100		$14,800	$4,800	$22,700
Cargo Bike	$9,900	$9,300			$19,200
Touring Bikes		$5,400			$5,400

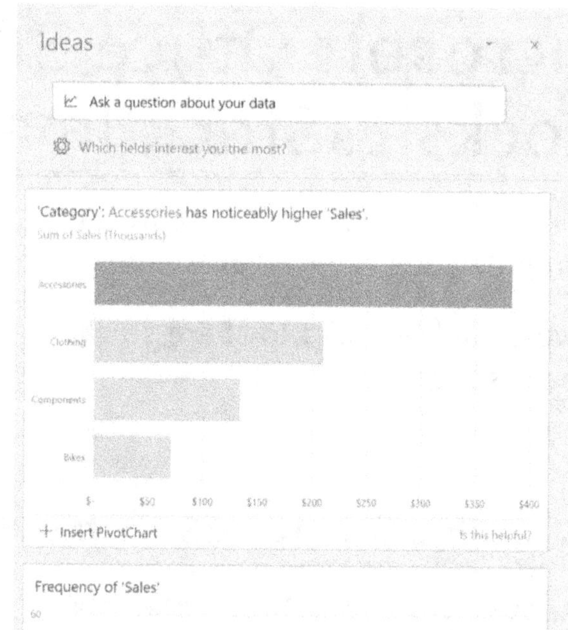

STEP 3: You can also type in a question. For example, we typed in ***"What are the Sales by region?"***

Once you are happy with what Excel has prepared, click **Insert PivotChart** and you will immediately have it ready with no setup!

FEATURE #2: Stocks Data Type

This is a new linked data type as you can get real stock data online in just a couple of steps.

STEP 1: Select your list of stocks

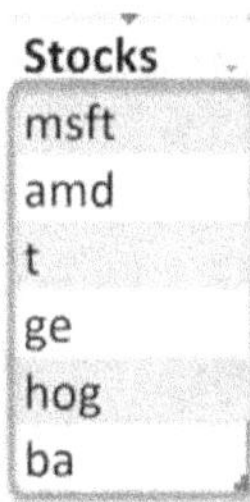

STEP 2: Go to ***Data > Data Types > Stocks***

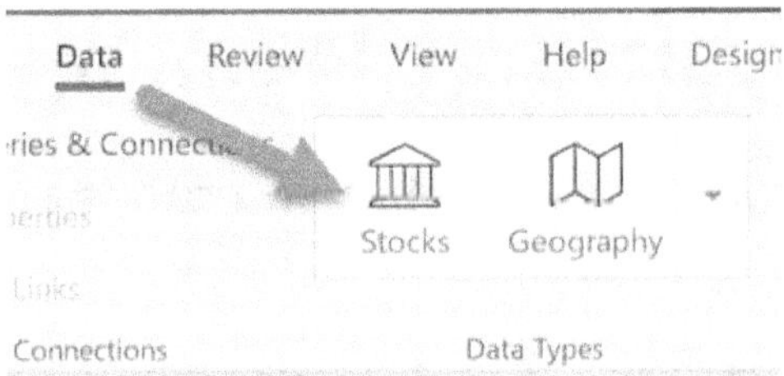

STEP 3: Let us get some online stock data!

Click the **Add Column** button and select **Previous close**

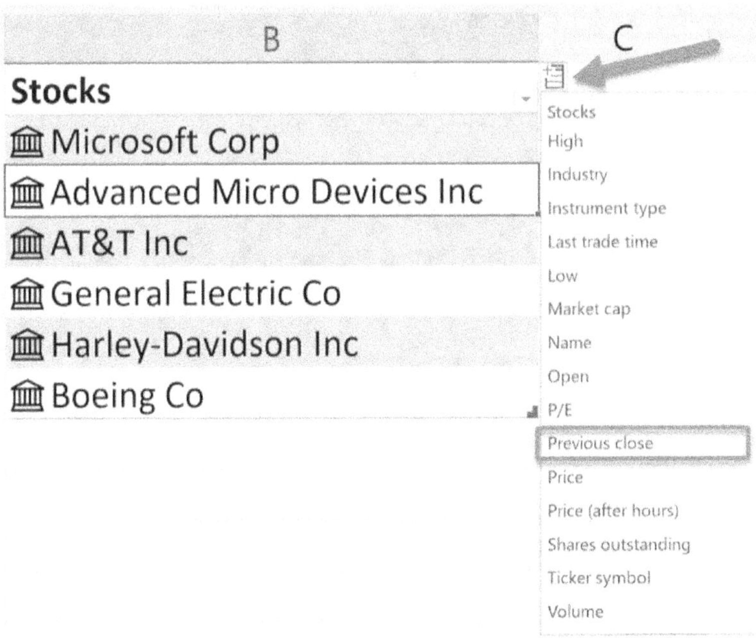

 Now you have your stock data! Keep on adding more columns as needed

B	C
Stocks	**Previous Close**
🏛 Microsoft Corp	$ 100.86
🏛 Advanced Micro Devices Inc	$ 17.11
🏛 AT&T Inc	$ 32.19
🏛 General Electric Co	$ 13.20
🏛 Harley-Davidson Inc	$ 45.57
🏛 Boeing Co	$ 354.70

FEATURE #3: Royalty-free Premium Images

Microsoft has added premium images that you can use for free and it is a blast to explore on what it has to offer.

STEP 1: Go to *Insert > Pictures > Stock Images*

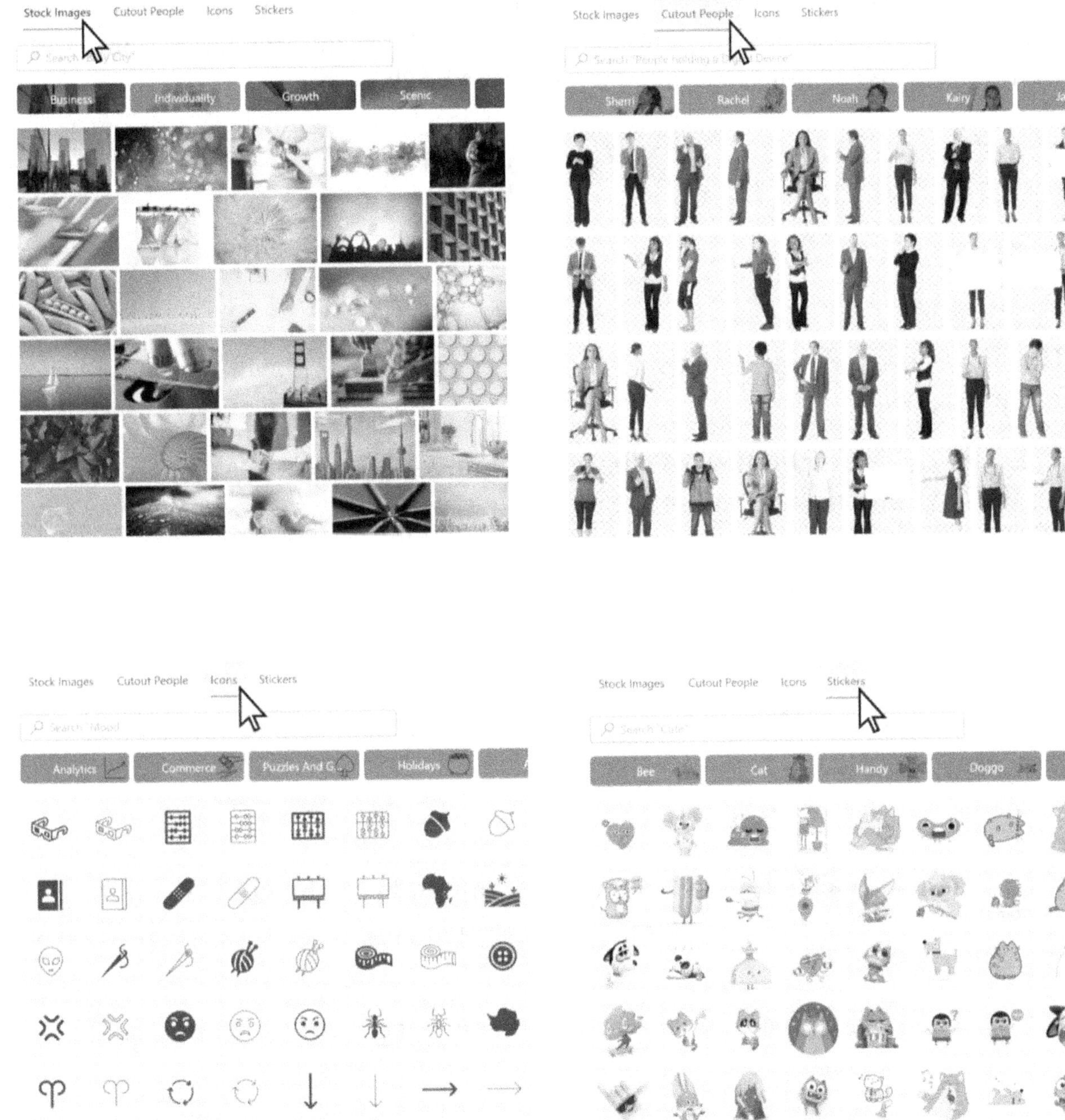

Quick Access Toolbar

The **Quick Access Toolbar (QAT)** is located at the top left-hand corner of the ribbon and has the most commonly used commands, like the Save, Undo and Redo. The QAT is unique to each user's workbook settings.

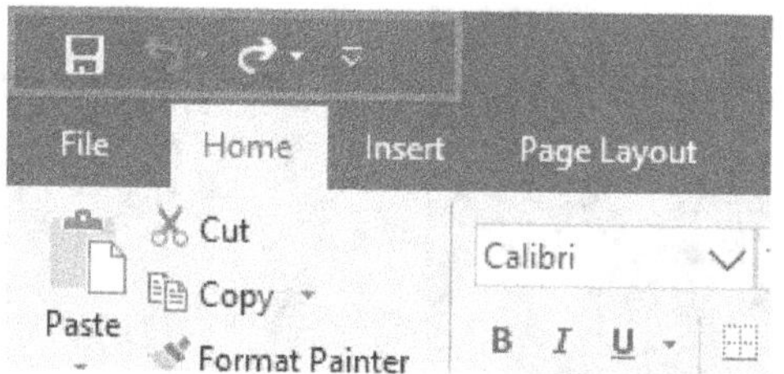

Did you know that you can customize this to your needs? I will show you how to do this below!

STEP 1: You can **move the QAT below or above the ribbon** by right clicking on the QAT and making the selection *Show Quick Access Toolbar Below the Ribbon.*

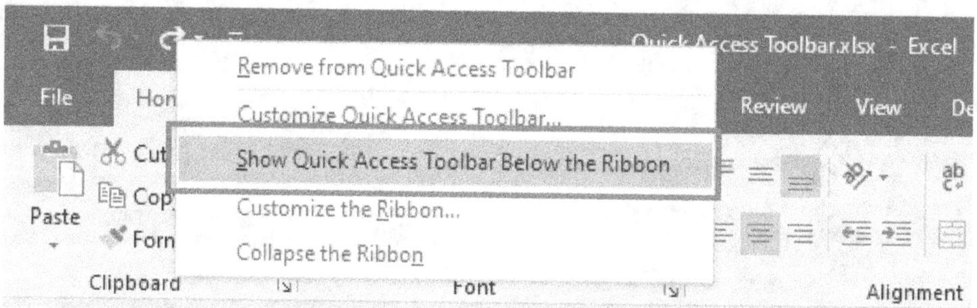

STEP 2: You can also **add your favorite commands to the QAT** by right clicking on your favorite command in the ribbon and selecting *Add to Quick Access Toolbar*.

For our example, let us right click on Bold and select *Add to Quick Access Toolbar.*

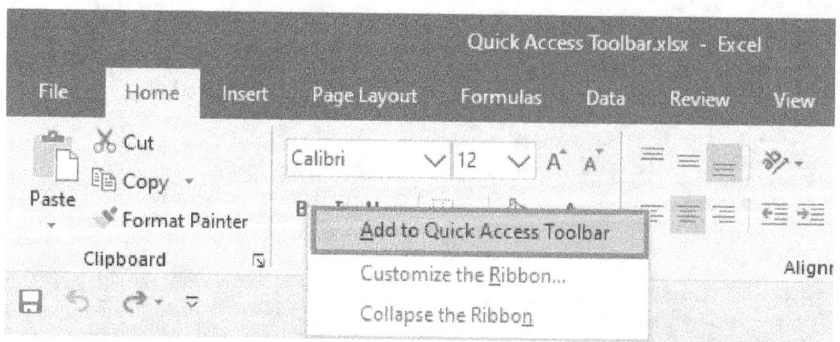

This will now add the Bold command to our QAT.

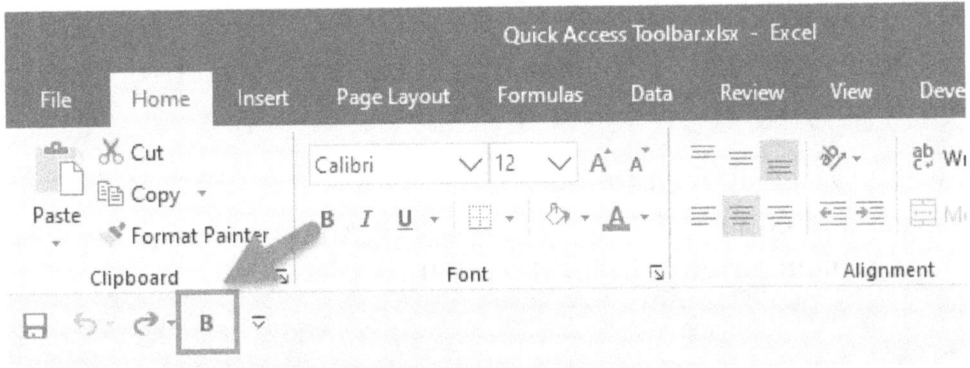

STEP 3: Finally, you can **activate your QAT commands** by pressing the *ALT* key on your keyboard and then pressing the number (e.g. 1,2,3 etc.) that appears at the bottom of that command.

In our example, you can use **ALT + 4** to activate the Bold command.

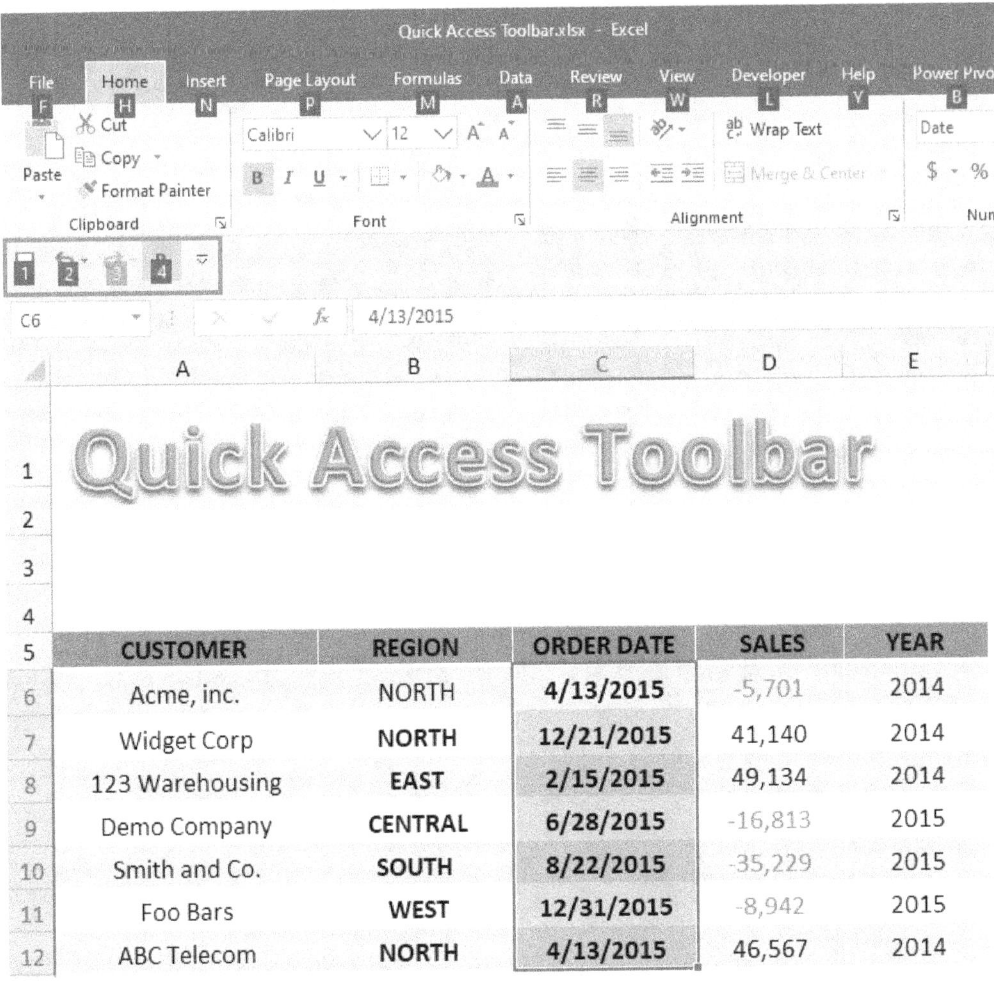

Status Bar Metrics

When you select a range of cells you can quickly see key metrics like the **_Sum, Count, Minimum, Maximum and Average._**

To activate this, you will need to Right Click on the Status Bar at the bottom of your workbook and choose the metrics that you want to show. Once selected, these options remain saved for all future workbooks.

STEP 1: Right click anywhere on the Status Bar to show the customization menu

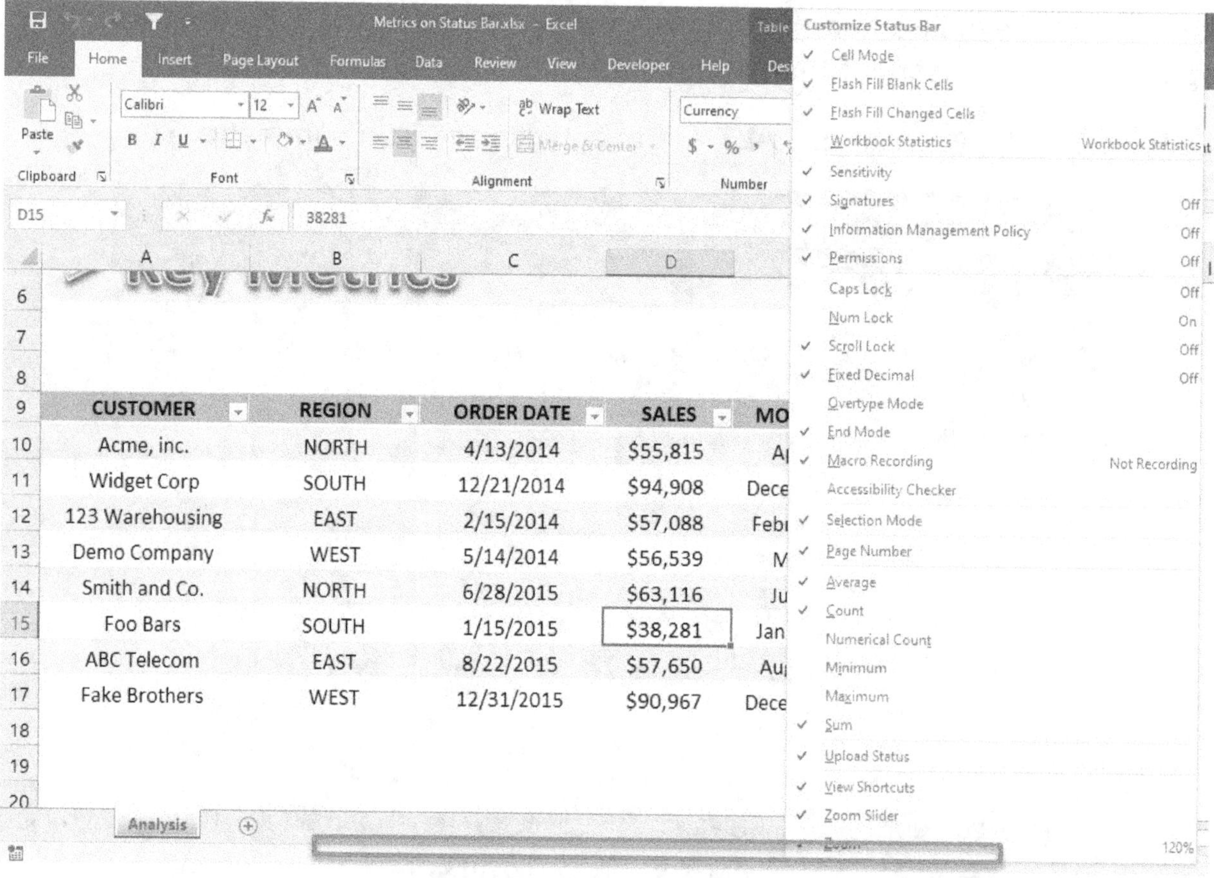

STEP 2: Tick the values that you want to be displayed in your Status Bar

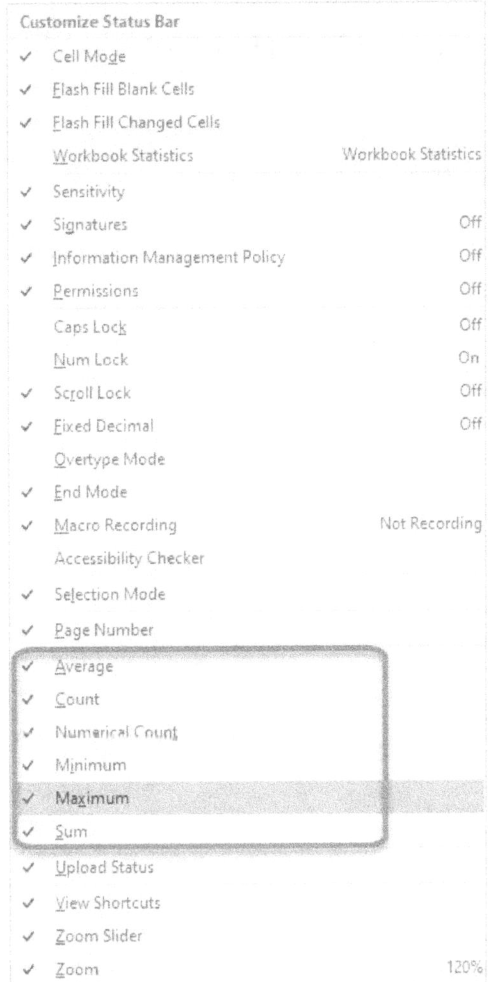

Now when you select and highlight numerical values, these auto-computed metrics will now show up in your status bar!

CUSTOMER	REGION	ORDER DATE	SALES	MONTH	YEAR
Acme, inc.	NORTH	4/13/2014	$55,815	April	2014
Widget Corp	SOUTH	12/21/2014	$94,908	December	2014
123 Warehousing	EAST	2/15/2014	$57,088	February	2014
Demo Company	WEST	5/14/2014	$56,539	May	2014
Smith and Co.	NORTH	6/28/2015	$63,116	June	2015
Foo Bars	SOUTH	1/15/2015	$38,281	January	2015
ABC Telecom	EAST	8/22/2015	$57,650	August	2015
Fake Brothers	WEST	12/31/2015	$90,967	December	2015

Synchronous Scrolling

When you have two workbooks or worksheets that you want to view side by side to do a quick check, Excel has you covered!

Here is a quick scenario wherein we have similar data however it is split across two tables inside a single workbook:

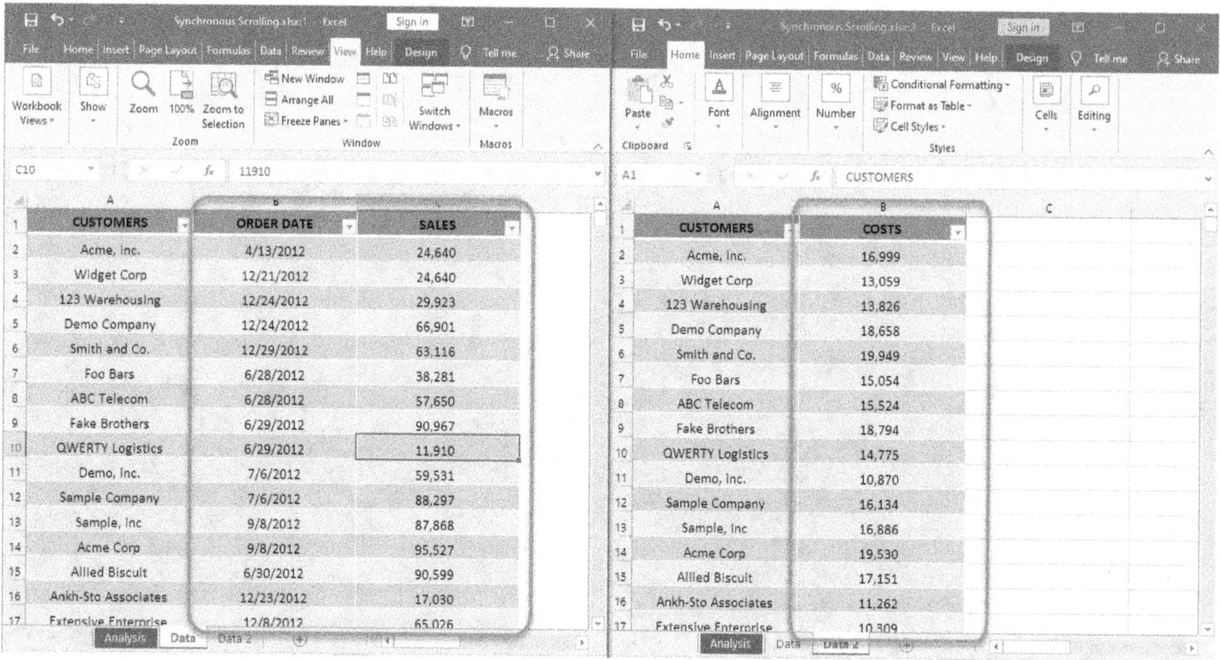

STEP 1: Since we want to view 2 worksheets from the same workbook, go to *View > Window > New Window*

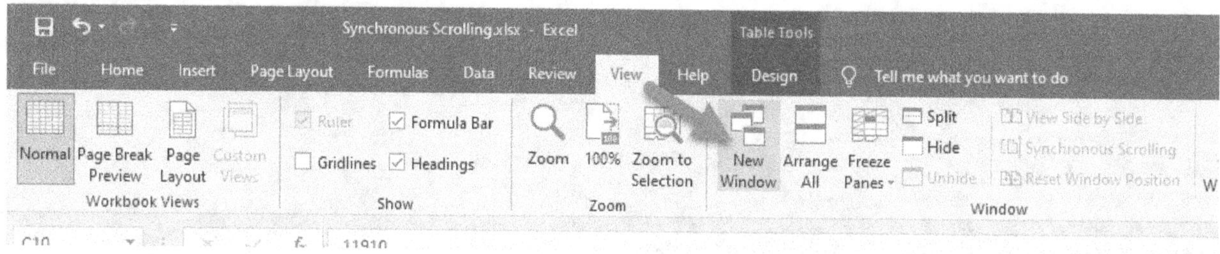

STEP 2: Now we have 2 views on the same workbook. On the first window, open **Data**, then select **Data 2** on the second one.

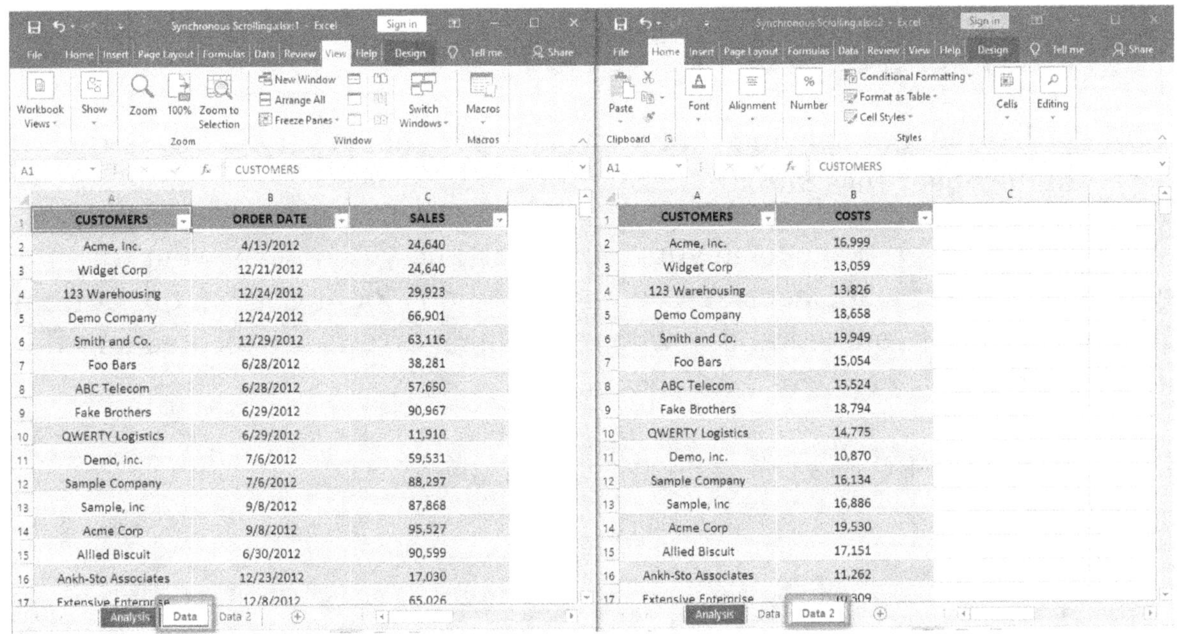

STEP 3: In any one of the windows, go to *View > Window > View Side by Side*

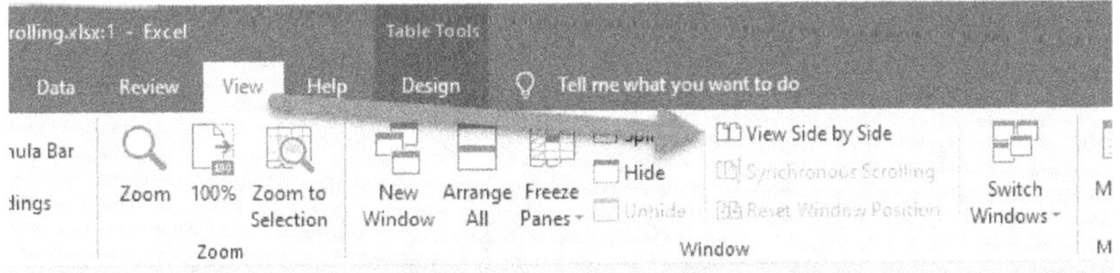

Now try scrolling up and down, you will see that the scrolling is synchronous for both windows!

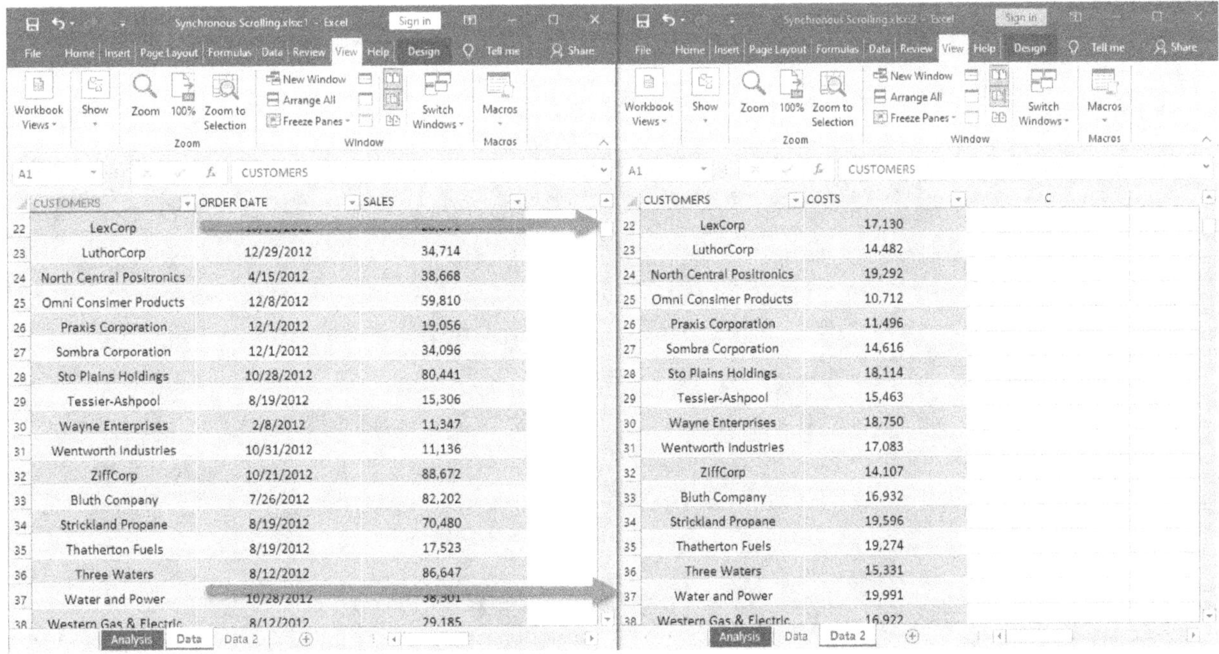

Worksheet Navigator

A cool tip that most people may not know and one that is very handy is the what I call the Sheet Navigator.

If you have lots of worksheets in your workbook and you quickly want to navigate to the last worksheets, all you need to do is Right Click in the bottom left-hand corner of your workbook where the sheet arrows are located and this will bring up a list of all your worksheets.

STEP 1: **Right-click** on the sheet arrows

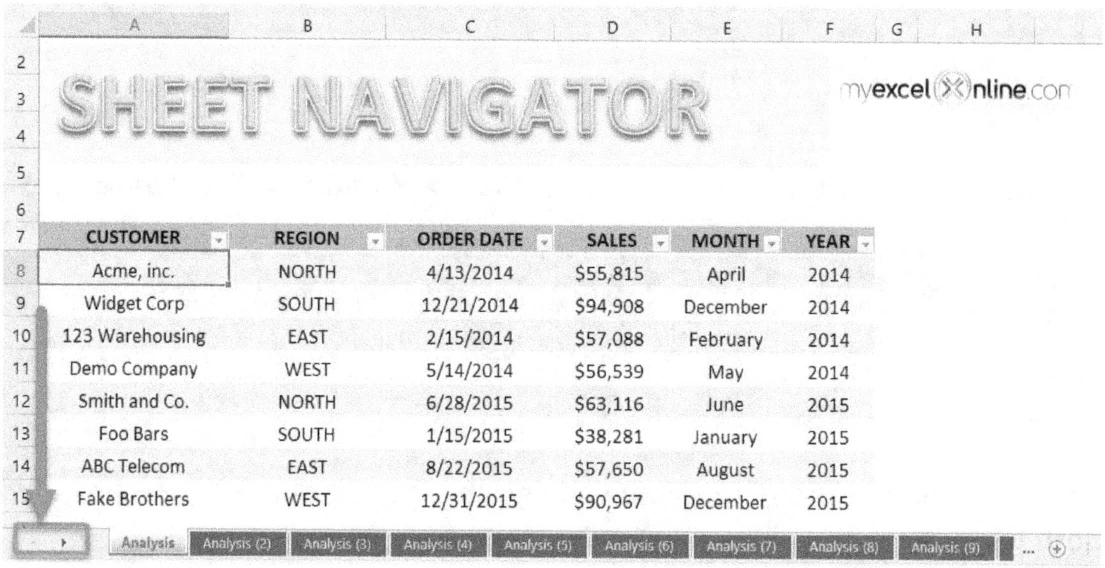

STEP 2: **Select the sheet** that you want to navigate to. Click **OK**

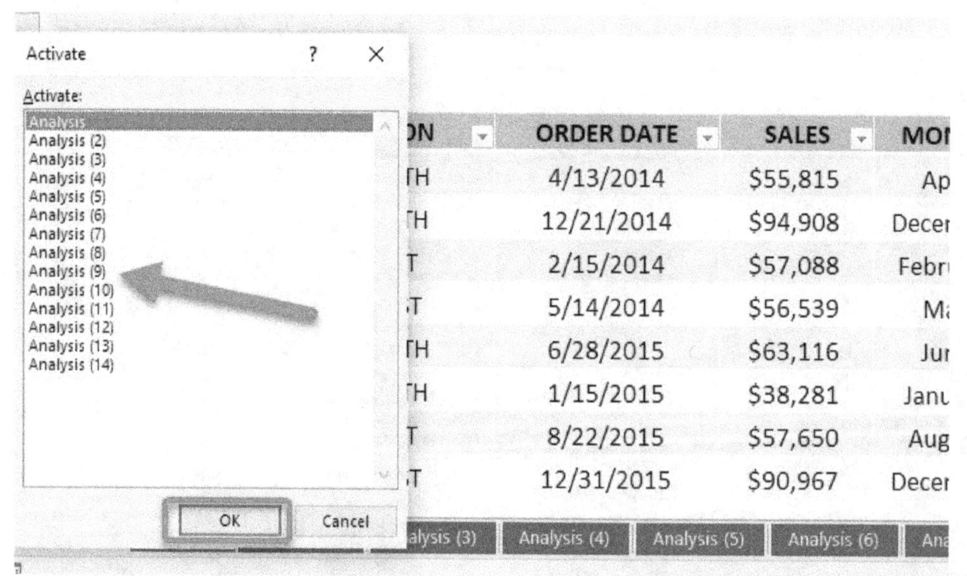

You have now jumped to your selected sheet in an instant!

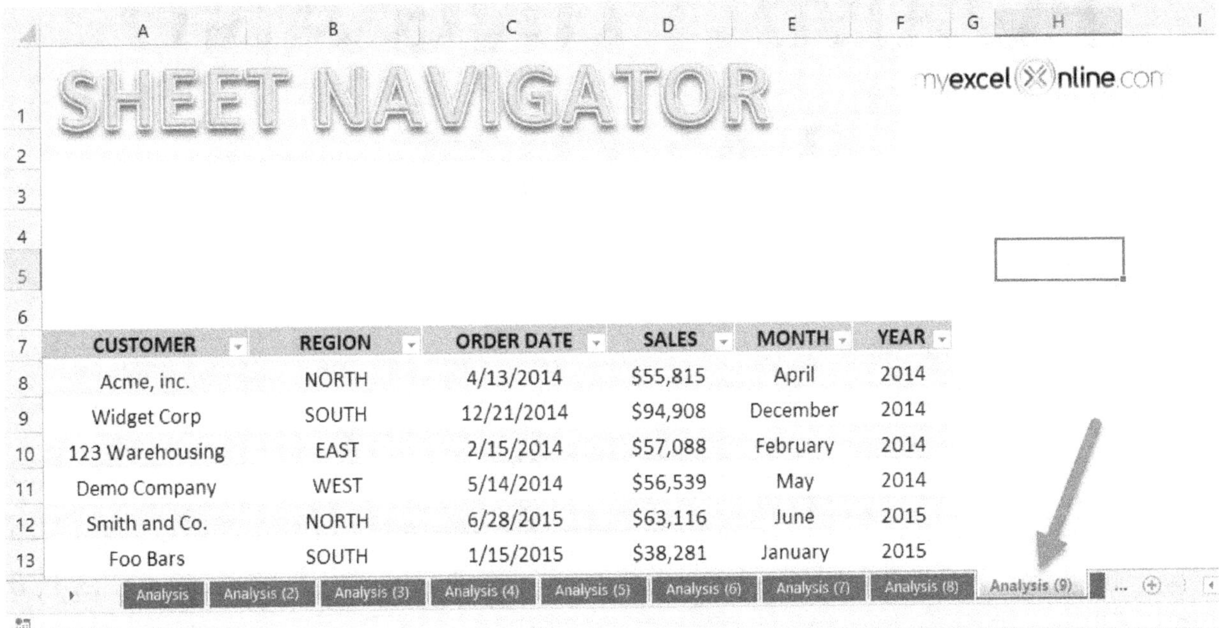

FORMATTING AND LAYOUT

6 Simple Ways to Merge Cells in Excel

While working in an Excel Worksheet, you will come across scenarios when you will have to merge cells or combine cells in Excel. Knowing how to merge cells in Excel can be useful when you want to create titles for your reports or combine various cells into one.

Excel has a number of approaches on how to merge cells in Excel that spans across rows and/or columns.

Let's take a look at how to merge cells in Excel.

We will go into detail about several approaches on how to merge cells in Excel. Each one will produce a different result and layout.

How to Use the Merge & Center button

A great way to customize the layout of your Excel worksheet is to use the **Merge & Center feature** in Excel.

It is a great way to create a label that spans several columns. This feature will retain the value in the upper-left cell but keep in mind that all data in the other merged cells will be deleted.

In the example below, you can see that the text "SALES REPORT" is located in a single cell in A1. Let us fix that!

	CUSTOMER	PRODUCTS	SALES PERSON	SALES REGION	ORDER DATE	SALES
	SALES REPORT					
	CUSTOMER	PRODUCTS	SALES PERSON	SALES REGION	ORDER DATE	SALES
3	LONG ISLANDS INC	SOFT DRINKS	Michael Jackson	AMERICAS	08/04/20	24,640
4	LONG ISLANDS INC	SOFT DRINKS	Michael Jackson	AMERICAS	19/04/20	24,640
5	LONG ISLANDS INC	SOFT DRINKS	Michael Jackson	AMERICAS	14/04/20	29,923
6	LONG ISLANDS INC	SOFT DRINKS	Michael Jackson	AMERICAS	13/04/20	66,901
7	LONG ISLANDS INC	SOFT DRINKS	Michael Jackson	AMERICAS	20/04/20	63,116
8	LONG ISLANDS INC	SOFT DRINKS	Michael Jackson	AMERICAS	14/04/20	38,281

STEP 1: Select the cells A1:F1 that you want to merge.

	CUSTOMER	PRODUCTS	SALES PERSON	SALES REGION	ORDER DATE	SALES
	SALES REPORT					
2	CUSTOMER	PRODUCTS	SALES PERSON	SALES REGION	ORDER DATE	SALES
3	LONG ISLANDS INC	SOFT DRINKS	Michael Rose	AMERICAS	08/04/20	24,640
4	LONG ISLANDS INC	SOFT DRINKS	John Lee	AMERICAS	19/04/20	13,850
5	LONG ISLANDS INC	SOFT DRINKS	David Smith	AMERICAS	14/04/20	29,923
6	LONG ISLANDS INC	SOFT DRINKS	Simson Jones	AMERICAS	13/04/20	66,901
7	LONG ISLANDS INC	SOFT DRINKS	Charles Spector	AMERICAS	20/04/20	63,116
8	LONG ISLANDS INC	SOFT DRINKS	George Brown	AMERICAS	14/04/20	38,281

STEP 2: Go to **Home > 'Alignment' group > Merge & Center** button

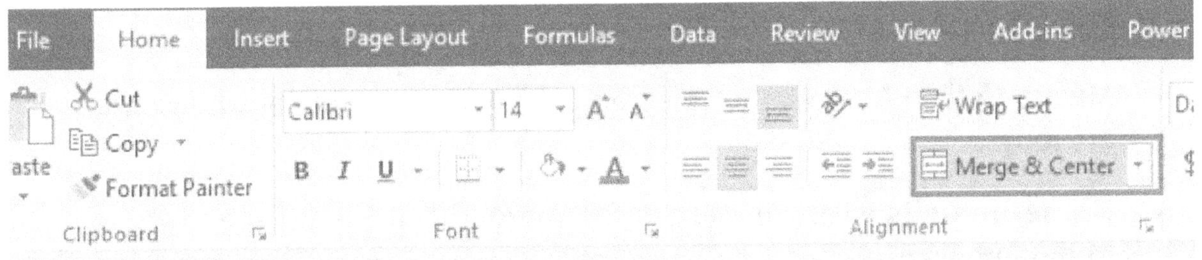

STEP 3: The currently selected cells will be merged, and their contents will be center aligned.

	CUSTOMER	PRODUCTS	SALES PERSON	SALES REGION	ORDER DATE	SALES
1	SALES REPORT					
2	CUSTOMER	PRODUCTS	SALES PERSON	SALES REGION	ORDER DATE	SALES
3	LONG ISLANDS INC	SOFT DRINKS	Michael Rose	AMERICAS	08/04/20	24,640
4	LONG ISLANDS INC	SOFT DRINKS	John Lee	AMERICAS	19/04/20	13,850
5	LONG ISLANDS INC	SOFT DRINKS	David Smith	AMERICAS	14/04/20	29,923
6	LONG ISLANDS INC	SOFT DRINKS	Simson Jones	AMERICAS	13/04/20	66,901
7	LONG ISLANDS INC	SOFT DRINKS	Charles Spector	AMERICAS	20/04/20	63,116
8	LONG ISLANDS INC	SOFT DRINKS	George Brown	AMERICAS	14/04/20	38,281

Notice that the reference for the 6 merged cells cell points at A1.

You can create headers/titles for your report that will make it much easier to understand.

Other Merge & Center Options

When you click on the drop down arrow beside the Merge & Center button in the Alignment group, you will see it contains a drop down list with additional options and each one produces a different result:

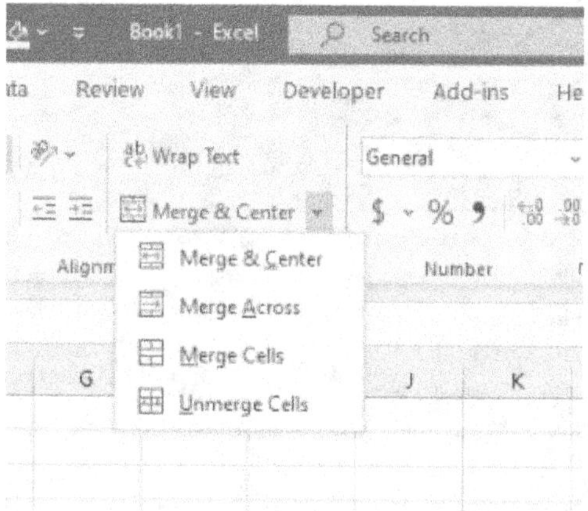

- **Merge Across** – When a multi-row range is selected, this command creates multiple merge cells in Excel — one for each row.

- **Merge Cells** – Merges the selected cells without applying the Center attribute.

- **Unmerge Cells** –This unmerges the merged cells in Excel and we explain in detail below.

Once you have learned how to merge cells in Excel, you should also know how to unmerge them:

STEP 1: Select the cells that you want to unmerge.

	CUSTOMER	PRODUCTS	SALES PERSON	SALES REGION	ORDER DATE	SALES
			SALES REPORT			
3	LONG ISLANDS INC	SOFT DRINKS	Michael Rose	AMERICAS	08/04/20	24,640
4	LONG ISLANDS INC	SOFT DRINKS	John Lee	AMERICAS	19/04/20	13,850
5	LONG ISLANDS INC	SOFT DRINKS	David Smith	AMERICAS	14/04/20	29,923
6	LONG ISLANDS INC	SOFT DRINKS	Simson Jones	AMERICAS	13/04/20	66,901
7	LONG ISLANDS INC	SOFT DRINKS	Charles Spector	AMERICAS	20/04/20	63,116
8	LONG ISLANDS INC	SOFT DRINKS	George Brown	AMERICAS	14/04/20	38,281

 Click the **Merge & Center** button or select the **Unmerge Cells** option from the drop down menu.

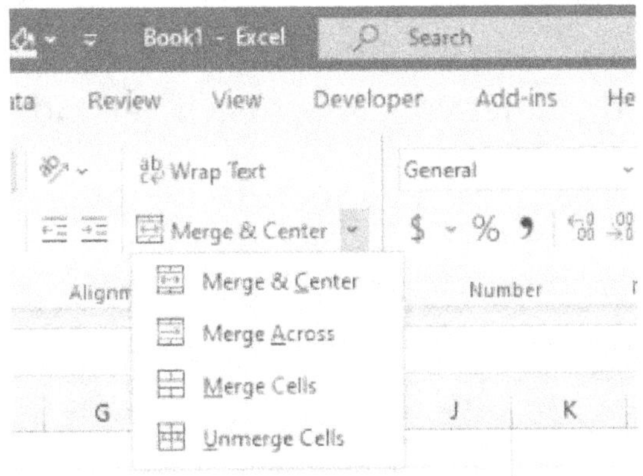

Your data is now unmerged.

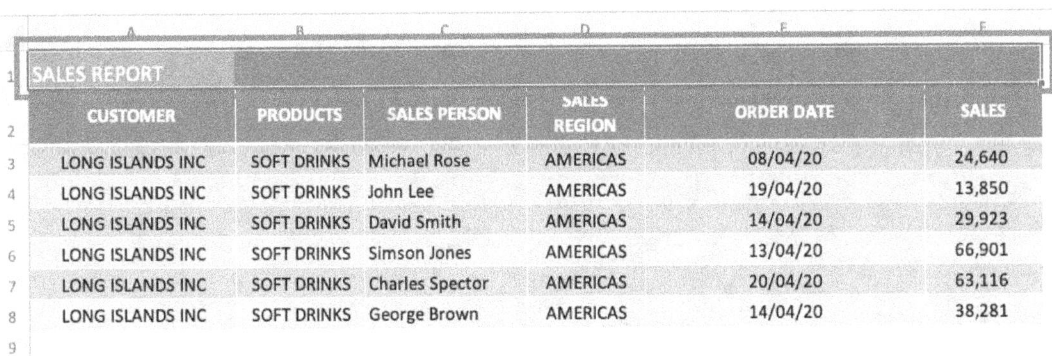

Even though this is a fairly simple process to know how to merge cells in Excel, it is not highly recommended, and further below we explain the alternatives to merge cells in Excel.

If any data was lost when the original cells were merged, they will not be restored (unless your press CTRL + Z to undo the last action).

Here are a couple of shortfalls once cells have been merged:

- Excel Functions won't work on merged cells

- Excel 'Sort' command will not work on ranges that contain the merged cells.

- Single column can't be selected if it contains any merged cells

- Excel Filters cannot be applied

- Dates cannot easily be copy-pasted elsewhere

Using Center Across Selection

To achieve the same result as Merge & Center without having the above restrictions, use the **Center Across Selection** feature. This would merge the cells across columns and still let you select each cell individually.

STEP 1: Select the cells A1:F1 that you want to merge.

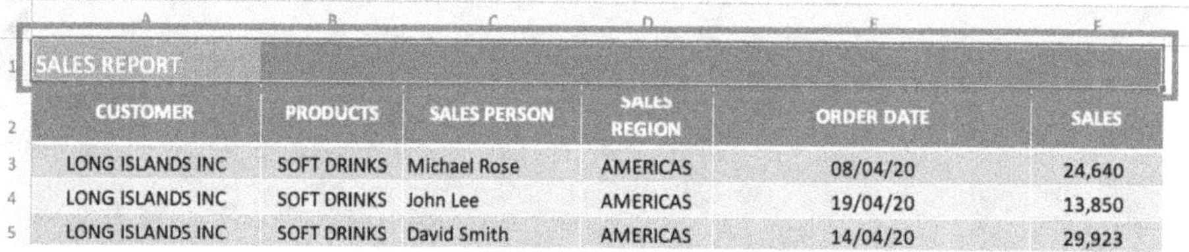

STEP 2: Press **Ctrl + 1** to bring up the *Format Cells* dialog box.

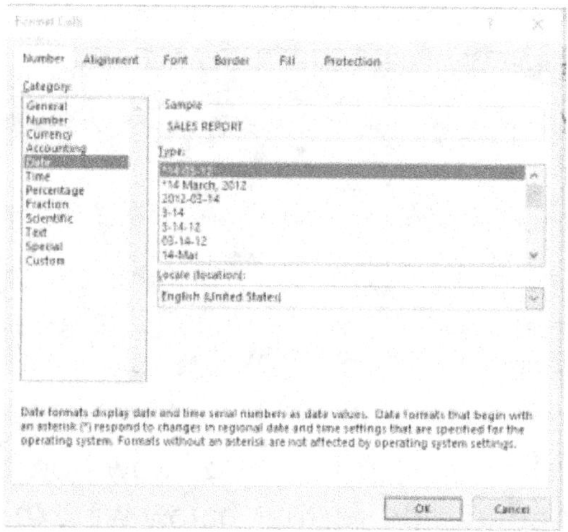

STEP 3: Under the **Alignment Tab**, in the **Horizontal** drop down box, select "**Center Across Selection**"

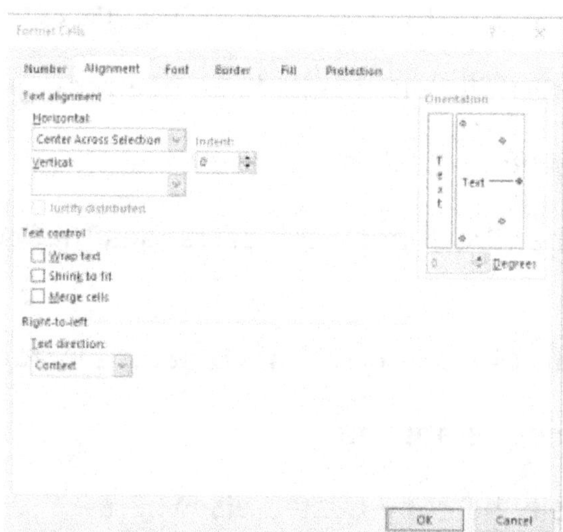

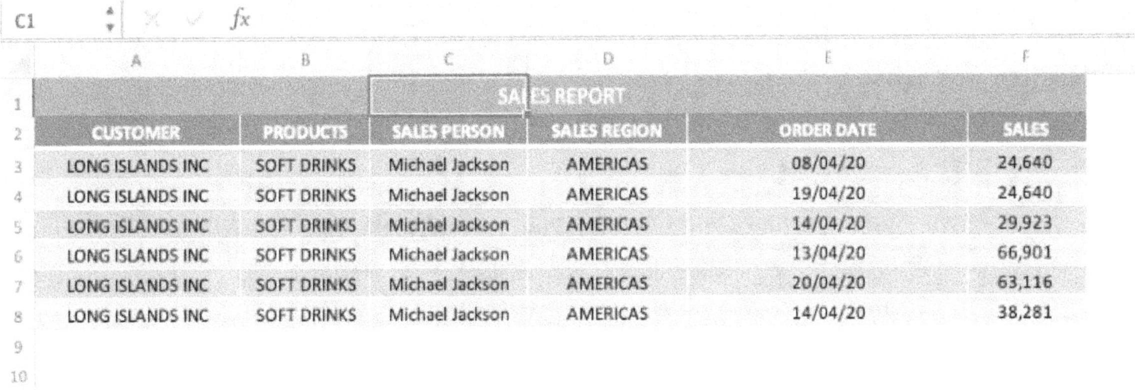

The selected cells are now merged. You can see that even though the data is merged across cell **A1: F1**, you can still select and refer to each cell individually!

Using the CONCATENATE Function

If you use the above options to merge cells in Excel, it will keep the text at the leftmost cell (A1 in this case) and remove the text from all other cells.

If you don't want to lose the text from the merged cells in Excel, use the **CONCATENATE Function** (pre Excel 2019), the **CONCAT Function** (Excel 2019 & Office 365) or the ampersand **&** operator. The CONCATENATE function combines cells in Excel quickly.

There may be times when you are dumped with data in Excel and it is not formatted quite the way you want. Say, you have the **First Name** and **Last Name** in different columns and you want to merge them in a single column containing First and Last Name.

Now, if you use **Merge & Center** or **Merge Across Selection**, it will delete the text in the second column and only display the First Name as a merged cell. But this is not what you were looking for. Right?

Let me introduce you to the **Concatenate Function** and the ampersand **&** operator that will merge cells in Excel! This feature should definitely be bookmarked as it will come in handy when cleaning, transforming and analyzing data in Excel.

The **Concatenate Function** will merge multiple cells into a single cell and keep both values. You can merge or join more than two cells together whether it contains text, numbers, or both.

In the SALES REPORT below, you have the First Name in **Column A** and Last Name in **Column B**. For reporting and further analysis, you need them to be combined into one column, so it's best to use the Concatenate function or the "&" Operator for this.

	FIRST NAME	LAST NAME	PRODUCTS	SALES REGION	ORDER DATE	SALES
1	SALES REPORT					
2	FIRST NAME	LAST NAME	PRODUCTS	SALES REGION	ORDER DATE	SALES
3	Michael	Rose	SOFT DRINKS	AMERICAS	08/04/20	24,640
4	John	Lee	SOFT DRINKS	AMERICAS	19/04/20	24,640
5	David	Smith	SOFT DRINKS	AMERICAS	14/04/20	29,923
6	Simson	Jones	SOFT DRINKS	AMERICAS	13/04/20	66,901
7	Charles	Spector	SOFT DRINKS	AMERICAS	20/04/20	63,116
8	George	Brown	SOFT DRINKS	AMERICAS	14/04/20	38,281
9	Emma	Miller	SOFT DRINKS	AMERICAS	22/04/20	42,150
10						

Before I get into how to merge cells in Excel, let's talk about exactly what happens when you try to use Merge & Center here. If you select cells A3 and B3 and then press the "**Merge & Center**" button, you will see that you end up with an Excel merged cell with only the upper-left cell's value (First Name).

To merge cells in Excel without losing any data, you should use the **Concatenate Function in Excel.** Follow the steps to know how to combine cells in Excel:

STEP 1: Select Column C and press **Ctrl +** to add a new column. Name this column as "**Full Name**".

	FIRST NAME	LAST NAME	FULL NAME	PRODUCTS	SALES REGION	ORDER DATE	SALES
1	SALES REPORT						
2	FIRST NAME	LAST NAME	FULL NAME	PRODUCTS	SALES REGION	ORDER DATE	SALES
3	Michael	Rose		SOFT DRINKS	AMERICAS	08/04/20	24,640
4	John	Lee		SOFT DRINKS	AMERICAS	19/04/20	24,640
5	David	Smith		SOFT DRINKS	AMERICAS	14/04/20	29,923
6	Simson	Jones		SOFT DRINKS	AMERICAS	13/04/20	66,901
7	Charles	Spector		SOFT DRINKS	AMERICAS	20/04/20	63,116
8	George	Brown		SOFT DRINKS	AMERICAS	14/04/20	38,281
9	Emma	Miller		SOFT DRINKS	AMERICAS	22/04/20	42,150
10							

STEP 2: Select Cell C3 and type the formula: **=CONCATENATE(A3, B3)**. Press Enter

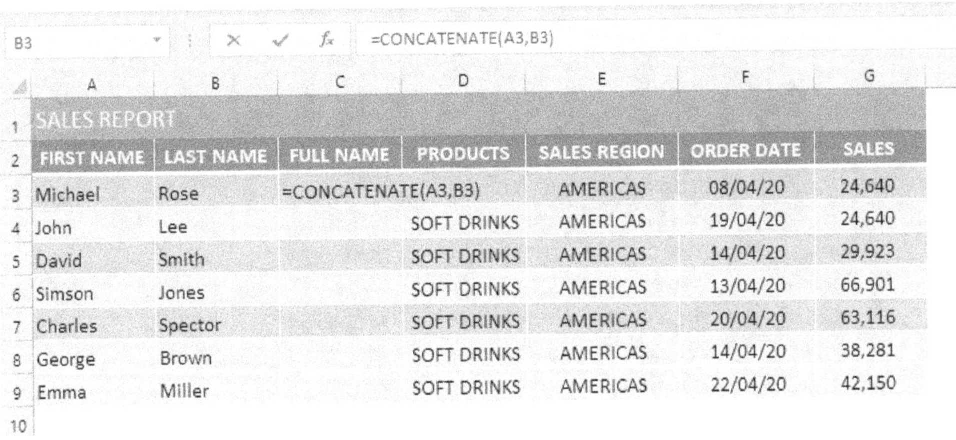

STEP 3: Copy cell C3 and paste it in remaining cells or drag the fill handle to copy the formula to the other cells below.

This will merge cells in Excel without losing the data! Below we show you how to make this merged cell look better by adding a space between the First & Last Names as well as a line break.

Adding a Space & Line Breaks while Merging Cells

In the FULL NAME column above, you can see that there is no space or any character between the FIRST NAME and the LAST NAME. This mashed-together value of the FULL NAME isn't a typographical mistake.

To **concatenate this information and include spaces**, in the 2nd CONCATENATE function argument, you need to type in double quotation marks and put a **space** between these quotations (**" "**)

The edited formula will be =CONCATENATE(A3," ", B3).

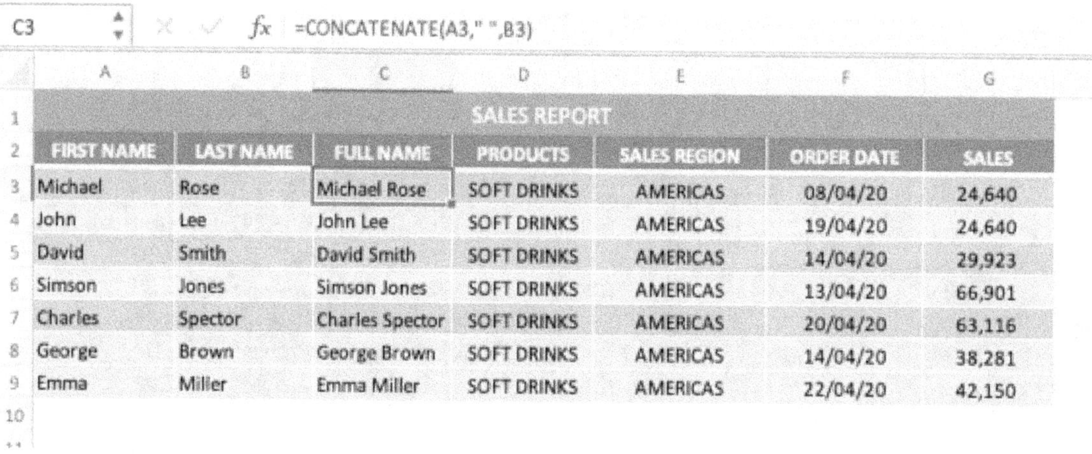

You can replace the space with a dot, comma, or any other character. Simply replace the space in this function with a character and make sure to enclose the character or text in double quotation marks.

With the Concatenate function you also have the option to amend the combination later, whereas you don't have any such option if you use Merge & Center.

You can also **use the ampersand sign, &, to combine cells** in Excel. The **&** operator works just like the CONCATENATE function where you can combine text, numbers, individual cells, etc. Both **CONCATENATE** and **&** produce the same results.

The following examples show the same SALES REPORT but this time I will use the **&** operator to merge cells in Excel.

The formula to be used is = **A3&" "&B3**

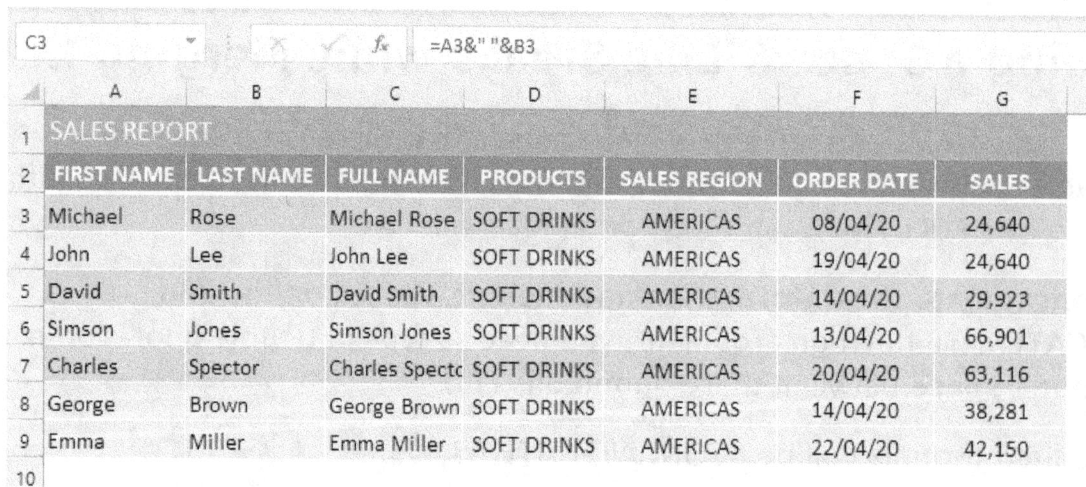

You can see that the result is the same and you can use either the ampersand sign **&** or the **CONCATENATE** function, it just depends on what you are more comfortable with.

You can also add line breaks while merging cells by using the **CHAR(10)** function in Excel.

The **CHAR(10)** function is used to add a line break between FULL NAME & SALES. You can use the formula: =CONCATENATE(B3, **CHAR(10)**, C3).

Also, make sure you select the "**Wrap Text**" option under the Home Tab, otherwise the result will be displayed in the same line only.

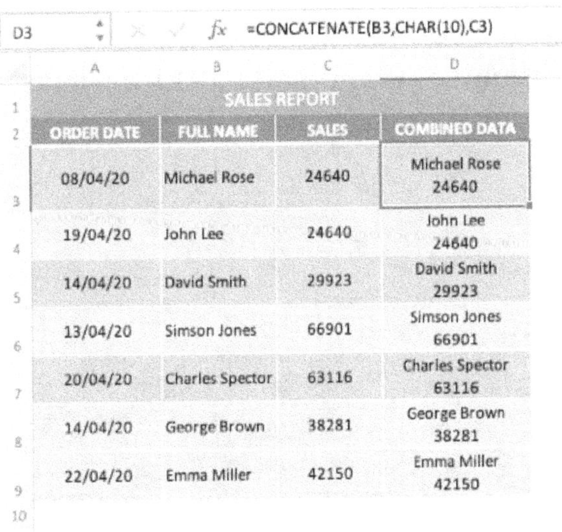

You can see that the FULL NAME is displayed on the first line and the second line contains SALES, which is another cool way you can create Excel merged cells.

Bonus Approach – Flash Fill

Lastly, **there is a BONUS approach** to merge cells in Excel with – **Flash Fill.** It is probably the simplest way to combine cells in Excel and is available in Excel 2013 or later.

Flash Fill is a special tool that analyses the pattern from the existing cells and then automatically extracts the data to the pattern that you set. We can combine the FIRST NAME and LAST NAME from the previous example using Flash Fill.

STEP 1: You should establish a pattern by typing the FULL NAME in cell C3. That will be "Michael Rose." This gives Flash Fill an example.

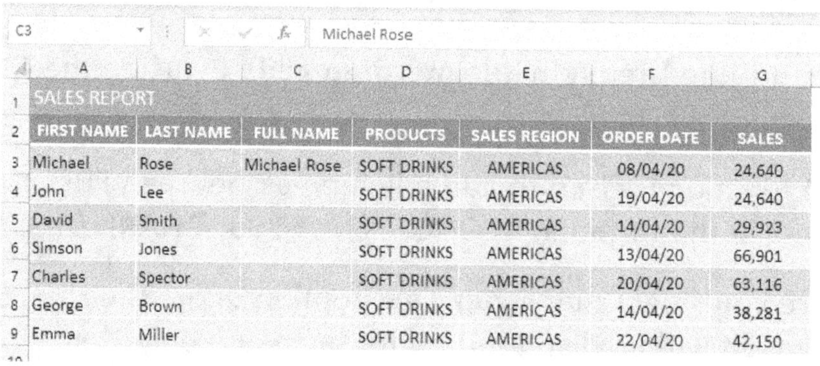

STEP 2: Highlight that value you just typed and press the keyboard shortcut **Ctrl + E** or go to the ribbon menu and select: **Data > Flash Fill**

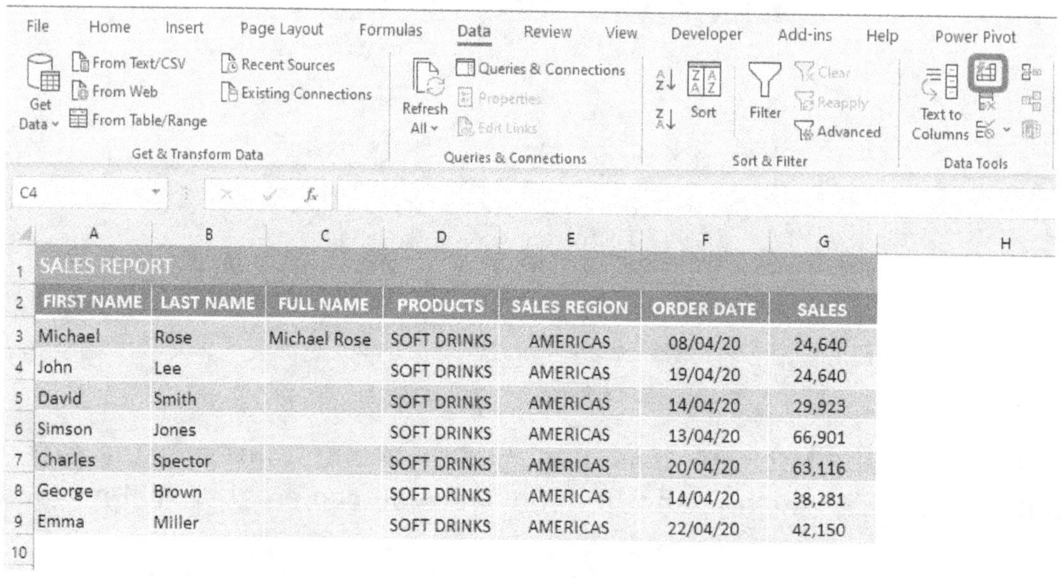

STEP 3: Excel will sense the pattern you provided in C3, and will fill in the empty cells below, merging the FIRST NAME with the LAST NAME.

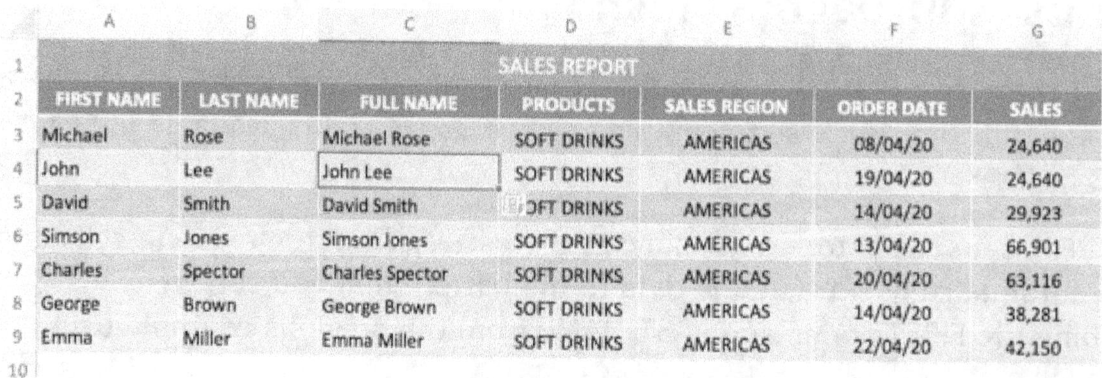

If the Flash Fill does not seem to be working for your data, make sure it is turned on.

To turn Flash Fill on, go to **Tools > Options > Advanced > Editing Options > check the "Automatically Flash Fill" box**.

Excel's Flash Fill feature is a versatile tool **that can be used to merge, split, or clean data.** You need to type the first entry for Excel to infer the pattern and then Excel fills in the rest of the data based on the pattern you provided.

Overall, the **Merge & Center** or **Center Across Selection** features in Excel makes data more visually presentable and highly organized. But it only keeps the contents of the top-left cell and deletes the rest.

This loss of data is a big disadvantage when you merge cells in Excel. To preserve your data in Excel, use the **&** operator, the **CONCATENATE** function, or **Flash Fill** to merge cell contents into one cell.

Add Custom Symbols With Numbers

Excel has several built in features to create custom formatting to your numbers. But if none of them meets your requirement, you will have to create your own.

The key benefit of adding custom formatting is that it only **controls how the number is displayed** without changing the underlying value of that number.

A cool feature within Excel is the ability to format a cell's value by pressing **CTRL + 1** on any cell. This brings up the **Format Cells** dialog box and under the **Custom** category, you can customize the Type to whatever you like.

You can even create custom symbols in Excel using this feature!

But before you understand how to **add a symbol to a number** in Excel, you need to first know how to **write a number format code.**

Understanding the Number Format Code

You can change the format of a cell's value by either using various formats available in Excel or creating a custom format using a number format code.

A number format code is created using symbols that tells Excel how you want to display the cell's value. When adding a custom format in Excel, there are four formatting sections that you have to follow:

Positive format; Negative format; Zero format; Text format.

Each of these sections is separated by a semicolon(;) and only the first section is required to create a custom format.

Create Custom Symbols in Excel

Now that you have understood the structure of how to use a number format code, let's use that knowledge and learn how to insert a symbol in an Excel formula based on the cell's value.

Working with an example will make this concept clearer. So, let's get started.

Example #1:

In the table below, we have daily temperatures recorded

DATE	TEMPERATURE
12-01-20	37.1
13-01-20	37.4
14-01-20	37.9
15-01-20	36.1
16-01-20	37.2
17-01-20	37
18-01-20	37.3
19-01-20	37.8
20-01-20	38
21-01-20	38
22-01-20	37.8
23-01-20	36.8

We want to add the symbol °C next to each temperature so it will look something like this:

DATE	TEMPERATURE
12-01-20	37.10 °C
13-01-20	37.40 °C
14-01-20	37.90 °C
15-01-20	36.10 °C
16-01-20	37.20 °C
17-01-20	37.00 °C
18-01-20	37.30 °C
19-01-20	37.80 °C
20-01-20	38.00 °C
21-01-20	38.00 °C
22-01-20	37.80 °C
23-01-20	36.80 °C

The following steps should be done to create custom symbols in Excel:

STEP 1: Select the "**Temperature**" column

DATE	TEMPERATURE
12-01-20	37.1
13-01-20	37.4
14-01-20	37.9
15-01-20	36.1
16-01-20	37.2
17-01-20	37
18-01-20	37.3
19-01-20	37.8
20-01-20	38
21-01-20	38
22-01-20	37.8
23-01-20	36.8

STEP 2: Go to **Home** > Under Format Dropdown, Select **More Number Formats** or press **CTRL + 1**

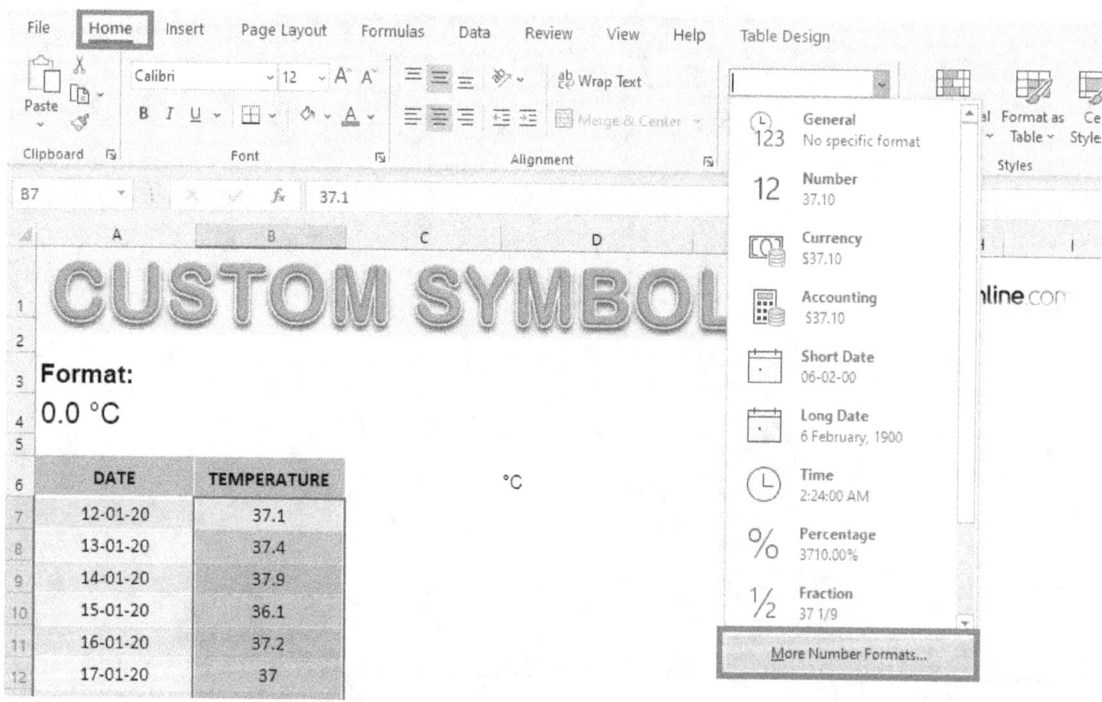

STEP 3: In the Format Cell dialog box, select Custom

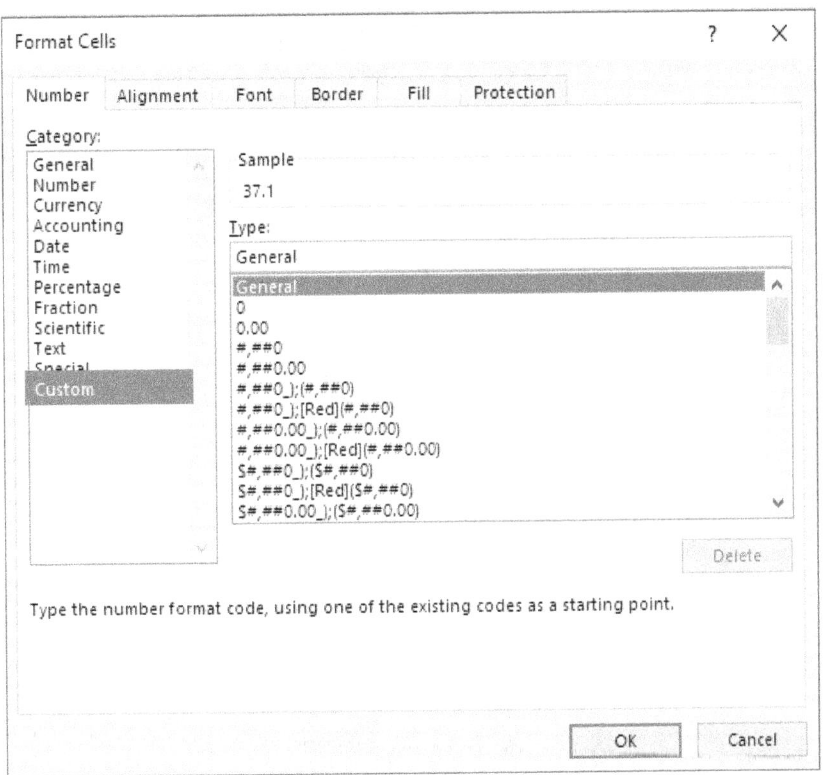

STEP 4: In the **Type** section, type **0.00 °C** and Click **OK**

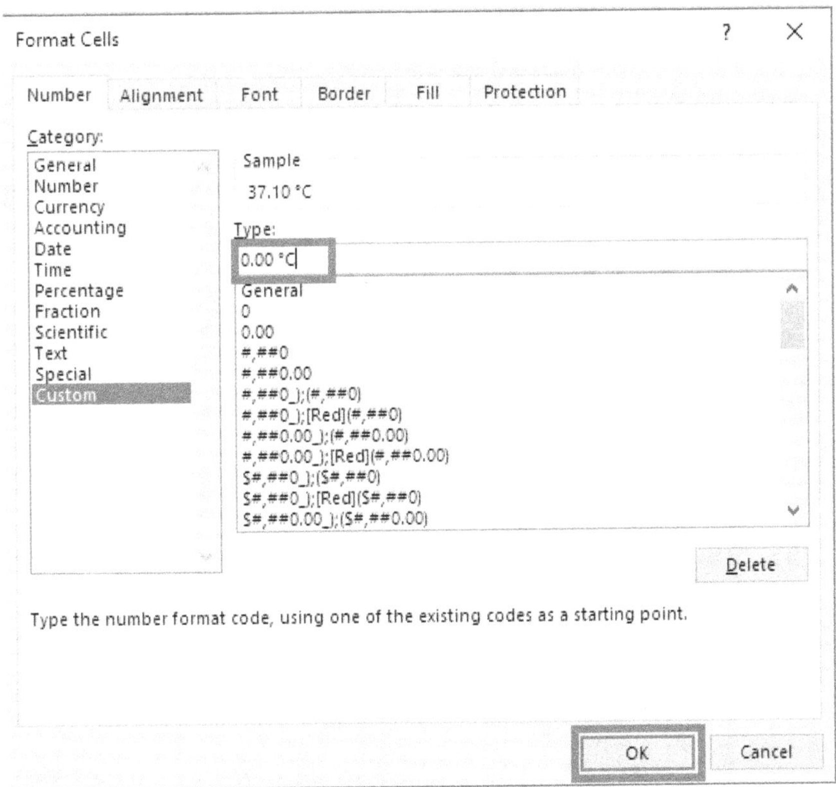

This is how the edited table will look like.

DATE	TEMPERATURE
12-01-20	37.10 °C
13-01-20	37.40 °C
14-01-20	37.90 °C
15-01-20	36.10 °C
16-01-20	37.20 °C
17-01-20	37.00 °C
18-01-20	37.30 °C
19-01-20	37.80 °C
20-01-20	38.00 °C
21-01-20	38.00 °C
22-01-20	37.80 °C
23-01-20	36.80 °C

Example #2:

In Example #1, you have learned how to add symbols in Excel irrespective of the cell's value. Now let's move forward and understand how to add symbols based on the number stored in the cell.

The symbols added would be based on the value stored in the cell.

In the table below, we have the status for different projects listed below with **0** indicating *Completed* and **-1 indicating** *Pending*.

PROJECT	STATUS
Project 1	0
Project 2	0
Project 3	-1
Project 4	-1
Project 5	0
Project 6	-1
Project 7	-1
Project 8	-1
Project 9	0
Project 10	0

Now you want to create custom symbols in Excel wherein you want to add these custom symbols:

√ Completed; **when status is 0**

✕ Pending; **when status is -1**

The table with custom symbols should look like this:

PROJECT	STATUS
Project 1	
Project 2	
Project 3	✕ Pending
Project 4	✕ Pending
Project 5	
Project 6	✕ Pending
Project 7	✕ Pending
Project 8	✕ Pending
Project 9	
Project 10	

STEP 1: Select the **Status Column**

PROJECT	STATUS
Project 1	0
Project 2	0
Project 3	-1
Project 4	-1
Project 5	0
Project 6	-1
Project 7	-1
Project 8	-1
Project 9	0
Project 10	0

STEP 2: Press **Ctrl +1** to open the **Format Cells** dialog box

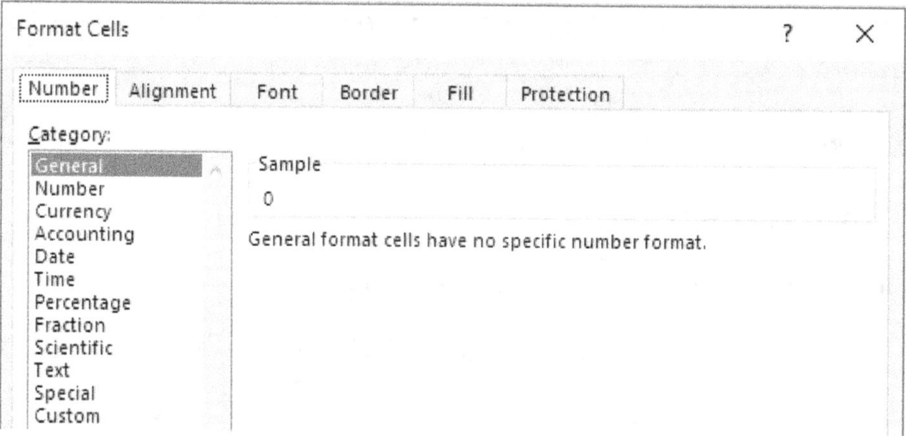

STEP 3: Select the **Custom** category and under **Type** enter this:

✓" Completed";✕" Pending"

This will change the format to ✓ **Completed** when cell value is 0 and ✕ **Pending** when cell value is -1.

You can also add colors to make the formatting more distinct. Under **Type** enter this:

[Green]✓" Completed";[Red]✕" Pending"

Which will add a green color to the completed project and a red color to pending projects.

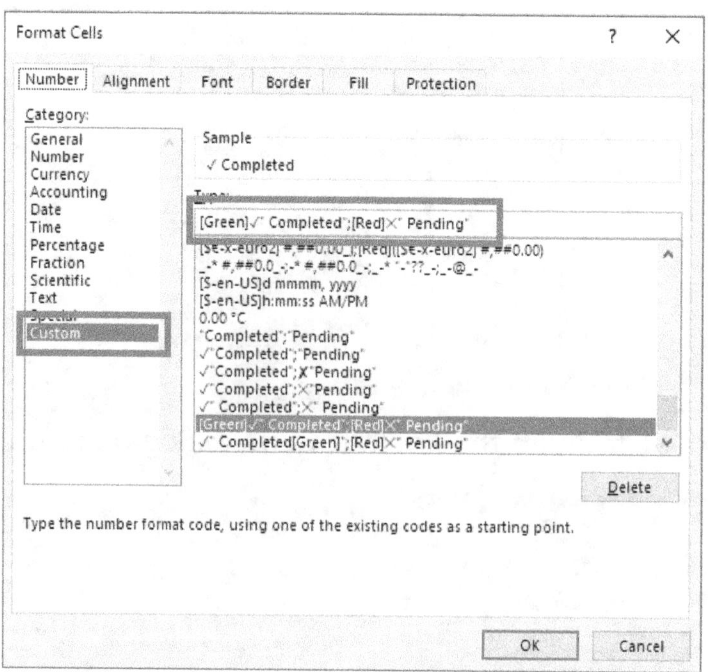

This is how the table will look like this.

PROJECT	STATUS
Project 1	
Project 2	
Project 3	✕ Pending
Project 4	✕ Pending
Project 5	
Project 6	✕ Pending
Project 7	✕ Pending
Project 8	✕ Pending
Project 9	
Project 10	

Example #3:

We have monthly sales, benchmark sales and variance in this table:

MONTH	SALES	BENCHMARK	VARIANCE
January	$125	$170	-26%
February	$330	$166	99%
March	$161	$240	-33%
April	$584	$291	101%
May	$455	$220	107%
June	$213	$167	28%
July	$345	$269	28%
August	$160	$152	5%
September	$441	$269	64%
October	$233	$237	-2%
November	$152	$125	22%
December	$105	$284	-63%

We want the % Variance column in our data to have symbols ▲▼ to show a negative and positive variance. So, you have the % variance value customized as below:

Green in color with ▲ symbol; when variance % is positive

Red in color with ▼ symbol; when variance % is negative

The table should look something like this:

MONTH	SALES	BENCHMARK	VARIANCE
January	$125	$170	▼-26%
February	$330	$166	▲99%
March	$161	$240	▼-33%
April	$584	$291	▲101%
May	$455	$220	▲107%
June	$213	$167	▲28%
July	$345	$269	▲28%
August	$160	$152	▲5%
September	$441	$269	▲64%
October	$233	$237	▼-2%
November	$152	$125	▲22%
December	$105	$284	▼-63%

STEP 1: Enter a Variance calculation in a column, select the column's variance numbers and press **CTRL + 1** to bring up the **Format Cells** dialog box

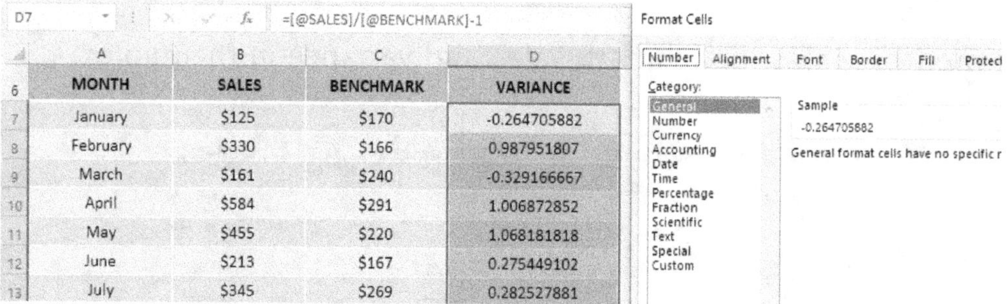

STEP 2: Select the **Custom** category and under **Type** enter this:

"#,##0;[Red]-#,##0

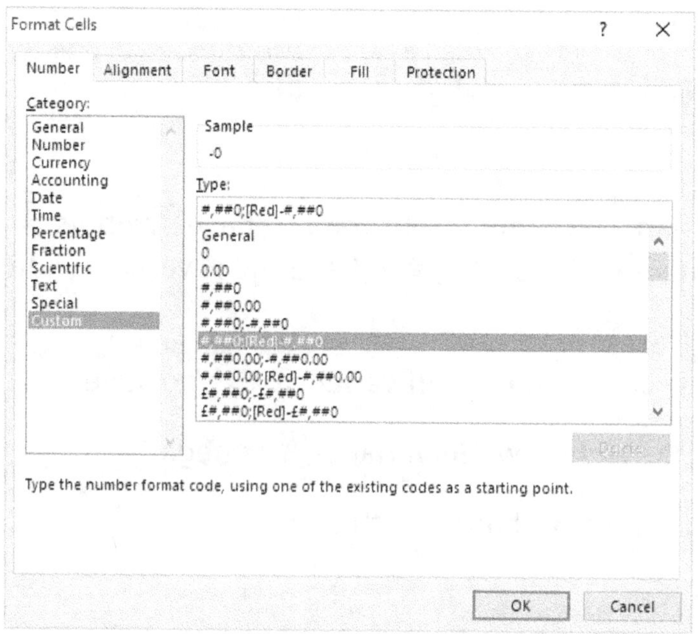

The first section of this code *#,##0* is for a **positive** number, and second code *[Red]-#,##0* is for a **negative** number.

To show the positive number in green color and add a % sign, follow **Step 3**.

STEP 3: Under the **Type:** area you will need to enter the text [green] at the start of the positive value string and enter the % sign at the end of the positive and negative value strings

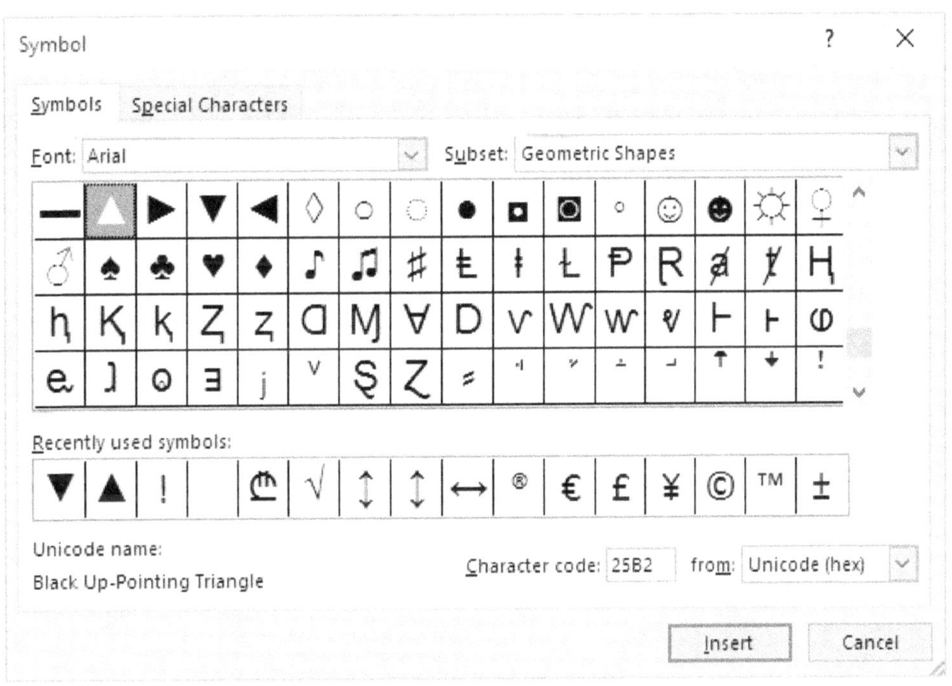

STEP 4: Now select a blank cell and go to **Insert > Symbol > Font: Arial > Subset: Geometric Shapes** and then **Insert** the *Up-Pointing Triangle* and then **Insert** the *Down-Pointing Triangle* and press **Cancel** to exit.

STEP 5: You will need to **copy the triangles**, select the variance numbers, press **CTRL + 1** and **paste the triangles before each positive and negative value string, then press OK**

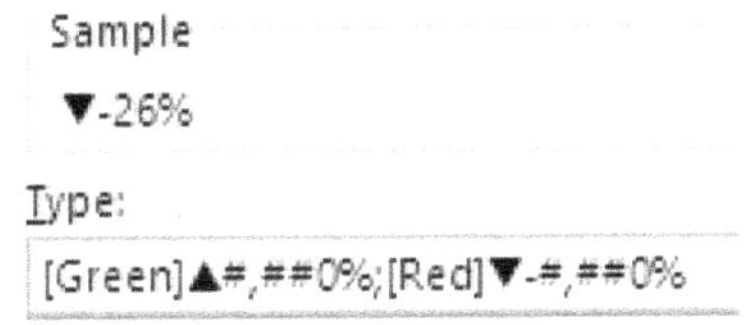

You now have your custom number formats with an upwards triangle for any positive %s and a downwards triangle for any negative %s

MONTH	SALES	BENCHMARK	VARIANCE
January	$125	$170	▼ -26%
February	$330	$166	[illegible]
March	$161	$240	▼ -33%
April	$584	$291	[illegible]
May	$455	$220	[illegible]
June	$213	$167	[illegible]
July	$345	$269	[illegible]
August	$160	$152	[illegible]

Clear a #REF! Error in Excel

Many times, you may have faced the problem that Excel is not returning the desired value, instead is showing an error. The most **common one amongst these is a #REF! error** in Excel.

A #REF error in Excel is shown when the **cell reference provided in a formula is not valid**. It is important to know why this error occurs and how to fix it.

What is a #REF! error in Excel?

What does #REF mean in Excel? #REF! error stands of reference.

This error is shown when the cell that is referenced in a formula is no longer valid or does not exist.

So, #REF error in Excel occurs when the reference used is invalid. It can happen due to one of the following reasons:

- Row, column or a sheet has been deleted.

- Formula contains an incorrect or invalid cell reference.

This means that Excel returns a #REF error when the formula refers to a cell that isn't valid.

Let's look at a few examples to see when this error occurs and how to fix it!

How to fix a #REF error in Excel?

Example #1:

In the table below, you will spot multiple #REF! errors within formulas used in several cells.

This has happened because we deleted a range that contains an explicit cell reference within the formula used.

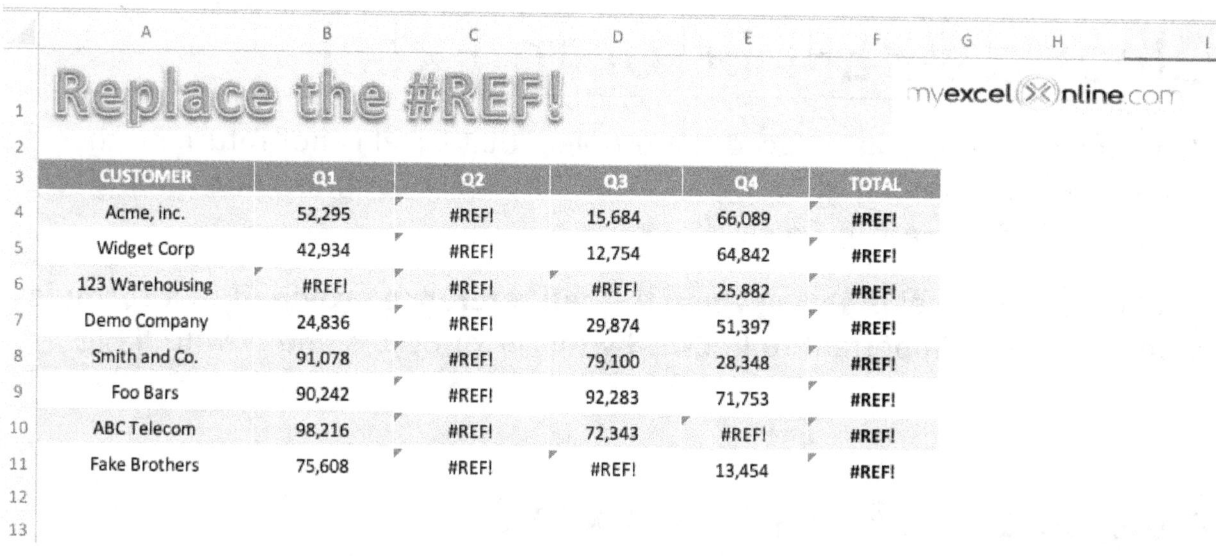

To get rid of this error message we have to select the cell(s) with this error, by using the **Find & Replace** dialog box and do the following:

Find What: #REF!

Replace With: (Leave this blank)

Press OK and it will clear the #REF error in Excel within the formula.

Let's look at the step-by-step tutorial below to understand how to remove #REF in Excel.

STEP 1: To check the cell containing the cell, simply click on the cell and press F2.

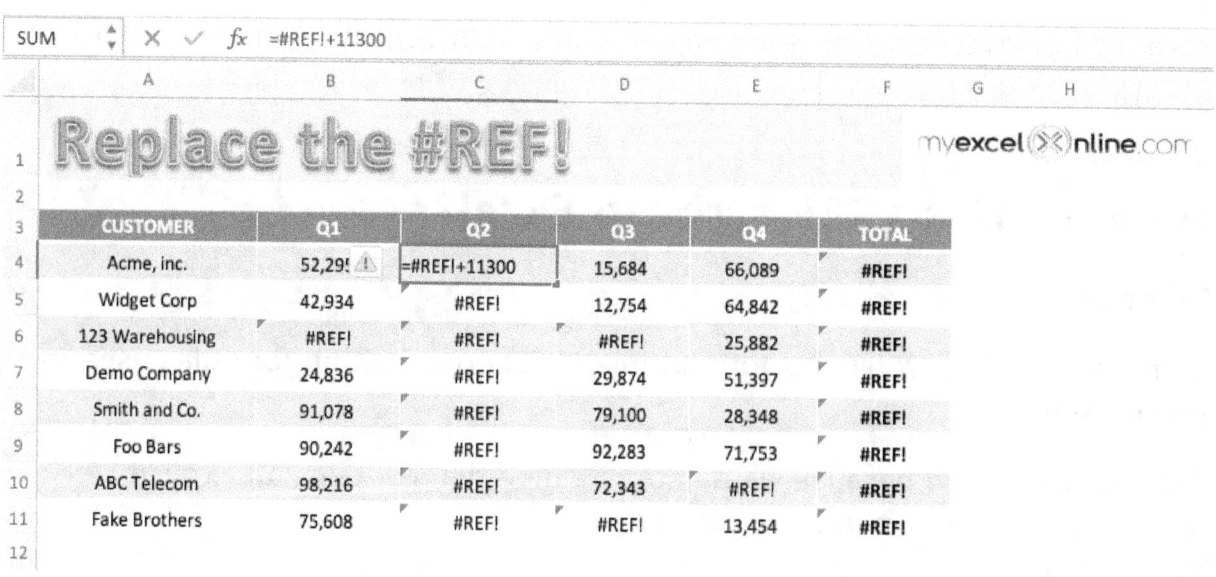

Here, since you have used an explicit cell reference and it was deleted, Excel is returning a #REF error.

 Highlight the table containing the errors.

CUSTOMER	Q1	Q2	Q3	Q4	TOTAL
Acme, inc.	52,295	#REF!	15,684	66,089	#REF!
Widget Corp	42,934	#REF!	12,754	64,842	#REF!
123 Warehousing	#REF!	#REF!	#REF!	25,882	#REF!
Demo Company	24,836	#REF!	29,874	51,397	#REF!
Smith and Co.	91,078	#REF!	79,100	28,348	#REF!
Foo Bars	90,242	#REF!	92,283	71,753	#REF!
ABC Telecom	98,216	#REF!	72,343	#REF!	#REF!
Fake Brothers	75,608	#REF!	#REF!	13,454	#REF!

STEP 3: Press **Ctrl + H** to open the **Find & Replace** dialog box.

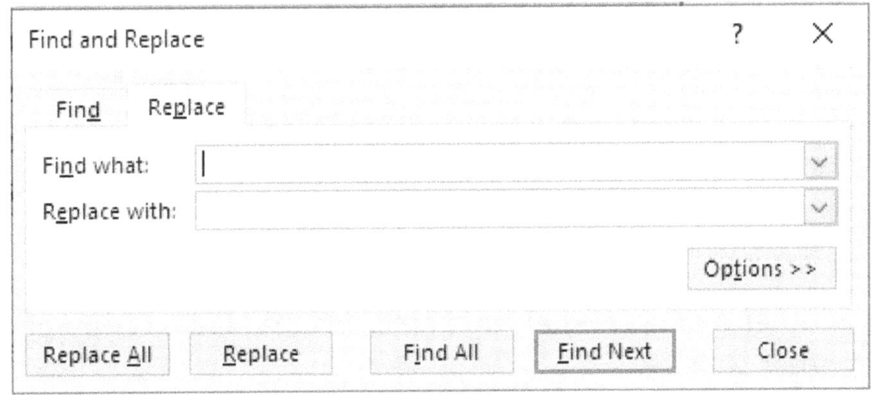

STEP 4: Under Find What, input #**REF!** and leave Replace as **blank**. This is done to replace all the #REF! errors with a blank.

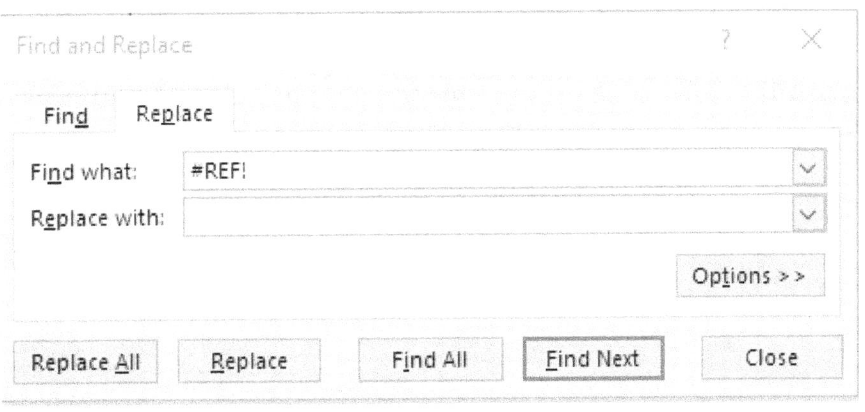

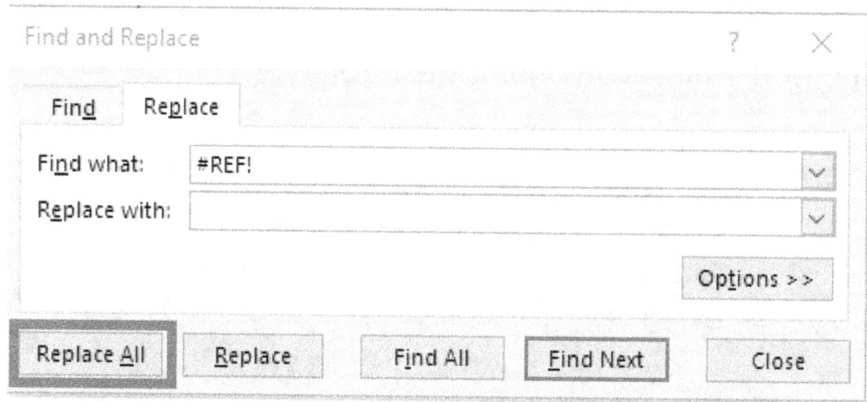

This is how your replaced data will look like:

CUSTOMER	Q1	Q2	Q3	Q4	TOTAL
Acme, inc.	52,295	11,300	15,684	66,089	145,368
Widget Corp	42,934	10,025	12,754	64,842	130,555
123 Warehousing	10,000	10,190	10,000	25,882	56,072
Demo Company	24,836	10,055	29,874	51,397	116,162
Smith and Co.	91,078	10,364	79,100	28,348	208,890
Foo Bars	90,242	12,600	92,283	71,753	266,878
ABC Telecom	98,216	13,000	72,343	10,000	193,559
Fake Brothers	75,608	15,000	10,000	13,454	114,062

Let's look at another example when this error occurs due to copy-pasting the formula from other cells.

Example #2:

In the table below, we have sales data for different customers for 4 quarters and a sum formula used to calculate the total sales. The formula used to calculate the total sales value is:

$$=SUM(B4, C4, D4, E4)$$

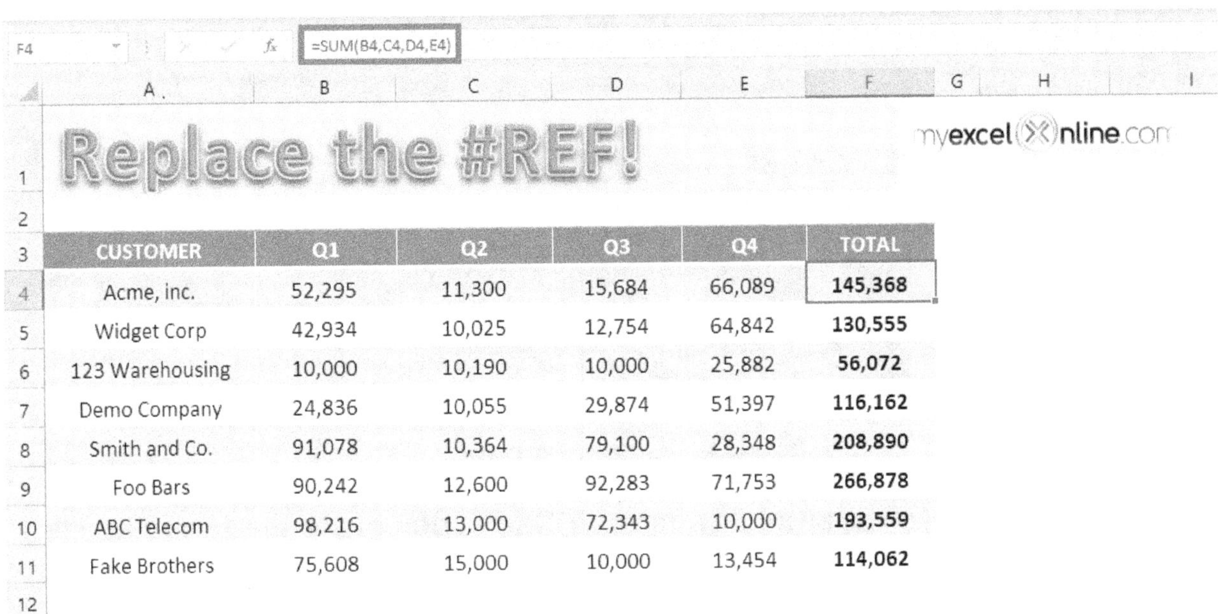

If you try and **delete Column E** (Quarter 4), the sum formula will change to =SUM(B4, C4, D4,#REF!) and return an error - #REF.

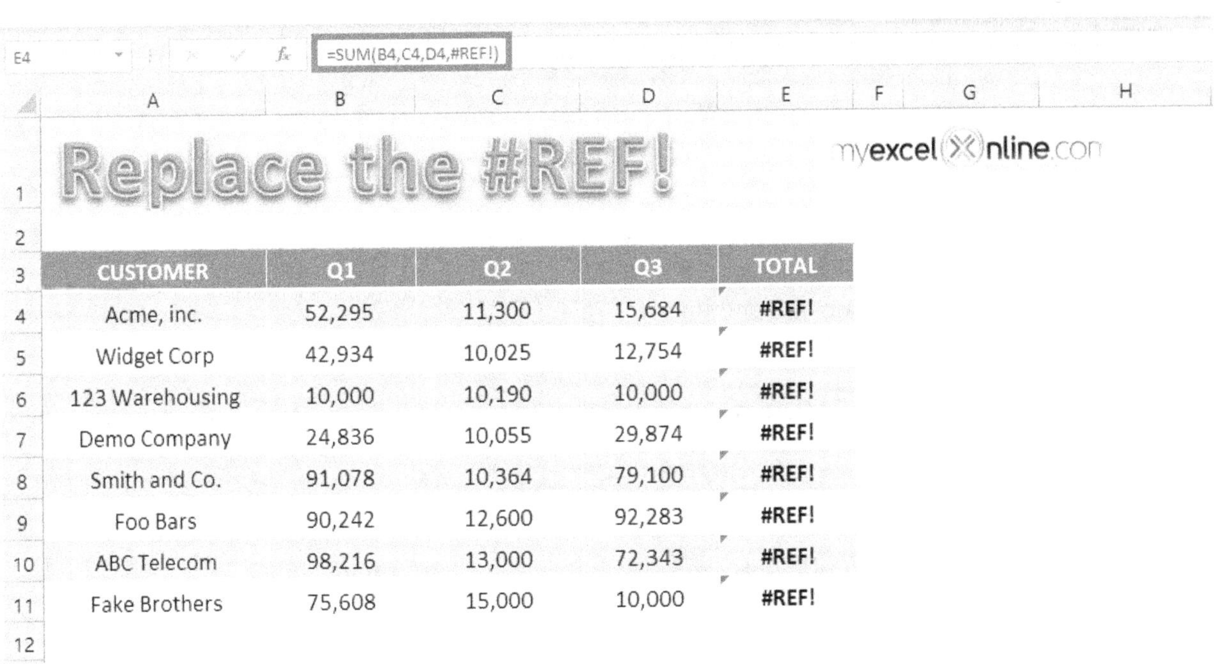

A simple fix to this problem is to use a **range** instead of an explicit cell reference. Let's look at the step-by-step tutorial to learn how:

Replace the #REF!

CUSTOMER	Q1	Q2	Q3	Q4	TOTAL
Acme, inc.	52,295	11,300	15,684	66,089	
Widget Corp	42,934	10,025	12,754	64,842	
123 Warehousing	10,000	10,190	10,000	25,882	
Demo Company	24,836	10,055	29,874	51,397	
Smith and Co.	91,078	10,364	79,100	28,348	
Foo Bars	90,242	12,600	92,283	71,753	
ABC Telecom	98,216	13,000	72,343	10,000	
Fake Brothers	75,608	15,000	10,000	13,454	

STEP 1: Use formula **=SUM(B4:E4)** in cell F4 and copy-paste the formula below to cells F5: F11.

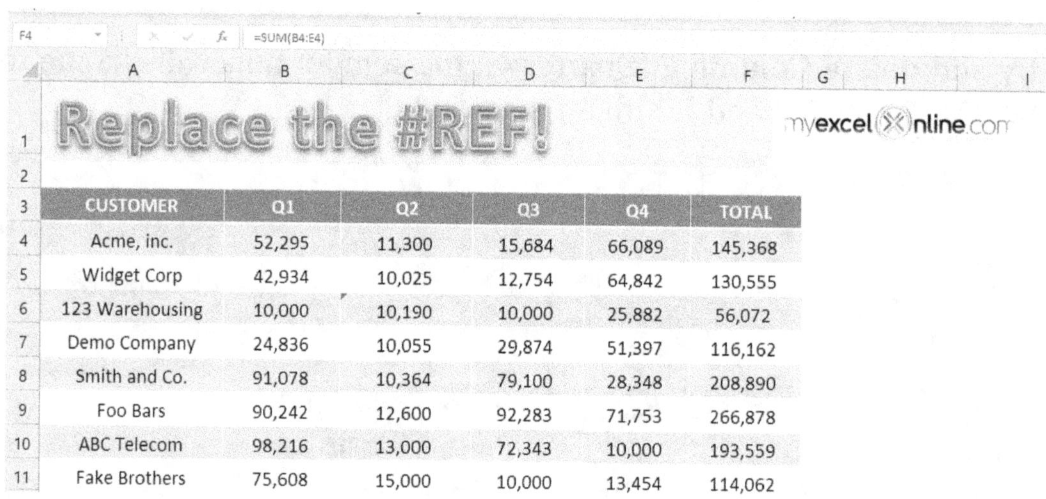

STEP 2: Now delete the **Column E** to get the total sales for only 3 quarters.

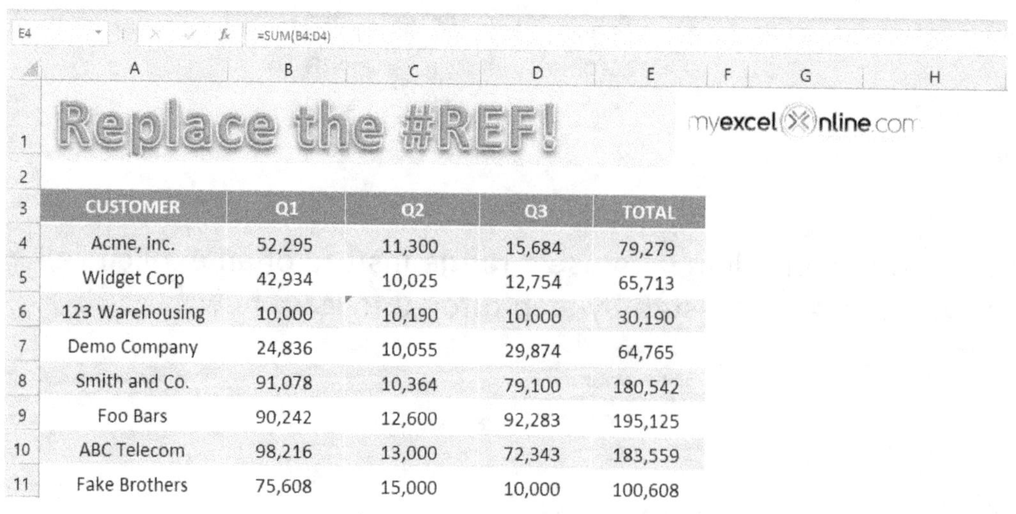

If you change the formula from **=SUM(B4, C4, D4, E4)** to **=SUM(B4: E4)**, you will no longer be vulnerable to #REF in Excel. This formula recalculates the total sales value by removing the deleted cell.

Hence, it is advised to use a range (if applicable) when writing a formula instead of an explicit cell reference.

Let's take a look at another example when the error occurred due to VLOOKUP containing invalid cell reference.

Example #3:

In the table below we have quarterly and total sales for different customers and using the VLOOKUP formula, we have tried to find out the total sales for the customer name mentioned.

CUSTOMER	Q1	Q2	Q3	Q4	TOTAL
Acme, inc.	52,295	11,300	15,684	66,089	145,368
Widget Corp	42,934	10,025	12,754	64,842	130,555
123 Warehousing	10,000	10,190	10,000	25,882	56,072
Demo Company	24,836	10,055	29,874	51,397	116,162
Smith and Co.	91,078	10,364	79,100	28,348	208,890
Foo Bars	90,242	12,600	92,283	71,753	266,878
ABC Telecom	98,216	13,000	72,343	10,000	193,559
Fake Brothers	75,608	15,000	10,000	13,454	114,062

CUSTOMER	TOTAL SALES
Foo Bars	#REF!

The formula used to find the total sales for customers mentioned in cell H4 is

=VLOOKUP(H4,$A$4:$F$11,7,0)

	A	B	C	D	E	F	G	H	I	J
1	Replace the #REF!									
2										
3	CUSTOMER	Q1	Q2	Q3	Q4	TOTAL		CUSTOMER	TOTAL SALES	
4	Acme, inc.	52,295	11,300	15,684	66,089	145,368		Foo Bars	#REF!	
5	Widget Corp	42,934	10,025	12,754	64,842	130,555				
6	123 Warehousing	10,000	10,190	10,000	25,882	56,072				
7	Demo Company	24,836	10,055	29,874	51,397	116,162				
8	Smith and Co.	91,078	10,364	79,100	28,348	208,890				
9	Foo Bars	90,242	12,600	92,283	71,753	266,878				
10	ABC Telecom	98,216	13,000	72,343	10,000	193,559				
11	Fake Brothers	75,608	15,000	10,000	13,454	114,062				
12										

If you look into the formula used in detail, you will see that the value used to indicate the column index number is incorrect.

The arguments for a VLOOKUP function are:

- **Lookup_value** = The value you want to look up in the first column of the table.

- **Table_array** = The table from which you need to retrieve the data.

- **Col_index_num** = The column number in the table array from which matching value should be returned.

- **Range_lookup** = Value should be 1 if you want an approximate match or 0 if you want an exact match of the return value.

Excel is returning an error in this formula because the VLOOKUP is looking to return a value from the 7th column but the reference $A$4:$F$11 contains only 6 columns. We choose 6 because the sales column is the sixth column in the range starting from the left.

To fix this error, use the formula =**VLOOKUP(H4,$A$4:$F$11,6,0)**.

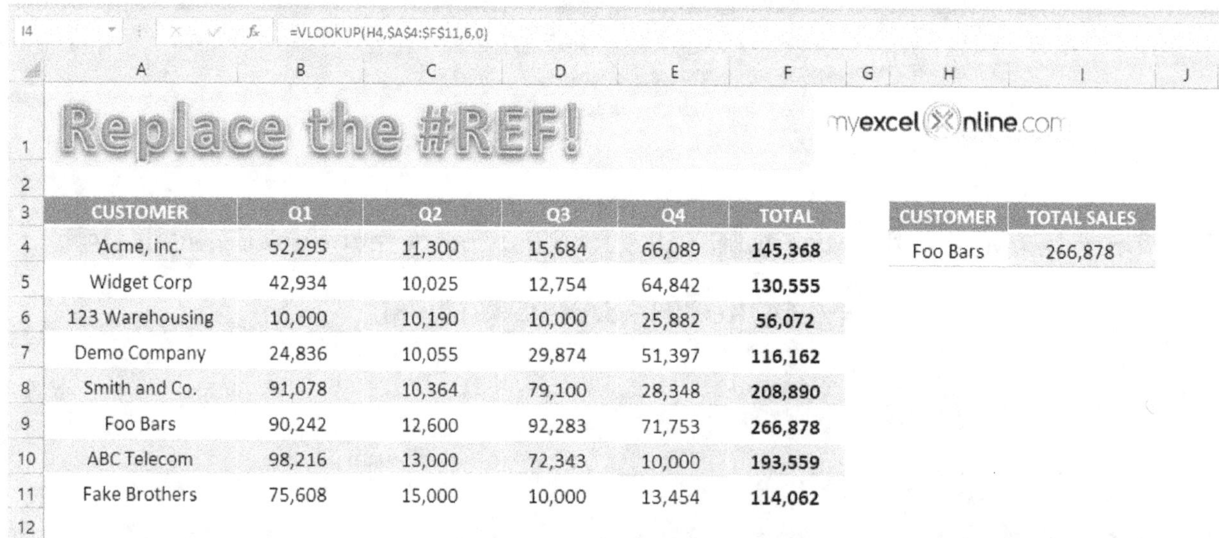

	CUSTOMER	Q1	Q2	Q3	Q4	TOTAL		CUSTOMER	TOTAL SALES
4	Acme, inc.	52,295	11,300	15,684	66,089	145,368		Foo Bars	266,878
5	Widget Corp	42,934	10,025	12,754	64,842	130,555			
6	123 Warehousing	10,000	10,190	10,000	25,882	56,072			
7	Demo Company	24,836	10,055	29,874	51,397	116,162			
8	Smith and Co.	91,078	10,364	79,100	28,348	208,890			
9	Foo Bars	90,242	12,600	92,283	71,753	266,878			
10	ABC Telecom	98,216	13,000	72,343	10,000	193,559			
11	Fake Brothers	75,608	15,000	10,000	13,454	114,062			

Conditional Formatting: Adding to Pivot Tables

Adding some Conditional Formatting to a Pivot Table allows a user to highlight key data in a split second.

See how easy it is to add some color to your analysis to make it visually appealing.

STEP 1: We want to create a rule that will **highlight values greater than 100,000**

Select any cell inside the Pivot Table

	B	C	D	E
5	**Sum of SALES**	Column Labels		
6	Row Labels	2013	2014	2015
7	⊟ EAST	134,146	157,847	89,747
8	123 Warehousing	66,826	49,562	75,088
9	ABC Telecom	67,320	108,285	14,659
10	⊟ NORTH	165,399	102,647	155,550
11	Acme, inc.	85,030	25,263	113,918
12	Smith and Co.	80,369	77,384	41,632
13	⊟ SOUTH	182,984	99,973	179,985
14	Widget Corp	129,462	68,797	94,378
15	Foo Bars	53,522	31,176	85,607
16	⊟ WEST	180,462	178,212	150,042
17	Demo Company	113,799	13,964	106,826
18	Fake Brothers	66,663	164,248	43,216
19	**Grand Total**	**662,991**	**538,679**	**575,324**

Pivot Table   Data   ⊕

STEP 2: Go to *Home > Conditional Formatting > New Rule*

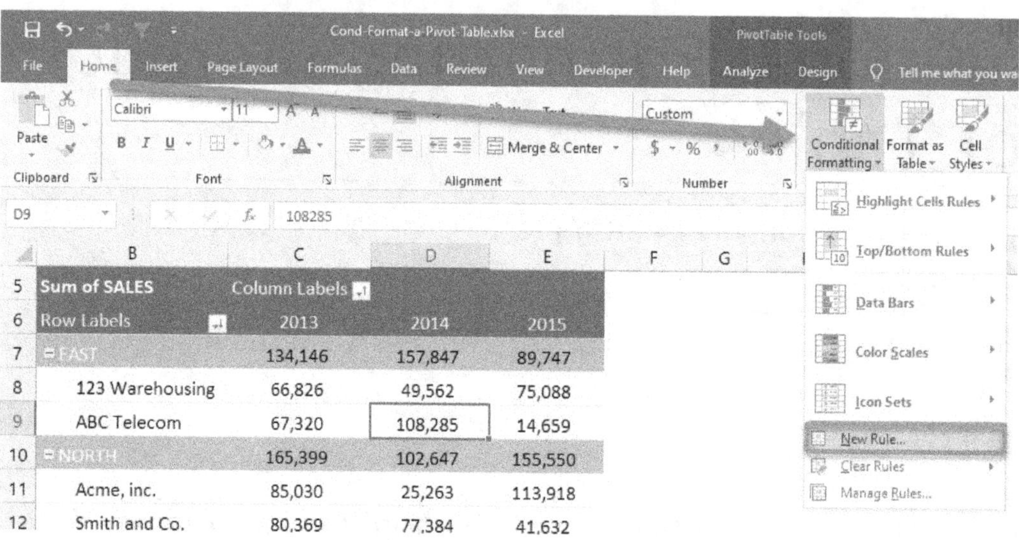

STEP 3: Select the following settings:

Apply Rule To: The 3rd option

Select a Rule Type: Format only cells that contain

Format only cells with: Cell Value > Grater than > 100000

Then click on the **Format** button.

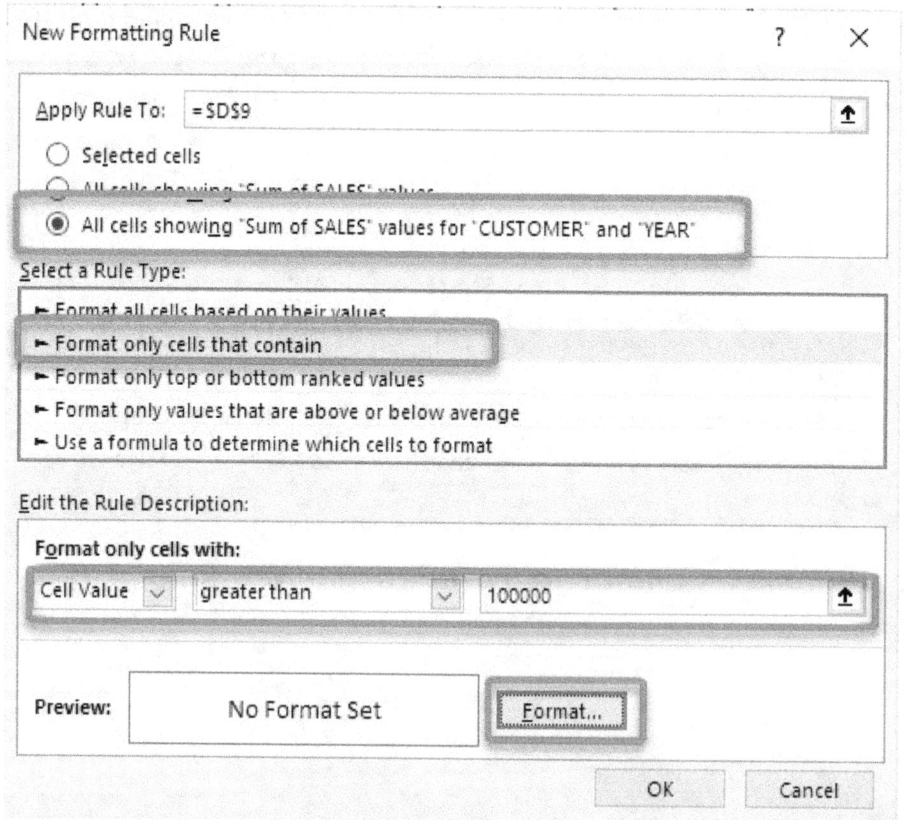

 FORMAT & LAYOUT

STEP 4: Select **Fill** and pick a color of your choice

Click **OK** twice

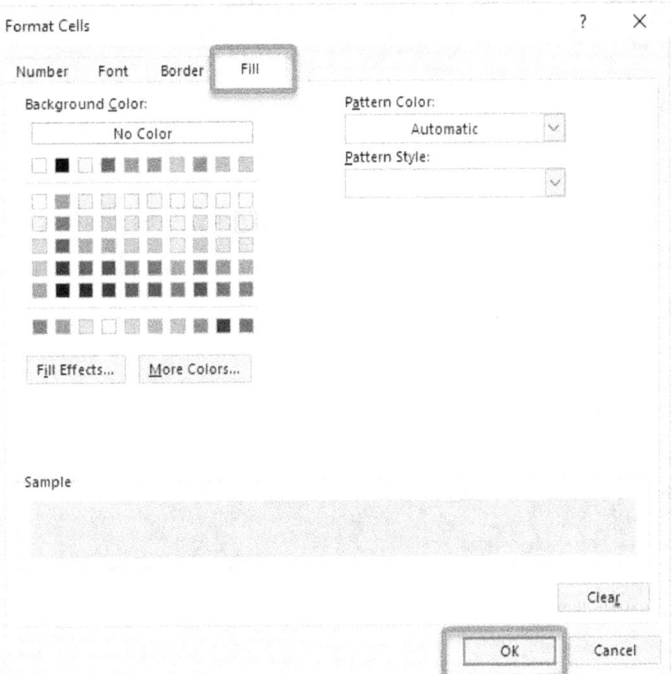

The formatting rule is now applied to your entire Pivot Table!

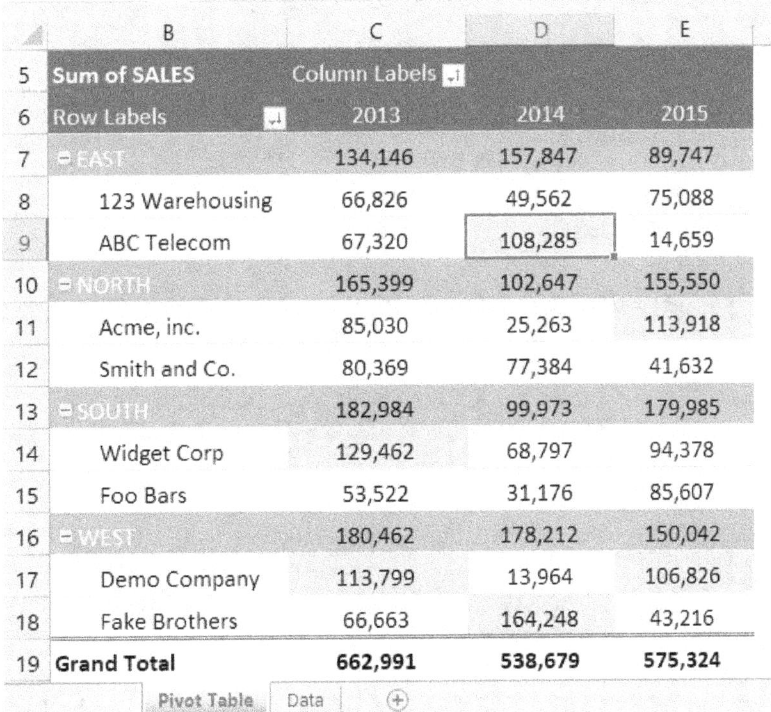

	B	C	D	E
5	**Sum of SALES**	Column Labels		
6	Row Labels	2013	2014	2015
7	⊟EAST	134,146	157,847	89,747
8	123 Warehousing	66,826	49,562	75,088
9	ABC Telecom	67,320	108,285	14,659
10	⊟NORTH	165,399	102,647	155,550
11	Acme, inc.	85,030	25,263	113,918
12	Smith and Co.	80,369	77,384	41,632
13	⊟SOUTH	182,984	99,973	179,985
14	Widget Corp	129,462	68,797	94,378
15	Foo Bars	53,522	31,176	85,607
16	⊟WEST	180,462	178,212	150,042
17	Demo Company	113,799	13,964	106,826
18	Fake Brothers	66,663	164,248	43,216
19	**Grand Total**	**662,991**	**538,679**	**575,324**

Conditional Formatting: Cell's Value

A great way to highlight values within your data set, Excel Table or Pivot Table is to use Conditional Formatting rules.

Formatting cells that contain a specific criterion, for example, *greater than X* or *less than X*, is a good way to visualize your results.

When your criteria references a cell, then you can make this conditional format interactive. So as you manually change the referenced cell's value, the conditional format gets updated and you can see the live results, as shown below.

STEP 1: Select a cell in your Pivot Table.

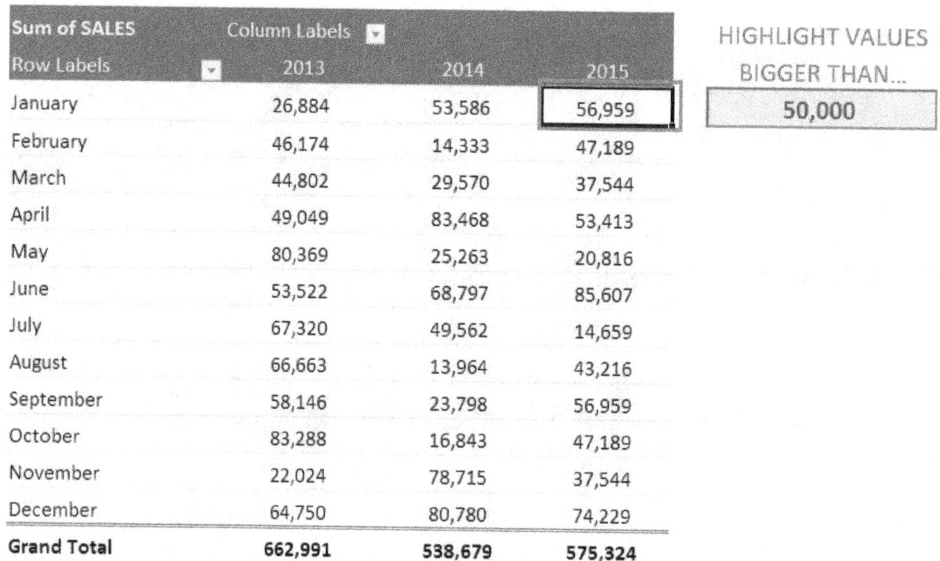

Sum of SALES	Column Labels				HIGHLIGHT VALUES
Row Labels	2013	2014	2015		BIGGER THAN...
January	26,884	53,586	56,959		50,000
February	46,174	14,333	47,189		
March	44,802	29,570	37,544		
April	49,049	83,468	53,413		
May	80,369	25,263	20,816		
June	53,522	68,797	85,607		
July	67,320	49,562	14,659		
August	66,663	13,964	43,216		
September	58,146	23,798	56,959		
October	83,288	16,843	47,189		
November	22,024	78,715	37,544		
December	64,750	80,780	74,229		
Grand Total	**662,991**	**538,679**	**575,324**		

STEP 2: Go to *Home > Conditional Formatting > New Rule*

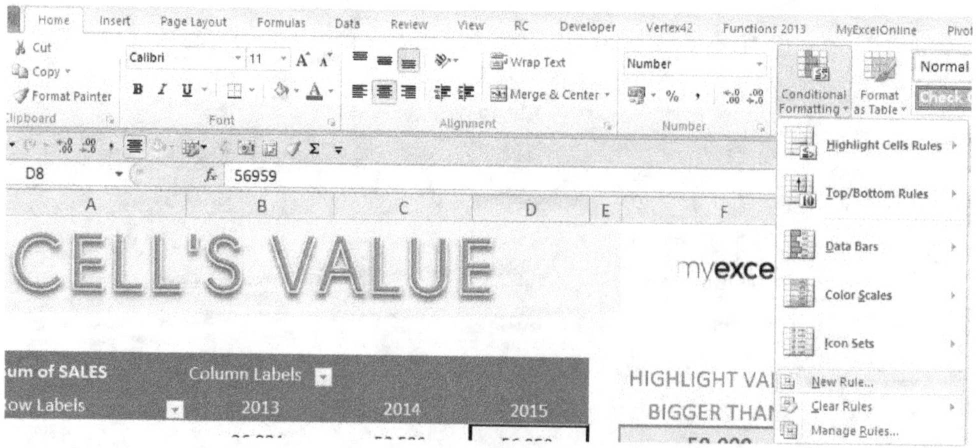

STEP 3: Set **Apply Rule** to the third option: All cells showing "Sum of SALES" values for "MONTH" and "YEAR"

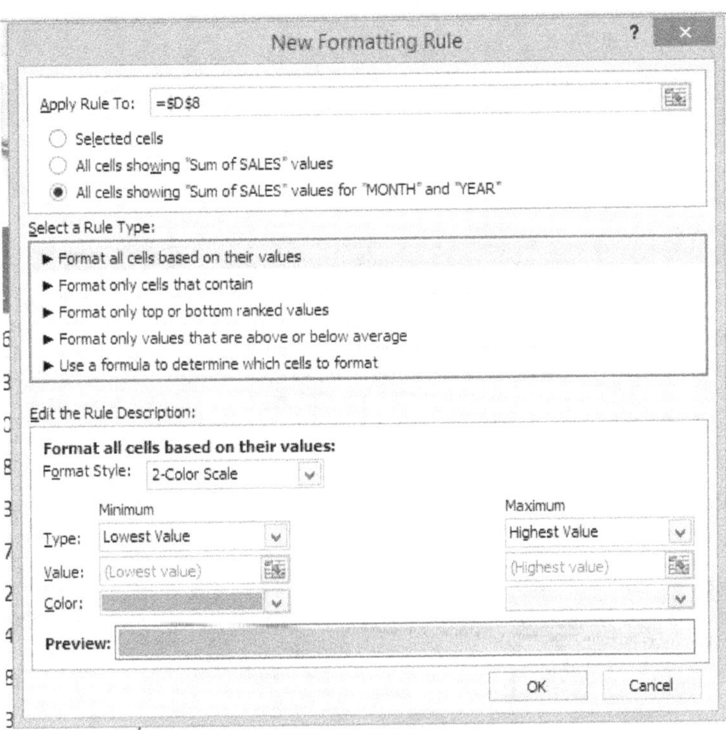

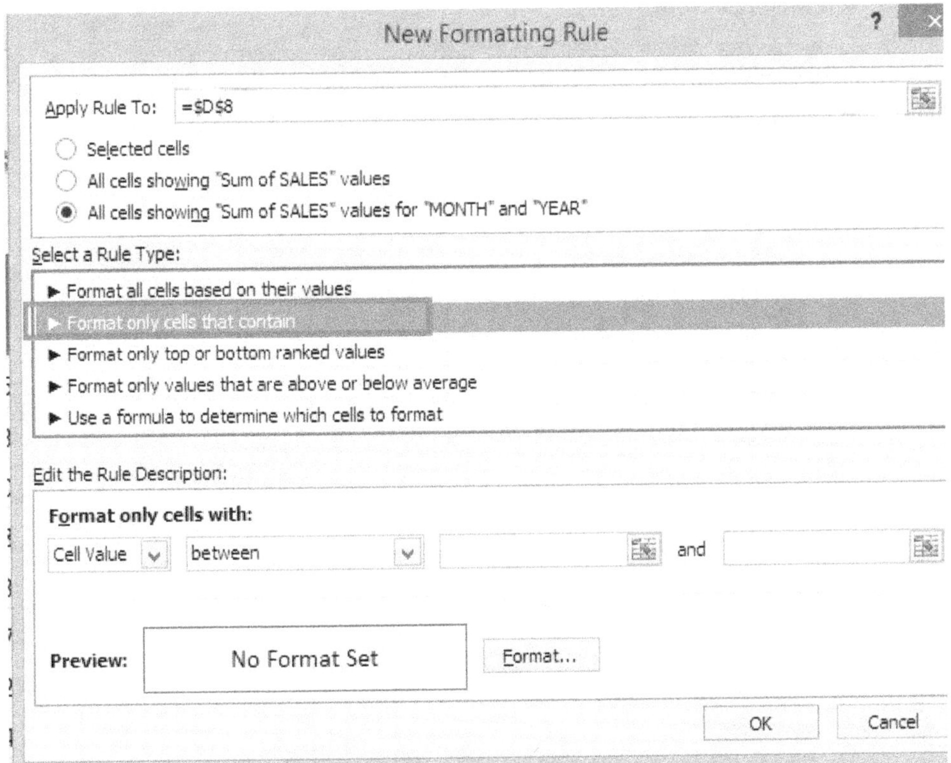

STEP 4: Select a rule type: **Format Only Cells That Contain**

 Edit the Rule Description. Go to *Cell Value > Greater Than > Select the cell F8*

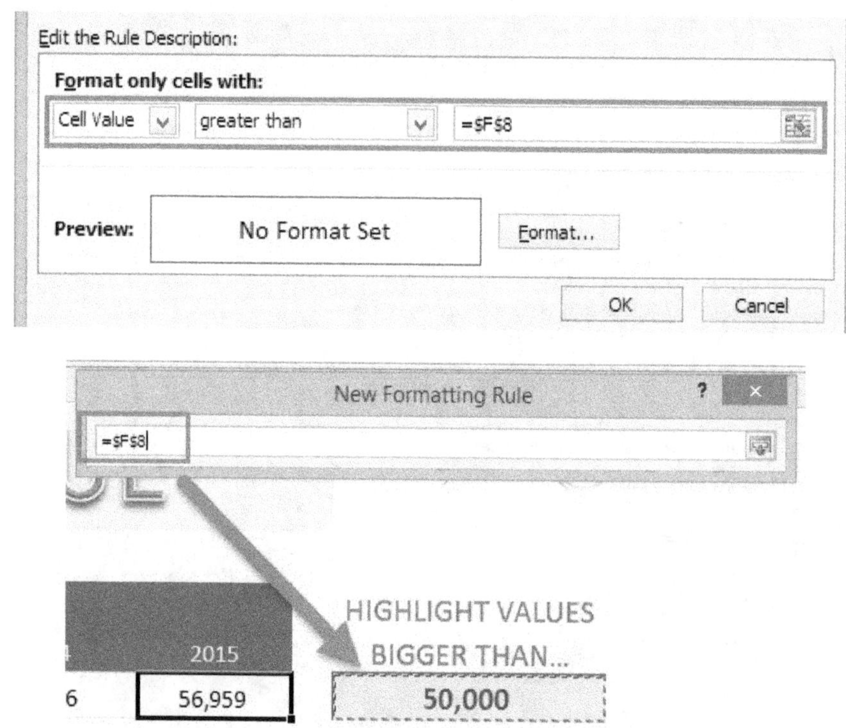

STEP 6: Select the cell format. Click **Format** and select the **Fill** tab and choose a **color (light red).** Click **OK.**

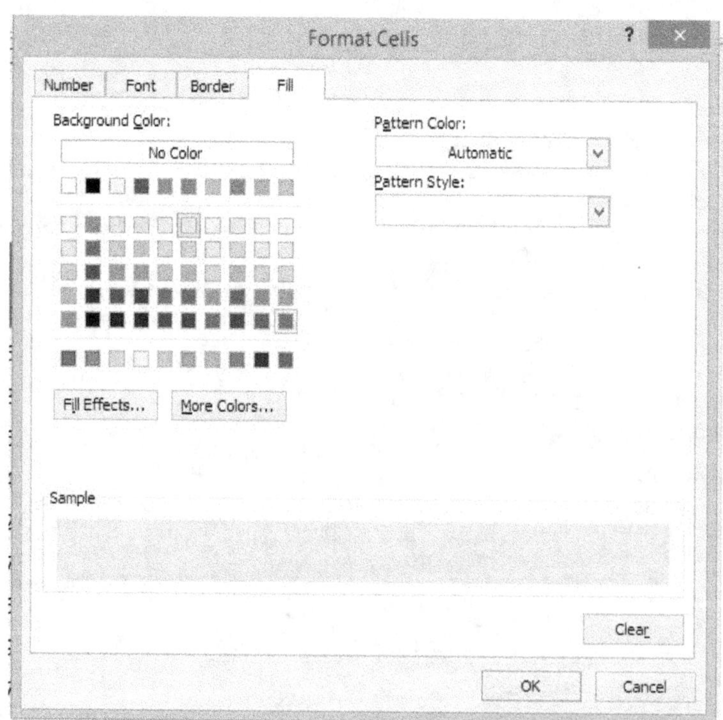

Try it out now! The highlight now happens dynamically when you update the value.

Sum of SALES	Column Labels		
Row Labels	2013	2014	2015
January	26,884	53,586	56,959
February	46,174	14,333	47,189
March	44,802	29,570	37,544
April	49,049	83,468	53,413
May	80,369	25,263	20,816
June	53,522	68,797	85,607
July	67,320	49,562	14,659
August	66,663	13,964	43,216
September	58,146	23,798	56,959
October	83,288	16,843	47,189
November	22,024	78,715	37,544
December	64,750	80,780	74,229
Grand Total	662,991	538,679	575,324

HIGHLIGHT VALUES BIGGER THAN...

80,000

Conditional Formatting: Data Bars, Color Scales & Icon Sets

Conditional Formatting improved with the release of Excel 2010 and the introduction of Data Bars, Color Scales & Icon Sets.

Data Bars: Includes graphic bars in a cell, proportional to the cell's value - Good for Financial Analysis.

Color Scales: Includes a background color, proportional to the cell's value - Good for Heat Maps.

Icon Sets: Shows icons in a cell. The icons depend on the cell's value - Good for Project Management reports.

STEP 1: Select the range that you want to apply the conditional formatting on.

CUSTOMER	2013	2014	2015
Acme, inc.	£85,030	£25,263	£113,918
Demo Company	£113,799	£13,964	£106,826
Widget Corp	£129,462	£68,797	£94,378
Foo Bars	£53,522	£31,176	£85,607
123 Warehousing	£66,826	£49,562	£75,088
Fake Brothers	£66,663	£164,248	£43,216
Smith and Co.	£80,369	£77,384	£41,632
ABC Telecom	£67,320	£108,285	£14,659

STEP 2: Go to *Home > Conditional Formatting*

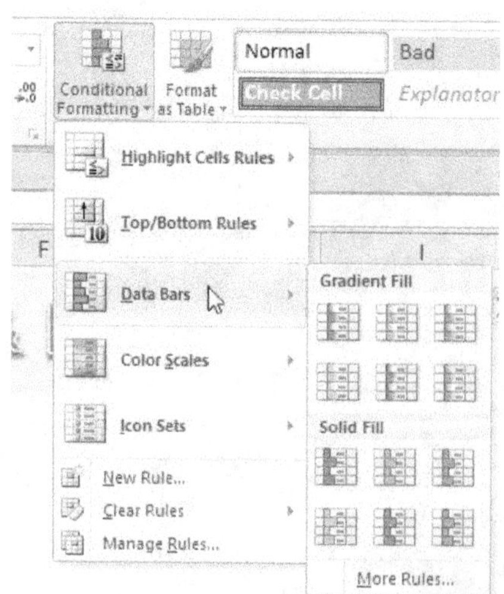

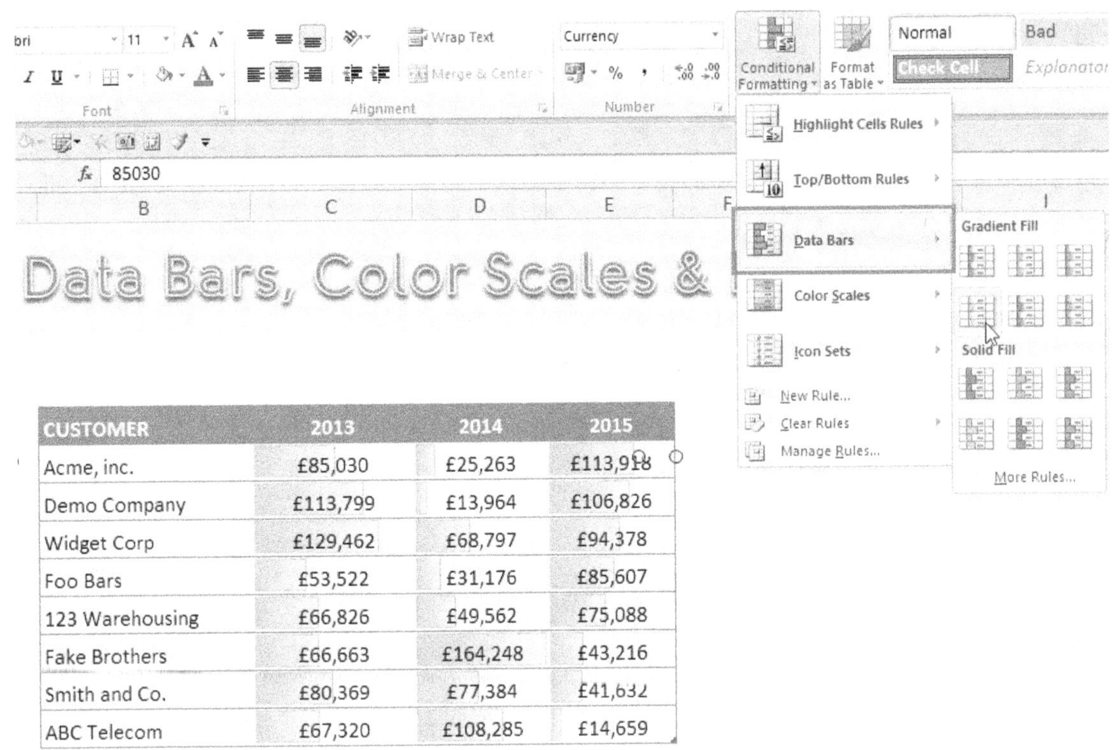

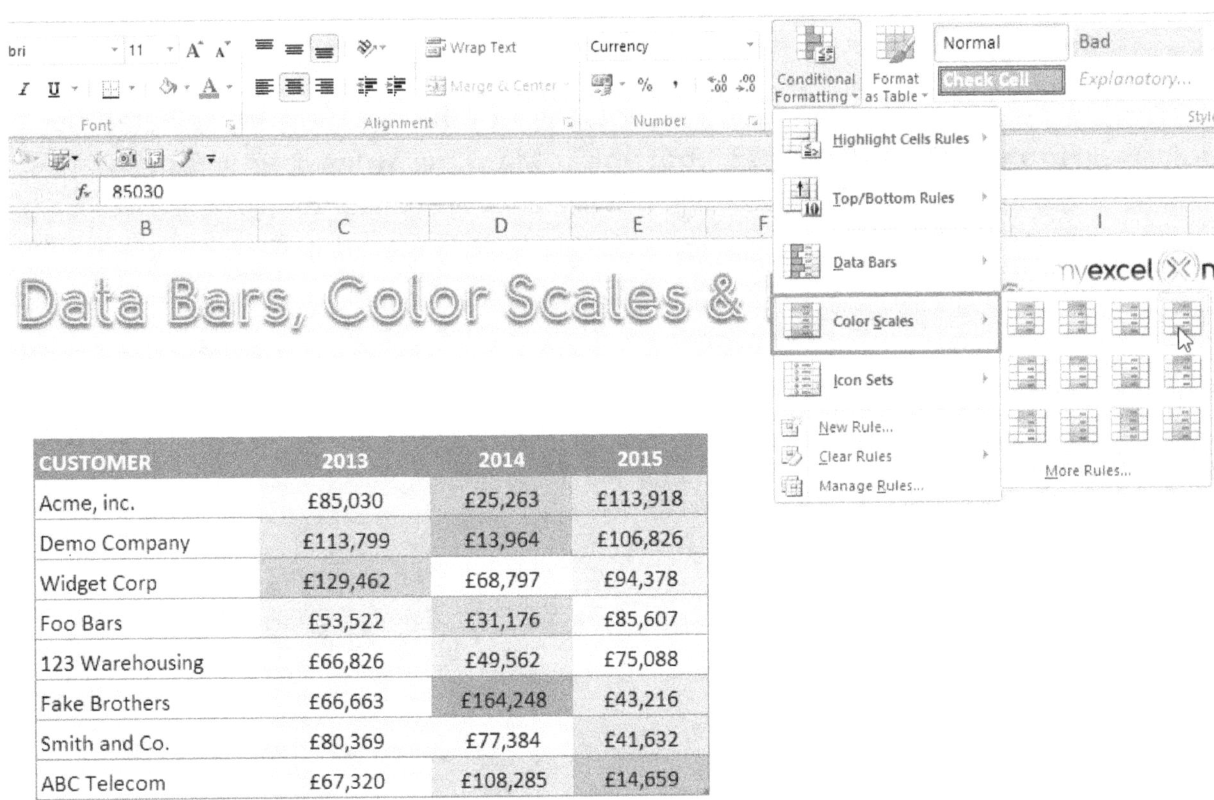

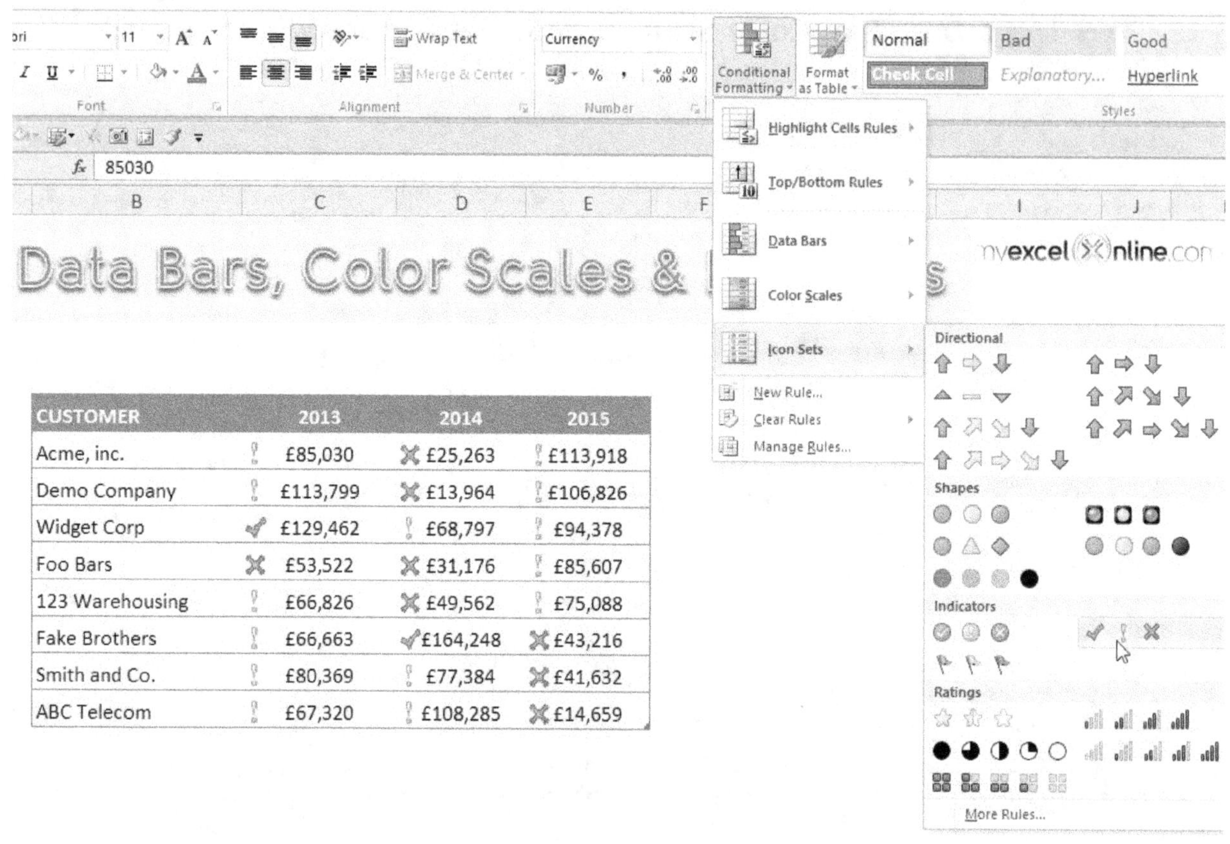

STEP 4: After your selection, you can edit the Conditional Format selected by going to **Home > Conditional Formatting > Manage Rules > Edit Rule**

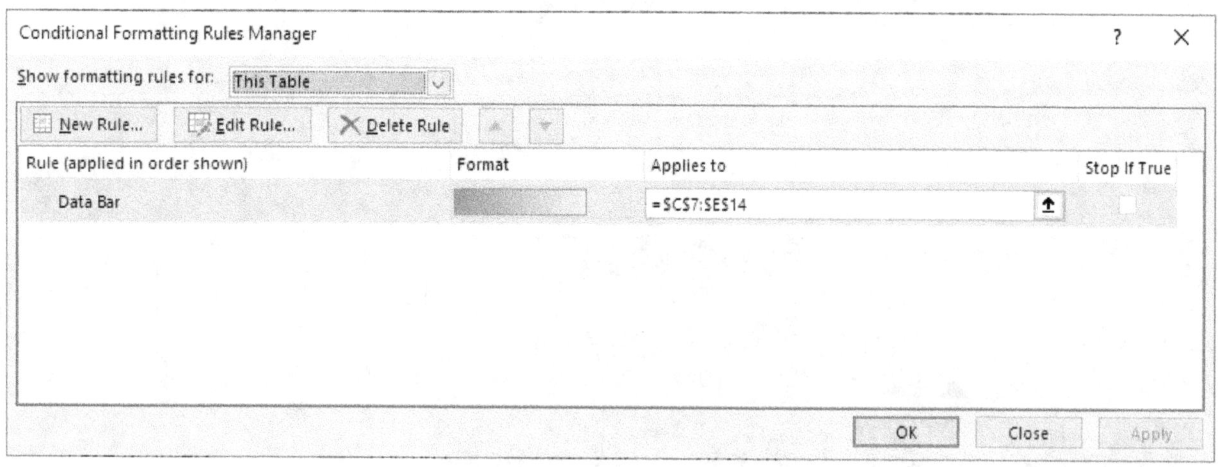

Conditional Formatting: Drop Down List

We are now going to take this concept one level further and apply some conditional formatting to a drop down data validation list.

This is useful if you want to highlight when a job is completed, check off items from a list or to evaluate risk in a project just like we have done in the example below.

STEP 1: Select the range that you want to apply the conditional formatting to.

	RISK TYPE	RISK REGION	DUE DATE	MONTH	YEAR
4	SMALL	NORTH	4/13/2014	April	2014
5	HIGH	SOUTH	12/21/2014	December	2014
6	MEDIUM	EAST	2/15/2014	February	2014
7	MEDIUM	WEST	5/14/2014	May	2014
8	SMALL	NORTH	6/28/2015	June	2015
9	HIGH	SOUTH	1/15/2015	January	2015
10	MEDIUM	EAST	8/22/2015	August	2015
11	SMALL	WEST	12/31/2015	December	2015

STEP 2: Go to *Home > Styles > Conditional Formatting > Manage Rules*

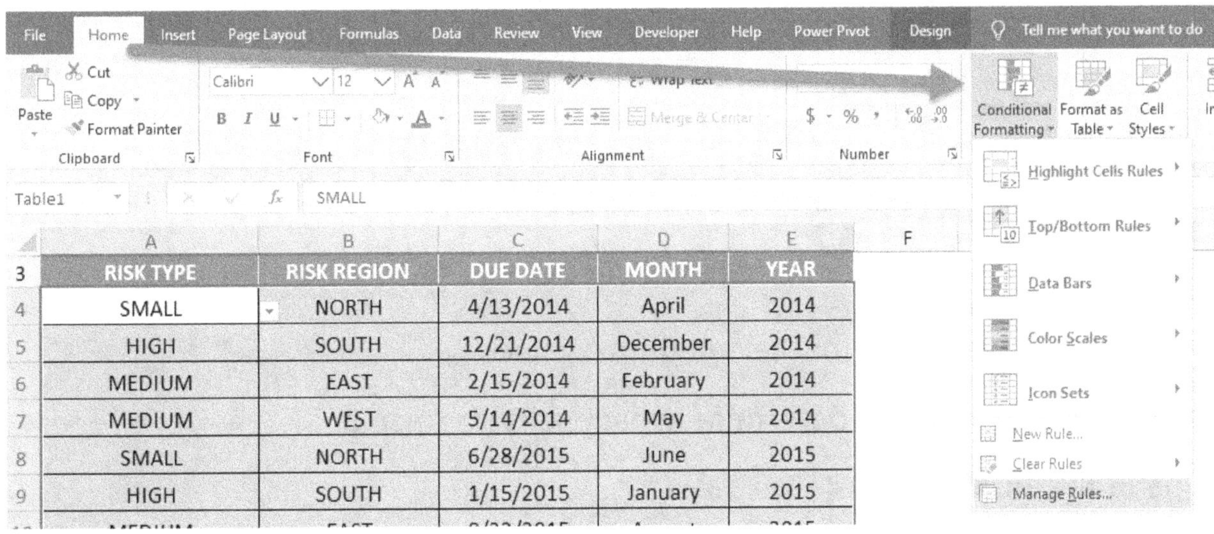

 Select **New Rule**

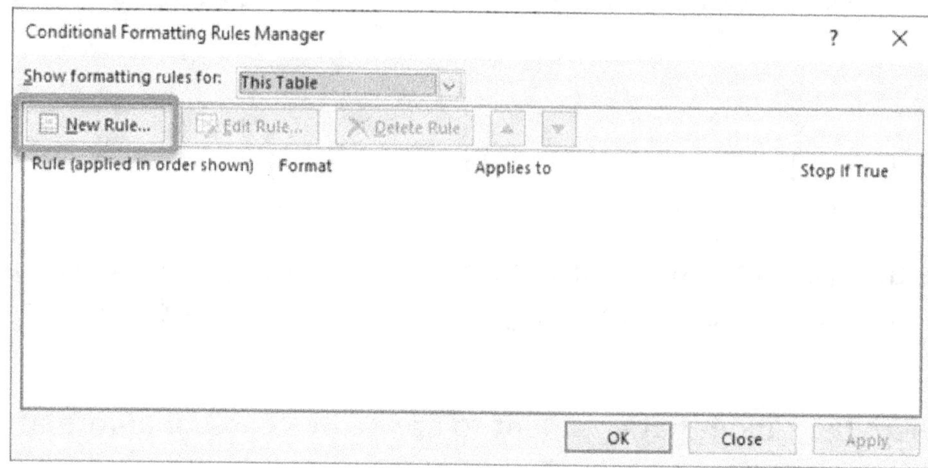

STEP 4: Create the new rule for the **"high"** values:

Select **Use a formula to determine which cells to format**

Type in the Formula *=$A4="high"*

This formula will ensure only the column is absolute or fixed.

Go to ***Format > Fill*** then select a color of your choosing. Click **OK.**

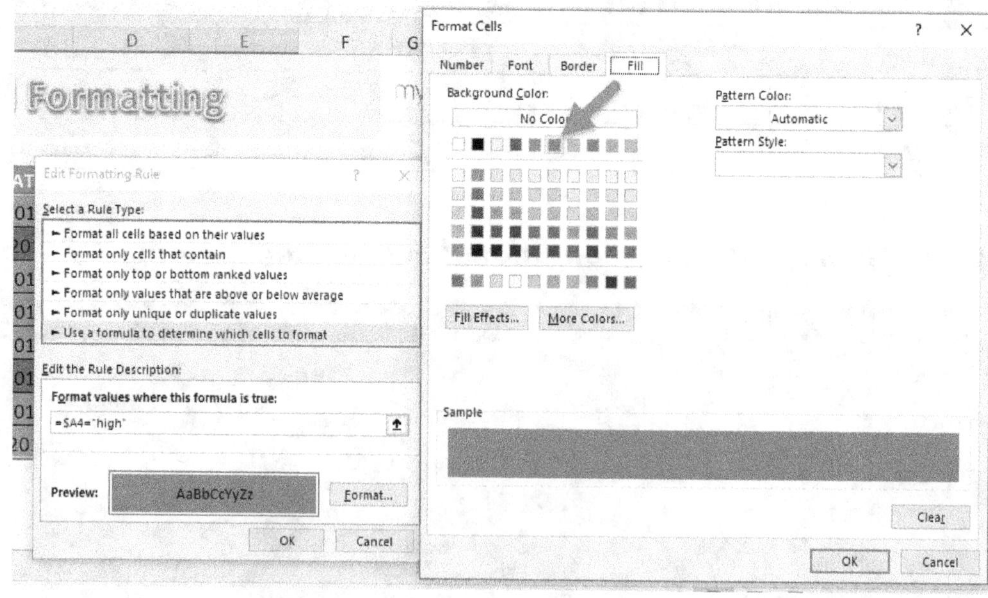

Repeat the **steps 1 to 3** for the **"medium"** values.

Select **Use a formula to determine which cells to format**

Type in the Formula *=$A4="medium"*

Go to *Format > Fill* then select a different color of your choosing. Click **OK.**

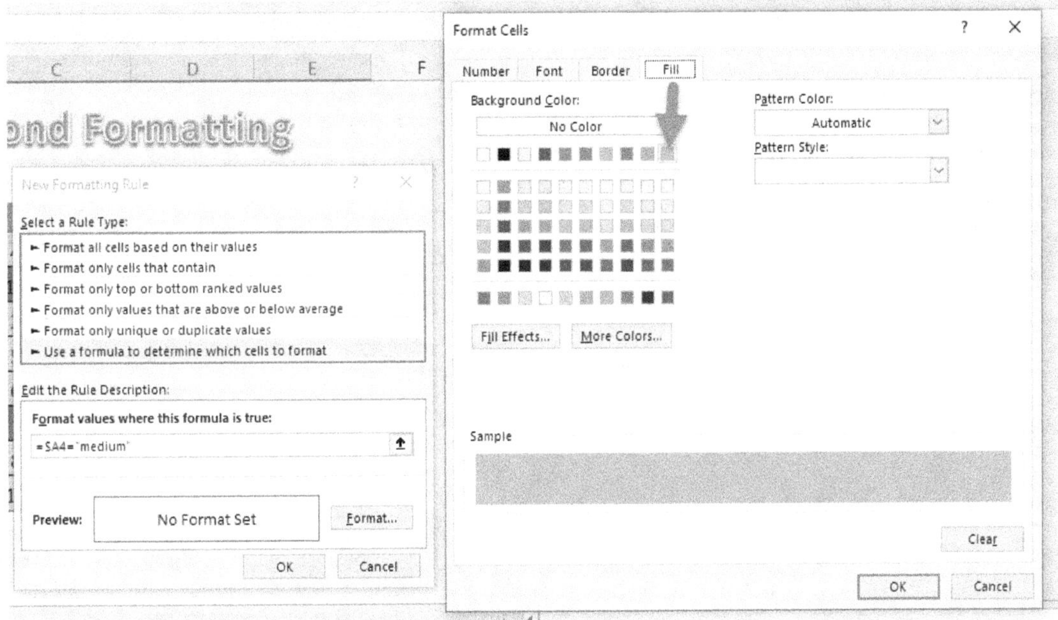

Repeat the **steps 1 to 3** for the **"low"** values.

Select **Use a formula to determine which cells to format**

Type in the Formula **=$A4="low"**

This formula will ensure only the column is absolute.

Go to *Format > Fill* then select a green color of your choosing. Click **OK.**

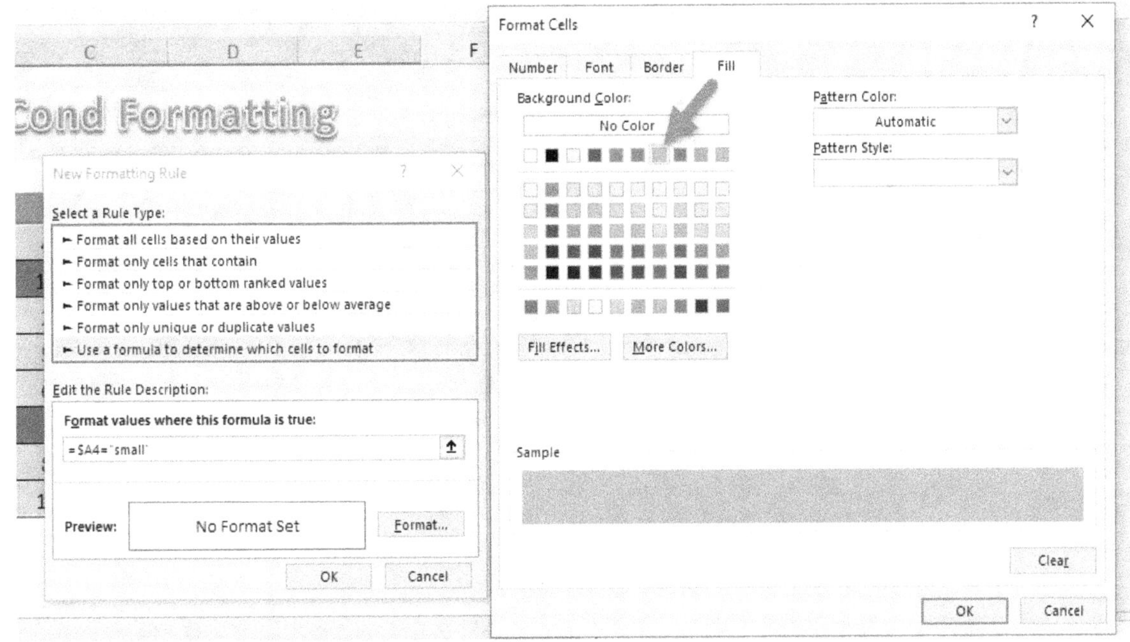

This is how our new set of rules will look like:

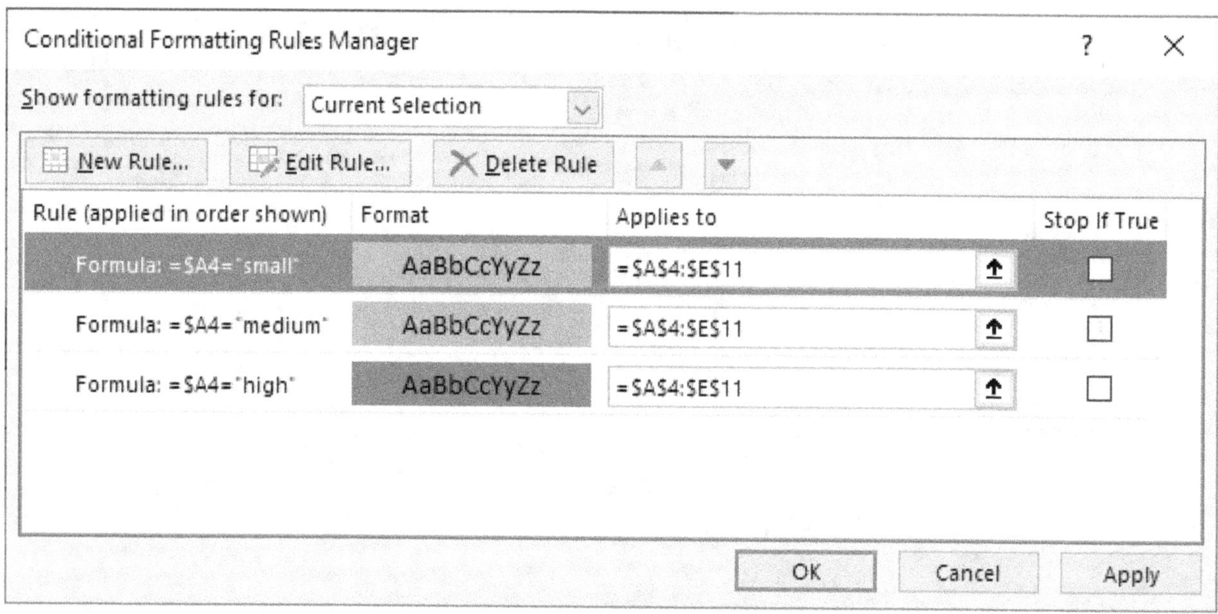

Now our table now has conditional formatting applied!

	A	B	C	D	E
1	Data Validation & Cond Formatting				
2					
3	**RISK TYPE**	**RISK REGION**	**DUE DATE**	**MONTH**	**YEAR**
4	SMALL	NORTH	4/13/2014	April	2014
5	HIGH	SOUTH	12/21/2014	December	2014
6	MEDIUM	EAST	2/15/2014	February	2014
7	MEDIUM	WEST	5/14/2014	May	2014
8	SMALL	NORTH	6/28/2015	June	2015
9	HIGH	SOUTH	1/15/2015	January	2015
10	MEDIUM	EAST	8/22/2015	August	2015
11	SMALL	WEST	12/31/2015	December	2015
12					

Conditional Formatting: Highlight Alternate Rows

Conditional formatting has a lot of cool applications and one of them is using it to highlight alternate rows. Plus we can use an Excel Formula to do this!

STEP 1: Select the range that you want to apply the conditional formatting to.

	RISK TYPE	RISK REGION	DUE DATE	MONTH	YEAR
3					
4	SMALL	NORTH	4/13/2014	April	2014
5	HIGH	SOUTH	12/21/2014	December	2014
6	MEDIUM	EAST	2/15/2014	February	2014
7	MEDIUM	WEST	5/14/2014	May	2014
8	SMALL	NORTH	6/28/2015	June	2015
9	HIGH	SOUTH	1/15/2015	January	2015
10	MEDIUM	EAST	8/22/2015	August	2015
11	SMALL	WEST	12/31/2015	December	2015

STEP 2: Go to *Home > Styles > Conditional Formatting > New Rule*

 Now let us populate the following:

- Select *Use a formula to determine which cells to format*

- Populate the formula as **=MOD(ROW(), 2)**

- Click **Format** to select the formatting that we want to apply

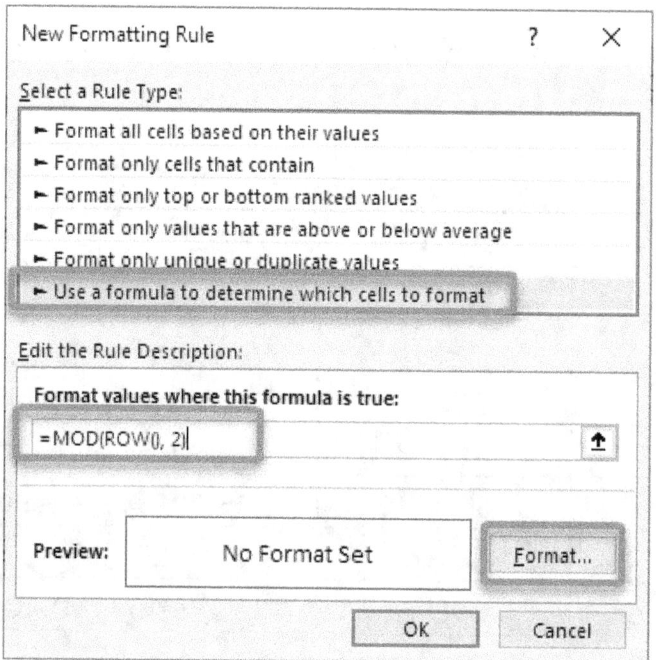

What does the formula do?

- The MOD formula gets the remainder of the division.

- The ROW formula then returns the row number.

- For example, for the 8th row, MOD (8, 2) gives 0. Since 8 divided by 2 equals 4 with the remainder of 0.

- Now if we take the 3rd row, MOD (3, 2) gives 1. Since 3 divided by 2 equals 1 with a remainder of 1.

- This means that all of our odd rows will return 1 which signifies TRUE, and they will all be shaded with our formatting rule.

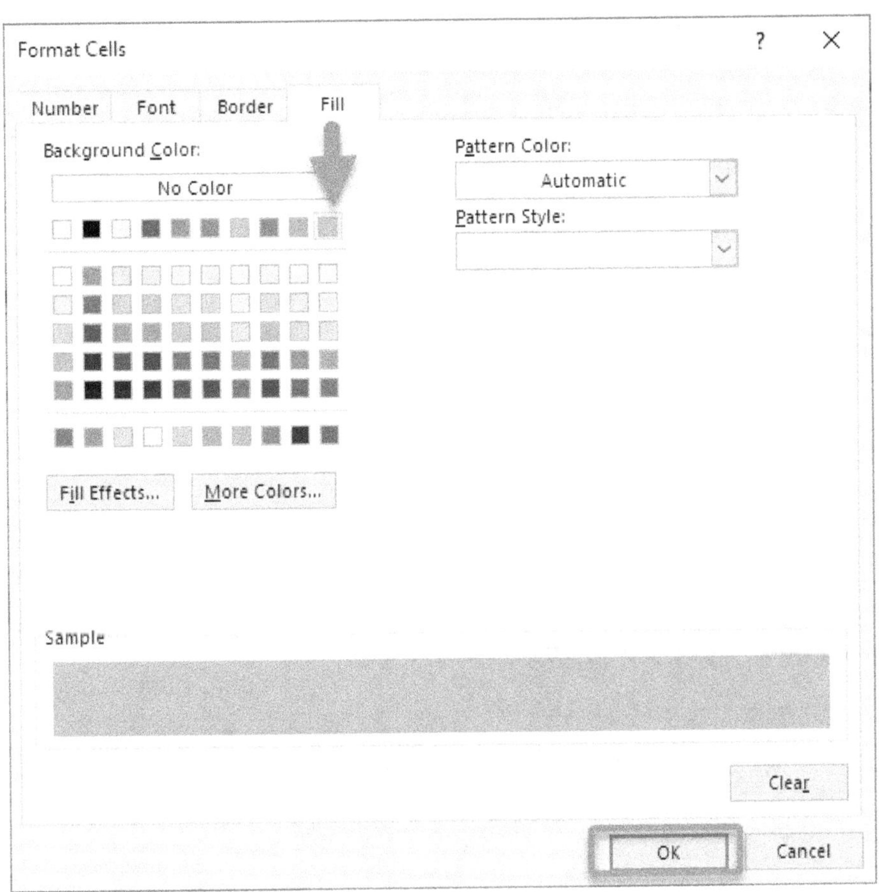

Now you have your alternative rows highlighted!

	A	B	C	D	E
3	RISK TYPE	RISK REGION	DUE DATE	MONTH	YEAR
4	SMALL	NORTH	4/13/2014	April	2014
5	HIGH	SOUTH	12/21/2014	December	2014
6	MEDIUM	EAST	2/15/2014	February	2014
7	MEDIUM	WEST	5/14/2014	May	2014
8	SMALL	NORTH	6/28/2015	June	2015
9	HIGH	SOUTH	1/15/2015	January	2015
10	MEDIUM	EAST	8/22/2015	August	2015
11	SMALL	WEST	12/31/2015	December	2015

Conditional Formatting: Pivot Table With Data Bars

Data Bars are a cool Conditional Formatting feature in Excel and they add a colored bar to your values.

The length of the data bar represents the value in the cell. A longer bar represents a higher value.

You have a Gradient Fill or a Solid Fill to choose from as well as different pre-determined colors.

If you select the **More Rules** option then you can select more colors as well as many different values types to format.

STEP 1: Select any value inside the Pivot Table. Go to *Home > Conditional Formatting > Data Bars > Gradient Fill*

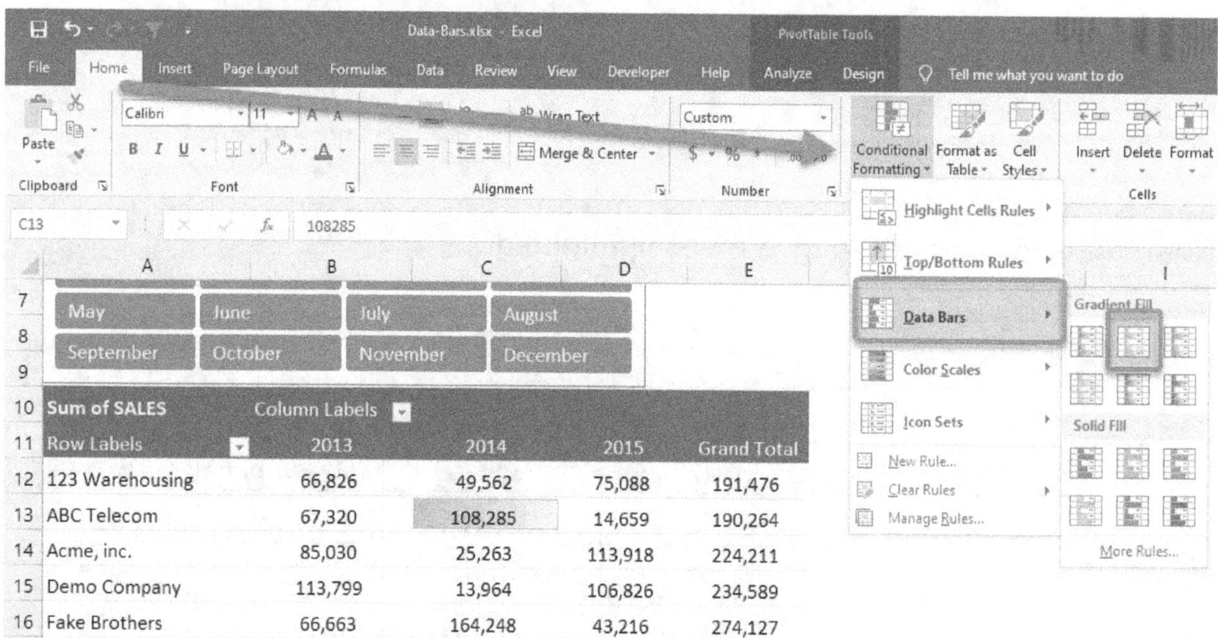

 Go to *Formatting Options Icon* and **select the second option** to apply the data bar formatting to the entire table.

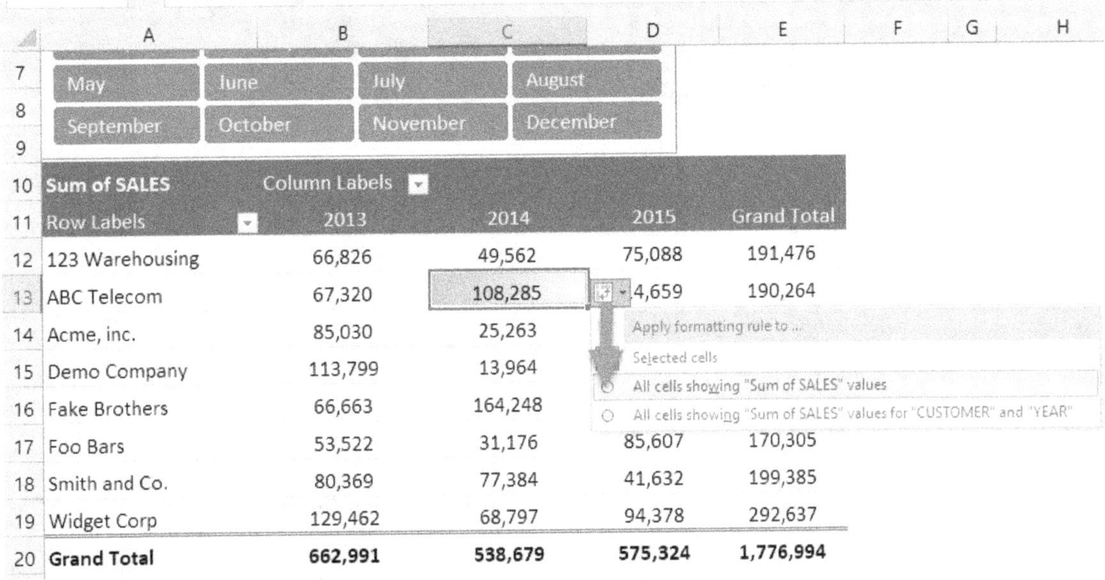

	A	B	C	D	E	F	G	H
7	May	June	July	August				
8	September	October	November	December				
9								
10	Sum of SALES	Column Labels						
11	Row Labels	2013	2014	2015	Grand Total			
12	123 Warehousing	66,826	49,562	75,088	191,476			
13	ABC Telecom	67,320	108,285	4,659	190,264			
14	Acme, inc.	85,030	25,263					
15	Demo Company	113,799	13,964					
16	Fake Brothers	66,663	164,248					
17	Foo Bars	53,522	31,176	85,607	170,305			
18	Smith and Co.	80,369	77,384	41,632	199,385			
19	Widget Corp	129,462	68,797	94,378	292,637			
20	Grand Total	662,991	538,679	575,324	1,776,994			

Now you have data bars showing up for the entire pivot table.

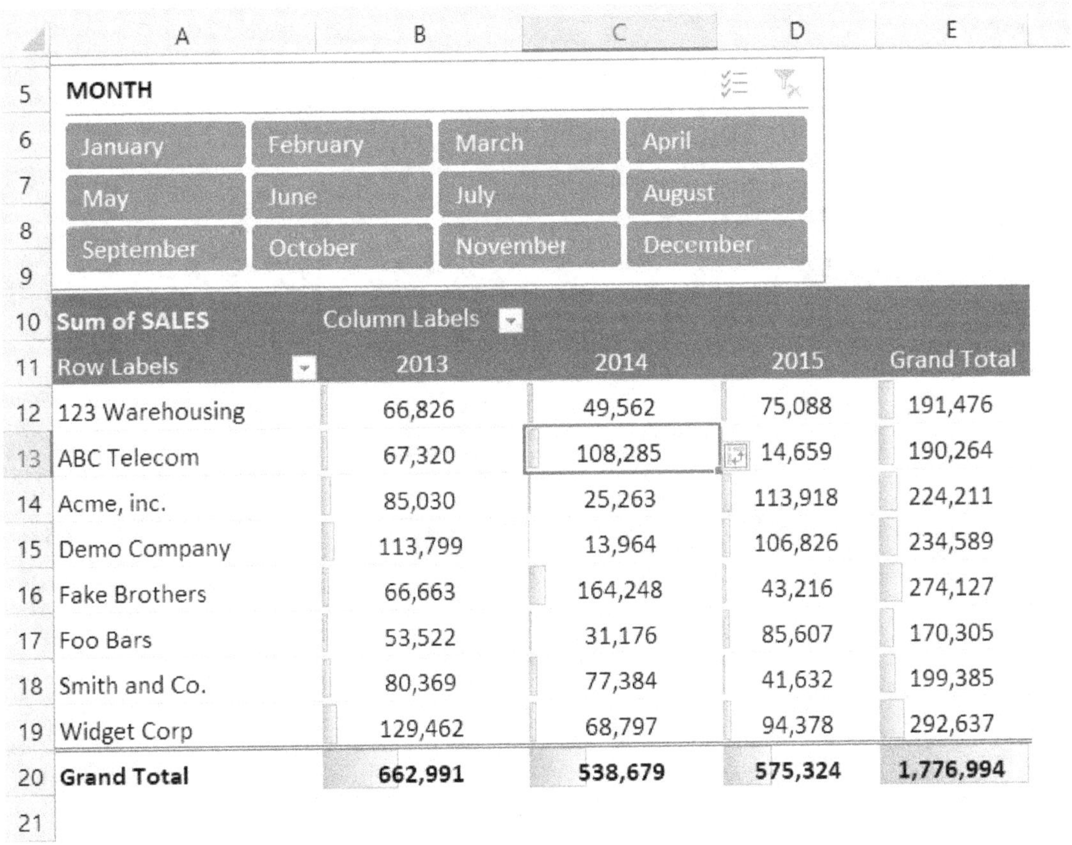

	A	B	C	D	E
5	MONTH				
6	January	February	March	April
7	May	June	July	August
8	September	October	November	December
9					
10	Sum of SALES	Column Labels			
11	Row Labels	2013	2014	2015	Grand Total
12	123 Warehousing	66,826	49,562	75,088	191,476
13	ABC Telecom	67,320	108,285	14,659	190,264
14	Acme, inc.	85,030	25,263	113,918	224,211
15	Demo Company	113,799	13,964	106,826	234,589
16	Fake Brothers	66,663	164,248	43,216	274,127
17	Foo Bars	53,522	31,176	85,607	170,305
18	Smith and Co.	80,369	77,384	41,632	199,385
19	Widget Corp	129,462	68,797	94,378	292,637
20	Grand Total	662,991	538,679	575,324	1,776,994
21					

 Go to *Formatting Options Icon* and **select the third option** which will apply the data bar formatting to the entire table while excluding the Grand Totals.

Sum of SALES	Column Labels			
Row Labels	2013	2014	2015	Grand Total
123 Warehousing	66,826	49,562	75,088	191,476
ABC Telecom	67,320	108,285	4,659	190,264
Acme, inc.	85,030	25,263		
Demo Company	113,799	13,964		
Fake Brothers	66,663	164,248		
Foo Bars	53,522	31,176	85,607	170,305
Smith and Co.	80,369	77,384	41,632	199,385
Widget Corp	129,462	68,797	94,378	292,637
Grand Total	**662,991**	**538,679**	**575,324**	**1,776,994**

Apply formatting rule to ...

- Selected cells
- All cells showing "Sum of SALES" values
- All cells showing "Sum of SALES" values for "CUSTOMER" and "YEAR"

You get a better visual representation as the Grand Totals are now excluded.

	A	B	C	D	E
5	**MONTH**				
6	January	February	March	April
7	May	June	July	August
8	September	October	November	December
9				

	A	B	C	D	E
10	**Sum of SALES**	Column Labels			
11	Row Labels	2013	2014	2015	Grand Total
12	123 Warehousing	66,826	49,562	75,088	191,476
13	ABC Telecom	67,320	108,285	14,659	190,264
14	Acme, inc.	85,030	25,263	113,918	224,211
15	Demo Company	113,799	13,964	106,826	234,589
16	Fake Brothers	66,663	164,248	43,216	274,127
17	Foo Bars	53,522	31,176	85,607	170,305
18	Smith and Co.	80,369	77,384	41,632	199,385
19	Widget Corp	129,462	68,797	94,378	292,637
20	**Grand Total**	**662,991**	**538,679**	**575,324**	**1,776,994**

Custom Date Formats in Excel

Custom date formats in Excel allow you to display only certain parts of the date.

Say you had a date of 18/02/1979, you can use the Format Cells dialog box to show only the number 18, the day that corresponds to that date (Sunday), the month as a number in abbreviated form and the year in two or four digits.

You can also mix and match to create a custom date formats or even enter a custom text that would show something like:

Today is Sunday

You can download the following workbook which shows you the different formats that you can use and see the tutorial below of how this can be easily achieved.

STEP 1: To see how the formatting works, pick any one on the table. Then press **CTRL + 1** to open the **Format Cells Dialog**.

CODE	OUTPUT	DATE/TIME	HOW IT APPEARS
m	Displays the month as a number	2/18/1979	2
mm	Displays the month as a number with leading zeros	2/18/1979	02
mmm	Displays the month in abbreviated form	2/18/1979	Feb
mmmm	Displays the month in full form	2/18/1979	February
mmmmm	Displays the first letter of the month	2/18/1979	F
d	Displays the day as a number	2/18/1979	18
dd	Displays the day as a number with leading zeros	2/1/1979	01
ddd	Displays the day in abbreviated form	2/18/1979	Thu
dddd	Displays the day in full form	2/18/1979	Thursday
yy	Displays the last two digits of the year	2/18/1979	79
yyyy	Displays all the digits of the year	2/18/1979	1979
mmmm d, yyyy	Displays the month, the date and the year	2/18/1979	February 18, 1979
mmmm-yyyy	Displays the month-year	2/18/1979	February-1979
"Today is" dddd	Displays a custom text for teh Today function	9/28/2020	Today is Monday
h	Displays the hour as a number	9:55:13	9
hh	Displays the hour as a number with leading zeros	9:55:13	09
AM/PM	Displays the hour indicating AM or PM	9:55:13	AM

Analysis ⊕

STEP 2: Over here you can see the Custom Date Format used, in our example, it's ***mmmm-yyyy*** and there is a sample of ***February-1979*** at the top to show you how it looks like.

Try it out for the different formats!

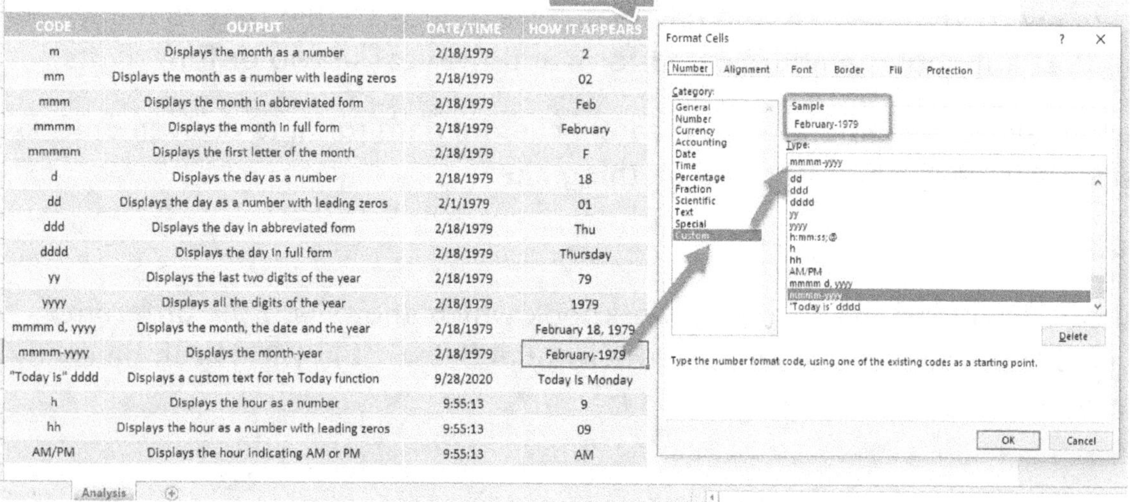

Here is the list of codes that you can use:

CODE	OUTPUT	DATE/TIME	APPEARS AS
m	Displays the month as a number	18/02/1979	2
mm	Displays the month as a number with leading zeros	18/02/1979	02
mmm	Displays the month in abbreviated form	18/02/1979	Feb
mmmm	Displays the month in full form	18/02/1979	February
mmmmm	Displays the first letter of the month	18/02/1979	F
d	Displays the day as a number	18/02/1979	18
dd	Displays the day as a number with leading zeros	01/02/1979	01
ddd	Displays the day in abbreviated form	18/02/1979	Thu
dddd	Displays the day in full form	18/02/1979	Thursday
yy	Displays the last two digits of the year	18/02/1979	79
yyyy	Displays all the digits of the year	18/02/1979	1979
mmmm d, yyyy	Displays the month, the date and the year	18/02/1979	February 18, 1979
mmmm-yyyy	Displays the month-year	18/02/1979	February-1979
"Today is" dddd	Displays a custom text for the Today function	11/06/2015	Today is Thursday
h	Displays the hour as a number	9:55:13	9
hh	Displays the hour as a number with leading zeros	9:55:13	09
AM/PM	Displays the hour indicating AM or PM	9:55:13	AM

Custom Number Formats in Excel

A custom number format in Excel can have up to four different sections in the following order:

Positive format; Negative format; Zero format; Text format

You can specify different format codes for each section as long as they are separated by a semicolon.

So you can display a positive number in black, a negative number in red, a zero in green and any text in blue.

The following table displays the different custom codes that you can enter in the Format Cells dialog box and how the values will appear. You can download the Excel workbook and press CTRL+1 in each cell to see the custom format entered.

CODE	OUTPUT	ORIGINAL VALUE	HOW IT APPEARS
General	General format display	123456	123456
#	Displays significant digits	123.456	123
#.00%	Displays percentage	0.6489	64.89%
$ - + / ( ) :	Displays this character	1234567890	-$1234567890
"text"	Displays the text in between the quotations	1234567890	1234567890 units
[Color n]	Displays the color in the Excel color palette (from 0 to 56)	1234567890	1234567890
[condition value]	Custom condition e.g. [If it meets this condition] True Format; False Format	0.01	1.00%

STEP 1: Copy the **custom number format**

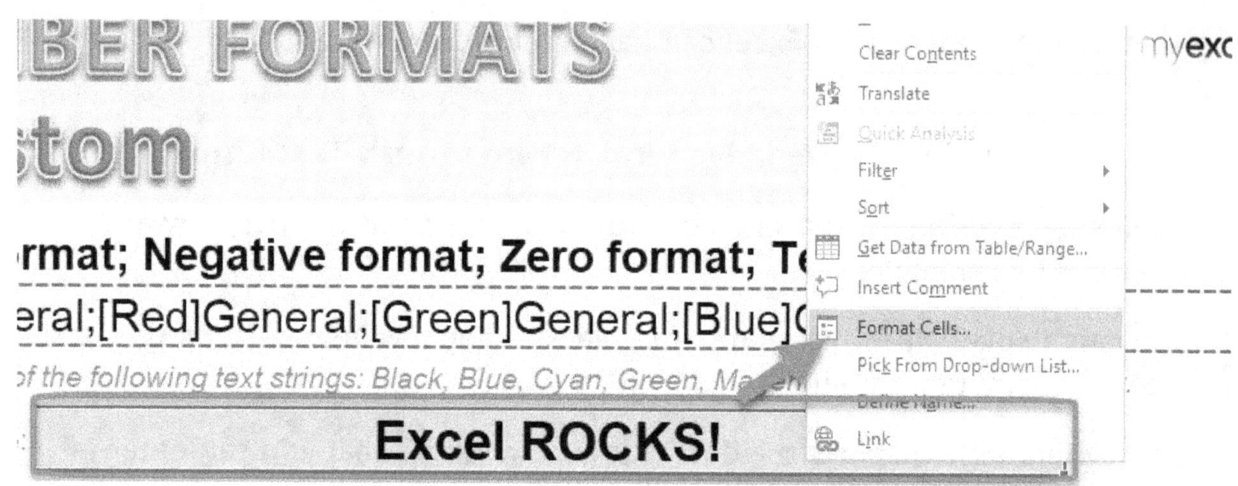

STEP 3: Choose **Custom** and paste the **custom number format** from Step 1 in the **Type** area. Then press **OK.**

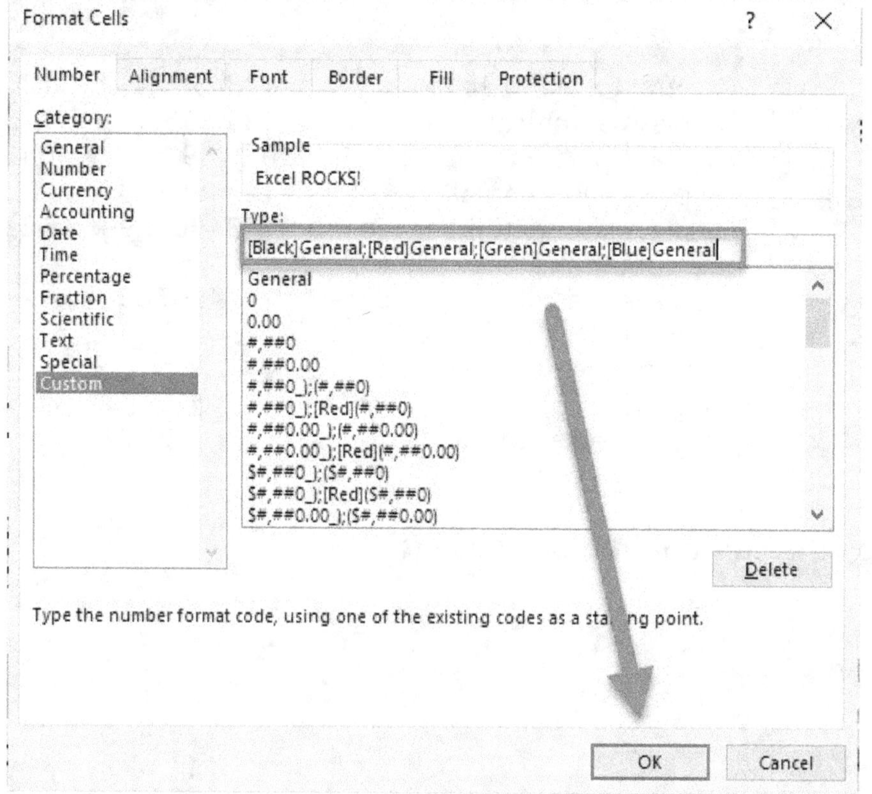

Change the cells to the following values and see the colors take effect:

- 100

- -200

- 0

- Excel ROCKS!

<table>
<tr><td align="center">100</td></tr>
<tr><td align="center">200</td></tr>
<tr><td align="center"></td></tr>
<tr><td align="center">Excel ROCKS!</td></tr>
</table>

Find Blank Cells In Excel With A Color

In Excel you can have a data set that comes from an external source which isn't always formatted to your liking.

One of the most common things you may encounter are blank cells in your Excel data which can hinder your analysis, especially if you are using a Pivot Table to analyze the data.

STEP 1: Make sure your entire table is selected. We will select all the blank cells or press the keyboard shortcut **CTRL + ***

STEP 2: Press *Ctrl + G* to open the **Go To Window**. Click **Special.**

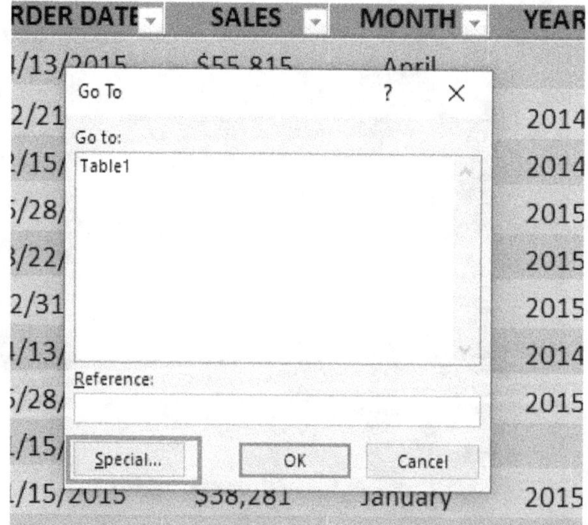

Select **Blanks.** Click **OK.**

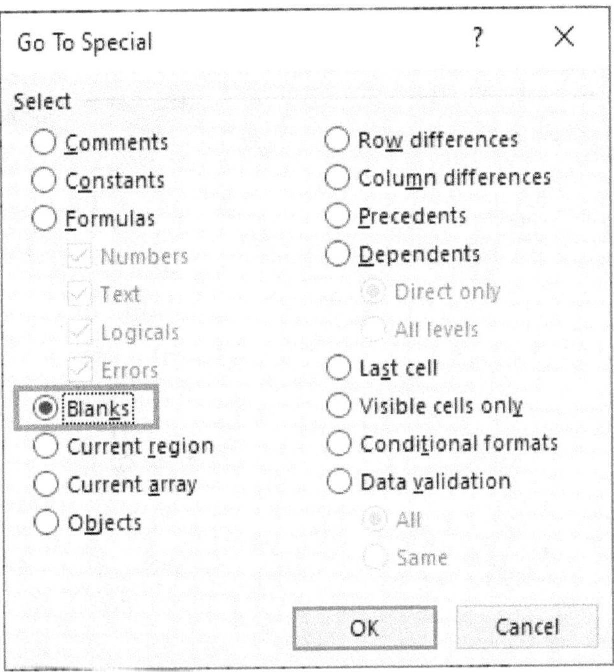

STEP 3: The blank cells are now selected. Go to *Home > Font > Fill > Red color*

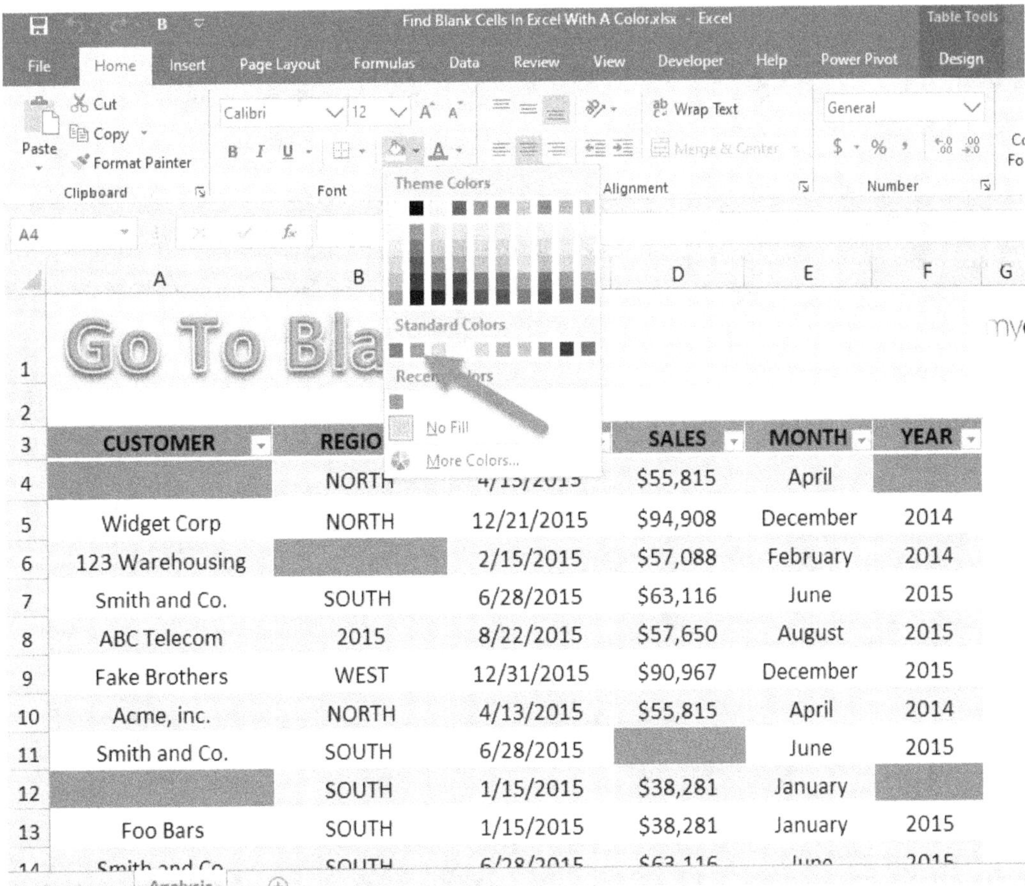

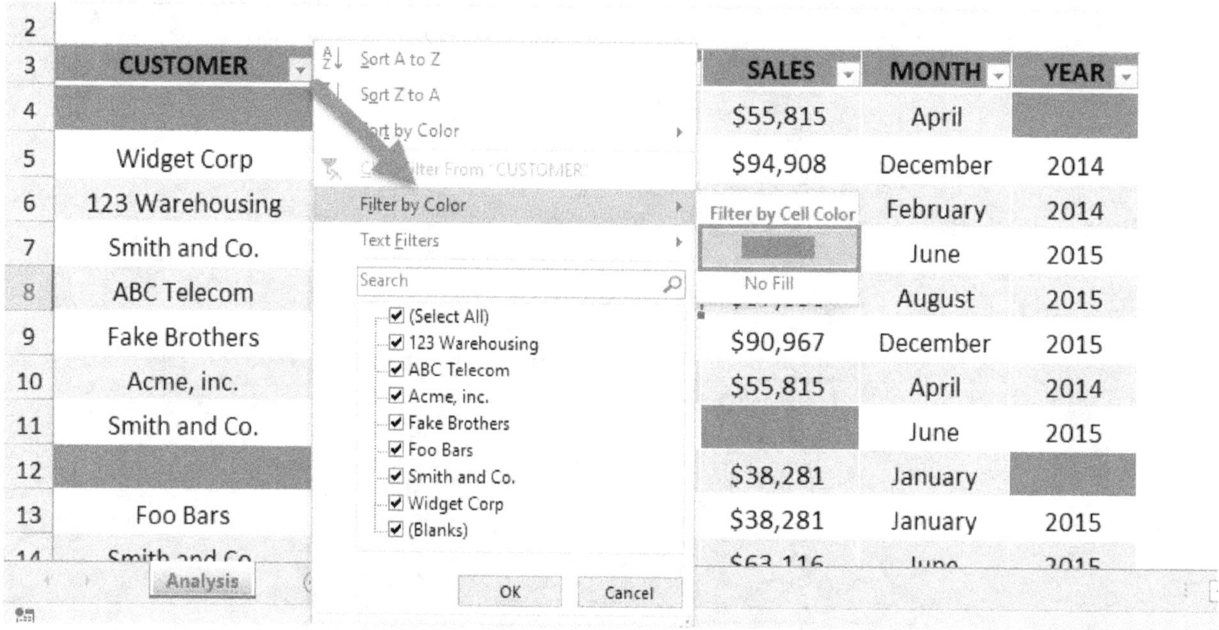

Our filtering has worked to show the blank cells which you can now manually fill in.

CUSTOMER	REGION	ORDER DATE	SALES	MONTH	YEAR
	NORTH	4/13/2015	$55,815	April	
	SOUTH	1/15/2015	$38,281	January	
	SOUTH	1/15/2015	$38,281	January	2015
	WEST	12/31/2015	$90,967	December	2015

Fill Justify Tool

An interesting tool within Excel is the Fill Justify. It allows you to select text from several rows and merge them in to one cell.

So if you have data that gets downloaded in to separate rows and want to join them up in to one sentence, then the Excel's Fill Justify option is your savior.

This is our text:

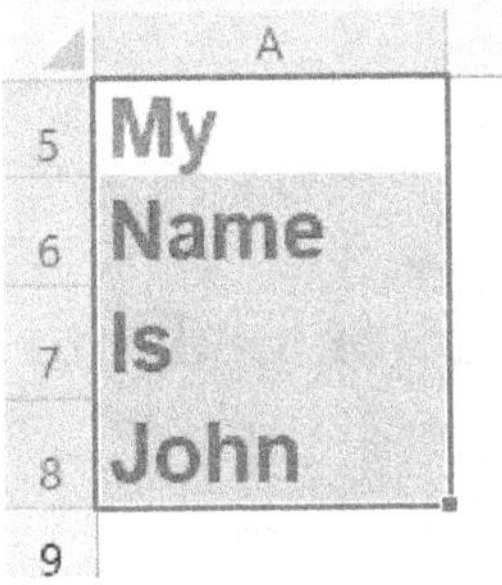

STEP 1: Adjust your column width so all the text could fit in one cell

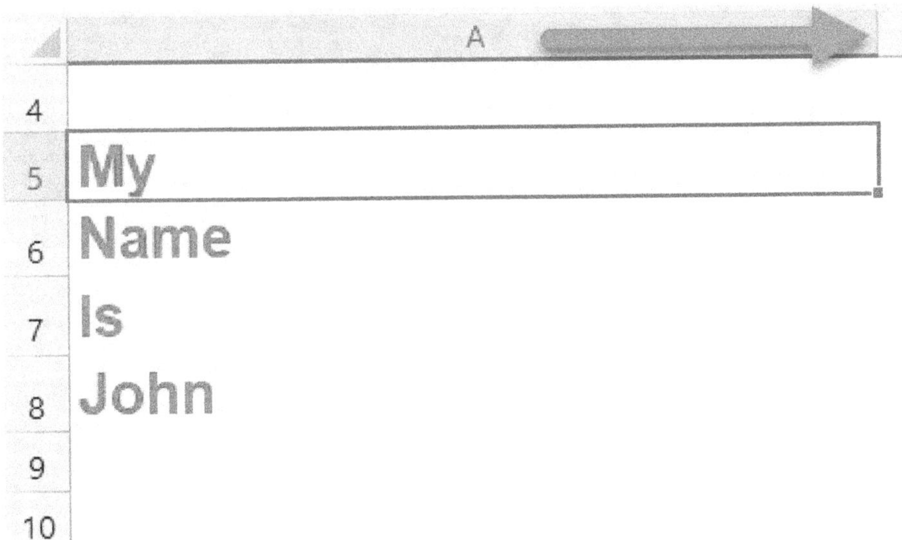

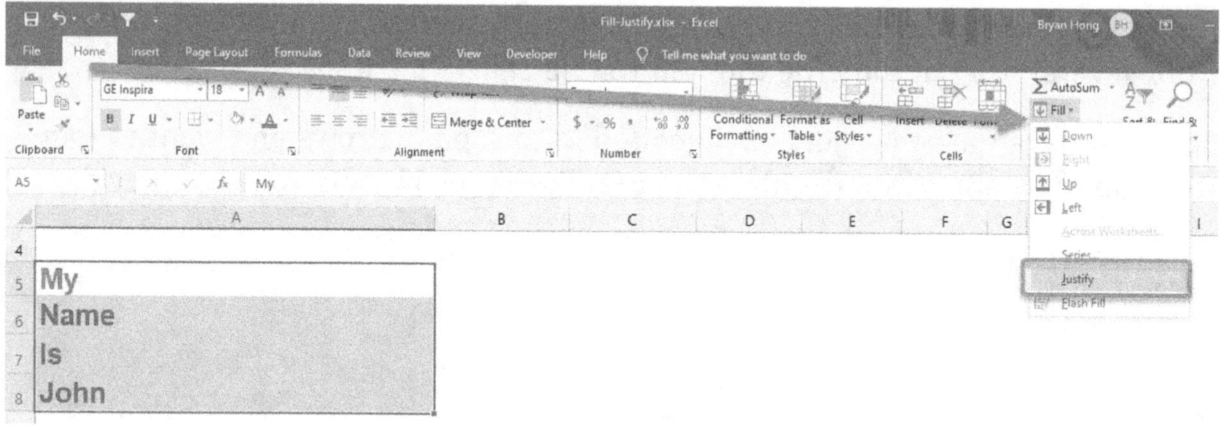

With just that, everything is now **combined into one single cell**!

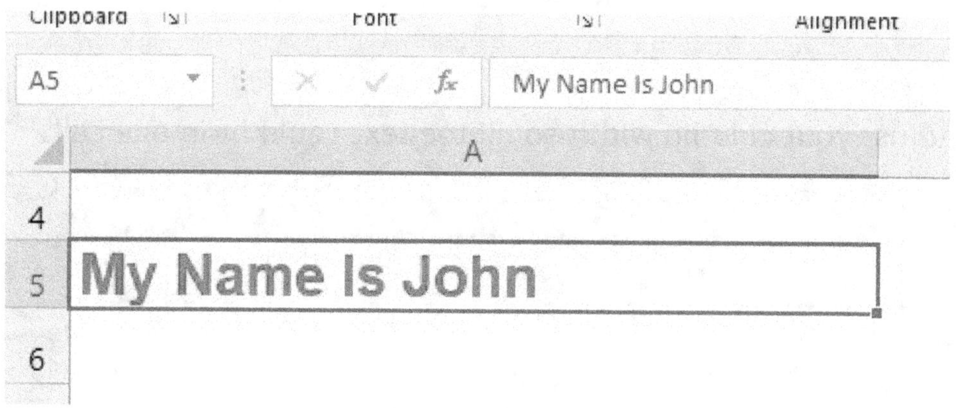

Format Cells: Special Numbers

If you have a list of values that come from a database and want to format them in Excel using a special number format like a Zip Code, Social Security Number or Phone Number, then this is possible using the Format Cells dialog box and choosing the "Special" number category.

See how easy this is achieved in just a few simple steps.

STEP 1: To format the **Zip Code**, select the cell containing the value and press *CTRL + 1*

Make sure that Locale has **English (United States)** selected.

Select *Special > Zip Code + 4* then click **OK.**

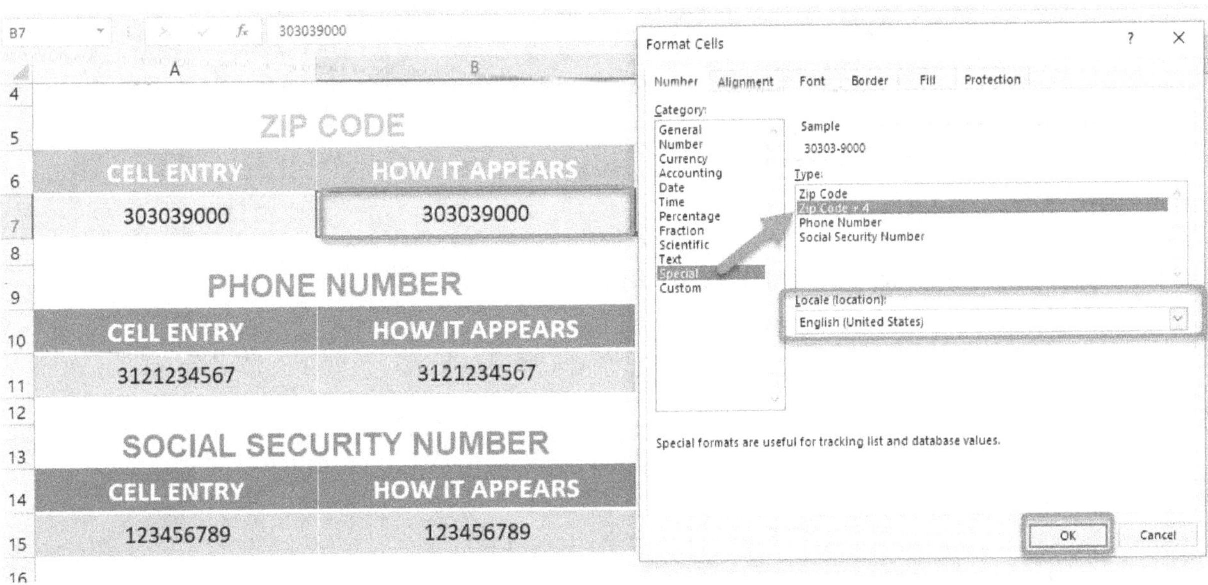

Your Zip Code is now formatted!

STEP 2: To format the **Phone Number**, select the cell containing the value and press *CTRL + 1*

Select *Special > Phone Number* then click **OK.**

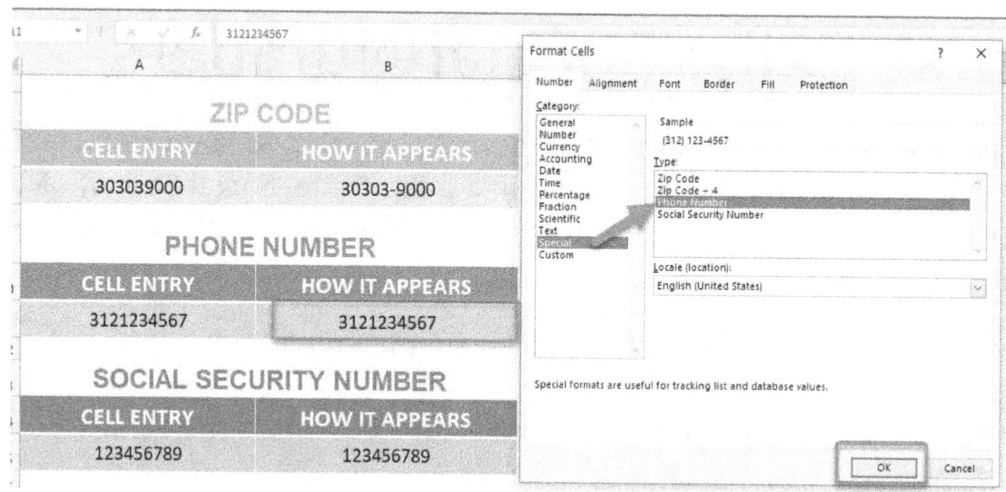

Your Phone Number is now formatted!

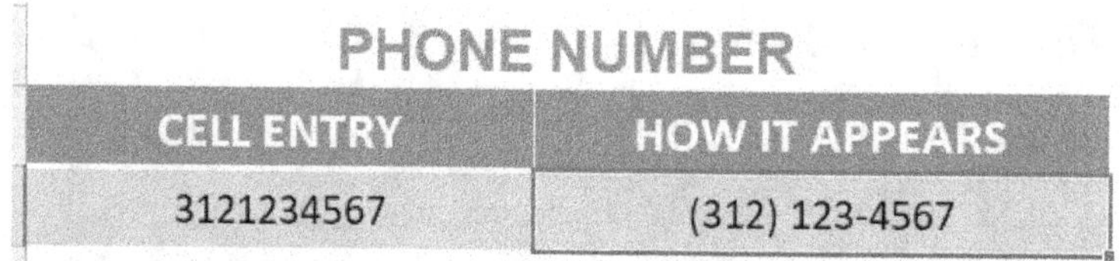

STEP 3: To format the **Social Security Number**, select the cell containing the value and press **CTRL + 1**

Select **Special > Social Security Number** then click **OK.**

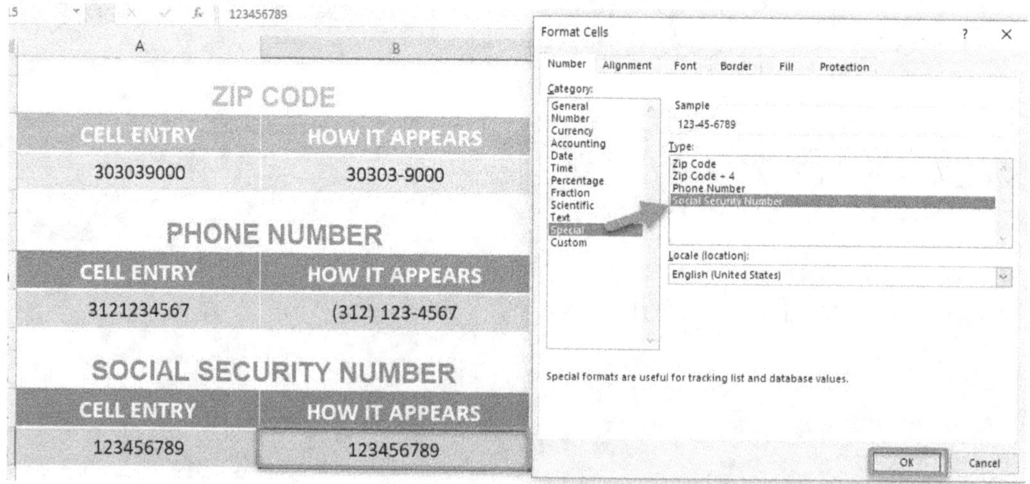

Your Social Security Number is now formatted!

SOCIAL SECURITY NUMBER	
CELL ENTRY	HOW IT APPEARS
123456789	123-45-6789

Format Painter Multiple Cells

The Format Painter copies formatting from one place and applies it to another but this can also be extended to multiple cells.

 Pick a cell that contains the formatting you want to copy

Go to **Home > Clipboard > Format Painter** and make sure to **double click** on the format painter icon

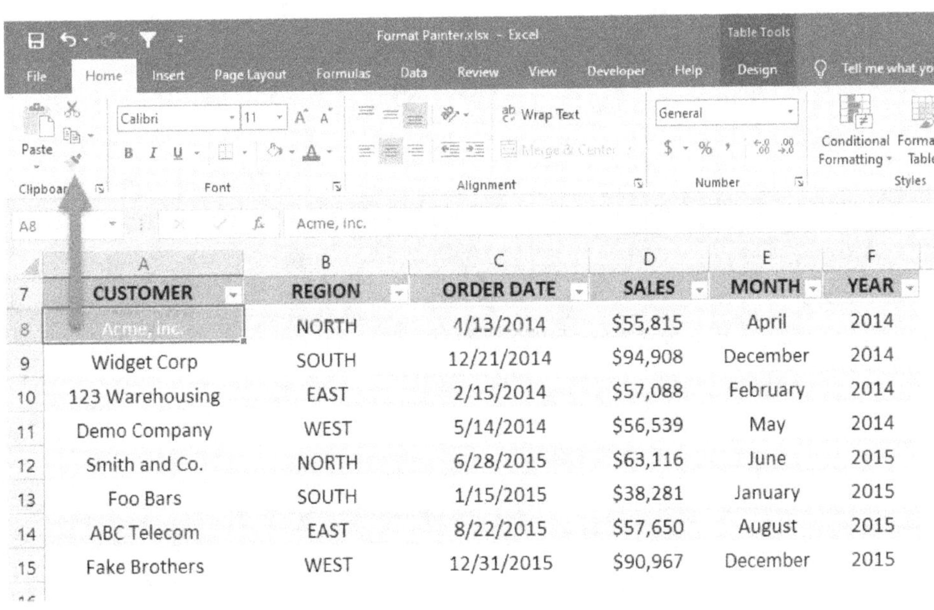

 These are the cells that we want to apply the same formatting. Click on all of them

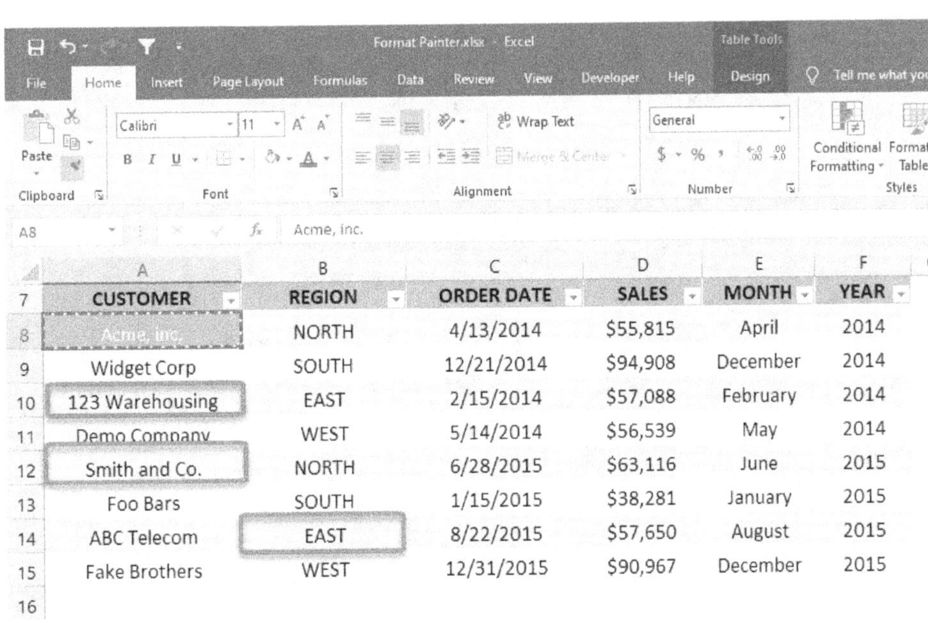

 The same formatting is applied with just a click. Now try applying it to the entire **YEAR Column** by highlighting the entire column

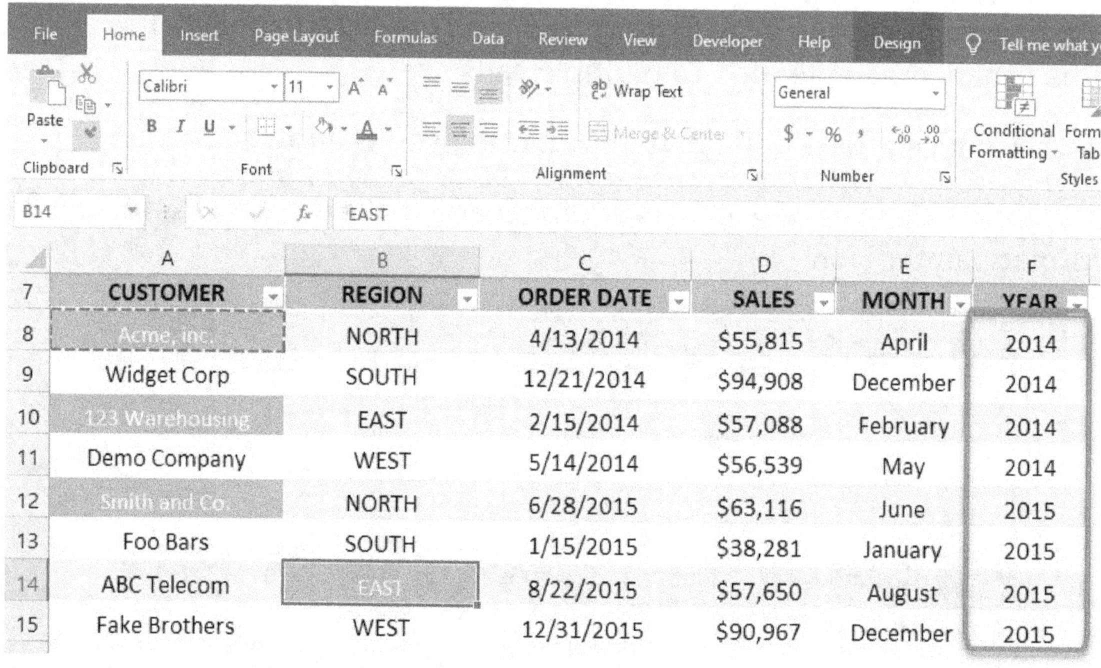

They now all have the same formatting!

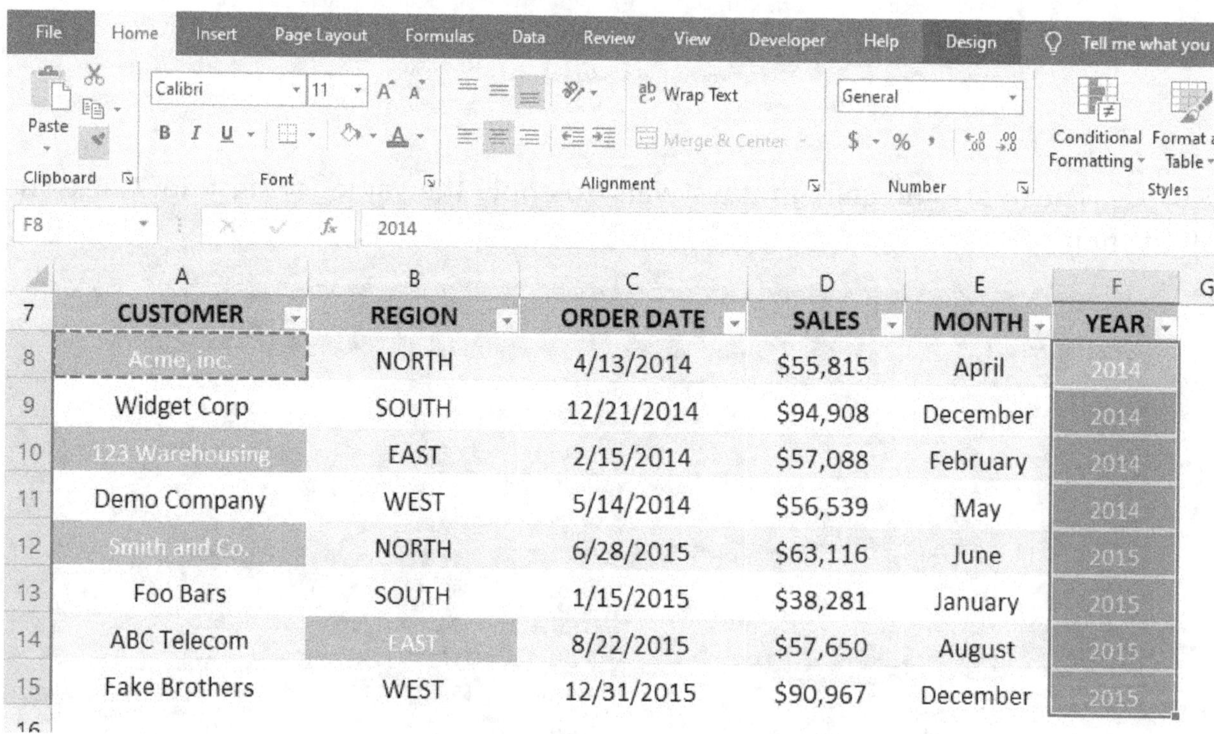

Freeze Panes in Excel

Have you ever encountered a situation where you had heaps of data with many rows and you needed to see the **headers** at all times?

Just like me, I am sure you have :)

There is a way in Excel that will allow us to freeze panes so that the column headings are visible whilst we are scrolling down our data.

STEP 1: Go to **View > Freeze Panes > Freeze Top Row**

This will freeze the Row 1 of your sheet:

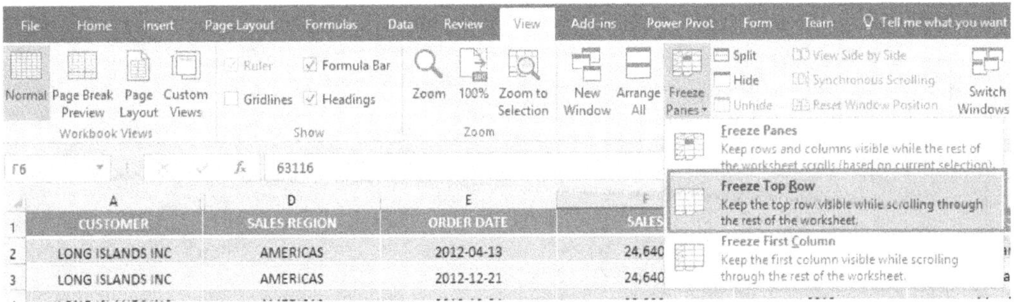

Try scrolling down, the **first row** is always visible!

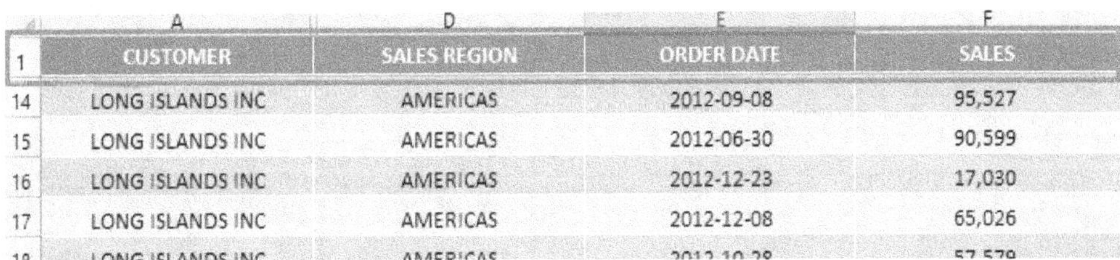

STEP 2: To be able to undo the freezing is very easy! Go to **View > Freeze Panes > Unfreeze Panes**

You should now be able to scroll normally.

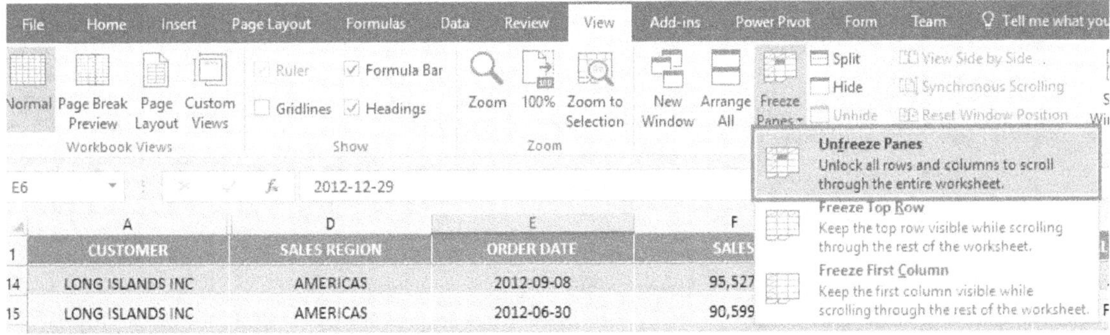

{ 197 }

STEP 3: The next question is, what if it's not the first row that you want to freeze? Say you want Rows 1 to 5 to be frozen?

Select the **sixth row:**

Go to **View > Freeze Panes > Freeze Panes**

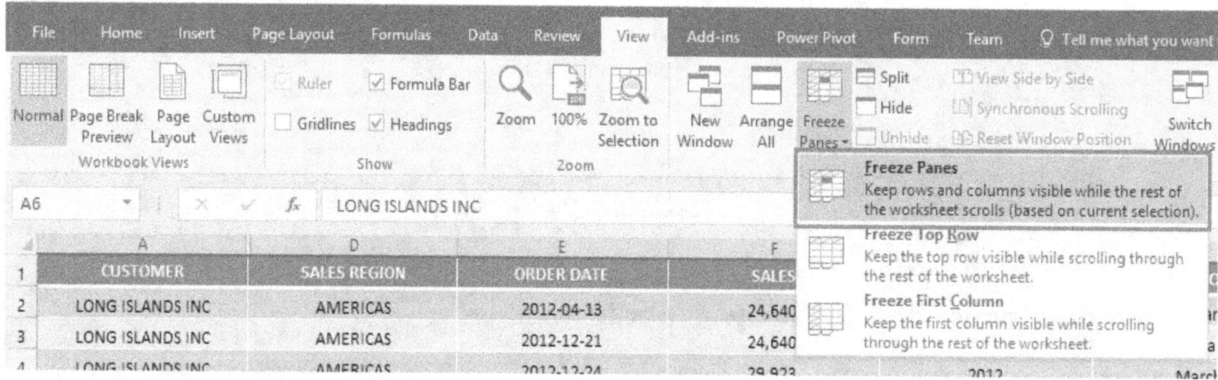

All of the rows above Row 6 are now frozen!

STEP 4: You can also freeze the first column! Go to **View > Freeze Panes > Freeze First Column**

This will freeze the Column 1 of your sheet:

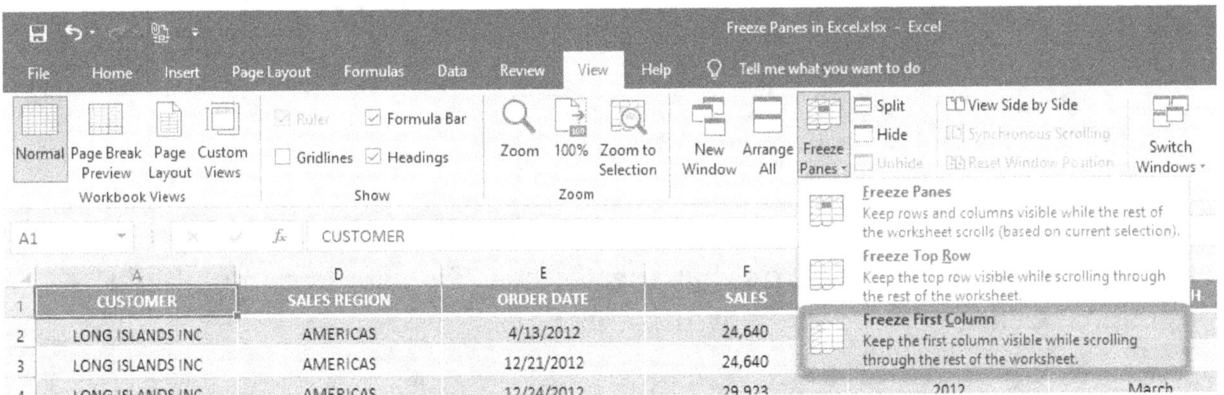

Try moving to the right, the **first column** is always visible!

STEP 5: You can also freeze your view from a specific cell! For example, let us try freezing from cell D4:

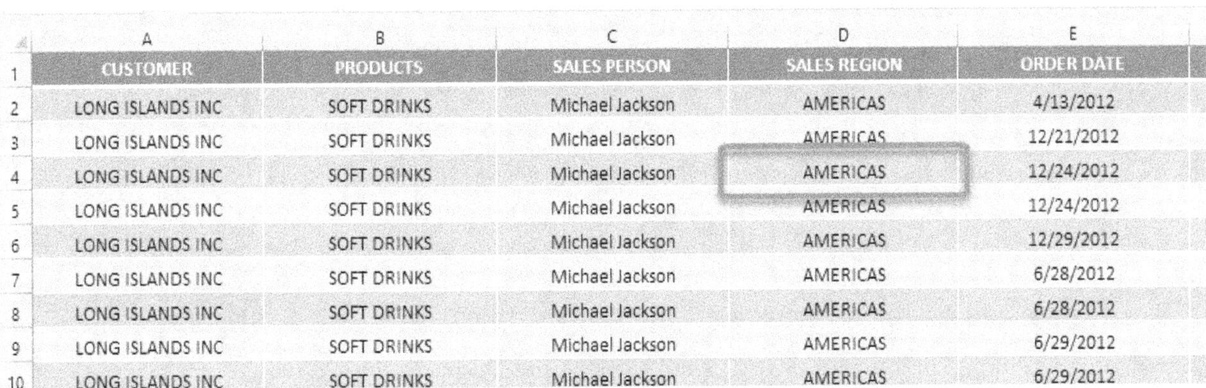

Select that cell. Go to **View > Freeze Panes > Freeze Panes**

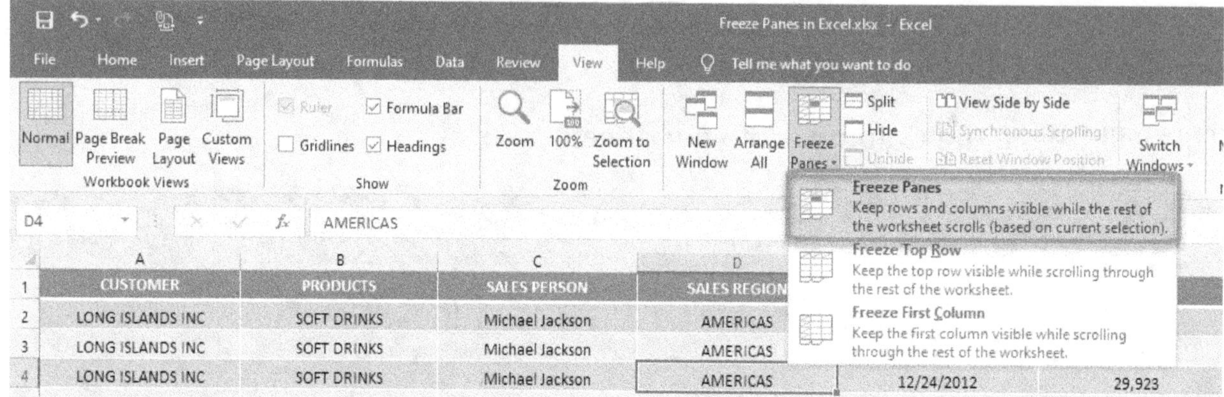

This will freeze panes based on that specific cell. Try scrolling in multiple directions. Cells A1 to C3 are now frozen!

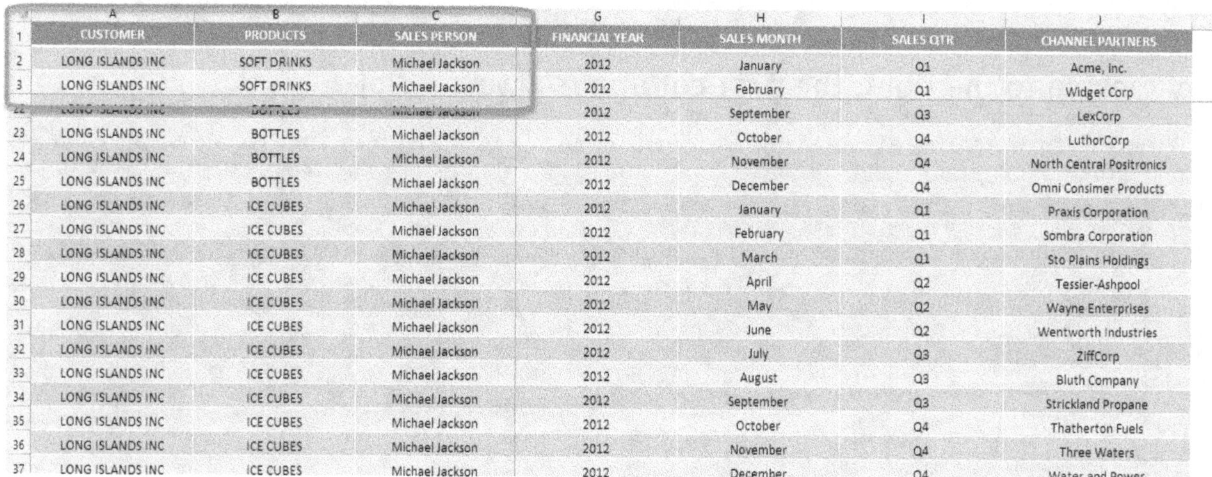

Lock Cells in Excel

Have you encountered a scenario where you do not want to lock the whole sheet, but just a couple of cells in your Excel worksheet?

Locking an entire sheet is straightforward, but **locking separate cells** is a different story.

Let us say, we have this single cell that we want to lock in our Excel worksheet:

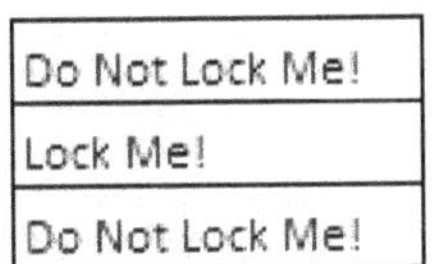

Here is the game plan:

- All of the cells are locked by default, however locked cells have no effect until you have **protected the worksheet**

- So we will **unlock all** of the cells

- Then select the single target cell and **lock it**

- After that, we will **protect the worksheet** and **our target cell will now be locked**!

STEP 1: Select all of the cells by **clicking the upper left corner:**

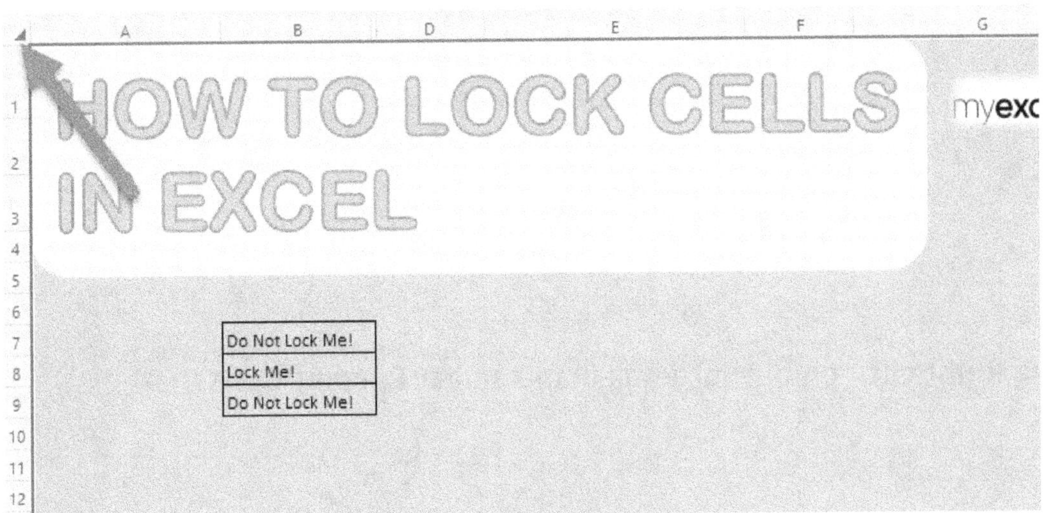

STEP 2: Right click any cell and select **Format Cells:**

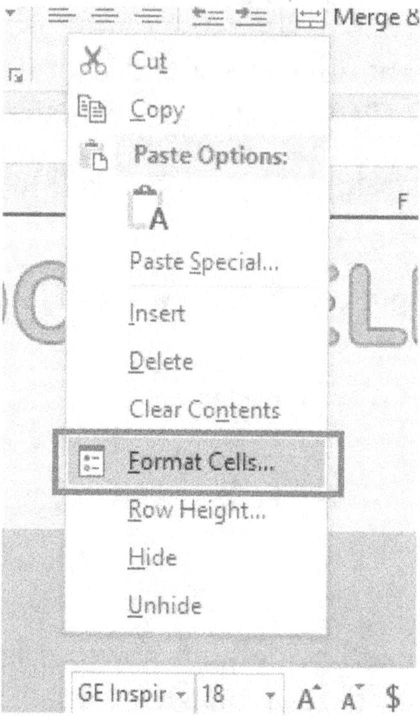

STEP 3: Ensure **Locked** is unticked. This will unlock our entire sheet. **Click OK.**

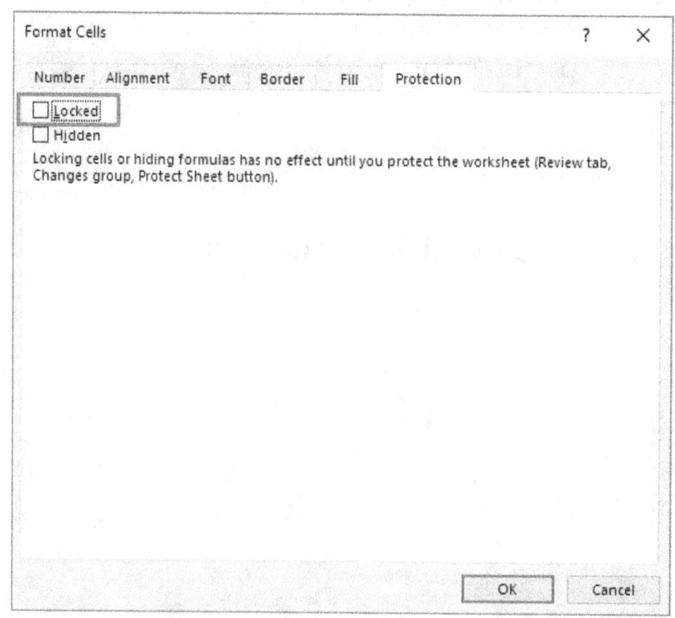

STEP 4: Right click on our target cell and select **Format Cells:**

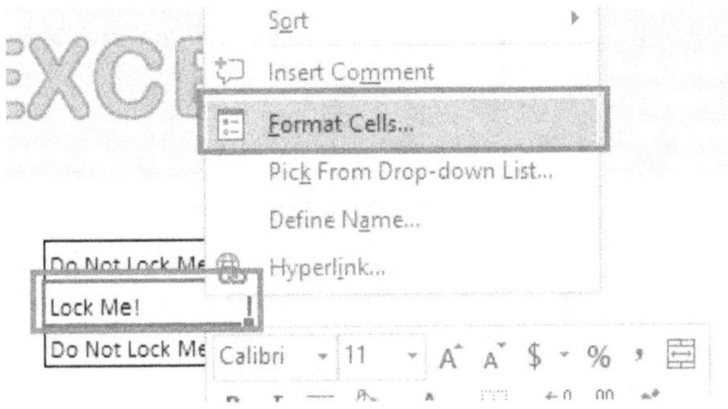

STEP 5: Ensure **Locked** is ticked this time. This will lock our target cell. **Click OK.**

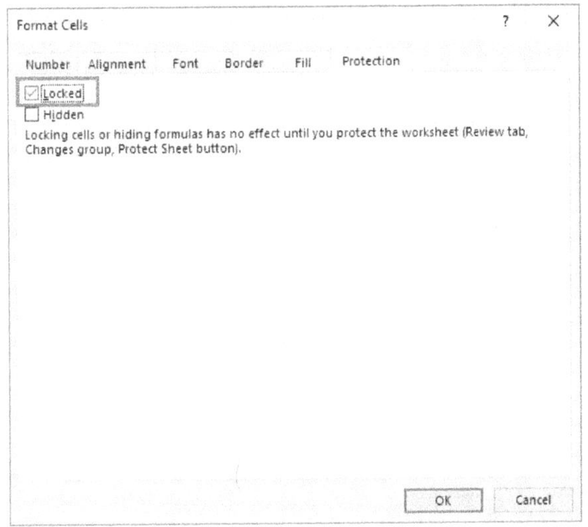

STEP 6: Now it is time to protect our Excel sheet and see the locking in action!

Right-click on the Worksheet Name and select **Protect Sheet** (or go to the ribbon menu and select **Review > Protect Sheet**)

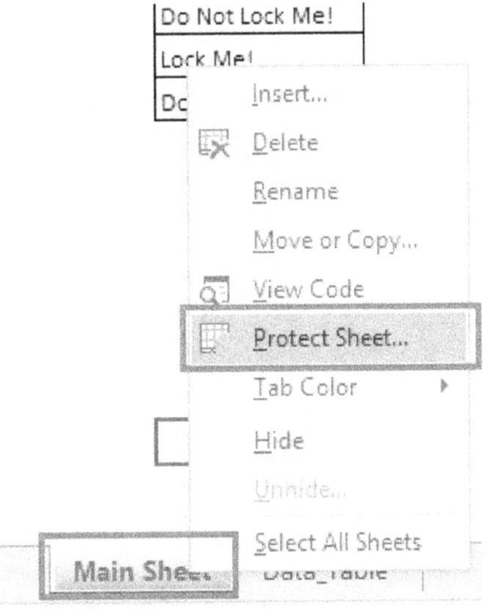

STEP 7: Type in a password and **Click OK.**   In our example, I typed in *excel* as the password.

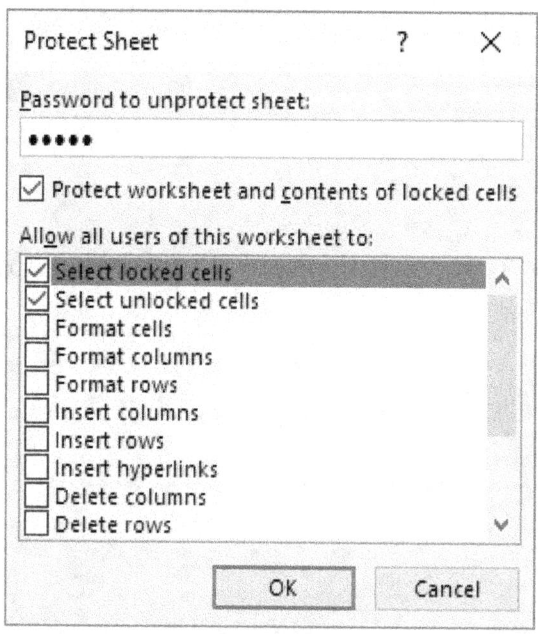

STEP 8: Retype the password and **Click OK.**

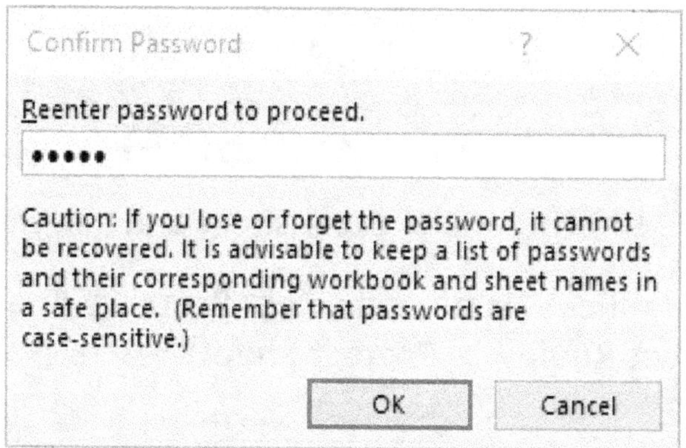

STEP 9: If you try editing your target cell now, Excel will not allow you to...And you are able to edit the other cells just fine!

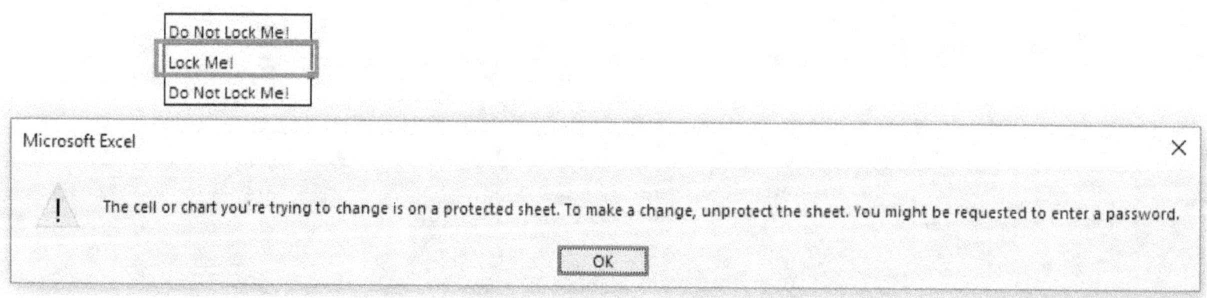

Lock & Protect Formula Cells

If you have a workbook with lots of formulas and you want to protect those formulas from being amended by other people who share your workbook, then you can!

STEP 1: Press the Go To Special shortcut **CTRL+G**

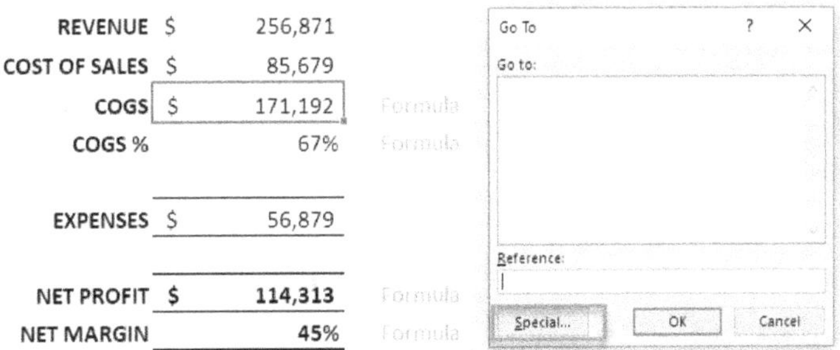

STEP 2: Select the **Constants** box and press **OK** (this highlights all the non-formula cells)

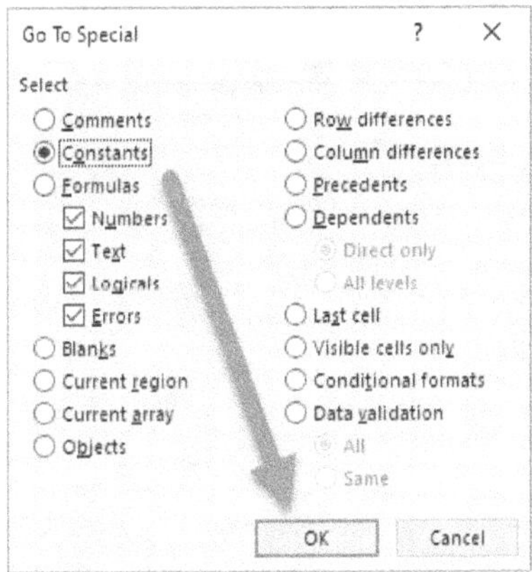

STEP 3: Press CTRL+1 to bring up the Format Cells dialog box

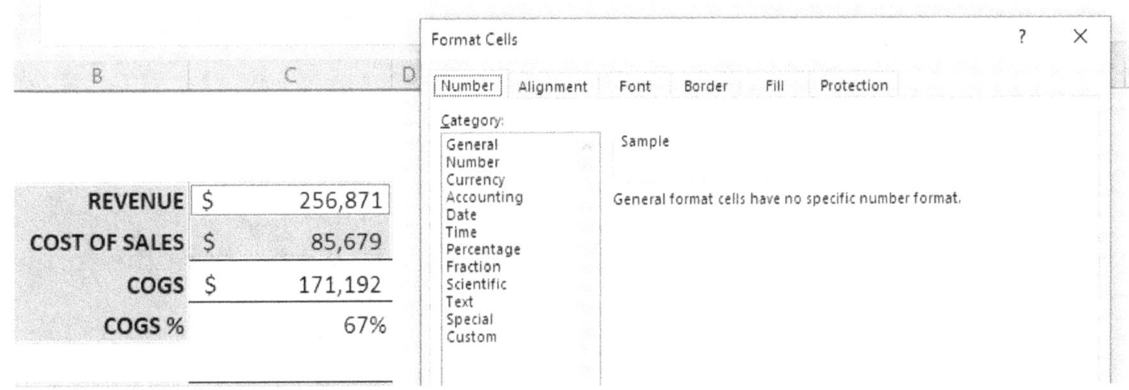

 Select the **Protection** tab and **Un-check the Locked box**

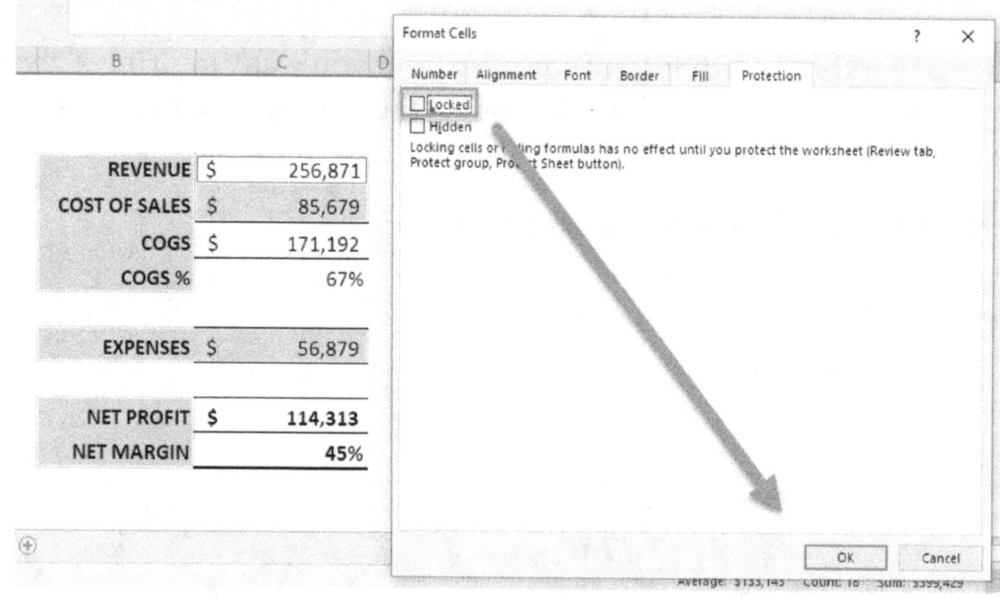

STEP 5: In the menu ribbon go to **Review > Protect Sheet > then enter your custom password** (optional)

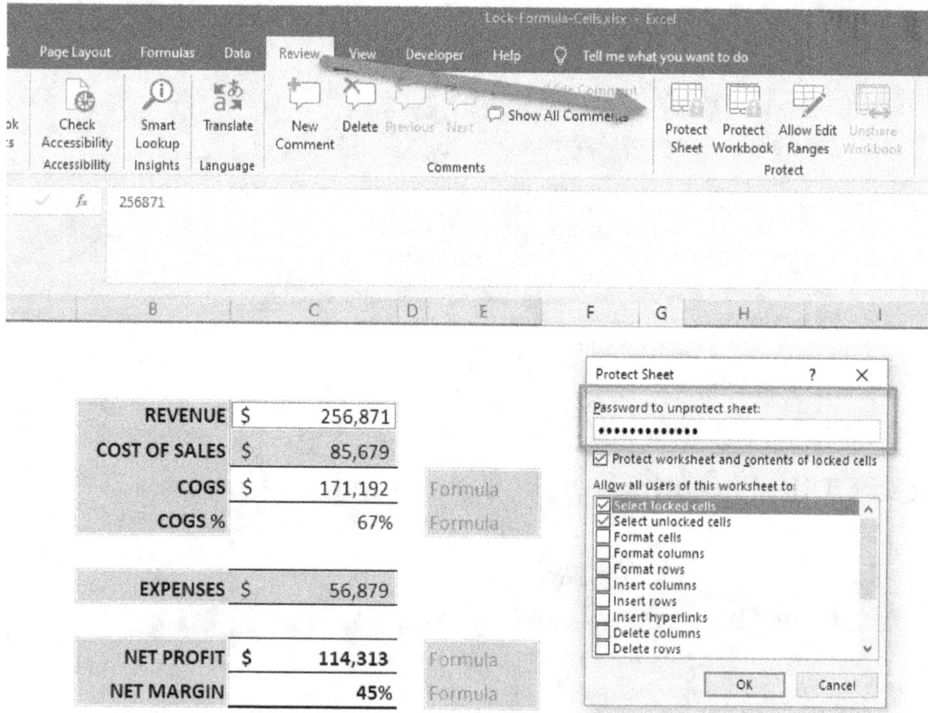

This will lock all the cells that are not constant, so this will be all of the formula cells!

Number Format: Make Negative Red Numbers

When you are working with lots of different numbers in Excel, you sometimes want your numbers to stand out by showing them in a negative red number enclosed in parenthesis.

STEP 1: Select the column that you want to apply the negative number formatting. Press *CTRL + 1* to open the **Format Dialog**.

STEP 2: Select **Number** as the category and select the formatting that you want to display for negative numbers. You can change the number of decimal places as well.

Click **OK**.

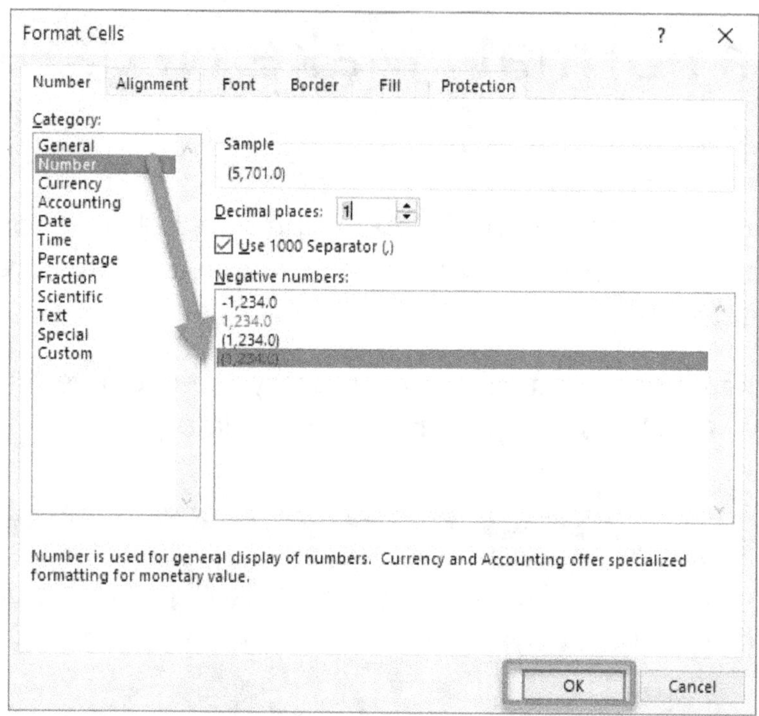

Now your negative numbers are now formatted!

Number Format - Thousands & Millions

Many times, you might have large numbers in an Excel report and it is hard to decipher and read the number at one glace.

The best way is to show the numbers in Thousands (K) or Millions (M).

In Excel you can display a number 45,200,000 as 45.2 Million.

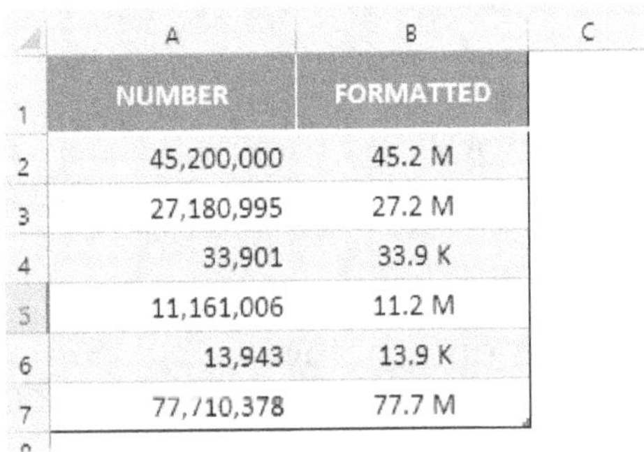

Custom Formatting

Before we move forward, it is important to know that **certain characters in custom formatting have specific meaning**:

- **0** *Display insignificant zeros*

- **#** *Display significant zeros*

- **,** *Thousand separator*

- **" "** *Add text within the quotes*

You can create Excel custom number formats for Millions and Thousands using either the placeholder zero or pound sign. Let's look at both of them one-by-one.

With Placeholder Pound Sign

#,##0, "ths"

#,##0,, "mills"

In the example below, we have sales data with the sales amount mentioned in columns D & E.

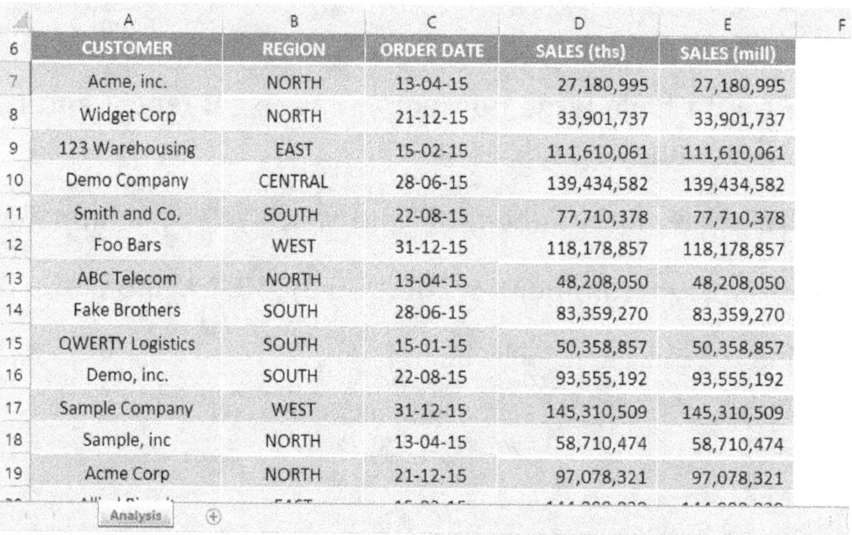

STEP 1: Select **Column D** in the data below.

STEP 2: Press **Ctrl + 1** to open the Format Cells dialog box.

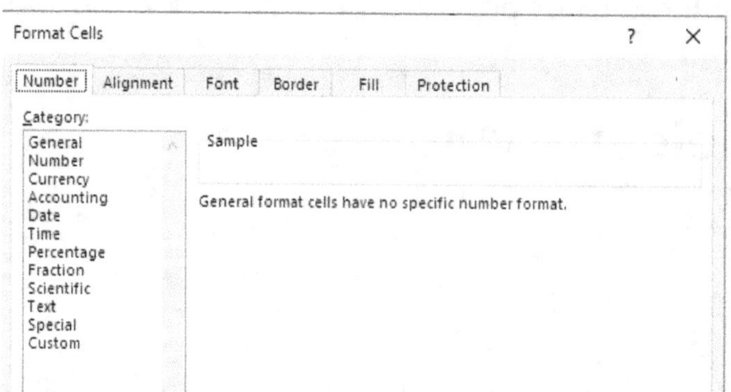

STEP 3: In the Format Cells dialog box, Under Number Tab select **Custom.**

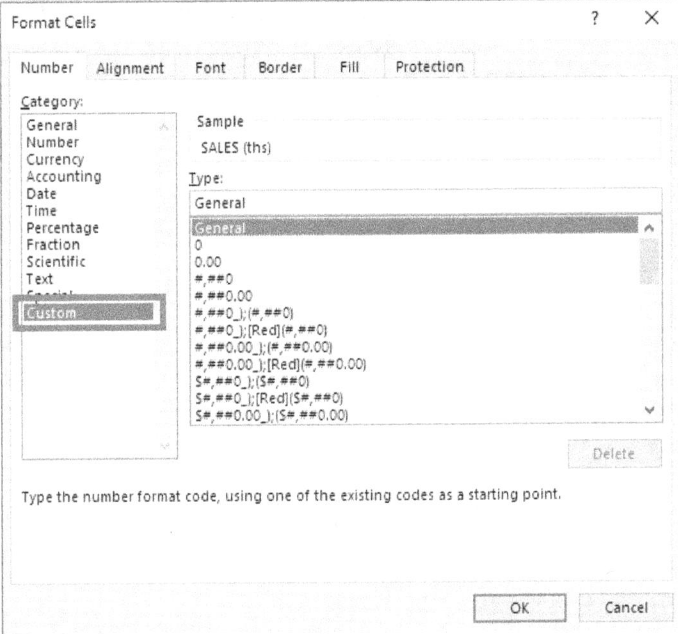

STEP 4: Type **#,##0**, **"ths"** and Click **OK**.

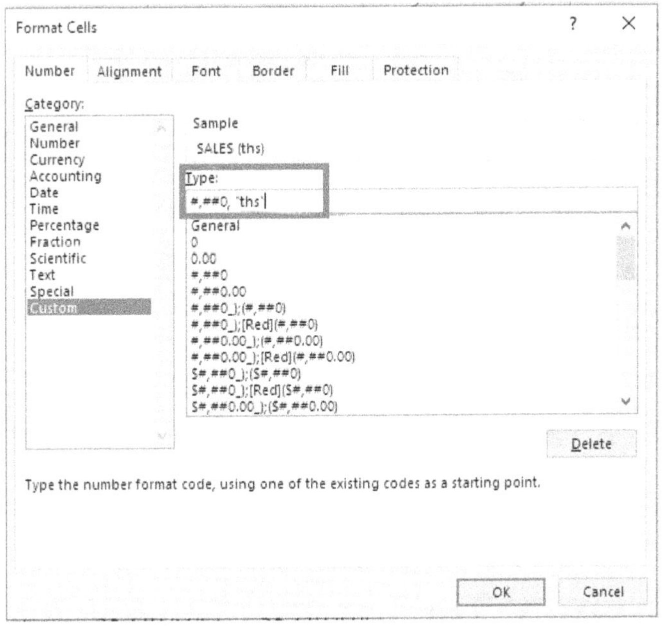

STEP 5: This is how the Column D after number formatting will look

	A	B	C	D	E	F
6	CUSTOMER	REGION	ORDER DATE	SALES (ths)	SALES (mill)	
7	Acme, inc.	NORTH	13-04-15	27,181 ths	27,180,995	
8	Widget Corp	NORTH	21-12-15	33,902 ths	33,901,737	
9	123 Warehousing	EAST	15-02-15	111,610 ths	111,610,061	
10	Demo Company	CENTRAL	28-06-15	139,435 ths	139,434,582	
11	Smith and Co.	SOUTH	22-08-15	77,710 ths	77,710,378	
12	Foo Bars	WEST	31-12-15	118,179 ths	118,178,857	
13	ABC Telecom	NORTH	13-04-15	48,208 ths	48,208,050	
14	Fake Brothers	SOUTH	28-06-15	83,359 ths	83,359,270	
15	QWERTY Logistics	SOUTH	15-01-15	50,359 ths	50,358,857	
16	Demo, inc.	SOUTH	22-08-15	93,555 ths	93,555,192	
17	Sample Company	WEST	31-12-15	145,311 ths	145,310,509	
18	Sample, inc	NORTH	13-04-15	58,710 ths	58,710,474	
19	Acme Corp	NORTH	21-12-15	97,078 ths	97,078,321	

STEP 6: Follow the same steps for Column E as well and type #,##0,, **"mills"** under the custom section.

	A	B	C	D	E	F
6	CUSTOMER	REGION	ORDER DATE	SALES (ths)	SALES (mill)	
7	Acme, inc.	NORTH	13-04-15	27,181 ths	27 mills	
8	Widget Corp	NORTH	21-12-15	33,902 ths	34 mills	
9	123 Warehousing	EAST	15-02-15	111,610 ths	112 mills	
10	Demo Company	CENTRAL	28-06-15	139,435 ths	139 mills	
11	Smith and Co.	SOUTH	22-08-15	77,710 ths	78 mills	
12	Foo Bars	WEST	31-12-15	118,179 ths	118 mills	
13	ABC Telecom	NORTH	13-04-15	48,208 ths	48 mills	
14	Fake Brothers	SOUTH	28-06-15	83,359 ths	83 mills	
15	QWERTY Logistics	SOUTH	15-01-15	50,359 ths	50 mills	
16	Demo, inc.	SOUTH	22-08-15	93,555 ths	94 mills	
17	Sample Company	WEST	31-12-15	145,311 ths	145 mills	
18	Sample, inc	NORTH	13-04-15	58,710 ths	59 mills	
19	Acme Corp	NORTH	21-12-15	97,078 ths	97 mills	

The only difference between the two custom formats (Thousands & Millions) is that you have to put **1 comma for Thousands** and **2 commas for Millions**.

Using Placeholder Zero 0 & Decimal Point

0.0, "K"

0.0,, "M"

Zero is used to display insignificant zeros when the number has fewer digits than the format represented using zero.

For example, a custom format **0.00** will display the numbers:

5 as 5.00

8.5 as 8.50

10.99 as 10.99

Also, you can round off the number using a decimal point symbol.

To get this formatting done, follow the steps below:

STEP 1: Select **Column D** in the data below.

	A	B	C	D	E
	CUSTOMER	**REGION**	**ORDER DATE**	**SALES (ths)**	**SALES (mill)**
7	Acme, inc.	NORTH	13-04-15	27,180,995	27,180,995
8	Widget Corp	NORTH	21-12-15	33,901,737	33,901,737
9	123 Warehousing	EAST	15-02-15	111,610,061	111,610,061
10	Demo Company	CENTRAL	28-06-15	139,434,582	139,434,582
11	Smith and Co.	SOUTH	22-08-15	77,710,378	77,710,378
12	Foo Bars	WEST	31-12-15	118,178,857	118,178,857
13	ABC Telecom	NORTH	13-04-15	48,208,050	48,208,050
14	Fake Brothers	SOUTH	28-06-15	83,359,270	83,359,270
15	QWERTY Logistics	SOUTH	15-01-15	50,358,857	50,358,857
16	Demo, inc.	SOUTH	22-08-15	93,555,192	93,555,192
17	Sample Company	WEST	31-12-15	145,310,509	145,310,509
18	Sample, inc	NORTH	13-04-15	58,710,474	58,710,474
19	Acme Corp	NORTH	21-12-15	97,078,321	97,078,321

STEP 2: Right-Click and then Select **Format Cells**.

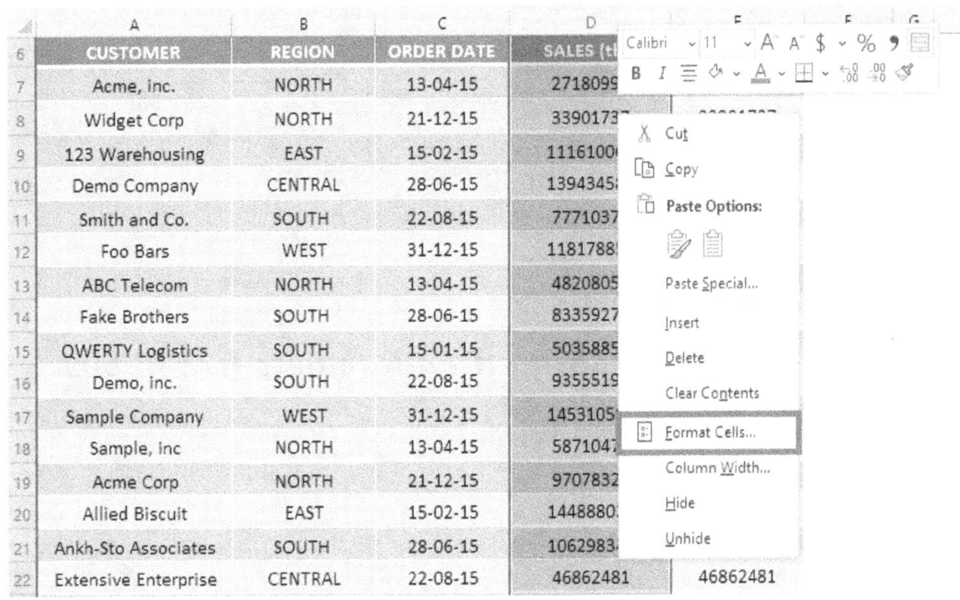

	A	B	C	D
	CUSTOMER	**REGION**	**ORDER DATE**	**SALES (t**
7	Acme, inc.	NORTH	13-04-15	2718099
8	Widget Corp	NORTH	21-12-15	3390173
9	123 Warehousing	EAST	15-02-15	1116100
10	Demo Company	CENTRAL	28-06-15	1394345
11	Smith and Co.	SOUTH	22-08-15	7771037
12	Foo Bars	WEST	31-12-15	1181788
13	ABC Telecom	NORTH	13-04-15	4820805
14	Fake Brothers	SOUTH	28-06-15	8335927
15	QWERTY Logistics	SOUTH	15-01-15	5035885
16	Demo, inc.	SOUTH	22-08-15	9355519
17	Sample Company	WEST	31-12-15	1453105
18	Sample, inc	NORTH	13-04-15	5871047
19	Acme Corp	NORTH	21-12-15	9707832
20	Allied Biscuit	EAST	15-02-15	1448880
21	Ankh-Sto Associates	SOUTH	28-06-15	1062983
22	Extensive Enterprise	CENTRAL	22-08-15	46862481	46862481

 In the Format Cells dialog box, Under Number Tab select **Custom.**

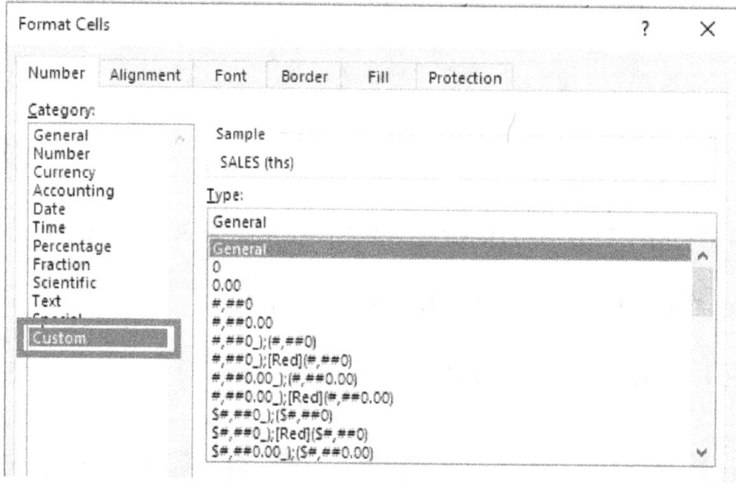

STEP 4: In the **Type** area enter this format:

0.0, "K"

Then click **OK.**

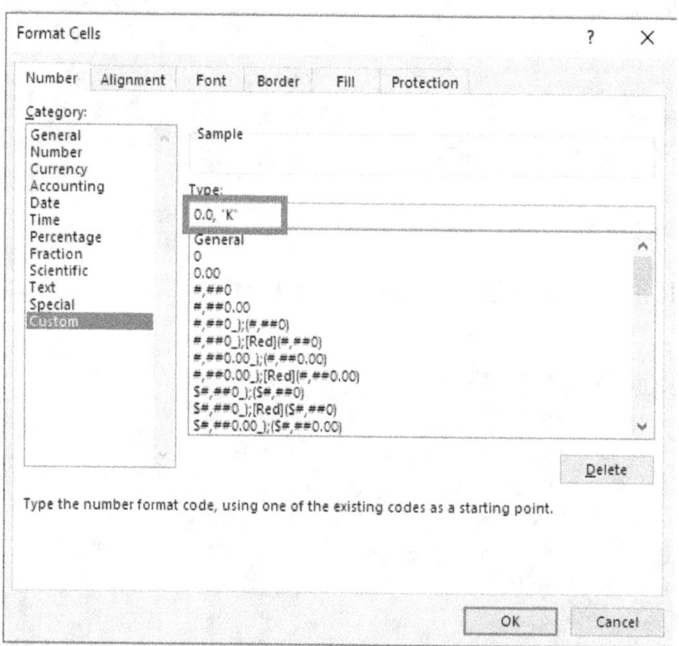

Follow the same process for formatting Numbers in Millions.

STEP 5: In the **Type** area enter this format:

0.0,, "M"

Then click **OK.**

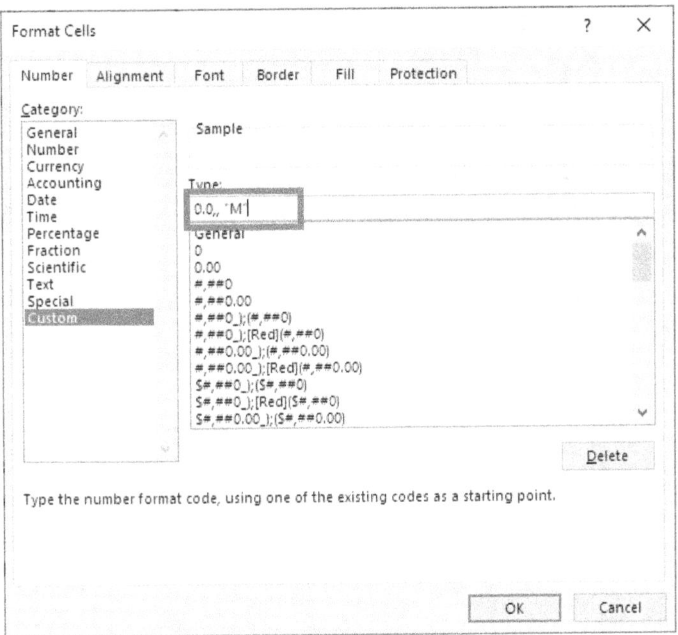

Excel number format millions & thousands is now ready!

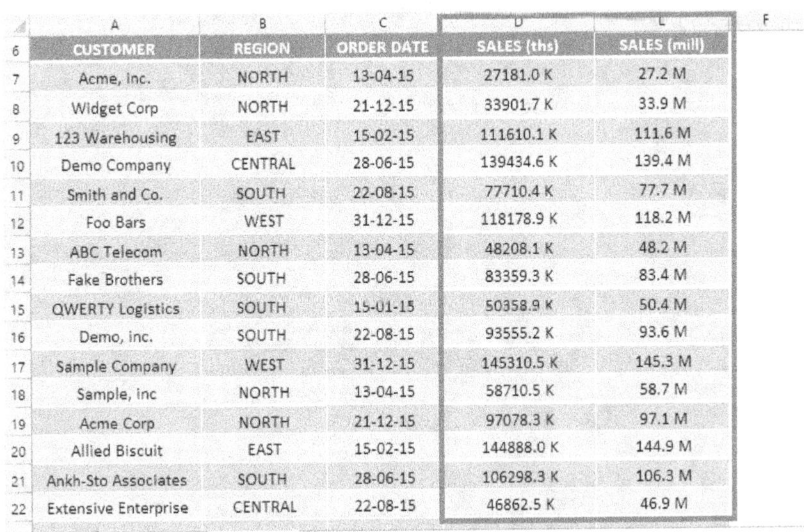

One thing to note is that this will **just format the way the number looks** like on the Worksheet. The number stored in the cell remains the same!

ROUND Function

You can use the ROUND function to change the formatting and also change the number as well.

In this method, you have to do three things:

- Divide the number by 1000,000

- Round off the decimal places

- Use & sign to add text "M"

In this example, you have the sales amount mentioned in Column D. Let's use the combination of division, round, and the **&** sign to get the formatting done.

 Select cell **E7**.

STEP 2: Start with the **division**. Type

=D7/1000000.

E7 =D7/1000000

	A	B	C	D	E	F
6	CUSTOMER	REGION	ORDER DATE	General Format	Using Round Formula	
7	Acme, inc.	NORTH	13-04-15	27180995	27.180995	
8	Widget Corp	NORTH	21-12-15	33901737		
9	123 Warehousing	EAST	15-02-15	111610061		
10	Demo Company	CENTRAL	28-06-15	139434582		
11	Smith and Co.	SOUTH	22-08-15	77710378		
12	Foo Bars	WEST	31-12-15	118178857		
13	ABC Telecom	NORTH	13-04-15	48208050		
14	Fake Brothers	SOUTH	28-06-15	83359270		
15	QWERTY Logistics	SOUTH	15-01-15	50358857		
16	Demo, inc.	SOUTH	22-08-15	93555192		
17	Sample Company	WEST	31-12-15	145310509		
18	Sample, inc	NORTH	13-04-15	58710474		
19	Acme Corp	NORTH	21-12-15	97078321		
20	Allied Biscuit	EAST	15-02-15	144888038		
21	Ankh-Sto Associates	SOUTH	28-06-15	106298344		
22	Extensive Enterprise	CENTRAL	22-08-15	46862481		

STEP 3: Add **Round** Function to this.

=ROUND(D7/1000000,1).

E7 =ROUND(D7/1000000,1)

	A	B	C	D	E	F
6	CUSTOMER	REGION	ORDER DATE	General Format	Using Round Formula	
7	Acme, inc.	NORTH	13-04-15	27180995	27.2	
8	Widget Corp	NORTH	21-12-15	33901737		
9	123 Warehousing	EAST	15-02-15	111610061		
10	Demo Company	CENTRAL	28-06-15	139434582		
11	Smith and Co.	SOUTH	22-08-15	77710378		
12	Foo Bars	WEST	31-12-15	118178857		
13	ABC Telecom	NORTH	13-04-15	48208050		
14	Fake Brothers	SOUTH	28-06-15	83359270		
15	QWERTY Logistics	SOUTH	15-01-15	50358857		
16	Demo, inc.	SOUTH	22-08-15	93555192		
17	Sample Company	WEST	31-12-15	145310509		
18	Sample, inc	NORTH	13-04-15	58710474		
19	Acme Corp	NORTH	21-12-15	97078321		
20	Allied Biscuit	EAST	15-02-15	144888038		
21	Ankh-Sto Associates	SOUTH	28-06-15	106298344		
22	Extensive Enterprise	CENTRAL	22-08-15	46862481		

STEP 4: Add **Text** to this formula using & sign.

=ROUND(D7/1000000,1)&" M".

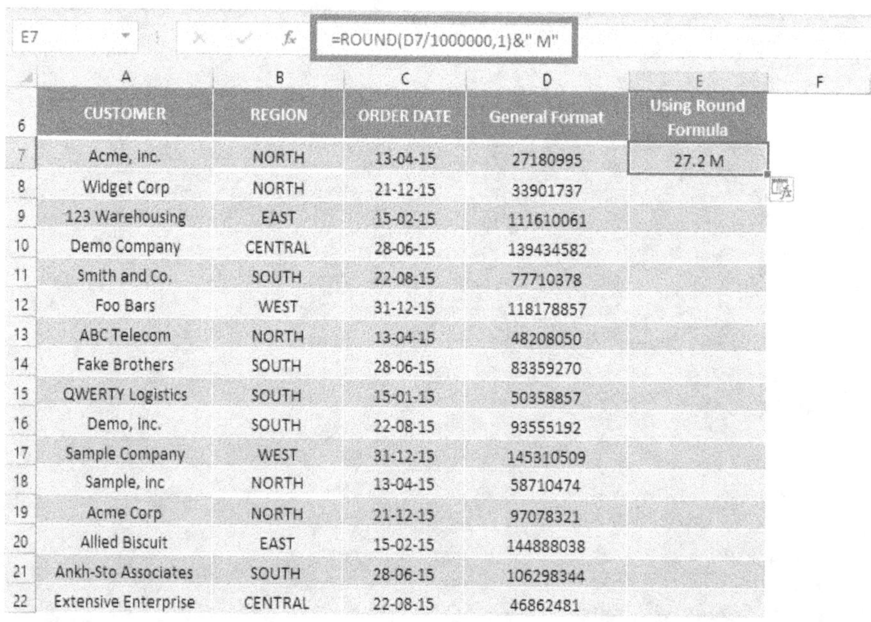

STEP 5: Copy the **formula down**.

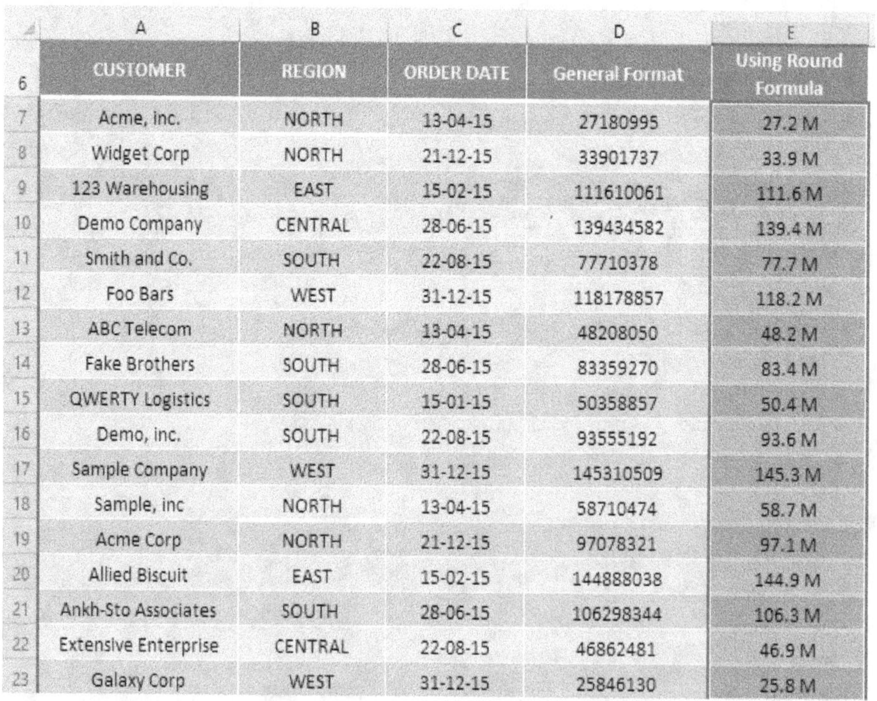

STEP 6: Copy the Column and the Press **Alt + E + S** to open the **Paste Special Box** and select **Values**. Then click **OK**.

This will hard code the values and get rid of the formula!

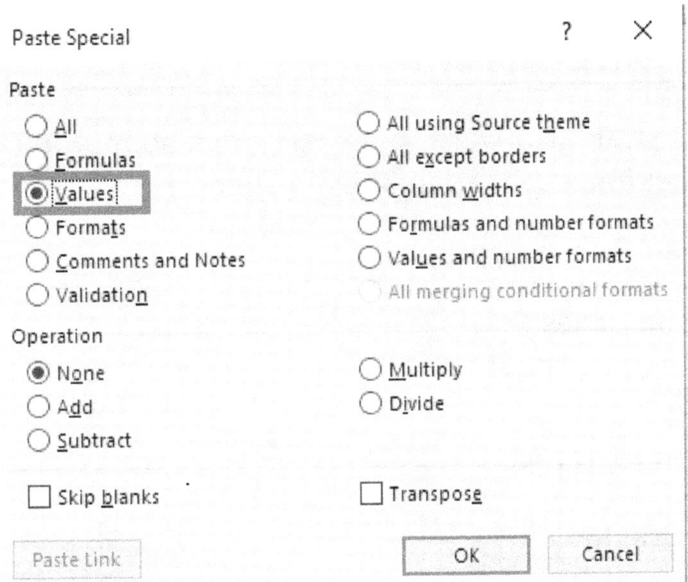

The only **difference between using Custom Format & Round Function** is that:

In **Custom Format**, only the formatting changes but the number stored remains the same.

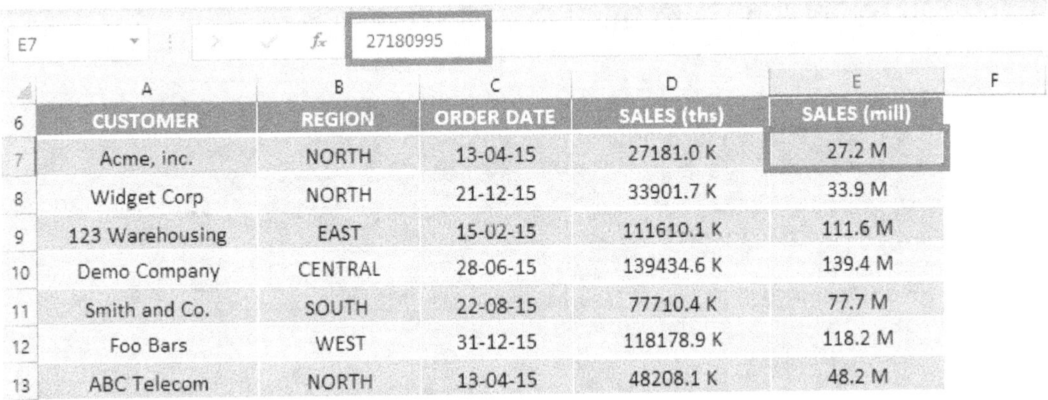

In **Round Function**, both the formatting and number changes.

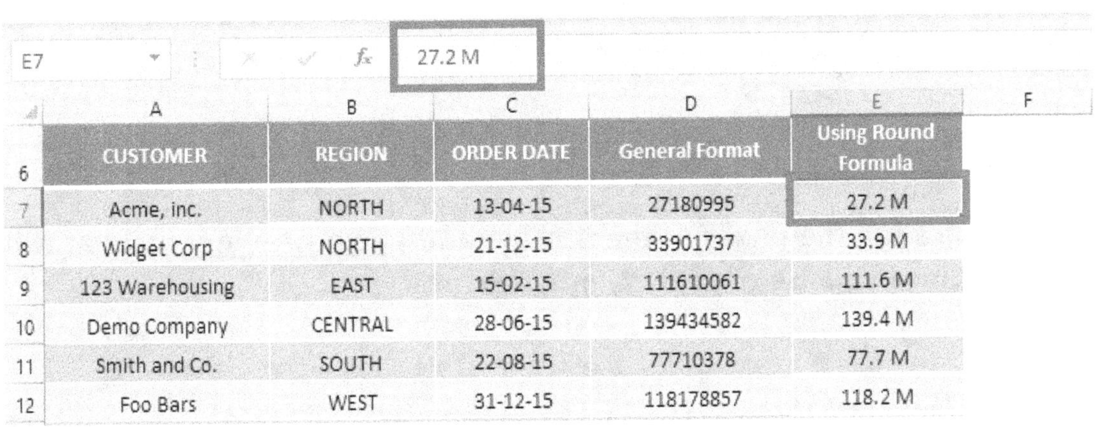

Printing Settings

Printing in Excel is straightforward, but there are also multiple settings that you need to learn to maximize its capabilities in Excel.

We will go over the following options:

- Previewing the pages

- Print selection

- Printing multiple copies

- Setting the Orientation

- Page Margins

- Scaling

STEP 1: We will be working with this table. Go to *File > Print*

	A	B	C	D	E	F
1	CUSTOMER	REGION	ORDER DATE	SALES	MONTH	YEAR
2	Acme, Inc.	NORTH	1/15/2013	$26,884	January	2013
3	Widget Corp	SOUTH	2/14/2013	$46,174	February	2013
4	123 Warehousing	EAST	3/16/2013	$44,802	March	2013
5	Demo Company	WEST	4/15/2013	$49,049	April	2013
6	Smith and Co.	NORTH	5/15/2013	$80,369	May	2013
7	Foo Bars	SOUTH	6/14/2013	$53,522	June	2013
8	ABC Telecom	EAST	7/14/2013	$67,320	July	2013
9	Fake Brothers	WEST	8/13/2013	$66,663	August	2013
10	Acme, Inc.	NORTH	9/12/2013	$58,146	September	2013
11	Widget Corp	SOUTH	10/12/2013	$83,288	October	2013
12	123 Warehousing	EAST	11/11/2013	$22,024	November	2013
13	Demo Company	WEST	12/11/2013	$64,750	December	2013
14	Smith and Co.	NORTH	1/10/2014	$53,586	January	2014
15	Foo Bars	SOUTH	2/9/2014	$14,333	February	2014
16	ABC Telecom	EAST	3/11/2014	$29,570	March	2014
17	Fake Brothers	WEST	4/10/2014	$83,468	April	2014
18	Acme, Inc.	NORTH	5/10/2014	$25,263	May	2014
19	Widget Corp	SOUTH	6/9/2014	$68,797	June	2014
20	123 Warehousing	EAST	7/9/2014	$49,562	July	2014
21	Demo Company	WEST	8/8/2014	$13,964	August	2014
22	Smith and Co.	NORTH	9/7/2014	$23,798	September	2014

You can go through the pages at the bottom and **see a preview** of what will be printed out. Once you are ok with it, press **Print**.

Print

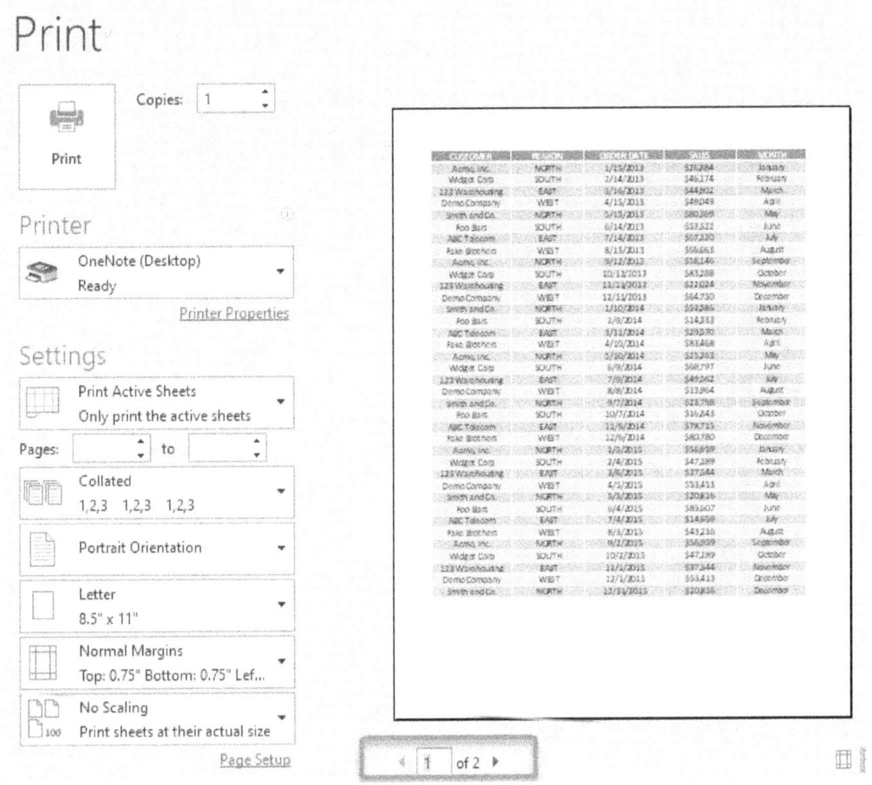

STEP 2: Another way to print is by **<u>printing a selection</u>**. For example, we have these range of cells selected:

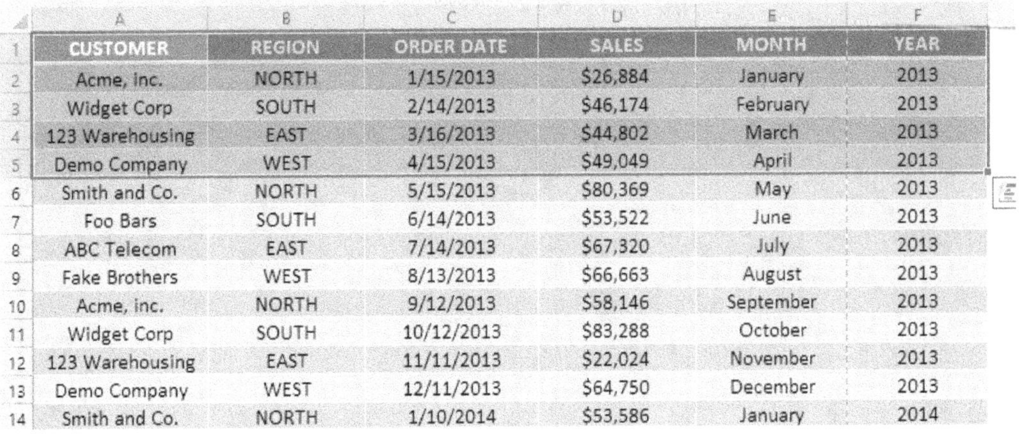

	CUSTOMER	REGION	ORDER DATE	SALES	MONTH	YEAR
1	CUSTOMER	REGION	ORDER DATE	SALES	MONTH	YEAR
2	Acme, inc.	NORTH	1/15/2013	$26,884	January	2013
3	Widget Corp	SOUTH	2/14/2013	$46,174	February	2013
4	123 Warehousing	EAST	3/16/2013	$44,802	March	2013
5	Demo Company	WEST	4/15/2013	$49,049	April	2013
6	Smith and Co.	NORTH	5/15/2013	$80,369	May	2013
7	Foo Bars	SOUTH	6/14/2013	$53,522	June	2013
8	ABC Telecom	EAST	7/14/2013	$67,320	July	2013
9	Fake Brothers	WEST	8/13/2013	$66,663	August	2013
10	Acme, inc.	NORTH	9/12/2013	$58,146	September	2013
11	Widget Corp	SOUTH	10/12/2013	$83,288	October	2013
12	123 Warehousing	EAST	11/11/2013	$22,024	November	2013
13	Demo Company	WEST	12/11/2013	$64,750	December	2013
14	Smith and Co.	NORTH	1/10/2014	$53,586	January	2014

Go to **File > Print.** Under Settings select **Print Selection.**

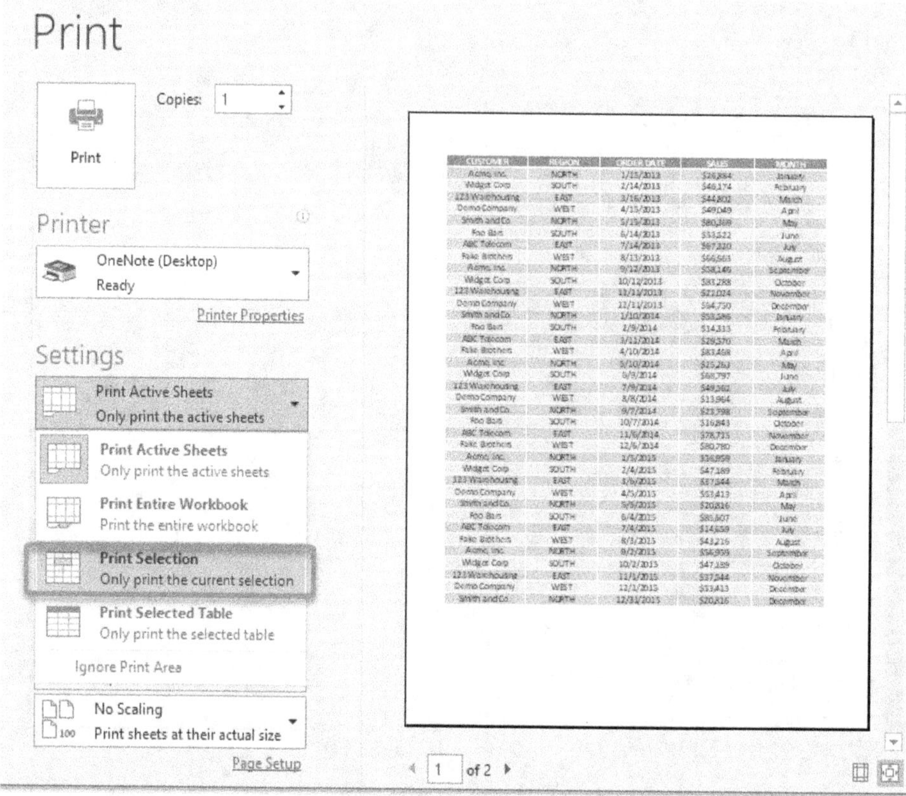

You will be shown a preview that only our selected cells will be printed out.

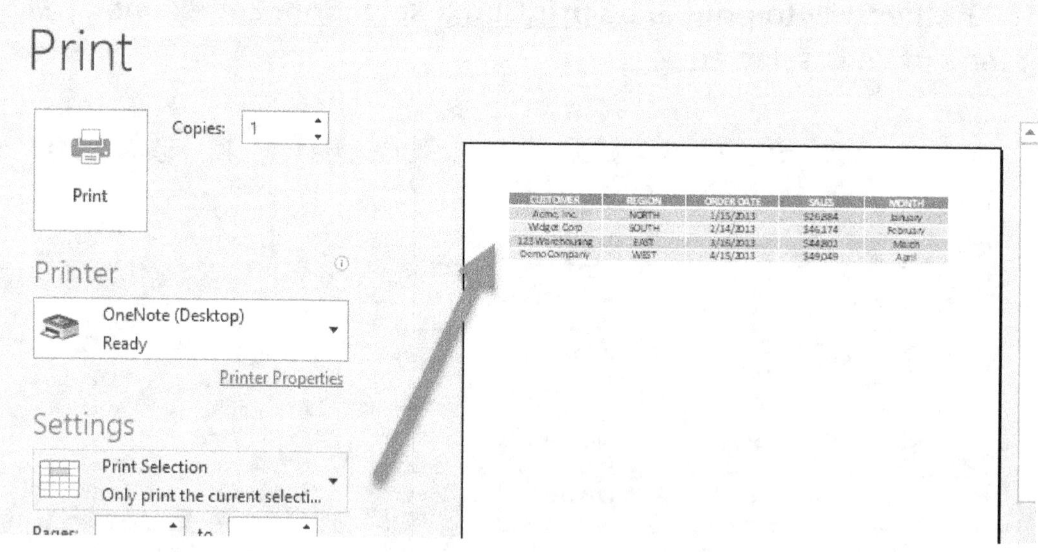

STEP 3: You can also specify <u>**how many copies are printed out**</u> by changing the number of **Copies**. You can also set if it is **Collated** or **Uncollated**.

Collated will print each set out completely, then onto the next set. While Uncollated prints all page 1s first, then followed by all page 2s and so on.

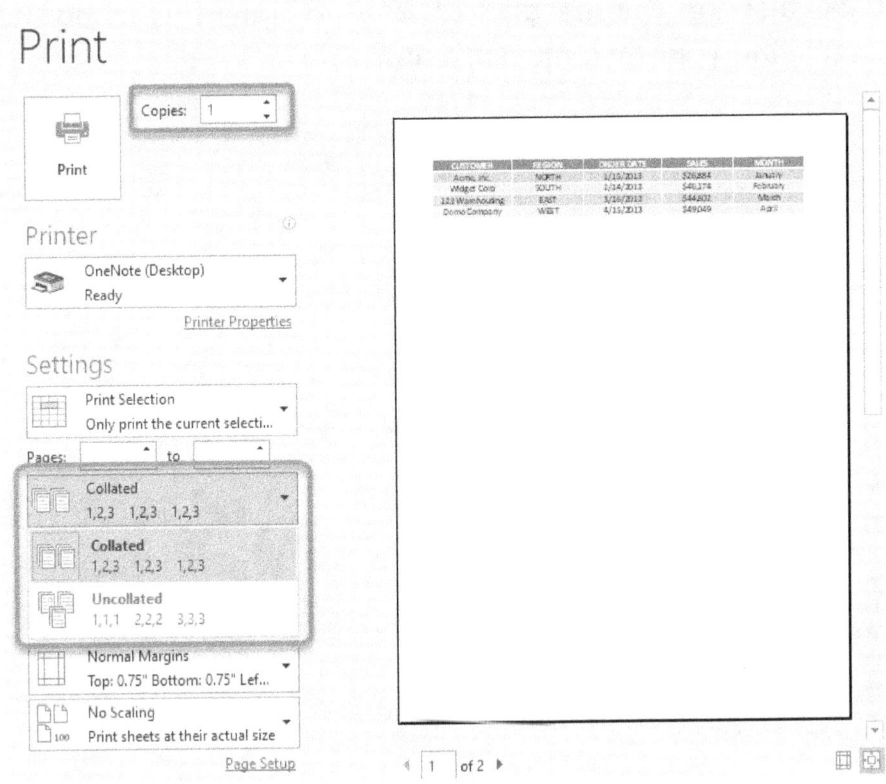

STEP 4: For <u>**Orientation**</u>, you can switch between **Portrait** or **Landscape** orientation depending on your spacing and printing needs.

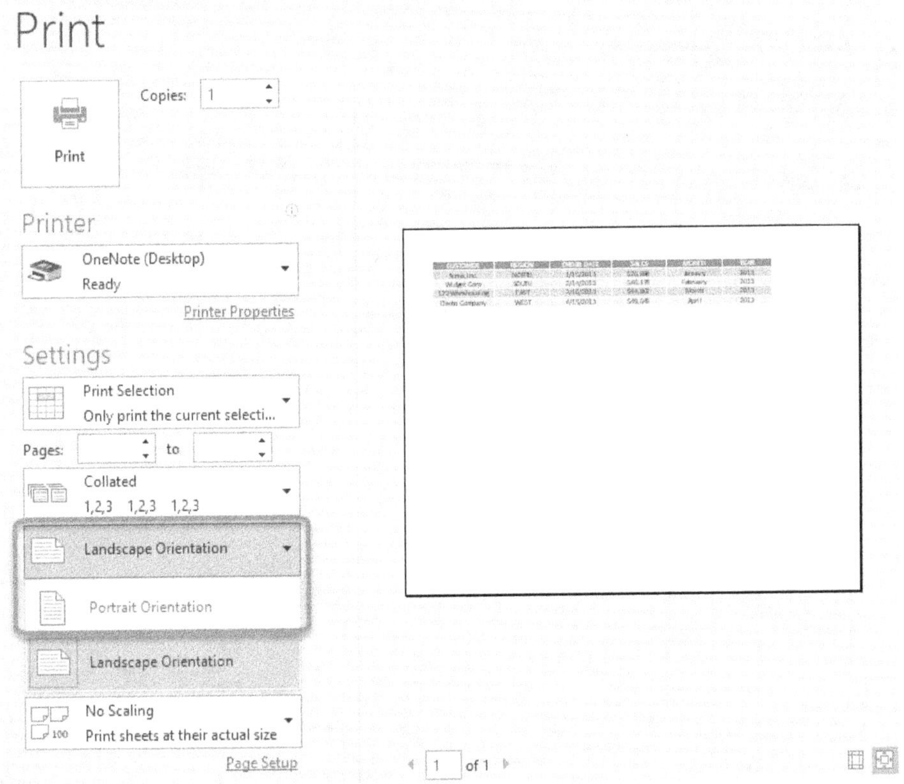

 You can also **set the margins** of your document by using the built-in options or specifying your own measurements.

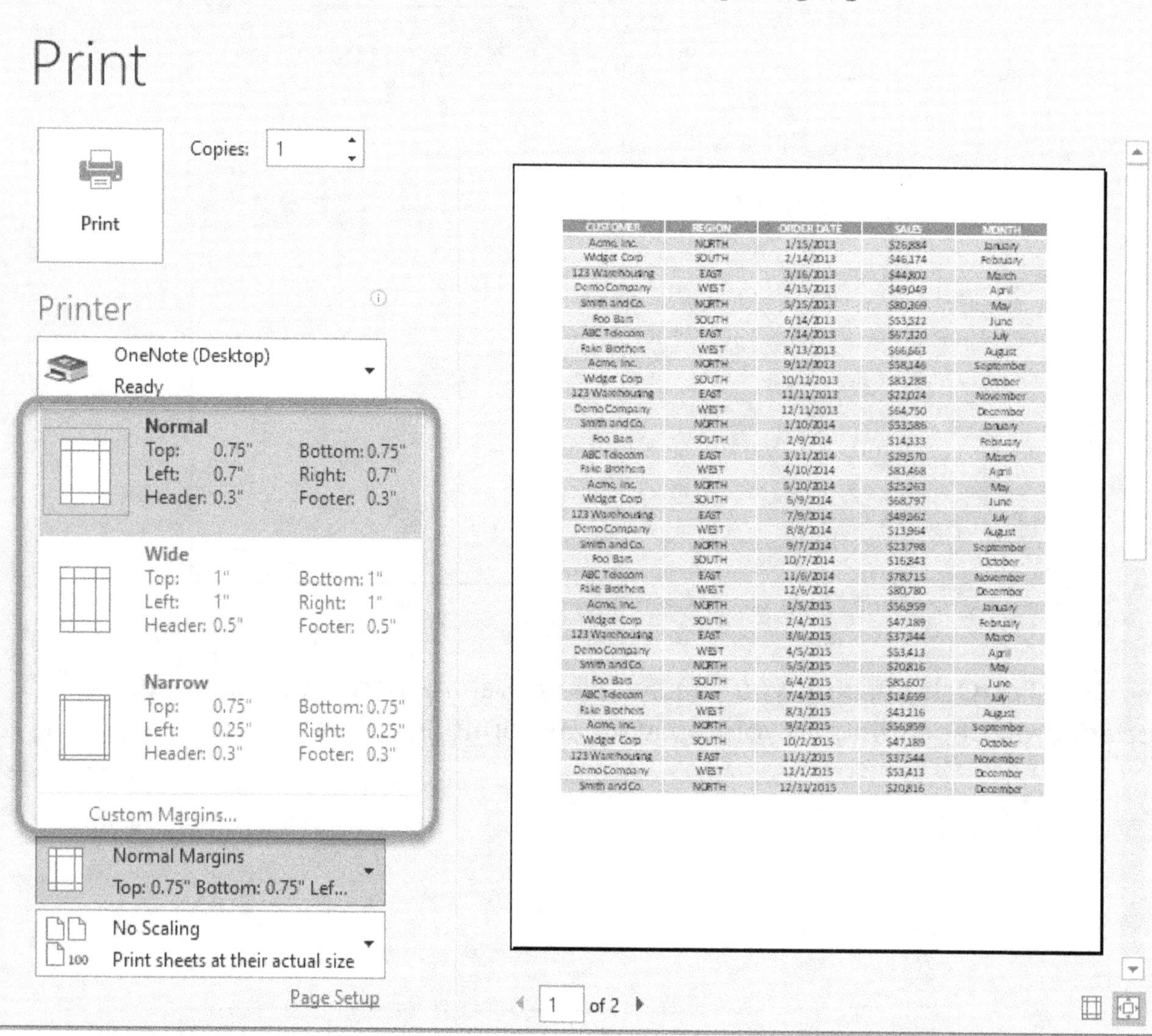

STEP 6: There are also **scaling options** if you want to fit more data into a page. For example, if we select **Fit Sheet on One Page**, then the entire table will be fit in that single page. I use this all the time!

You can also choose to either shrink only all of the columns or all of the rows in a single page.

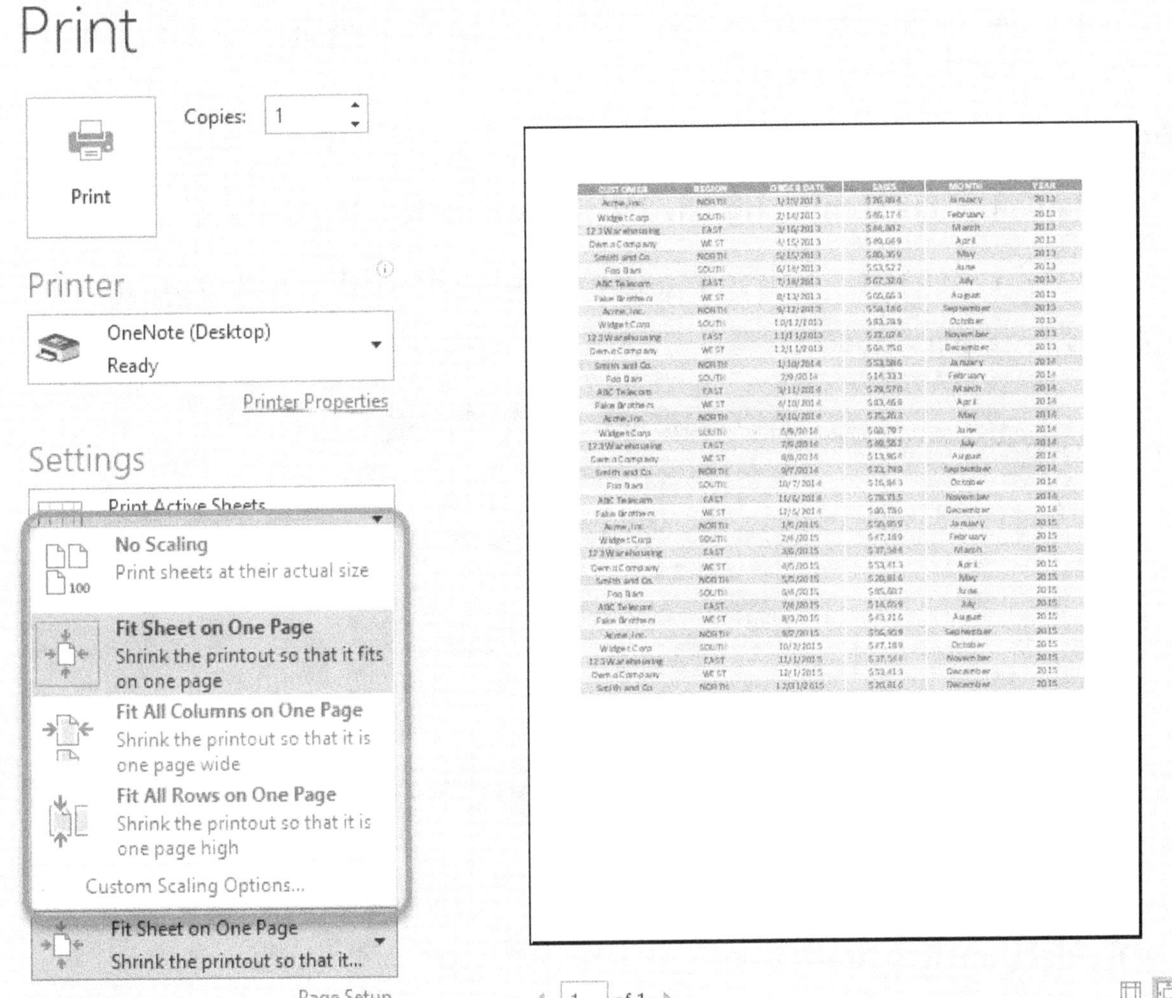

Replace a Format with Another Format

Imagine this, you have a table full of bold text. The bold text could also be all over your worksheet in random cells.

Then you decide that the **bold** text does not suit your expected design and prefer red colored text instead.

What would you do?

Changing all of the formatting one by one would be a big pain!

Thankfully, Excel allows you to **replace formatting with another formatting**!

This is our initial Table:

Unformatted SSN	Formatted SSN
123456789	123-45-6789
478923744	478-92-3744
980412833	980-41-2833
491823821	491-82-3821
239842394	239-84-2394
123981293	123-98-1293

STEP 1: Go to *Home > Find & Select*

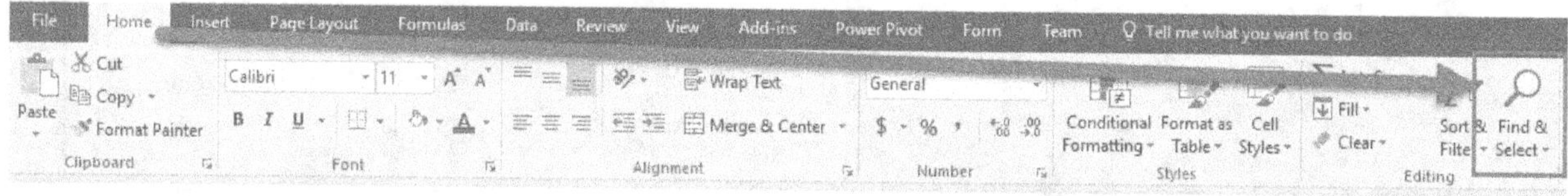

Then select the **Replace** option.

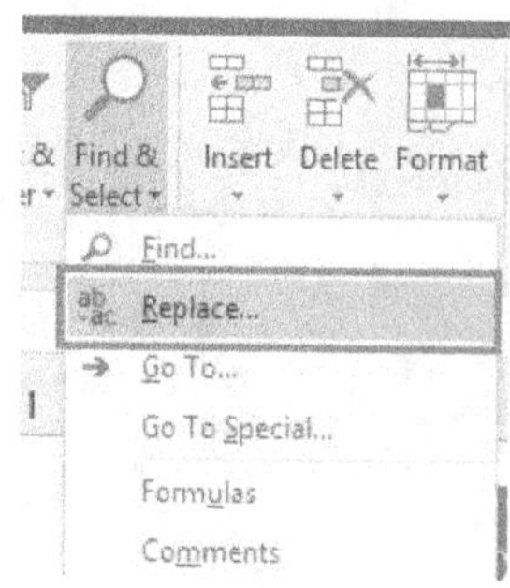

 Select **Options**.

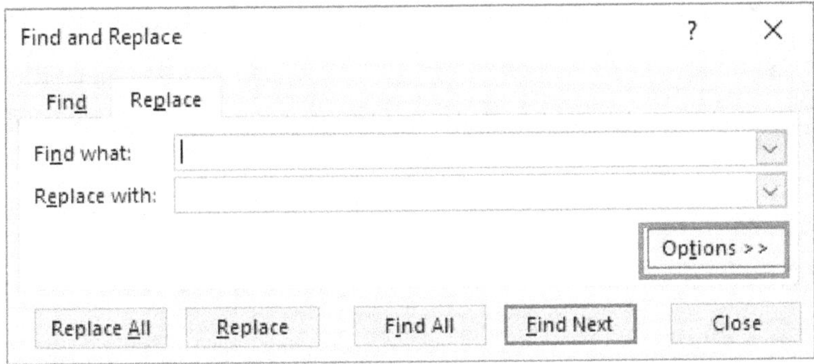

 Select **Format**. We will set the format that we want to change.

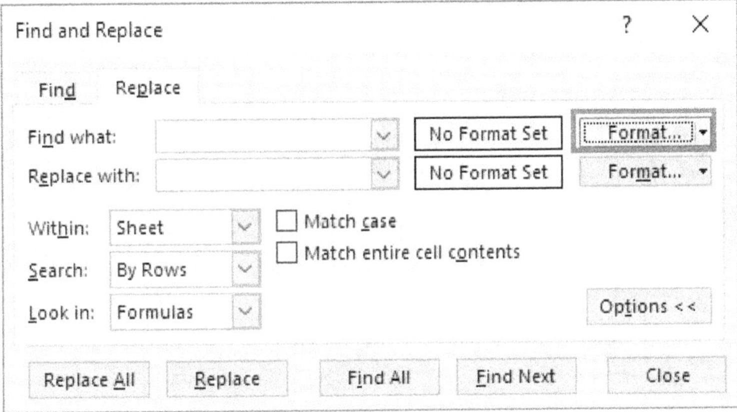

Make sure **Bold** is selected. Click **OK.**

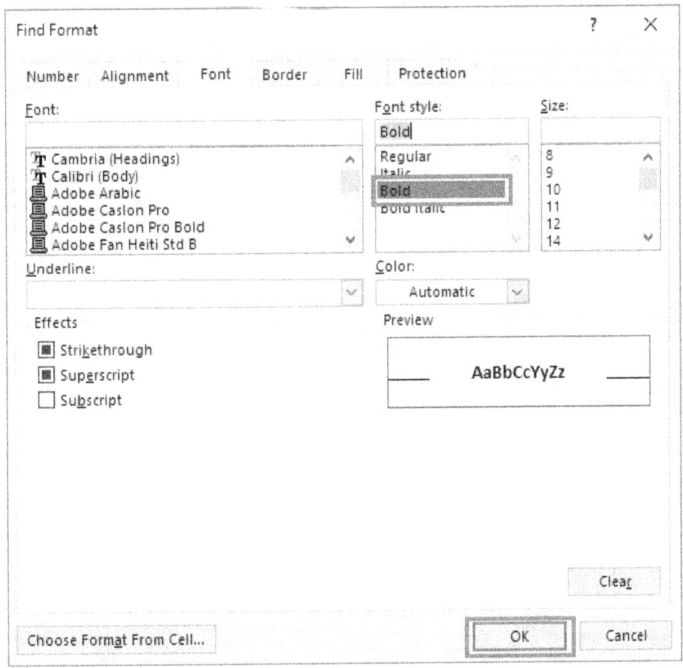

STEP 4: Select the second **Format**. We will set the format that we want to be the final formatting.

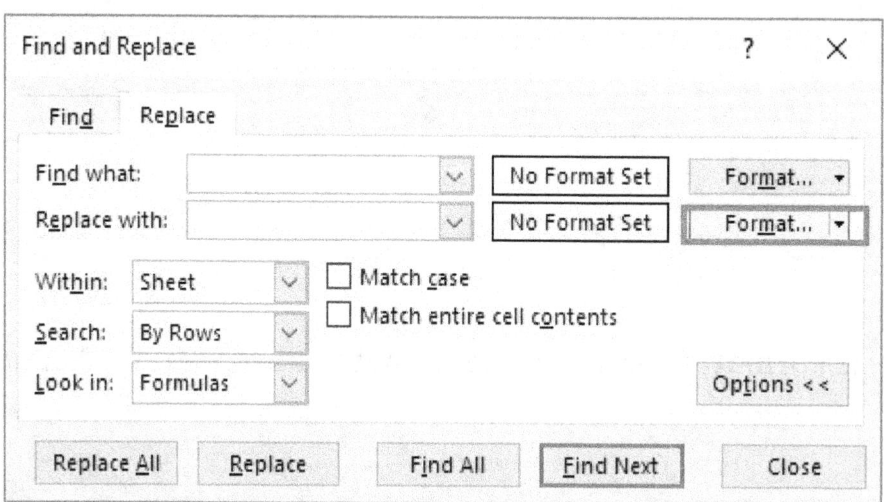

Make sure the color Red is selected. Click **OK.**

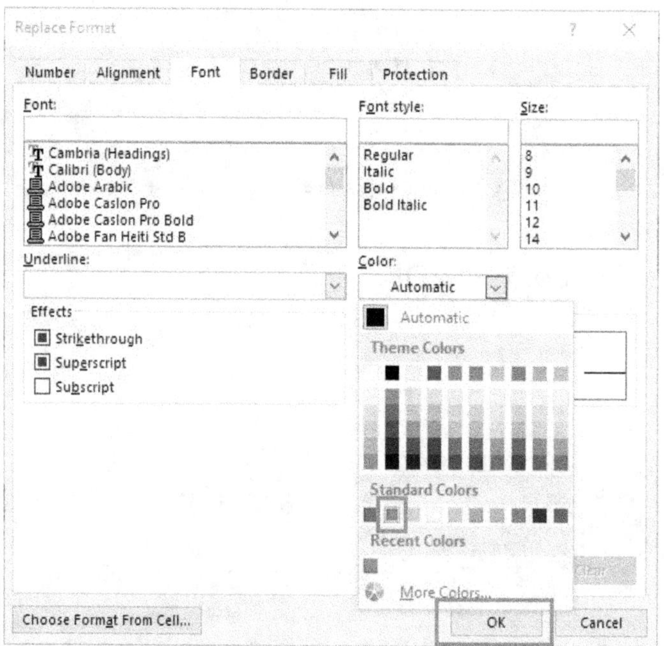

 Click **Replace All** and see the magic happen!

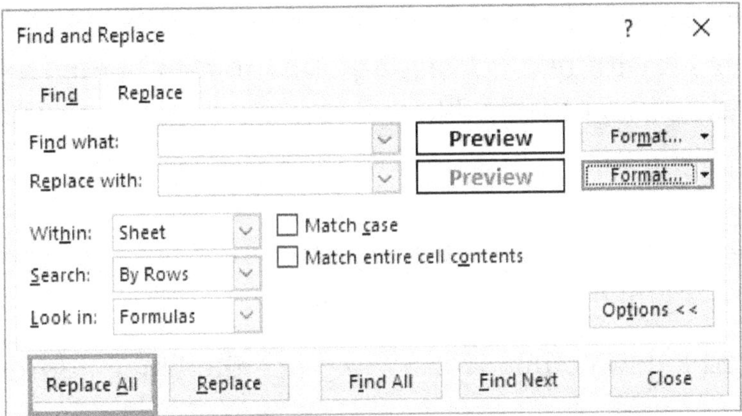

The formatting is now replaced with the color Red!

Unformatted SSN	Formatted SSN
123456789	123-45-6789
478923744	478-92-3744
980412833	980-41-2833
491823821	491-82-3821
239842394	239-84-2394
123981293	123-98-1293

Text to Columns - Emails

If you have a data set with text consisting of names and email addresses that are wrapped inside a parenthesis, like:

John (john@email.com)

...then you can use the *Text to Columns* feature in Excel to take out the email addresses and put them in a separate column.

STEP 1: Let us add a new column for us to place the Email addresses in.

Right-click on the **Year Column header**. Go to *Insert > Table Columns to the Left*

Make sure to rename the new column header to **Email**.

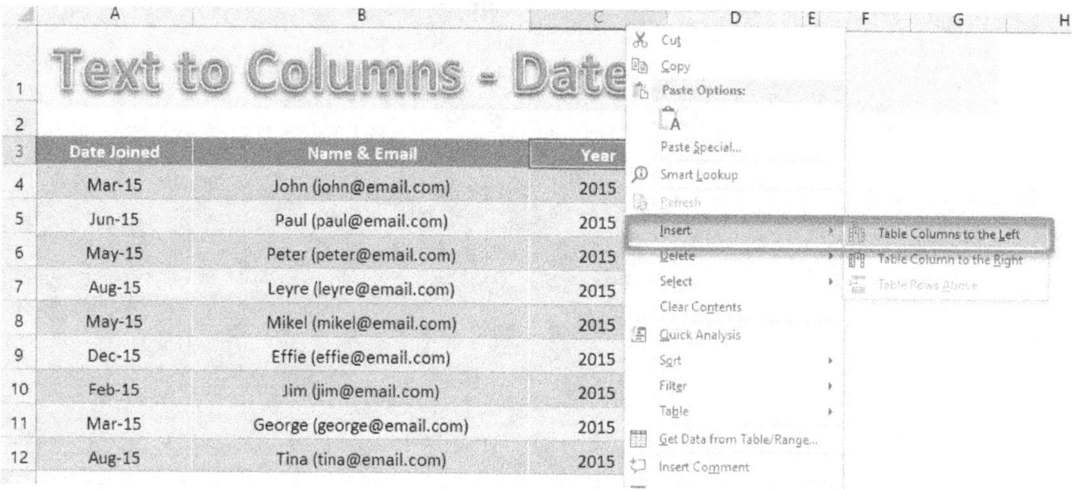

STEP 2: Now we have a blank Email column. Select the values of the **Name & Email column.**

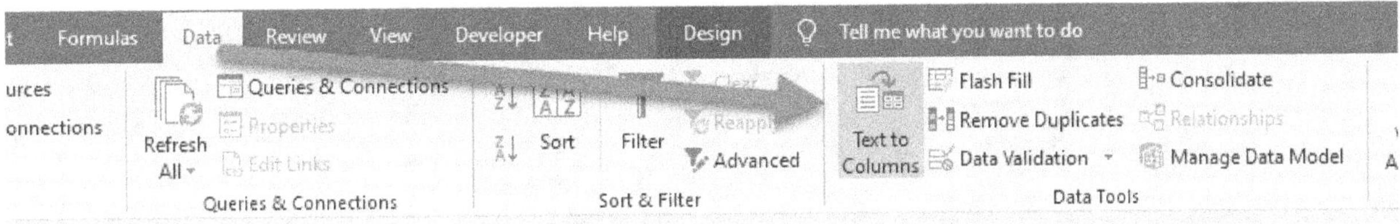

STEP 4: Click **Next**.

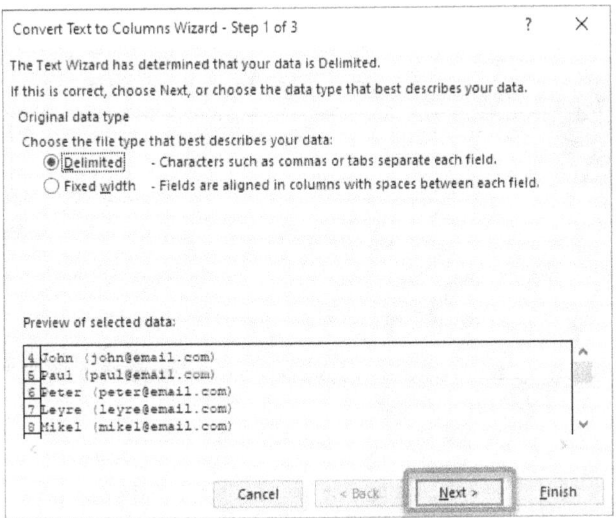

We want to split the Name & Email value by the open parenthesis (

To do this select **Other** and enter the open parenthesis in the box:

(

Then click **Next**.

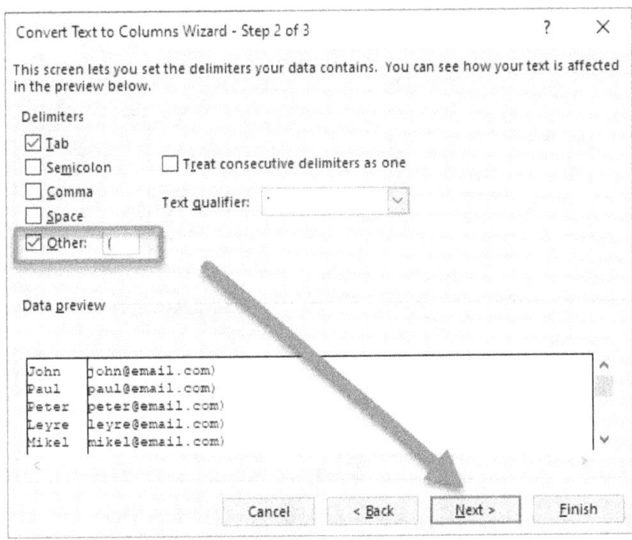

The preview of the conversion looks good. Click **Finish.**

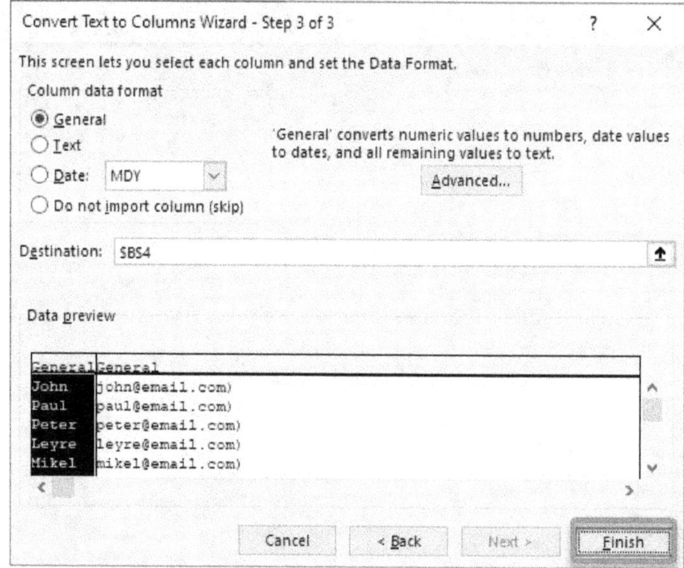

Click **OK.**

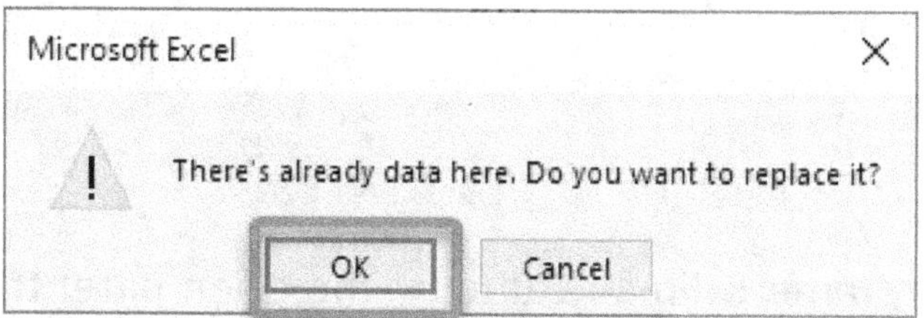

STEP 5: Now we have the **Email** column populated. The last step is to remove the) at the end. Select the values of the **Email** column.

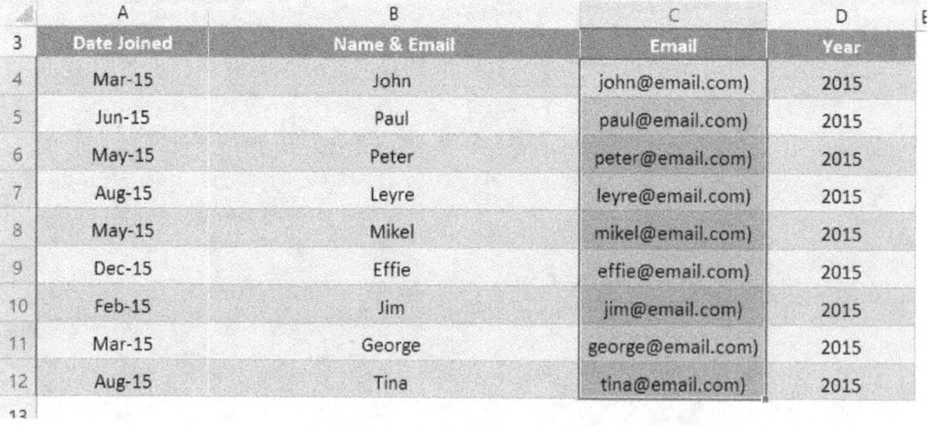

STEP 6: Let us do a replacement of the values. Press **CTRL + H.**

Place) in the **Find what** and click **Replace All**. This will replace the) with a blank value, resulting in it getting completely removed.

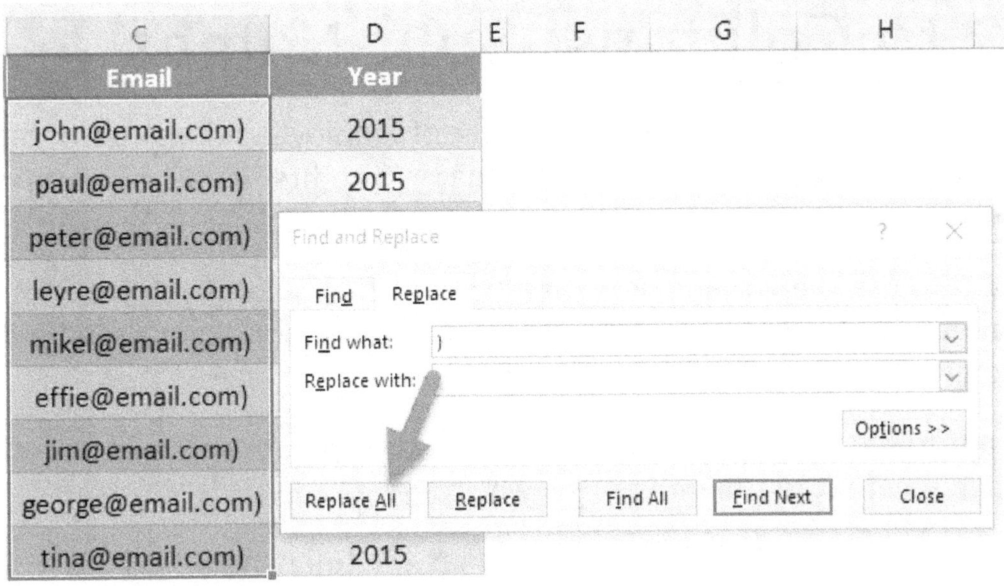

Now we have our names and emails separated!

	Date Joined	Name & Email	Email	Year
3				
4	Mar-15	John	john@email.com	2015
5	Jun-15	Paul	paul@email.com	2015
6	May-15	Peter	peter@email.com	2015
7	Aug-15	Leyre	leyre@email.com	2015
8	May-15	Mikel	mikel@email.com	2015
9	Dec-15	Effie	effie@email.com	2015
10	Feb-15	Jim	jim@email.com	2015
11	Mar-15	George	george@email.com	2015
12	Aug-15	Tina	tina@email.com	2015

Text to Columns: Split Names

There are times when you receive a data set of employee full names in one column and you want to separate the full name into first name and surname in separate columns.

One way is to use the Power Query method, which is great if you have lots of data that gets added each day, week or month and simply want to Refresh your Query to get the output needed each time.

If you want to quickly split a cell's full name into separate columns on an ad-hoc basis, then the Text to Columns is the way to go.

STEP 1: Highlight your column's data that has the full names

STEP 2: Go to **Data > Text to Columns**

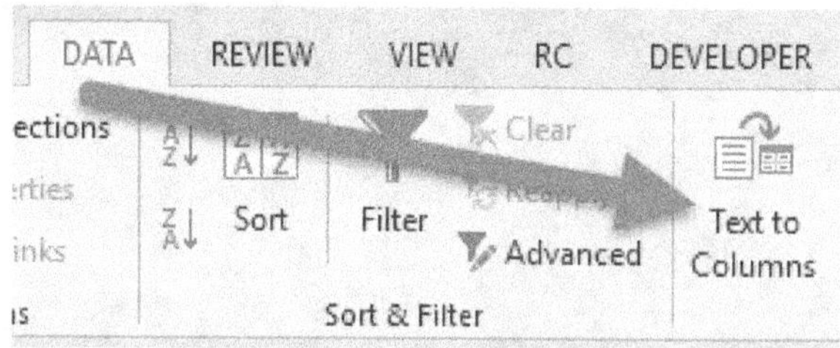

STEP 3: In Step 1 of 3 you need to select the **Delimited** button and press **Next**

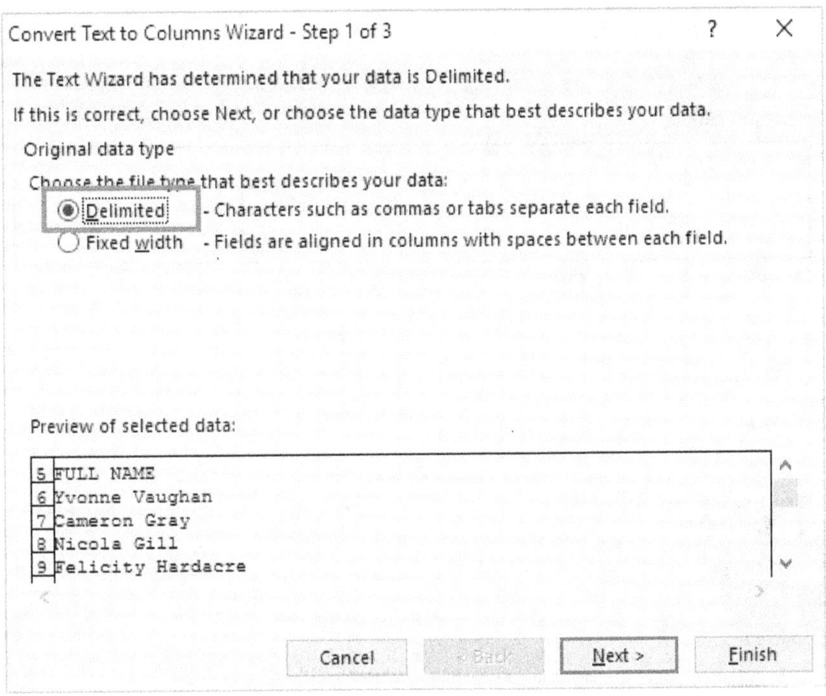

STEP 4: In Step 2 of 3, you need to "check" the **Tab** and **Space** boxes and press **Next** (since we are splitting the full name at each space)

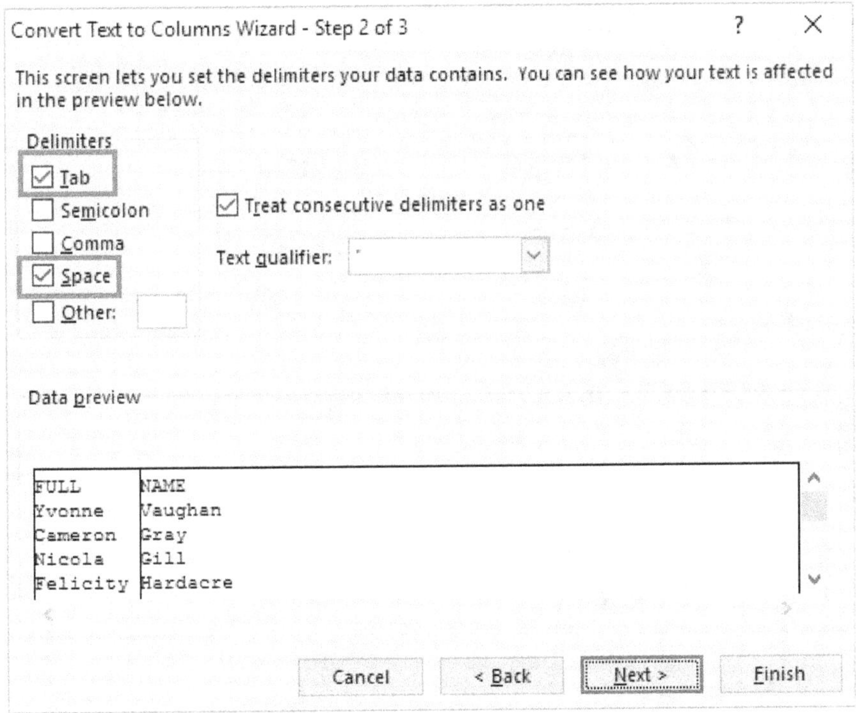

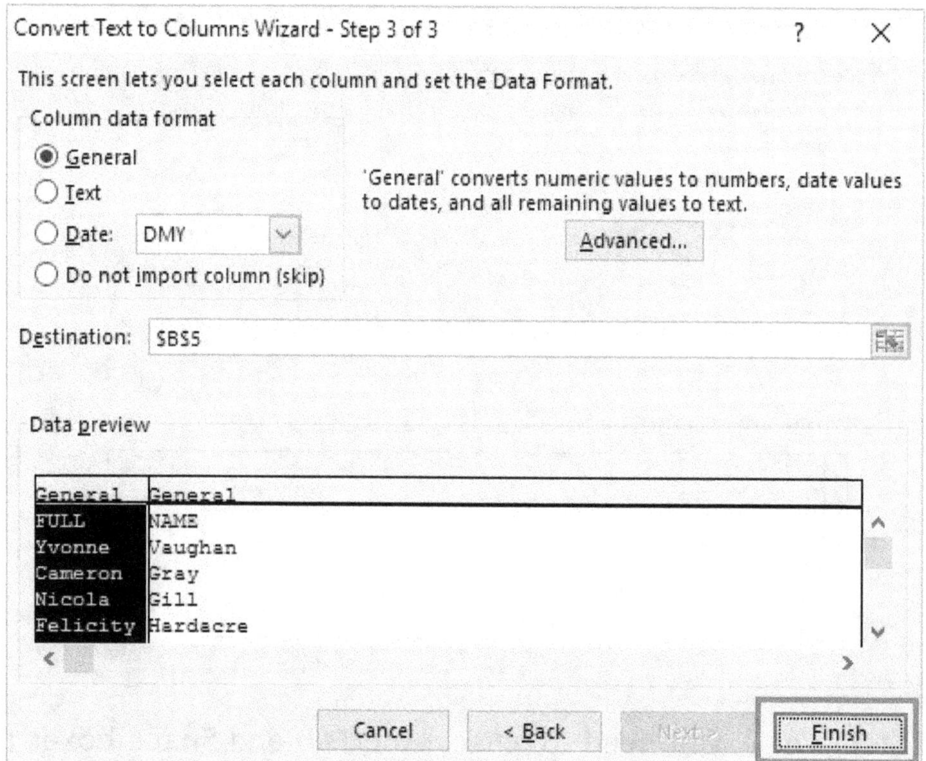

This will split the column into two columns, separating the first from the second name. You can go ahead and change the column headings to get the following result:

FIRST NAME	SURNAME
Yvonne	Vaughan
Cameron	Gray
Nicola	Gill
Felicity	Hardacre
Jan	Taylor
Yvonne	Gill
Bernadette	Duncan
Benjamin	Hughes
Austin	Clarkson
Ian	Smith

Turn Text Dates To Excel Dates

Whenever you import data from your company's server, ERP system or any other source for that matter, the Dates usually come in a TEXT format.

I will show you a cool trick where you can turn the TEXT Date to an Excel Date that Excel can read and work with.

STEP 1: Let's confirm that the Dates are in TEXT format by including the **ISTEXT function**.

A TRUE means that it is a TEXT format:

Date	Value	
20-Dec-15	20	=ISTEXT(A5)
21-Dec-15	21	ISTEXT(value)
22-Dec-15	22	TRUE
23-Dec-15	23	TRUE
24-Dec-15	24	TRUE
25-Dec-15	24	TRUE
26-Dec-15	26	TRUE

STEP 2: Now that we know that our Dates are in TEXT format, we can **highlight the whole Dates column**

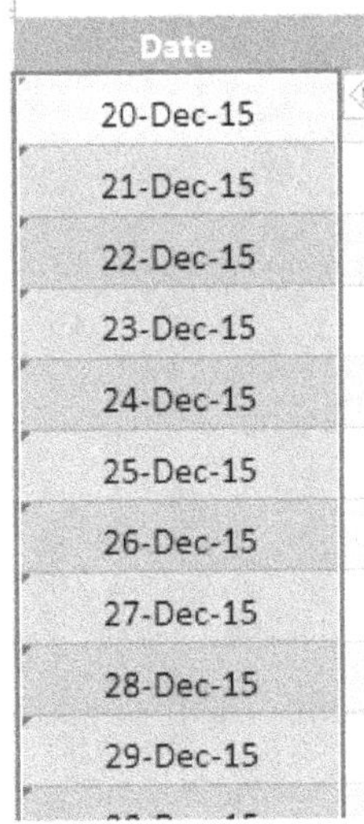

STEP 3: Go to *Data > Text to Columns > Finish*

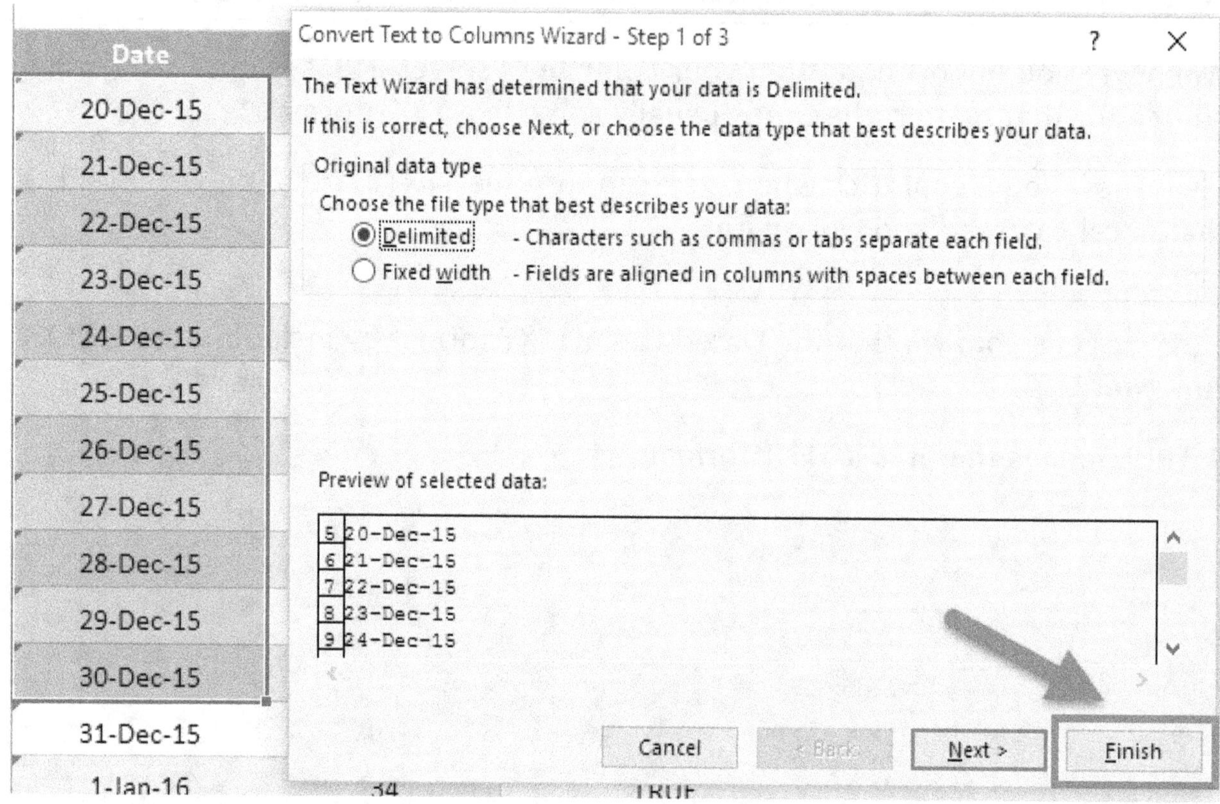

This will turn the TEXT Date into an Excel Date! How quick was that?

Date	Value	
20/12/2015	20	FALSE
21-Dec-15	21	FALSE
22-Dec-15	22	FALSE
23-Dec-15	23	FALSE
24-Dec-15	24	FALSE
25-Dec-15	24	FALSE
26-Dec-15	26	FALSE
27-Dec-15	28	FALSE
28-Dec-15	29	FALSE
29-Dec-15	30	FALSE
30-Dec-15	32	FALSE

Turn Text To Values With Paste Special

Many times, you would have received data from your IT system which is formatted wrong! Well a gazillion times if you work in a big corporate!

When you try and sum the values you get a count rather than a sum. That is because Excel reads the data as **text** rather than a **value**.

You can press **F2** in the cell to see why it is in text format.

An apostrophe ´ before the number converts values to text, as you can see below:

SALES $
'13941.3
152484.3
1105964.1
160671.6

You can also use the **ISTEXT** function to confirm a cell's format:

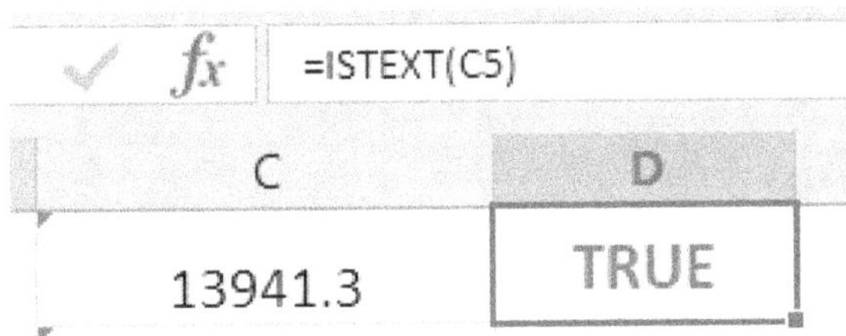

Now you can easily convert the text into values by using the *Paste Special > Values > Multiply* combination. Here is how...

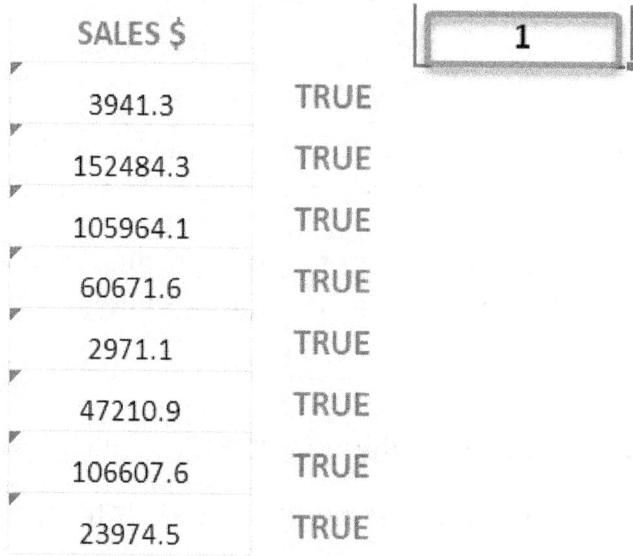

STEP 2: **Copy** that cell

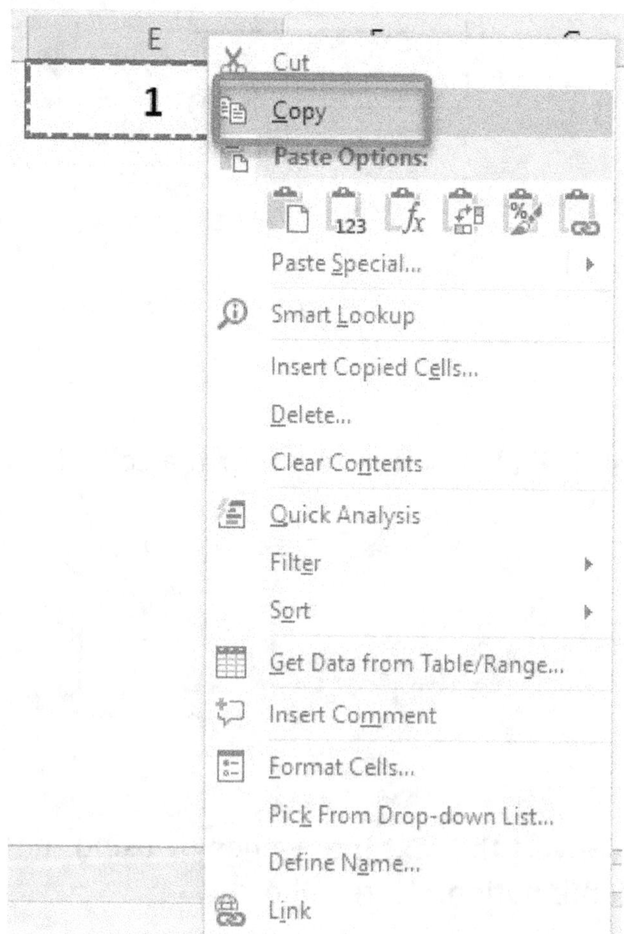

STEP 3: Select the data range, **Right Click and select Paste Special**

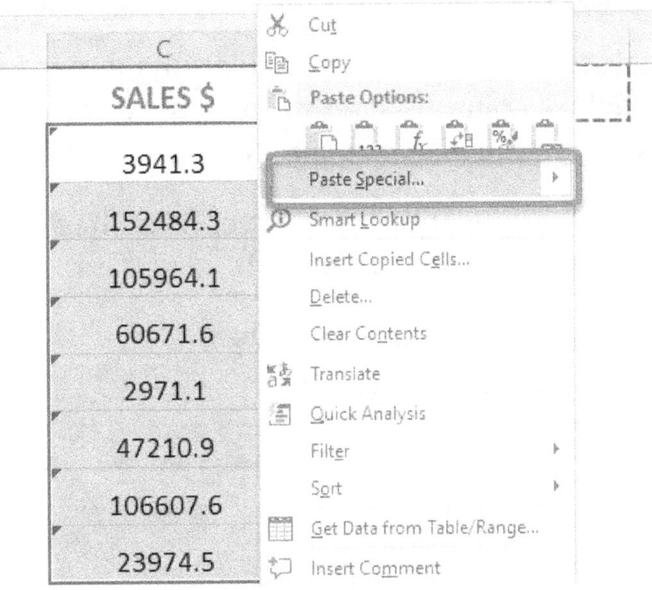

STEP 4: Select **Values & Multiply** and press **OK**

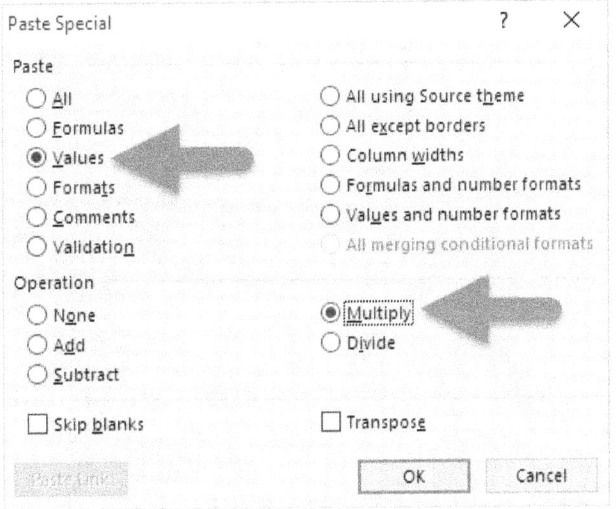

Your data will be transformed into values:

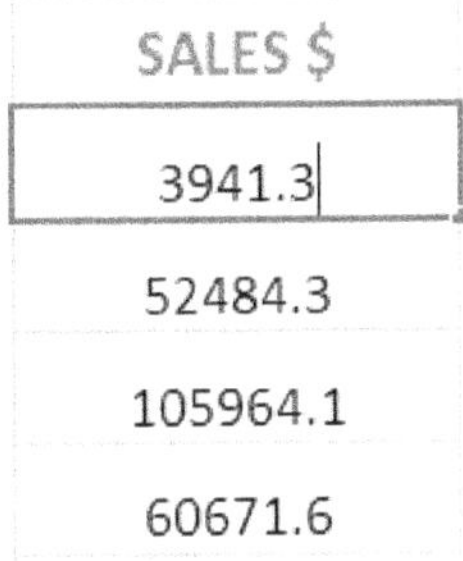

Unhide Columns in Excel

We normally use "helper columns" to do calculations in our Excel worksheet. These "helper columns" are for our own internal use and we usually hide these columns so no one else can see them, like our boss!

But once we are done with presenting our Excel worksheet to our boss, we can **unhide these Excel columns** very easily!

For our example, **Columns B and C are hidden**:

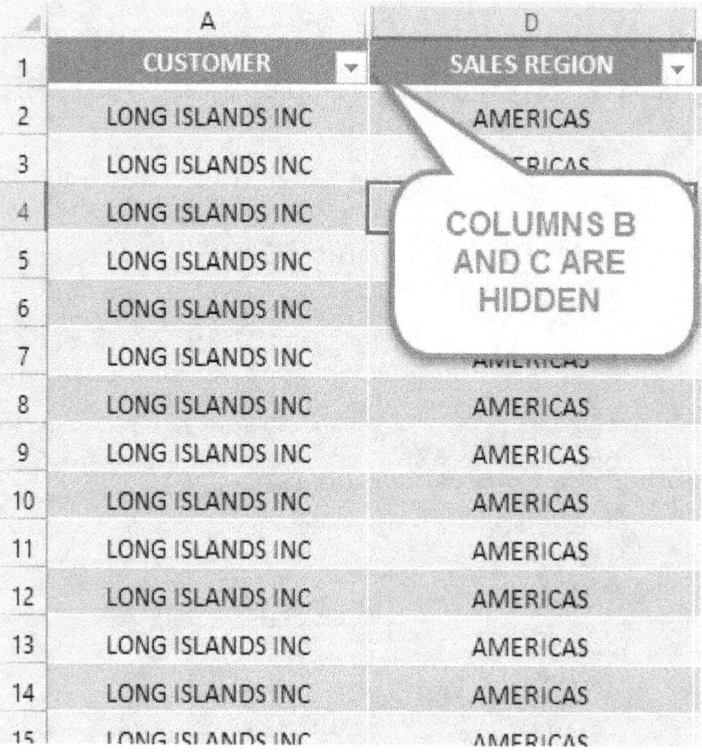

STEP 1: Select the columns that is both on the left and right of the hidden columns.

For our example, since our hidden columns are **B and C**, then we need to highlight columns **A (left of B) and D (right of C).**

Right-click and select **Unhide:**

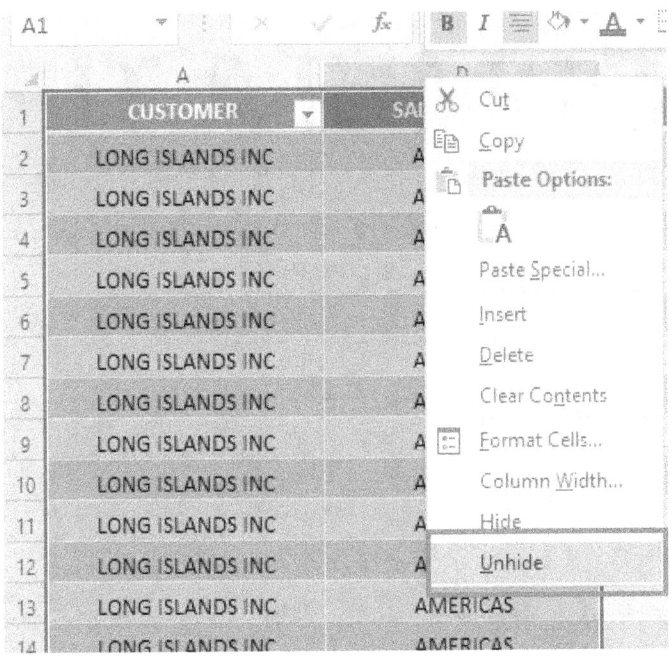

STEP 2: Your hidden columns are **now displayed**!

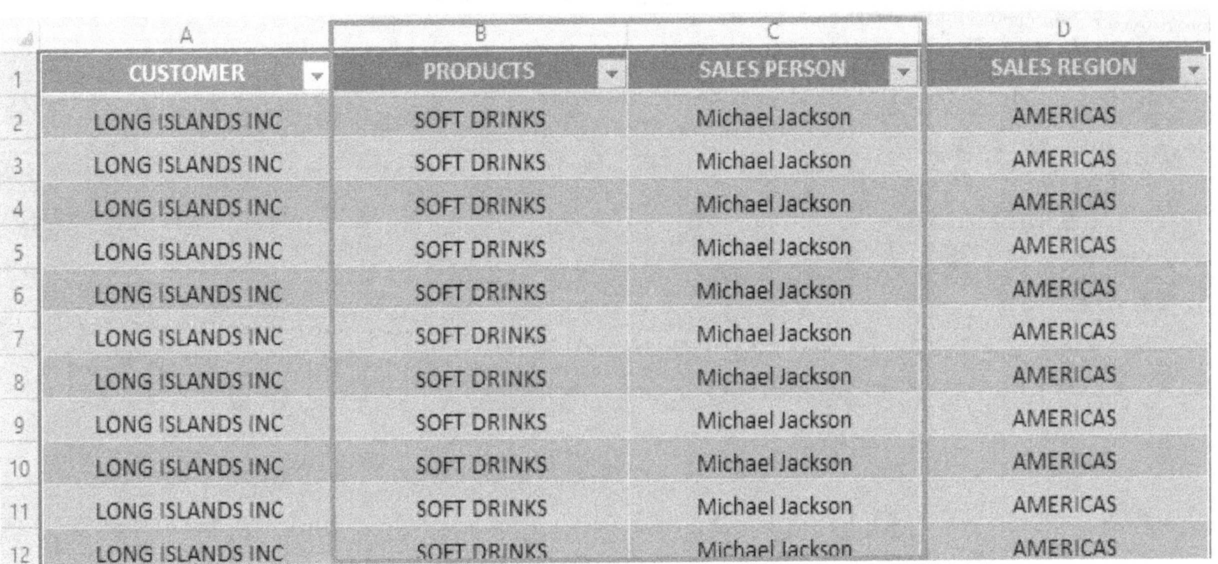

FORMULA TIPS

Add Leading Zeros in Excel

Many times you may have faced a situation where you need to **add a leading zero** in Excel.

This tutorial will help you do exactly that! Do you have a lot of numbers with an uneven number of digits in your Excel list?

Do you want to make them uniform by adding leading zeros to them?

When adding **zip codes, security numbers, or employee IDs** in Excel, you may have seen that Excel removes any leading zeros in the cell. For example, if you type "007845" in Excel it will immediately turn it into "7845".

This is because Excel automatically **treats these values as numbers** and tosses the leading zeros out.

There are various ways to add a leading zero in Excel. Let's look at those options one by one.

Make sure to download the exercise workbook to follow along and learn how to add a leading zero in Excel.

Change format to Text

Since the reason why the zeros are tossed out is that Excel treats these values as numbers. The best option to add a leading zero in Excel would be to just change the format to the cell from "Number" to "Text".

To change the cell format to text, follow the steps below:

STEP 1: Select the cell in which you want to add prefix "0".

Number	Added Leading Zeros
1	1
12	12
123	123
1234	1234
12345	12345

STEP 2: Go to the **Home** tab > Number Group.

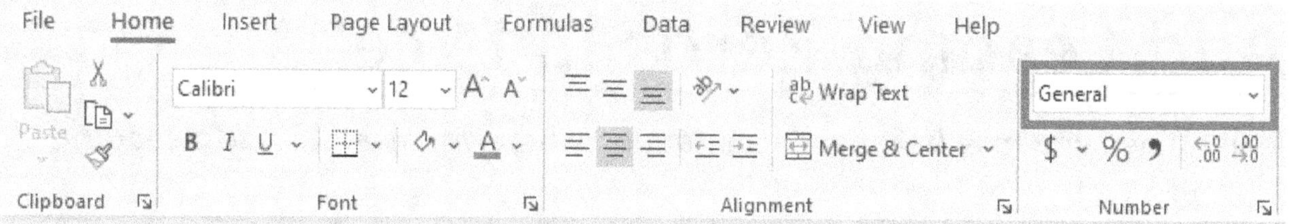

STEP 3: From the dropdown select "**Text**".

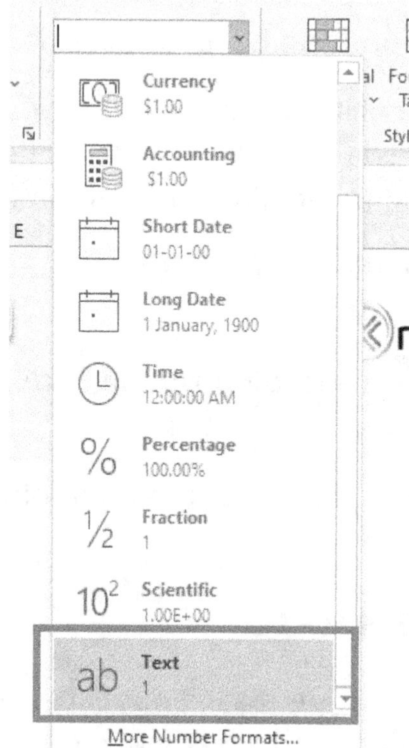

Now when you add the zeros in front of the number, the zeros will remain intact.

Number	Added Leading Zeros
1	00001
12	00012
123	00123
1234	01234
12345	12345

You might notice a small yellow triangle on that cell. It is simply indicated that you have stored a number as a text format.

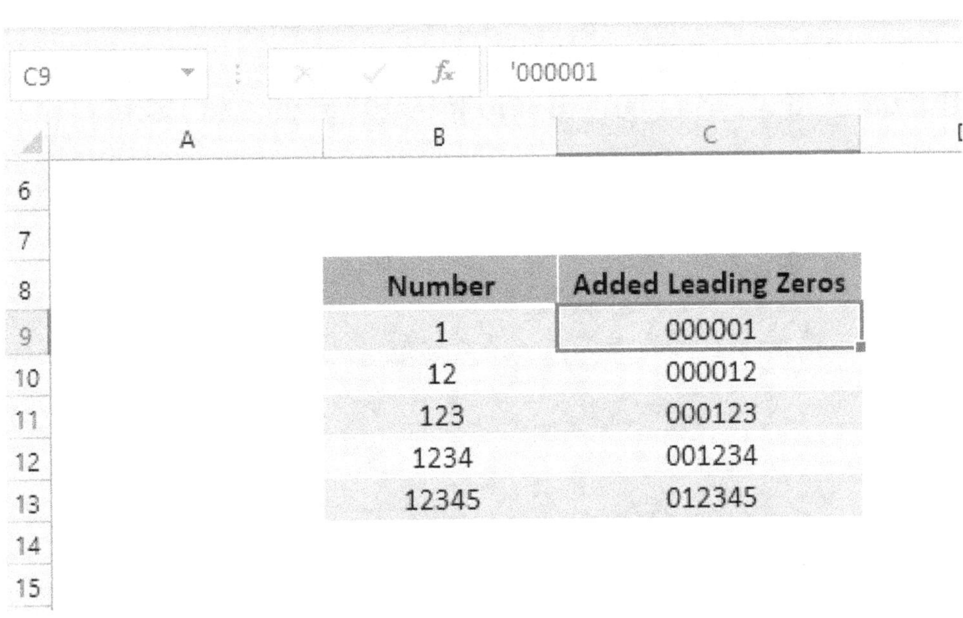

To remove that message, click on the triangle, and select **"Ignore Error"**.

Add an apostrophe '

You can simply add an apostrophe ' in front of the number which will convert it to text. So, you can type **'000001** instead of just **000001**. This way, the number will be shown as you want it to without having to change the format.

You can see in the formula bar that an apostrophe is added as a prefix to the number.

Use the TEXT formula

Even though the above options get the work done, it's a pain to add zeros in front of them one by one!

Follow the steps below to understand how to add a leading zero with **one single formula**!

STEP 1: We need to **enter the *TEXT* function in a blank cell**:

=TEXT(

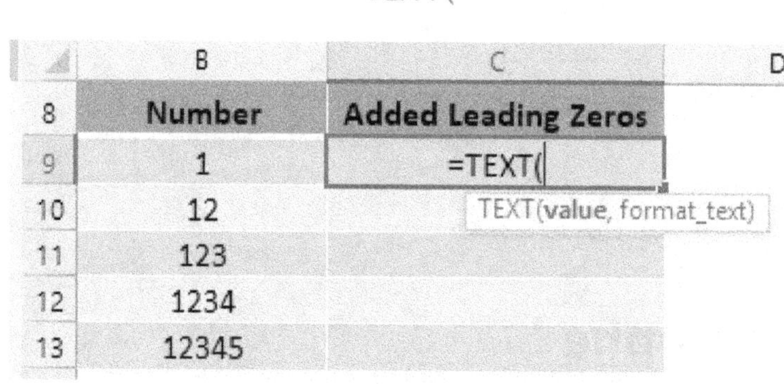

STEP 2: The **TEXT** arguments:

value

What is the value that you want to add a leading zero in Excel on?

=TEXT(B9,

How many leading zeros do you need?

If we want our number to be 6 digits long, then type in 6 zeros: "000000"

$$=TEXT(B9, "000000")$$

	B	C
8	**Number**	**Added Leading Zeros**
9	1	=TEXT(B9, "000000")
10	12	
11	123	
12	1234	
13	12345	

Apply the same formula to the rest of the cells by dragging the lower right corner downwards. Your leading zeros are now ready!

	B	C
8	**Number**	**Added Leading Zeros**
9	1	000001
10	12	000012
11	123	000123
12	1234	001234
13	12345	012345
14		

You should keep in mind that all of these methods add a leading zero in Excel by actually converting the cell format to **text**.

These methods will add the zeros in front of the numbers but the resulting value will be a text string, not a number.

You will not be able to use them to do any calculations or use them in numeric formulas.

This brings us to the last method to add leading zeros in Excel - Using a Custom Format.

Using a Custom Format

You can add leading zeros in Excel by using a custom format. This will only change the display and not the value of the cell. The value in the cell will still be a number but the display will contain leading zeros.

Let's see how it can be done!

STEP 1: Select the column in which you want to add leading zeros

Number	Added Leading Zeros
1	1
12	12
123	123
1234	1234
12345	12345

STEP 2: Press Ctrl +1 to open the **Format Cells** dialog box

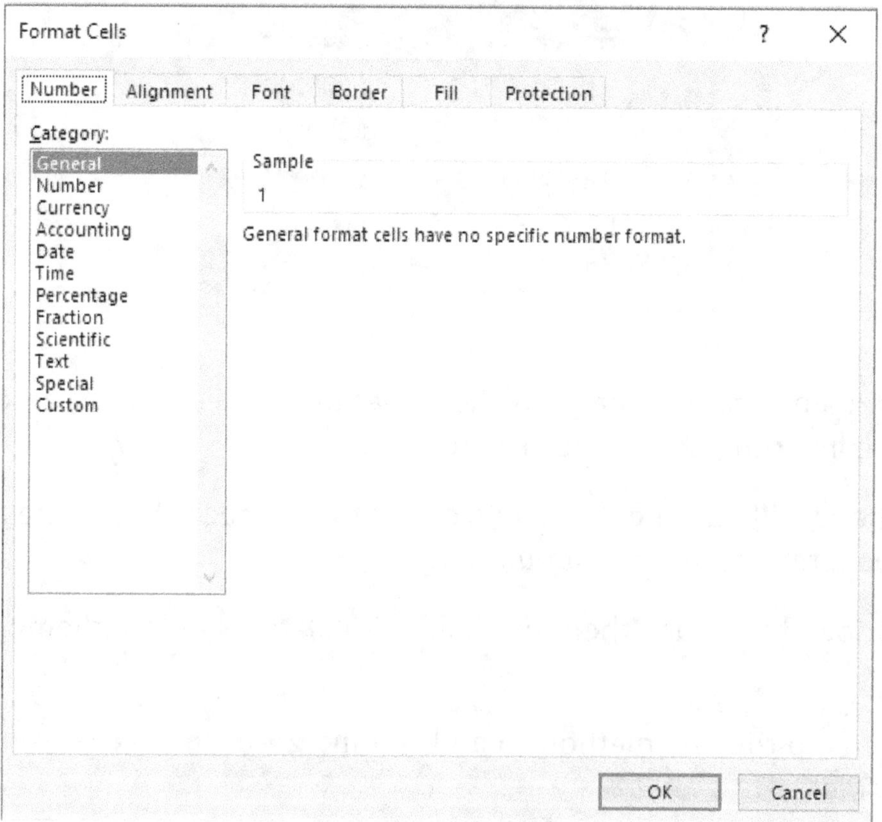

STEP 3: Select Custom and fill the type with **000000.** Click OK.

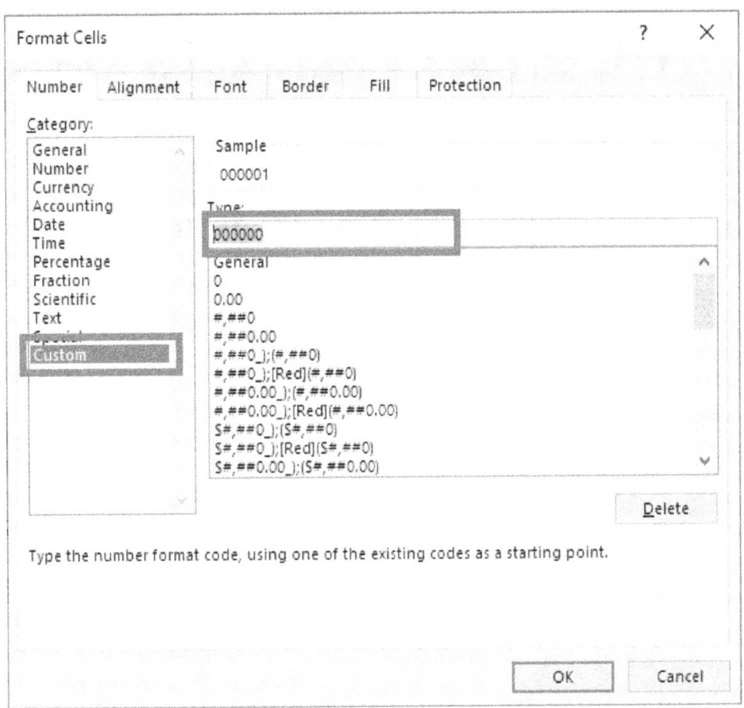

Leading zeros will be added to all the numbers. If you select a cell containing these numbers and look at the formula bar, you will see that the underlying value in the formula bar remains unchanged.

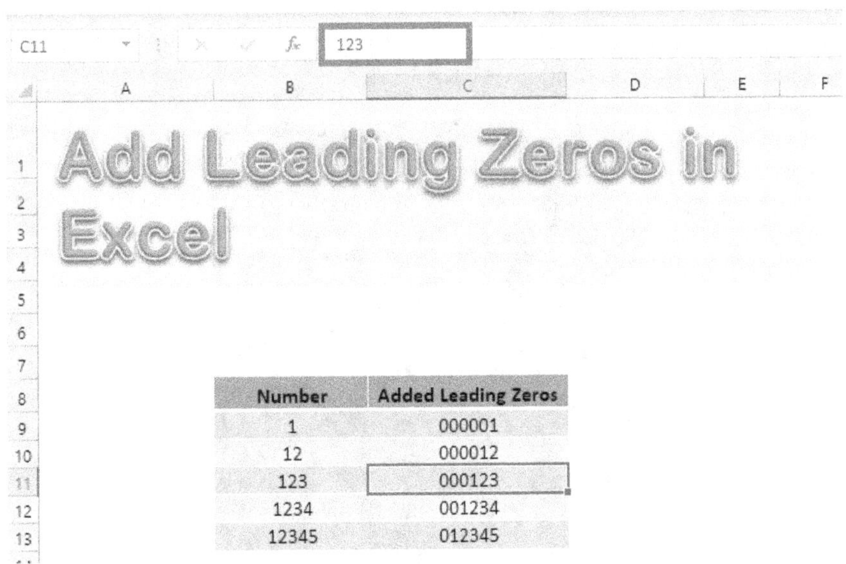

Number	Added Leading Zeros
1	000001
12	000012
123	000123
1234	001234
12345	012345

Now all 6 digits are displayed and the leading zeros will be added to numbers containing less than 6 digits. Also, the value will still be a number and will not be converted to a text string.

Charts: In-Cell Bar Charts with the REPT Function

When you are creating an Excel Dashboard and are limited by space and do not want to insert a chart, you can easily create an in-cell bar chart using the REPT (repeat) function.

The REPT function uses the **vertical bar character | as the first argument:** *text* and **references the value cell for the second argument:** *number_times*

So it enters the vertical bar character by the number of times of the value cell, looking something like this:

||||||||||||||||||||||||||||||||||||||||||||||||||||||||||||||||||||||||||||||||

STEP 1: Enter the REPT function in a column next to your values

=REPT

STEP 2: **Enter the vertical bar** keyboard character in the first argument

=REPT("|")

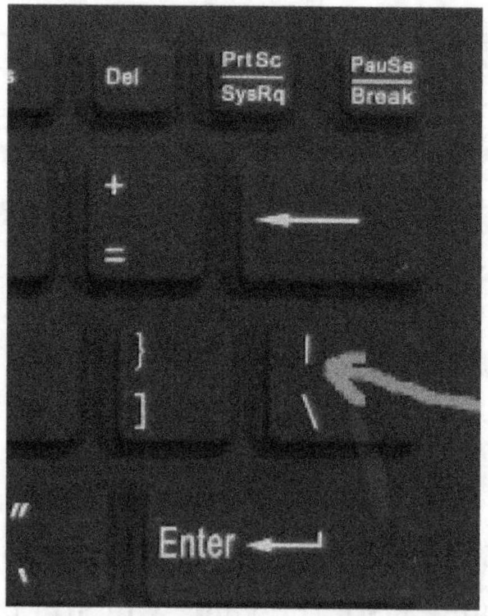

STEP 3: **Reference the value cell** for the second argument

=REPT("|", B6)

STEP 4: Highlight the formula column and **insert the** *Stencil* **font** from the Home menu and choose a font color

STEP 5: If your value cells are high, the bar will go out of your screen. To fix this, you need to enter a divisor in the second argument of your formula which will reduce the length

$$=REPT("|",\ B6/5)$$

MONTH	SALES	CHART
January	$125	=REPT("|",[@SALES]/5)
February	$330	
March	$161	
April	$584	
May	$455	
June	$213	
July	$345	
August	$160	

Check Your Math with F9

If you are ever writing a big formula and it doesn't give you the result that you are after, you can use the **F9 shortcut** to check the result of each part of your formula.

Our formula calculates the Average of Sales, let us check out if the calculation came out as intended!

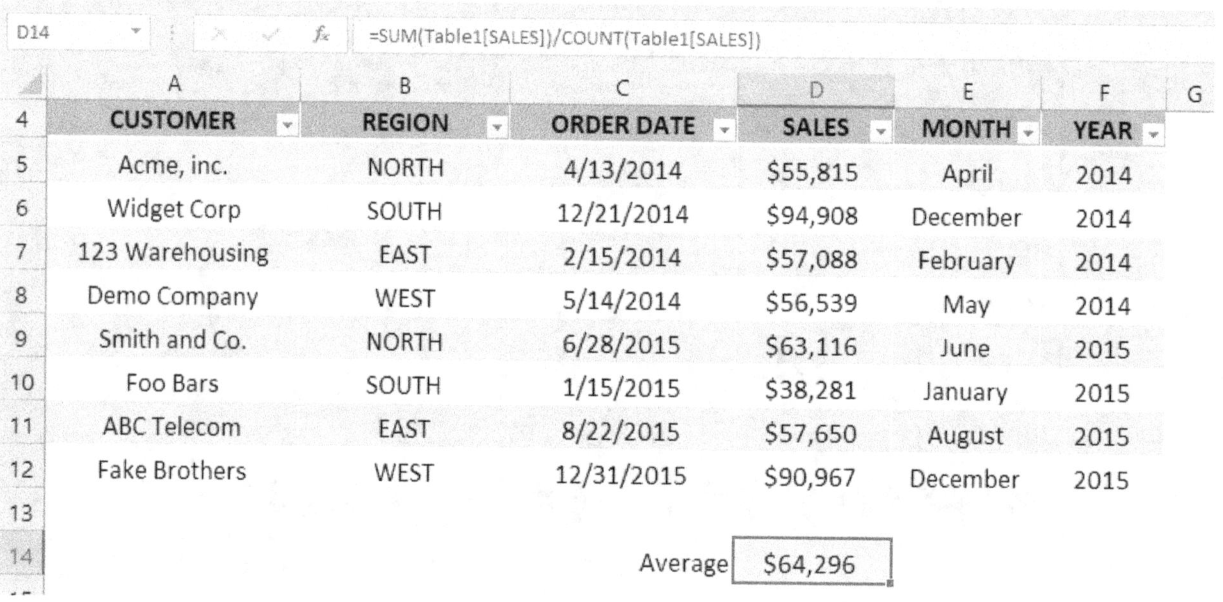

STEP 1: Edit the cell containing your formula by double clicking on it or pressing the **F2** shortcut

STEP 2: Let us highlight the first half of the formula.

	A	B	C	D	E	F
4	CUSTOMER	REGION	ORDER DATE	SALES	MONTH	YEAR
5	Acme, inc.	NORTH	4/13/2014	$55,815	April	2014
6	Widget Corp	SOUTH	12/21/2014	$94,908	December	2014
7	123 Warehousing	EAST	2/15/2014	$57,088	February	2014
8	Demo Company	WEST	5/14/2014	$56,539	May	2014
9	Smith and Co.	NORTH	6/28/2015	$63,116	June	2015
10	Foo Bars	SOUTH	1/15/2015	$38,281	January	2015
11	ABC Telecom	EAST	8/22/2015	$57,650	August	2015
12	Fake Brothers	WEST	12/31/2015	$90,967	December	2015
13						
14			=SUM(Table1[SALES])/COUNT(Table1[SALES])			
15						

STEP 3: Press **F9**. This will show the result of the SUM formula.

	A	B	C	D	E	F	G
4	CUSTOMER	REGION	ORDER DATE	SALES	MONTH	YEAR	
5	Acme, inc.	NORTH	4/13/2014	$55,815	April	2014	
6	Widget Corp	SOUTH	12/21/2014	$94,908	December	2014	
7	123 Warehousing	EAST	2/15/2014	$57,088	February	2014	
8	Demo Company	WEST	5/14/2014	$56,539	May	2014	
9	Smith and Co.	NORTH	6/28/2015	$63,116	June	2015	
10	Foo Bars	SOUTH	1/15/2015	$38,281	January	2015	
11	ABC Telecom	EAST	8/22/2015	$57,650	August	2015	
12	Fake Brothers	WEST	12/31/2015	$90,967	December	2015	
13							
14			=514364/COUNT(Table1[SALES])				
15							

You can see that the total is 514,364. Now press **CTRL+Z** to revert to the original Formula

STEP 4: Let us highlight the second half of the formula.

	CUSTOMER	REGION	ORDER DATE	SALES	MONTH	YEAR
4	CUSTOMER	REGION	ORDER DATE	SALES	MONTH	YEAR
5	Acme, inc.	NORTH	4/13/2014	$55,815	April	2014
6	Widget Corp	SOUTH	12/21/2014	$94,908	December	2014
7	123 Warehousing	EAST	2/15/2014	$57,088	February	2014
8	Demo Company	WEST	5/14/2014	$56,539	May	2014
9	Smith and Co.	NORTH	6/28/2015	$63,116	June	2015
10	Foo Bars	SOUTH	1/15/2015	$38,281	January	2015
11	ABC Telecom	EAST	8/22/2015	$57,650	August	2015
12	Fake Brothers	WEST	12/31/2015	$90,967	December	2015
13						
14			=SUM(Table1[SALES])/COUNT(Table1[SALES])			

STEP 5: Press **F9.** This will show the result of the COUNT formula.

	CUSTOMER	REGION	ORDER DATE	SALES	MONTH	YEAR
4	CUSTOMER	REGION	ORDER DATE	SALES	MONTH	YEAR
5	Acme, inc.	NORTH	4/13/2014	$55,815	April	2014
6	Widget Corp	SOUTH	12/21/2014	$94,908	December	2014
7	123 Warehousing	EAST	2/15/2014	$57,088	February	2014
8	Demo Company	WEST	5/14/2014	$56,539	May	2014
9	Smith and Co.	NORTH	6/28/2015	$63,116	June	2015
10	Foo Bars	SOUTH	1/15/2015	$38,281	January	2015
11	ABC Telecom	EAST	8/22/2015	$57,650	August	2015
12	Fake Brothers	WEST	12/31/2015	$90,967	December	2015
13						
14			=SUM(Table1[SALES])/8			

You can see that the count is 8. Now press **CTRL+Z** to revert to the original Formula

You can use this technique to quickly check any part of a complicated formula that needs auditing!

Create a Named Range in Excel

Whenever I work with spreadsheets, there's no escaping the fact that I have to work with a lot of ranges.

Some of these ranges I have to reuse time and time again to create different calculations!

Good thing there are **Named Ranges** in Excel!

By using a **Named Range**, you can make your formulas much easier to understand and maintain.

You can define a name for a cell range, function, constant, or table.

Let us work with the following table below. We want to populate the **Euro Amounts** and the **Sum of the USD** columns:

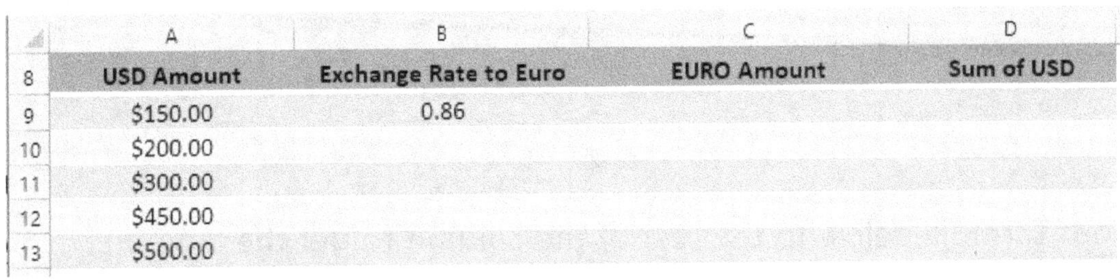

Let us go over how to do this in the tutorial below:

STEP 1: Let us create our first **Named Range.**

Highlight the USD Amounts and type in the **Name Box** a name: *Amounts*

Make sure that there are no spaces. Press **Enter.**

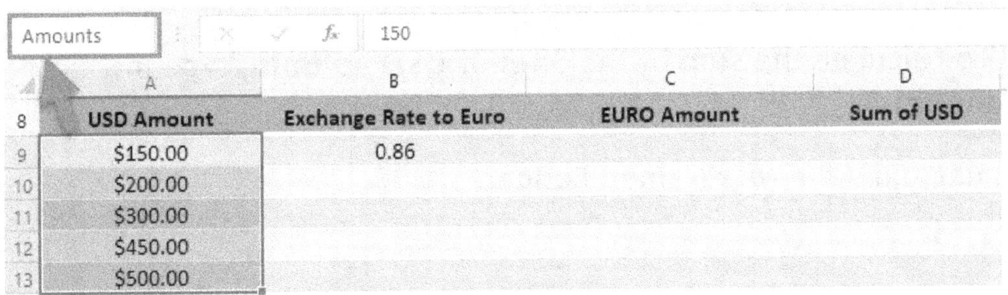

Let us do the same to our **Euro Exchange Rate**. Highlight the exchange rate, and type in the **Name Box** a name: *EuroRate*

Press **Enter.**

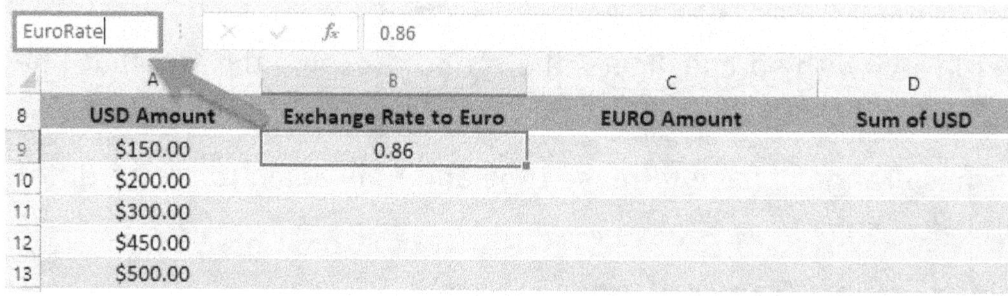

STEP 2: Let us see our Named Ranges in action!

To calculate the **Euro Amount column**, type in: **=A9 * EuroRate**.

This will use our *EuroRate* Named Range!

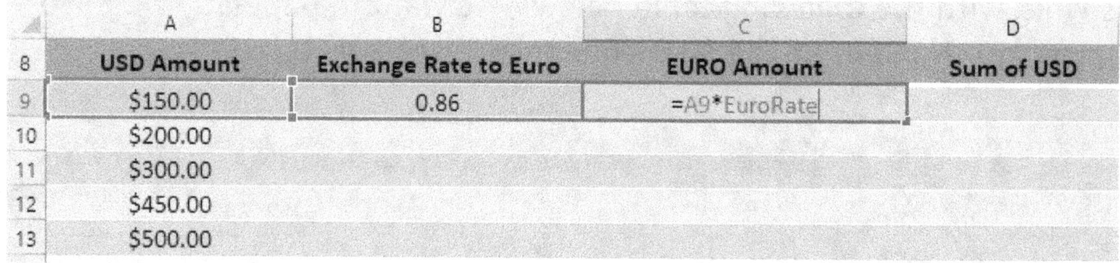

Drag your formula below to the rest of the column to get the amounts calculated:

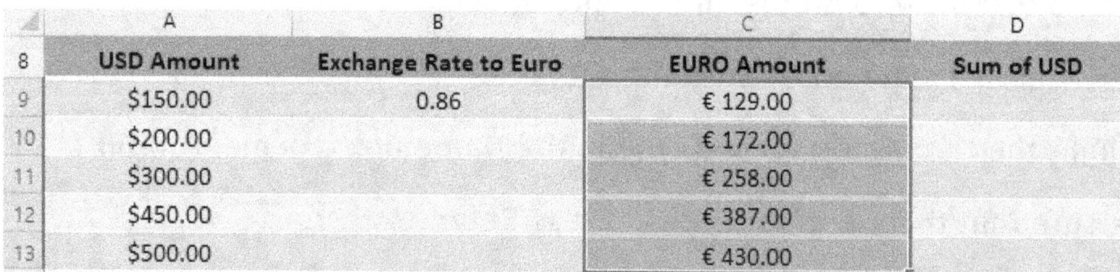

STEP 3: To calculate the sum of the **Sum of USD column**, type in: **=SUM(Amounts).**

This will use our *Amounts* Named Range!

	A	B	C	D
8	**USD Amount**	**Exchange Rate to Euro**	**EURO Amount**	**Sum of USD**
9	$150.00	0.86	€ 129.00	=SUM(Amounts)
10	$200.00		€ 172.00	
11	$300.00		€ 258.00	
12	$450.00		€ 387.00	
13	$500.00		€ 430.00	

And now you have your total!

	A	B	C	D
8	**USD Amount**	**Exchange Rate to Euro**	**EURO Amount**	**Sum of USD**
9	$150.00	0.86	€ 129.00	$1,600.00
10	$200.00		€ 172.00	
11	$300.00		€ 258.00	
12	$450.00		€ 387.00	
13	$500.00		€ 430.00	

STEP 4: If you want to check all the Named Ranges you created, go to *Formulas > Defined Names > Name Manager*

You can edit your Named Ranges in here or delete them as well.

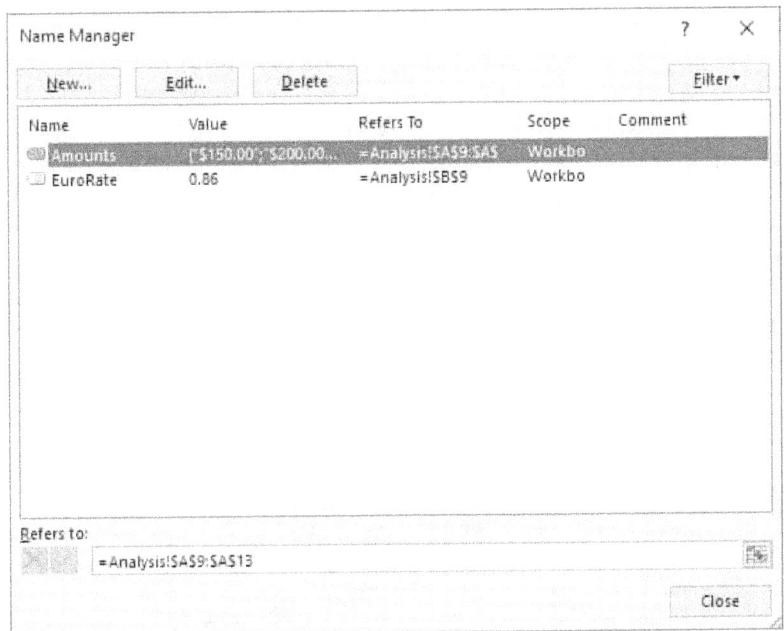

Evaluate Formulas Step By Step in Excel

This is one of the coolest tricks I have seen in Excel, as there are countless times where I had a hard time understanding formulas. Especially long and complex ones!

Excel provides the way to evaluate your formula, and break it down step by step so that you can understand it!

Let us take the formulas I've created below in the **IS THE VALUE IN BETWEEN** column. We will see how this formula is resolved in a series of steps:

	A	B	C	D	E
6	START OF RANGE	END OF RANGE	VALUE TO BE EVALUATED	IS THE VALUE IN BETWEEN?	FORMULA
7	20	60	50	Yes	=IF(C7=MEDIAN(A7:C7), "Yes", "No")
8	10	40	50	No	=IF(C8=MEDIAN(A8:C8), "Yes", "No")

STEP 1: You can see our formula uses both the **If formula** and the **Median formula.**

The goal of this formula is to evaluate if a value (**VALUE TO BE EVALUATED**) is in between the range (**START OF RANGE to VALUE TO BE EVALUATED**)

For example: Is 50 the median of the range 20; 60; 50?

$$=IF(C7=MEDIAN(A7:C7), \text{"Yes"}, \text{"No"})$$

To start understanding our formula, highlight the formula, then go to *Formulas > Evaluate Formula*:

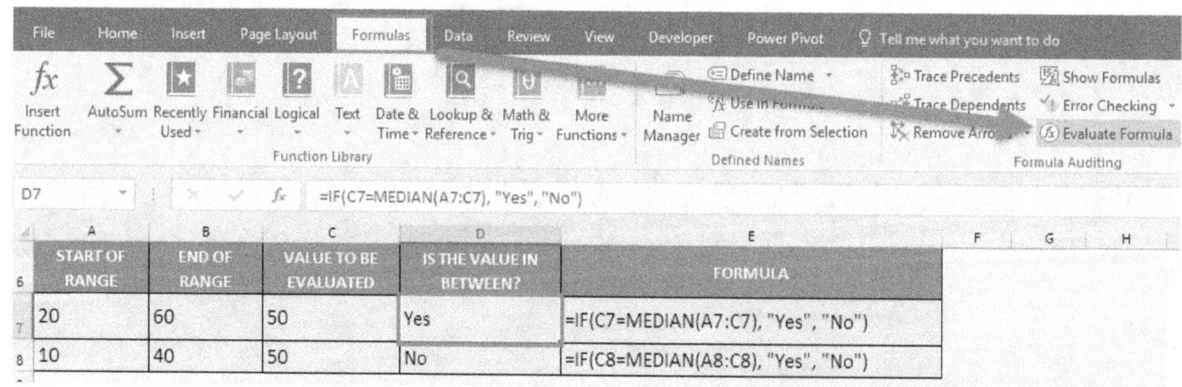

	A	B	C	D	E	F	G	H
6	START OF RANGE	END OF RANGE	VALUE TO BE EVALUATED	IS THE VALUE IN BETWEEN?	FORMULA			
7	20	60	50	Yes	=IF(C7=MEDIAN(A7:C7), "Yes", "No")			
8	10	40	50	No	=IF(C8=MEDIAN(A8:C8), "Yes", "No")			

STEP 2: Our formula is now shown on screen, and the part that is <u>underlined</u> is the one to be evaluated first. Click **Evaluate**.

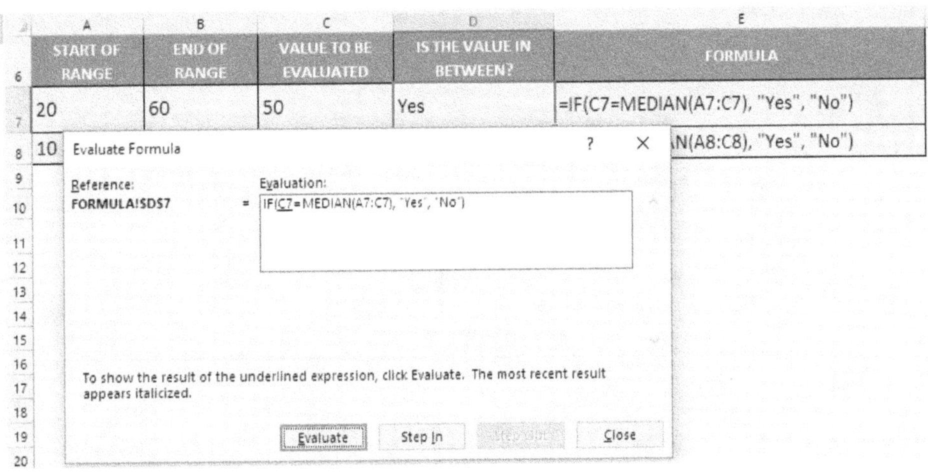

STEP 3: **C7** has been evaluated to **50**. Click **Evaluate**.

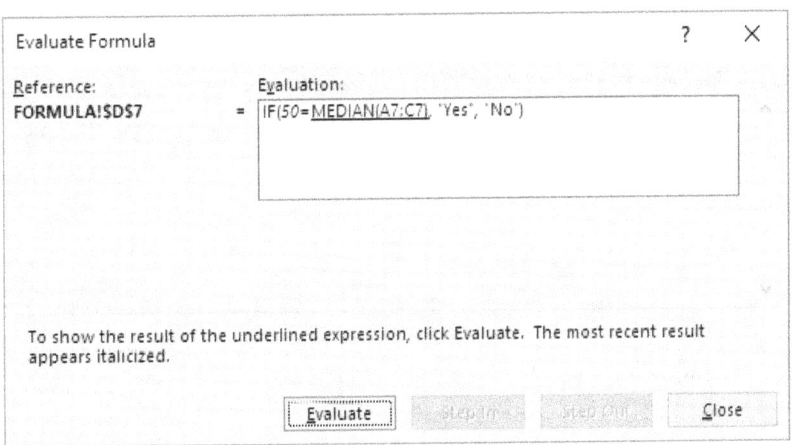

STEP 4: The median of the values from A7 to C7 (20, 60, 50) is evaluated as **50**. Click **Evaluate**.

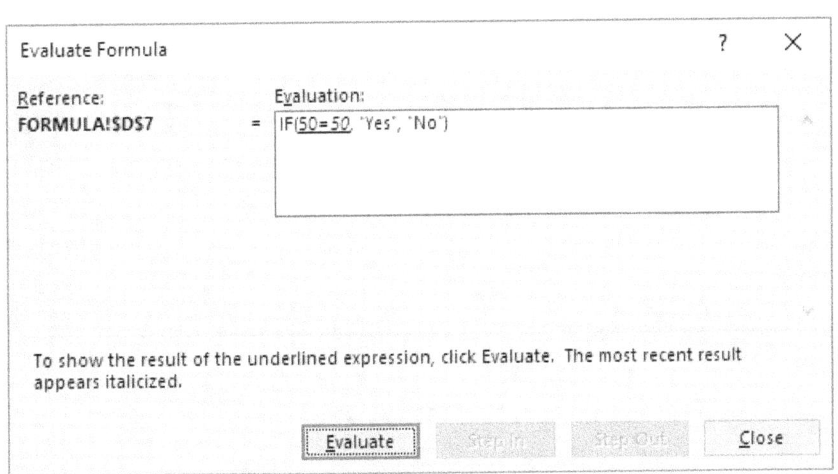

STEP 5: Is 50 equal to 50?

Excel has evaluated it to *TRUE*. Click **Evaluate**.

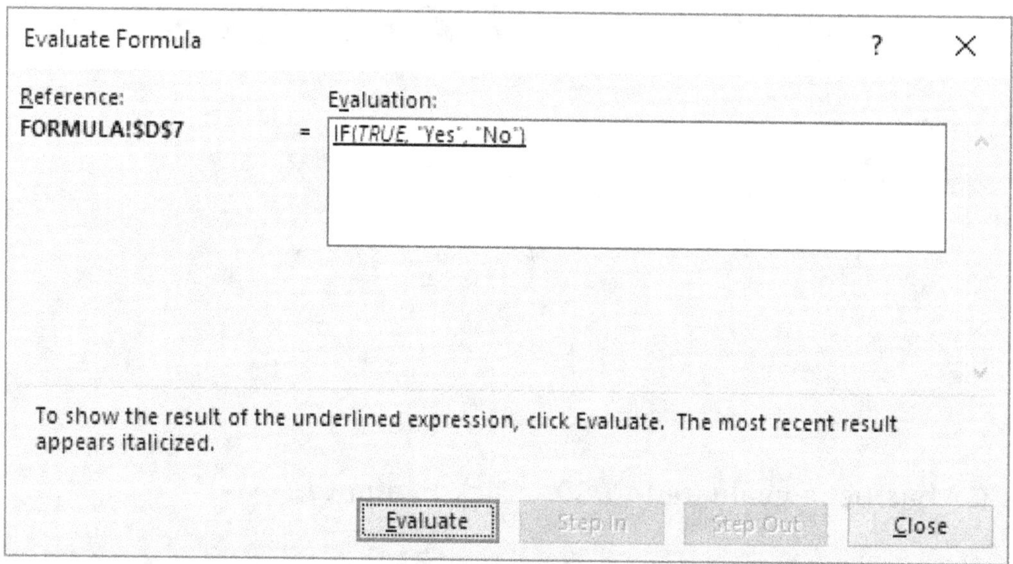

STEP 6: Since the **If formula** received a *TRUE*, Excel evaluated it as a **Yes**. We have seen how the formula gave us the result in a few easy steps!

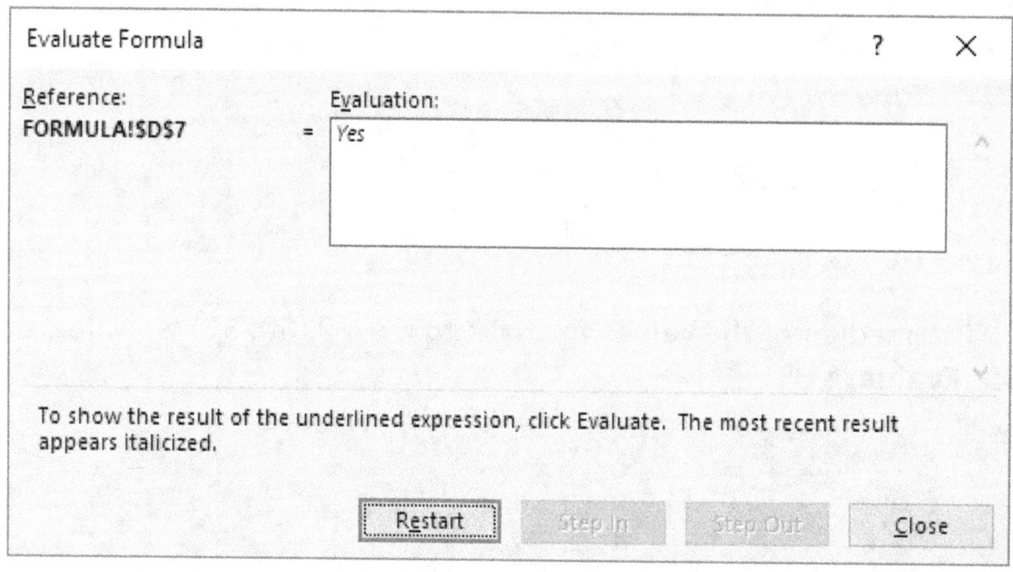

Fill Down Formulas

If you have a formula that you want to copy down your table quickly, you can do it the slow way by dragging down the bottom right-hand corner of the cell, or the quick way, which is to double click the bottom right-hand corner of the cell.

As long as there is **data to the left-hand side of the formula** that you want to copy downwards, this trick will work!

STEP 1: Type in your **Excel Formula**

	A	B	C	D	E	F	G
7	CUSTOMER	REGION	ORDER DATE	SALES	MONTH	YEAR	FORMULA
8	Acme, inc.	NORTH	Sunday, April 13, 2014	$55,815	April	2014	=D8/10
9	Widget Corp	SOUTH	Sunday, December 21, 2014	$94,908	December	2014	
10	123 Warehousing	EAST	Saturday, February 15, 2014	$57,088	February	2014	
11	Demo Company	WEST	Wednesday, May 14, 2014	$56,539	May	2014	
12	Smith and Co.	NORTH	Sunday, June 28, 2015	$63,116	June	2015	
13	Foo Bars	SOUTH	Thursday, January 15, 2015	$38,281	January	2015	
14	ABC Telecom	EAST	Saturday, August 22, 2015	$57,650	August	2015	
15	Fake Brothers	WEST	Thursday, December 31, 2015	$90,967	December	2015	

STEP 2: **Double click on the lower right corner of the cell** to apply the same formula to the rest of the column

	A	B	C	D	E	F	G
7	CUSTOMER	REGION	ORDER DATE	SALES	MONTH	YEAR	FORMULA
8	Acme, inc.	NORTH	Sunday, April 13, 2014	$55,815	April	2014	$5,582
9	Widget Corp	SOUTH	Sunday, December 21, 2014	$94,908	December	2014	
10	123 Warehousing	EAST	Saturday, February 15, 2014	$57,088	February	2014	
11	Demo Company	WEST	Wednesday, May 14, 2014	$56,539	May	2014	
12	Smith and Co.	NORTH	Sunday, June 28, 2015	$63,116	June	2015	
13	Foo Bars	SOUTH	Thursday, January 15, 2015	$38,281	January	2015	
14	ABC Telecom	EAST	Saturday, August 22, 2015	$57,650	August	2015	
15	Fake Brothers	WEST	Thursday, December 31, 2015	$90,967	December	2015	

The same Excel formula is applied to the entire column in a flash!

	A	B	C	D	E	F	G
7	CUSTOMER	REGION	ORDER DATE	SALES	MONTH	YEAR	FORMULA
8	Acme, inc.	NORTH	Sunday, April 13, 2014	$55,815	April	2014	$5,582
9	Widget Corp	SOUTH	Sunday, December 21, 2014	$94,908	December	2014	$9,491
10	123 Warehousing	EAST	Saturday, February 15, 2014	$57,088	February	2014	$5,709
11	Demo Company	WEST	Wednesday, May 14, 2014	$56,539	May	2014	$5,654
12	Smith and Co.	NORTH	Sunday, June 28, 2015	$63,116	June	2015	$6,312
13	Foo Bars	SOUTH	Thursday, January 15, 2015	$38,281	January	2015	$3,828
14	ABC Telecom	EAST	Saturday, August 22, 2015	$57,650	August	2015	$5,765
15	Fake Brothers	WEST	Thursday, December 31, 2015	$90,967	December	2015	$9,097
16							

Find the Best Formula

This is one of the coolest tricks I have seen in Excel, as there are countless times where I had a hard time finding the right Excel formula for my task!

The best part is with this trick, there is no need for you to memorize Excel formulas.

Let us say we have this horizontal table that we want to search for values:

Stock List	Television	Laptop	Tablet
Price	$ 150.00	$ 185.00	$ 245.00
Cost	$ 85.00	$ 95.00	$ 90.00

Here is our main target: How do we lookup and return the **price** of a **television?**

STEP 1: Let us look for that perfect formula! Go to *Formulas > Insert Function*

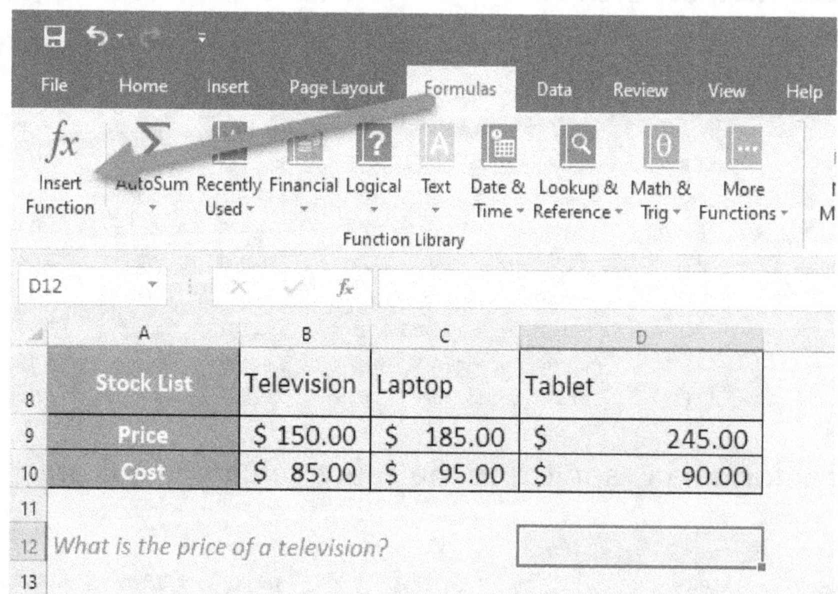

STEP 2: Let us type in **lookup** as that is what we want to do. Click **Go** and we will see a couple of formulas.

You can also see a description of each formula and **HLOOKUP** is perfect for the job! Select that and click **OK**.

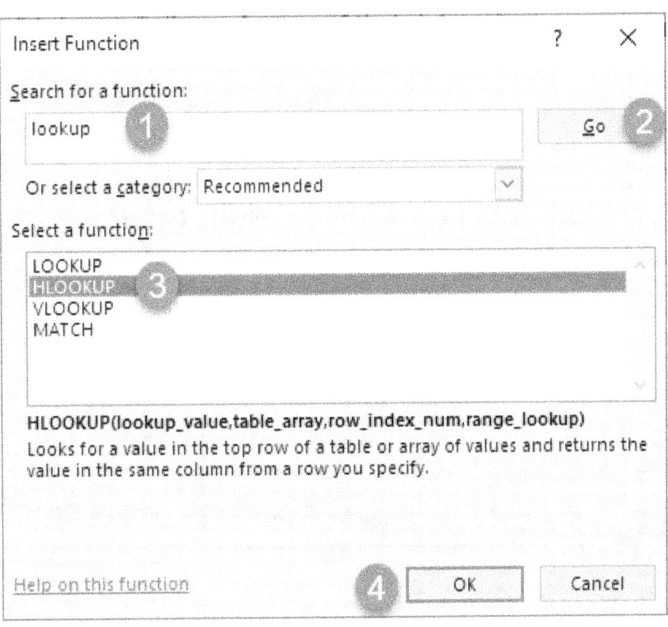

STEP 3: Now this is the fun part, Excel explains each argument to us on how to properly utilize the formula. There is also a description on each argument as you click through each one.

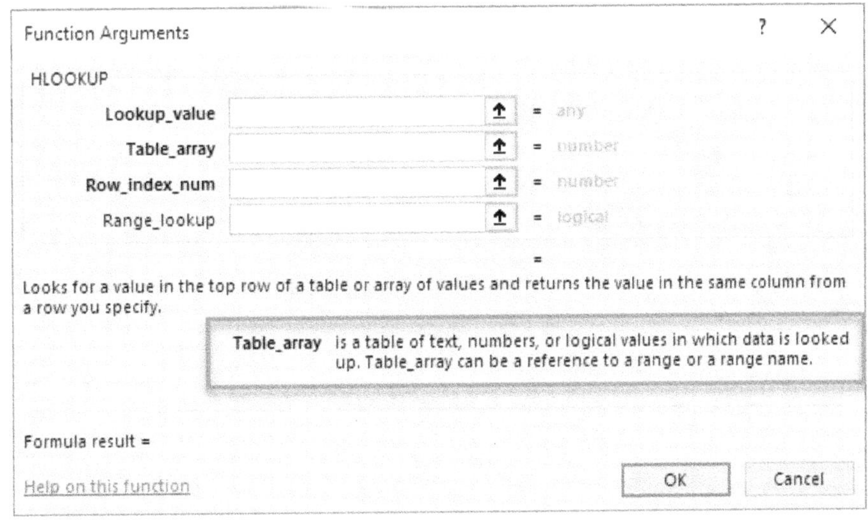

Let us now start filling up the values! Click **OK** afterwards.

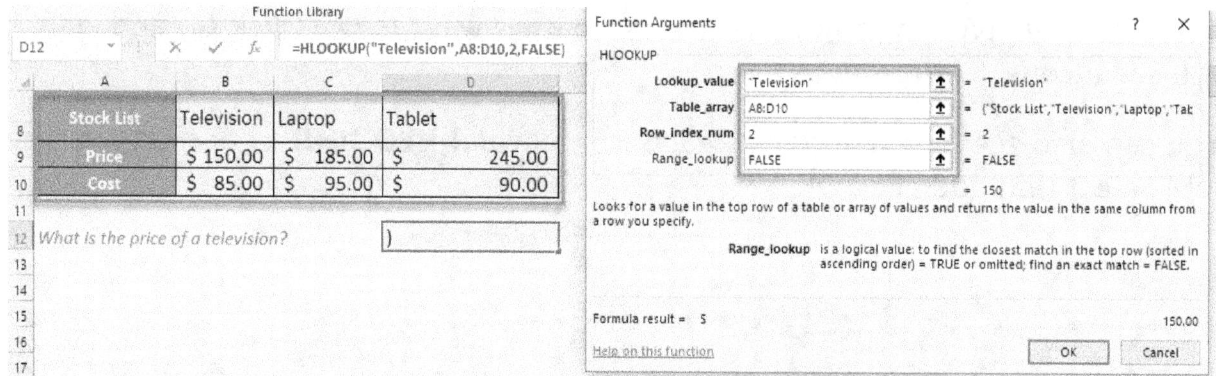

You now have your correct formula with the right result!

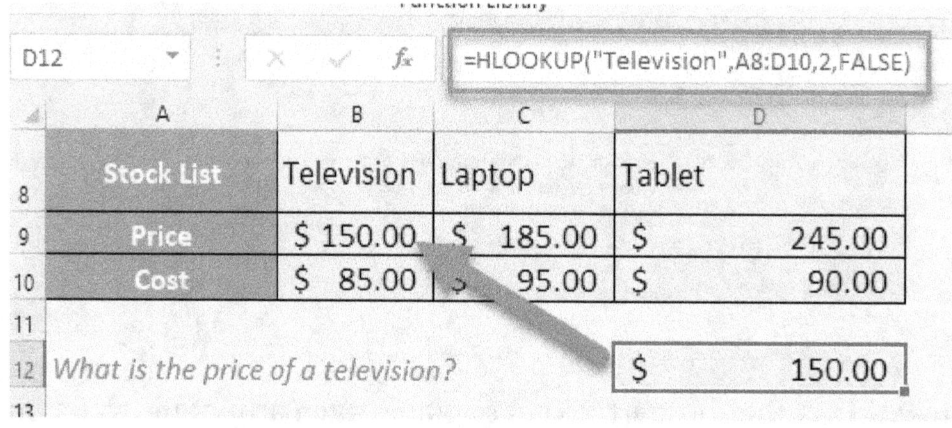

Highlight All Excel Formula Cells

Whenever you are auditing an Excel worksheet and need to know where all the formulas are located, a great way is to highlight the formula cells in a distinctive color. This is how it is done:

STEP 1: Select all the cells in your Excel worksheet by clicking on the top left-hand corner of your worksheet.

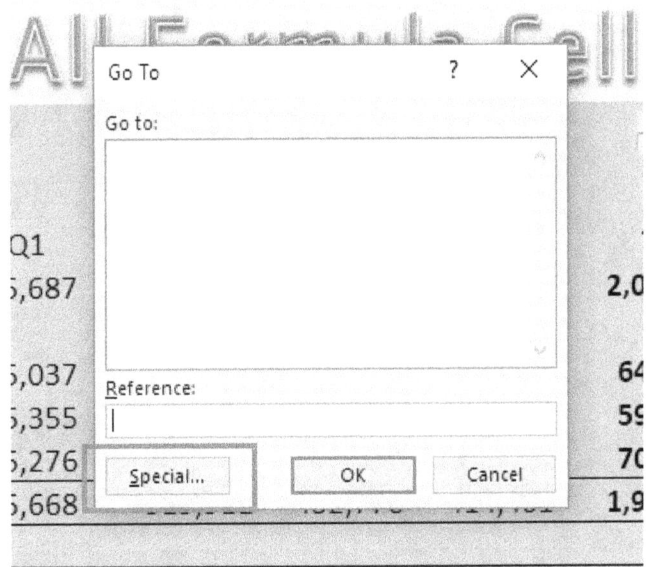

STEP 2: Press the **CTRL+G** shortcut which will open up the **Go To** dialog box and select the *Special* button.

 Select the ***Formulas*** radio button and press ***OK***.

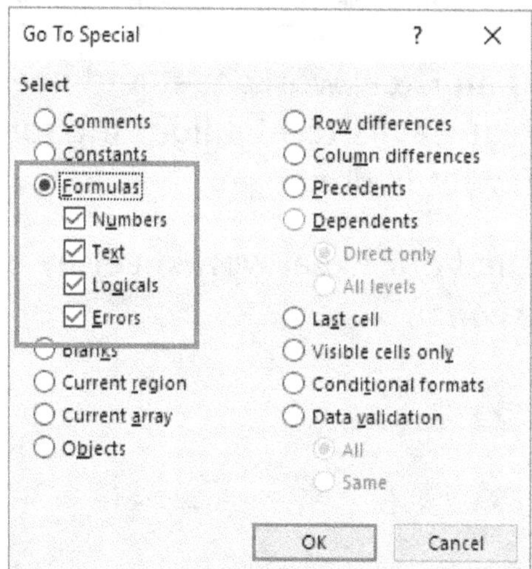

STEP 4: This will highlight all the formulas in your Excel worksheet and you can use the ***Fill Color*** to color in the formula cells.

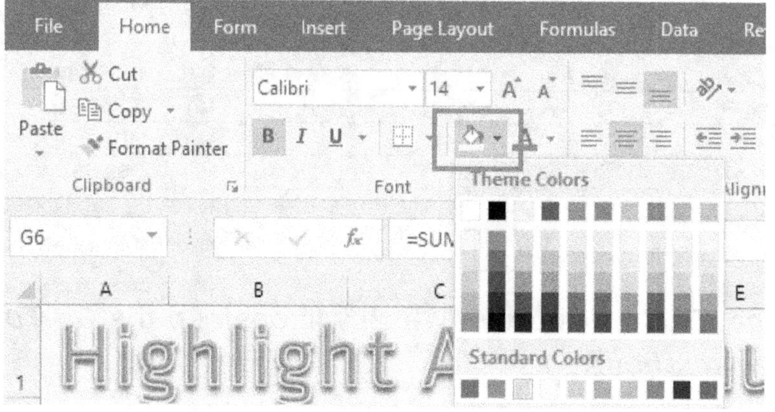

And now all your cells containing formulas are now highlighted!

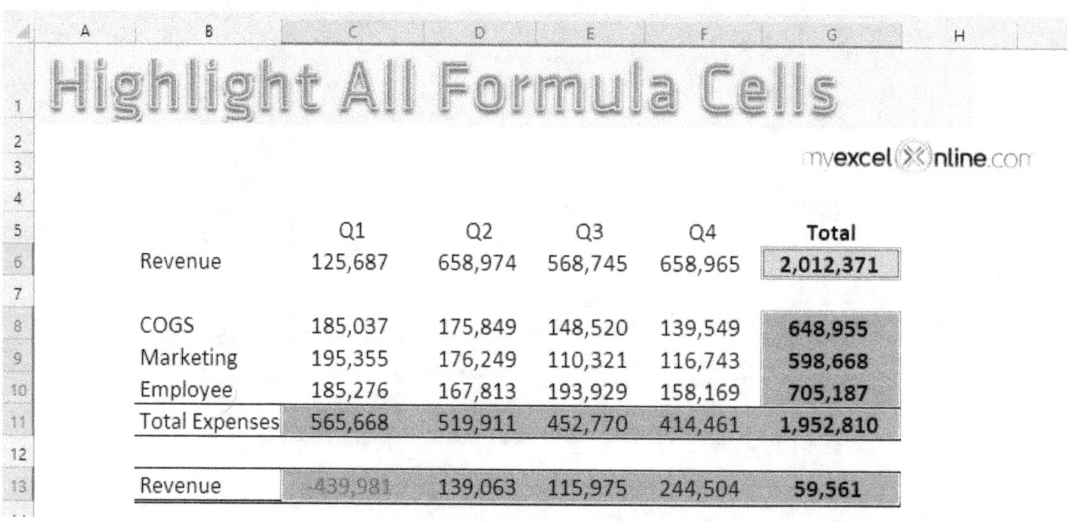

	Q1	Q2	Q3	Q4	Total
Revenue	125,687	658,974	568,745	658,965	2,012,371
COGS	185,037	175,849	148,520	139,549	648,955
Marketing	195,355	176,249	110,321	116,743	598,668
Employee	185,276	167,813	193,929	158,169	705,187
Total Expenses	565,668	519,911	452,770	414,461	1,952,810
Revenue	-439,981	139,063	115,975	244,504	59,561

Remove Formulas in Excel

There are times when I have an Excel worksheet full of formulas and I want to hard code the results and remove the formulas completely.

This is very easy to do in Excel!

Here is our sample worksheet which has the following formulas in **Column E**:

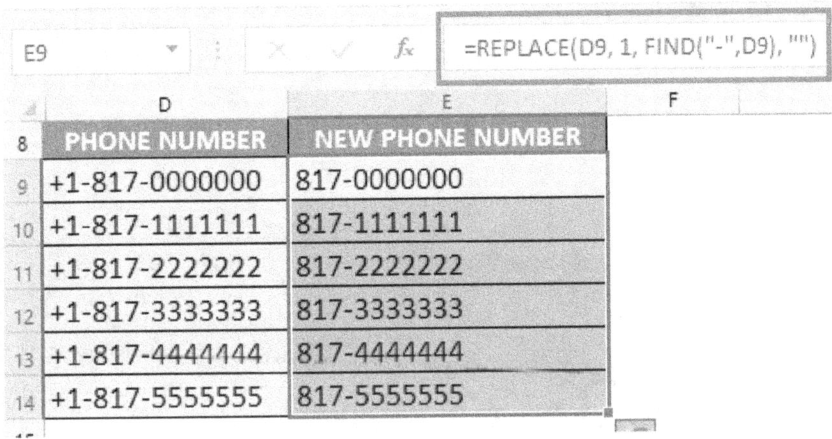

STEP 1: Select all the cells that have formulas:

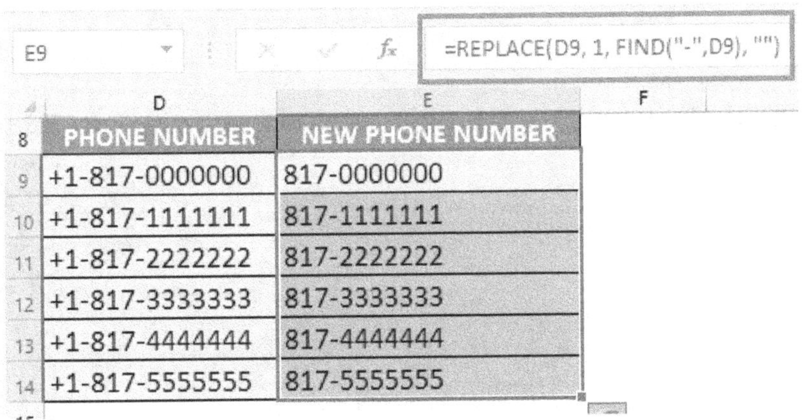

STEP 2: Right click and select **Copy:**

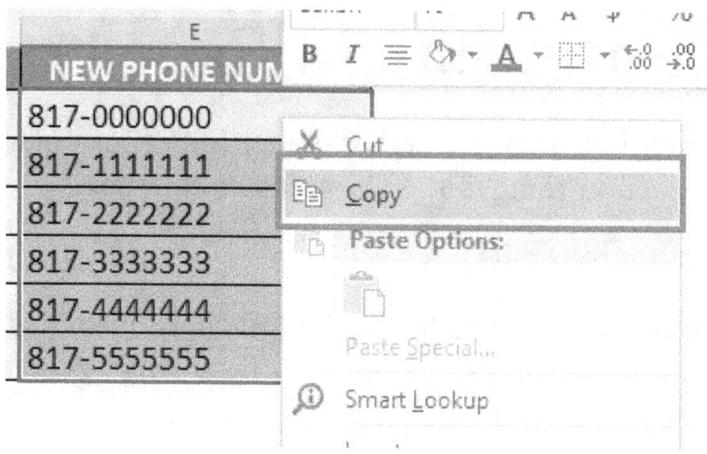

STEP 3: Right click again and select **Paste Values**:

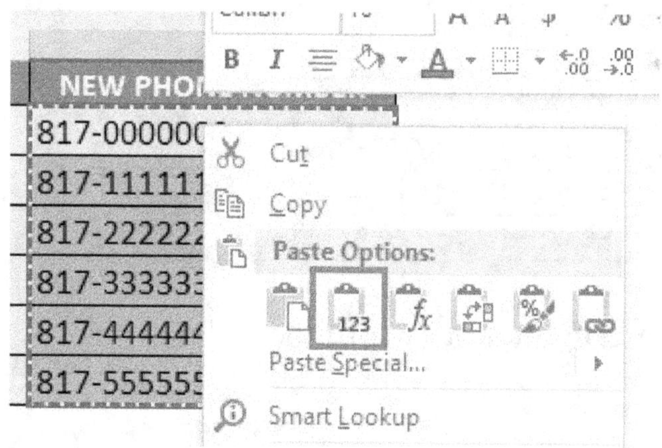

Now you will see that the values are only retained and the formulas are now gone!

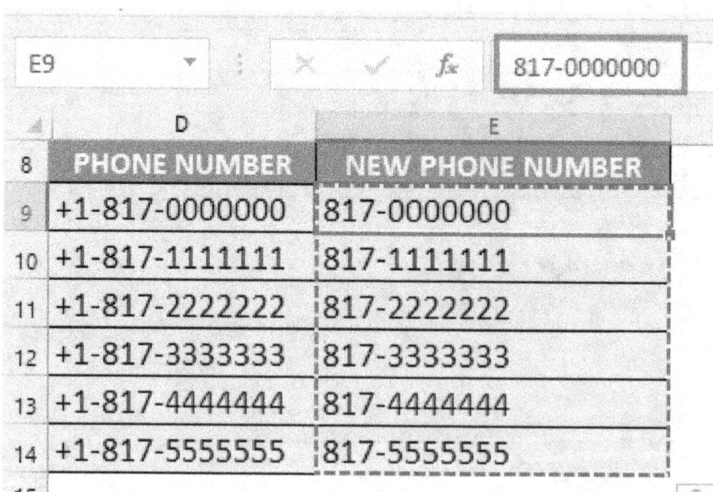

Remove Leading and Trailing Spaces

Leading spaces (at the start of the text) and *Trailing spaces* (at the end of the text) usually get in the way when we want to perform operations in Excel.

Whether it be leading or trailing spaces, we have a couple of ways how to clean them in Excel.

Let's use the TRIM formula to remove leading & trailing spaces:

	TEXT	CLEANED TEXT	
6			
7	With normal spaces	=TRIM(C7)	
8	With non-breaking spaces		
9	With non-breaking spaces		

The spaces get removed with no issues:

	TEXT	CLEANED TEXT	
6			
7	With normal spaces	With normal spaces	
8	With non-breaking spaces		
9	With non-breaking spaces		

However if we have **non-breaking spaces**, the **TRIM formula will not remove these spaces:**

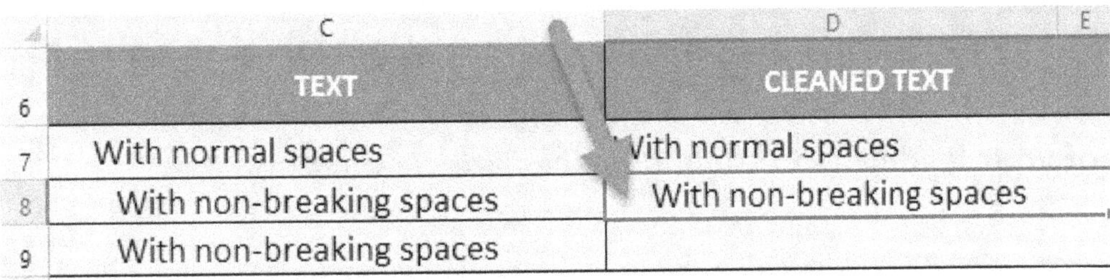

	TEXT	CLEANED TEXT	
6			
7	With normal spaces	With normal spaces	
8	With non-breaking spaces	With non-breaking spaces	
9	With non-breaking spaces		

The leading space is still there!

What are non-breaking spaces you ask?

Sometimes data downloaded as text uses non-breaking spaces for formatting purposes. It prevents an automatic line break in between these spaces.

This is represented by **CHAR(160)**:

```
=CHAR(160) & CHAR(160) &CHAR(160) &CHAR(160) &"   With non-breaking spaces  "&CHAR(160) &CHAR(160) &CHAR(160) &CHAR(160)
```

This looks like a pain! How do we clean these? I explain how you can do this below:

STEP 1: We will use the SUBSTITUTE Formula to remove the non-breaking spaces depicted by **CHAR(160)**

The goal is to replace the non-breaking spaces with normal spaces.

=SUBSTITUTE(C9, CHAR(160), " ")

	C	D	E
6	TEXT	CLEANED TEXT	
7	With normal spaces	With normal spaces	
8	With non-breaking spaces	With non-breaking spaces	
9	With non-breaking spaces	=SUBSTITUTE(C9,CHAR(160)," ")	

STEP 2: Now that we do not have the non-breaking spaces anymore, let us nest the TRIM Formula:

=TRIM(SUBSTITUTE(C9, CHAR(160), " "))

	C	D	E	F
6	TEXT	CLEANED TEXT		
7	With normal spaces	With normal spaces		
8	With non-breaking spaces	With non-breaking spaces		
9	With non-breaking spaces	=TRIM(SUBSTITUTE(C9,CHAR(160)," "))		

Now all of your leading and trailing spaces are cleaned up!

	C	D	E
6	TEXT	CLEANED TEXT	
7	With normal spaces	With normal spaces	
8	With non-breaking spaces	With non-breaking spaces	
9	With non-breaking spaces	With non-breaking spaces	

Separate Formula into Rows

When I have a complex or long formula, sometimes I wish there was a way to make it more readable and easier on the eyes. And guess what, there is a way in Excel!

Let us say we have a SWITCH Formula wherein we want to return the following:

- A rating of 1 is Bad

- A rating of 2 is Average

- A rating of 3 is Great

- Otherwise, show Unknown

This is our complete SWITCH Formula. We can do some formatting magic to make it more readable!

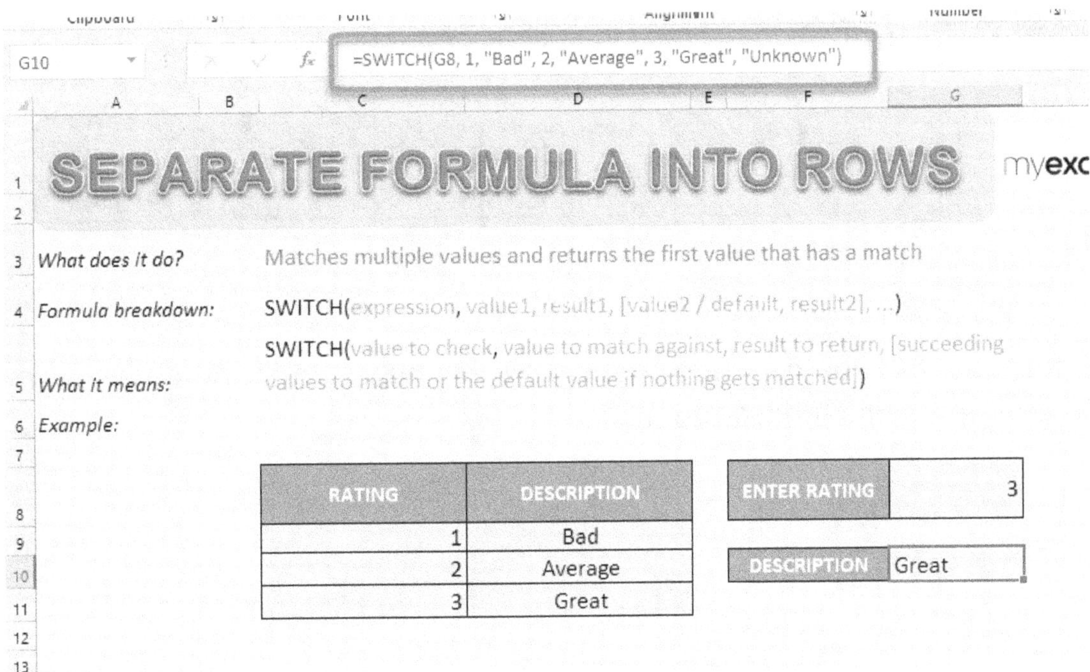

STEP 1: Start editing your formula by double clicking on the cell that has the formula.

We will use the **ALT + ENTER keyboard shortcut** to add new lines to our formula, then you can add spaces as well to have indentation inside your Excel formula.

Functionally speaking there is no additional functionality that you have added in your Excel Formula but you have made it easier to read and understand!

Here is the result:

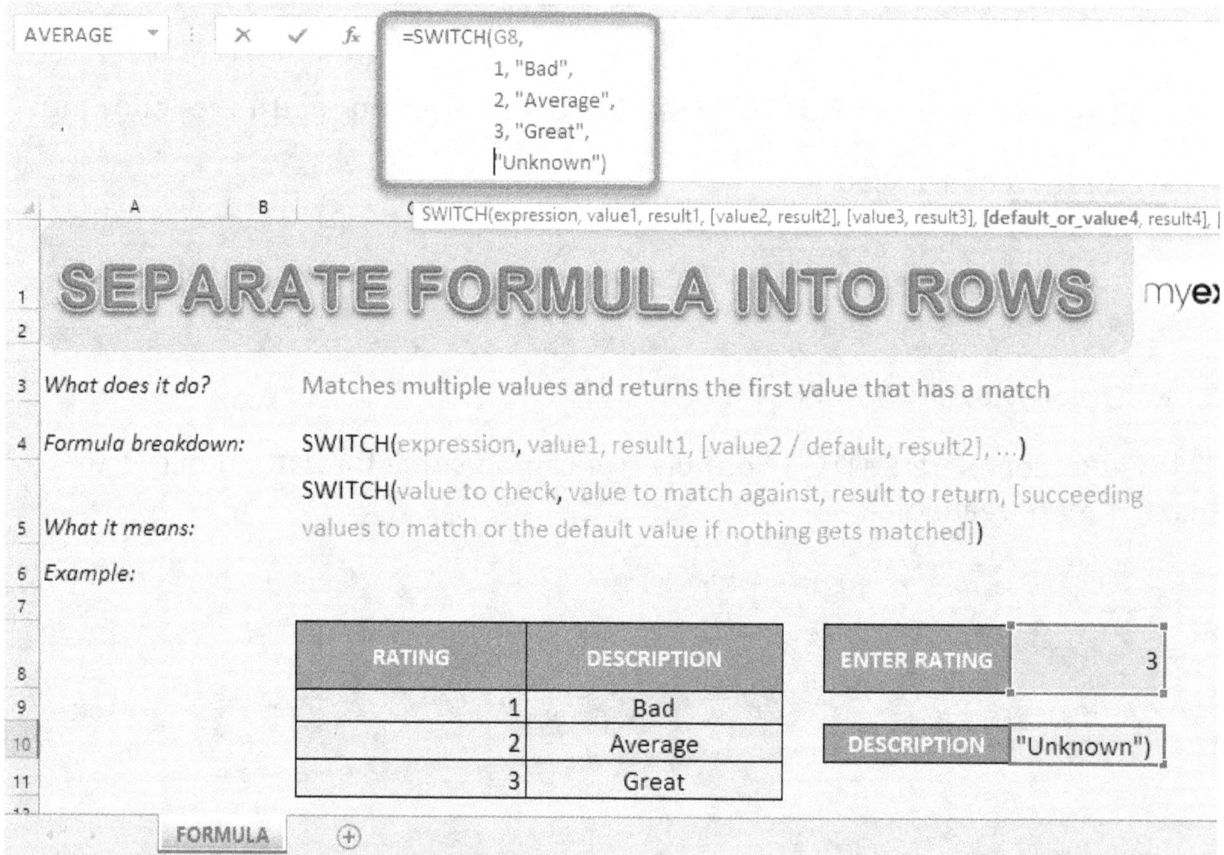

Same formula, but you can quickly see with this new formatting on which rating would end up to which description.

Show & Hide Formulas in Excel

When I have a sheet full of Excel formulas, sometimes I want to quickly check how each formula looks like. This is great for spreadsheet auditing.

Here is our sample worksheet with formulas:

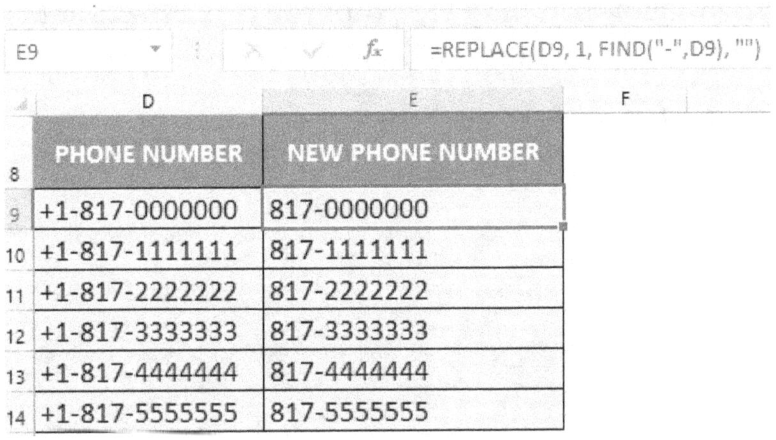

STEP 1: Press on your keyboard the following keys: **Ctrl + `**

The ` key is usually located on the upper left part of your keyboard. This will show all your Excel formulas in your worksheet!

	D	E
	PHONE NUMBER	**NEW PHONE NUMBER**
9	+1-817-0000000	=REPLACE(D9, 1, FIND("-",D9), "")
10	+1-817-1111111	=REPLACE(D10, 1, FIND("-",D10), "")
11	+1-817-2222222	=REPLACE(D11, 1, FIND("-",D11), "")
12	+1-817-3333333	=REPLACE(D12, 1, FIND("-",D12), "")
13	+1-817-4444444	=REPLACE(D13, 1, FIND("-",D13), "")
14	+1-817-5555555	=REPLACE(D14, 1, FIND("-",D14), "")

Press the **Ctrl + `** combination again to hide the formulas.

STEP 2: If you prefer to set this via Excel Options, another way is to go to **File > Options**

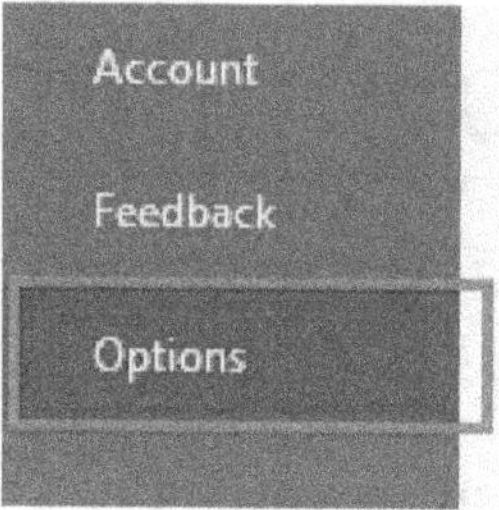

STEP 3: Go to **Advanced> Display Options for this Worksheet > Show formulas in cells instead of their calculated fields**

Ensure this is checked.

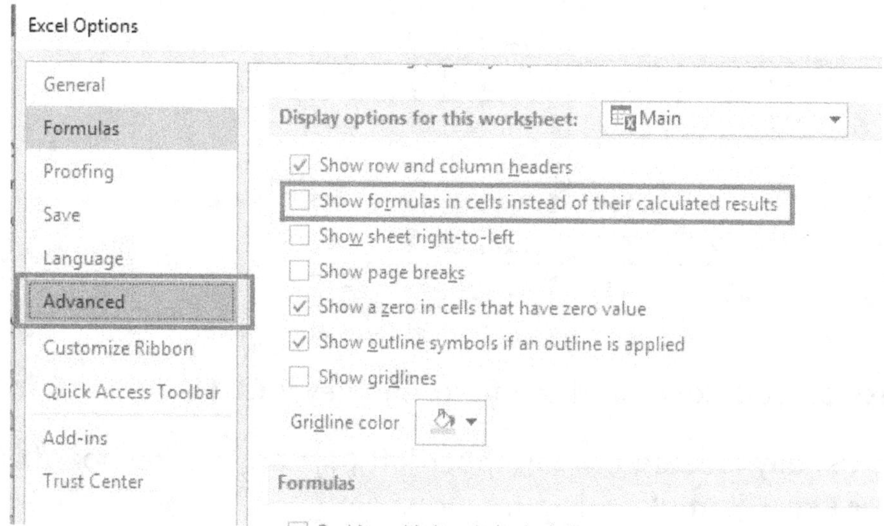

The formulas are all shown now too! You can uncheck it to hide the formulas again.

PHONE NUMBER	NEW PHONE NUMBER
+1-817-0000000	=REPLACE(D9, 1, FIND("-",D9), "")
+1-817-1111111	=REPLACE(D10, 1, FIND("-",D10), "")
+1-817-2222222	=REPLACE(D11, 1, FIND("-",D11), "")
+1-817-3333333	=REPLACE(D12, 1, FIND("-",D12), "")
+1-817-4444444	=REPLACE(D13, 1, FIND("-",D13), "")
+1-817-5555555	=REPLACE(D14, 1, FIND("-",D14), "")

Vlookup in an Excel Table

What does it do?

Searches for a value in the first column of a table array and returns a value in the same row from another column (to the right) in the table array.

Formula breakdown:

=VLOOKUP(lookup_value, table_array, col_index_num, [range_lookup])

What it means:

=VLOOKUP(this value, TableName, and get me value in this column, Exact Match/FALSE/0])

Excel Tables are just amazing and should be used all the time, whether you have 2 rows or 200,000 rows of data!

When you use a Vlookup formula to lookup in an Excel Table then your formula becomes dynamic due to its structured referencing.

What that means is that as the Excel Table expands with more data added to it, your Vlookup formula's 2nd argument (***table_array***) does not need to be updated as it **refers to the Excel Table as a whole** by referring to its name like ***Table1, Table2, Table3*** etc.

In the example below our Excel Table name is ***Table2*** and as we add more rows of data to it, the Vlookup formula does not need to be adjusted. How bloody cool is that?

STEP 1: We need to convert the data into an Excel Table. Press Ctrl + T then press OK.

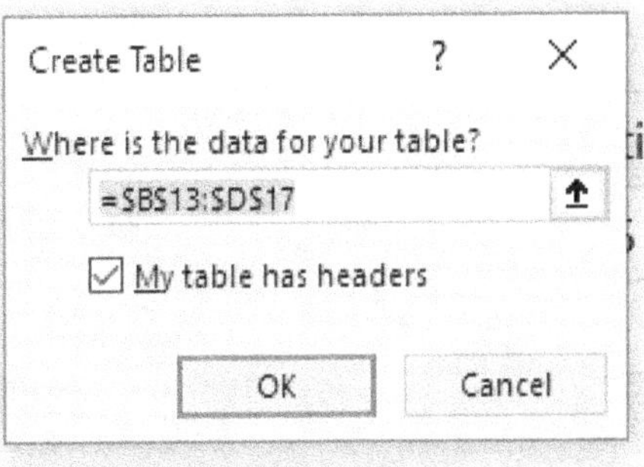

Stock List	Price	Cost
Television	$150	$85
Laptop	$185	$95
Tablet	$245	$90
Keyboard	$55	$5

STEP 2: Now let us create the formula to get the price of the Laptop. Let us use the **VLOOKUP** formula:

$$=VLOOKUP(G15, Table1, 2, FALSE)$$

This will get the lookup value (**Laptop** in Cell G15), then search in the **first column of Table1**.

Afterwards it will get the value in **Column #2** which is the **price**. The FALSE means is we want to get the exact match.

Stock List	Price	Cost		Item	Quantity	Price	Total Price
Television	$150	$85					
Laptop	$185	$95		lookup_value Laptop	125	=VLOOKUP(G15,Table1,2,FALSE)	$23,125
Tablet	$245	$90		lookup_value Mouse	35	VLOOKUP(lookup_value, table_array, col_index_num, [range_lookup]) 0
Keyboard	$55	$5					Total **$23,125**

STEP 3: Drag down the formula to copy it across the table. Notice that the second row is looking for the price of **Mouse**. This does not exist in our data table yet.

	Item	Quantity	Price	Total Price
lookup_value	Laptop	125	185	$23,125
lookup_value	Mouse	35		$0
			Total	**$23,125**

STEP 4: Now add and type in a new row in our table for the price of the mouse.

Stock List	Price	Cost
Television	$150	$85
Laptop	$185	$95
Tablet	$245	$90
Keyboard	$55	$5
Mouse	$100	$50

The beauty with this is our VLOOKUP formula still works fine. Since we are using the Table1, there is no need to update the range of values that our VLOOKUP will use. It is now automatically included and the price of the mouse is retrieved right away.

Stock List	Price	Cost
Television	$150	$85
Laptop	$185	$95
Tablet	$245	$90
Keyboard	$55	$5
Mouse	$100	$50

Item	Quantity	Price	Total Price
lookup_value Laptop	125	185	$23,125
lookup_value Mouse	35	100	$3,500
		Total	$26,625

Watch Window in Excel

The Watch Window feature in Excel is great to track specific formula results. Imagine you have the resulting cell in a separate worksheet, it would be cumbersome to go back and forth checking the results!

Here is our sample worksheet with our target result:

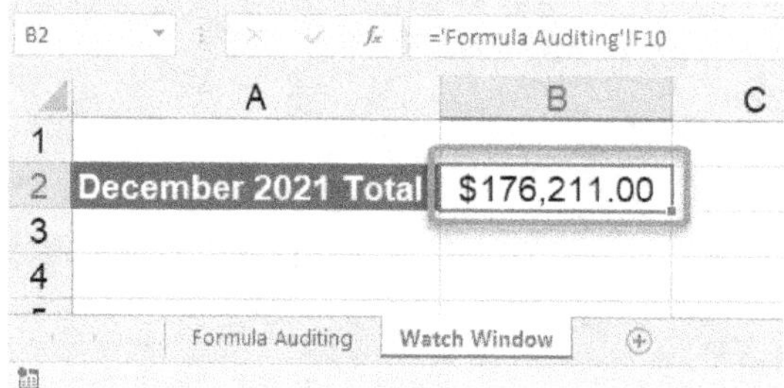

The actual calculations happen in the **_Formula Auditing_** worksheet:

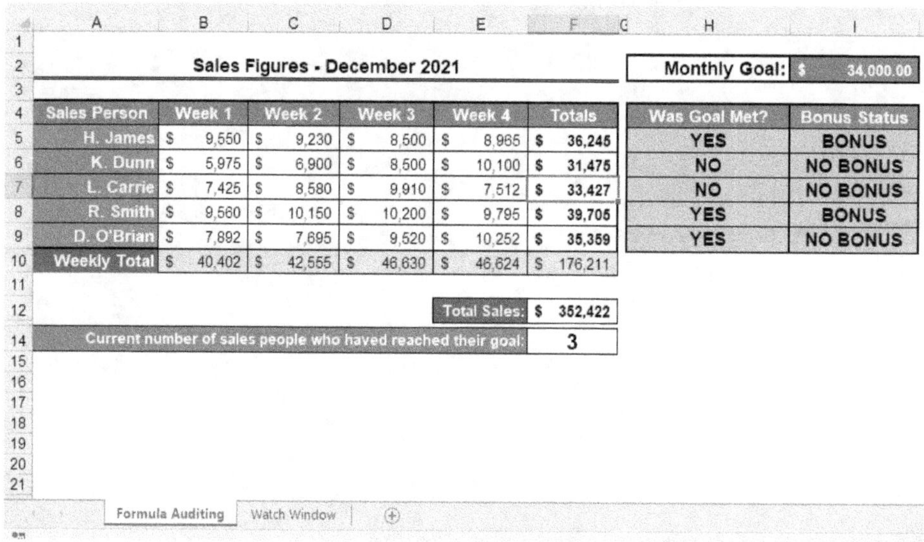

STEP 1: Select the cell that you want to monitor.

Go to **_Formulas > Formula Auditing > Watch Window_**

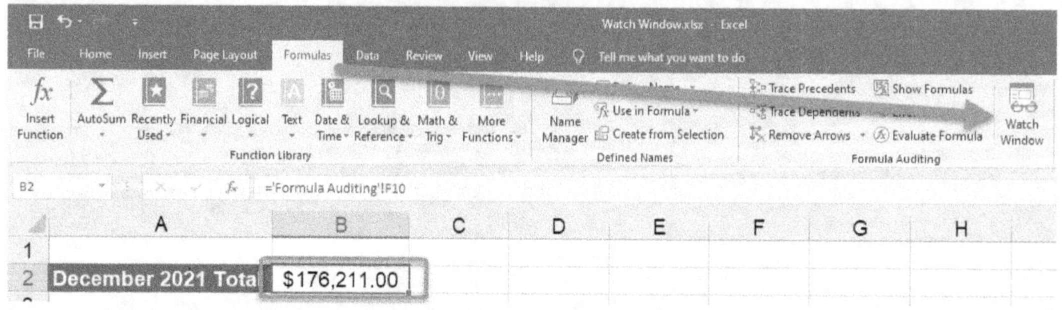

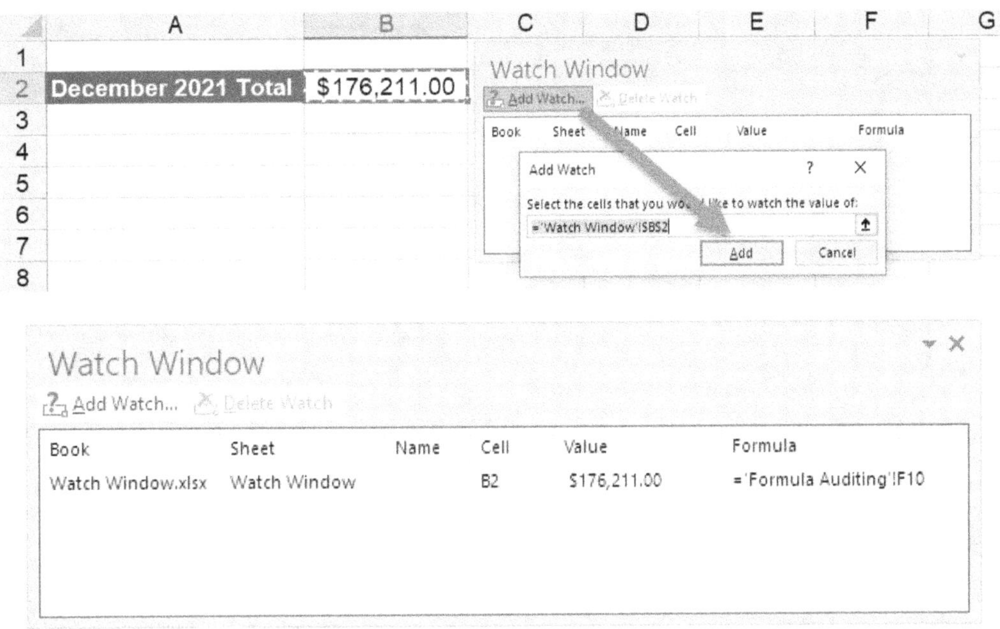

STEP 3: Now let us see this in action! Jump over to the **Formula Auditing** Worksheet. And change any value inside the Sales Table.

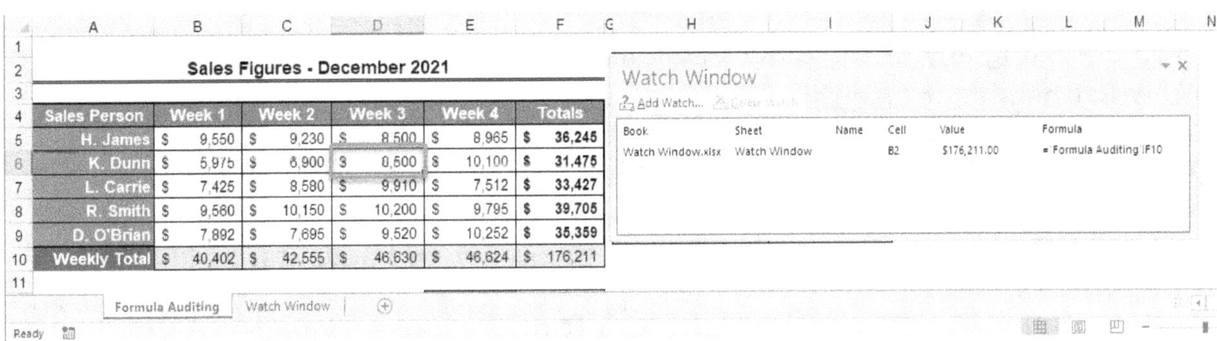

I've increased the value to 120,000 and you can see the Formula cell we have tracked in the Watch Window has updated too! No need to jump back forth and forth between worksheets anymore!

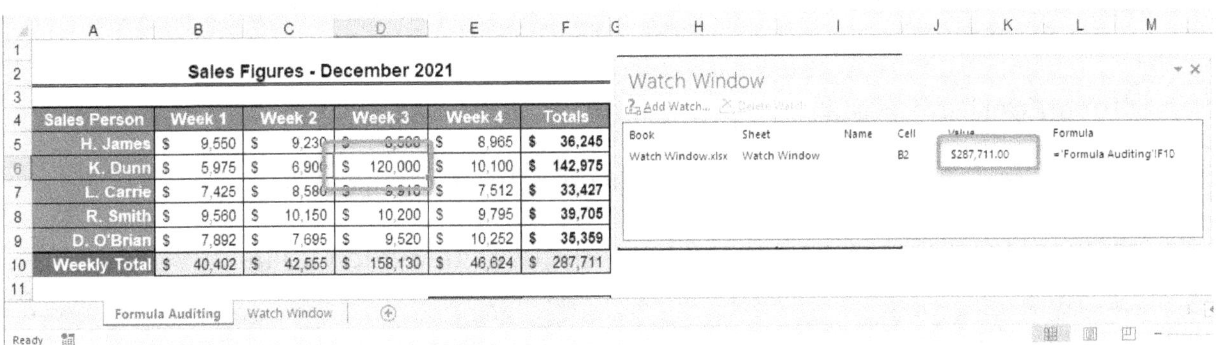

XLOOKUP Function in Excel

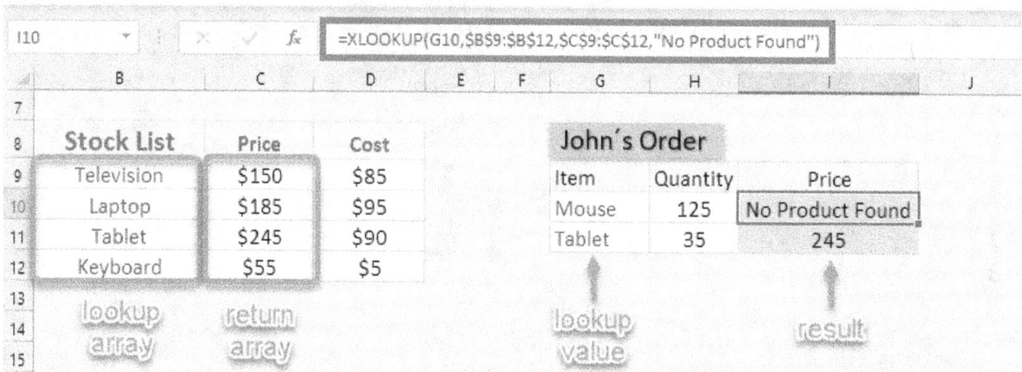

Ever wanted to lookup values in Excel? Which of the following Excel function did you use:

The dynamic one - VLOOKUP? The horizontal one - HLOOKUP? The complicated one - INDEX MATCH?

Even though the above Excel functions can get the job done, they come with their own limitations. The solution to this is to use the brand new Excel function **introduced in Microsoft Office 365 - XLOOKUP!**

If you are using any of the older versions of Excel (2010, 2013, 2016, 2019) you won't be able to use this function.

XLOOKUP is a **versatile and outstanding replacement** for the above-mentioned Excel functions. It allows you to quickly lookup values in a data set (just like VLOOKUP Excel) with additional flexibility and advantages like:

- It can lookup data to the **right or left** of the lookup values.

- It looks for an **exact match by default**. You do not have to enter an additional argument for it.

- It allows you to provide a custom value or text if your **search result is not found**.

- It can perform a **partial match lookup using wildcards**.

- It can search for values **both horizontally and vertically**.

- It can **return a range** instead of a single value which spills out the results.

- It allows you to **find the last occurrence** in your data.

Excited? Read on to learn more about XLOOKUP!

XLOOKUP - An Introduction

What does it do?

Excel XLOOKUP can be used to search an array for a specific value and returns the value in the same row from another array.

- It can search the value both horizontally and vertically,

- Perform an exact or approximate match,

- Use wildcards,

- Return a custom text when no result is found,

- Doesn't even have the restriction of the return array to be on the right of the lookup array.

Isn't that AMAZING? It is a **power-packed function** with so many advantages!

Formula breakdown:

=XLOOKUP (lookup_value, lookup_array, return_array, [if_not_found], [match_mode], [search_mode])

where:

- lookup_value - the value you want to search;

- lookup_array - the range or array where you want to search the value;

- return_array - the range or array from which you want the result;

- [if_not_found] - the value you want to display if there are no results found;

- [match_mode]

    - **0** - Exact Match (if no result found, then error)

    - **-1** - Exact or next smaller (if no result found, then the next smaller value will be displayed)

- o **1** - Exact or next larger (if no result found, then the next larger value will be displayed)

- o **2** - Wildcards

- [search_mode]

  - o **1** - to search from first

  - o **-1** - to search from last

  - o **2** - binary search ascending

  - o **-2** - binary search descending

How to use XLOOKUP in Excel?

In this example below, there are two tables:

- o **Stocklist** containing the product's SKU, name, price, and cost.

- o **Orders Table** with its quantity mentioned

You want to extract the price of the products from the stock list table using XLOOKUP.

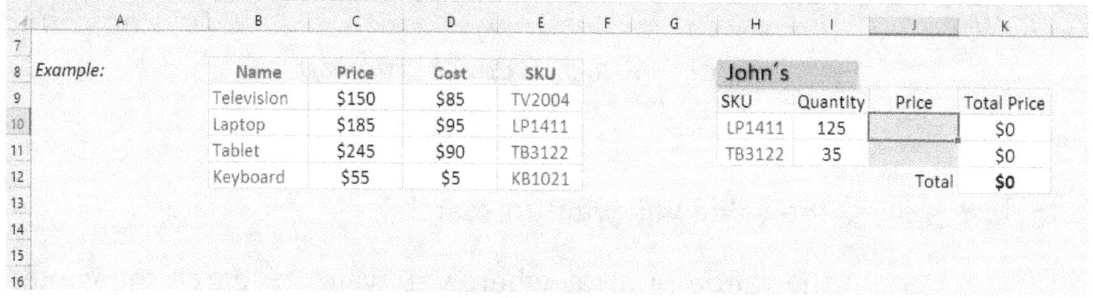

STEP 1: We need to enter the **XLOOKUP** function in a blank cell

=XLOOKUP(

STEP 2: Enter the first **XLOOKUP** argument - *Lookup_value (product's SKU that you are looking for)*

=XLOOKUP(H10,

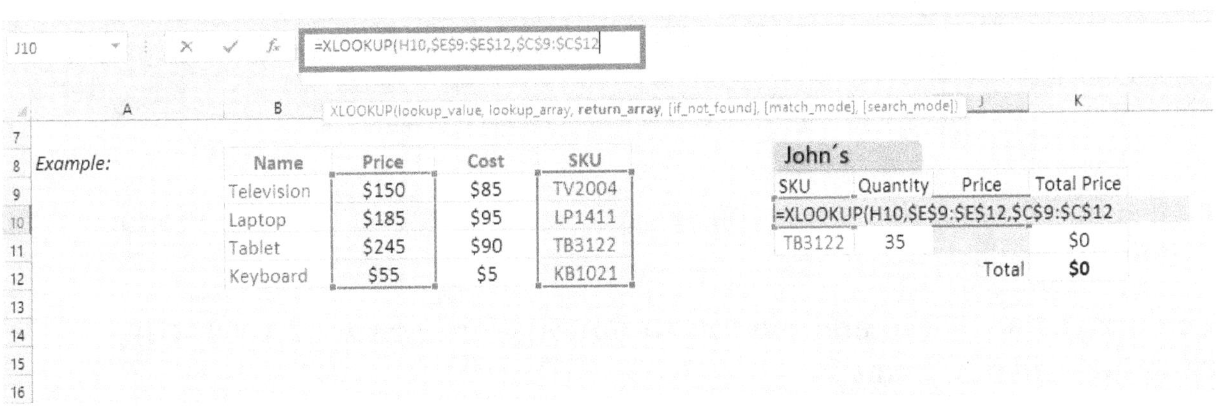

STEP 3: Enter the second **XLOOKUP** argument - ***Lookup_array (the array that contains all product SKUs)***

=XLOOKUP(H10,$E$9:$E$12

Ensure that you press F4 so that you can lock the table range

STEP 4: Enter the third **XLOOKUP** argument - ***return_array (the array that contains price)***

=XLOOKUP(H10,$E$9:$E$12,$C$9:$C$12)

As you will see, **Excel has pulled the price of the SKU** *LP1411* from the stock list and provided the result ($185) in the cell.

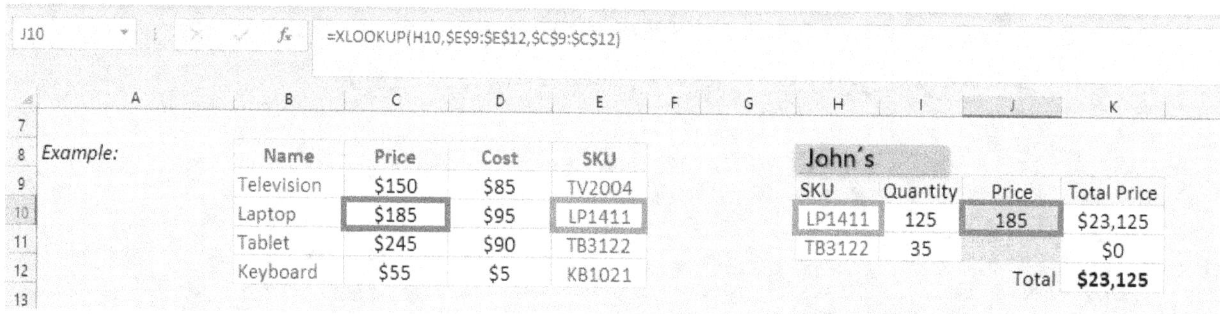

Apply the same formula to the rest of the cells by dragging the lower right corner downwards.

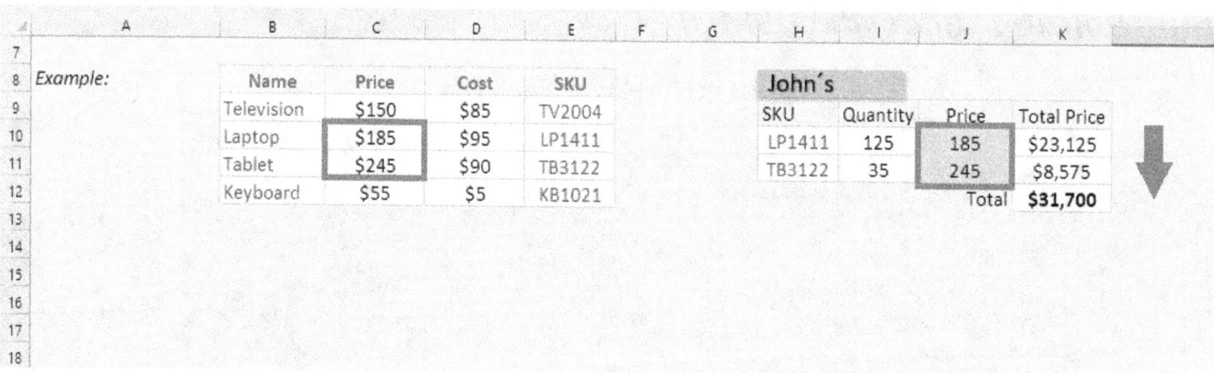

What if you are trying to search for a product name that is not available in the stock list table?

Excel will provide you with an **error**!

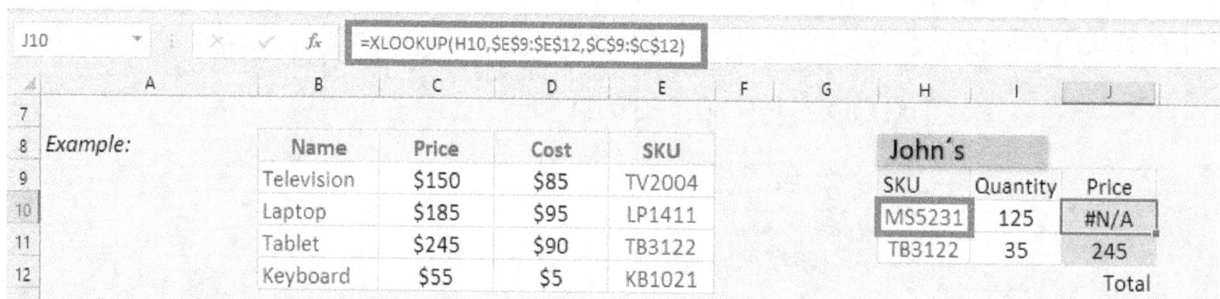

Instead of showing this error, you can **add a custom text** (say, No Product Found) to display!

To do that, simply can **add the fourth optional argument of XLOOKUP function - [if_not_found]**

$$=XLOOKUP(H10,\$E\$9:\$E\$12,\$C\$9:\$C\$12,"No Product Found")$$

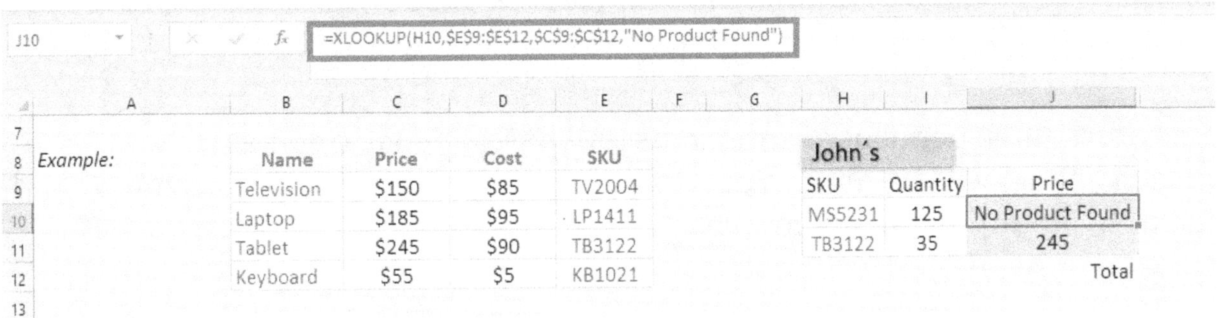

This was a basic example of how to use XLOOKUP in Excel. Let's **explore the advanced uses of this function** in detail!

Approximate Match

In this example, Excel will **look for the income entered** in cell F14 and **find the matching tax rate** from column C.

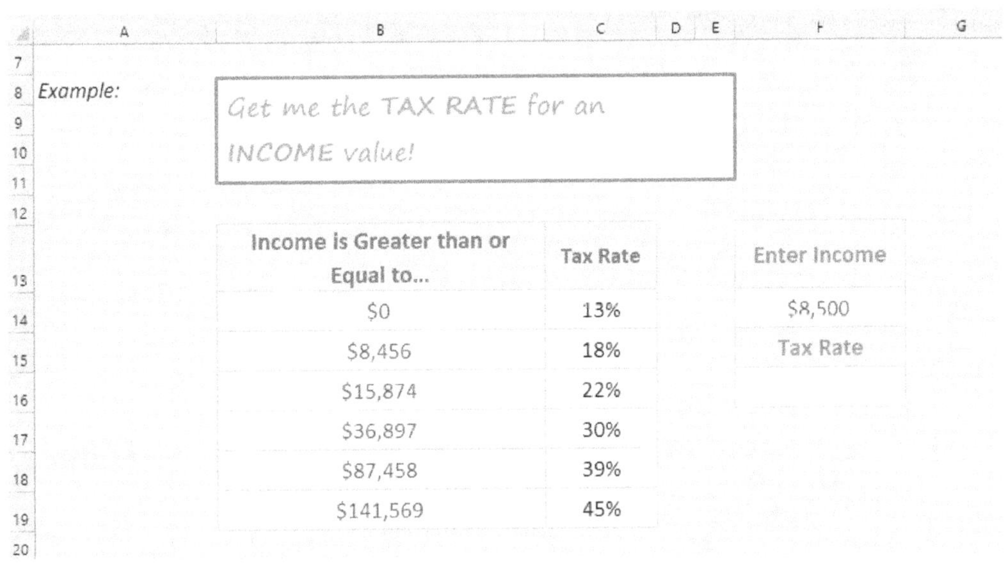

Income is Greater than or Equal to...	Tax Rate	Enter Income
$0	13%	$8,500
$8,456	18%	Tax Rate
$15,874	22%	
$36,897	30%	
$87,458	39%	
$141,569	45%	

Instead of looking for an exact match, it will now look for an approximate match. If an exact match is not found it will look for the next smaller or larger item based on the input provided.

If the **income is greater than or equal** to $0, the tax rate will be 13%. Similarly, if the income is greater than or equal to $8,456, the tax rate will be 18%, and so on.

So, let's **use this function to determine the tax rate for the income amount** mentioned in cell F14.

=XLOOKUP *(lookup_value, lookup_array, return_array, [if_not_found], [match_mode], [search_mode])*

Here, the three permanent arguments and one optional argument [match_mode] will be used. You can ignore arguments - [if_not_found] and [search_mode] for this example.

Follow the step-by-step tutorial below to **perform an approximate match** using the XLOOKUP function:

STEP 1: Enter the first argument **lookup_value** - the income amount mentioned in cell E5.

=XLOOKUP(E5

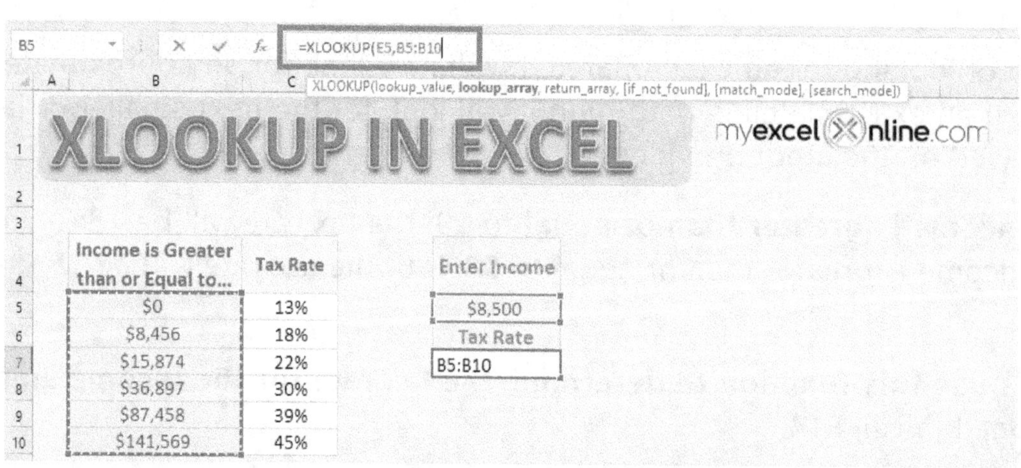

STEP 2: Enter the lookup_array - the **range containing income range** (B5: B10).

=XLOOKUP(E5,B5:B10

$$=XLOOKUP(E5,B5:B10,C5:C10$$

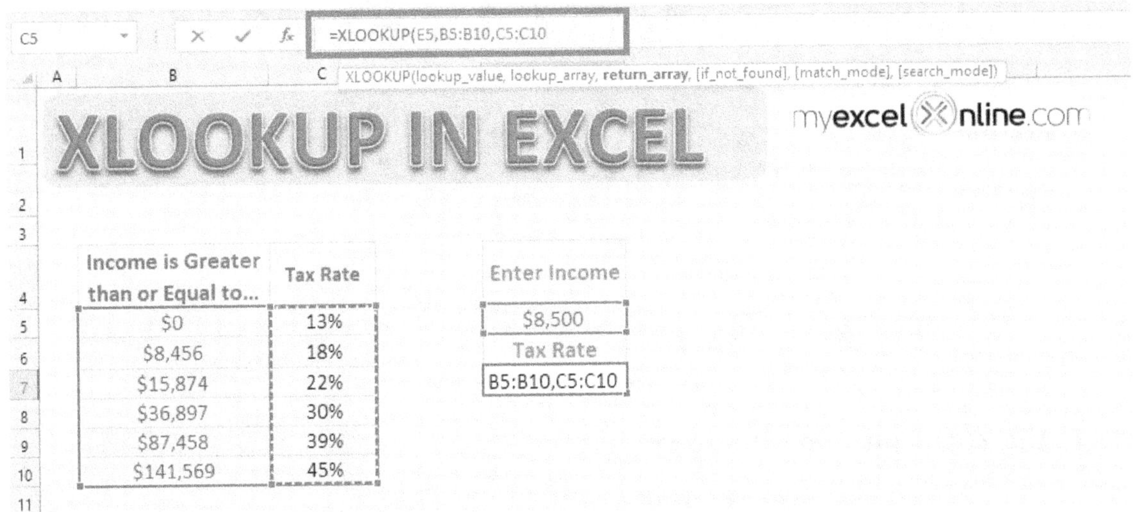

STEP 4: Enter the 5th argument[**match_mode**]. The accepted values for this argument are:

- **0** - Exact Match (if no result found, then error)

- **-1** - Exact or next smaller (if no result found, then the next smaller value will be displayed)

- **1** - Exact or next larger (if no result found, then the next larger value will be displayed)

- **2** - Wildcards

In this example, the value will be -1.

$$=XLOOKUP(E5,B5:B10,C5:C10,,-1)$$

We will ignore the 4th argument.

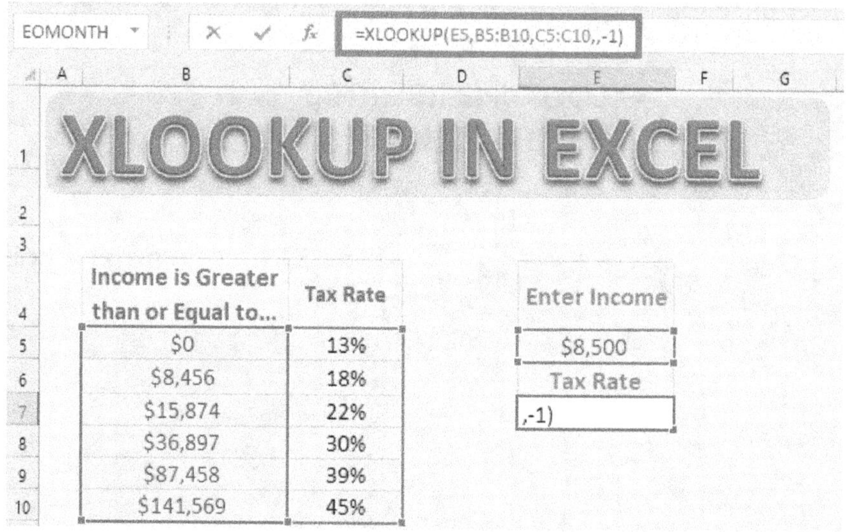

Below is the **formula** that should be used:

=XLOOKUP(E5,B5:B10,C5:C10,,-1)

As you know this function will perform an exact match by default, you need to **use the optional argument of the function - [match_mode]**. So, if Excel fails to find an exact match, it will look for the next smaller income range mentioned in the table.

One of the **advantages** of using this function over Excel VLOOKUP for an approximate match is that **you do not need to sort the data in ascending order.** Excel will do that on its own!

In the example below, you will see that the data is not arranged in ascending order.

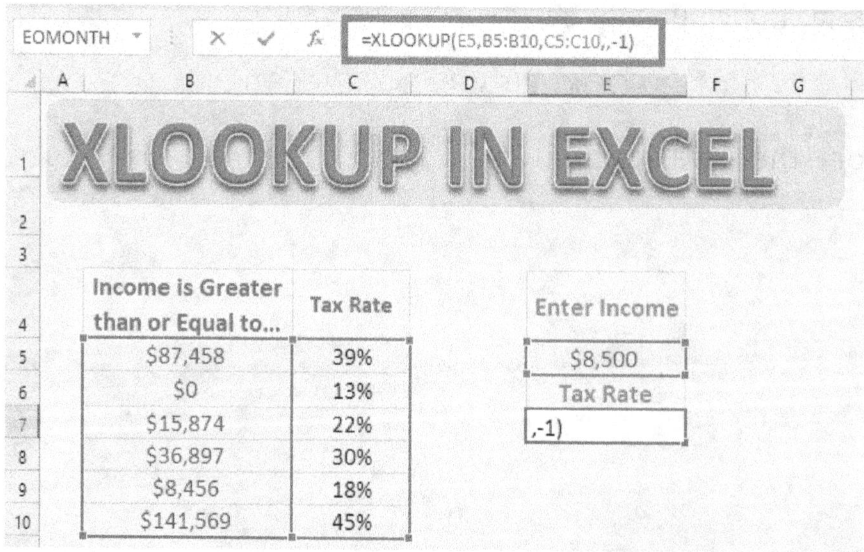

You can use the same formula in **randomly arranged data** and Excel will **provide you with the same (correct) result.**

Horizontal Lookup

The syntax for performing a horizontal lookup using XLOOKUP is the same as for vertical lookup.

You just need to **provide Excel with the lookup and return an array,** the table's orientation is irrelevant to the XLOOKUP function.

In this example, the product name is displayed on Row 5 and the price is displayed on Row 6. You need to perform a **horizontal lookup** to get your results.

STEP 1: Enter the lookup value - the product name mentioned in cell H6.

=XLOOKUP(H6

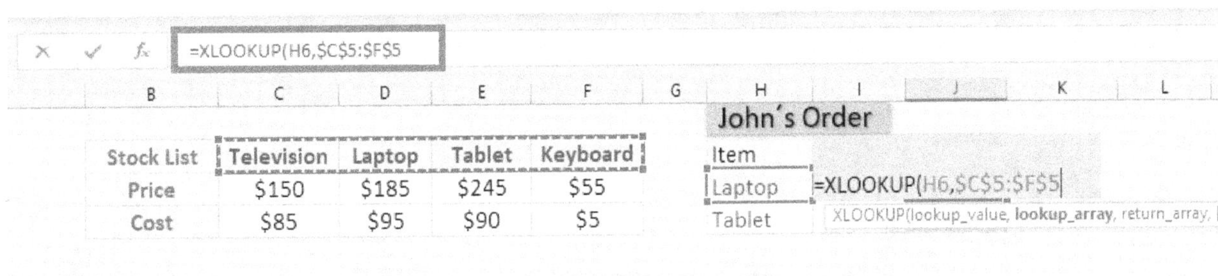

STEP 2: Enter the lookup array - the array containing the product name.

=XLOOKUP(H6,$C$5:$F$5

STEP 3: Enter the return array - the array containing prices of the product.

=XLOOKUP(H6,$C$5:$F$5,$C$6:$F$6)

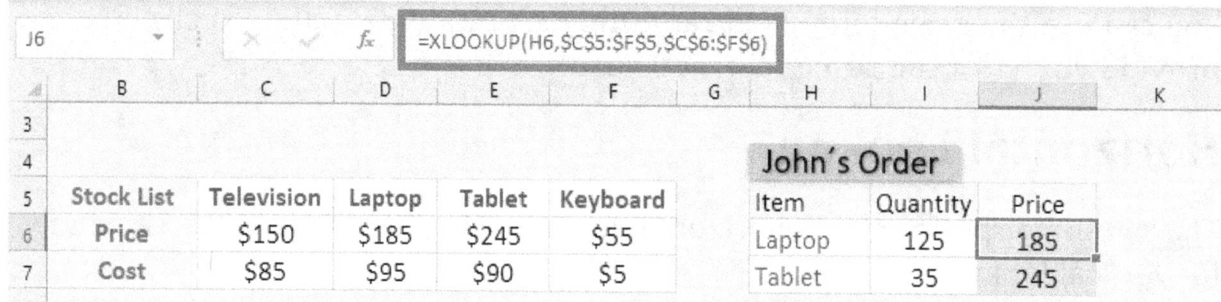

It's that easy to do a horizontal lookup using the new XLOOKUP function in Excel!

Return a Range instead of Value

Excel XLOOKUP has the ability to return multiple values instead of just one for a correct match. It can be done without making any change in the syntax, simply input the entire range in the function instead of just a single column or row.

In this example, we want to **retrieve all the details related to the product name** mentioned in cell G5.

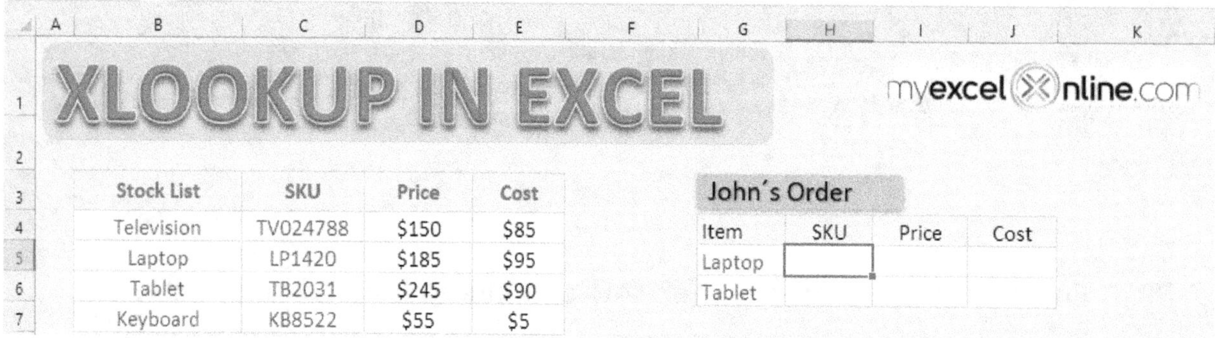

STEP 1: Select the cell containing the lookup value.

=XLOOKUP(G5

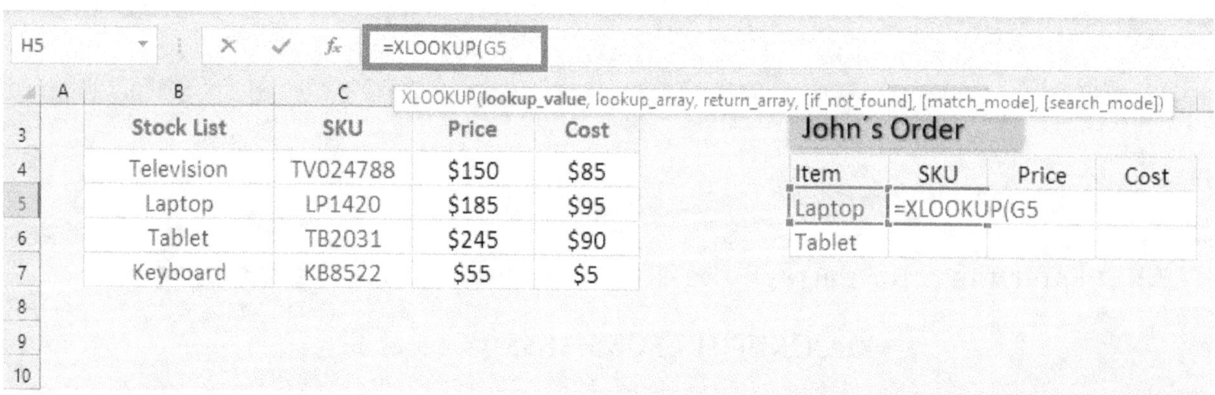

 Select the range containing the product list.

$$=XLOOKUP(G5,\$B\$4:\$B\$7$$

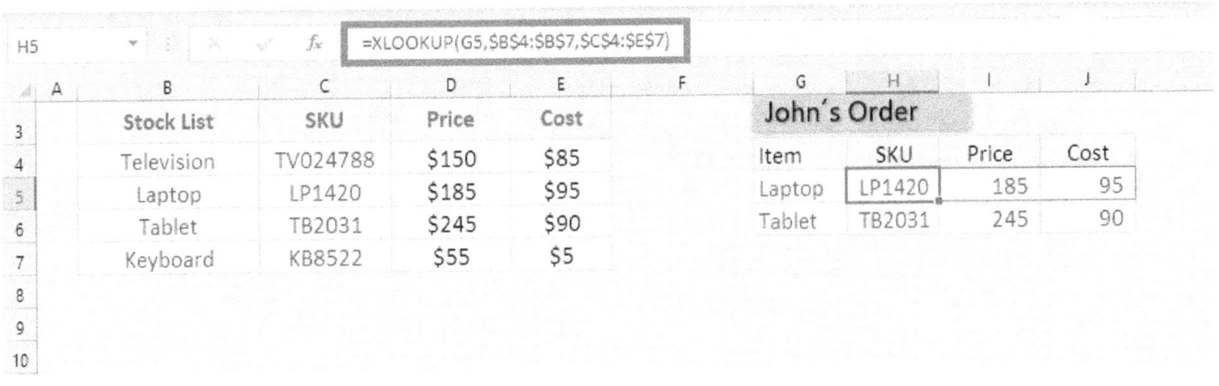

STEP 3: Select the entire range containing columns for SKU, price, and cost.

$$=XLOOKUP(G5,\$B\$4:\$B\$7,\$C\$4:\$E\$7)$$

Excel will extract or "spill" all the values with the help of the XLOOKUP formula!

Using Wildcards

Xlookup in Excel allows you to search for a partial match **using wildcards** characters like: * ? ~

This can be done using Excel VLOOKUP as well. But the problem arises when you are actually trying to search the wildcard character itself in the data.

For XLOOKUP, you can use wildcards in the **lookup_value argument** and specify that in the **[match_mode] argument**. Enter **2 as the match_mode** value to let Excel know that you are trying to do a partial match.

The three wildcards in Excel are:

- **Asterisk mark (*)** represents any number of characters. For example, Jo* could mean Joanne, John, Joe, etc.

- **Question mark (?)** represents one character. For example, Jo?n could mean John, Joan, etc.

- **Tilde (~)** can be used when you want the asterisk or question mark to not be a wildcard. Simply place a tilde just before * or ?.

In these **examples below**, you can use wildcard characters (* or ?) to search for a partial match and return the corresponding email address.

Joa* will search for the first match starting with Joa and any number of characters after that **(Joan)** and return the corresponding email address **(joan_ferguson@gmail.com)**.

$$=XLOOKUP(E5,\$B\$4:\$B\$10,\$C\$4:\$C\$10,,2)$$

Jo?n will search for the first match starting with **Jo** followed by **one character** and then **n** (John) and return the corresponding email address **(john_doe@gmail.com)**.

$$=XLOOKUP(E6,\$B\$4:\$B\$10,\$C\$4:\$C\$10,,2)$$

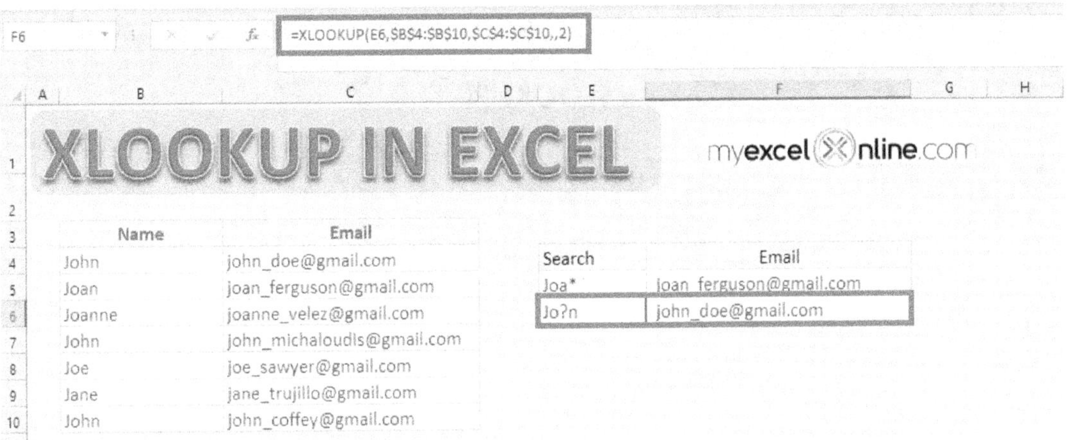

Search from bottom to top

In this example, we will **search the value from bottom to top** instead of the default direction (top to bottom). This can be achieved by **using the 6th argument of the function - [search_mode].**

It is an amazing feature if you wish to **find the last occurrence of something in your data**. Let's dive into this XLOOKUP example to learn how.

In this **example**, you have sales data with the Sales date, Product name and Price mentioned. You have to **find out the latest price at which a particular product** was sold.

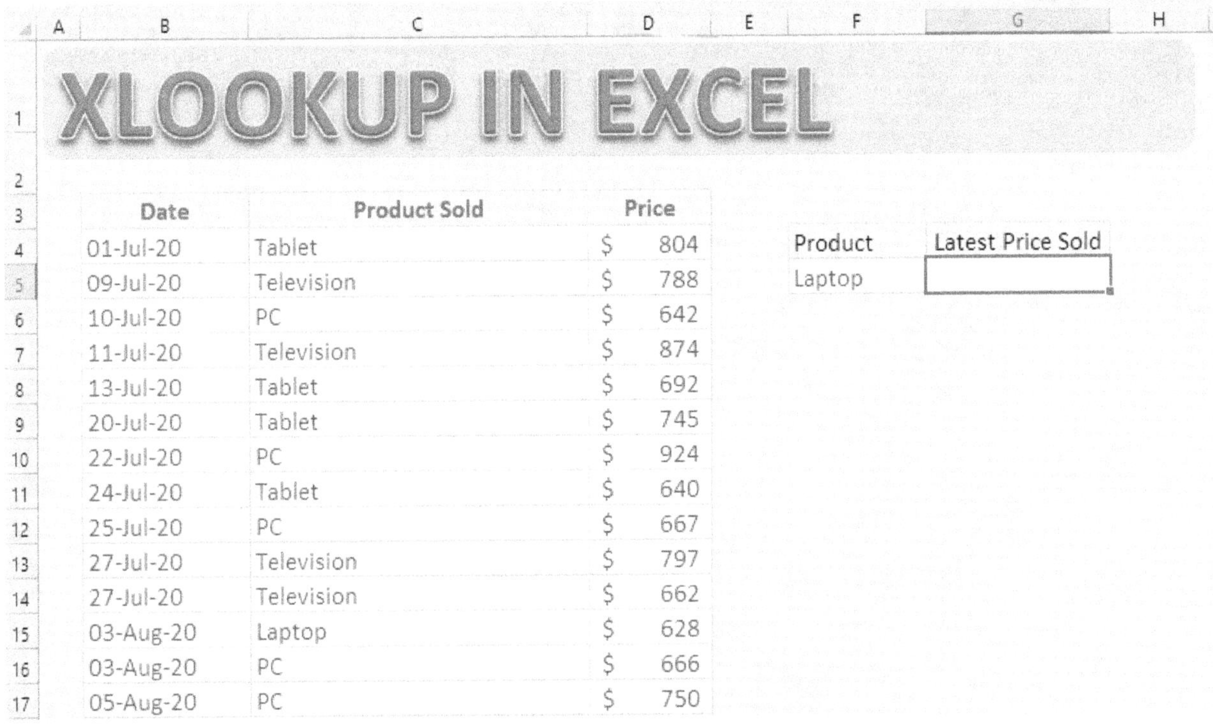

STEP 1: Enter the lookup value - the product name mentioned in cell F5.

=XLOOKUP(F5

	Date	Product Sold	Price		Product	Latest Price Sold
4	01-Jul-20	Tablet	$ 804		Laptop	=XLOOKUP(F5
5	09-Jul-20	Television	$ 788			
6	10-Jul-20	PC	$ 642			
7	11-Jul-20	Television	$ 874			
8	13-Jul-20	Tablet	$ 692			
9	20-Jul-20	Tablet	$ 745			
10	22-Jul-20	PC	$ 924			
11	24-Jul-20	Tablet	$ 640			
12	25-Jul-20	PC	$ 667			
13	27-Jul-20	Television	$ 797			
14	27-Jul-20	Television	$ 662			
15	03-Aug-20	Laptop	$ 628			

STEP 2: Enter the lookup array - the array containing the product name.

=XLOOKUP(F5,C4:C30

	Date	Product Sold	Price		Product	Latest Price Sold
4	01-Jul-20	Tablet	$ 804		Laptop	C4:C30,
5	09-Jul-20	Television	$ 788			
6	10-Jul-20	PC	$ 642			
7	11-Jul-20	Television	$ 874			
8	13-Jul-20	Tablet	$ 692			
9	20-Jul-20	Tablet	$ 745			
10	22-Jul-20	PC	$ 924			
11	24-Jul-20	Tablet	$ 640			
12	25-Jul-20	PC	$ 667			
13	27-Jul-20	Television	$ 797			
14	27-Jul-20	Television	$ 662			
15	03-Aug-20	Laptop	$ 628			
16	03-Aug-20	PC	$ 666			
17	05-Aug-20	PC	$ 750			

 Enter the return array - the array containing prices of the product.

=XLOOKUP(F5,C4:C30,D4:D30

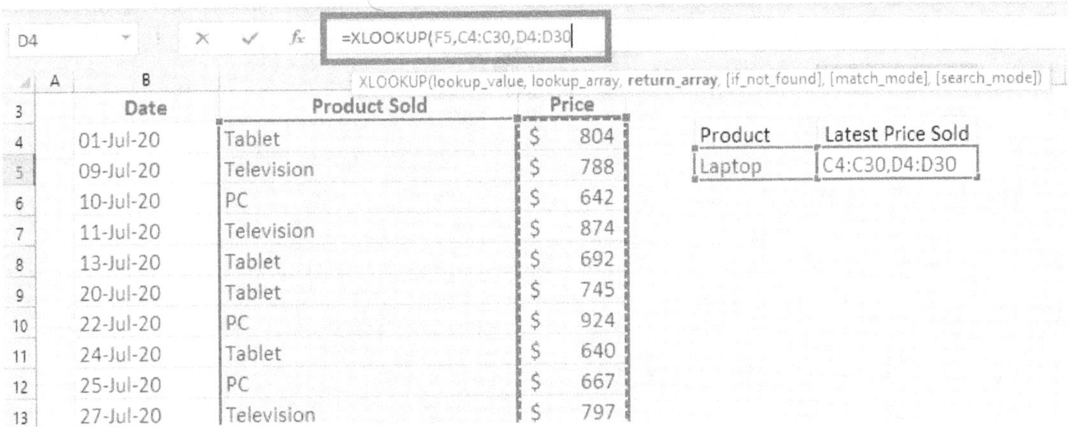

	A	B	Product Sold	Price				
		Date					Product	Latest Price Sold
3								
4		01-Jul-20	Tablet	$	804		Laptop	C4:C30,D4:D30
5		09-Jul-20	Television	$	788			
6		10-Jul-20	PC	$	642			
7		11-Jul-20	Television	$	874			
8		13-Jul-20	Tablet	$	692			
9		20-Jul-20	Tablet	$	745			
10		22-Jul-20	PC	$	924			
11		24-Jul-20	Tablet	$	640			
12		25-Jul-20	PC	$	667			
13		27-Jul-20	Television	$	797			

The formula bar shows: =XLOOKUP(F5,C4:C30,D4:D30 and the ScreenTip XLOOKUP(lookup_value, lookup_array, **return_array**, [if_not_found], [match_mode], [search_mode])

STEP 4: Enter the **6th argument [search_mode]**. It will be **-1** for this example as you want to search from bottom to top.

=XLOOKUP(F5,C4:C30,D4:D30,,,-1)

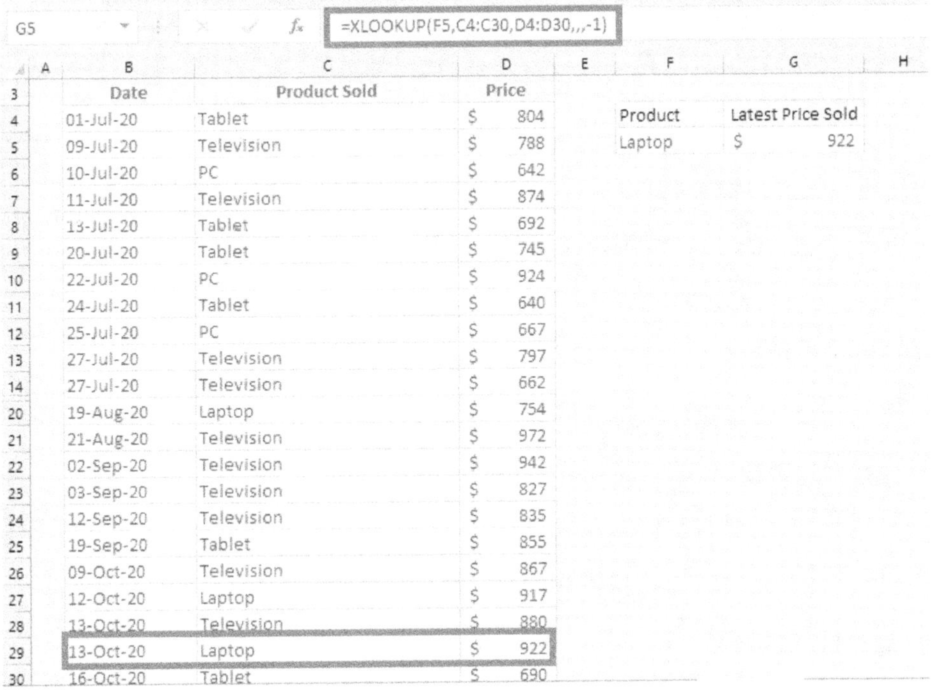

	A	B	C	D	E	F	G	H
3		Date	Product Sold	Price				
4		01-Jul-20	Tablet	$ 804		Product	Latest Price Sold	
5		09-Jul-20	Television	$ 788		Laptop	$ 922	
6		10-Jul-20	PC	$ 642				
7		11-Jul-20	Television	$ 874				
8		13-Jul-20	Tablet	$ 692				
9		20-Jul-20	Tablet	$ 745				
10		22-Jul-20	PC	$ 924				
11		24-Jul-20	Tablet	$ 640				
12		25-Jul-20	PC	$ 667				
13		27-Jul-20	Television	$ 797				
14		27-Jul-20	Television	$ 662				
20		19-Aug-20	Laptop	$ 754				
21		21-Aug-20	Television	$ 972				
22		02-Sep-20	Television	$ 942				
23		03-Sep-20	Television	$ 827				
24		12-Sep-20	Television	$ 835				
25		19-Sep-20	Tablet	$ 855				
26		09-Oct-20	Television	$ 867				
27		12-Oct-20	Laptop	$ 917				
28		13-Oct-20	Television	$ 880				
29		13-Oct-20	Laptop	$ 922				
30		16-Oct-20	Tablet	$ 690				

Excel will **start the search from the bottom** and the first match will be produced as a result!

TABLE AND PIVOT TABLE TIPS

Excel Tables: Autofill Formulas

One of the advantages of using an Excel Table is the ability to autofill a formula all the way down your data without having to copy and paste.

When you write a formula anywhere in your Excel Table, it will **automatically fill down and up** within that column.

As you add extra rows to your Excel Table, the formula fills in to the extra rows added, so you do not need to copy and paste.

How efficient is that!

This is our starting data and has been converted into an Excel Table. Our goal is to compute the **percentage of costs in our sales amount** then put it in the blank column.

CUSTOMER	REGION	ORDER DATE	SALES	COSTS	COGS
Acme, inc.	NORTH	4/13/2014	$55,815	$9,932	
Widget Corp	SOUTH	12/21/2014	$94,908	$7,859	
123 Warehousing	EAST	2/15/2014	$57,088	$18,986	
Fake Brothers	WEST	12/31/2015	$90,967	$5,033	
Demo Company	WEST	5/14/2014	$56,539	$17,276	
Smith and Co.	NORTH	6/28/2015	$63,116	$18,311	
Foo Bars	SOUTH	1/15/2015	$38,281	$1,654	
ABC Telecom	EAST	8/22/2015	$57,650	$12,982	

STEP 1: Type in this formula to get the percentage of costs in sales. We are using **IFERROR** to account for blank values.

=IFERROR([@COSTS]/[@SALES], "")

AVERAGE | × ✓ fx | =IFERROR([@COSTS]/[@SALES],"")

	CUSTOMER	REGION	ORDER DATE	SALES	COSTS	COGS
5	CUSTOMER	REGION	ORDER DATE	SALES	COSTS	COGS
6	Acme, inc.	NORTH	4/13/2014	$55,815	$9,932	=IFERROR([@COSTS]/[@SALES],"")
7	Widget Corp	SOUTH	12/21/2014	$94,908	$7,859	
8	123 Warehousing	EAST	2/15/2014	$57,088	$18,986	
9	Fake Brothers	WEST	12/31/2015	$90,967	$5,033	
10	Demo Company	WEST	5/14/2014	$56,539	$17,276	
11	Smith and Co.	NORTH	6/28/2015	$63,116	$18,311	
12	Foo Bars	SOUTH	1/15/2015	$38,281	$1,654	
13	ABC Telecom	EAST	8/22/2015	$57,650	$12,982	
14						
15						

STEP 2: Pick on any random row and notice that the formula has been applied to that as well. This is the power of using **Excel Tables** and your formula has been applied to the entire column! No more copy pasting!

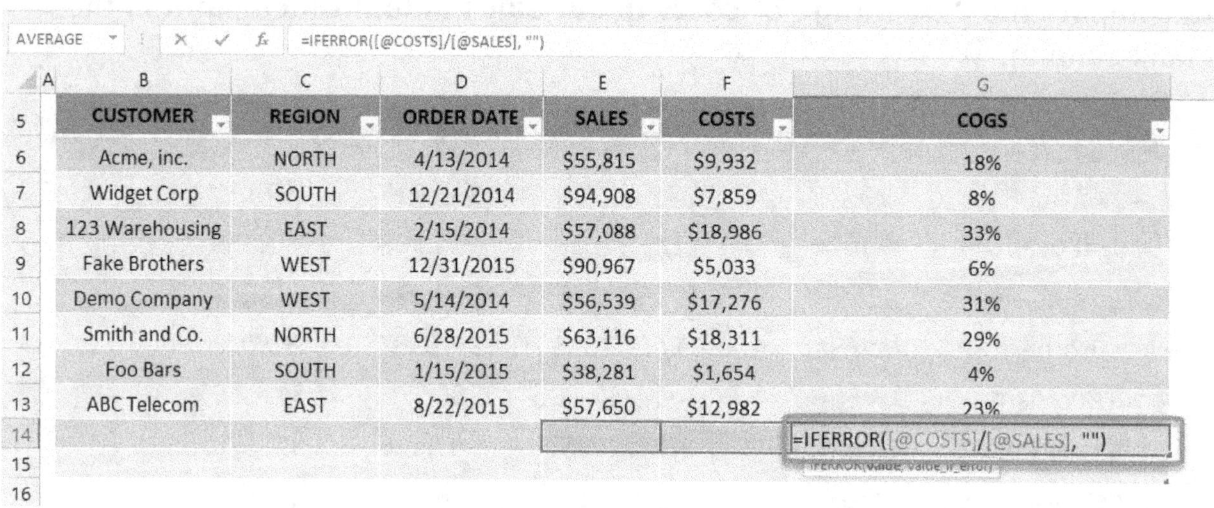

AVERAGE | × ✓ fx | =IFERROR([@COSTS]/[@SALES], "")

	CUSTOMER	REGION	ORDER DATE	SALES	COSTS	COGS
5	CUSTOMER	REGION	ORDER DATE	SALES	COSTS	COGS
6	Acme, inc.	NORTH	4/13/2014	$55,815	$9,932	18%
7	Widget Corp	SOUTH	12/21/2014	$94,908	$7,859	8%
8	123 Warehousing	EAST	2/15/2014	$57,088	$18,986	33%
9	Fake Brothers	WEST	12/31/2015	$90,967	$5,033	6%
10	Demo Company	WEST	5/14/2014	$56,539	$17,276	31%
11	Smith and Co.	NORTH	6/28/2015	$63,116	$18,311	29%
12	Foo Bars	SOUTH	1/15/2015	$38,281	$1,654	4%
13	ABC Telecom	EAST	8/22/2015	$57,650	$12,982	23%
14						=IFERROR([@COSTS]/[@SALES], "")
15						IFERROR(value, value_if_error)
16						

Excel Tables: Extra Styles

The Excel Table Styles give a user a choice of different styles ranging from Light, Medium and Dark.

There are over 50 choices depending on your favorite style or company standard but you are not only limited to those.

You have extra Table styles in the **Page Layout** tab in your Ribbon menu. Click on that and select the **Colors drop down** and you can choose from an array of combinations.

Go crazy with this to brighten up your dull data :)

STEP 1: Select anywhere in the table. Go to *Table Tools > Design > Table Styles*

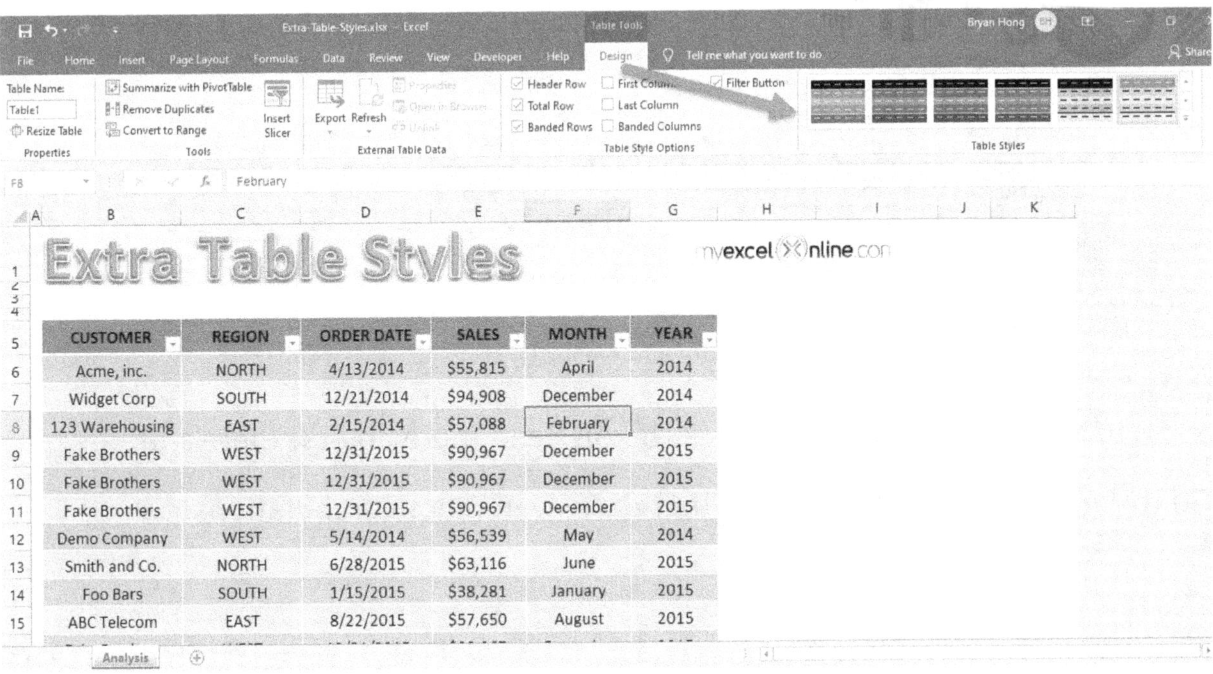

There are a lot of styles to choose from! Pick any that you prefer.

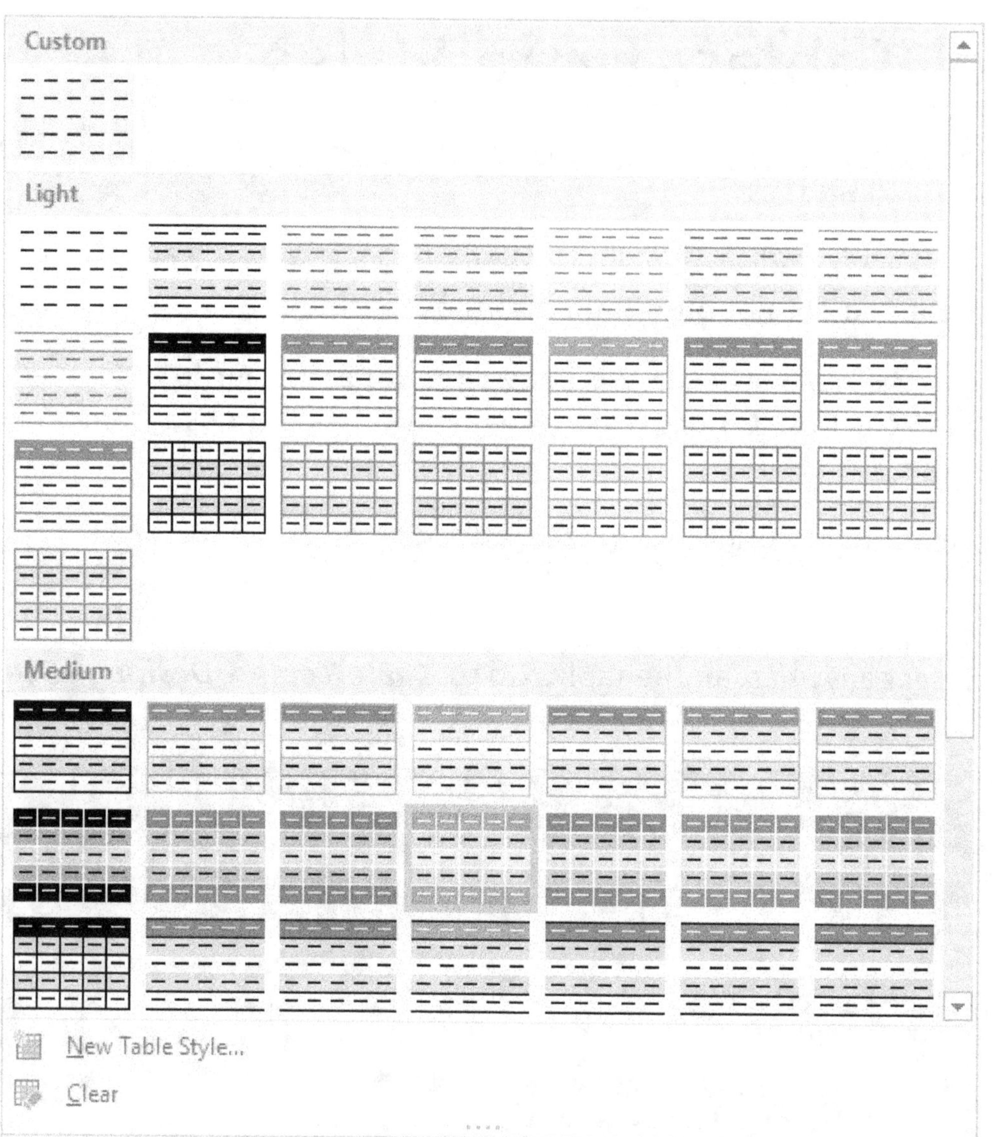

STEP 2: Now here is the magic trick, if you need more colors, there's more!

Go to **Page Layout > Colors** and there are even more combinations!

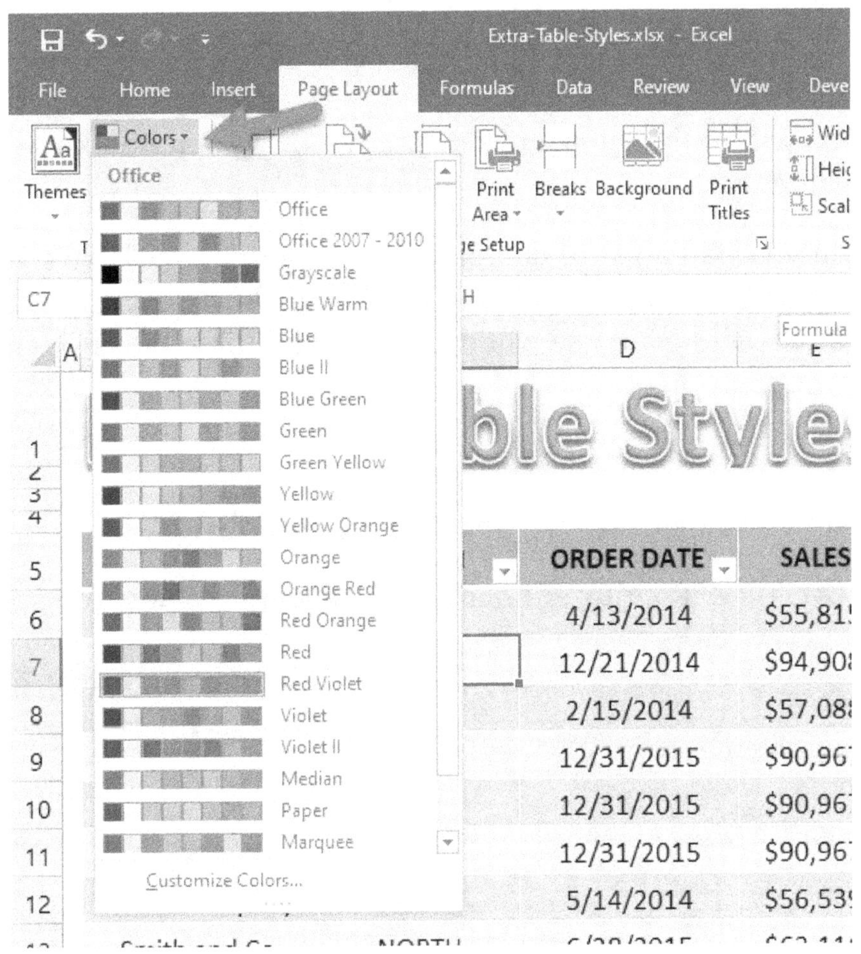

After picking one, here is the final result for the Excel Table Style!

CUSTOMER	REGION	ORDER DATE	SALES	MONTH	YEAR
Acme, inc.	NORTH	4/13/2014	$55,815	April	2014
Widget Corp	SOUTH	12/21/2014	$94,908	December	2014
123 Warehousing	EAST	2/15/2014	$57,088	February	2014
Fake Brothers	WEST	12/31/2015	$90,967	December	2015
Fake Brothers	WEST	12/31/2015	$90,967	December	2015
Fake Brothers	WEST	12/31/2015	$90,967	December	2015
Demo Company	WEST	5/14/2014	$56,539	May	2014
Smith and Co.	NORTH	6/28/2015	$63,116	June	2015
Foo Bars	SOUTH	1/15/2015	$38,281	January	2015
ABC Telecom	EAST	8/22/2015	$57,650	August	2015

Excel Tables: Filter & Search

The Search box within the Filter button is very powerful if you know how to use it to your advantage.

For example, if you had a list of customers, the Search box allows you to find specific customers by typing in a few letters only, allows you to add a selection to your filtered list and even use wildcard symbols - like the asterisk * to drill down to specific customers.

STEP 1: We will do some basic filtering to set our table up

Click on the **CUSTOMER column header** and select 2 values to display only

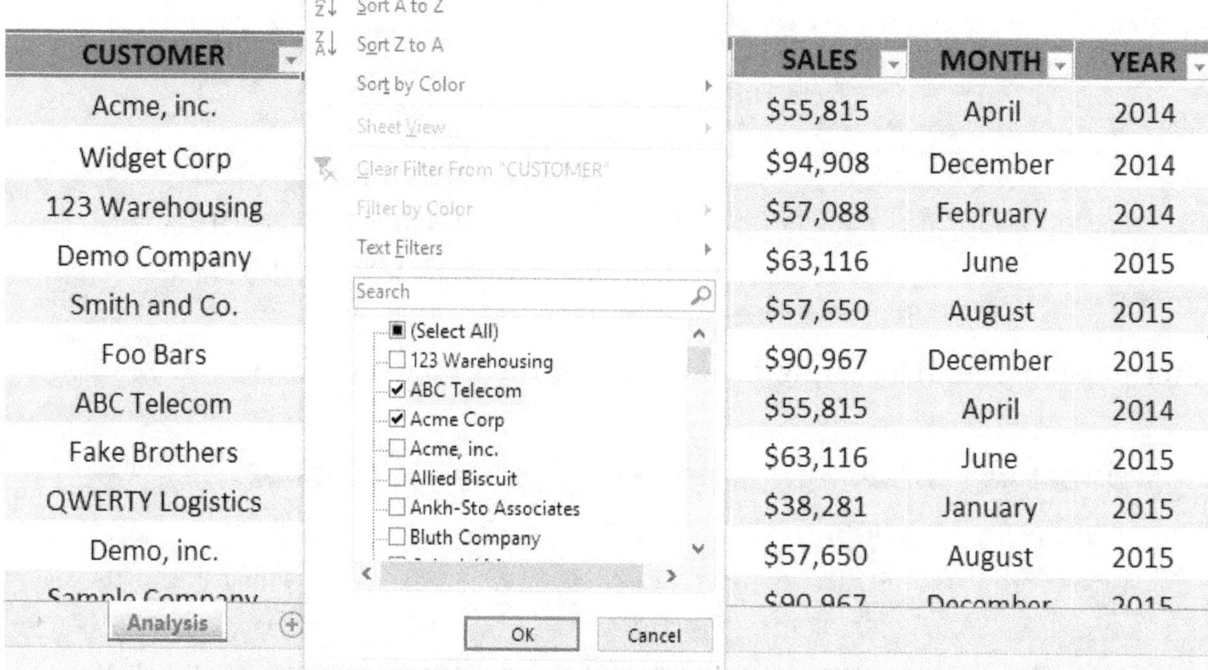

Now we have these 2 values only being displayed:

CUSTOMER	REGION	ORDER DATE	SALES	MONTH	YEAR
ABC Telecom	NORTH	4/13/2015	$55,815	April	2014
Acme Corp	NORTH	12/21/2015	$94,908	December	2014

STEP 2: Now click on the **CUSTOMER column header** and type "the" in the search box

Once you tick *Add current selection to filter,* this will include the Customers with the word "the" in the text

This will be included to your filter. Click **OK**

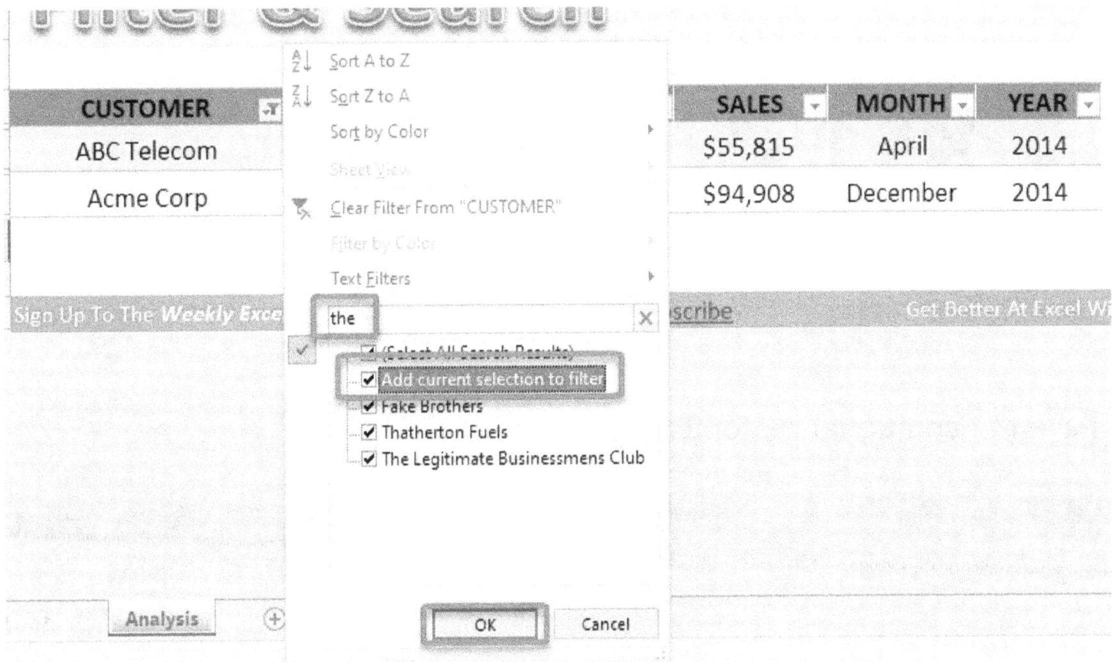

You have 3 additional customers added now:

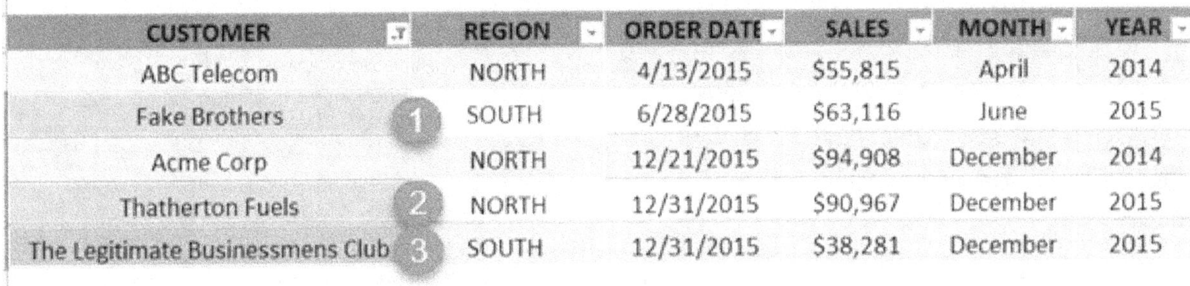

CUSTOMER	REGION	ORDER DATE	SALES	MONTH	YEAR
ABC Telecom	NORTH	4/13/2015	$55,815	April	2014
Fake Brothers	SOUTH	6/28/2015	$63,116	June	2015
Acme Corp	NORTH	12/21/2015	$94,908	December	2014
Thatherton Fuels	NORTH	12/31/2015	$90,967	December	2015
The Legitimate Businessmens Club	SOUTH	12/31/2015	$38,281	December	2015

STEP 3: Now click on the **CUSTOMER column header** and type **w*** in the search box

The **asterisk** * is a wildcard character, this means this will search for all text starting with **w** only

Once you tick *Add current selection to filter,* this will include the Customers with the letter **w** in the beginning

This will be included to your filter. Click **OK**

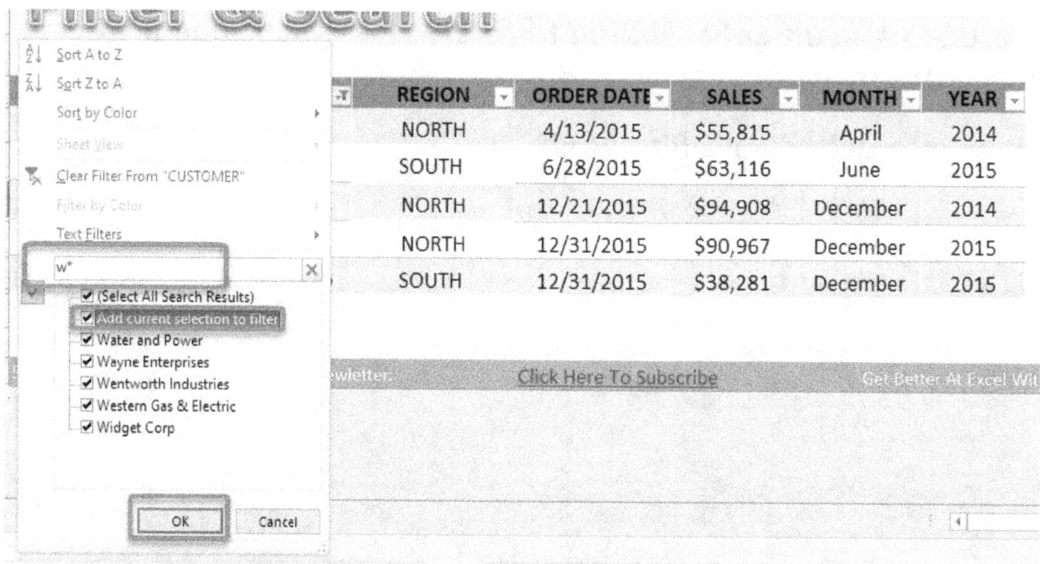

You have the additional customers added now:

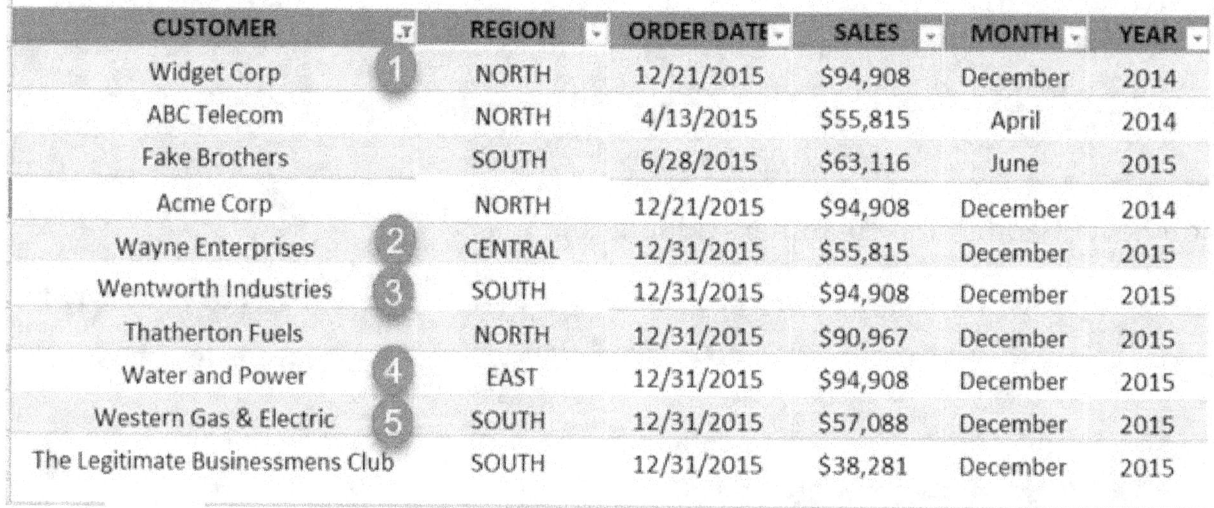

CUSTOMER	REGION	ORDER DATE	SALES	MONTH	YEAR
Widget Corp	NORTH	12/21/2015	$94,908	December	2014
ABC Telecom	NORTH	4/13/2015	$55,815	April	2014
Fake Brothers	SOUTH	6/28/2015	$63,116	June	2015
Acme Corp	NORTH	12/21/2015	$94,908	December	2014
Wayne Enterprises	CENTRAL	12/31/2015	$55,815	December	2015
Wentworth Industries	SOUTH	12/31/2015	$94,908	December	2015
Thatherton Fuels	NORTH	12/31/2015	$90,967	December	2015
Water and Power	EAST	12/31/2015	$94,908	December	2015
Western Gas & Electric	SOUTH	12/31/2015	$57,088	December	2015
The Legitimate Businessmens Club	SOUTH	12/31/2015	$38,281	December	2015

BONUS TIP: Here is an additional tip, you can also use the **question mark ?** as a wildcard character, it represents one single character. For example **m?n** could match both **man** and **men**.

Give it a try!

Excel Tables: Filter Unique Records

The **Advanced Filter** in Excel allows you to filter unique records and copy them to another location outside the data set. This is useful when you want to use a filtered list for further analysis.

Let's see how we can do this using the Advanced Filter.

 We want to create a **list of unique values** for the **REGION column.**

Go to *Data > Sort & Filter > Advanced*

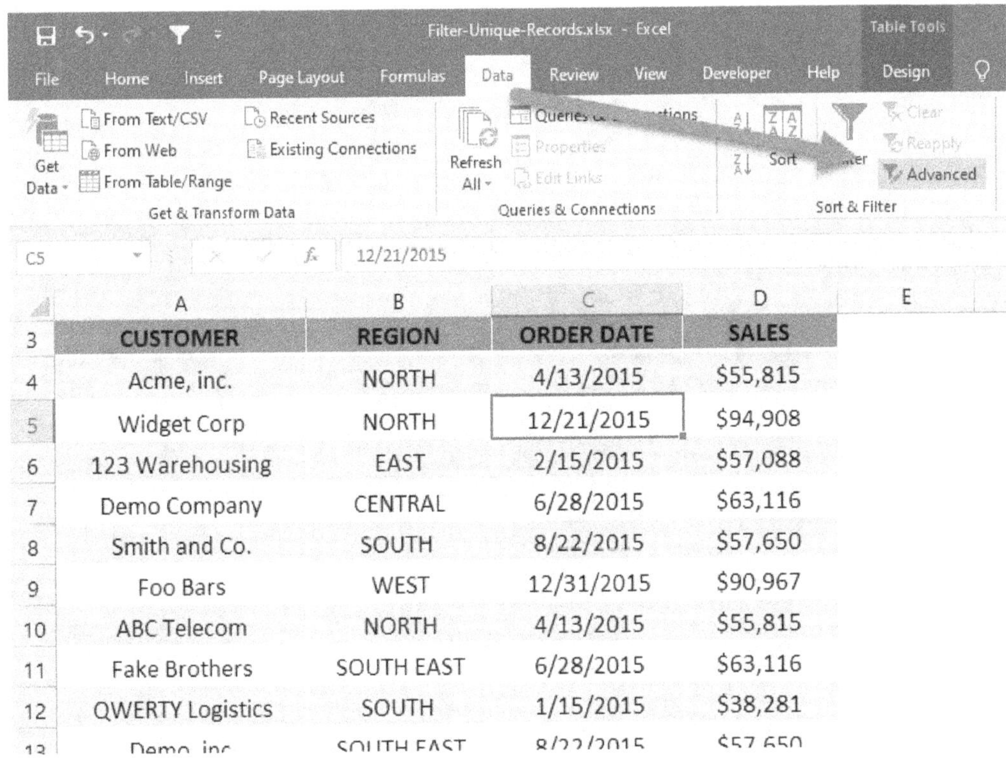

	A	B	C	D	E
3	**CUSTOMER**	**REGION**	**ORDER DATE**	**SALES**	
4	Acme, inc.	NORTH	4/13/2015	$55,815	
5	Widget Corp	NORTH	12/21/2015	$94,908	
6	123 Warehousing	EAST	2/15/2015	$57,088	
7	Demo Company	CENTRAL	6/28/2015	$63,116	
8	Smith and Co.	SOUTH	8/22/2015	$57,650	
9	Foo Bars	WEST	12/31/2015	$90,967	
10	ABC Telecom	NORTH	4/13/2015	$55,815	
11	Fake Brothers	SOUTH EAST	6/28/2015	$63,116	
12	QWERTY Logistics	SOUTH	1/15/2015	$38,281	
13	Demo, inc.	SOUTH EAST	8/22/2015	$57,650	

STEP 2: Select the following:

- **Copy to another location** - this will create the unique list on your chosen location

- **List range** - select the REGION column and include the column header

- **Copy to** - place it in a cell where you want the unique list to be generated

- **Unique records only** - make sure this is ticked to create a unique list

Click **OK**

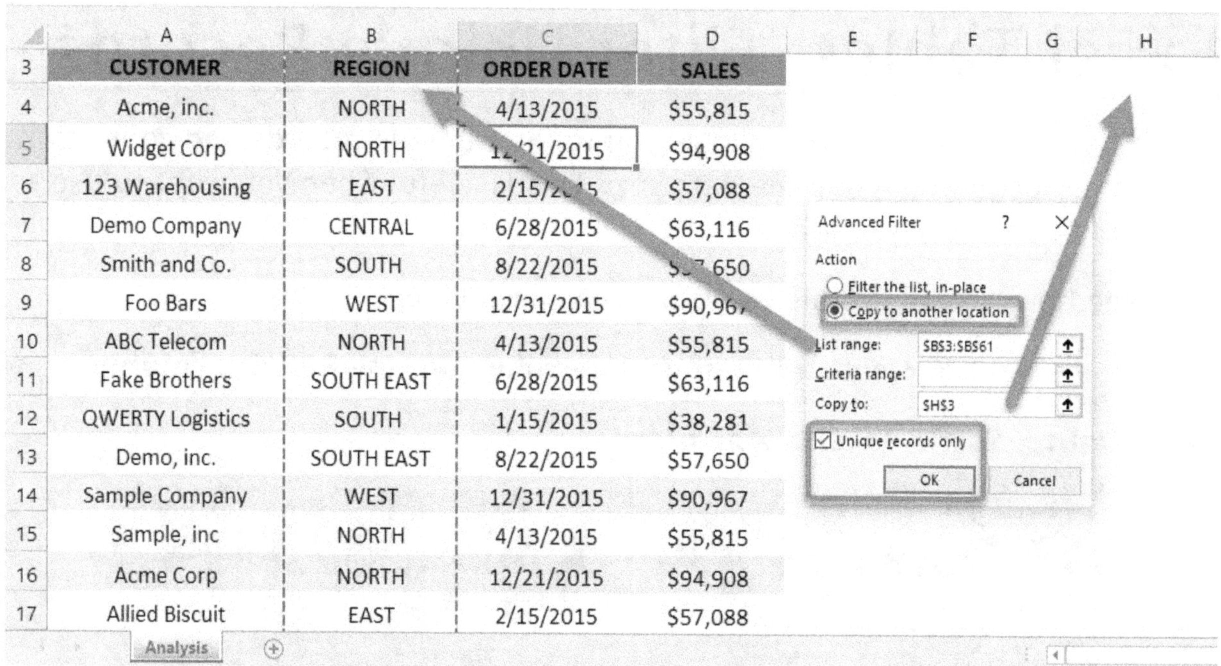

You now have your list of unique values generated!

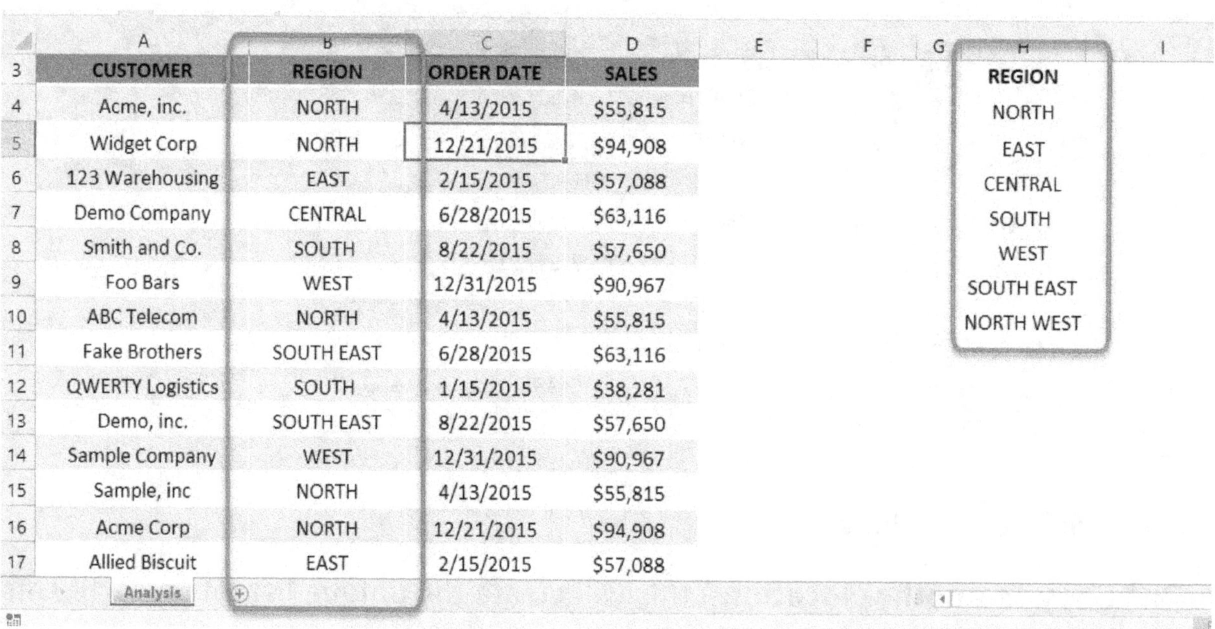

Excel Tables: Go to Blanks

The *Go To Special* tool within Excel is a must for any serious Excel user as it has an array of useful spreadsheet formatting and clean up tools.

One that I use all the time is the *Go To Special > Blanks*. This allows you to delete multiple blank rows/columns within seconds. I show you how below.

STEP 1: STEP 1: Select the entire table containing your data

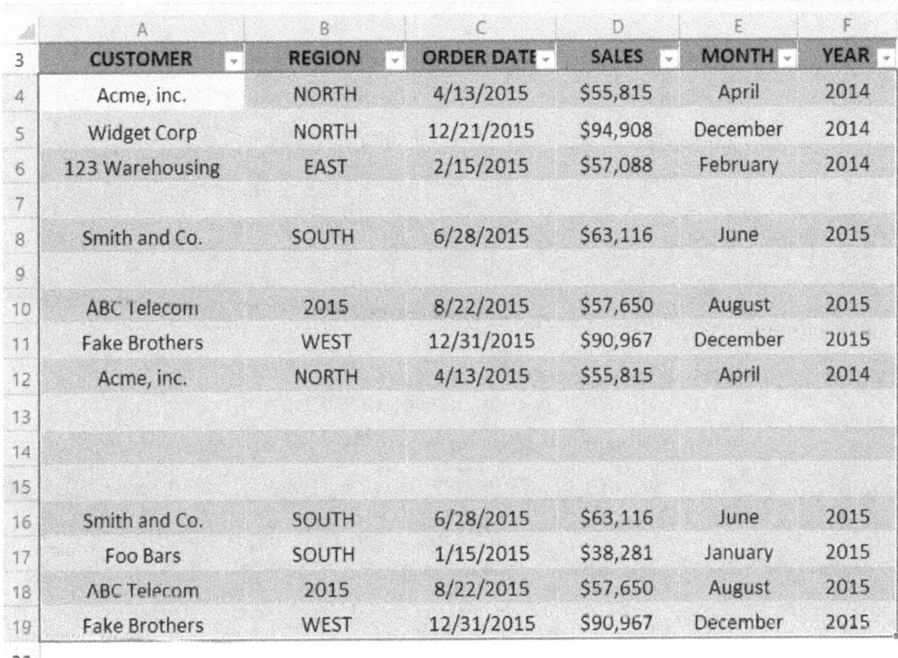

STEP 2: Press **CTRL + G** to open the **Go To Dialog**. Click **Special**

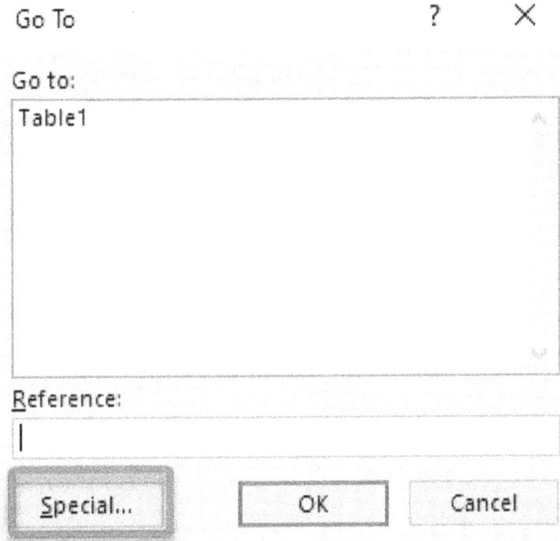

STEP 3: Select **Blanks** and click **OK**

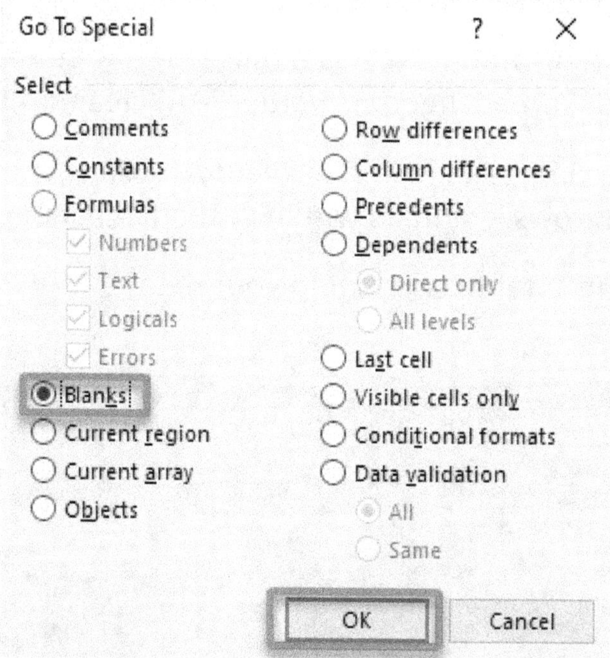

STEP 4: Now we have the blank rows selected

	A	B	C	D	E	F
3	**CUSTOMER**	**REGION**	**ORDER DATE**	**SALES**	**MONTH**	**YEAR**
4	Acme, inc.	NORTH	4/13/2015	$55,815	April	2014
5	Widget Corp	NORTH	12/21/2015	$94,908	December	2014
6	123 Warehousing	EAST	2/15/2015	$57,088	February	2014
7						
8	Smith and Co.	SOUTH	6/28/2015	$63,116	June	2015
9						
10	ABC Telecom	2015	8/22/2015	$57,650	August	2015
11	Fake Brothers	WEST	12/31/2015	$90,967	December	2015
12	Acme, inc.	NORTH	4/13/2015	$55,815	April	2014
13						
14						
15						
16	Smith and Co.	SOUTH	6/28/2015	$63,116	June	2015
17	Foo Bars	SOUTH	1/15/2015	$38,281	January	2015
18	ABC Telecom	2015	8/22/2015	$57,650	August	2015
19	Fake Brothers	WEST	12/31/2015	$90,967	December	2015

Right click on a blank row, and go to ***Delete > Table Rows***

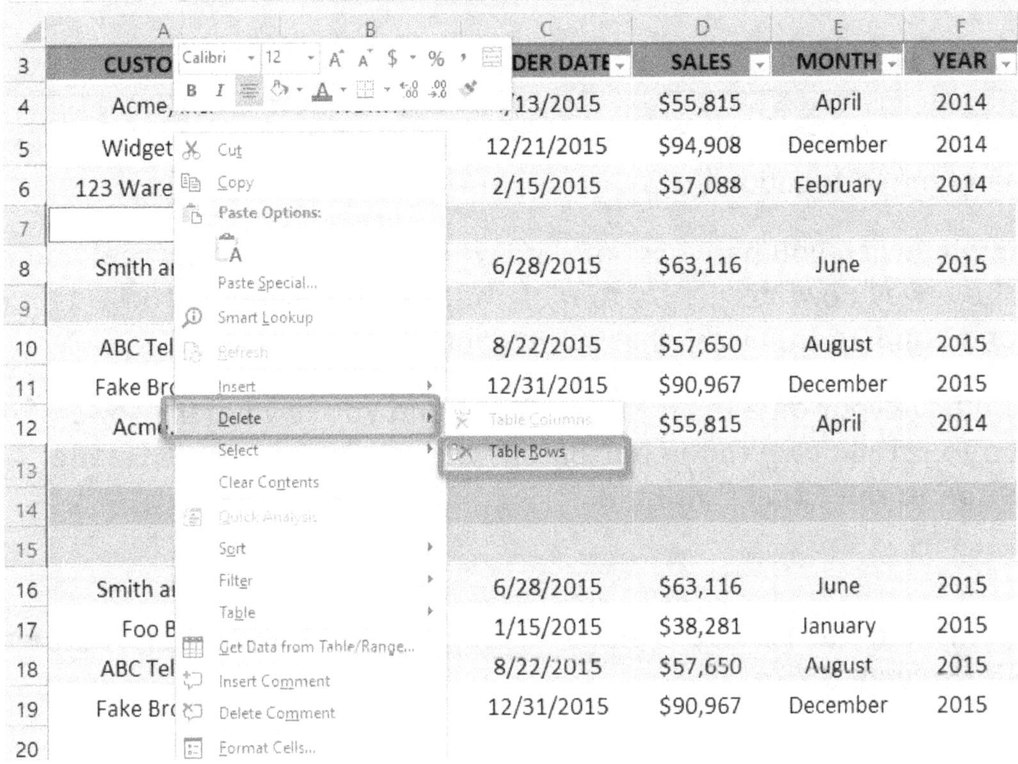

Now your blank rows are now deleted in a blink of an eye!

	A	B	C	D	E	F
3	CUSTOMER	REGION	ORDER DATE	SALES	MONTH	YEAR
4	Acme, inc.	NORTH	4/13/2015	$55,815	April	2014
5	Widget Corp	NORTH	12/21/2015	$94,908	December	2014
6	123 Warehousing	EAST	2/15/2015	$57,088	February	2014
7	Smith and Co.	SOUTH	6/28/2015	$63,116	June	2015
8	ABC Telecom	2015	8/22/2015	$57,650	August	2015
9	Fake Brothers	WEST	12/31/2015	$90,967	December	2015
10	Acme, inc.	NORTH	4/13/2015	$55,815	April	2014
11	Smith and Co.	SOUTH	6/28/2015	$63,116	June	2015
12	Foo Bars	SOUTH	1/15/2015	$38,281	January	2015
13	ABC Telecom	2015	8/22/2015	$57,650	August	2015
14	Fake Brothers	WEST	12/31/2015	$90,967	December	2015

Excel Tables: Headers Show in Columns

Before *Excel Tables* were introduced in Excel 2007, there were *Excel Lists* which had limited functionality.

For example, when you had a list of data with hundreds of rows and you had to scroll all the way down to the bottom of your list, the Headers row was not visible and you had to guess what some columns related to.

When you have your data in an *Excel Table* and you have many rows of data and need to scroll down to the bottom of your Excel Table, the **Header names stay visible in the Excel Columns.**

STEP 1: This is our Excel Table. Have a look of the **Table Header values** then **scroll all the way down**.

CUSTOMER	REGION	ORDER DATE	SALES	MONTH	YEAR
Acme, inc.	NORTH	4/13/2014	$55,815	April	2014
Widget Corp	SOUTH	12/21/2014	$94,908	December	2014
123 Warehousing	EAST	2/15/2014	$57,088	February	2014
Demo Company	WEST	5/14/2014	$56,539	May	2014
Smith and Co.	NORTH	6/28/2015	$63,116	June	2015
Foo Bars	SOUTH	1/15/2015	$38,281	January	2015
ABC Telecom	EAST	8/22/2015	$57,650	August	2015
Fake Brothers	WEST	12/31/2015	$90,967	December	2015
Fake Brothers	WEST	12/31/2015	$90,967	December	2015
Total	9	2/6/2015	$605,331		

	CUSTOMER	REGION	ORDER DATE	SALES	MONTH	YEAR
7	Demo Company	WEST	5/14/2014	$56,539	May	2014
8	Smith and Co.	NORTH	6/28/2015	$63,116	June	2015
9	Foo Bars	SOUTH	1/15/2015	$38,281	January	2015
10	ABC Telecom	EAST	8/22/2015	$57,650	August	2015
11	Fake Brothers	WEST	12/31/2015	$90,967	December	2015
12	Fake Brothers	WEST	12/31/2015	$90,967	December	2015
13	**Total**	**9**	**2/6/2015**	**$605,331**		
14						
15						

Excel Tables: How to Insert

Excel Tables are very powerful and have many advantages when using them. You should start using them asap regardless of the size of your data set, as their benefits are HUUUGE:

- Structured referencing;

- Many different built in **Table Styles** with color formatting;

- Use of a **Total Row** which uses built in functions to calculate the contents of a particular column;

- Drop down lists that allows you to Sort & Filter;

- When you scroll down from the Table, its Headers replace the Column Letters in the worksheet;

- Remove Duplicate Rows automatically;

- Summarize the Table with a **Pivot Table**;

- Supports calculated Columns so you can create dynamic formulas outside the Table;

STEP 1: Select a cell in your table

CUSTOMER	REGION	ORDER DATE	SALES	MONTH	YEAR
Acme, inc.	NORTH	2014-04-13	$55,815	April	2014
Widget Corp	SOUTH	2014-12-21	$94,908	December	2014
123 Warehousing	EAST	2014-02-15	$57,088	February	2014
Demo Company	WEST	2014-05-14	$56,539	May	2014
Smith and Co.	NORTH	2015-06-28	$63,116	June	2015
Foo Bars	SOUTH	2015-01-15	$38,281	January	2015
ABC Telecom	EAST	2015-08-22	$57,650	August	2015
Fake Brothers	WEST	2015-12-31	$90,967	December	2015

STEP 2: Let us insert our table! To do that press **Ctrl + T** or go to *Insert > Table:*

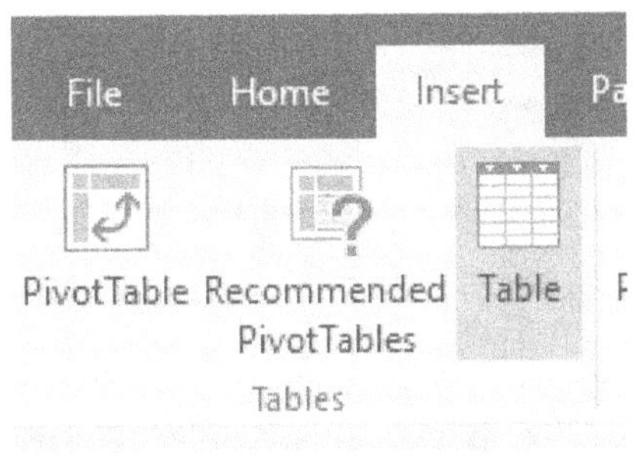

STEP 3: Click **OK.**

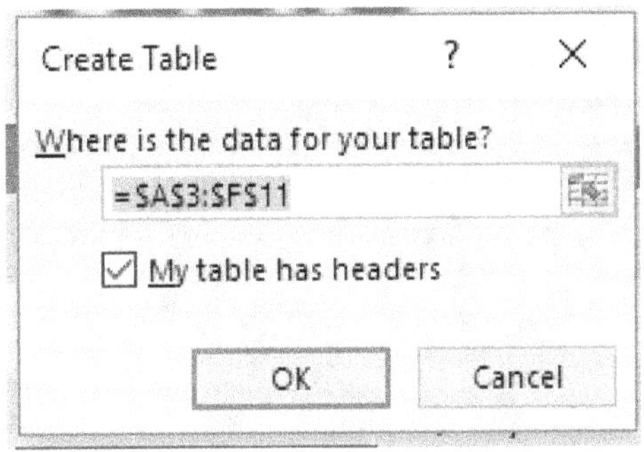

Your cool table is now ready!

CUSTOMER	REGION	ORDER DATE	SALES	MONTH	YEAR
Acme, inc.	NORTH	2014-04-13	$55,815	April	2014
Widget Corp	SOUTH	2014-12-21	$94,908	December	2014
123 Warehousing	EAST	2014-02-15	$57,088	February	2014
Demo Company	WEST	2014-05-14	$56,539	May	2014
Smith and Co.	NORTH	2015-06-28	$63,116	June	2015
Foo Bars	SOUTH	2015-01-15	$38,281	January	2015
ABC Telecom	EAST	2015-08-22	$57,650	August	2015
Fake Brothers	WEST	2015-12-31	$90,967	December	2015

Excel Tables: Remove Duplicates

When you have duplicates values within your Excel Table there is a quick and easy way to remove those values.

The duplicate values could be all over your Excel Table and sometimes it takes valuable time trying to locate those duplicates and then deleting them.

Not to worry, Remove Duplicates to the rescue!

STEP 1: Click inside your **Excel Table** and select *Table Tools > Design > Remove Duplicates*

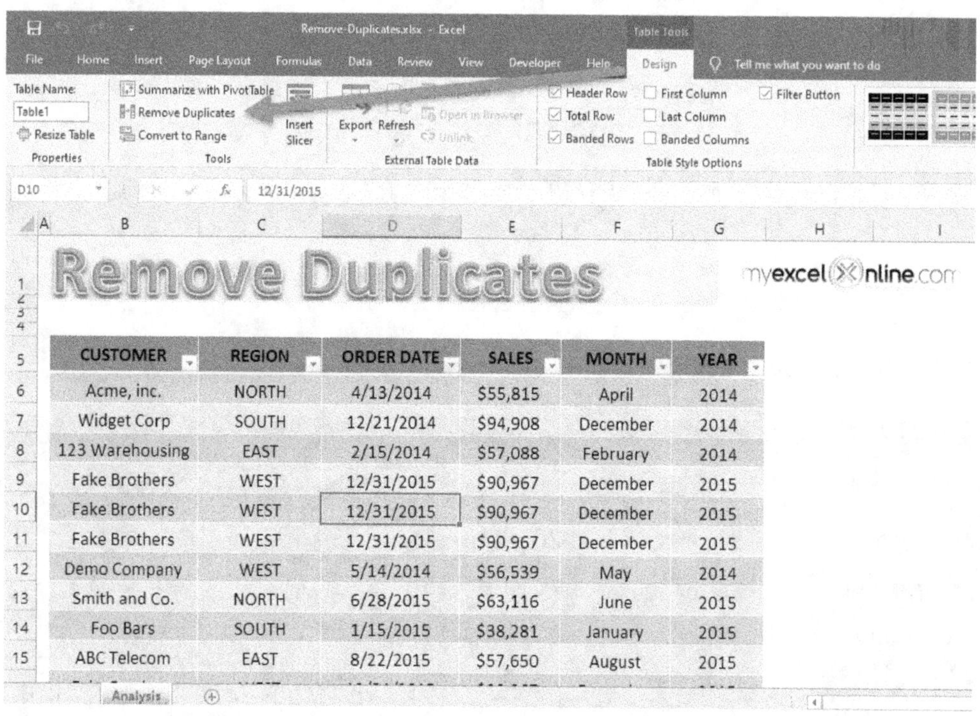

STEP 2: This will bring up the Remove Duplicates dialog box. **Select only the Columns box that contains the duplicates** that you want to remove and press **OK**

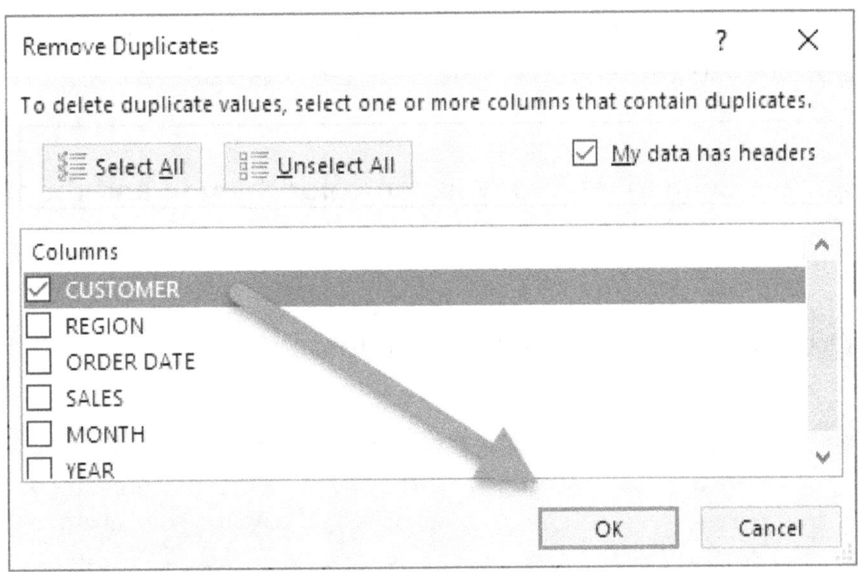

Your duplicates are now removed from the CUSTOMER column!

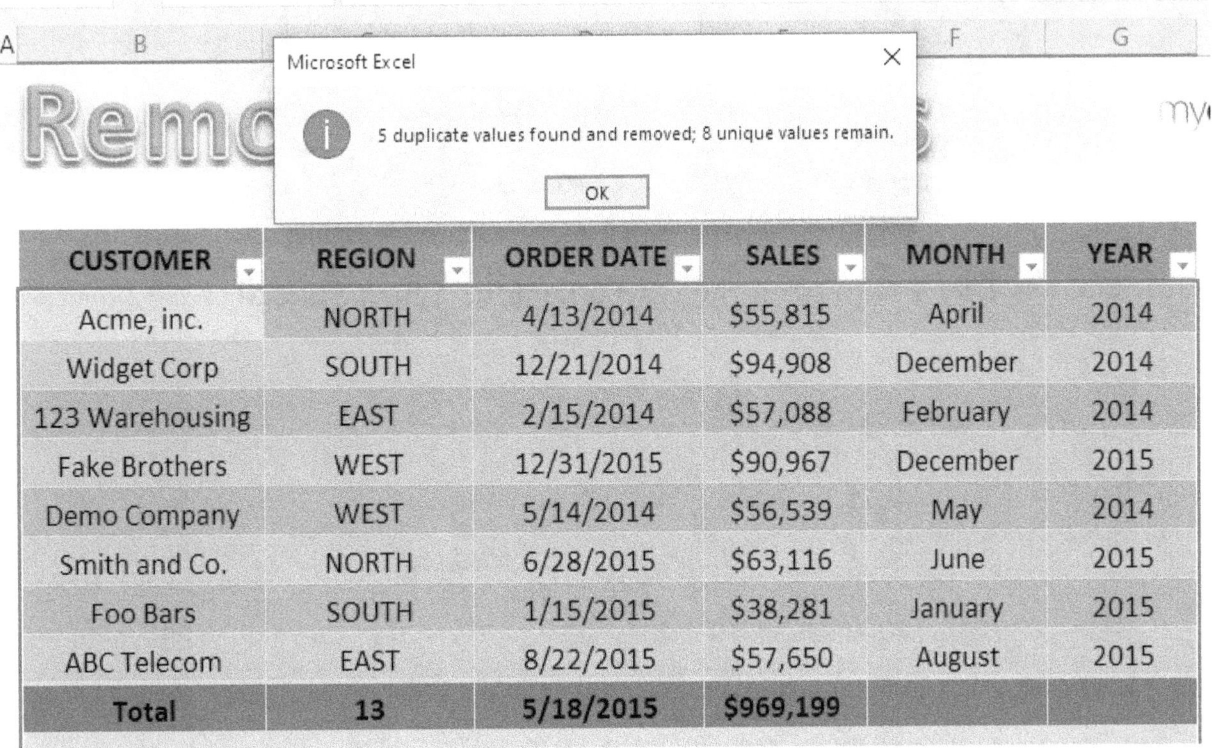

CUSTOMER	REGION	ORDER DATE	SALES	MONTH	YEAR
Acme, inc.	NORTH	4/13/2014	$55,815	April	2014
Widget Corp	SOUTH	12/21/2014	$94,908	December	2014
123 Warehousing	EAST	2/15/2014	$57,088	February	2014
Fake Brothers	WEST	12/31/2015	$90,967	December	2015
Demo Company	WEST	5/14/2014	$56,539	May	2014
Smith and Co.	NORTH	6/28/2015	$63,116	June	2015
Foo Bars	SOUTH	1/15/2015	$38,281	January	2015
ABC Telecom	EAST	8/22/2015	$57,650	August	2015
Total	13	5/18/2015	$969,199		

Excel Tables: Row Differences

If you have two rows that you want to compare, for example, sale amount versus amount paid, you can easily filter the differences between these two columns by going in to the ***Find & Select > Go To Special > Row Differences***.

Once the cells have been identified, you can color them in and then filter to see each transaction.

STEP 1: Select the rows that you want to compare

	CUSTOMER	REGION	ORDER DATE	INVOICED	PAID
4	Acme, inc.	NORTH	4/13/2015	$55,815	$55,815
5	Widget Corp	NORTH	12/21/2015	$94,908	$94,908
6	123 Warehousing	EAST	2/15/2015	$57,088	$57,000
7	Smith and Co.	SOUTH	6/28/2015	$63,116	$63,116
8	ABC Telecom	2015	8/22/2015	$57,650	$50,000
9	Fake Brothers	WEST	12/31/2015	$90,967	$95,600
10	Acme, inc.	NORTH	4/13/2015	$55,815	$55,815
11	Smith and Co.	SOUTH	6/28/2015	$63,116	$63,000
12	Foo Bars	SOUTH	1/15/2015	$38,281	$38,281
13	ABC Telecom	2015	8/22/2015	$57,650	$57,650
14	Fake Brothers	WEST	12/31/2015	$90,967	$45,415

STEP 2: Press ***Ctrl + G*** to open the **Go To Dialog.** Select **Special**

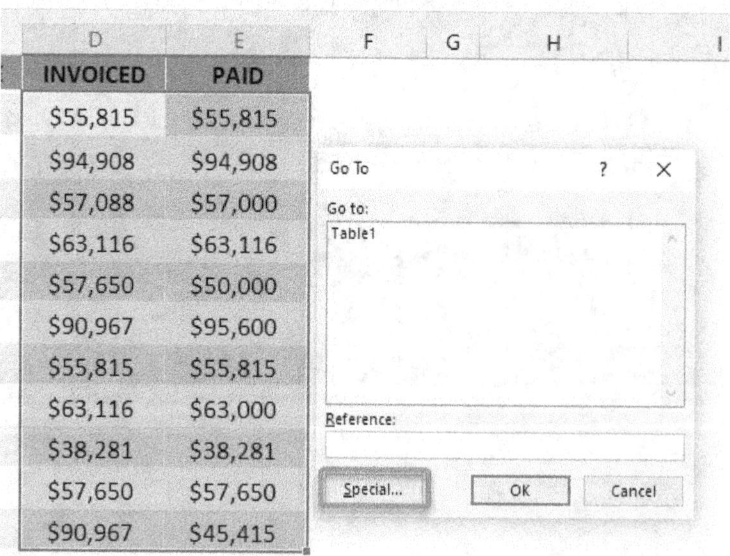

STEP 3: Select **Row Differences** and click **OK**.

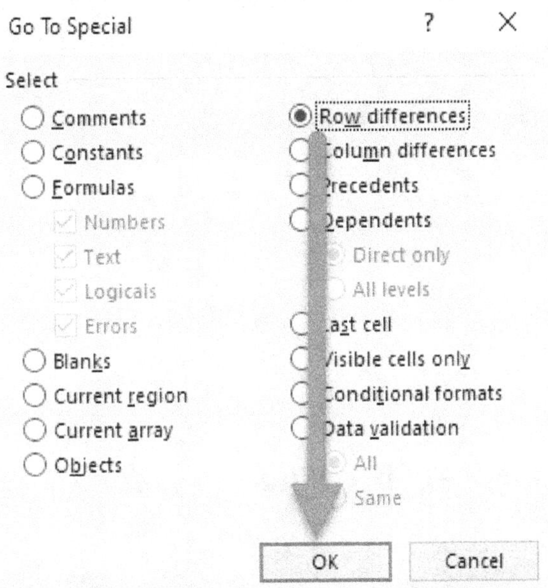

STEP 4: Color the selected cells

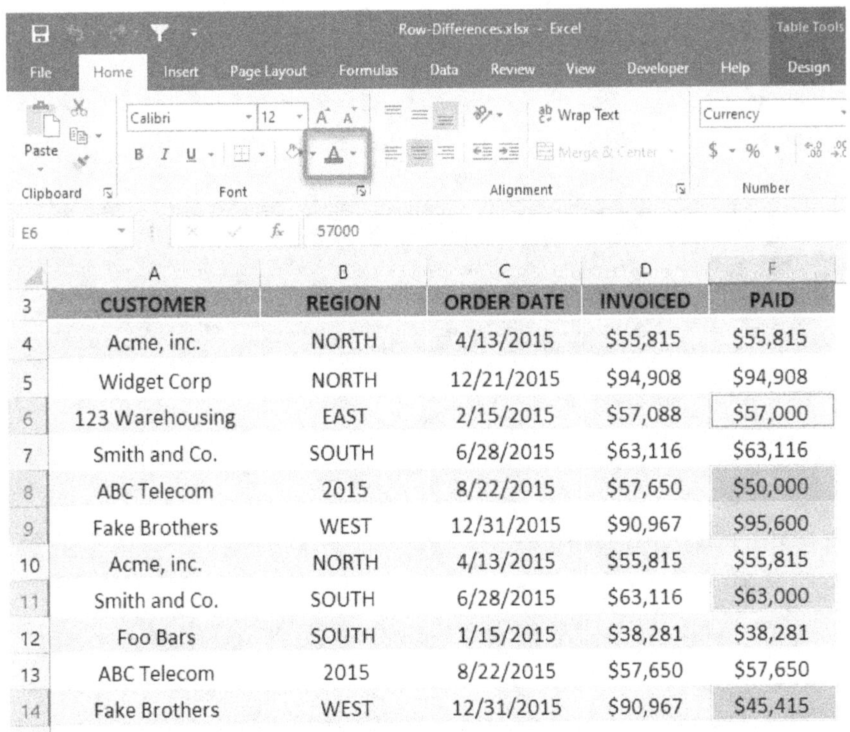

STEP 5: Now let's filter and leave these rows! Go to **Home > Sort & Filter > Filter**

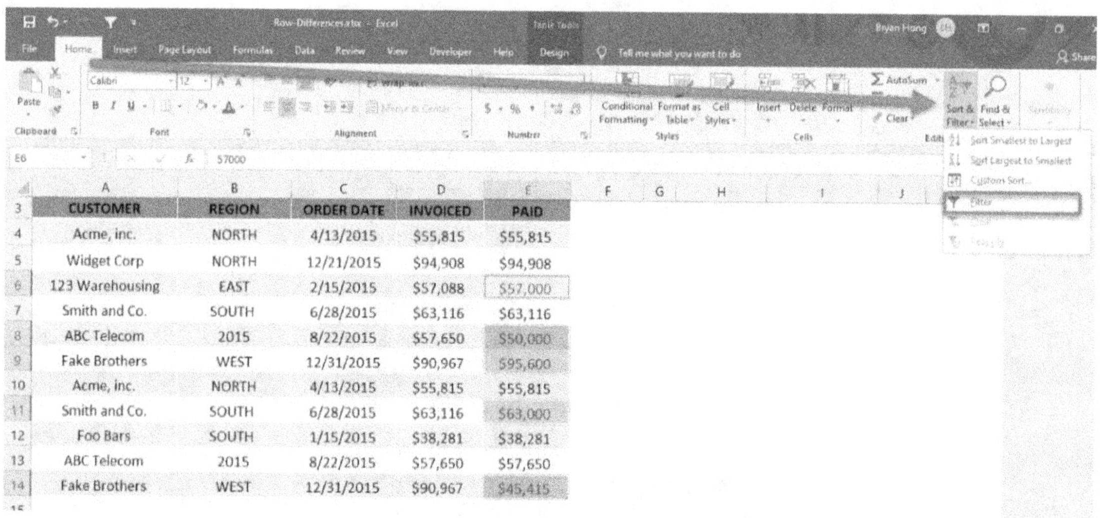

STEP 6: Go to *Paid Column Filter > Filter by Color > Red Color*

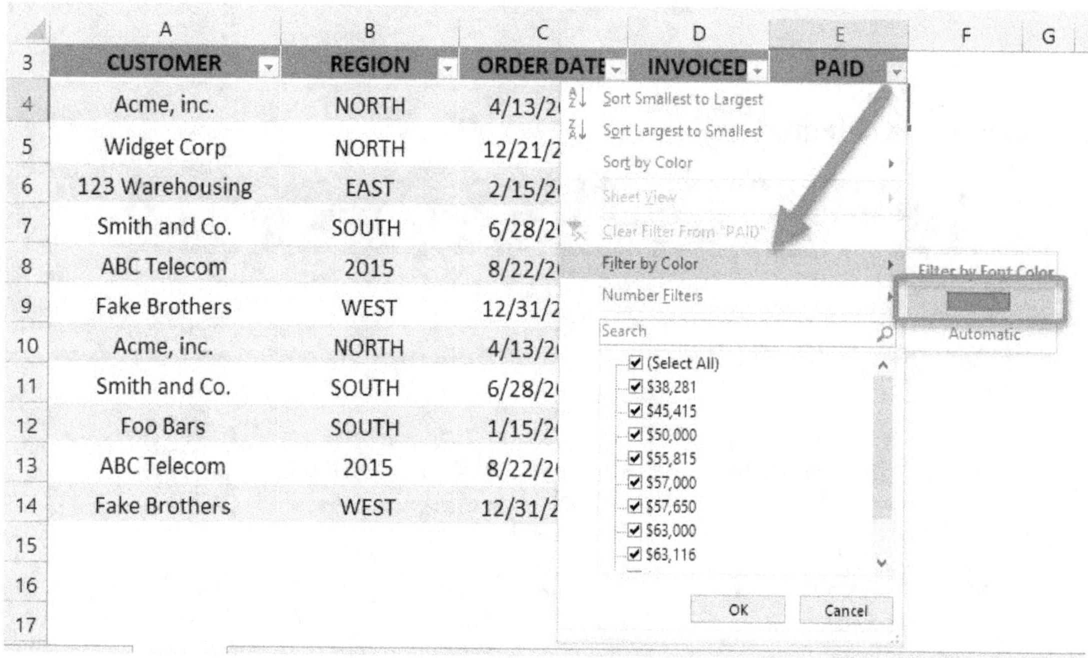

Now you have your row differences!

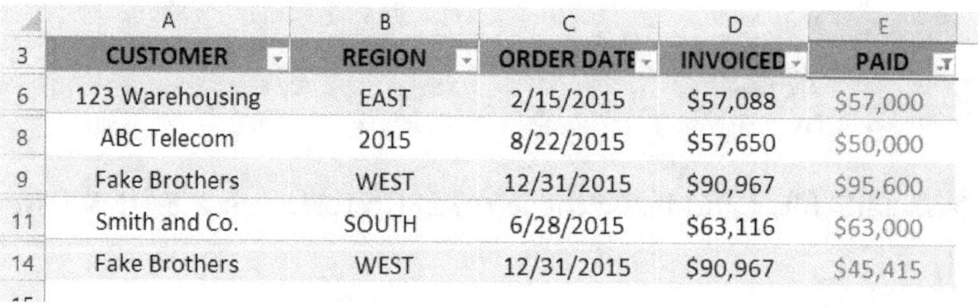

Excel Tables: Slicers

Slicers were introduced with Pivot Tables in Excel 2010 and they allow us to select items to filter with beautiful interactive buttons.

You can see the power of Slicers and the different ways you can format them in these posts: https://www.myexcelonline.com/category/pivot-tables/slicers/

In Excel 2013, Slicers were introduced in Excel Tables!

To insert a Slicer in an Excel Table you have to follow these short steps:

STEP 1: Click inside the Excel Table

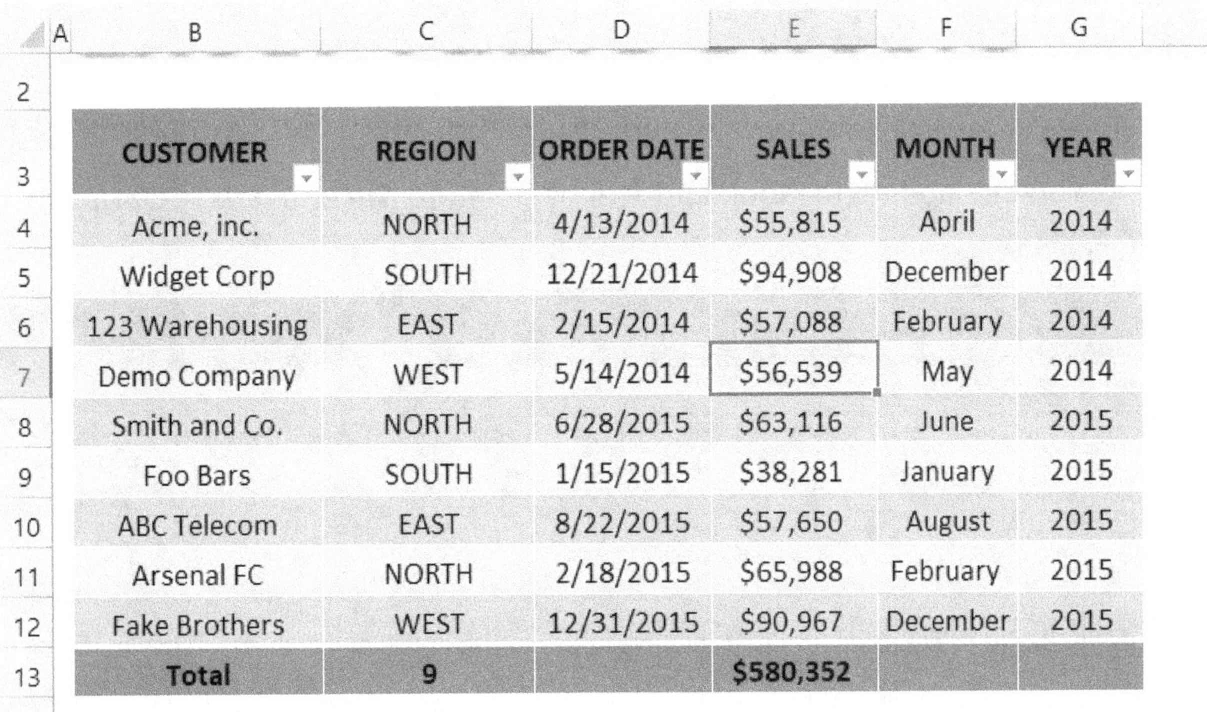

CUSTOMER	REGION	ORDER DATE	SALES	MONTH	YEAR
Acme, inc.	NORTH	4/13/2014	$55,815	April	2014
Widget Corp	SOUTH	12/21/2014	$94,908	December	2014
123 Warehousing	EAST	2/15/2014	$57,088	February	2014
Demo Company	WEST	5/14/2014	$56,539	May	2014
Smith and Co.	NORTH	6/28/2015	$63,116	June	2015
Foo Bars	SOUTH	1/15/2015	$38,281	January	2015
ABC Telecom	EAST	8/22/2015	$57,650	August	2015
Arsenal FC	NORTH	2/18/2015	$65,988	February	2015
Fake Brothers	WEST	12/31/2015	$90,967	December	2015
Total	9		$580,352		

STEP 2: Select *Table Tools > Design > Insert Slicer*

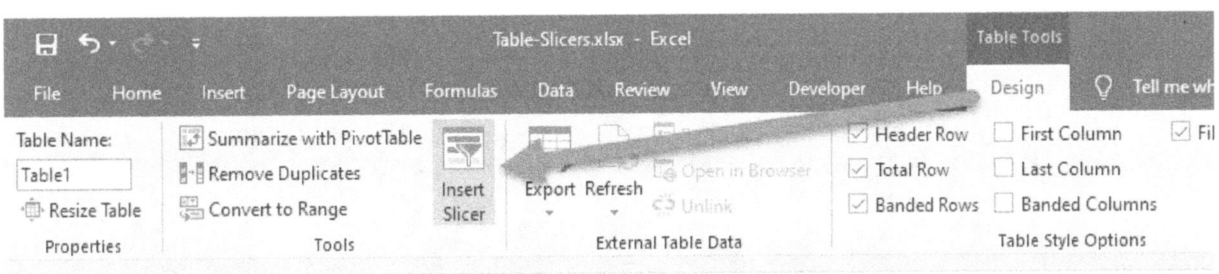

 Tick the Table Headers that you want to include in your Slicer and press **OK**

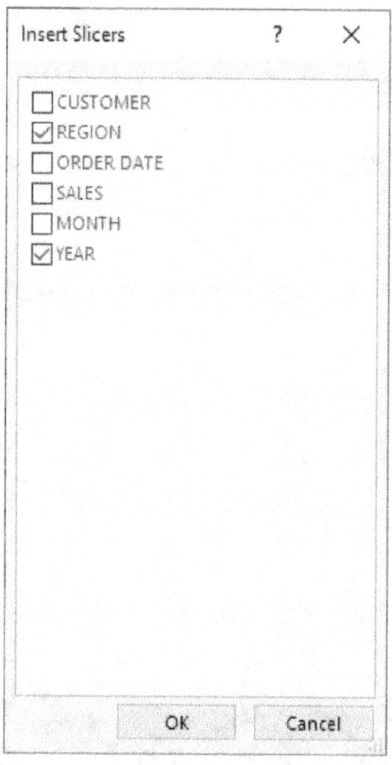

STEP 4: You can update the look and feel by going to *Slicer Tools > Options > Slicer Styles*

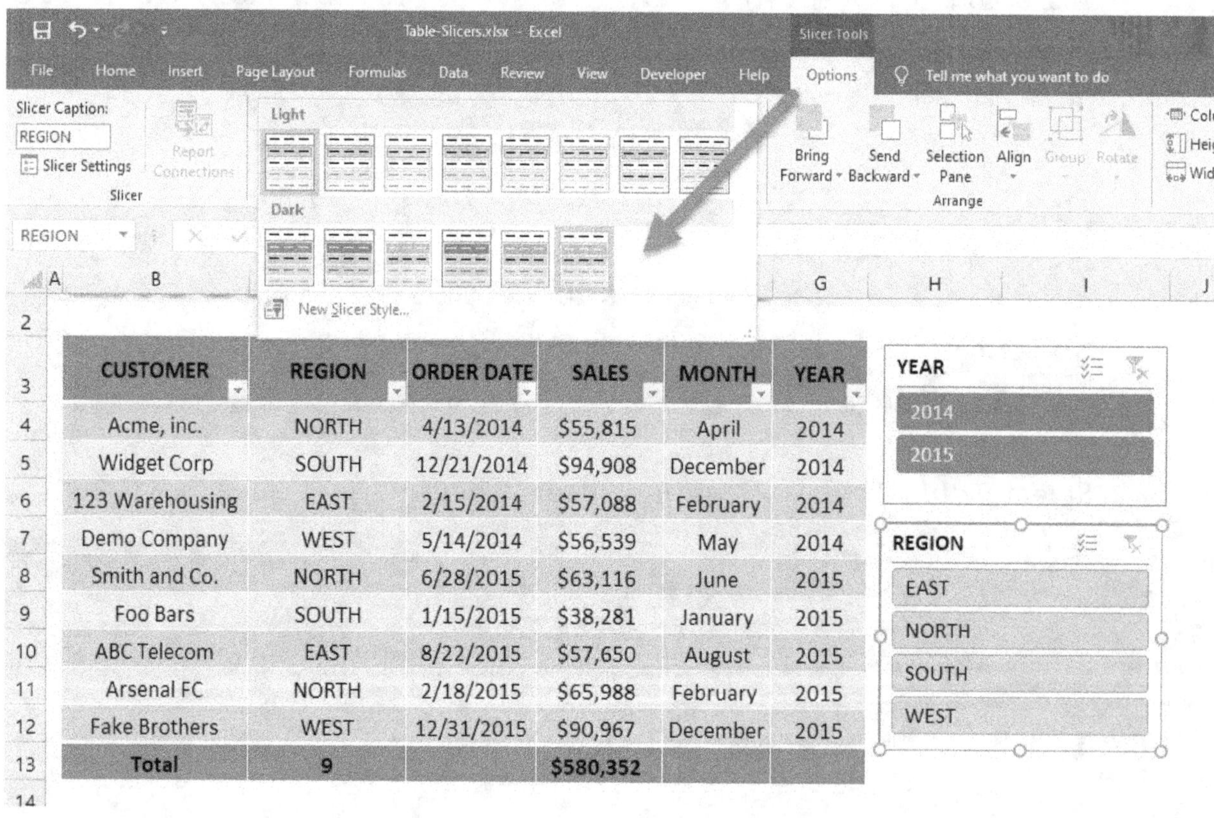

CUSTOMER	REGION	ORDER DATE	SALES	MONTH	YEAR
Acme, inc.	NORTH	4/13/2014	$55,815	April	2014
Widget Corp	SOUTH	12/21/2014	$94,908	December	2014
123 Warehousing	EAST	2/15/2014	$57,088	February	2014
Demo Company	WEST	5/14/2014	$56,539	May	2014
Smith and Co.	NORTH	6/28/2015	$63,116	June	2015
Foo Bars	SOUTH	1/15/2015	$38,281	January	2015
ABC Telecom	EAST	8/22/2015	$57,650	August	2015
Arsenal FC	NORTH	2/18/2015	$65,988	February	2015
Fake Brothers	WEST	12/31/2015	$90,967	December	2015
Total	9		$580,352		

Click on the Slicer buttons and see how your Excel Table gets filtered without needing to select the filter drop down.

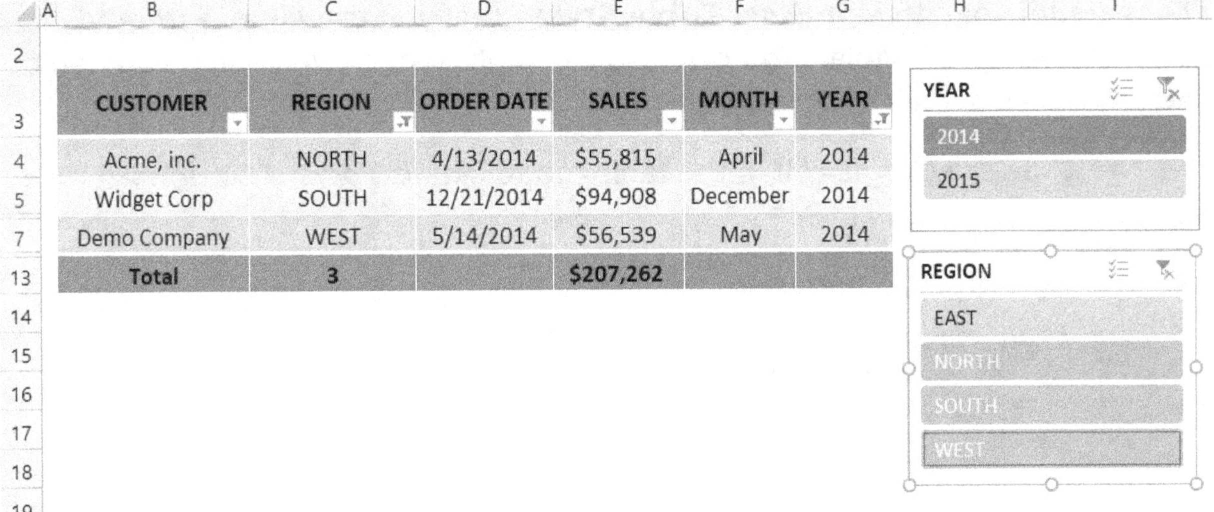

Excel Tables: Styles

There are lots of different **Excel Table Styles** that you can choose from to spice up your Excel Table. You can also customize your own style if you don't like any of the default Excel styles.

STEP 1: While selecting a cell in the table, go to ***Table Tools > Design > Table Styles***

Pick any style that you prefer

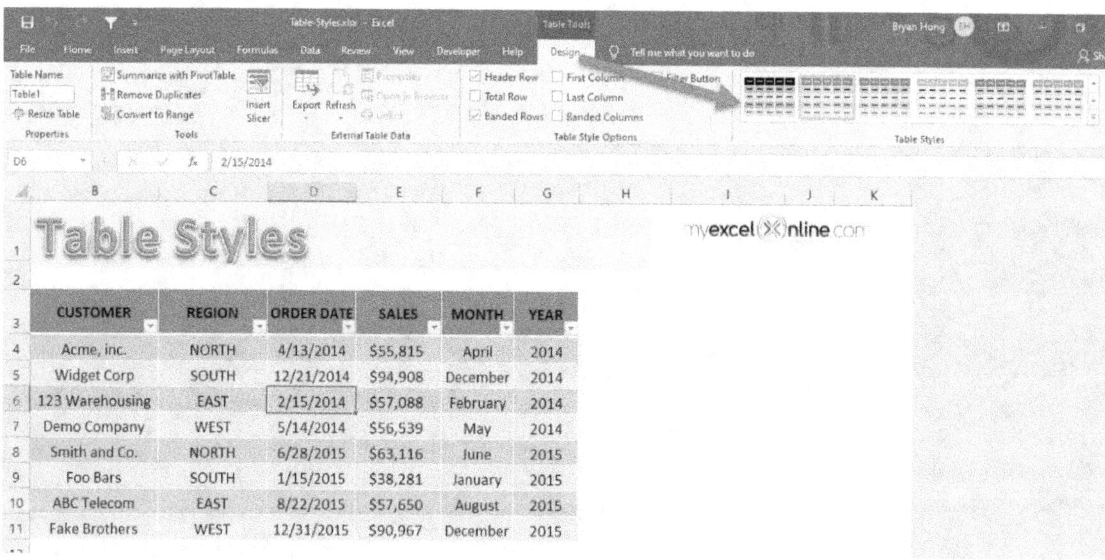

You now have your updated table.

CUSTOMER	REGION	ORDER DATE	SALES	MONTH	YEAR
Acme, inc.	NORTH	4/13/2014	$55,815	April	2014
Widget Corp	SOUTH	12/21/2014	$94,908	December	2014
123 Warehousing	EAST	2/15/2014	$57,088	February	2014
Demo Company	WEST	5/14/2014	$56,539	May	2014
Smith and Co.	NORTH	6/28/2015	$63,116	June	2015
Foo Bars	SOUTH	1/15/2015	$38,281	January	2015
ABC Telecom	EAST	8/22/2015	$57,650	August	2015
Fake Brothers	WEST	12/31/2015	$90,967	December	2015

STEP 2: You can also create your own style! Go to ***Table Tools > Design > Table Styles > New Table Style***

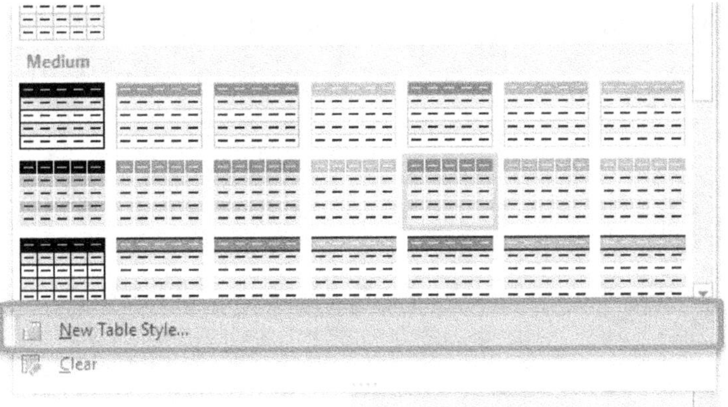

STEP 3: You can give the new table style a name. Click **Format**

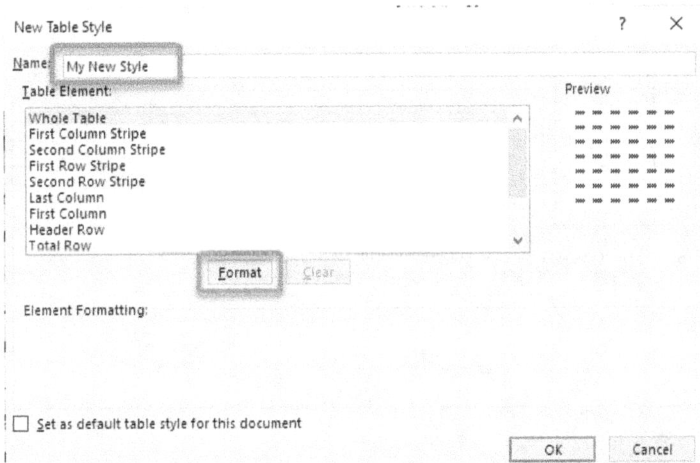

STEP 4: Let us select **Fill** and pick a color. Click OK twice.

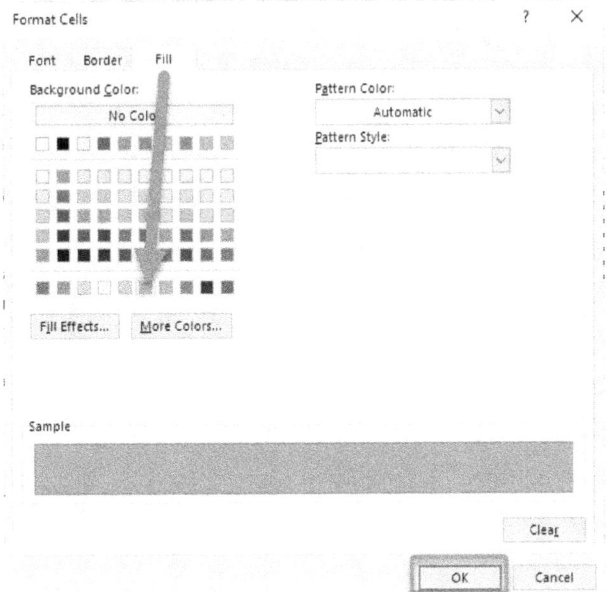

Pick your newly created style

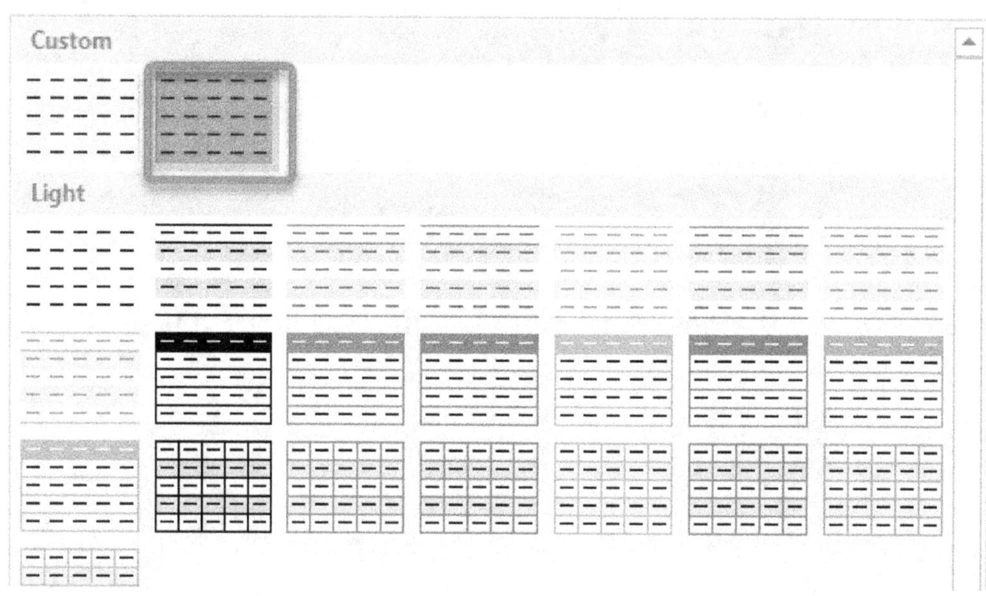

It is now reflected in your Excel Table!

CUSTOMER	REGION	ORDER DATE	SALES	MONTH	YEAR
Acme, inc.	NORTH	4/13/2014	$55,815	April	2014
Widget Corp	SOUTH	12/21/2014	$94,908	December	2014
123 Warehousing	EAST	2/15/2014	$57,088	February	2014
Demo Company	WEST	5/14/2014	$56,539	May	2014
Smith and Co.	NORTH	6/28/2015	$63,116	June	2015
Foo Bars	SOUTH	1/15/2015	$38,281	January	2015
ABC Telecom	EAST	8/22/2015	$57,650	August	2015
Fake Brothers	WEST	12/31/2015	$90,967	December	2015

Excel Tables: Subtotal Feature

Excel's Subtotal feature is a great way to automatically insert a **_Sum/Count/Average/Max/Min_** subtotal to your data set with a press of a button.

This feature is located under the Excel Data tools menu: **_Data > Subtotal_**. To insert this feature, you need to follow these quick steps:

STEP 1: Highlight your data and go to *Data > Subtotal*

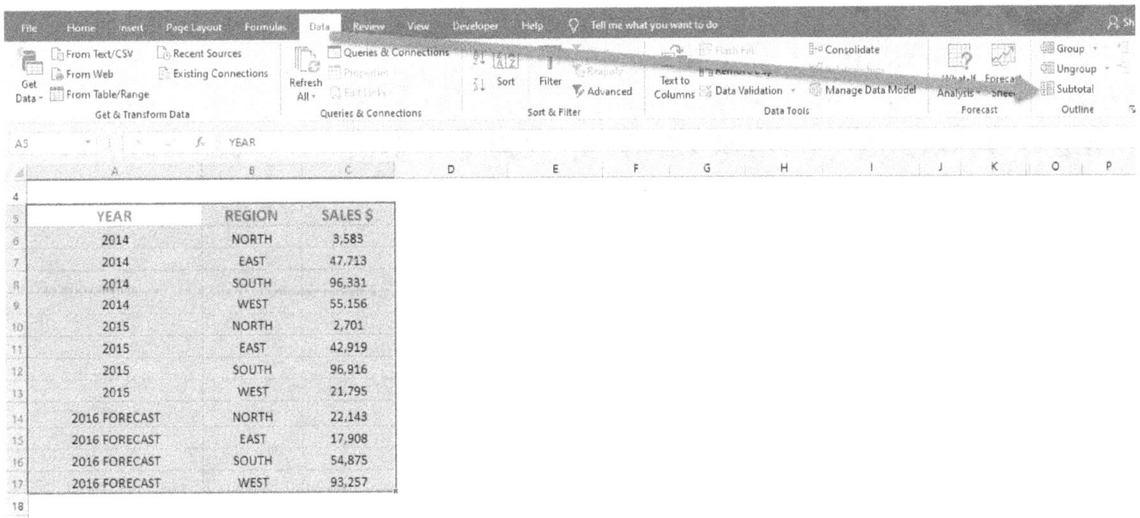

STEP 2: This will open up the **Subtotal dialog box**

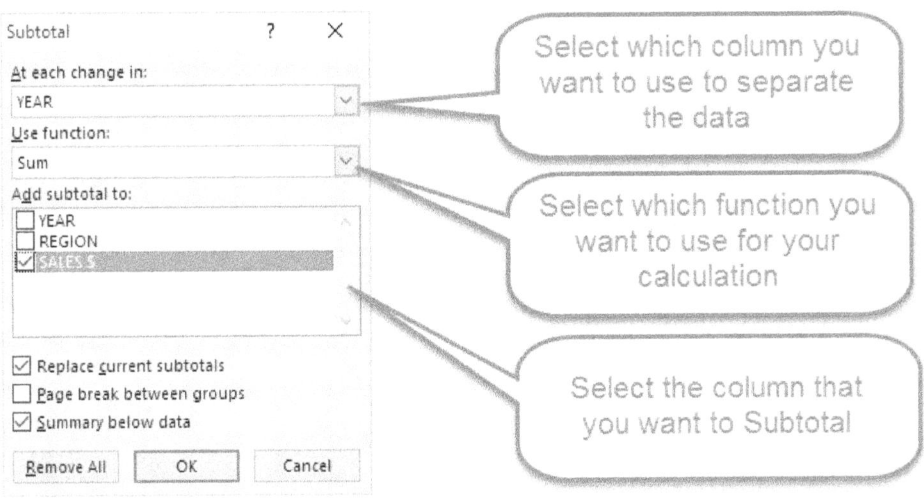

STEP 3: **At each change:** Select which column you want to use to separate the data. Make sure that the data in the selected column is in ascending/descending order

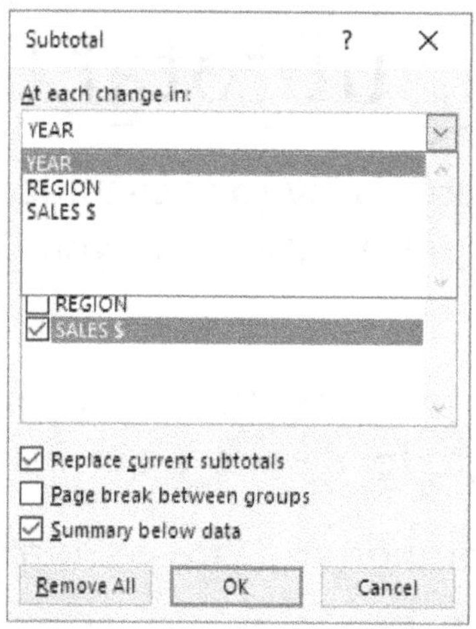

STEP 4: Use function: Select which function you want to use for your calculation. You can select from ***Sum, Count, Average, Maximum, Minimum, Product, Count Numbers, StdDev, StdDevp, Var, Varp***

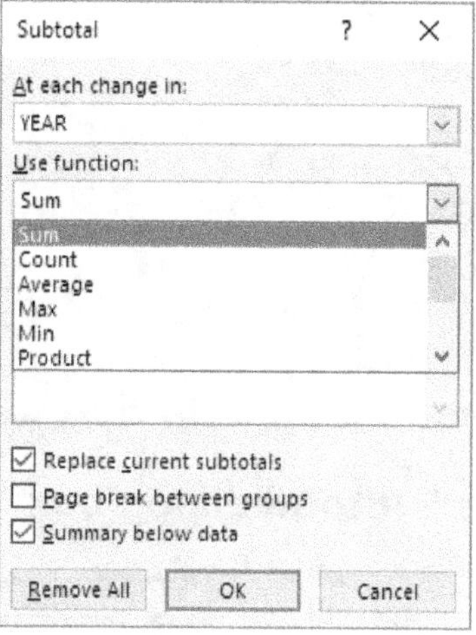

STEP 5: Add subtotal to: Select the column that you want to Subtotal

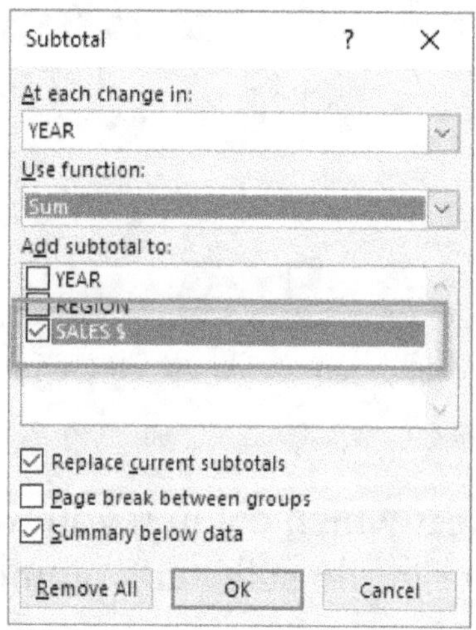

STEP 6: Press OK and this will add extra lines to your data with the chosen Subtotal

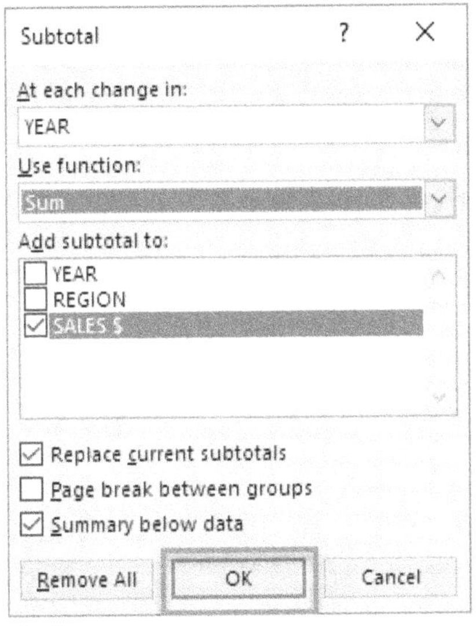

STEP 7: **If you want to change the Subtotal** (say from a Sum to an Average) all you have to do is click in your data and go to *Data > Subtotal* and it will bring up the Subtotal dialog box once again. Under *Use function* select *Average* and press *OK*.

	YEAR	REGION	SALES $
5	YEAR	REGION	SALES $
6	2014	NORTH	3,583
7	2014	EAST	47,713
8	2014	SOUTH	96,331
9	2014	WEST	55,156
10	**2014 Total**		202,783
11	2015	NORTH	2,701
12	2015	EAST	42,919
13	2015	SOUTH	96,916
14	2015	WEST	21,795
15	**2015 Total**		164,331
16	2016 FORECAST	NORTH	22,143
17	2016 FORECAST	EAST	17,908
18	2016 FORECAST	SOUTH	54,875
19	2016 FORECAST	WEST	93,257
20	**2016 FORECAST Total**		188,183
21	**Grand Total**		555,297

Analysis ⊕

Excel Tables: Summarize Data With Subtotals

What does it do?

It returns a Subtotal in a list or database

Formula breakdown:

=SUBTOTAL(function_num, ref1)

What it means:

=SUBTOTAL(function number 1-11 includes manually-hidden rows & 101-111 excludes them, your list or range of data)

The Subtotal function can become dynamic when we combine it with a drop down list.

This is a great trick and one that can be used when creating an Excel Dashboard that summarizes key data metrics on one page.

STEP 1:   We need to **list the Subtotal summary functions** in our Excel worksheet

AVERAGE
COUNT
COUNTA
MAX
MIN
PRODUCT
STDEV
STDEVP
SUM
VAR
VARP

STEP 3: With your mouse **select the region where you want to insert the Combo Box**

STEP 4: Right Click on the Combo Box and select **Format Control...**

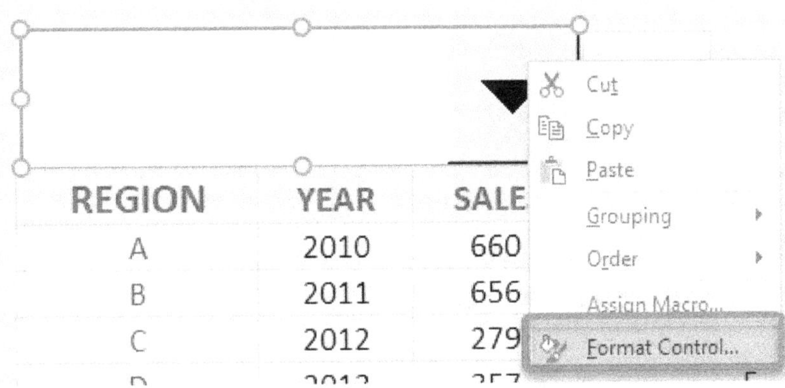

STEP 5: For the **Input Range**, you need to **select the range with the Subtotal summary names from STEP 1**

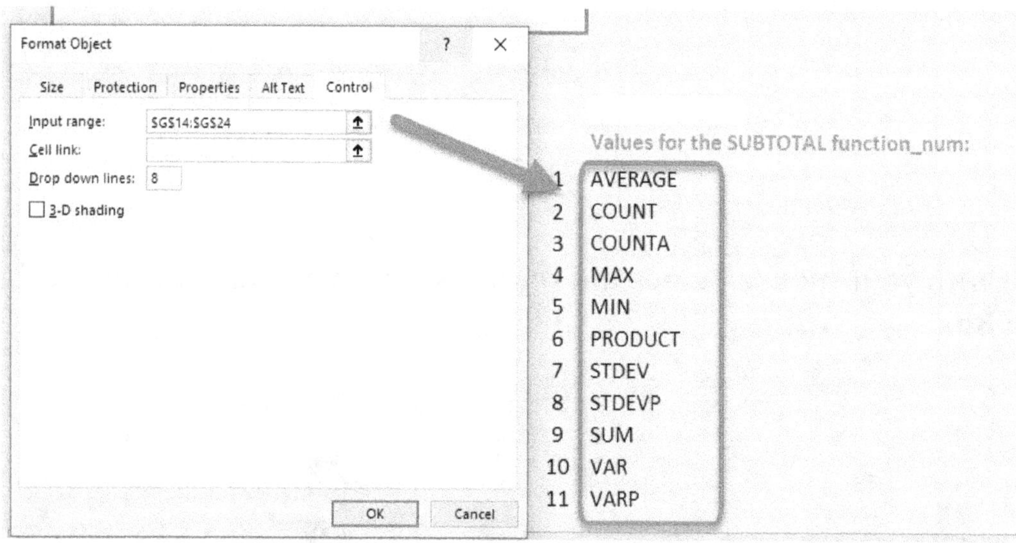

STEP 6: For the **Cell Link**, you need to **select a cell where you want to show the output** and press **OK**

(The Cell Link increments by 1 depending on the order of the list and the name chosen. We will use this value as our first argument in the SUBTOTAL function)

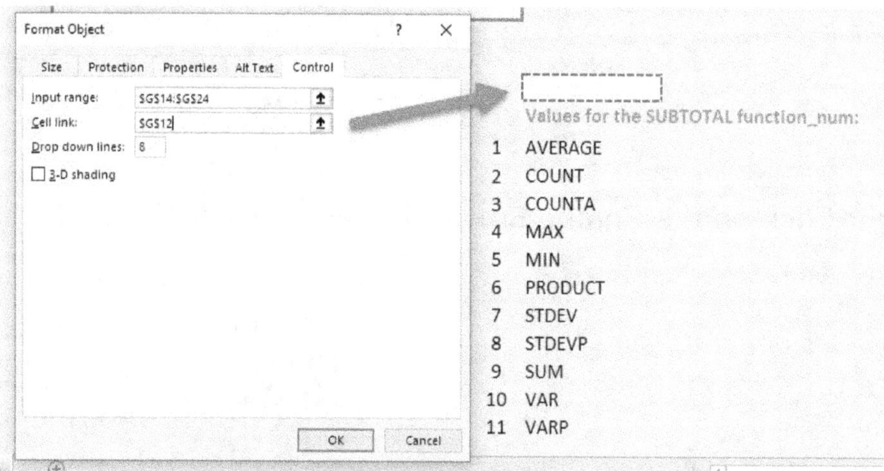

STEP 7: Enter the Subtotal function and for the **first argument** *function_num* **we will reference the Cell Link from STEP 6**

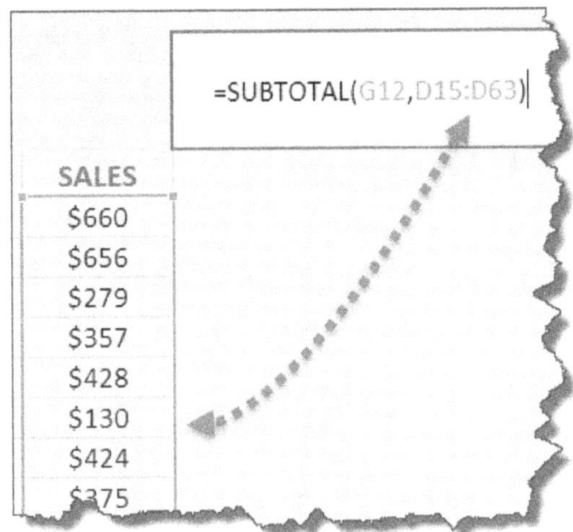

So you can see as you choose a summary name from the drop down list, it gives us a value for the Cell Link which equals to the *function_num* for that summary name!

Let us give it a try! Select **MAX** and you will get the maximum value:

REGION	YEAR	SALES
A	2010	660
B	2011	656
C	2012	279
D	2013	357
E	2014	428
F	2015	130
G	2016	424
A	2010	375

Now let us try **COUNT** and you get the number of records:

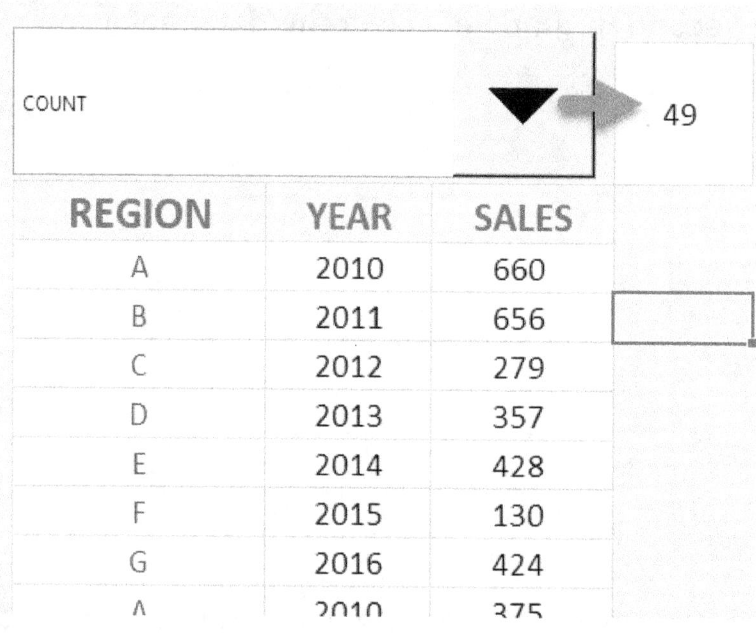

Here are the values for the **SUBTOTAL** *function_num*:

Function	Includes hidden values	Ignores hidden values
AVERAGE	1	101
COUNT	2	102
COUNTA	3	103
MAX	4	104
MIN	5	105
PRODUCT	6	106
STDEV	7	107
STDEVP	8	108
SUM	9	109
VAR	10	110
VARP	11	111

Excel Tables: Total Row Calculations

One of the most powerful features of an Excel Table is the use of formulas to calculate its Column contents.

This will add a *Totals Row* at the bottom of your Table and by clicking in any of the boxes, a list of formulas will appear! You can use the default formulas like *Average, Count, Count Numbers, Max, Min, Sum* plus you can click on *More Functions* which will let you choose any of Excel's many formulas.

STEP 1: Select any cell in your table. Go to *Table Tools > Design > Table Style Options > Total Row*

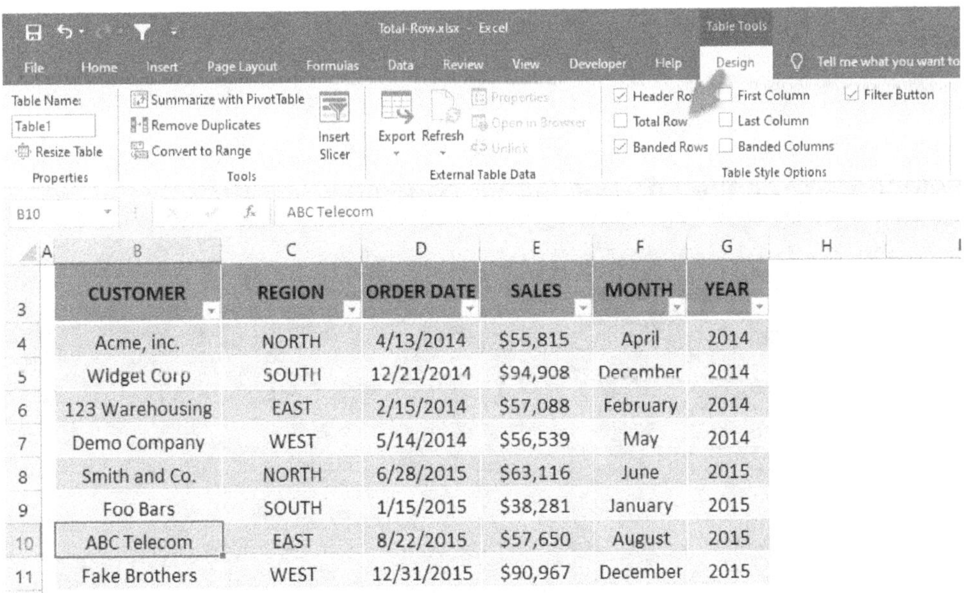

STEP 2: A new row has been added at the bottom of the data. Select **Count** for the **REGION column**

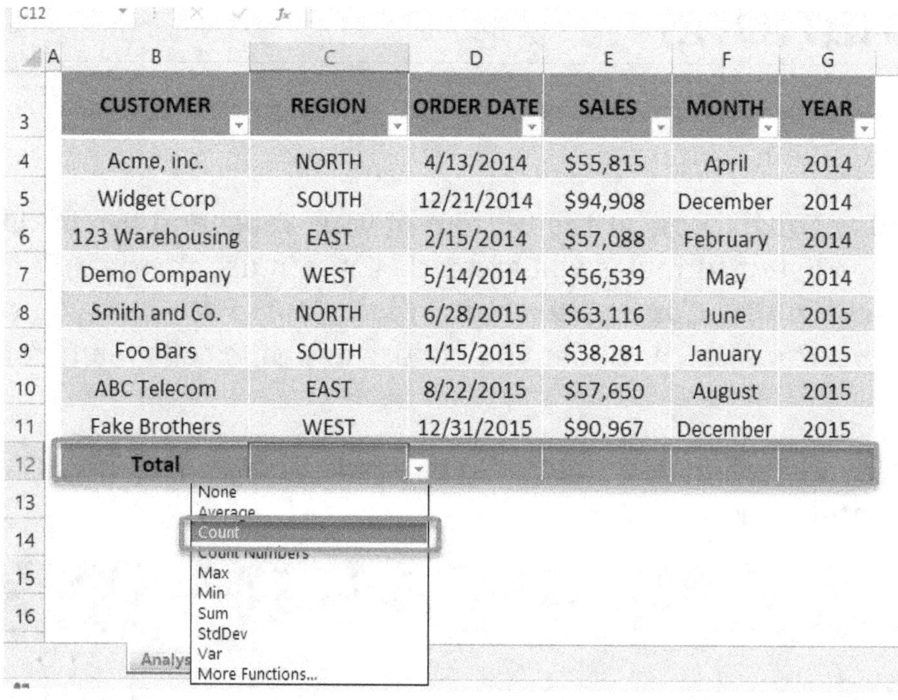

STEP 3: Select **Max** for the **ORDER DATE column**

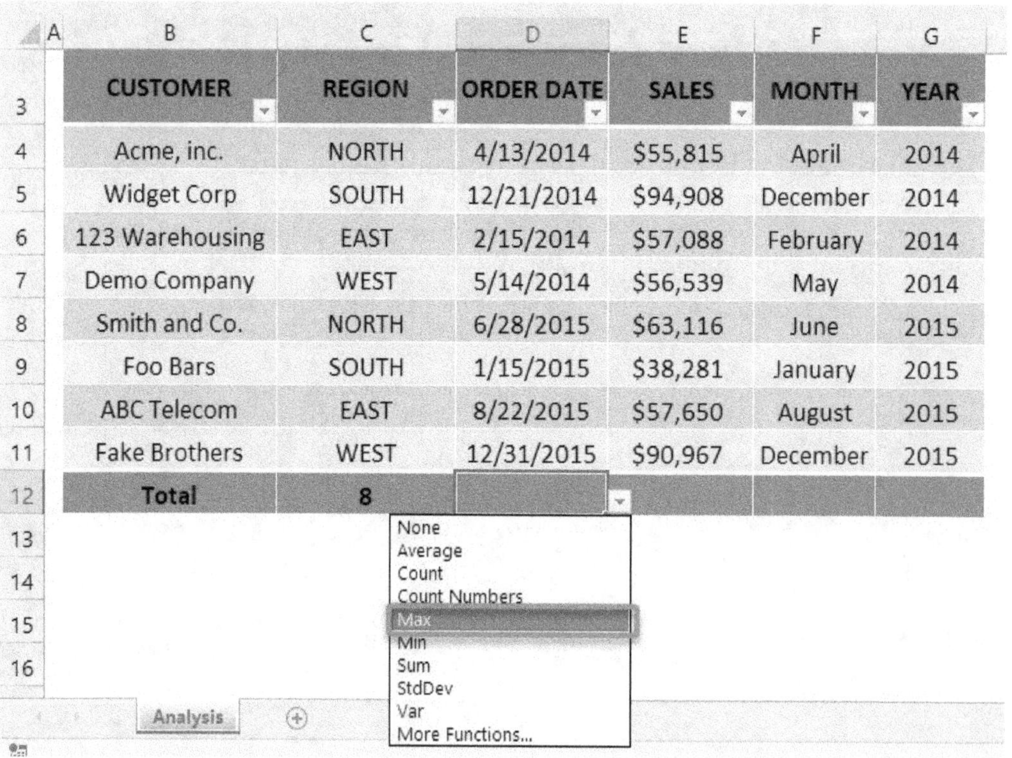

	CUSTOMER	REGION	ORDER DATE	SALES	MONTH	YEAR
4	Acme, inc.	NORTH	4/13/2014	$55,815	April	2014
5	Widget Corp	SOUTH	12/21/2014	$94,908	December	2014
6	123 Warehousing	EAST	2/15/2014	$57,088	February	2014
7	Demo Company	WEST	5/14/2014	$56,539	May	2014
8	Smith and Co.	NORTH	6/28/2015	$63,116	June	2015
9	Foo Bars	SOUTH	1/15/2015	$38,281	January	2015
10	ABC Telecom	EAST	8/22/2015	$57,650	August	2015
11	Fake Brothers	WEST	12/31/2015	$90,967	December	2015
12	**Total**	**8**	**12/31/2015**			

None
Average
Count
Count Numbers
Max
Min
Sum
StdDev
Var
More Functions...

Now you have your updated values! They get updated automatically as you add new rows and change values!

	CUSTOMER	REGION	ORDER DATE	SALES	MONTH	YEAR
4	Acme, inc.	NORTH	4/13/2014	$55,815	April	2014
5	Widget Corp	SOUTH	12/21/2014	$94,908	December	2014
6	123 Warehousing	EAST	2/15/2014	$57,088	February	2014
7	Demo Company	WEST	5/14/2014	$56,539	May	2014
8	Smith and Co.	NORTH	6/28/2015	$63,116	June	2015
9	Foo Bars	SOUTH	1/15/2015	$38,281	January	2015
10	ABC Telecom	EAST	8/22/2015	$57,650	August	2015
11	Fake Brothers	WEST	12/31/2015	$90,967	December	2015
12	**Total**	**8**	**12/31/2015**	**$514,364**		

Pivot Tables: Connect Slicers to Multiple Pivot Tables

When you insert an Excel Pivot Table Slicer it is **only connected to the Pivot Table that you are inserting it from**.

What about if you had multiple Pivot Tables from the same data set and wanted to control them using one Slicer, so when you press a button all the Pivot Tables change?

Well this is possible with the Report Connections (*Excel 2013, 2016, 2019 & Office 365*) / PivotTable Connections (Excel 2010) option within the Slicer.

STEP 1: Create 2 Pivot Tables by clicking in your data set and selecting *Insert > Pivot Table > New Worksheet/Existing Worksheet*

Setup Pivot Table #1:

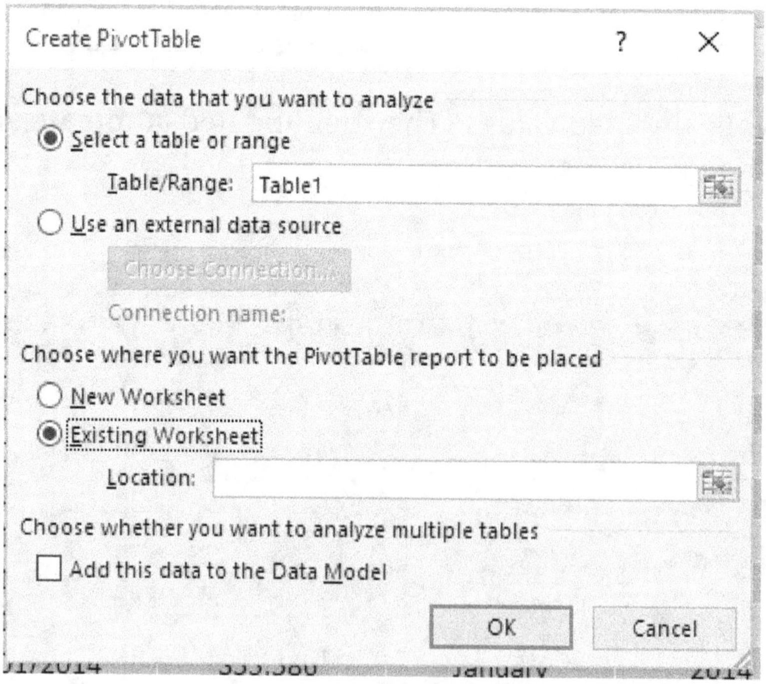

ROWS: Region

VALUES: Sum of Sales

	A	B
5	Row Labels	Sum of SALES
6	EAST	381740
7	NORTH	423596
8	SOUTH	462942
9	WEST	508716
10	**Grand Total**	**1776994**

Setup Pivot Table #2:

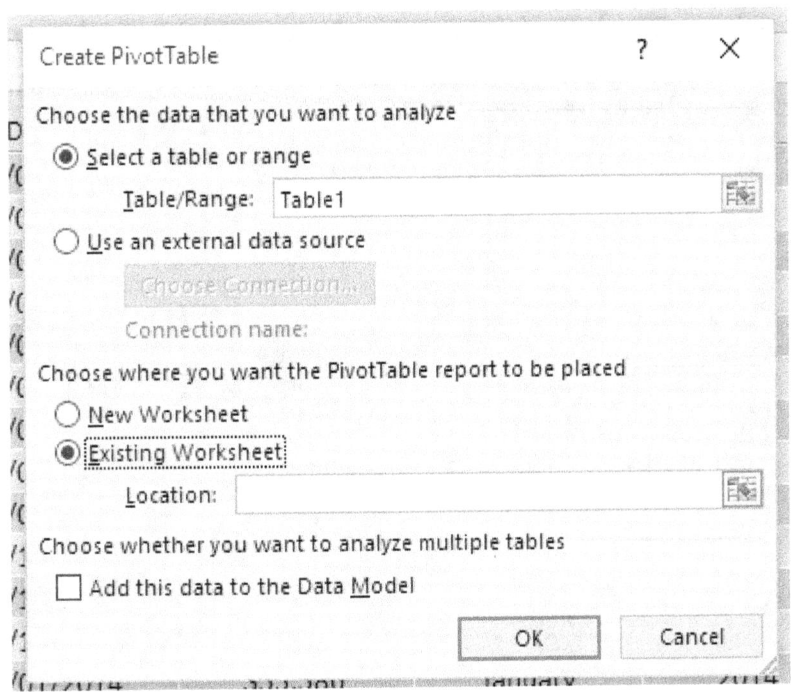

ROWS: Customer

VALUES: Sum of Sales

STEP 2: **Click in Pivot Table #1 and insert a <u>MONTH Slicer</u>** by going to *PivotTable Tools > Analyze/Options > Insert Slicer > Month > OK*

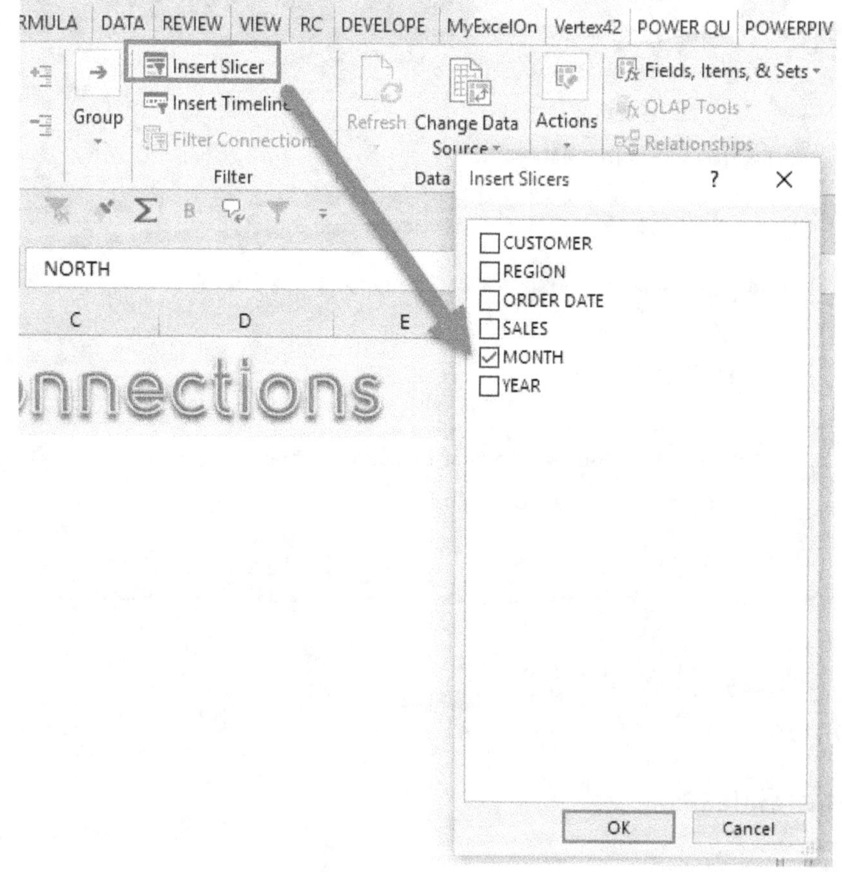

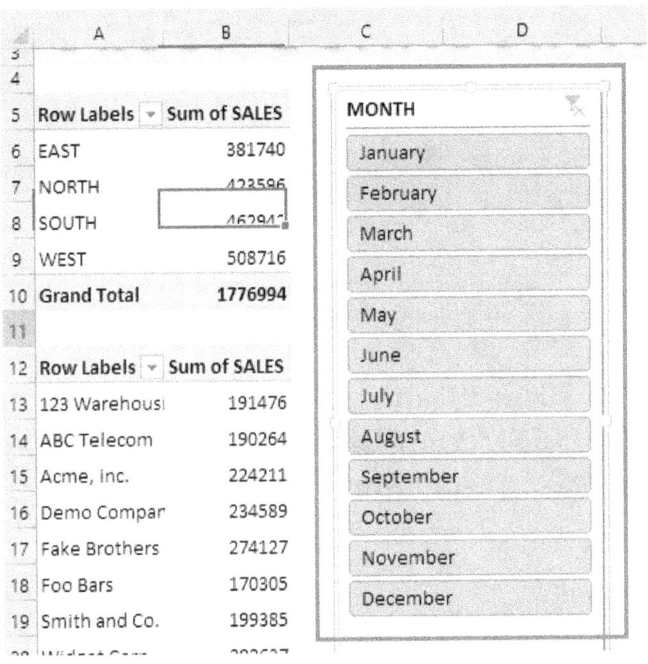

STEP 3: Click in Pivot Table #2 and insert a <u>YEAR Slicer</u> by going to
PivotTable Tools > Analyze/Options > Insert Slicer > Year > OK

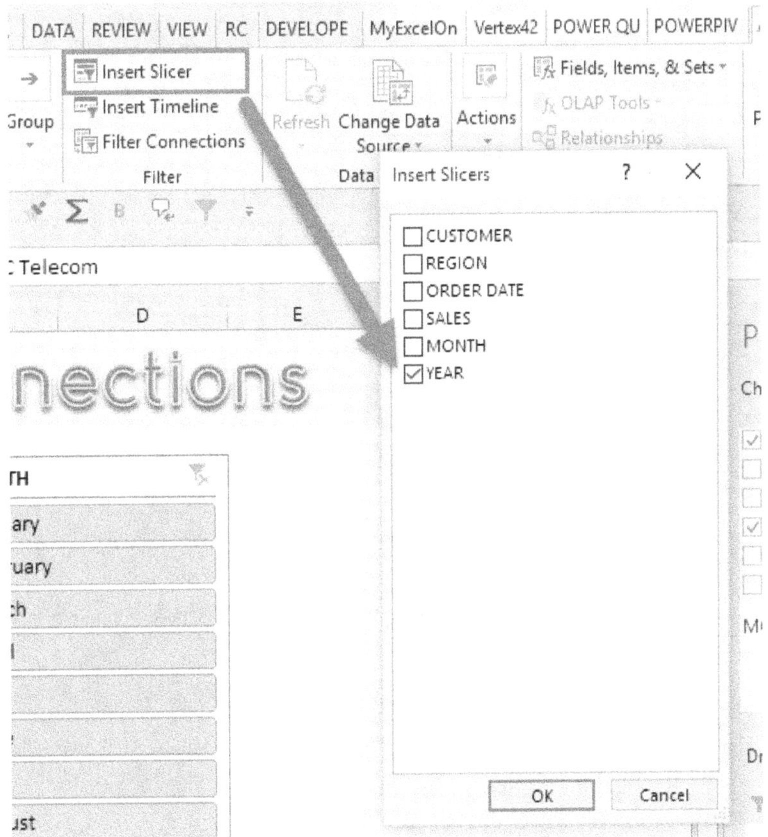

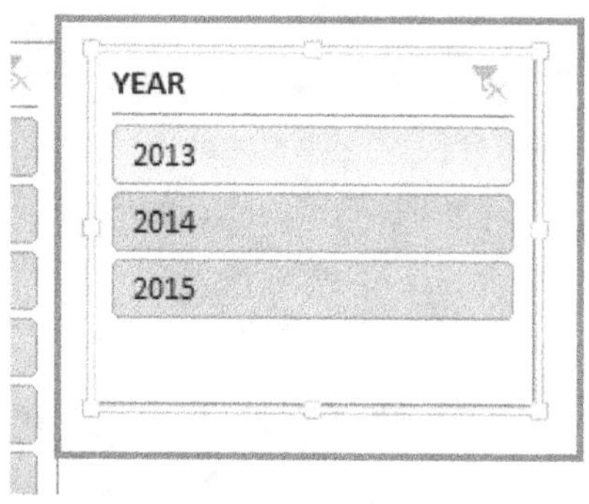

STEP 4: Right Click on Slicer #1 and go to ***Report Connections(Excel 2013, 2016, 2019 & Office 365)/PivotTable Connections (Excel 2010)* >** *"check"* the ***PivotTable2*** **box** and press **OK**

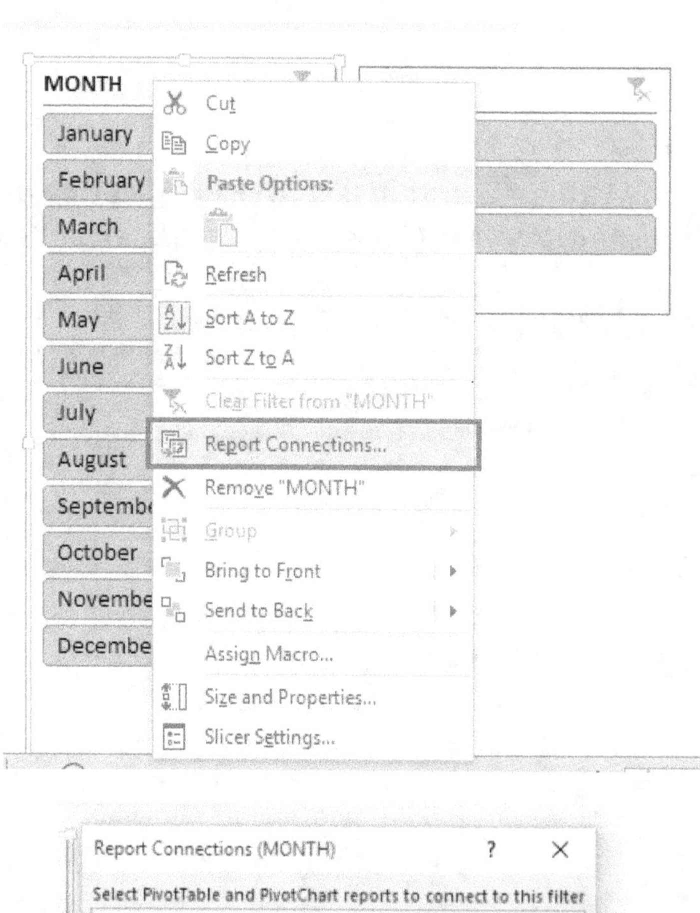

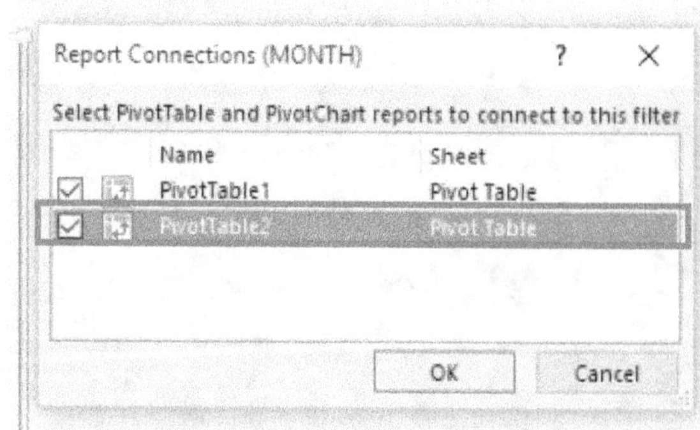

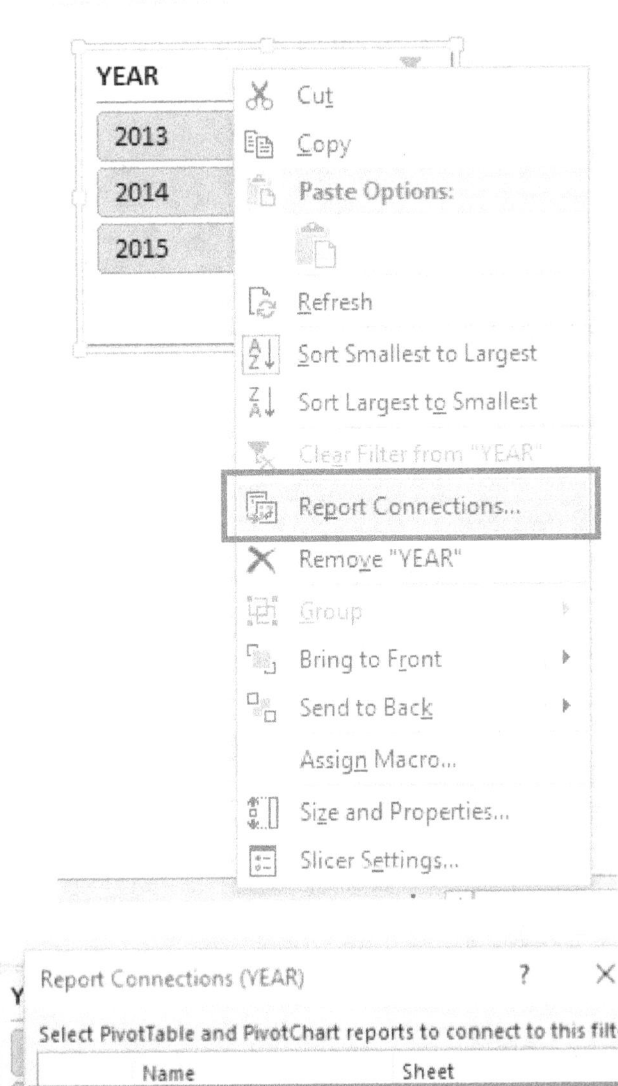
YEAR
2013
2014
2015
Cut
Copy
Paste Options:
Refresh
Sort Smallest to Largest
Sort Largest to Smallest
Clear Filter from "YEAR"
Report Connections...
Remove "YEAR"
Group
Bring to Front
Send to Back
Assign Macro...
Size and Properties...
Slicer Settings...
Report Connections (YEAR)
?
Select PivotTable and PivotChart reports to connect to this filter
Name
Sheet
PivotTable1
Pivot Table
PivotTable2
Pivot Table
OK
Cancel

Now as you select each Slicer's items, both Pivot Tables will change!

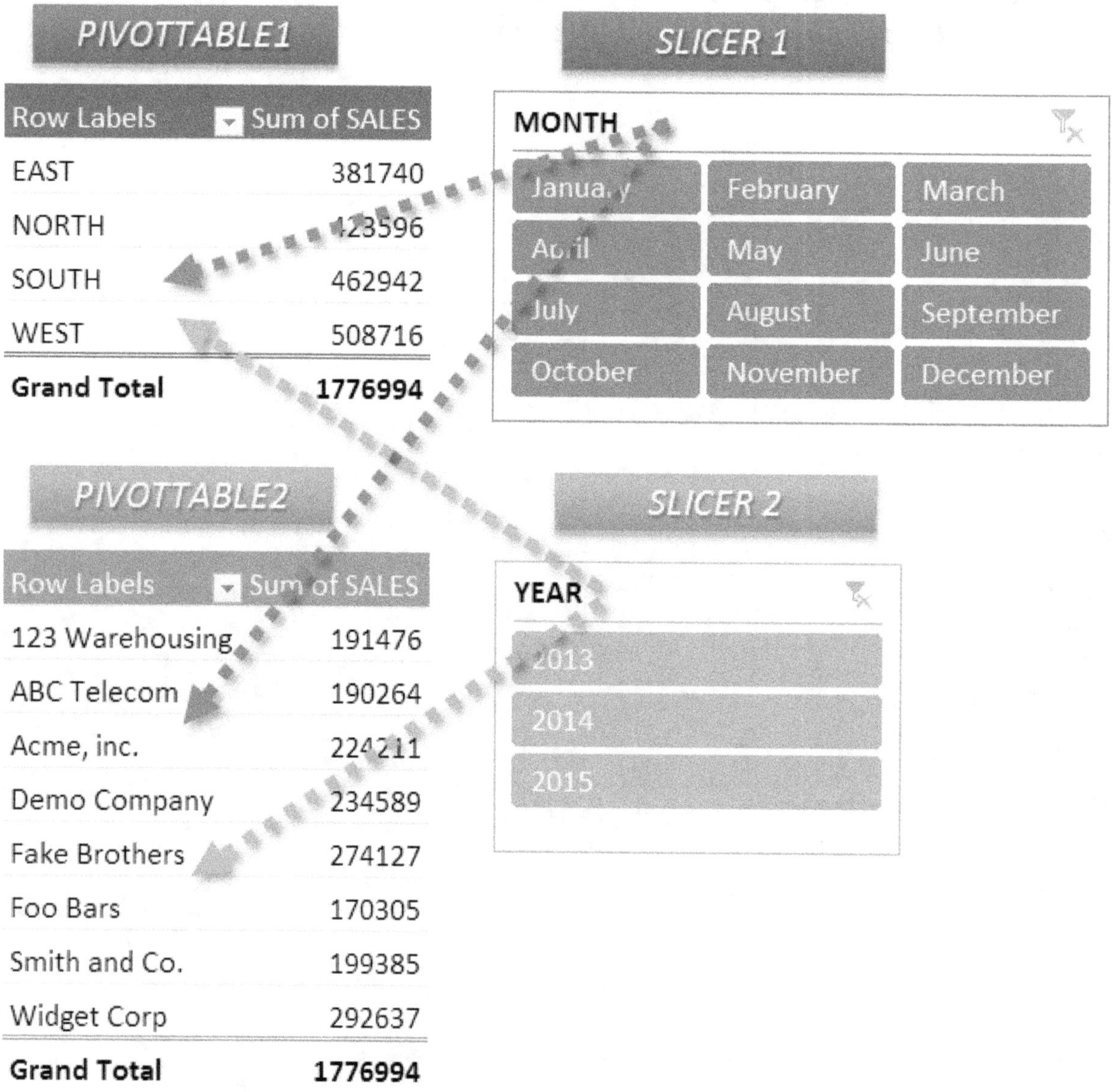

PIVOTTABLE1

Row Labels	Sum of SALES
EAST	381740
NORTH	423596
SOUTH	462942
WEST	508716
Grand Total	**1776994**

SLICER 1

MONTH

January	February	March
April	May	June
July	August	September
October	November	December

PIVOTTABLE2

Row Labels	Sum of SALES
123 Warehousing	191476
ABC Telecom	190264
Acme, inc.	224211
Demo Company	234589
Fake Brothers	274127
Foo Bars	170305
Smith and Co.	199385
Widget Corp	292637
Grand Total	**1776994**

SLICER 2

YEAR

2013
2014
2015

Pivot Tables: Data Model and Relationships

Ever had multiple related tables and wondered how to create a report that connects them together in a single Pivot Table? We have just the thing with **Data Model** and Relationships!

Below is our data that we will use. What we want to do is create a report that shows the First Name of the student and the Number of Classes that the student has taken.

The tricky part here is the First Name is in the **Students Table (on the right)**, while the number of classes are in the **Classes Table (on the left)**.

Both Tables have a **StudentId column** which we will use to create our relationship.

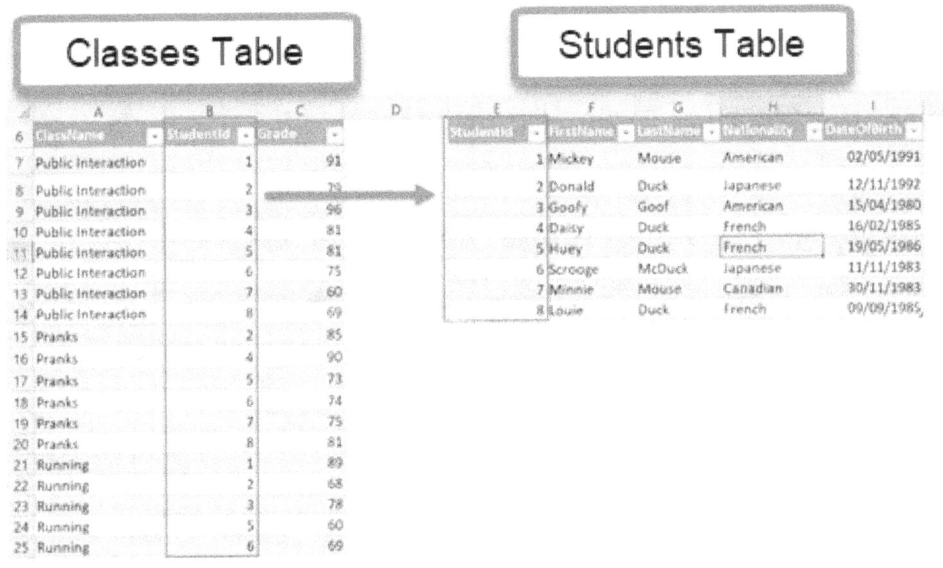

STEP 1: Select the *Classes Table*. Go to *Insert > Pivot Table > New Worksheet*

Make sure to tick **Add this data to the Data Model**. Click OK.

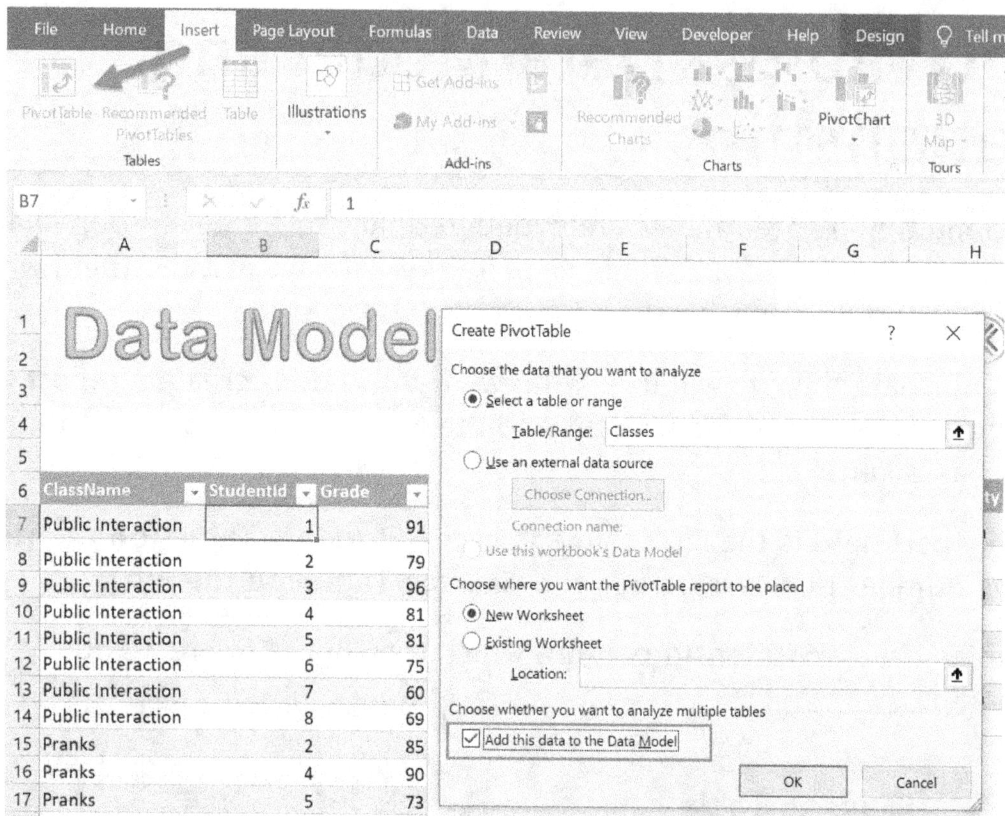

STEP 2: Select the ***Students Table***. Go to ***Insert > Pivot Table > New Worksheet***

Make sure to tick **Add this data to the Data Model**. Click OK.

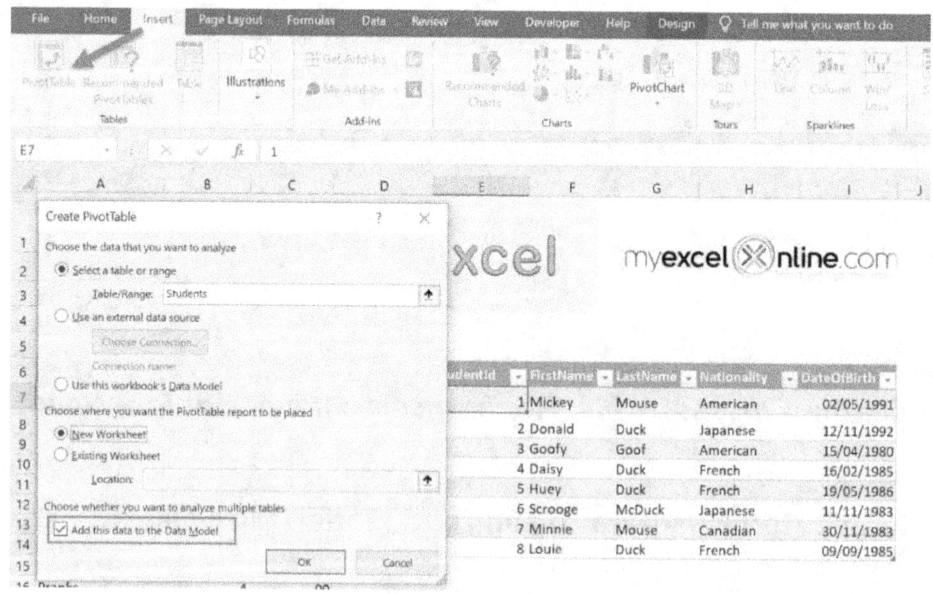

 Click **All** in **PivotTable Fields** and you should see both Tables there.

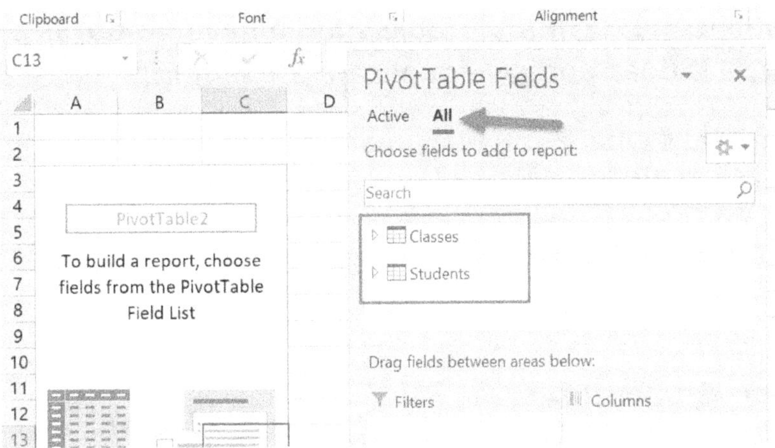

STEP 4: Now we need to link them together! Go to *PivotTable Tools > Analyze > Calculations > Relationships*

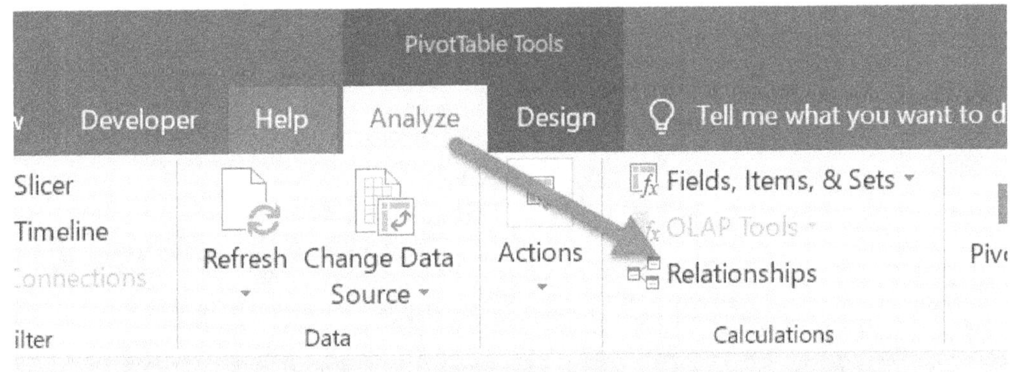

Click **New.**

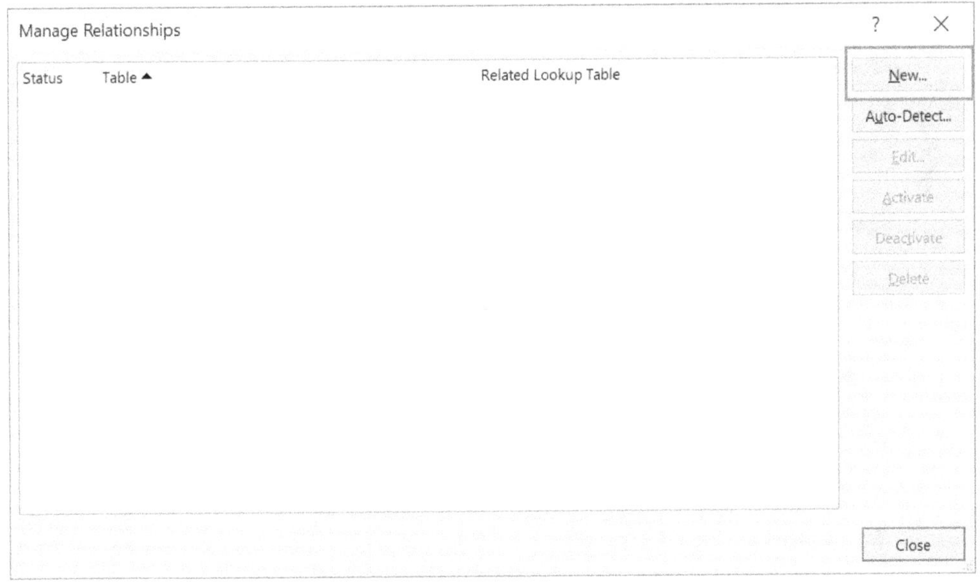

 There are 2 sides of a relationship when we want to link them together.

The rule of thumb is the "**Primary**" Table should have **no duplicates**. This is the *Students Table* as it does not have duplicate *Student Ids*.

The "**Foreign**" Table is where you have many transactions with duplicate values. This is the *Classes Table* as it has duplicate *Student Ids*.

Set the following then Click **OK**:

Table - **Classes**

Column (foreign) - **StudentId**

Related Table - **Students**

Related Column (Primary) - **StudentId**

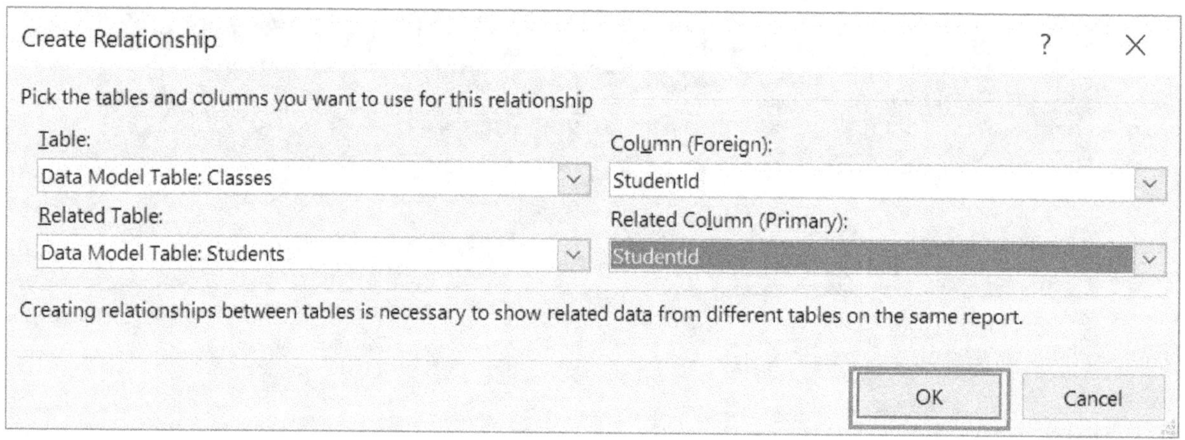

Click **Close**.

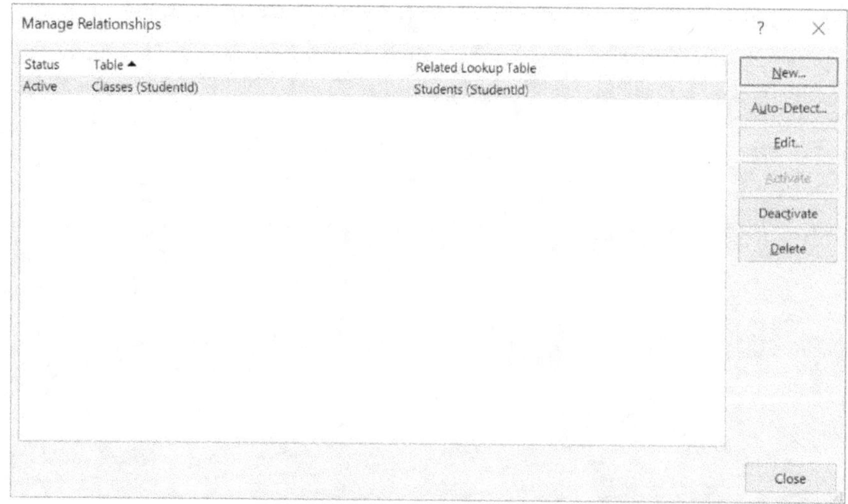

 In the **ROWS** section put in the *Students(FirstName)* field. In the **VALUES** section put in the *Classes (ClassName)* field.

With just that, you can see that Excel was able to show the results in a merged fashion without the need to use the VLOOKUP formula!

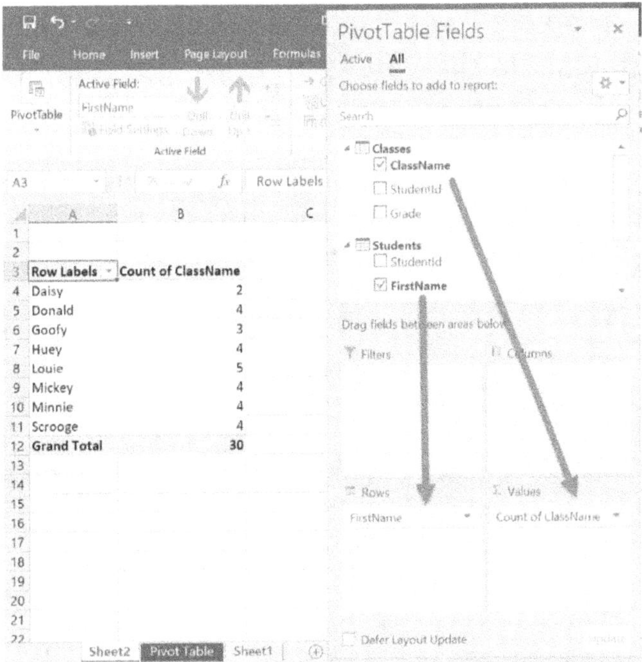

Pivot Tables: Distinct Count

When Pivot Table features were updated in Excel 2013, one that had been well overdue was the distinct or unique count.

Previously when we created a Pivot Table and dropped a *Customers* field in the Row Labels and then again in the Values area, we got the **"Total number of transactions"** for each customer.

But what about if we want to show the total unique customers?

STEP 1: Click in your data source and go to *Insert > Pivot Table*

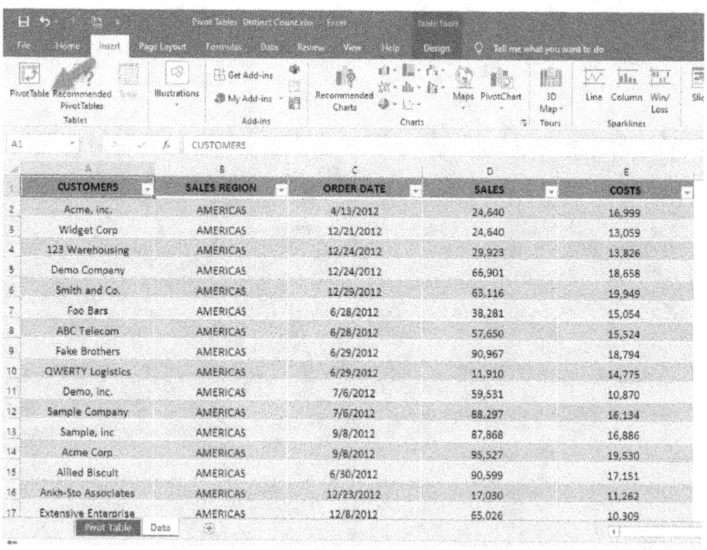

STEP 2: The important step here is to **check** the **Add this data to the Data Model** box and press **OK**

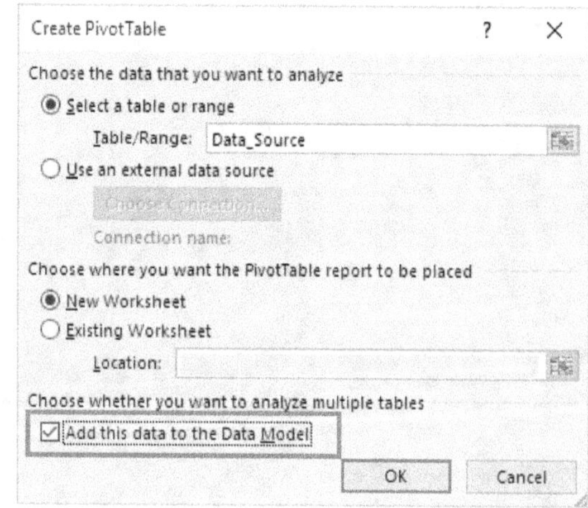

 This will create a Pivot Table. Now **drop the *Customers* field in the Row and Values areas** which will give you the "total transactions" for each customer.

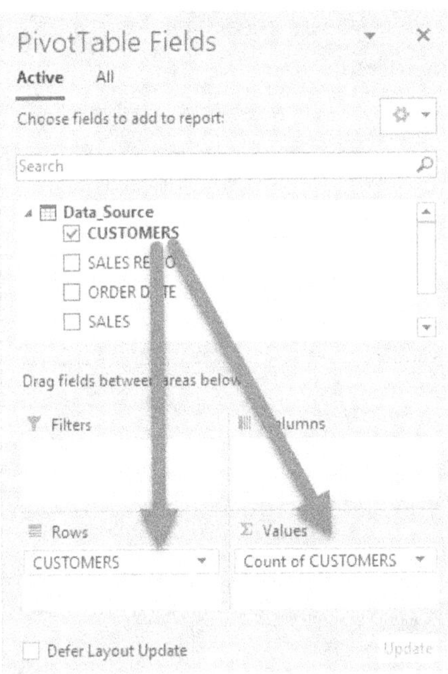

STEP 4: To get a Distinct Count, you need to click on the **Values drop down** for the *Count of Customers* and select the **Value Field Settings**

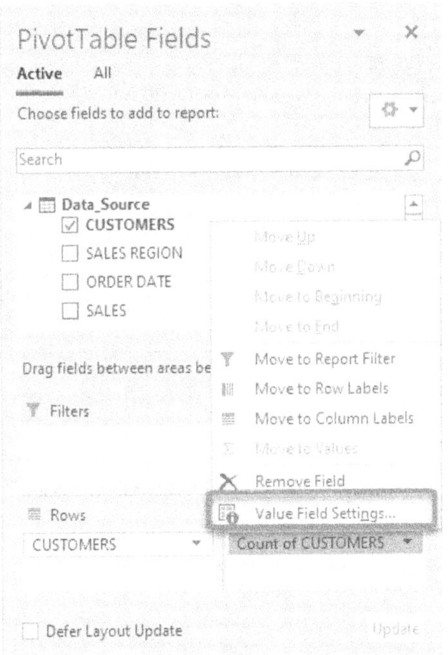

STEP 5: Under **Summarize Values By** tab, select the last option, **Distinct Count** and press **OK**

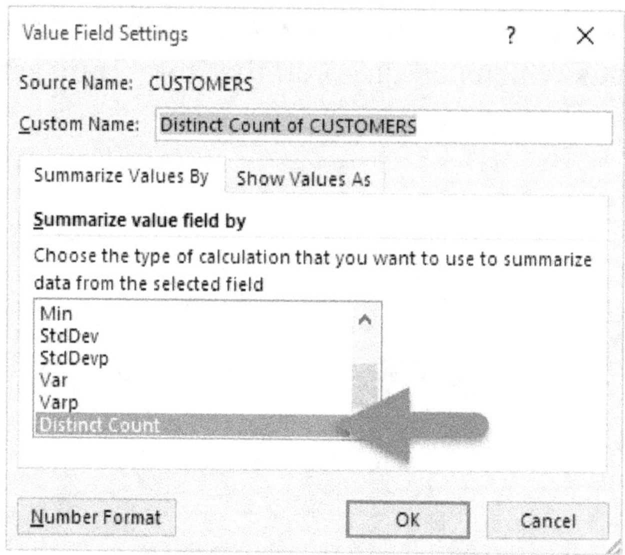

You now have your distinct counts!

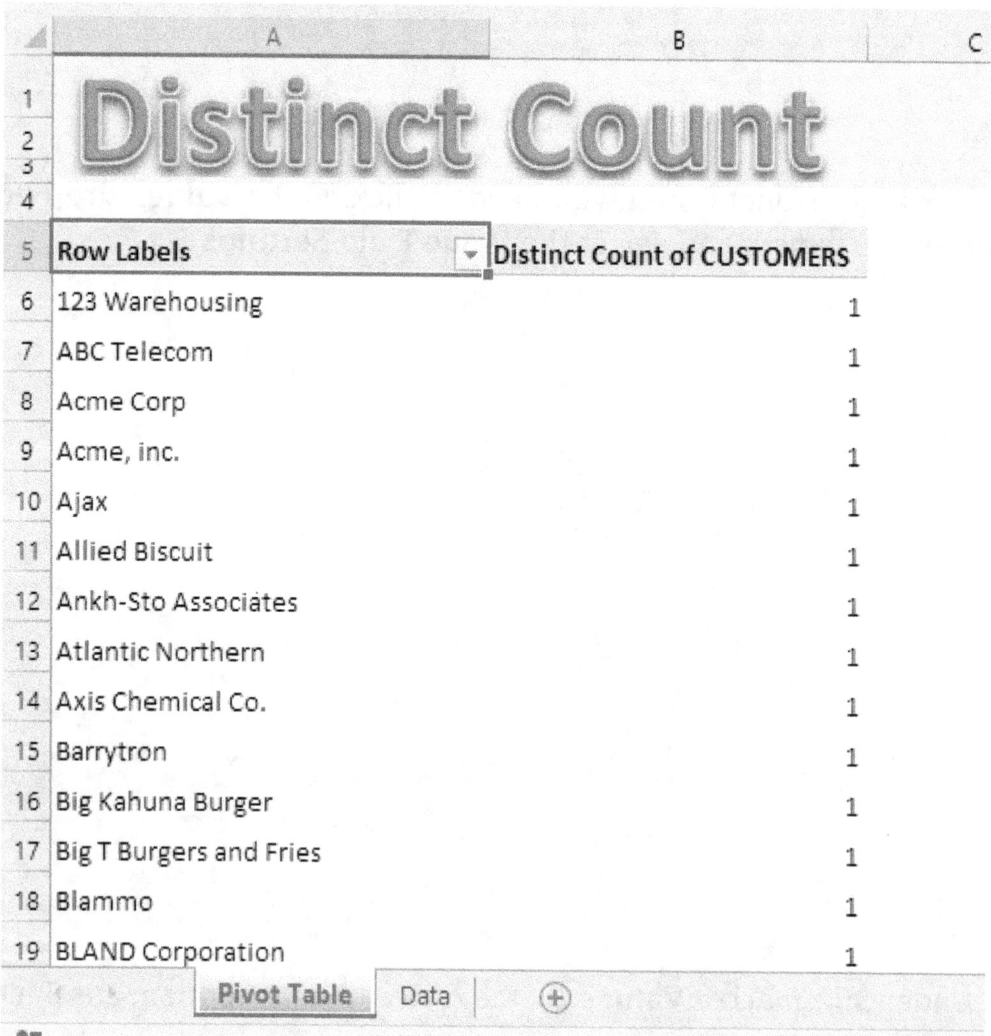

Pivot Tables: Filter by Dates

There is an array of different *Date* filters in a Pivot Table. You can filter by a particular date range, for example: *by this week, next month, next quarter, next year, last year, year to date* and the list goes on and on. This is useful if you want to see what invoices are due to be paid this month or what sales transactions were included in a particular quarter.

Below I show you a few quick Pivot Table filter examples.

STEP 1: Go to **Row Labels** and select *Date Filters > Between*

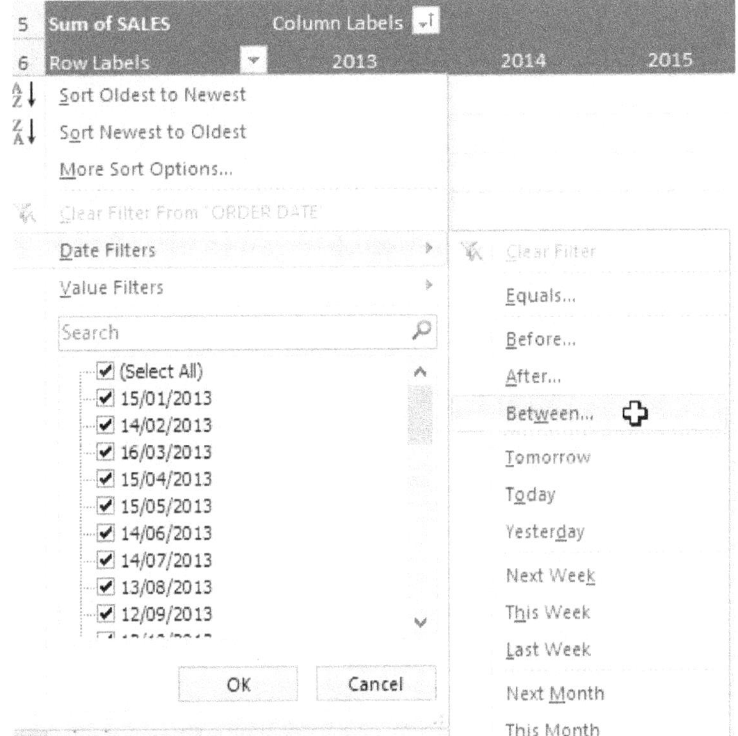

STEP 2: Place a date range. Click **OK.**

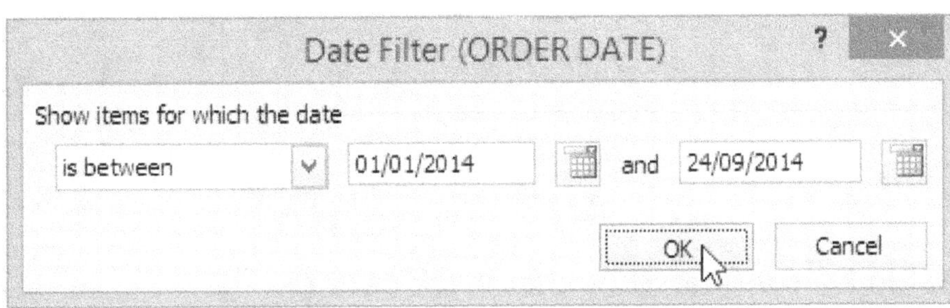

Your Pivot Table is now filtered by the dates!

Sum of SALES	Column Labels
Row Labels	2014
10/01/2014	53,586
09/02/2014	14,333
11/03/2014	29,570
10/04/2014	83,468
10/05/2014	25,263
09/06/2014	68,797
09/07/2014	49,562
08/08/2014	13,964
07/09/2014	23,798
Grand Total	362,341

STEP 3: Let us try another one. Go to **Row Labels** and select *Date Filters > Next Quarter*

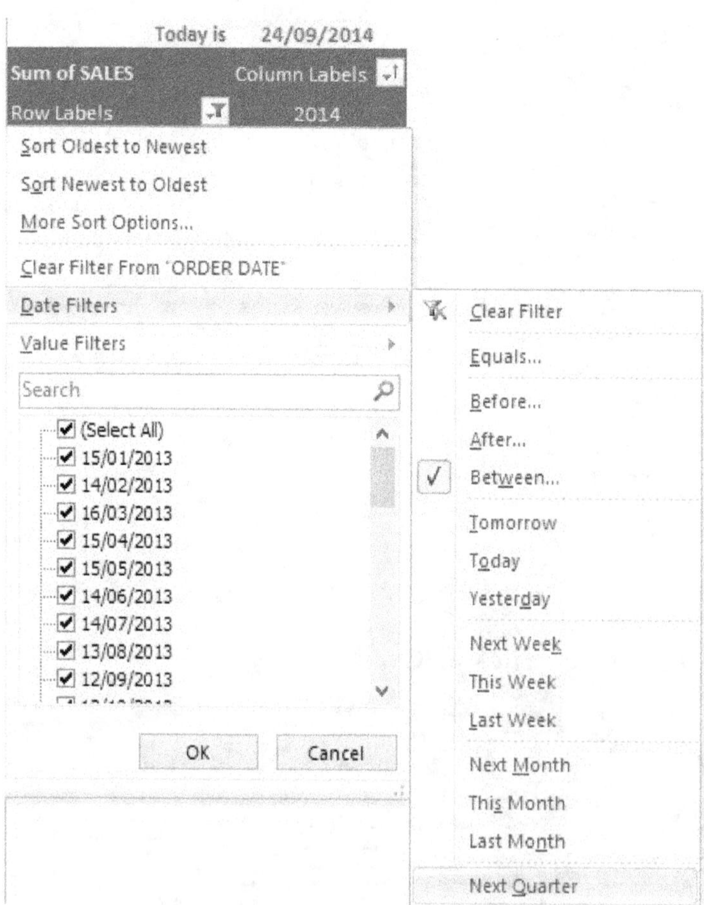

Your Pivot Table is now filtered by the next quarter!

(This tip only works if your Pivot Table's dates and the today's date are within the same year)

Sum of SALES	Today is	24/09/2014
	Column Labels	
Row Labels		2014
07/10/2014		16,843
06/11/2014		78,715
06/12/2014		80,780
Grand Total		176,338

Pivot Tables: Filter Top 5 Customers

You can easily *Filter* your Pivot Table to show your Top X customers. There are lots of different *Value Filters* to choose from and one of my favorites is the Top 10 Filter.

Here is our Pivot Table:

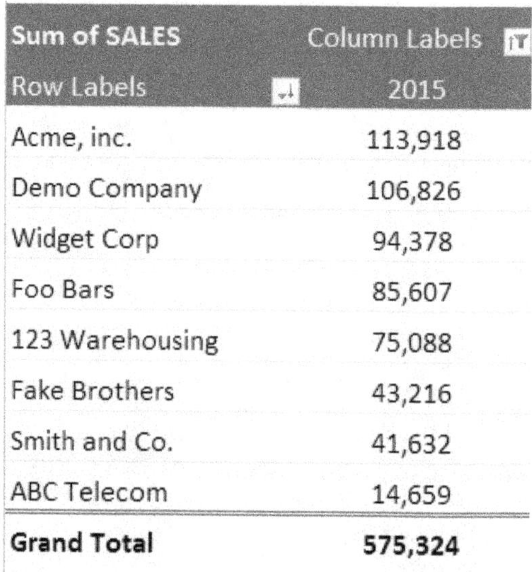

STEP 1: Go to **Row Labels > Value Filters > Top 10**

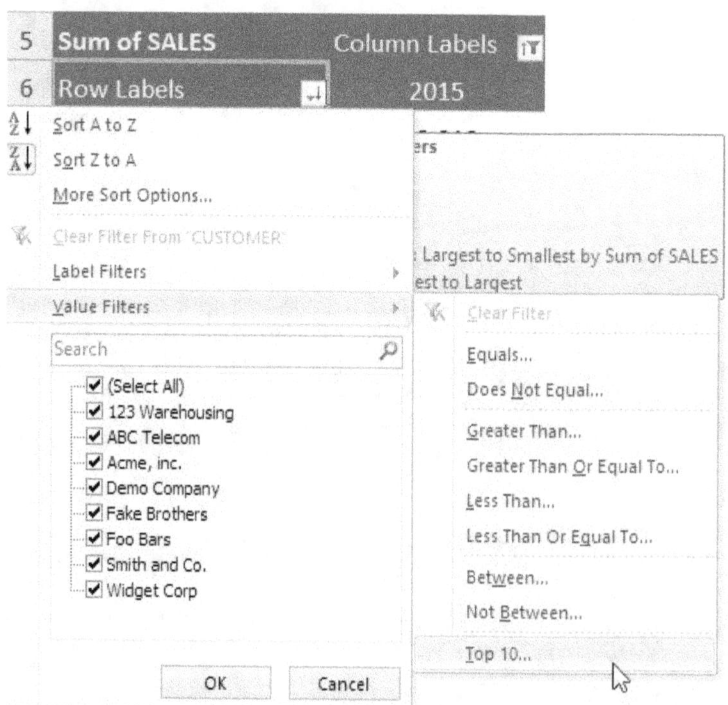

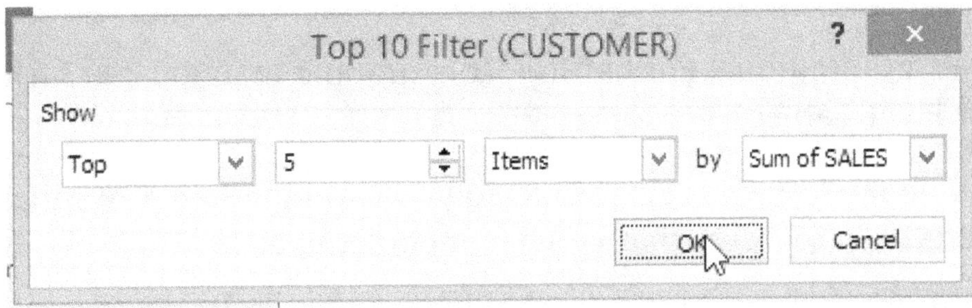

Your pivot table is now filtered!

Sum of SALES	Column Labels
Row Labels	2015
Acme, inc.	113,918
Demo Company	106,826
Widget Corp	94,378
Foo Bars	85,607
123 Warehousing	75,088
Grand Total	**475,817**

Pivot Tables: Icon Sets

An Icon Set is a Conditional Formatting icon/graphic that you can include in your cells or Pivot Tables.

The icon will depend on the cell's value so you can highlight key variances or trends. There are a few sets that you can include, like:

DIRECTIONAL (Change in values)

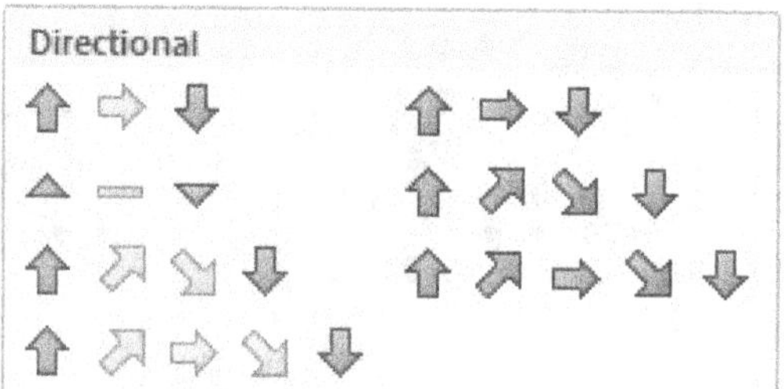

SHAPES (Milestones)

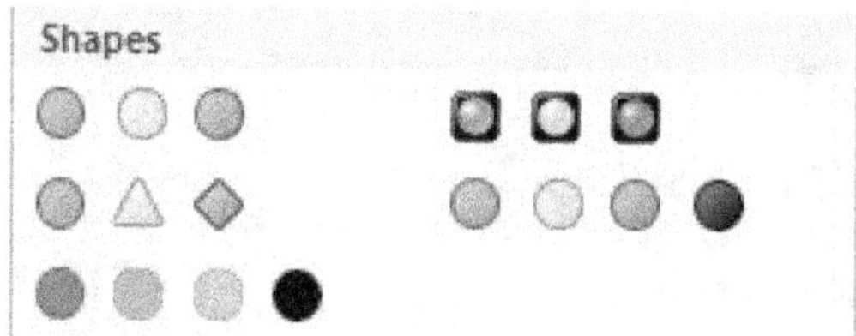

INDICATORS (Positive/Negative)

RATINGS (Scores)

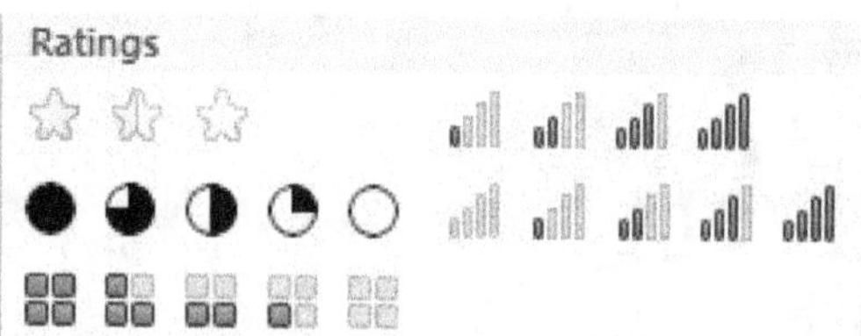

I show you how easy it is to insert an Icon Set within a Pivot Table that will show a "directional icon" depending on the change of the monthly sales values.

So when monthly sales increase from the previous month, a green up arrow is shown and when monthly sales decrease, a red down arrow is shown.

STEP 1: Place the **SALES** Field in the **Values** area, the **MONTH** Field in the **Rows** area and the **YEAR** Field in the **Columns** area.

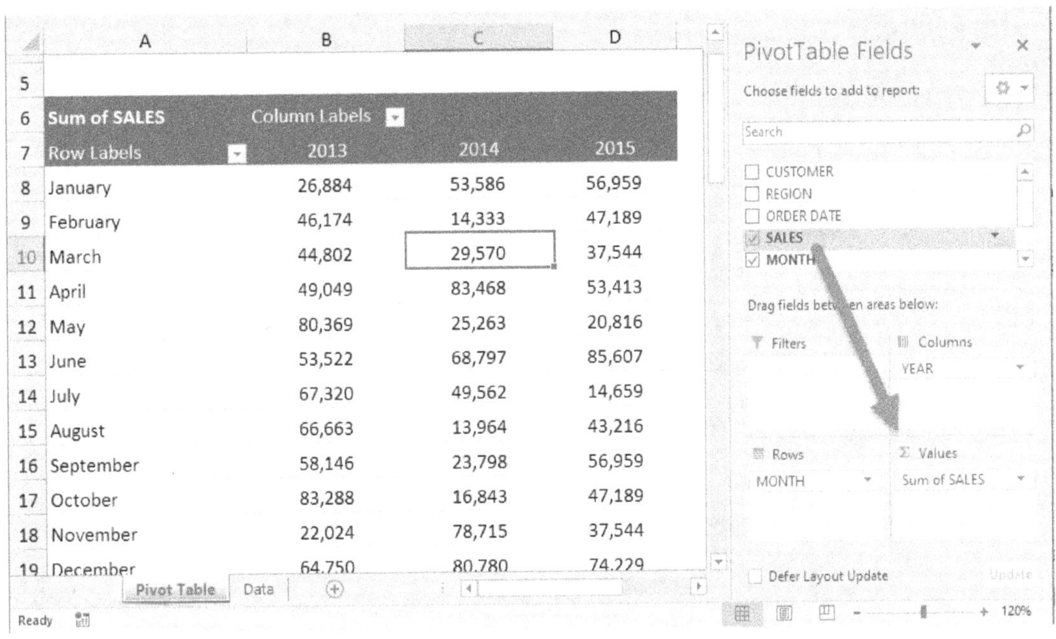

STEP 2: Place the **SALES** Field in the **Values** area a second time. Click on the *Sum of SALES2* field and select **Value Field Settings**

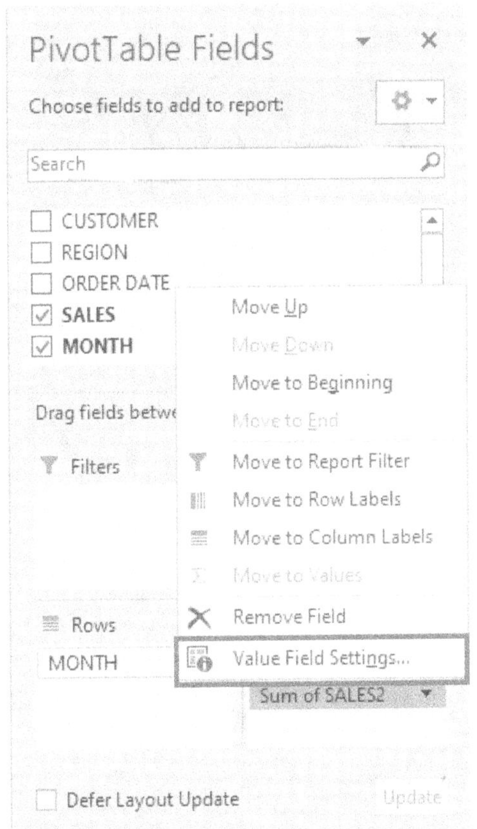

Go to **Show Values as** and from the from down select **Difference From.** Select these parameters:

Base field: MONTH

Base item: (previous)

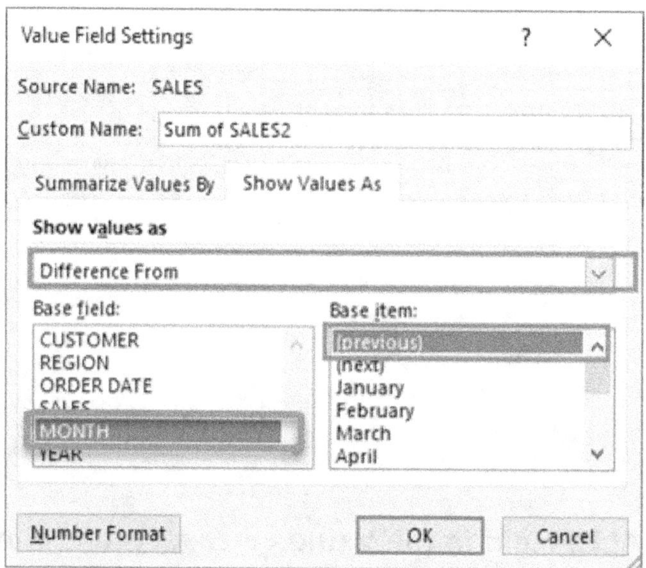

STEP 3: Click in a variance cell. Go to ***Home > Styles > Conditional Formatting > Icon Sets > The First Icon Set***

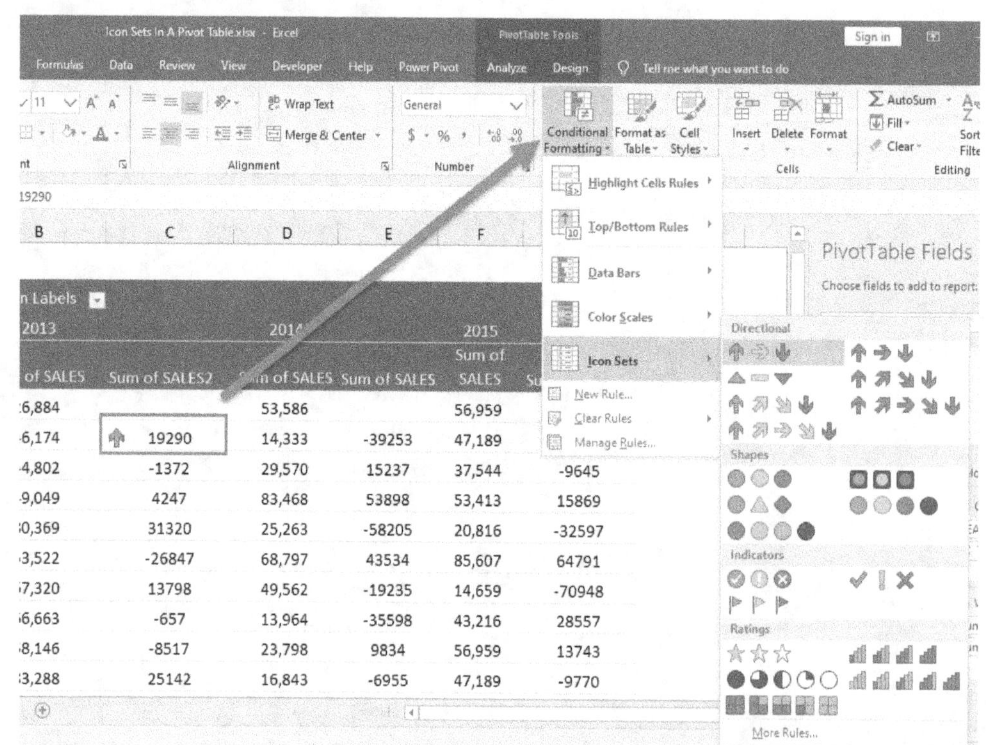

STEP 4: Make sure to select the third option. This excludes the Subtotals and Grand Totals.

Row Labels	2013		2014		2015	
	Sum of SALES	Sum of SALES2	Sum of SALES	Sum of SALES.	Sum of SALES	Sum of SALES2
January	26,884		53,586		56,959	
February	46,174	19290	4,333	-39253	47,189	-9770
March	44,802	-1372				
April	49,049	4247				
May	80,369	31320				
June	53,522	-26847	68,797	43534	85,607	64791
July	67,320	13798	49,562	-19235	14,659	-70948
August	66,663	-657	13,964	-35598	43,216	28557
September	58,146	-8517	23,798	9834	56,959	13743
October	83,288	25142	16,843	-6955	47,189	-9770

Apply formatting rule to …

○ Selected cells
○ All cells showing "Sum of SALES2" values
○ All cells showing "Sum of SALES2" values for "MONTH" and "YEAR"

STEP 5: Go to *Home > Styles > Conditional Formatting > Manage Rules*

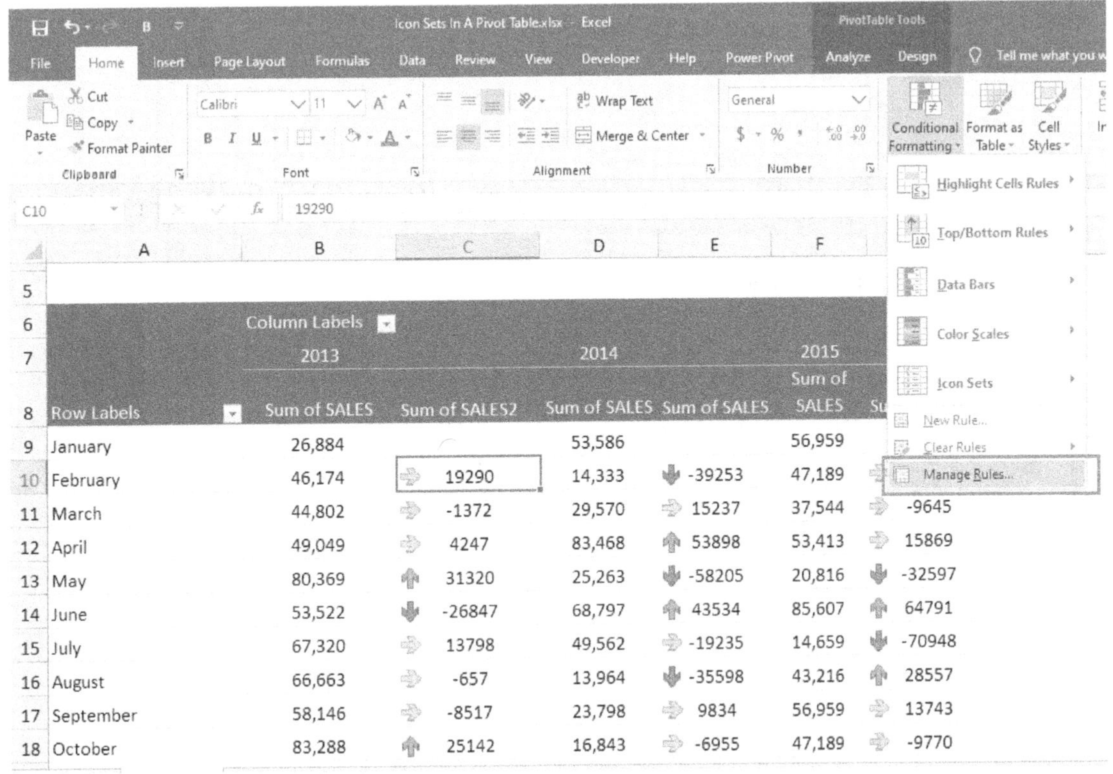

Select **Edit Rule.**

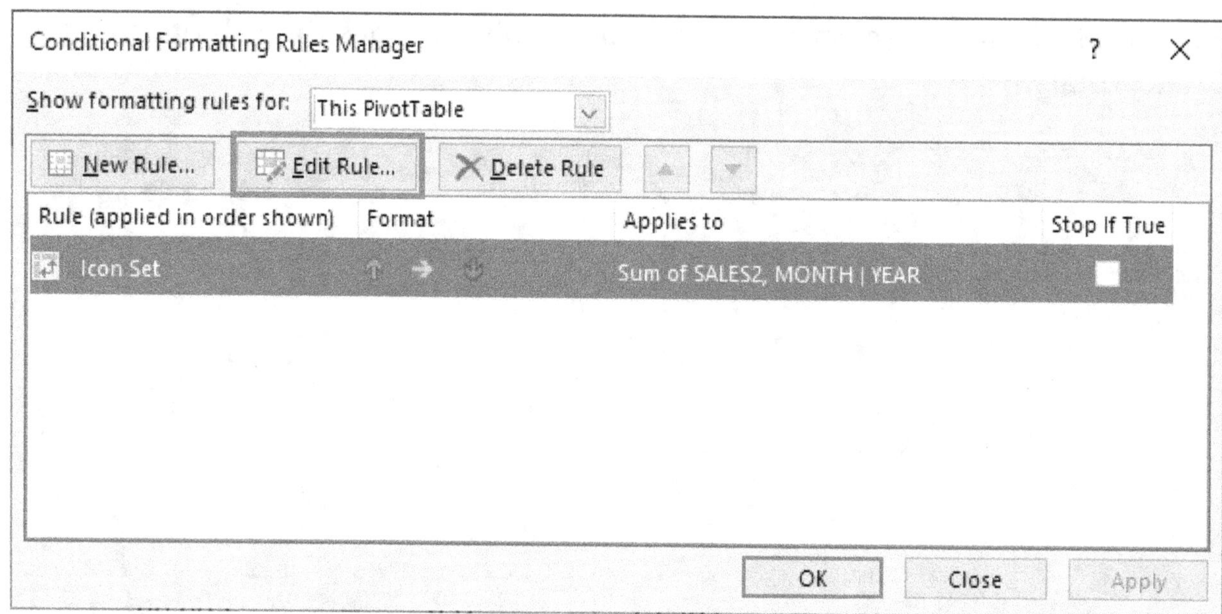

Set the settings to the ones shown below. This will set the column to show the **arrow icons** only - *A green arrow for positive, an orange for zero and a red arrow for negative.*

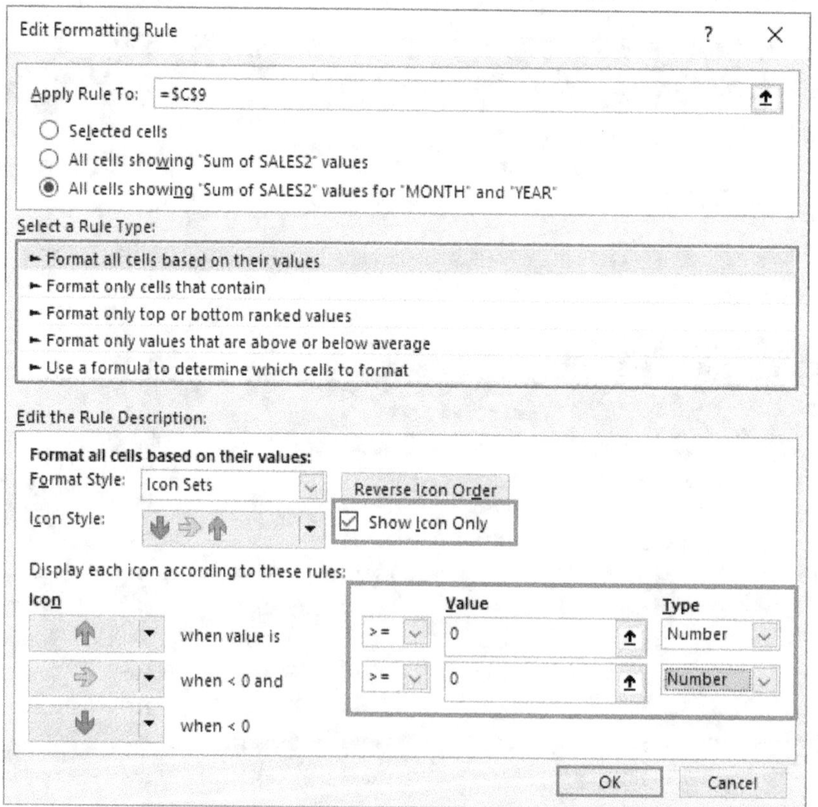

Your icons are now ready in your Pivot Table!

Bonus Tip: Click on the cell with the title *Sum of SALES2* and manually change the name to *Variance*.

	Column Labels					
	2013		2014		2015	
Row Labels	Sum of SALES	Sum of SALES2	Sum of SALES	Sum of SALES	Sum of SALES	Sum of SALES2
January	26,884		53,586		56,959	
February	46,174	↑	14,333	↓	47,189	↓
March	44,802	↓	29,570	↑	37,544	↓
April	49,049	↑	83,468	↑	53,413	↑
May	80,369	↑	25,263	↓	20,816	↓
June	53,522	↓	68,797	↑	85,607	↑
July	67,320	↑	49,562	↓	14,659	↓
August	66,663	↓	13,964	↓	43,216	↑
September	58,146	↓	23,798	↑	56,959	↑
October	83,288	↑	16,843	↓	47,189	↓
November	22,024	↓	78,715	↑	37,544	↓
December	64,750	↑	80,780	↑	74,229	↑
Grand Total	**662,991**		**538,679**		**575,324**	

Pivot Tables: Show Report Filter Pages

When you are using an Excel Pivot Table you can show the items within the Report Filter on separate sheets inside your workbook.

Say that you have created an awesome Pivot Table which shows total sales and number of transactions per region.

You can drop in your *Customer* field in the Report Filter and replicate the Pivot Table for each of your customers in a separate *Sheet*.

See how you can do this below.

Here is our data:

CUSTOMER	REGION	ORDER DATE	SALES	MONTH	YEAR
Acme, inc.	NORTH	13/04/2014	$1,000,000	April	2014
Widget Corp	SOUTH	21/12/2014	$1,500,000	December	2014
123 Warehousing	EAST	15/02/2014	$2,000,000	February	2014
Demo Company	WEST	14/05/2014	$2,500,000	May	2014
Smith and Co.	NORTH	28/06/2015	$63,116	June	2015
Foo Bars	SOUTH	15/01/2015	$38,281	January	2015

Here is our Pivot Table:

Row Labels	Sum of SALES	Count of SALES2
EAST	2,000,000	1
NORTH	1,063,116	2
SOUTH	1,538,281	2
WEST	2,500,000	1
Grand Total	**7,101,397**	**6**

STEP 1: Drop the **Customer** Field in the report filter.

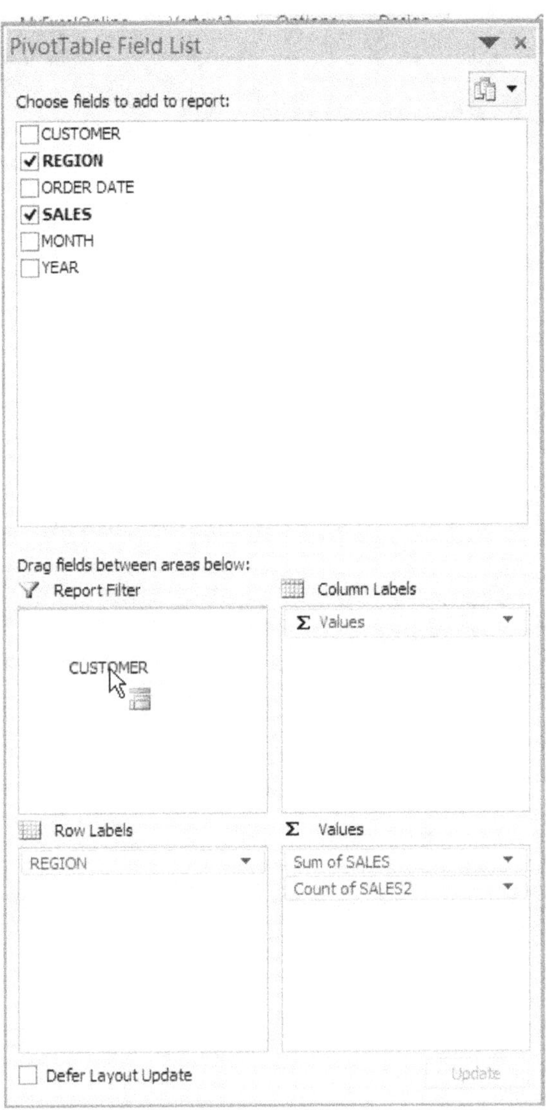

STEP 2: Go to *Options > Options Drop Down > Show Report Filter Pages*

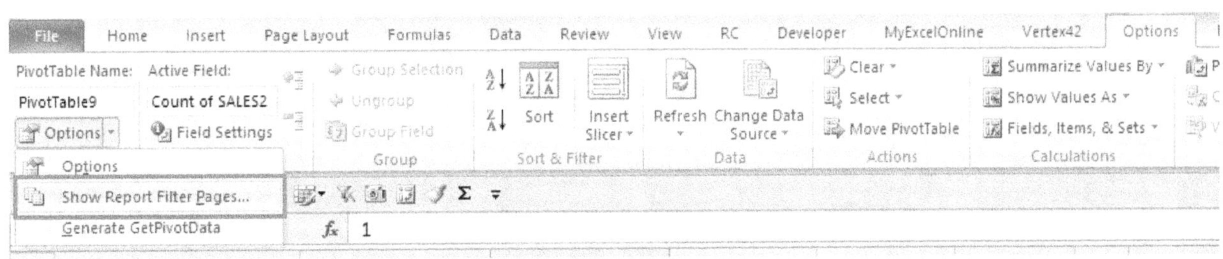

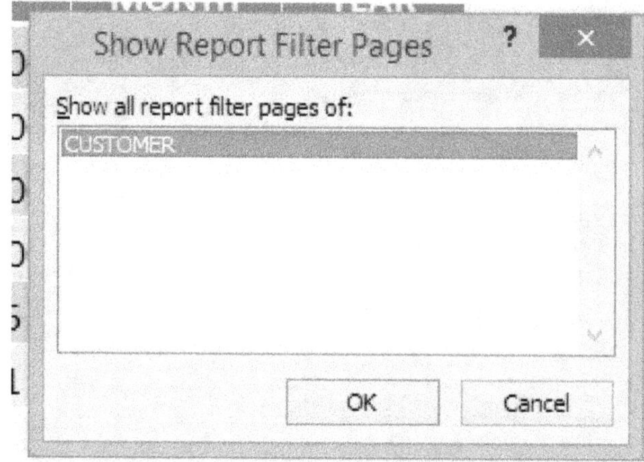

Each customer's pivot table will show in a unique sheet!

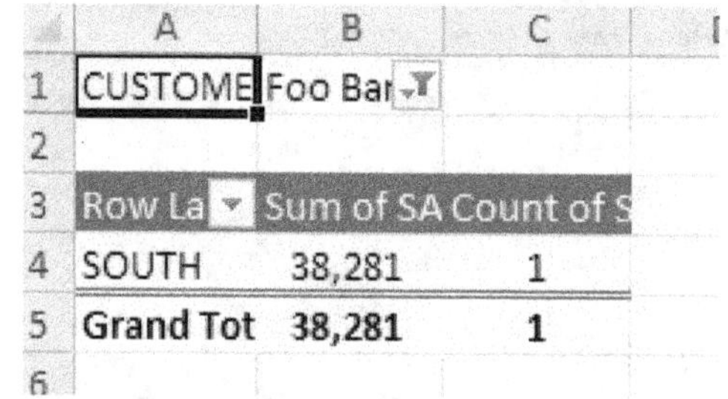

Pivot Tables: Sorting a Pivot Table

There are a few ways that you can *Sort* a Pivot Table. You can Sort the Row/Column Labels as well as Values within a Pivot Table. Below I show you three quick ways.

STEP 1: You can sort by **clicking a cell & dragging each row item up or down**

Sum of SALES	Column Labels			
Row Labels	2014	2015	2013	Grand Total
Widget Corp	68,797	94,378	129,462	292,637
Fake Brothers	164,248	43,216	66,663	274,127
Demo Company	13,964	106,826	113,799	234,589
Acme, inc.	25,263	113,918	85,030	224,211
Smith and Co.	77,384	41,632	80,369	199,385
123 Warehousing	49,562	75,088	66,826	191,476
ABC Telecom	108,285	14,659	67,320	190,264
Foo Bars	31,176	85,607	53,522	170,305
Grand Total	538,679	575,324	662,991	1,776,994

This is now the sorted result:

Sum of SALES	Column Labels			
Row Labels	2014	2015	2013	Grand Total
123 Warehousing	49,562	75,088	66,826	191,476
ABC Telecom	108,285	14,659	67,320	190,264
Acme, inc.	25,263	113,918	85,030	224,211
Demo Company	13,964	106,826	113,799	234,589
Foo Bars	31,176	85,607	53,522	170,305
Fake Brothers	164,248	43,216	66,663	274,127
Smith and Co.	77,384	41,632	80,369	199,385
Widget Corp	68,797	94,378	129,462	292,637
Grand Total	538,679	575,324	662,991	1,776,994

STEP 2: You can also sort by **typing an existing cell value**

In our example, we are typing Widget Corp, which is currently located at the last row.

Sum of SALES	Column Labels			
Row Labels	2014	2015	2013	Grand Total
Widget Corp	49,562	75,088	66,826	191,476
ABC Telecom	108,285	14,659	67,320	190,264
Acme, inc.	25,263	113,918	85,030	224,211
Demo Company	13,964	106,826	113,799	234,589
Foo Bars	31,176	85,607	53,522	170,305
Fake Brothers	164,248	43,216	66,663	274,127
Smith and Co.	77,384	41,632	80,369	199,385
Widget Corp	68,797	94,378	129,462	292,637
Grand Total	**538,679**	**575,324**	**662,991**	**1,776,994**

123 Warehousing gets pushed down, and Widget Corp moves to the top row.

Sum of SALES	Column Labels			
Row Labels	2014	2015	2013	Grand Total
Widget Corp	68,797	94,378	129,462	292,637
123 Warehousing		75,088	66,826	191,476
ABC Telecom		14,659	67,320	190,264
Acme, inc.		113,918	85,030	224,211
Demo Company	13,964	106,826	113,799	234,589
Foo Bars	31,176	85,607	53,522	170,305
Fake Brothers	164,248	43,216	66,663	274,127
Smith and Co.	77,384	41,632	80,369	199,385
Grand Total	**538,679**	**575,324**	**662,991**	**1,776,994**

Sum of SALES
Value: 68,797
Row: Widget Corp
Column: 2014

Try it on any company name and select *Sort > Sort A to Z*

Our table will be sorted in alphabetical order based on the company name.

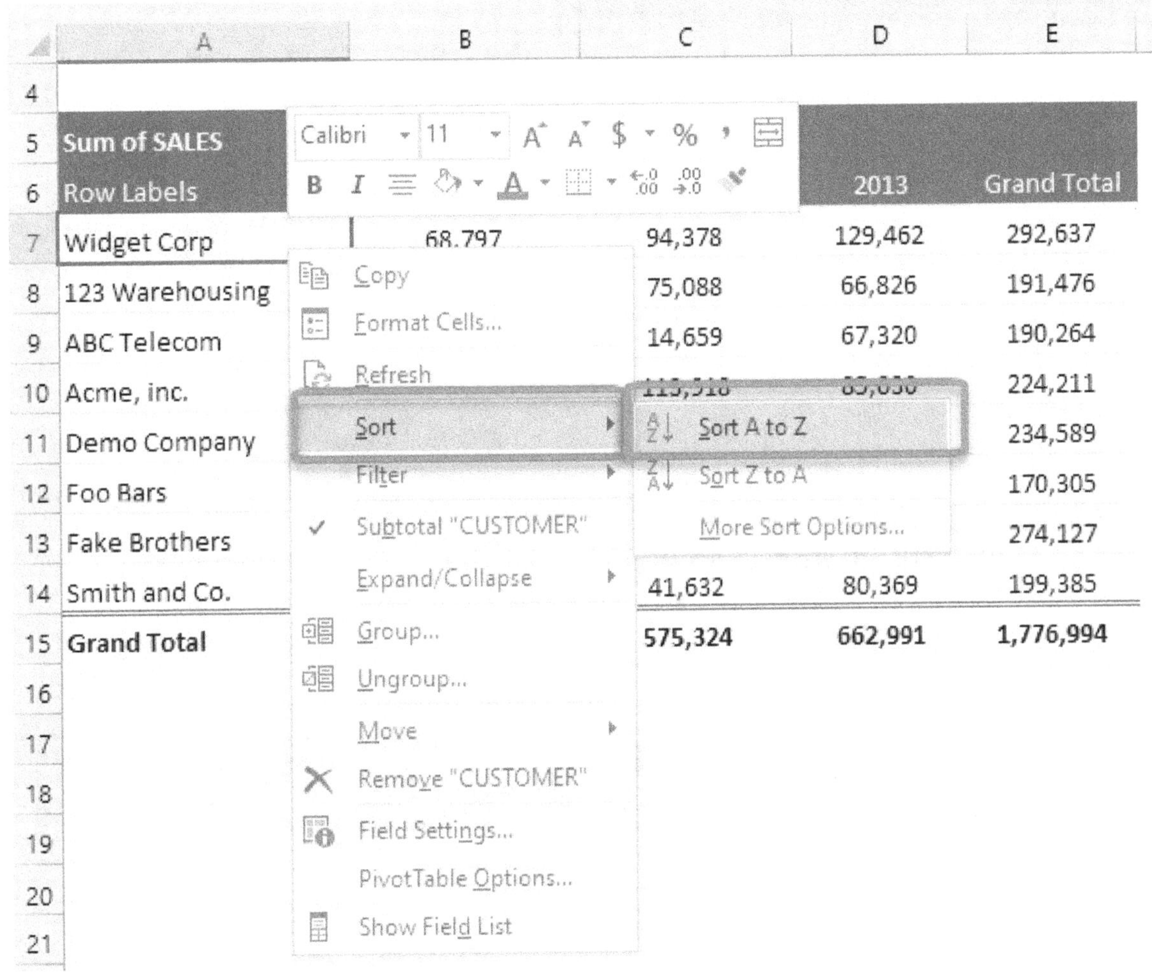

Try it also on the Grand Total column. **Right click** and select *Sort > Sort Smallest to Largest*

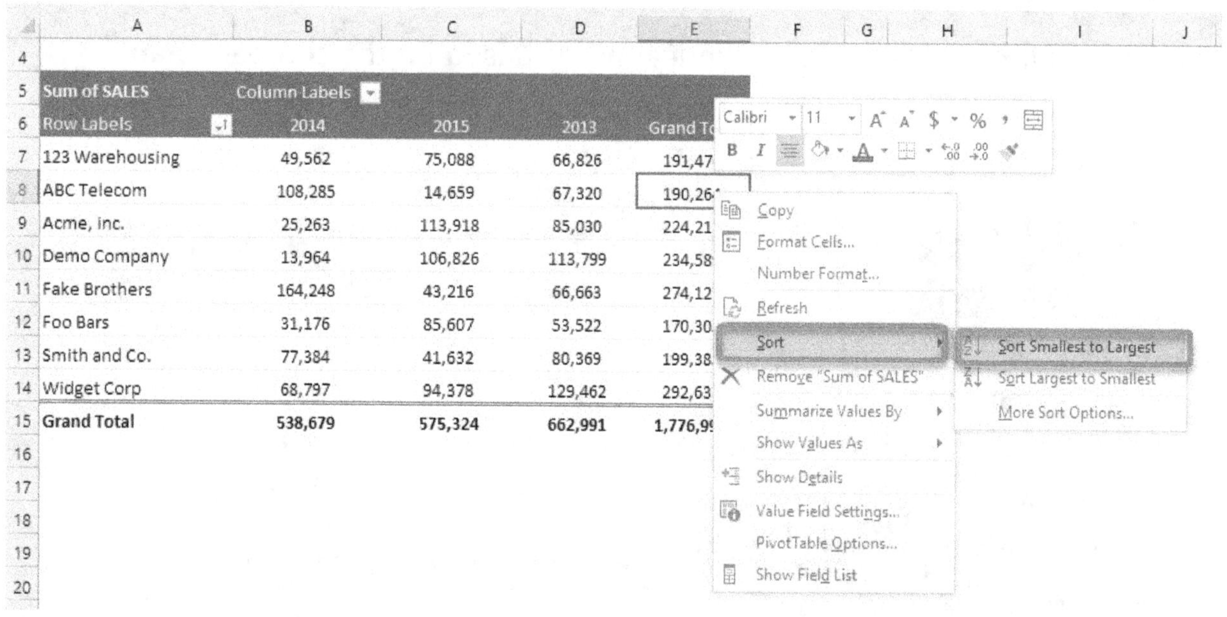

Our table is now sorted in ascending order by the Grand Total values!

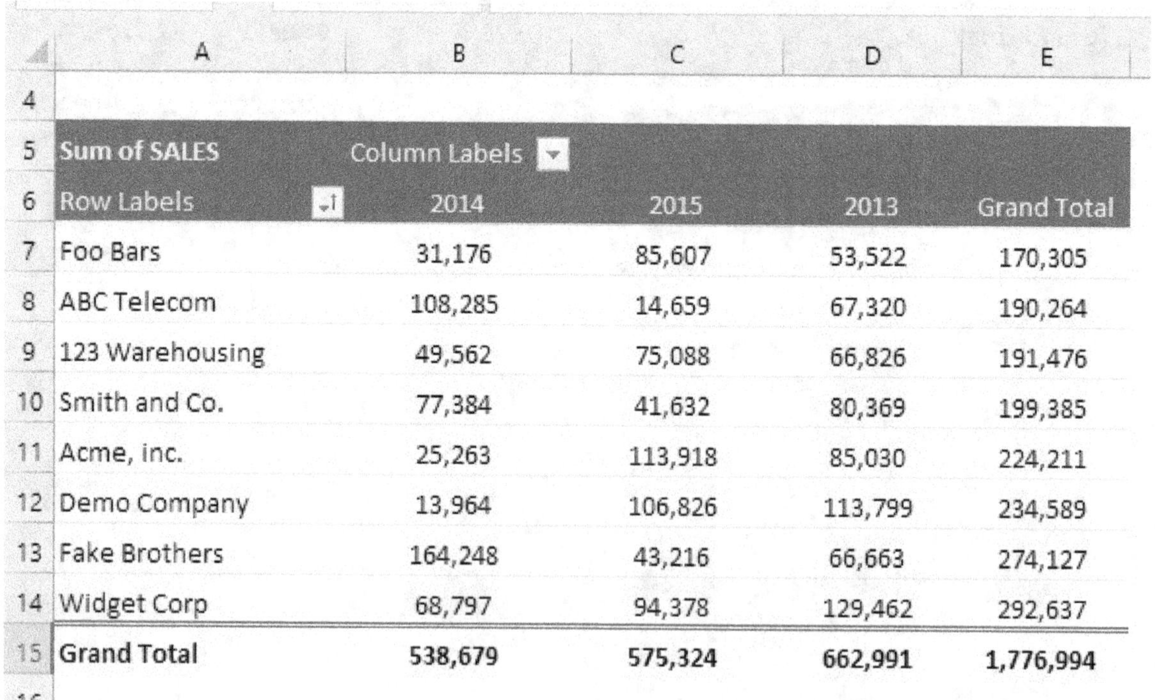

Sum of SALES	Column Labels			
Row Labels	2014	2015	2013	Grand Total
Foo Bars	31,176	85,607	53,522	170,305
ABC Telecom	108,285	14,659	67,320	190,264
123 Warehousing	49,562	75,088	66,826	191,476
Smith and Co.	77,384	41,632	80,369	199,385
Acme, inc.	25,263	113,918	85,030	224,211
Demo Company	13,964	106,826	113,799	234,589
Fake Brothers	164,248	43,216	66,663	274,127
Widget Corp	68,797	94,378	129,462	292,637
Grand Total	538,679	575,324	662,991	1,776,994

WORKING WITH DATA

11 Excel Data Entry Form Tips

Data Entry Forms is an **extremely useful feature** if inputting data is part of your daily work.

It can help you **avoid the mistakes** and make the **data entry process faster**. It also helps you focus on **one record at a time**!

It is a convenient and faster way to input records in Excel by displaying one row of information at a time without having to move from one column to another.

Whenever I wanted to enter data in Excel, it would take me a very long time to input these records one by one, but I discovered a handy trick that can turn my Excel Table into a handy Excel **Data Entry Form**!

Create Form in Excel

Say goodbye to inputting entering data into this Table row by row by row by row....

Follow the steps below:

STEP 1: Convert your Column names into a Table, go to *Insert> Table*

Make sure **My table has headers** is also checked.

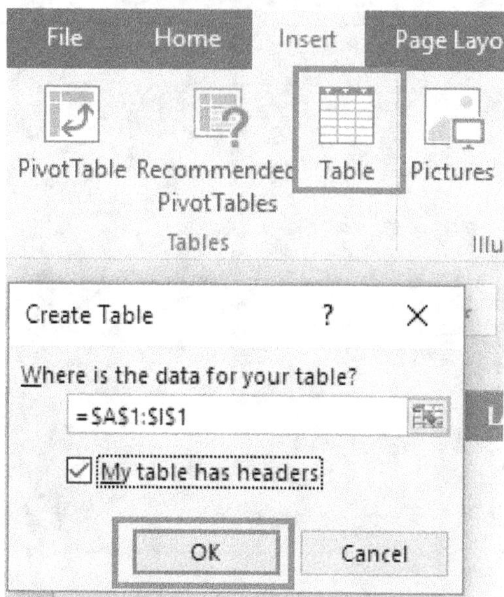

STEP 2: Let us add the **Form** Creation functionality to understand how to make a fillable form in Excel.

Go to ***File > Options***

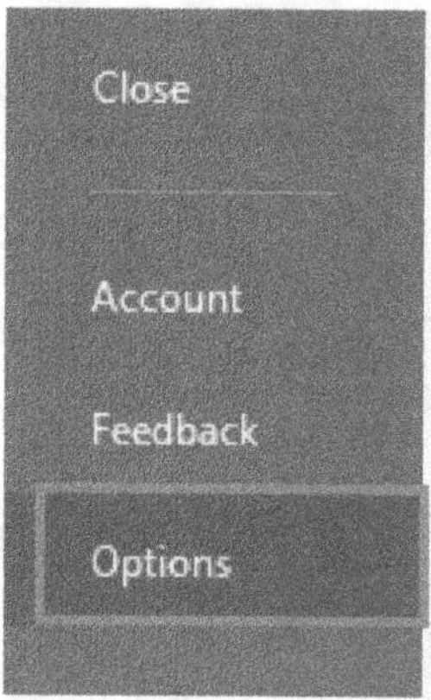

STEP 3: Go to ***Customize Ribbon.***

Select **Commands Not in the Ribbon** and **Form.** This is the functionality we need. Click **New Tab.**

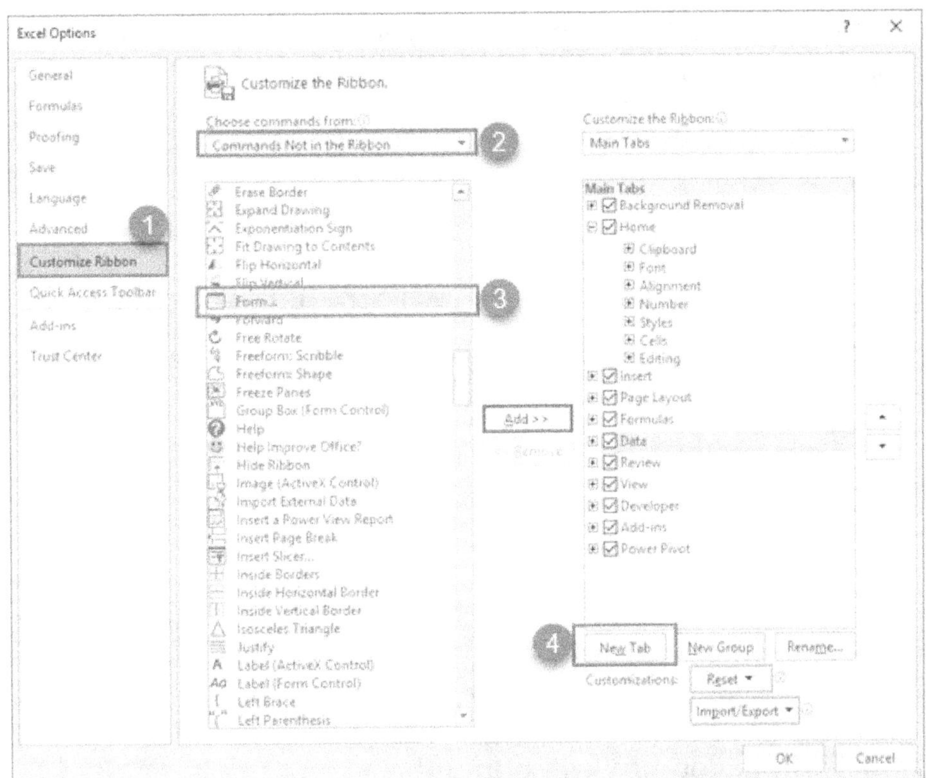

STEP 4: Under the **New Tab**, select **New Group,** and click **Add.**

This will add **Forms** to a New Tab in our Ribbon.

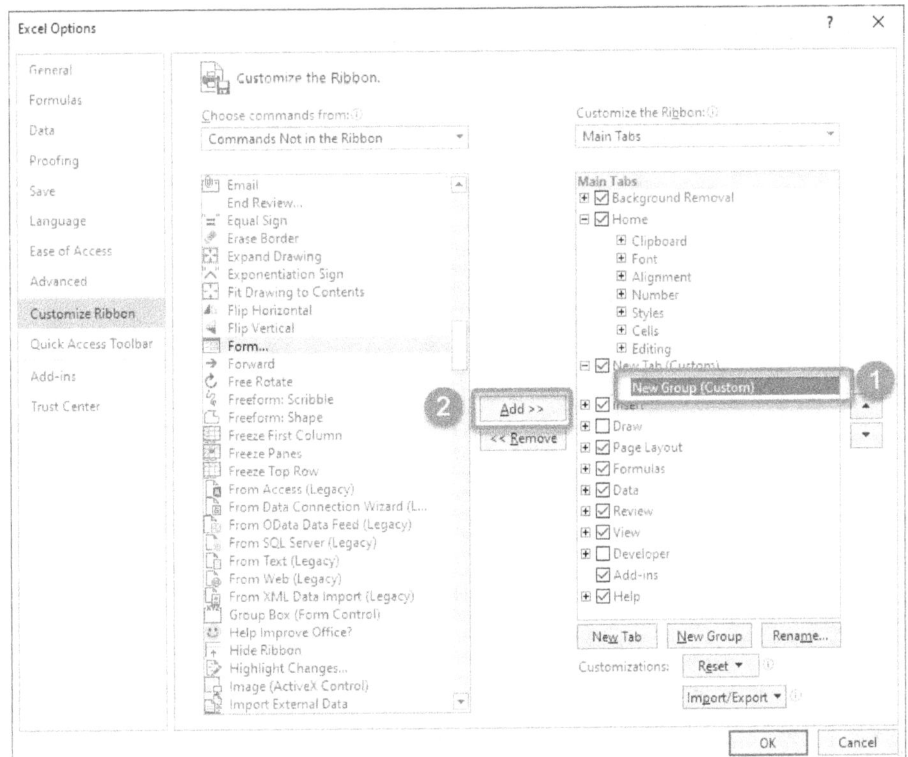

Notice that there is also a **Rename** button, you can use it to rename the **New Tab** and **New Group** into something more descriptive, like *Form*:

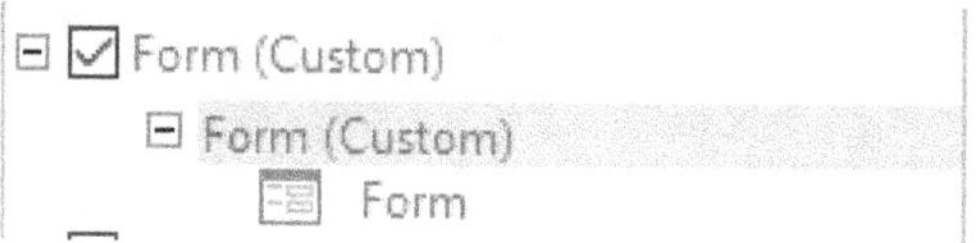

STEP 5: Select your Table, and on your new **Form** tab, select **Form**.

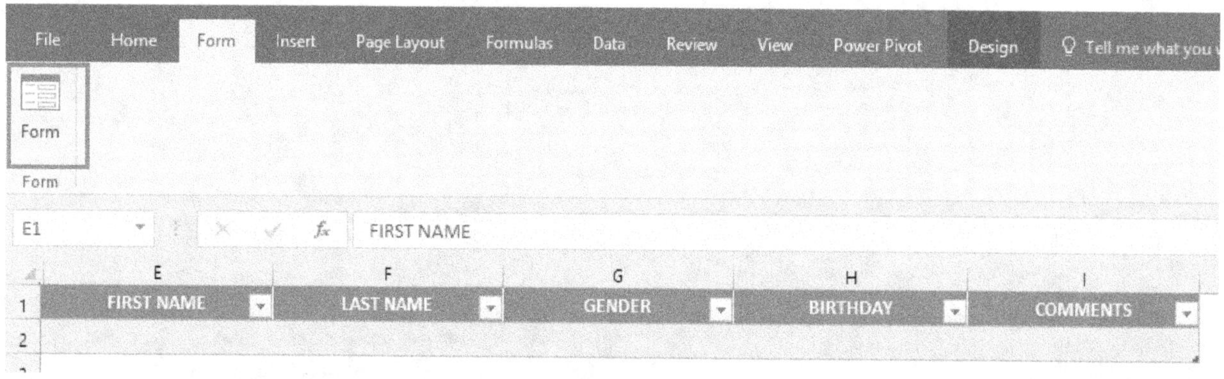

STEP 6: A new Form dialog box will pop up!

Input your data into each section.

Click **New** to save it. Repeat this process for all the records you want to add.

Press **Close** to get out of this screen and see the data in your Excel Table.

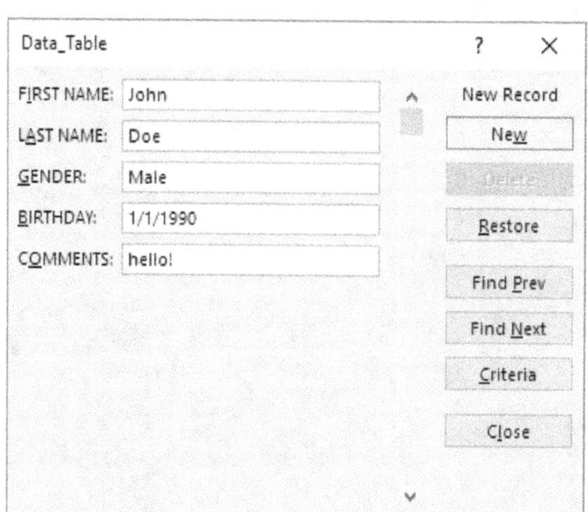

You can now use this new form to continually input data into your Excel Table!

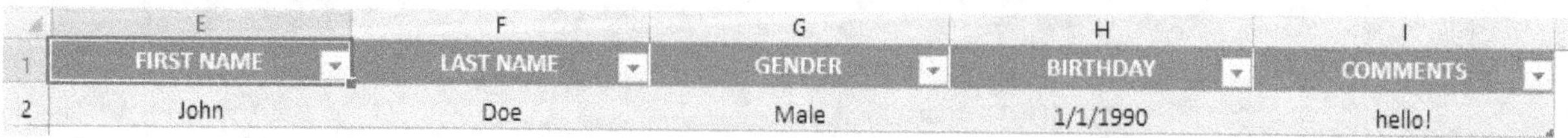

Add to Quick Access Toolbar (QAT)

Now that you have learned how to create a form in Excel, let's put them on your QAT for easy access.

To add to the Quick Access Toolbar (QAT), follow the steps below:

STEP 1: Click on the **small arrow right next to QAT**.

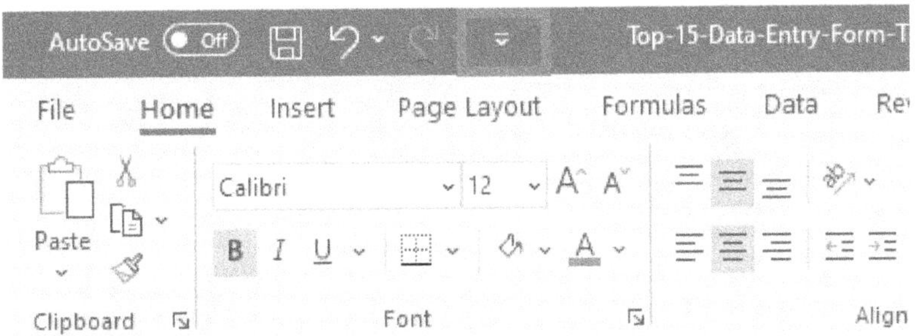

STEP 2: Click on **More Commands** from the dropdown list.

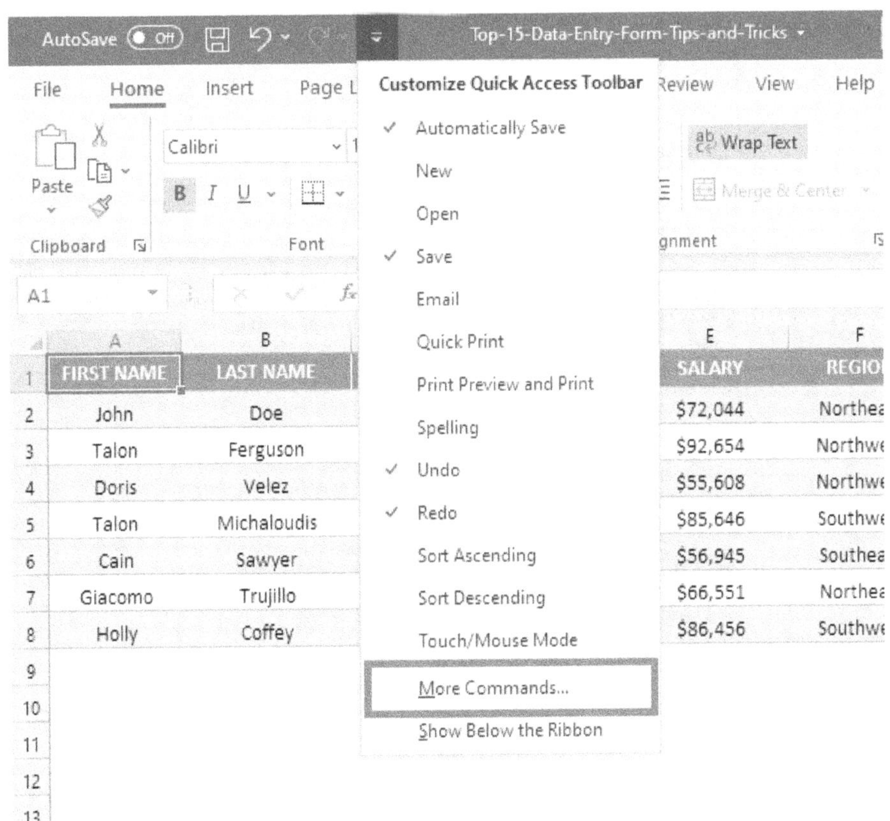

STEP 3: In the Excel Options dialog box, select **All Commands** from *Choose commands from* list.

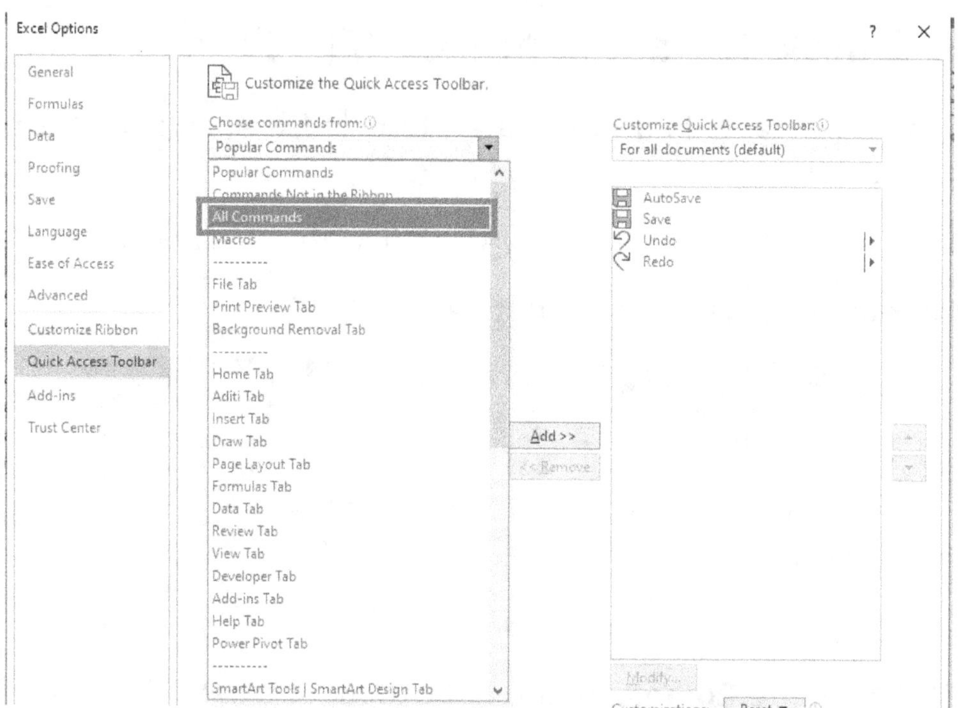

STEP 4: Select **Form** from the list and then click on **Add>>**.

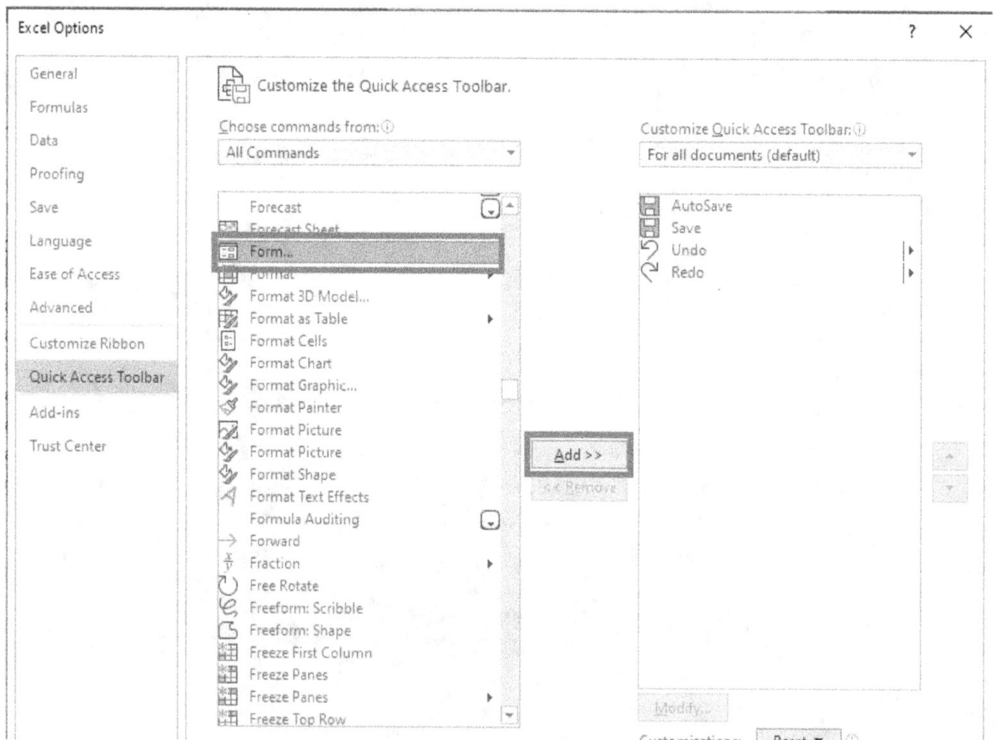

STEP 5: Form is now available in the *Customize Quick Access Toolbar*. Click **OK**.

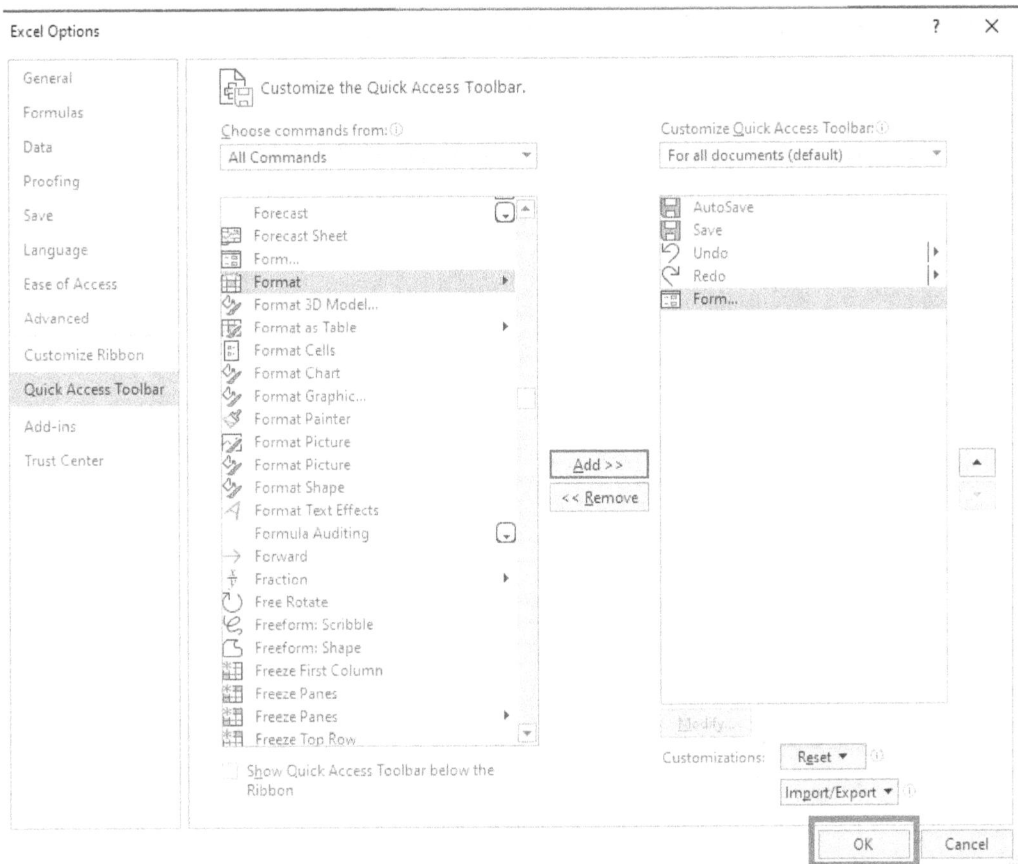

Data Entry Form is now part of your Quick Access Toolbar.

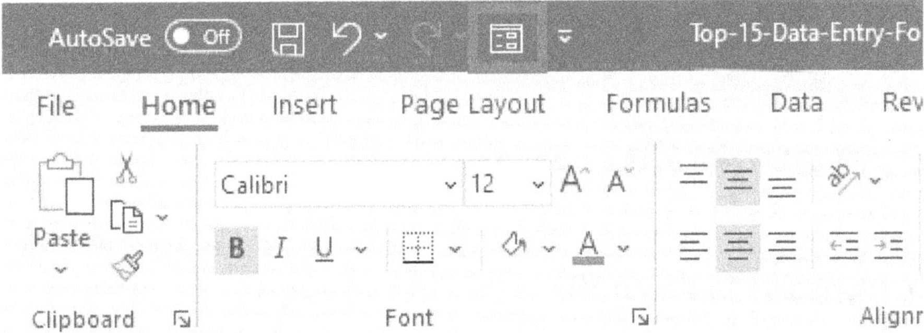

Access the Form anytime

To access the Excel Data Entry Form, **click on any cell** in the table and click on the **Form icon** in Quick Access Toolbar.

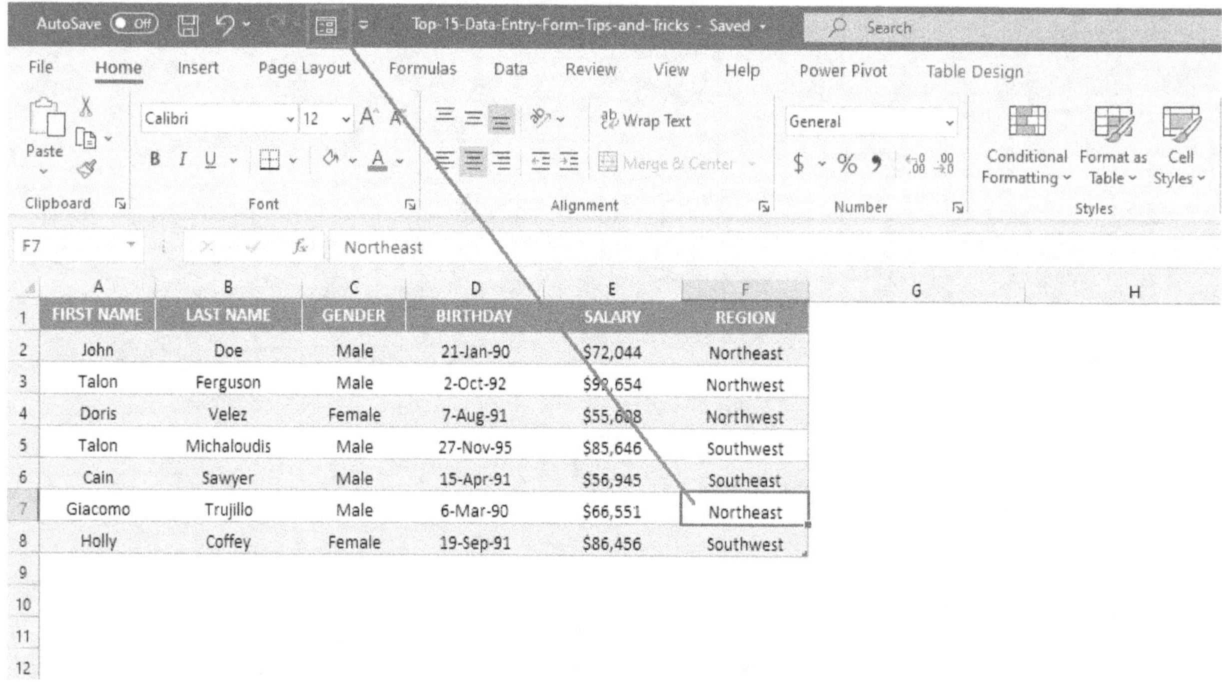

If you try to access the form when **you haven't selected a cell within the data table**, you will receive an **error message** like the one shown below:

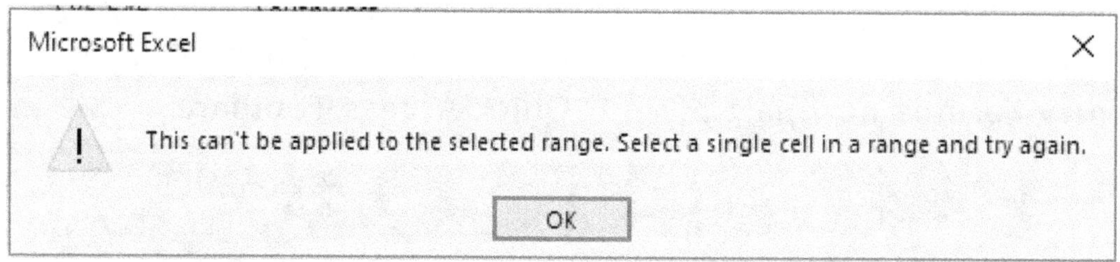

Browse through Records

To navigate through the existing records, simply use the **Find Previous** and **Find Next** buttons available on the Data Entry Form.

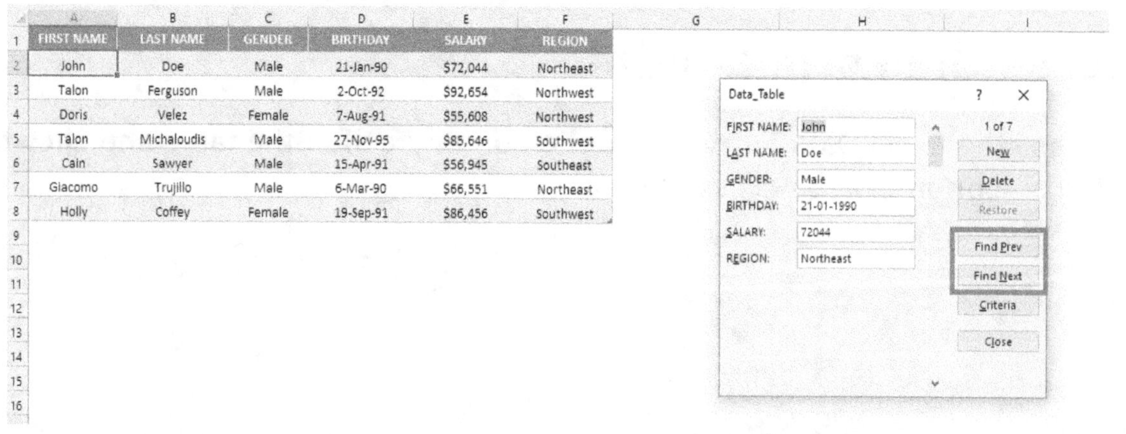

{ 380 }

You can also **use the scroll bar** to go through the records one after the other.

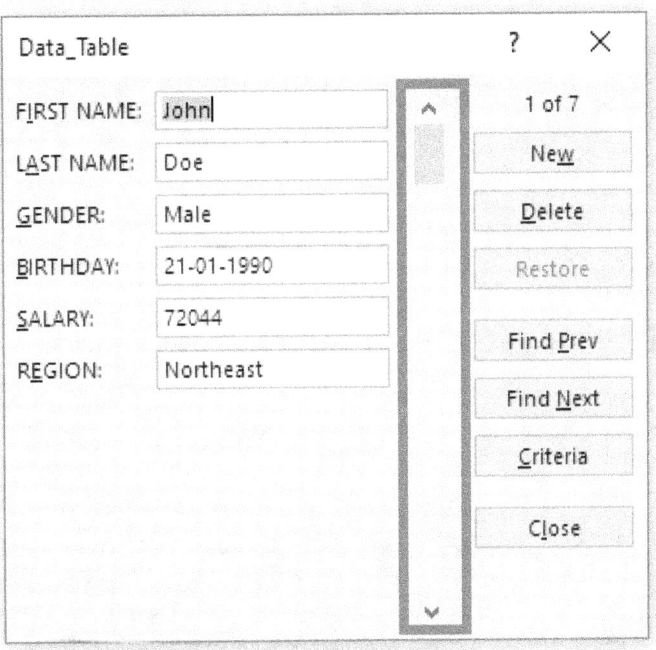

This will save time when you have a data with multiple columns and records.

Edit Existing Record

Use the **Find Previous** and **Find Next** buttons to **search for the record** you want to edit.

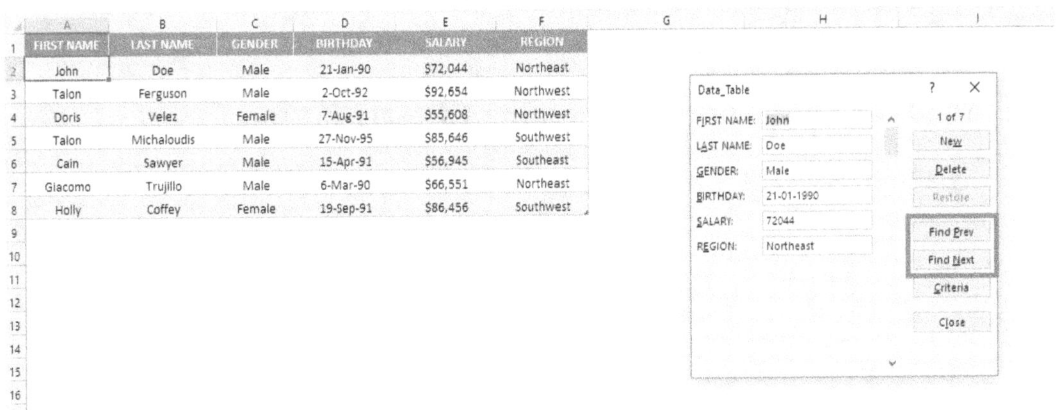

Once you find the desired record, simply **make the necessary changes** and hit **Enter** in Excel.

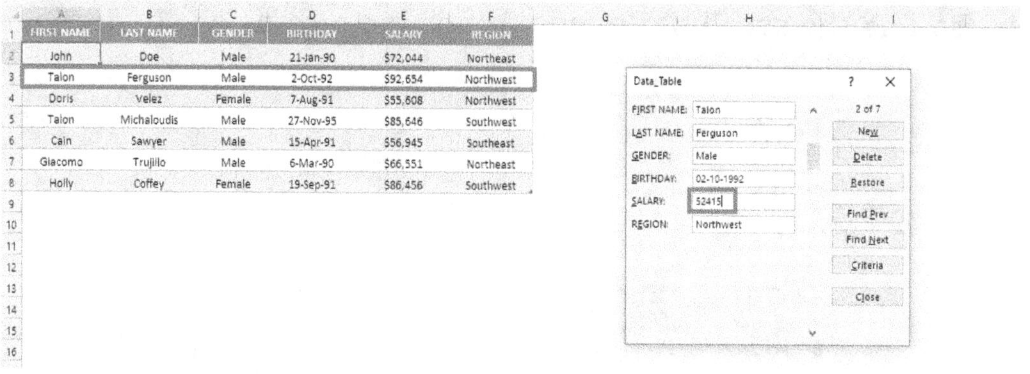

The data table will be updated with the changes made.

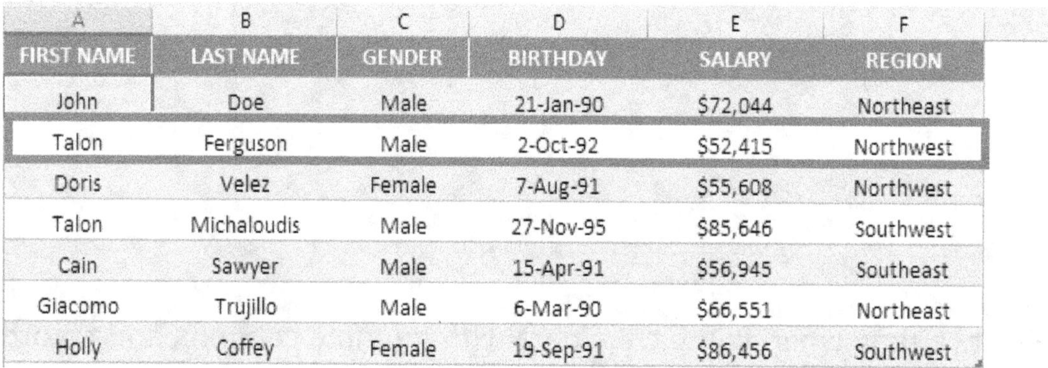

Search Criteria

Using Wildcards

If you wish to search all entries containing the word "east" in the Region Column, you can do that by using the wildcard asterisk *.

STEP 1: In the Data Entry Form, click on the **Criteria** button

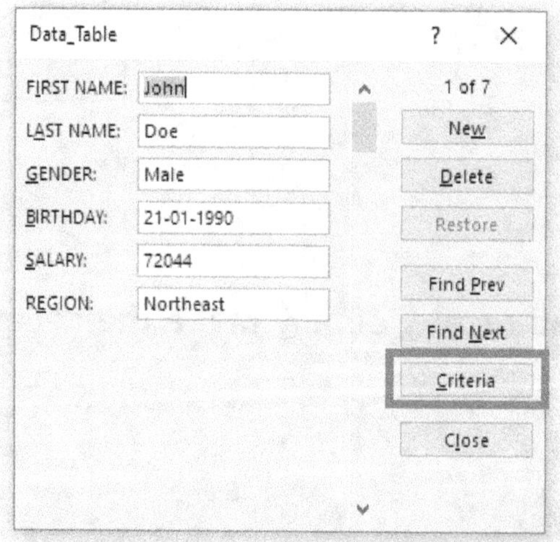

STEP 3: Click **Find Next** to find the entries containing the word *east*.

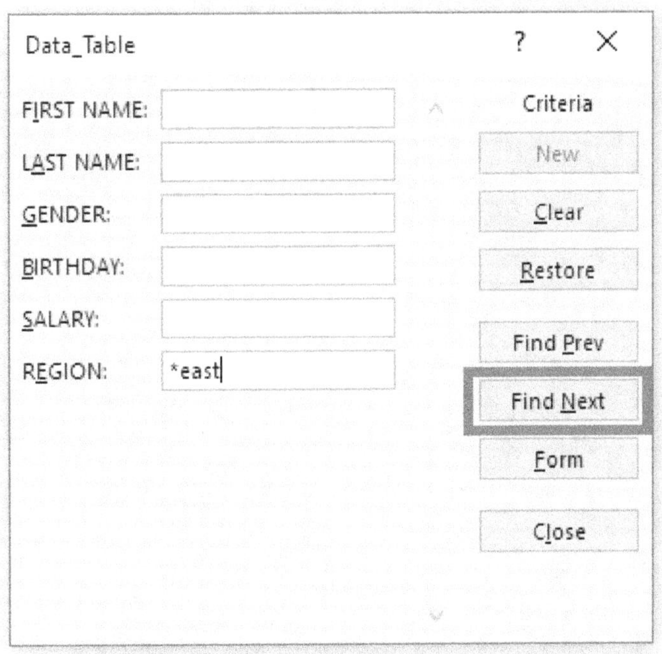

The Data Entry Form will find the three entries for you in this scenario!

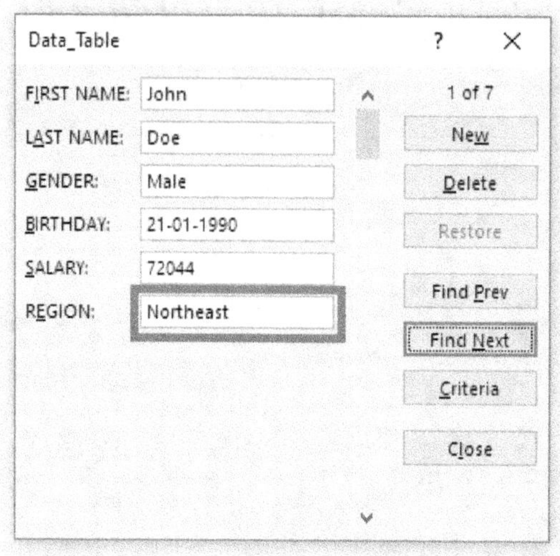

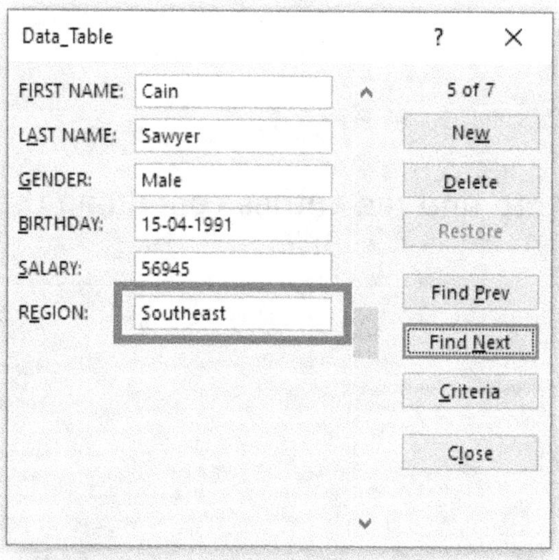

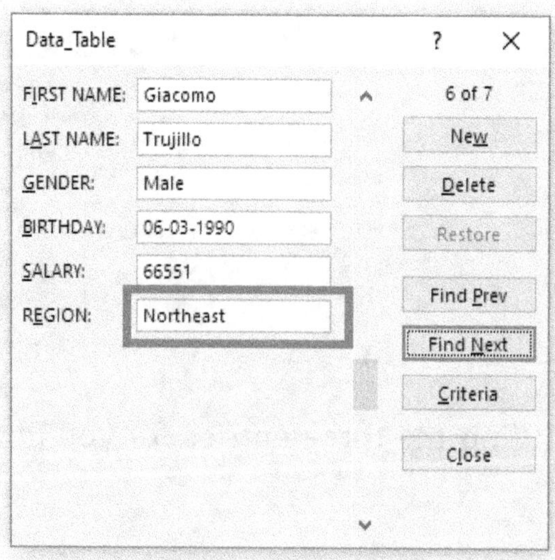

Using greater or less than sign

If you want to search for people having a salary greater than or equal to $75,000, you can do so by following the steps below:

STEP 1: In the Data Entry Form, click on the **Criteria** button

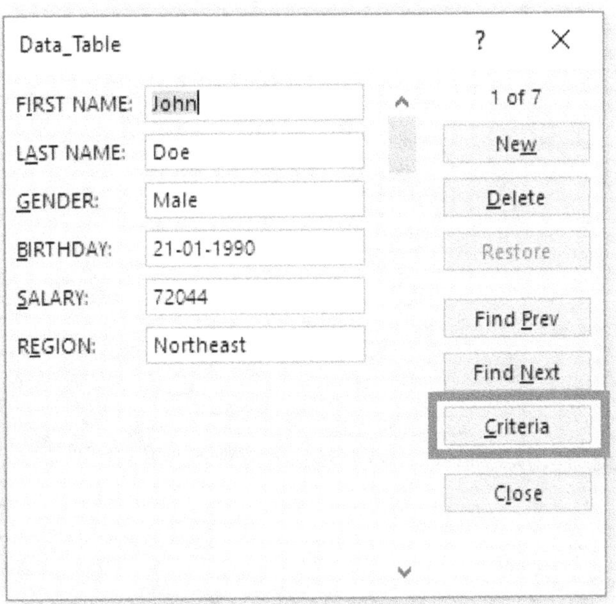

STEP 2: In the **Salary** field, type *>=75000.*

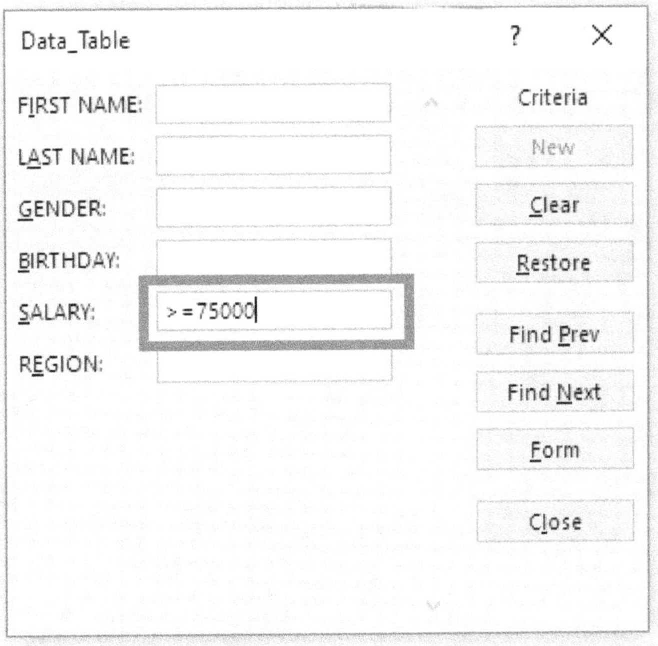

STEP 3: Click **Find Next** to find all entries with a salary *greater than or equal to $75,000*.

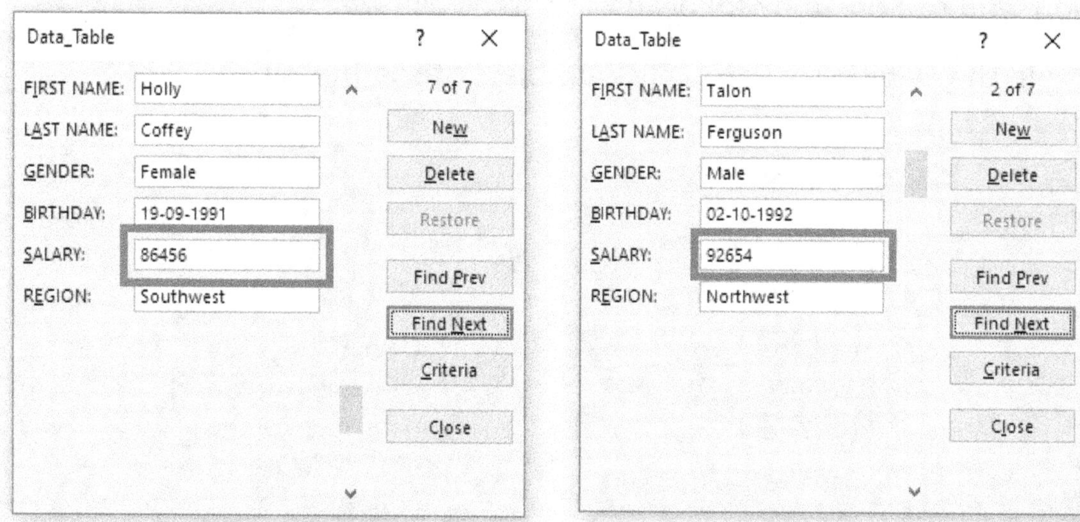

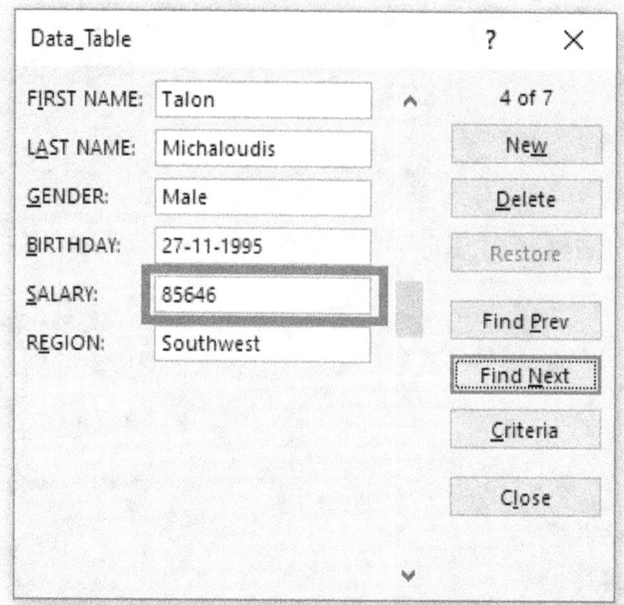

Restore a Record

Suppose you have **accidentally deleted** the first name of a record.

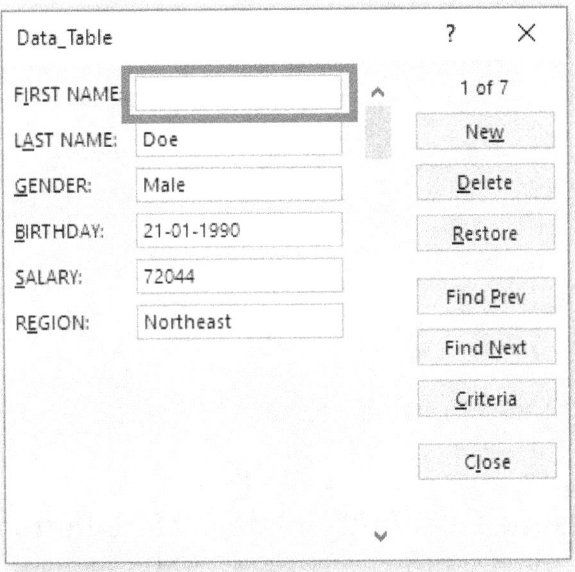

And you don't remember what was written in that field! Don't panic.

You can use the **Restore** button in the Excel Data Entry Form and **retrieve the data lost** accidentally.

The data will reappear in the respective field.

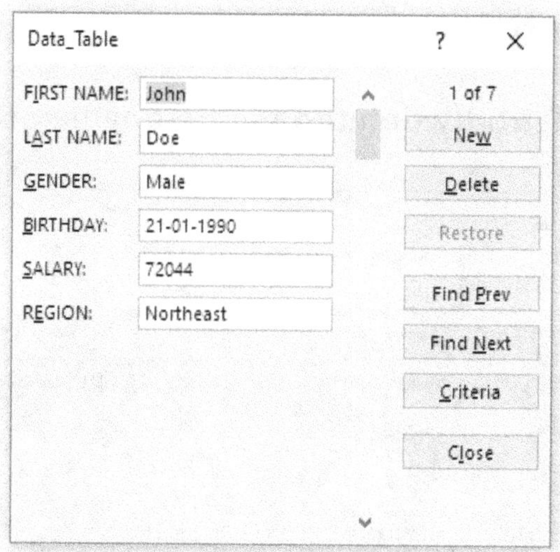

One thing you need to keep in mind is that the Restore button is **only useful if you haven't pressed Enter.**

The moment you press the Enter button, the Restore button will become inactive and you won't be able to revert back to the original data.

Data Validation in Forms

Even though you cannot directly add any data validation to the form, any **restriction created on the data table will still be in effect within the Forms.**

Let's see how!

Say, you add a list rule to the Region Column using Data Validation.

STEP 1: Select the **Region** Column.

	A	B	C	D	E	F
1	FIRST NAME	LAST NAME	GENDER	BIRTHDAY	SALARY	REGION
2	John	Doe	Male	21-Jan-90	$72,044	Northeast
3	Talon	Ferguson	Male	2-Oct-92	$52,415	Northwest
4	Doris	Velez	Female	7-Aug-91	$55,608	Northwest
5	Talon	Michaloudis	Male	27-Nov-95	$85,646	Southwest
6	Cain	Sawyer	Male	15-Apr-91	$56,945	Southeast
7	Giacomo	Trujillo	Male	6-Mar-90	$66,551	Northeast
8	Holly	Coffey	Female	19-Sep-91	$86,456	Southwest
9						
10						

STEP 2: Go to **Data Tab** > **Data Tools (Group)** > **Data Validation.**

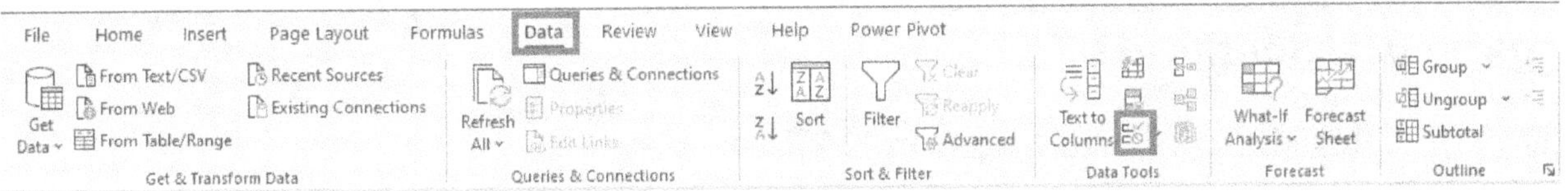

STEP 3: In the Data Validation dialog box, click on the *Allow* dropdown and select **List**.

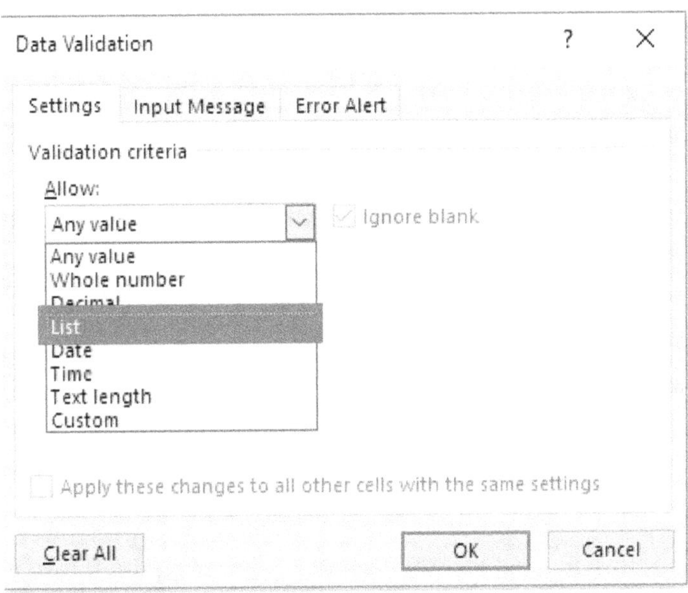

STEP 4: In the *Source* field, type **Northeast, Northwest, Southeast, Southwest,** and click **OK.**

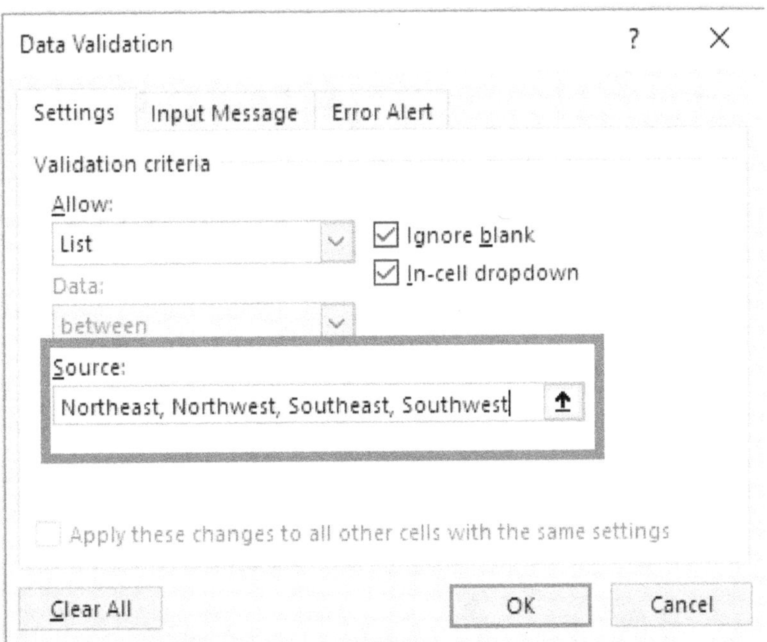

Data Validation has now been inserted in the Region Column where you are only allowed to enter values present in the list *(Northeast, Northwest, Southeast, Southwest).*

STEP 5: Click on the **Forms icon** in QAT.

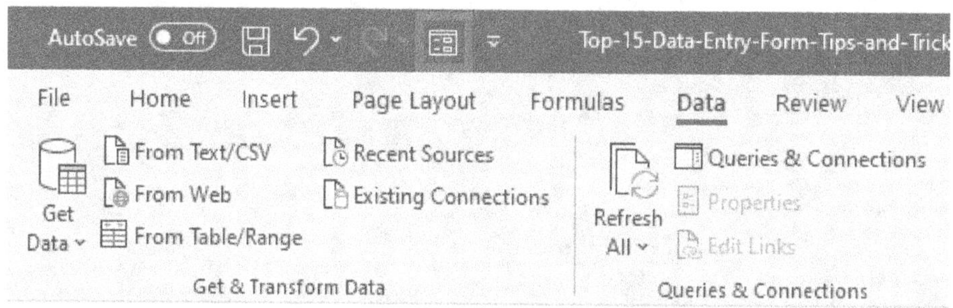

STEP 6: Change the Region for Record 1 from **Northeast to East** and Click **OK**.

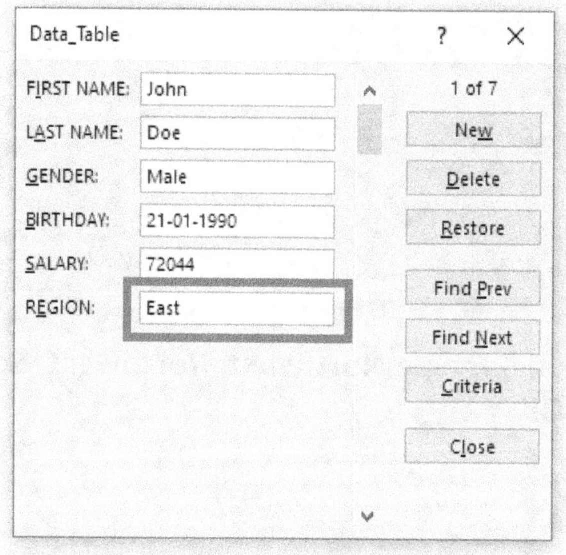

Once you click OK, you will see an ***error message*** as below:

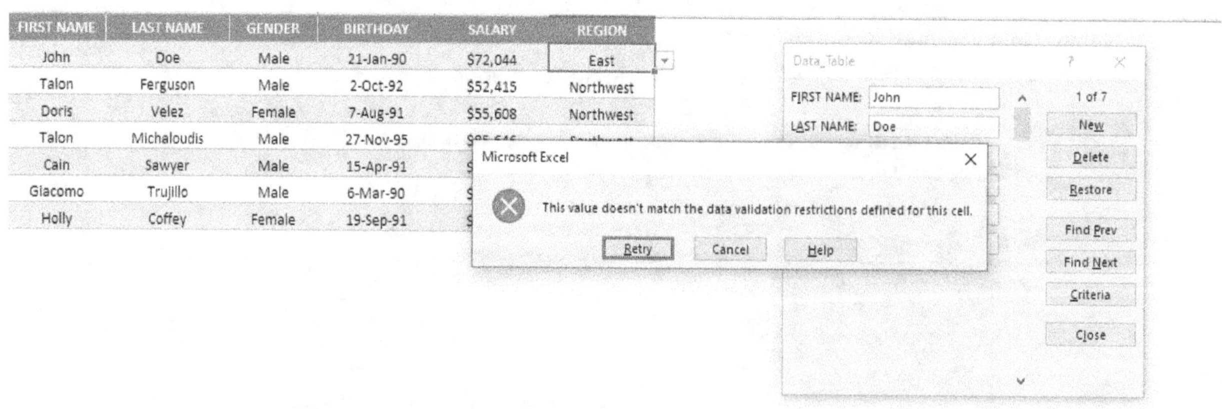

Delete a Record

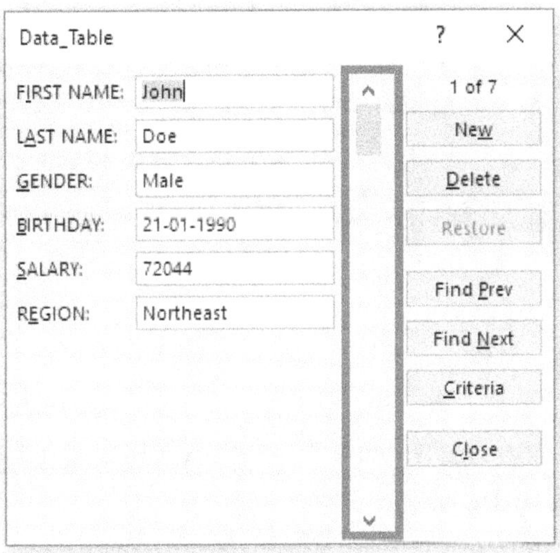

	A	B	C	D	E	F
1	FIRST NAME	LAST NAME	GENDER	BIRTHDAY	SALARY	REGION
2	John	Doe	Male	21-Jan-90	$72,044	Northeast
3	Talon	Ferguson	Male	2-Oct-92	$52,415	Northwest
4	Doris	Velez	Female	7-Aug-91	$55,608	Northwest
5	Talon	Michaloudis	Male	27-Nov-95	$85,646	Southwest
6	Cain	Sawyer	Male	15-Apr-91	$56,945	Southeast
7	Giacomo	Trujillo	Male	6-Mar-90	$66,551	Northeast
8	Holly	Coffey	Female	19-Sep-91	$86,456	Southwest

STEP 1: Use the Scroll Bar to navigate to find the entry you want to delete.

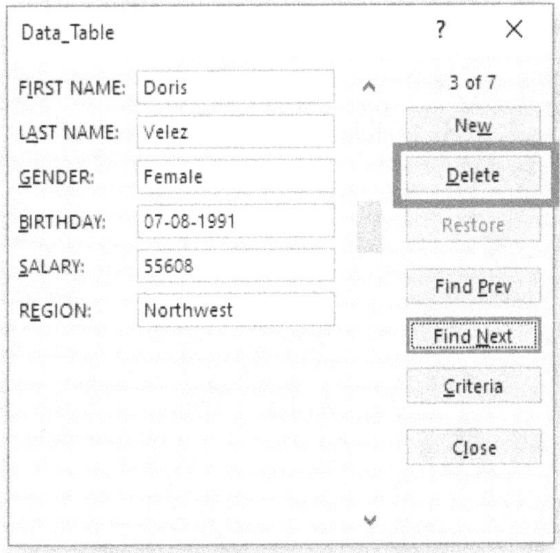

STEP 2: Click on the **Delete** button.

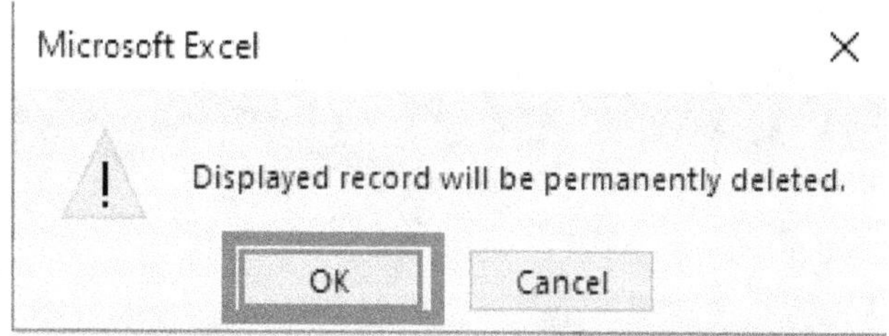

The desired entry will be removed from the data table.

FIRST NAME	LAST NAME	GENDER	BIRTHDAY	SALARY	REGION
John	Doe	Male	21-Jan-90	$72,044	Northeast
Talon	Ferguson	Male	2-Oct-92	$52,415	Northwest
Talon	Michaloudis	Male	27-Nov-95	$85,646	Southwest
Cain	Sawyer	Male	15-Apr-91	$56,945	Southeast
Giacomo	Trujillo	Male	6-Mar-90	$66,551	Northeast
Holly	Coffey	Female	19-Sep-91	$86,456	Southwest

Close the Form

To close the dialog box for Data Forms, simply click on the **Close button (X)** on the top-right corner of the box.

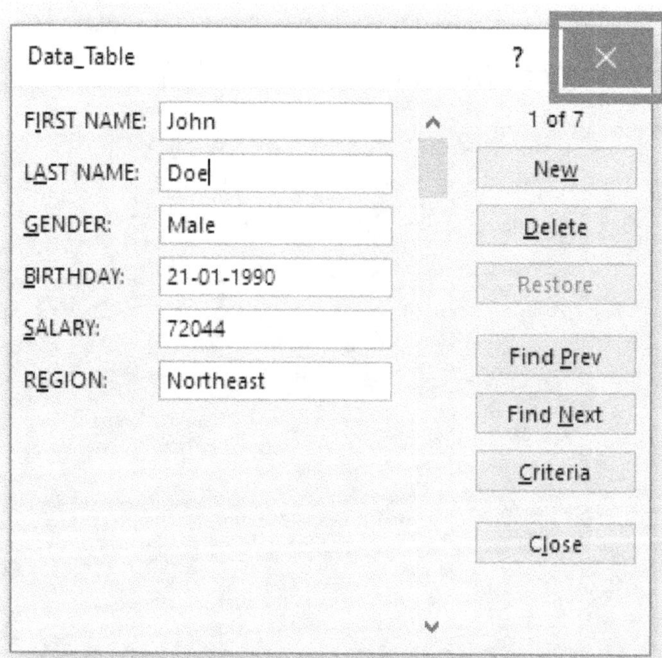

Keyboards Shortcuts for Data Entry Forms

You can use the **following keyboard shortcuts to work faster** when using Data Entry Forms:

- Press **Tab** to go to the next field in the Excel Forms.

- Press **Enter** to go to the next record in the Excel Forms.

- Hit the **Esc** button on your keyboard to close the Excel Form.

This concludes the **top 11 things you should know** about Excel Data Entry Forms. It will not only make the process **faster but also a lot easier** and fun!

Few things to keep in mind when using the Excel Data Entry Form are:

- You can add a **maximum of 32 fields** per record.

- You **cannot print** a data form record.

- Before you hit Enter, you can **restore any changes** made to the data.

So, give it a try! I am sure you are going to love it!

Autocorrect to Input Complex Text

Autocorrect has its uses in Excel, and when we have fat fingers it's very handy to have it correct our commonly typed mistakes. But did you know that autocorrect in Excel can be used to type in complicated text values?

If you have a list of complex text that you type often (I could think of long medical terms), then you can use autocorrect to change a shortcut version to the text that you want!

For example, we can change the initials **"JM"** to **"John Michaloudis."** Autocorrect can do this for us!

STEP 1: Go to *File > More > Options*

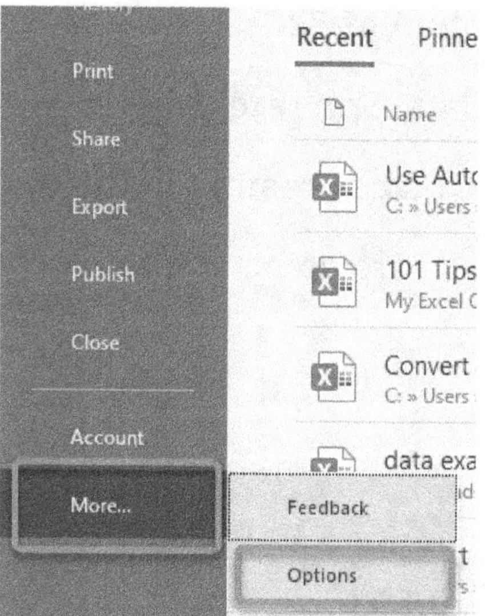

STEP 2: Go to *Proofing > AutoCorrect Options*

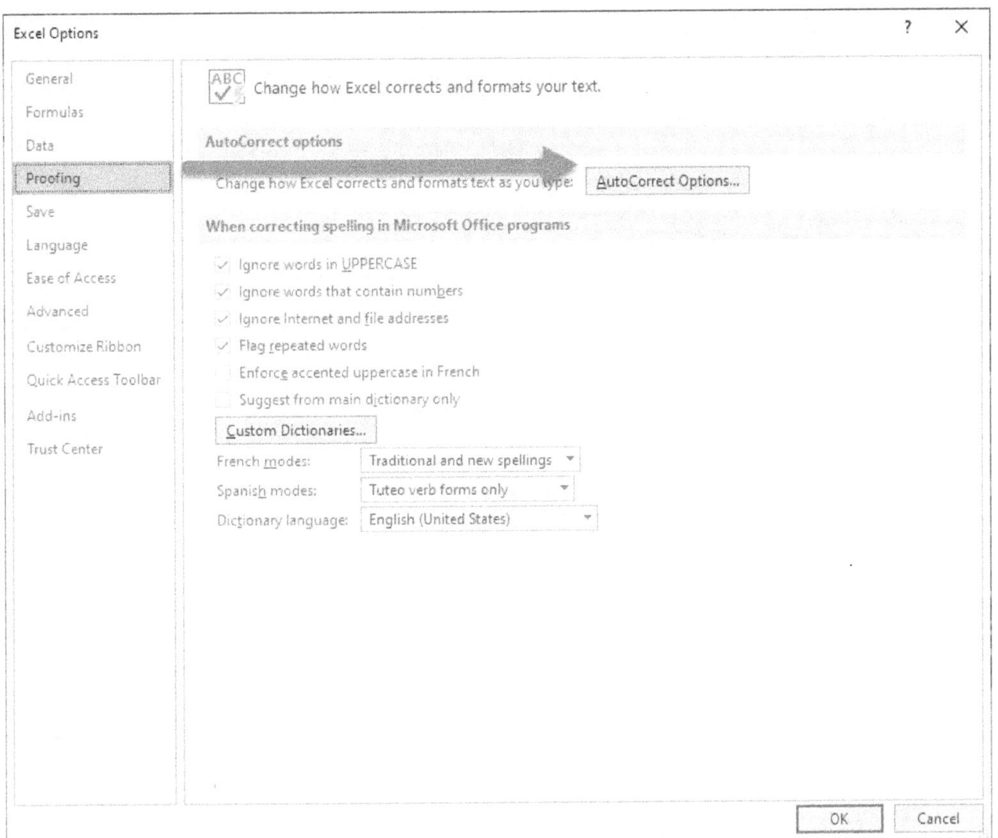

STEP 3: Type in the **Replace** and **With** fields the values that you want AutoCorrect to change

Once done, **click Add and OK twice**

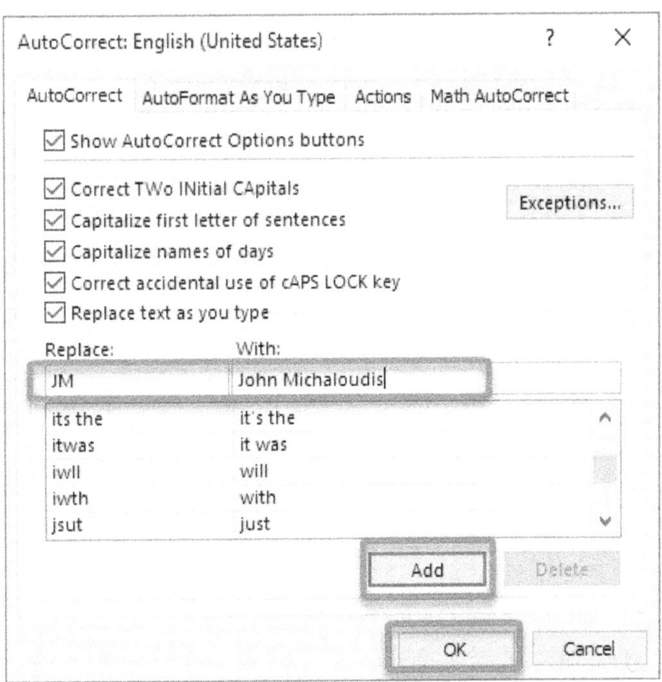

Let us test it out! Type in "**JM**"

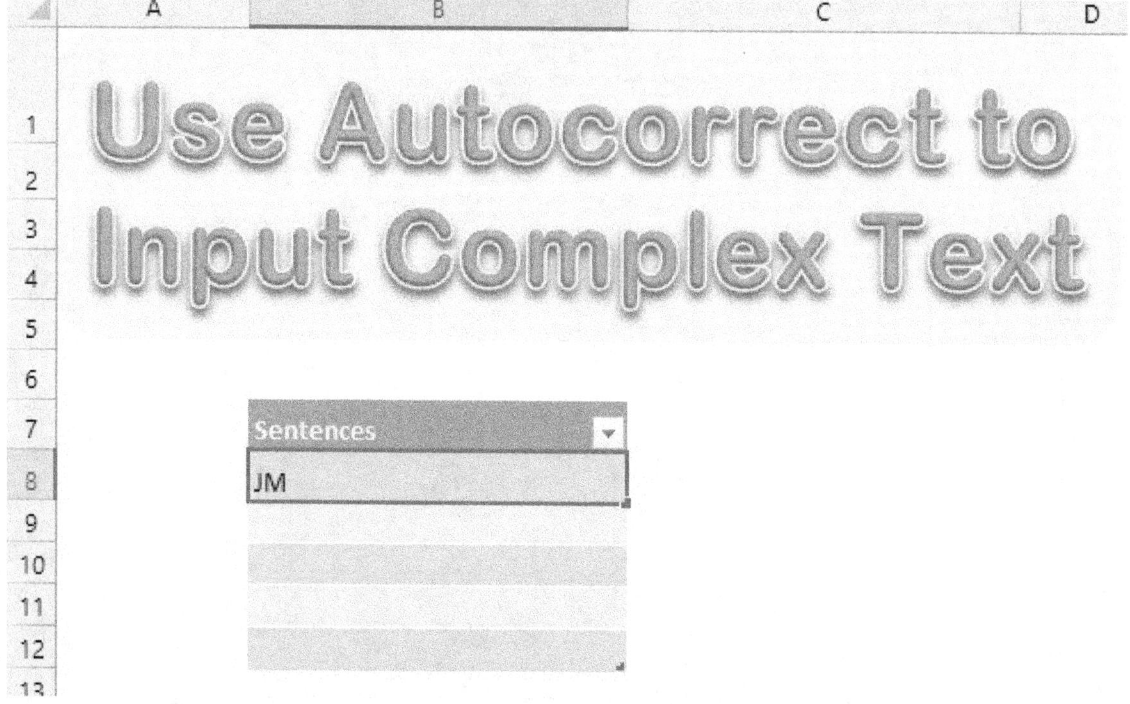

After you press Enter, AutoCorrect gets to work and changes it to **John Michaloudis!**

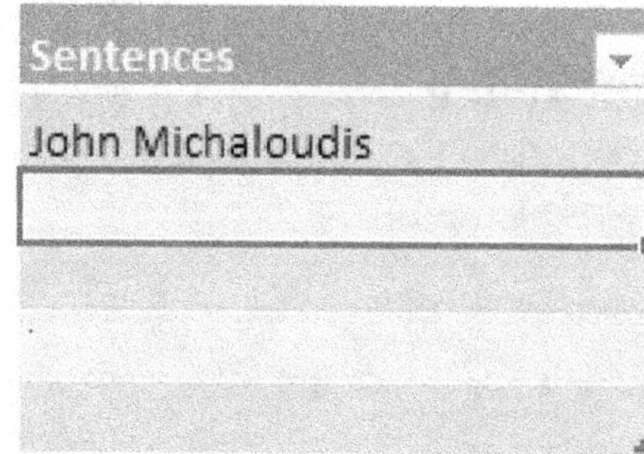

Add the Calculator to the Excel Toolbar

You might have found using the Windows in-built **Calculator** in Excel when you want to do some quick and basic calculations that did not require formulas. Many of the times, the Calculator app and Excel go hand-in-hand.

Did you know that instead of scrambling for the Calculator Application, you can actually have a Calculator in Excel itself!

Excel has a lot of customizations and one handy tool is to include the Calculator in the Excel toolbar.

You can literally place it on your Excel window, and it is very easy and handy to open it whenever needed:

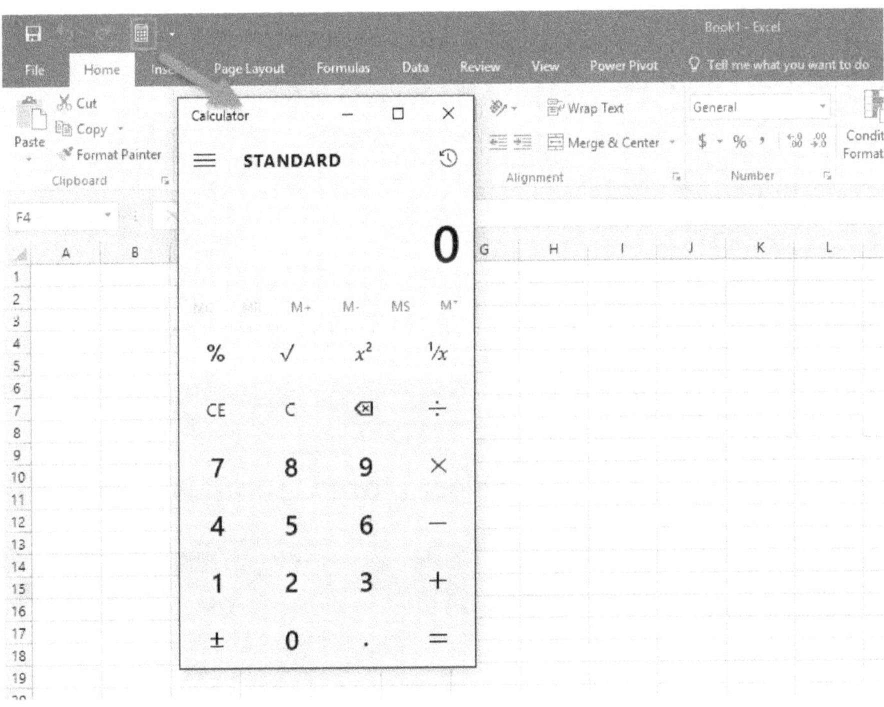

Adding Excel Calculator to the Quick Access Toolbar would save you a lot of time and could prove to be extremely helpful.

Quick Access Toolbar (QAT) is located at the top-left portion of the Ribbon where you can access the commonly used functions and commands of Excel.

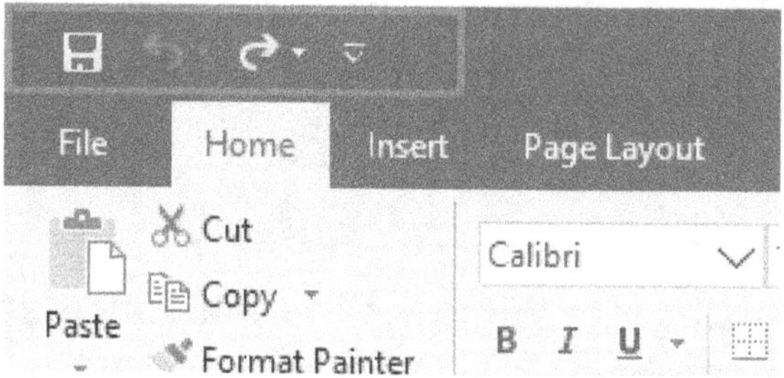

By default, the only options available in QAT are Save, Undo, and Redo. But it can be customized individually by Excel users. So, if you are one who frequently uses Calculator App with Excel. Adding a calculator to your QAT would be the perfect step!

How to Add Calculator to QAT

The steps for how to create a calculator in Excel are very straightforward. They are outlined below:

STEP 1: Go to the top-left corner of the Excel Ribbon and click the **down arrow** on the Excel Toolbar.

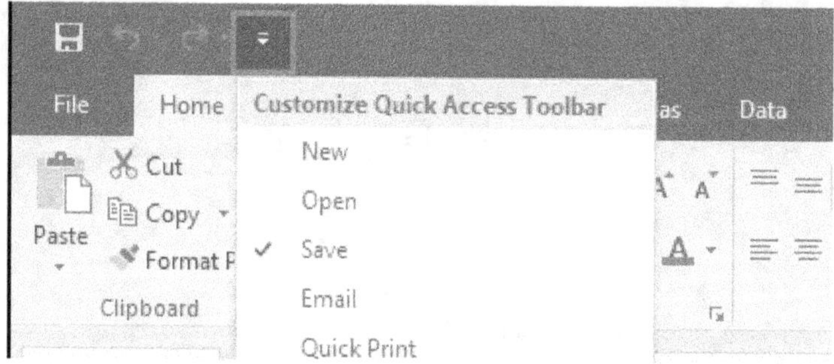

STEP 2: From the drop down menu, select **More Commands** from the list.

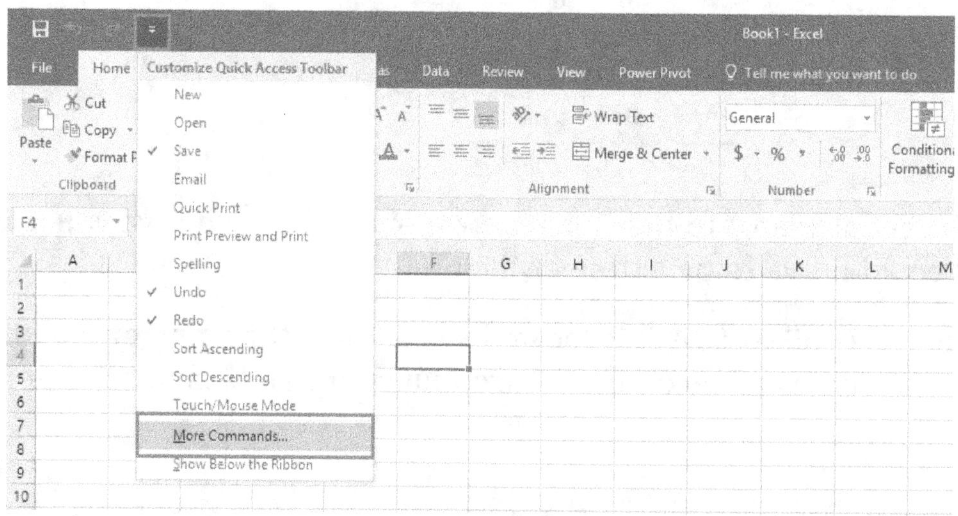

STEP 3: Select **Commands Not in the Ribbon.**

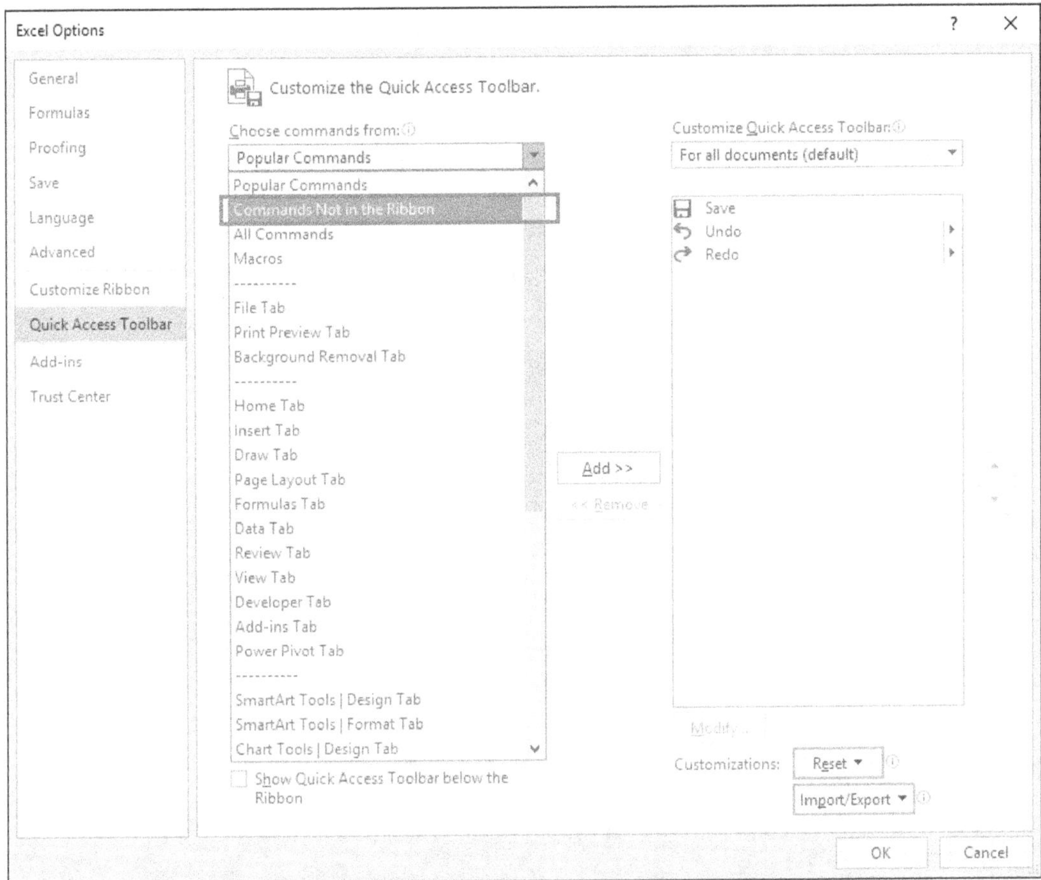

STEP 4: Scroll down and select **Calculator.**   Click **Add.**

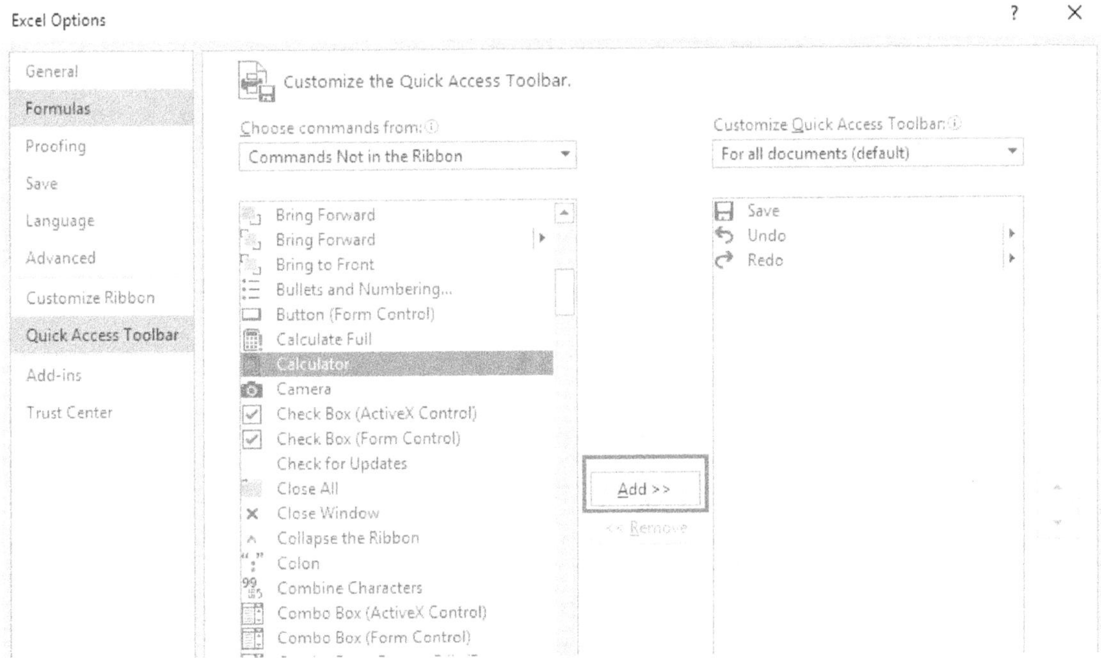

STEP 5: Click **OK.**

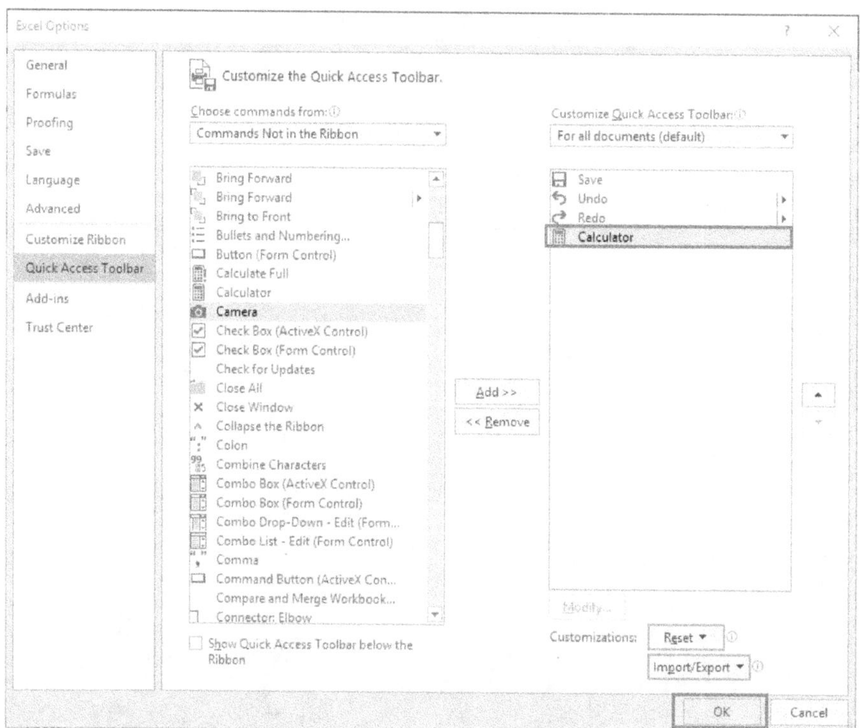

STEP 6: Your Calculator icon is now ready.

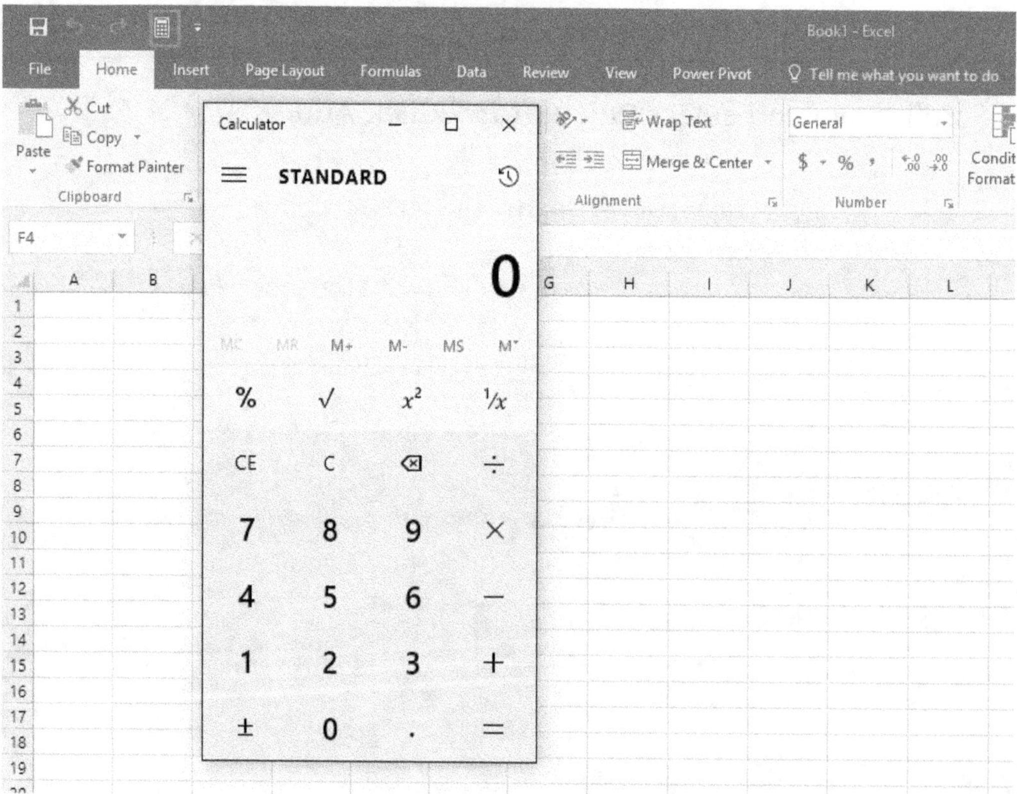

How to Remove Calculator from QAT

Now that you know how to make a calculator in excel, you should also learn how to remove it from the QAT. Follow the steps below to do so:

STEP 1: Go to the top-left corner of the Excel Ribbon and click the **down arrow** on the Excel Toolbar.

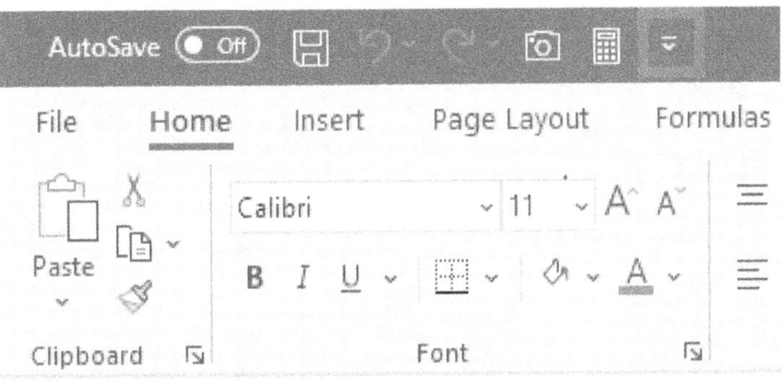

STEP 2: From the drop down menu, select **More Commands** from the list.

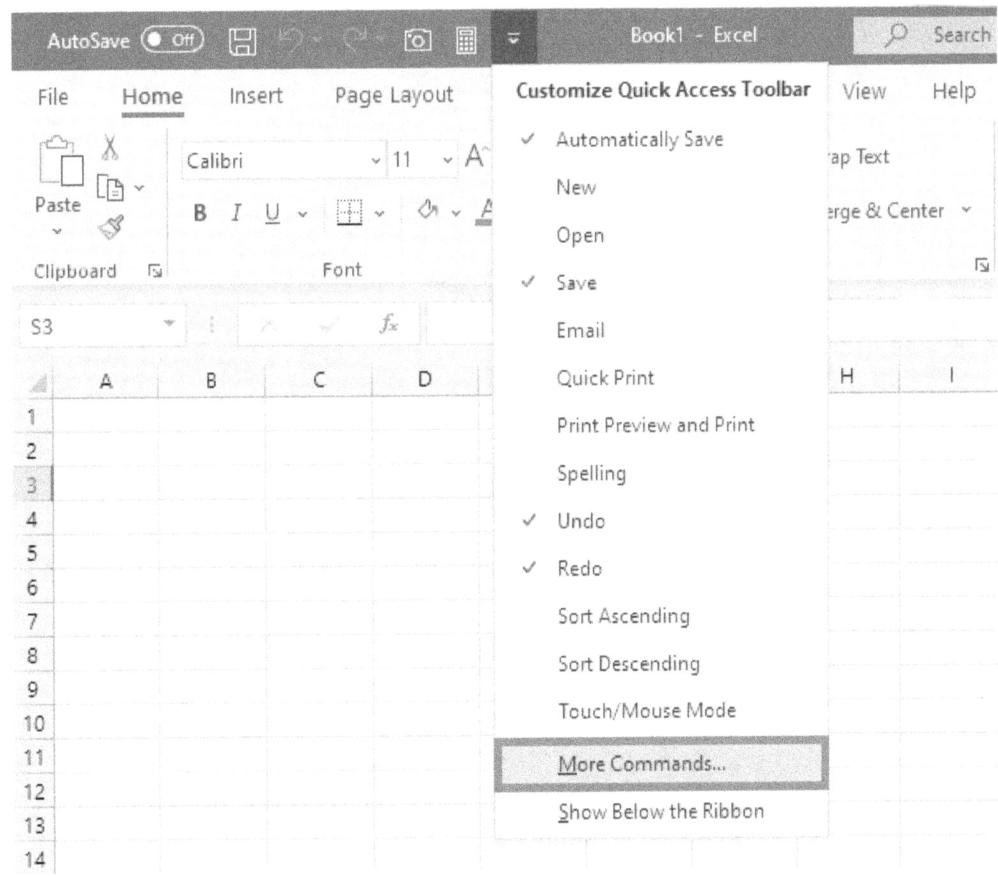

STEP 3: Under Customize Quick Access Toolbar, select Calculator and click on Remove.

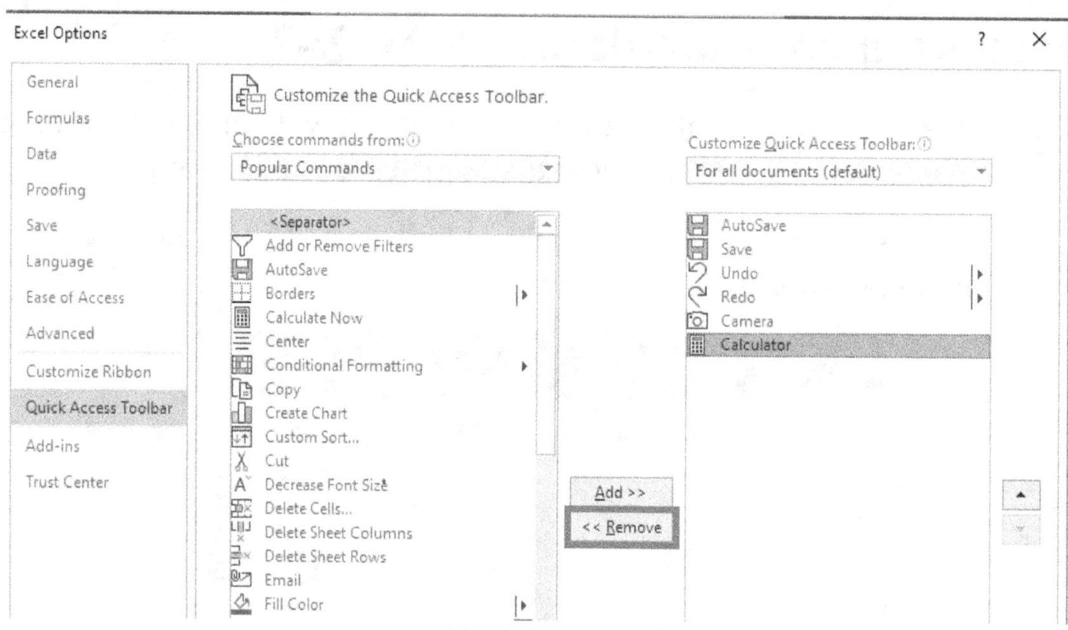

STEP 4: Click **OK.**

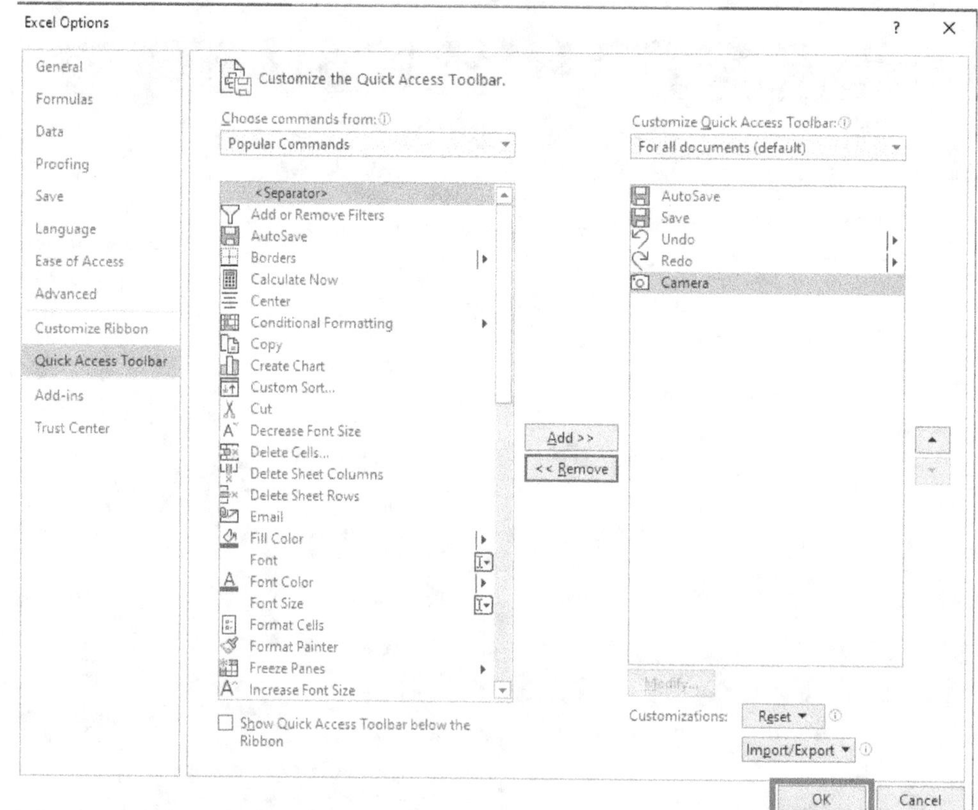

This brings us back to the original QAT setup.

How to Use Calculator in Excel

This calculator tool is an extremely useful tool and does a lot more than just addition and subtraction. There are 4 modes available to use - Standard, Scientific, Programmer, and Date Calculation.

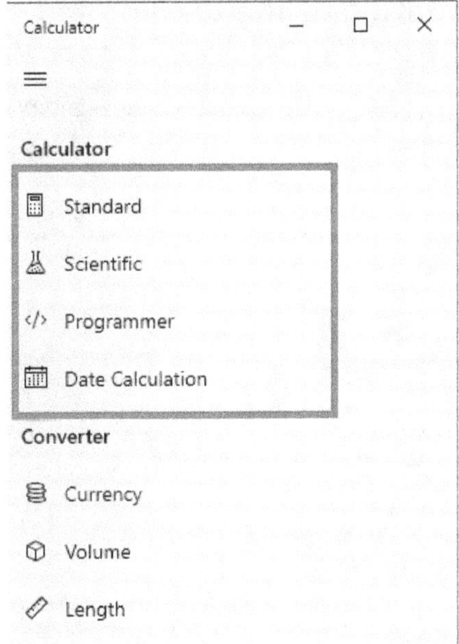

- **Standard** - It is used for basic math calculations like add, subtract, divide, multiple, finding square root, calculating percentages, and working with fractions.

- **Scientific** - It is used for functions like log, modulus, exponent, trigonometric calculations, sin, cos, tan, etc.

- **Programmer** - It is used to switch between different number systems— binary, decimal, hexadecimal, and octal.

- **Date Calculation** - It is used to calculate the difference between two specific dates.

Now, let's give it a try and learn how to use a Calculator in Excel.

Say, you have to input the difference between two dates - 12th April 2020 and 2nd June 2020 without using any Excel formulas.

STEP 1: Click on the **calculator icon** in QAT

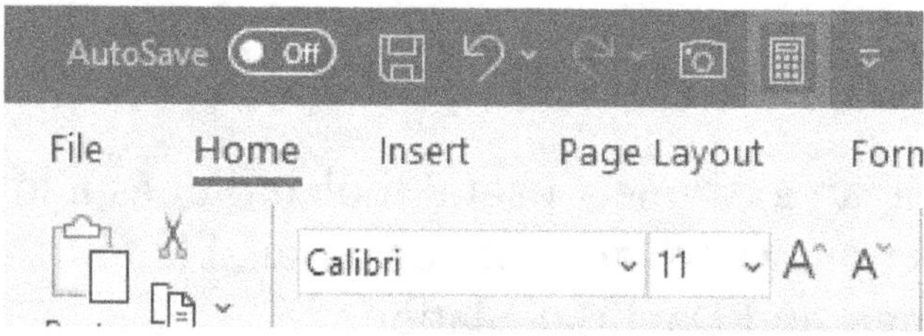

STEP 2: Click on the menu button at the top left and then select **Date Calculation**.

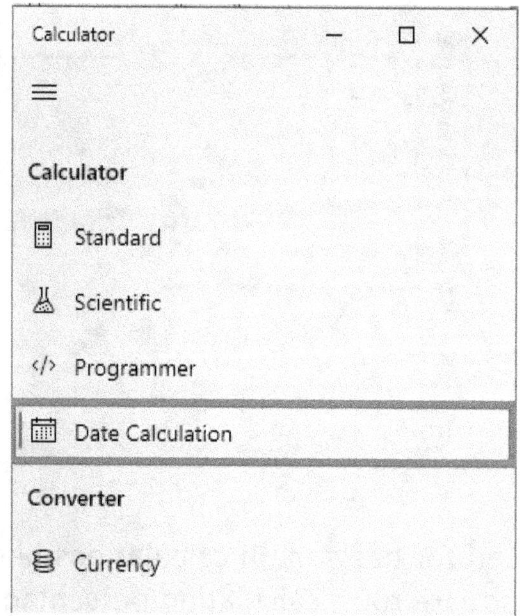

STEP 3: Insert the two dates - 12th April 2020 and 2nd June 2020

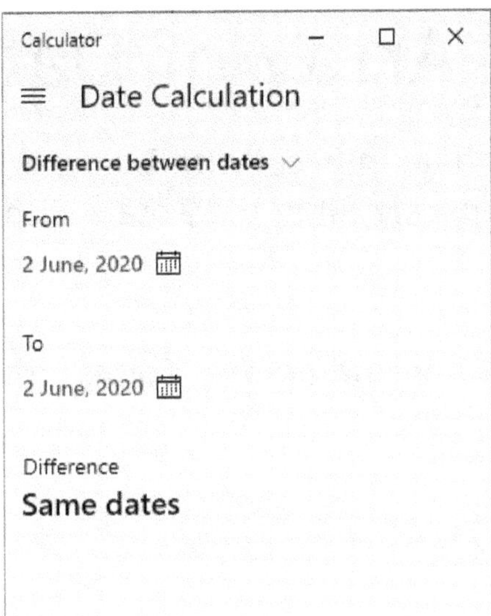

STEP 4: The difference between the two dates will be displayed.

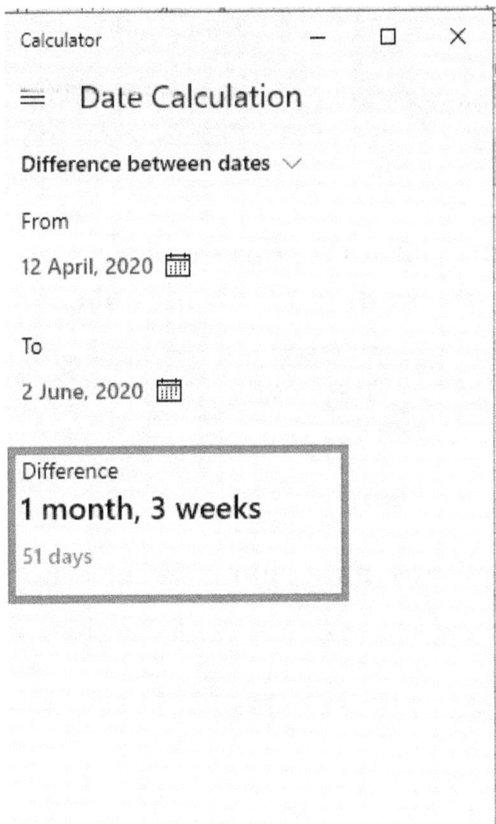

Autosum an Array of Data in Excel

When you have an array of data in Excel with Totals at the bottom and to the right of the data, you can quickly fill in the Totals with the Autosum button.

STEP 1: **Highlight your data** including the "Totals" row and column;

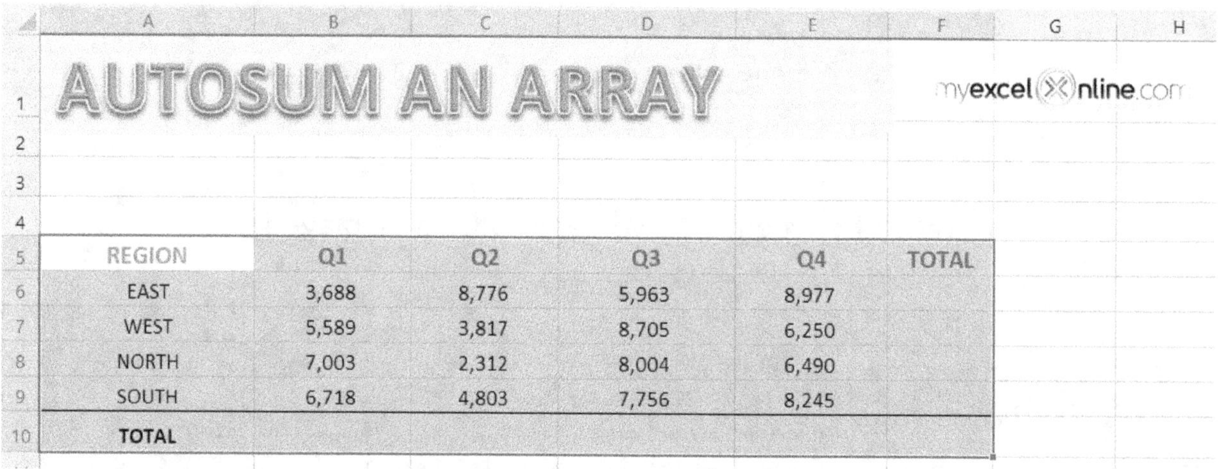

REGION	Q1	Q2	Q3	Q4	TOTAL
EAST	3,688	8,776	5,963	8,977	
WEST	5,589	3,817	8,705	6,250	
NORTH	7,003	2,312	8,004	6,490	
SOUTH	6,718	4,803	7,756	8,245	
TOTAL					

STEP 2: Click the **Autosum** button (under the **Home** or **Formulas** tabs) and this will fill in the Totals cells with the **Sum** formula.

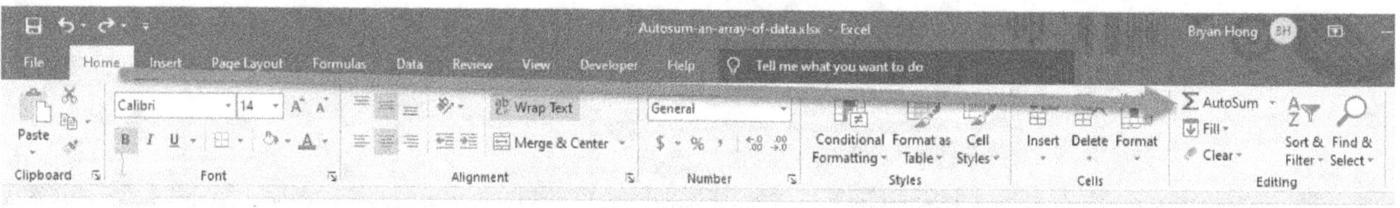

Afterwards both your Total row and column are now populated!

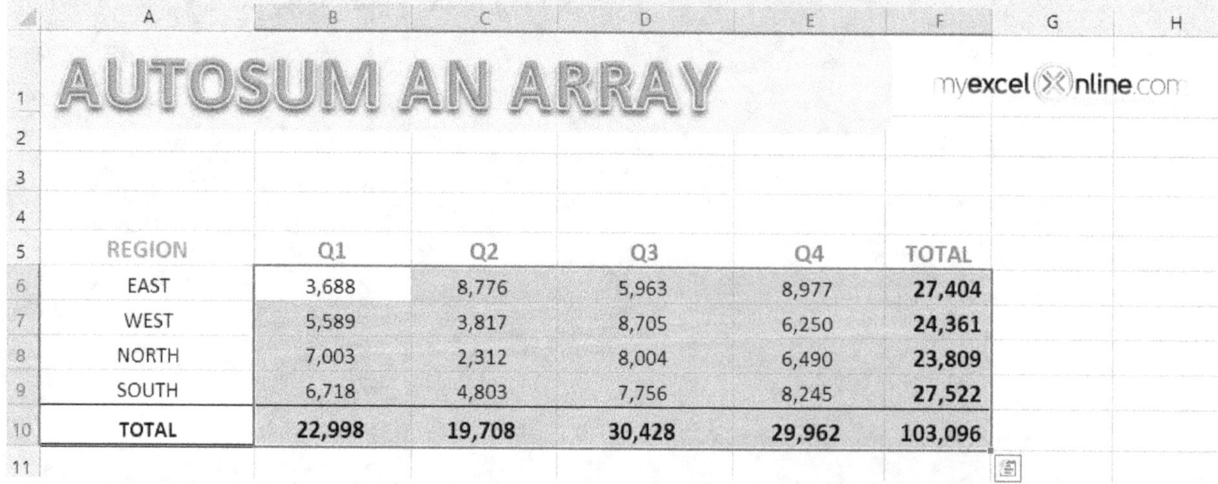

REGION	Q1	Q2	Q3	Q4	TOTAL
EAST	3,688	8,776	5,963	8,977	27,404
WEST	5,589	3,817	8,705	6,250	24,361
NORTH	7,003	2,312	8,004	6,490	23,809
SOUTH	6,718	4,803	7,756	8,245	27,522
TOTAL	22,998	19,708	30,428	29,962	103,096

Change & Convert UK Dates to US

Have you ever come across a scenario where your dates in Excel are in the wrong format?

Say you type in **01/05/2018** which actually means **January 5, 2018** in the US but it shows as **May 1, 2018!**   It drives me nuts because the entire spreadsheet of dates is interpreted incorrectly by Excel!

That happens because your **computer's region settings** are in UK format and need to be changed to a US format.

Thankfully, there is an easy way to change your **Windows region & date settings** so that the dates will be interpreted correctly by **Excel!**

Here I show you how you can do this.

STEP 1: For Windows 10, go to your Search Bar and type **Date & Time Settings.**

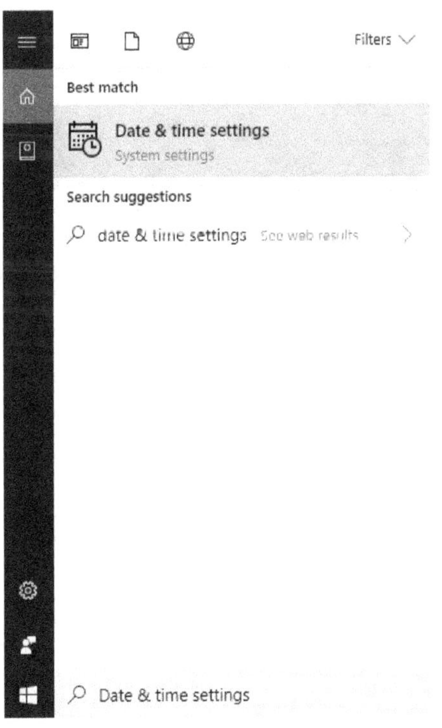

STEP 2: Scroll to the very bottom, and select **Change date and time formats.**

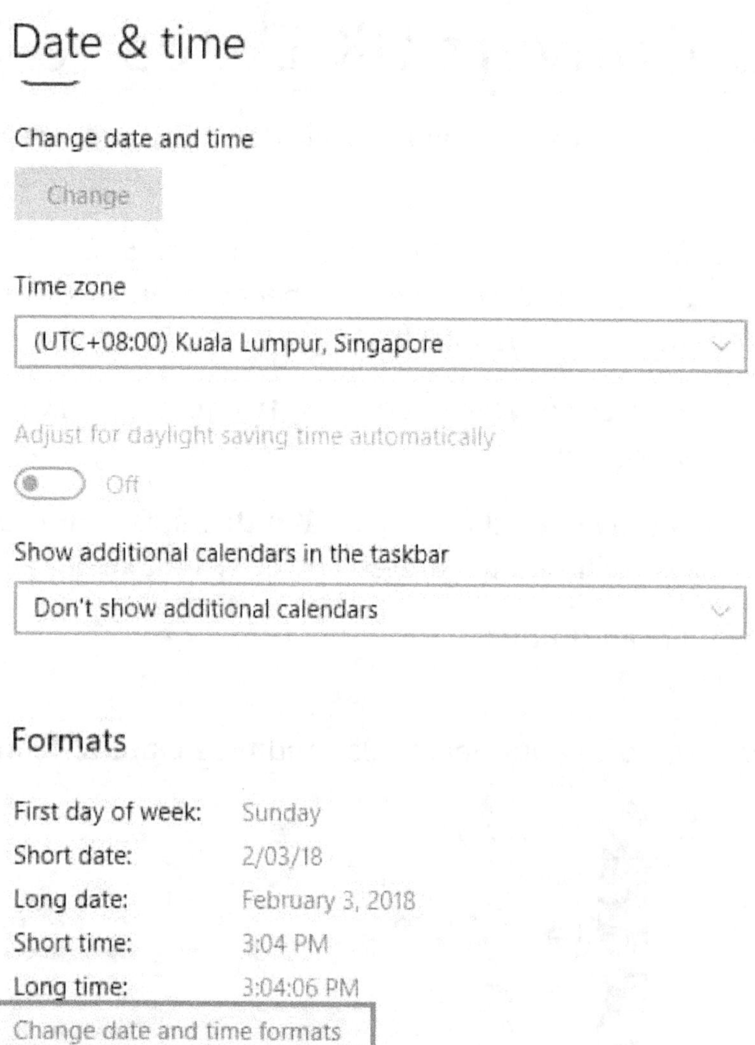

STEP 3: You can see the current **Short date** setting is Day-Month-Year.

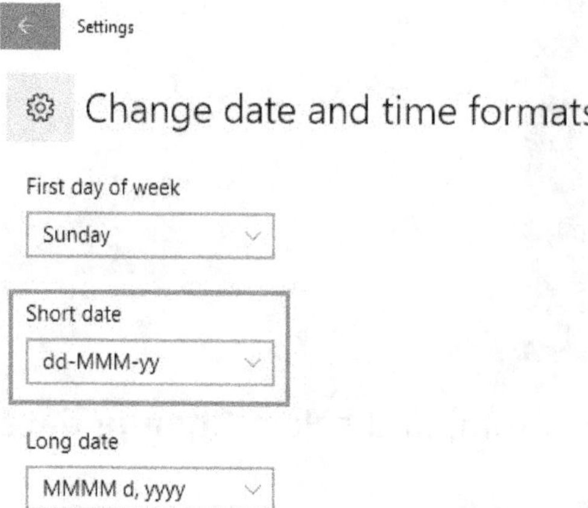

Change it to **M/dd/yy** which is the **US Date Format.**

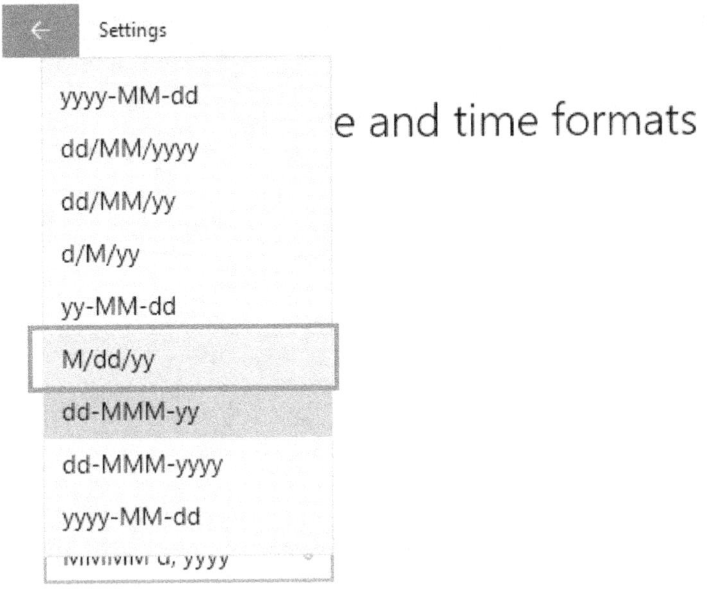

STEP 4: Now go to Excel and type in **01/05/2018.**

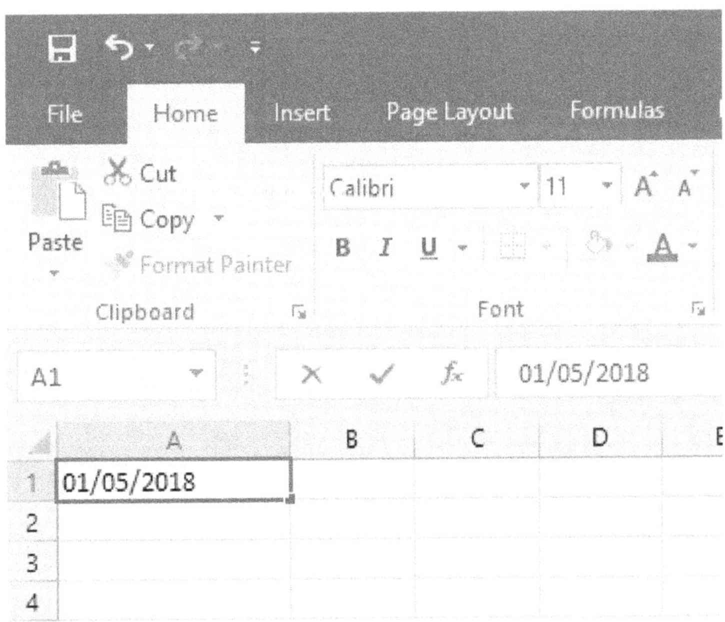

It is now correctly interpreted as **January 5, 2018!**

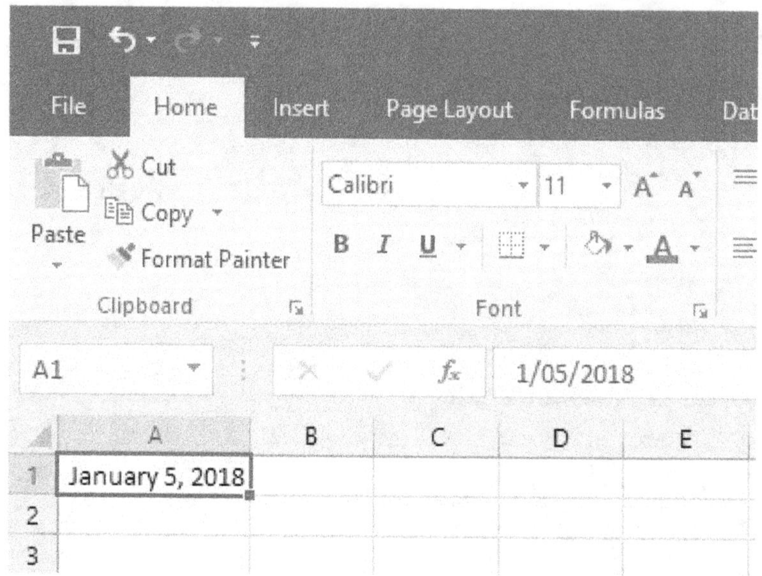

Bonus Tip: If you are still unable to make this work, you will need to change your computer's Region settings:

Settings > Region > Additional date, time & regional settings (top right) > Change date, time or number formats > Format: English (United States) > Apply

Charts: Change the Axis Units

Whenever you create a chart in Excel, it gives you the default vertical Axis based on the values that are in your data set.

If you have large numbers in your data, like tens or hundreds of millions of dollars, then the vertical axes will take up lots of real estate space in your chart.

A great way to overcome this problem is to display the axis units in "Thousands" or "Millions", thus making your chart much cleaner.

STEP 1: Select the vertical axis.

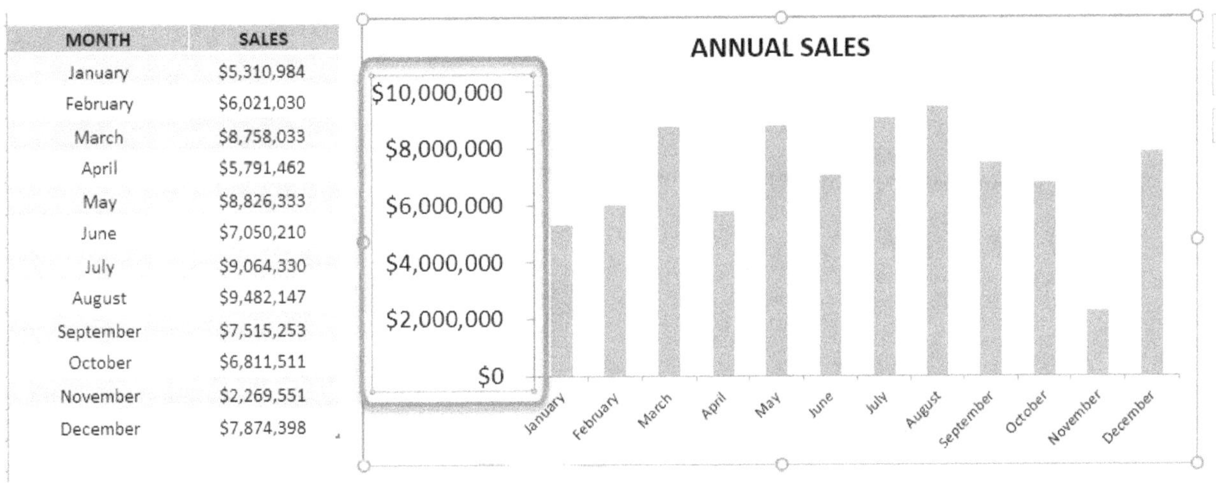

STEP 2: Right click and select **Format Axis**

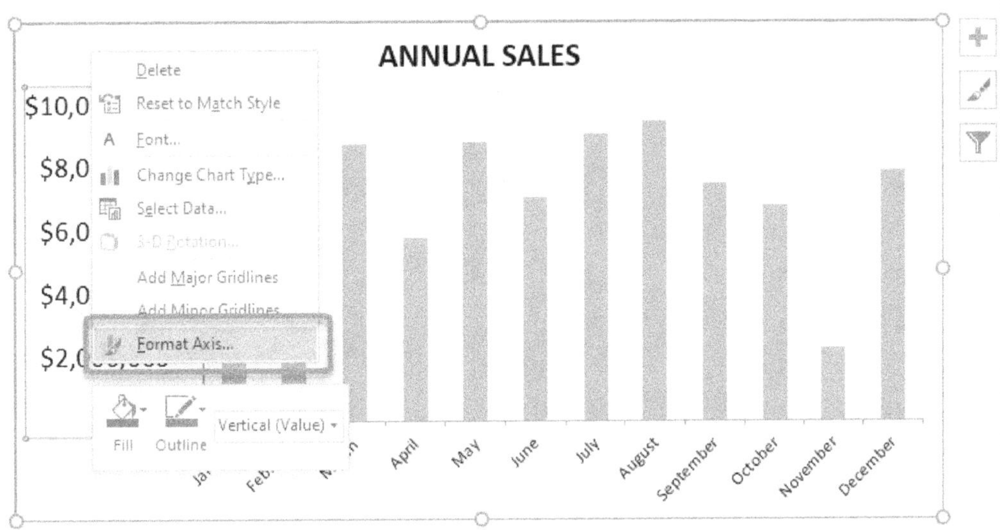

STEP 3: Select **Millions** for the **Display units** and tick **Show display units label on chart**

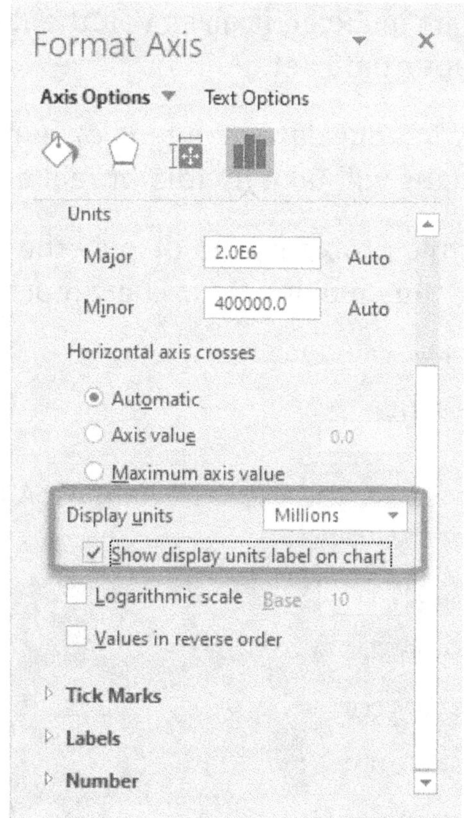

Your updated chart is now ready!

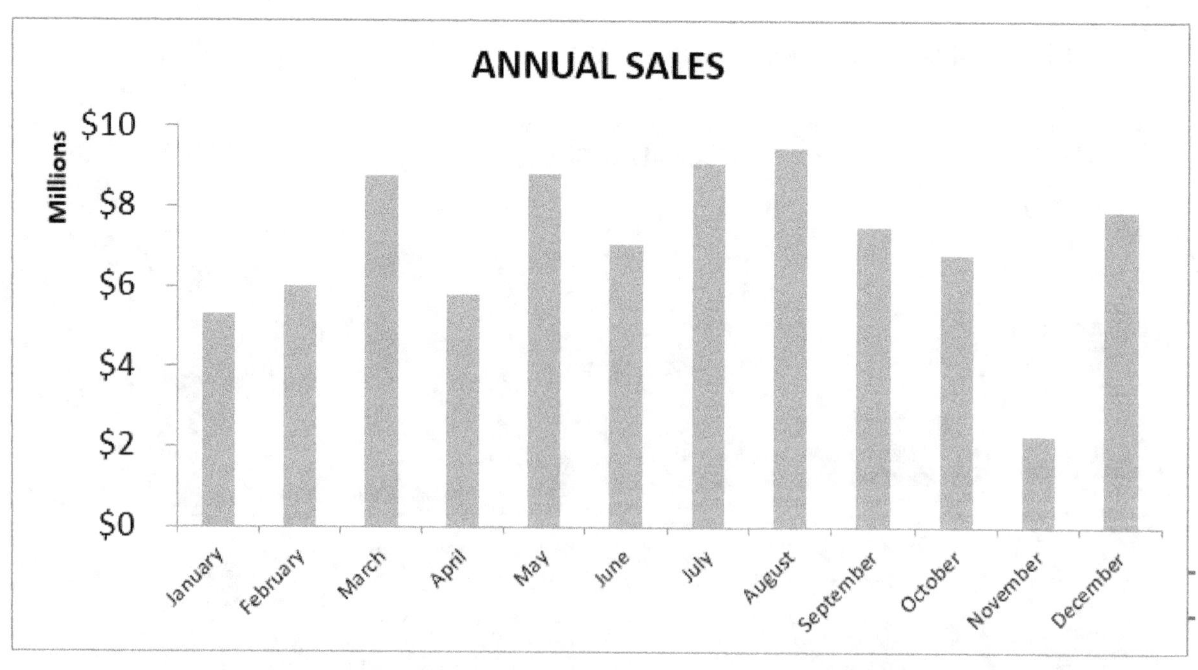

Charts: Copying and Moving Charts

I am going to show your three quick ways to copy and move your Excel charts.
You will be surprised on these additional tricks with Excel charts!

#1 - COPYING A CHART

Click on the chart with your left mouse key and at the same time hold down the
CTRL key to copy it and move the chart to wherever you want.

When you are done, let go of the mouse key to paste it.

MONTH	SALES
January	$5,310,984
February	$6,021,030
March	$8,758,033
April	$5,791,462
May	$8,826,333
June	$7,050,210
July	$9,064,330
August	$9,482,147
September	$7,515,253
October	$6,811,511
November	$2,269,551
December	$7,874,398

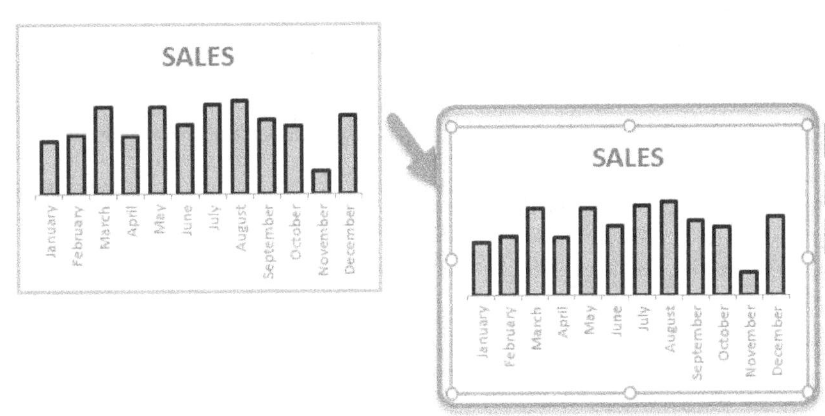

#2 - COPYING A CHART IN THE SAME ALIGNMENT

Click on the chart with your left mouse key and at the same time hold down the
CTRL+SHIFT keys to copy and move the chart to wherever you want (notice that
it stays fixed in the same alignment as the original chart!)

When you are done, let go of the mouse key to paste it.

MONTH	SALES
January	$5,310,984
February	$6,021,030
March	$8,758,033
April	$5,791,462
May	$8,826,333
June	$7,050,210
July	$9,064,330
August	$9,482,147
September	$7,515,253
October	$6,811,511
November	$2,269,551
December	$7,874,398

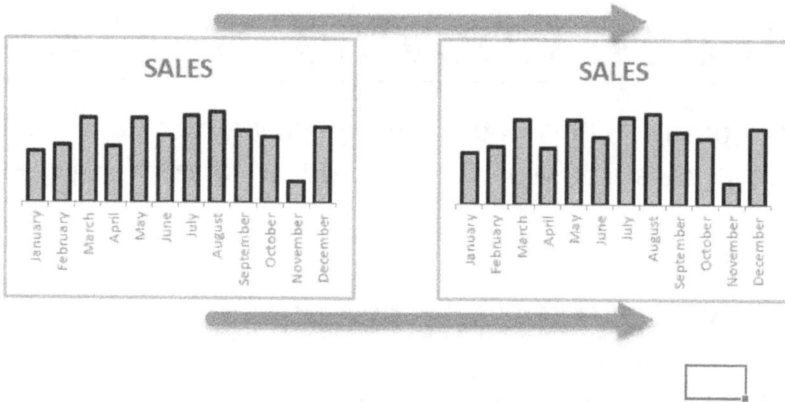

#3 - MOVING A CHART IN THE SAME ALIGNMENT

Click on the chart with your left mouse key and at the same time hold down the **SHIFT** key to move it to wherever you want.

When you are done, let go of the mouse key to place it.

MONTH	SALES
January	$5,310,984
February	$6,021,030
March	$8,758,033
April	$5,791,462
May	$8,826,333
June	$7,050,210
July	$9,064,330
August	$9,482,147
September	$7,515,253
October	$6,811,511
November	$2,269,551
December	$7,874,398

Charts: Logarithmic Scale

When you have a large numerical range of data and you want to plot a graph, you will most probably end up with a skewed looking chart like the one below:

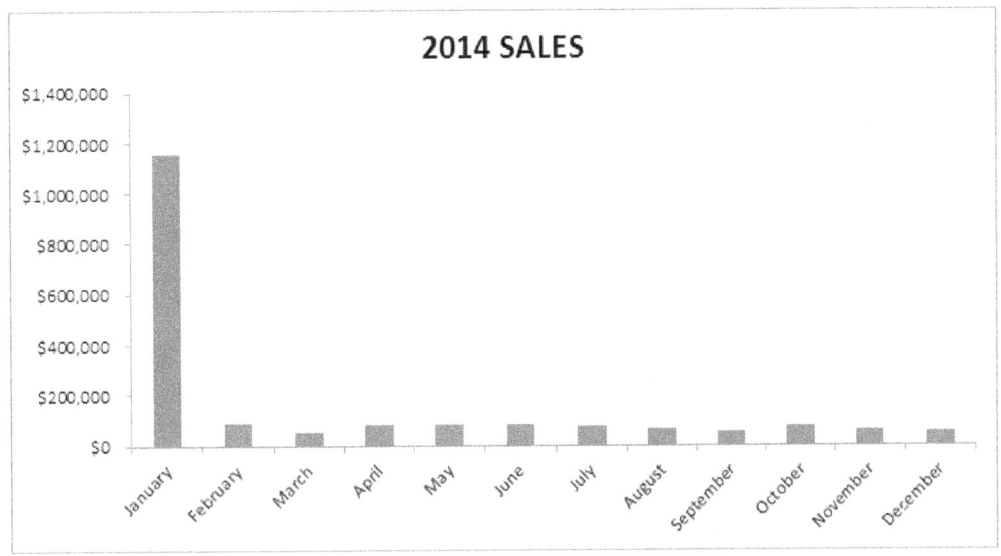

You can use the **logarithmic scale (log scale)** in the Format Axis dialogue box to scale your chart by a base of **10**.

What this does is it multiplies the vertical axis units by 10, so it starts at 1, 10, 100, 1000, 10000, 100000, 1000000 etc. This scales the chart to show a more even spread, like the image below:

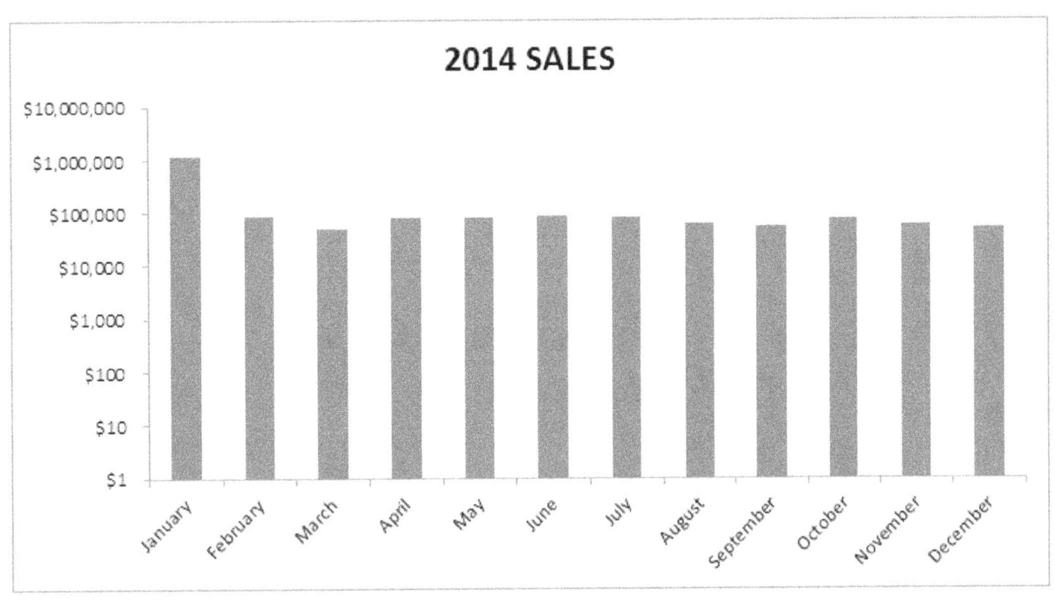

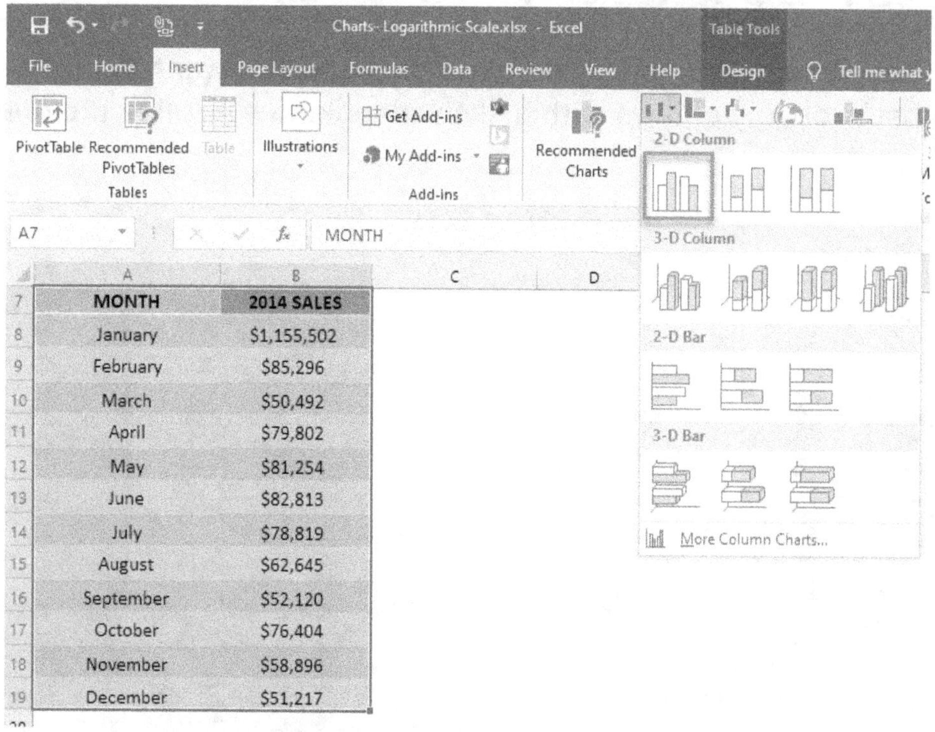

STEP 2: Select the vertical axis of your chart

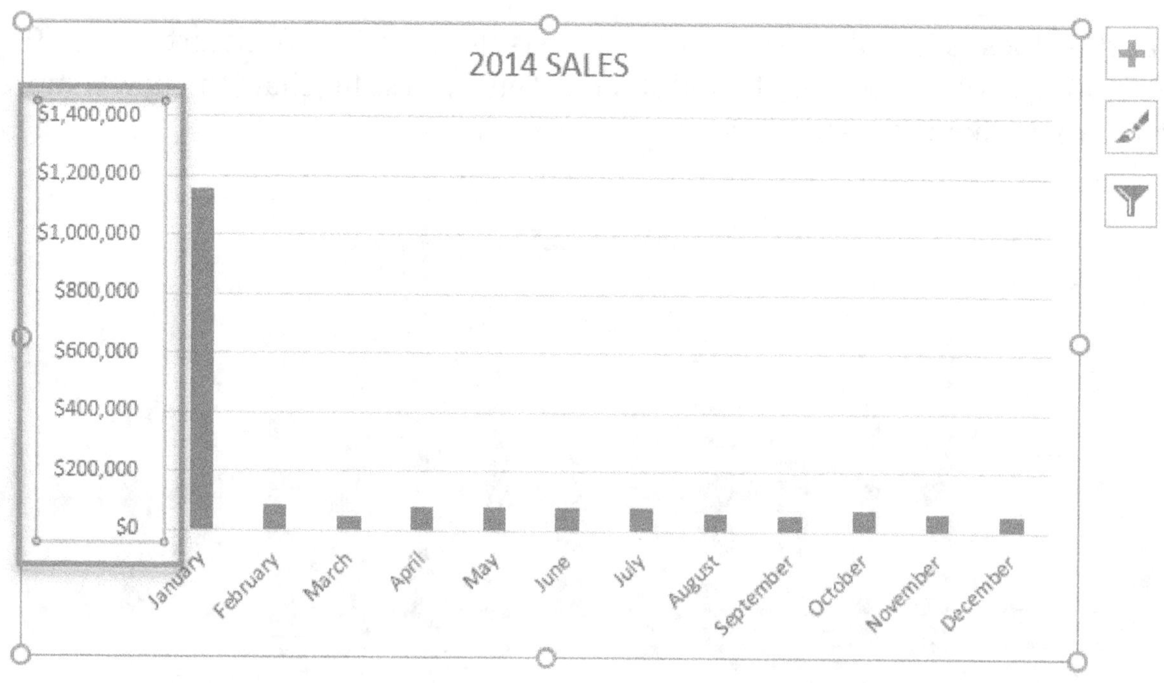

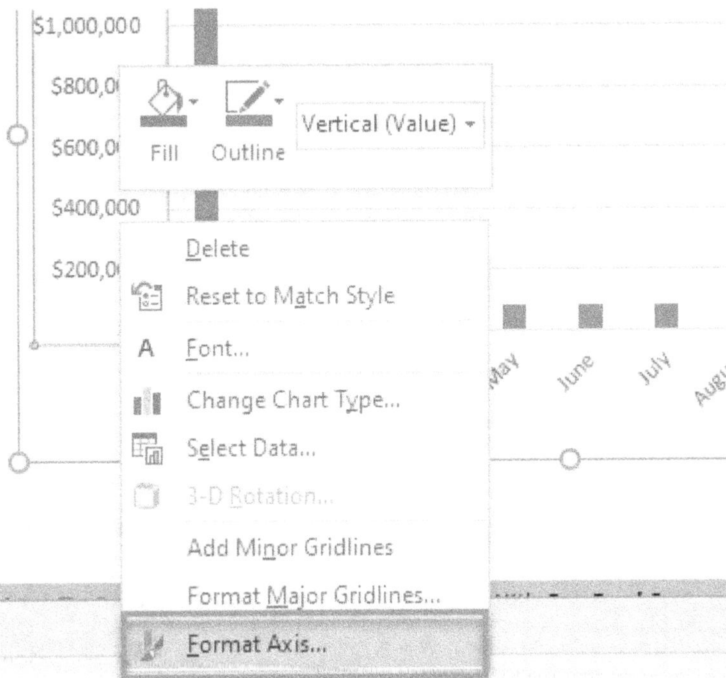

STEP 4: Check the **Logarithmic scale** and set it to a **Base of 10**

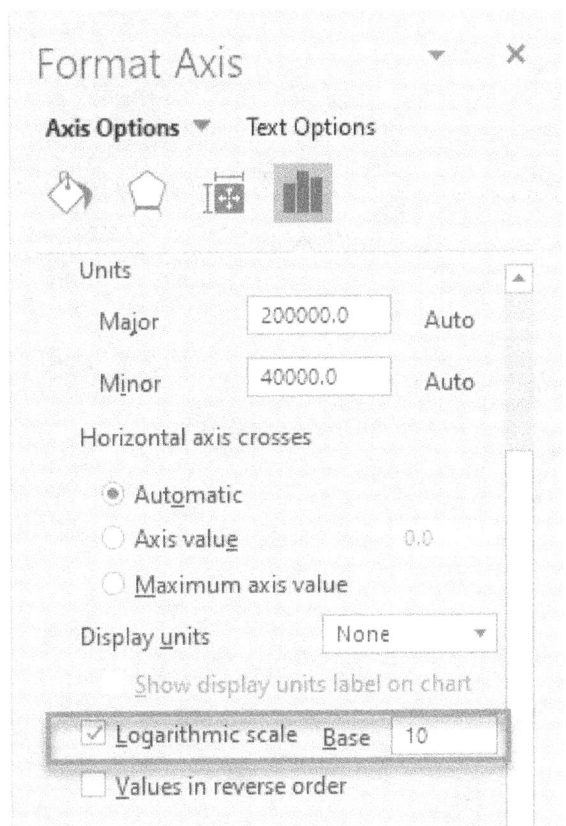

Your updated chart is now ready!

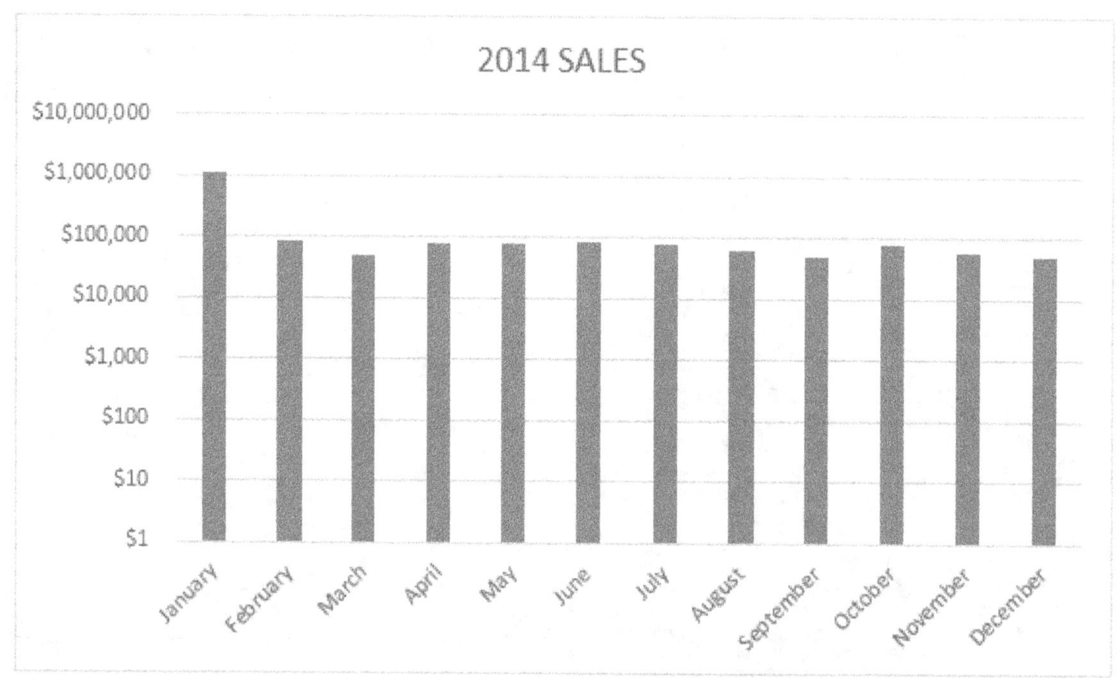

Charts: Save Templates

Saving a Chart template in Excel is an efficient way to reuse your favorite or your company's standard chart template.

So whenever you have new data and want to create a chart with your (company's) standard formatting, all you need is a couple of clicks and you will have it seconds!

STEP 1: First you need to customize a chart to your liking and then Save it by right clicking on your chart and clicking *Save As Template*

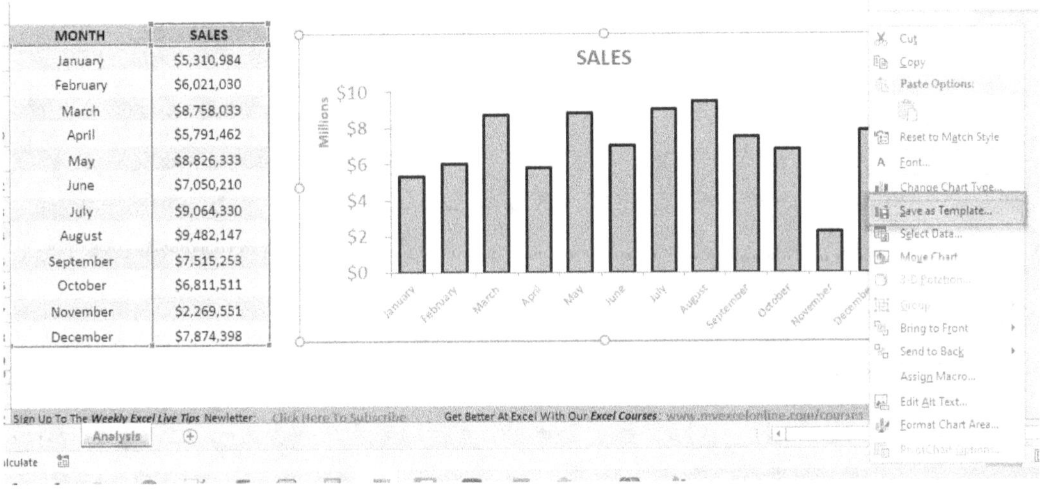

STEP 2: Name your template and click **Save**

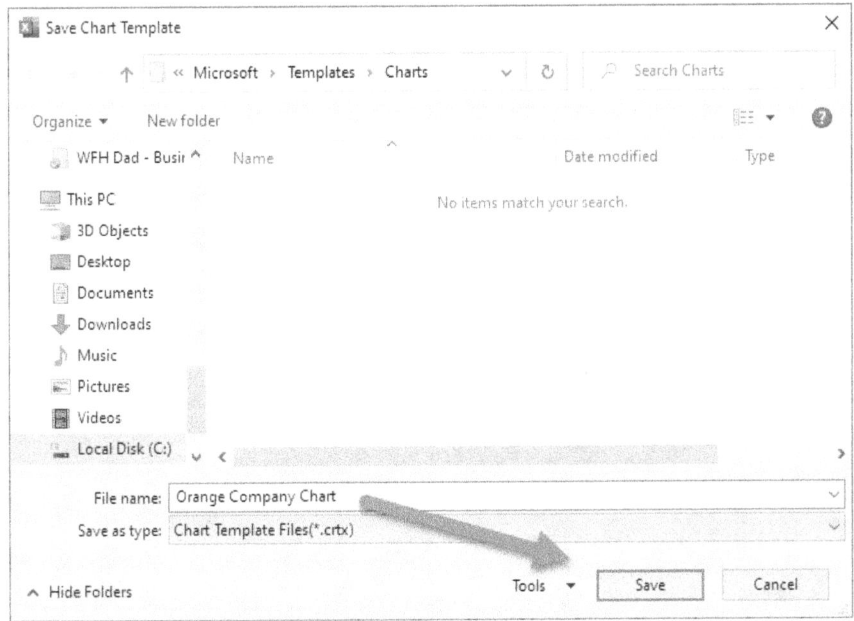

STEP 3: The next time you create a chart all you have to do is click on your data, select *Insert > Recommended Charts > All Charts* and choose your custom template from the selection.

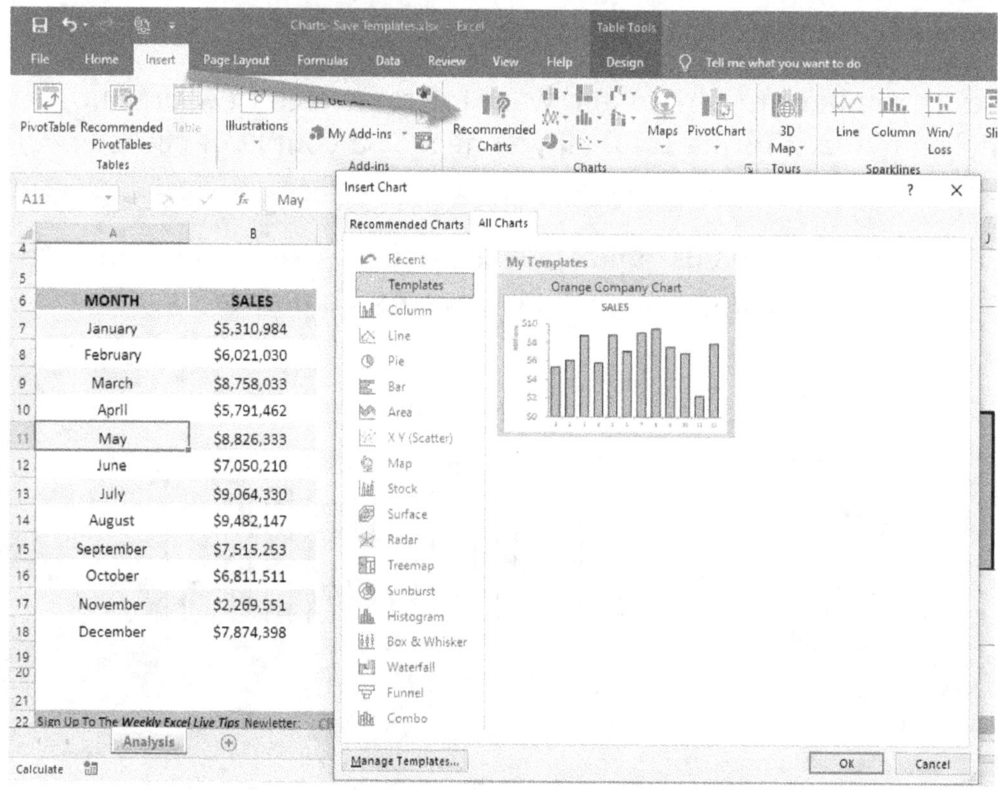

Consolidate Tool in Excel

The Consolidate tool in Excel is located in the Data menu and combines values from multiple ranges into one new range.

You would use this feature when you have a single text column on the left with duplicate values and sales on a separate column.

 Select a cell outside your data table.

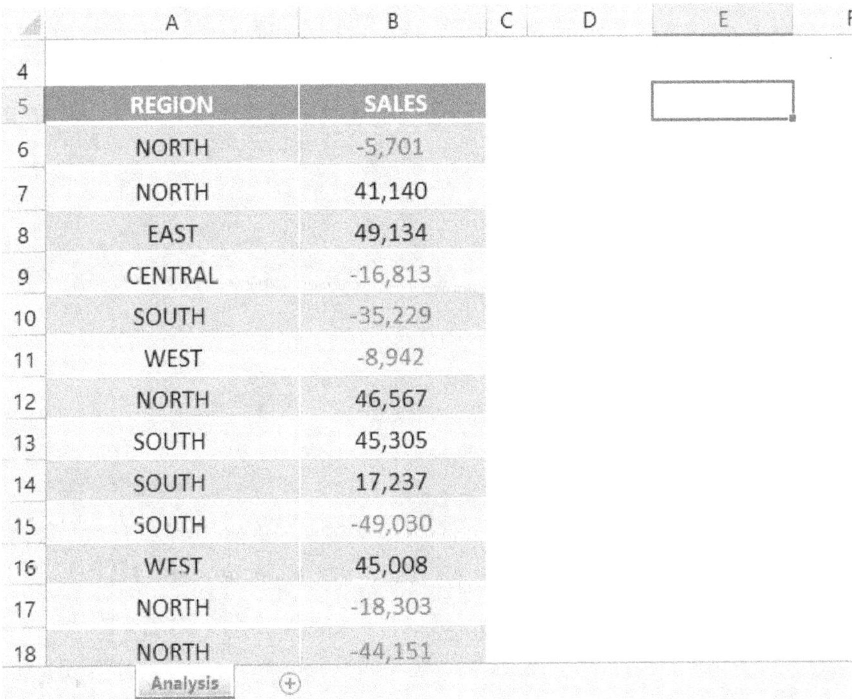

STEP 2: Go to **Data > Consolidate**

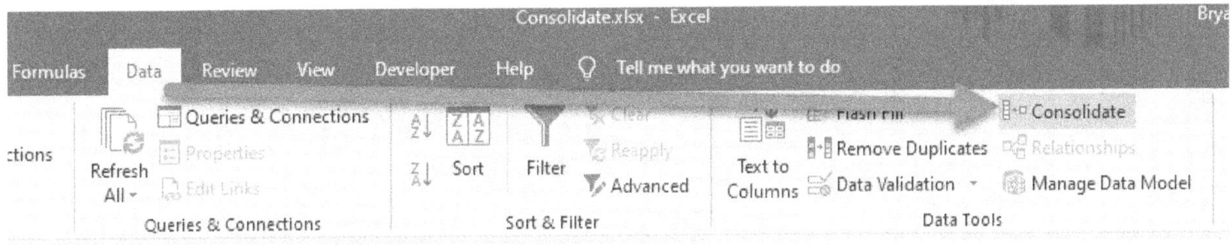

STEP 3: For the **Reference**, make sure to select the entire table.

Then ensure **Use Labels in** has both **Top Row** and **Left Column** selected.

Press **OK.**

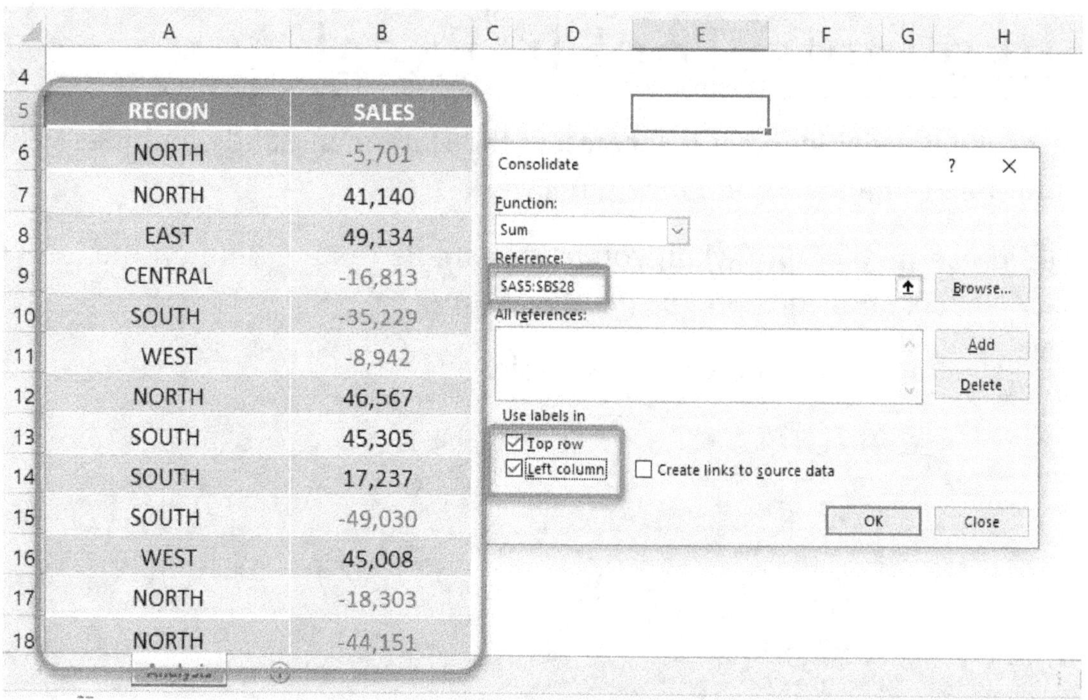

Your consolidated data table is now ready!

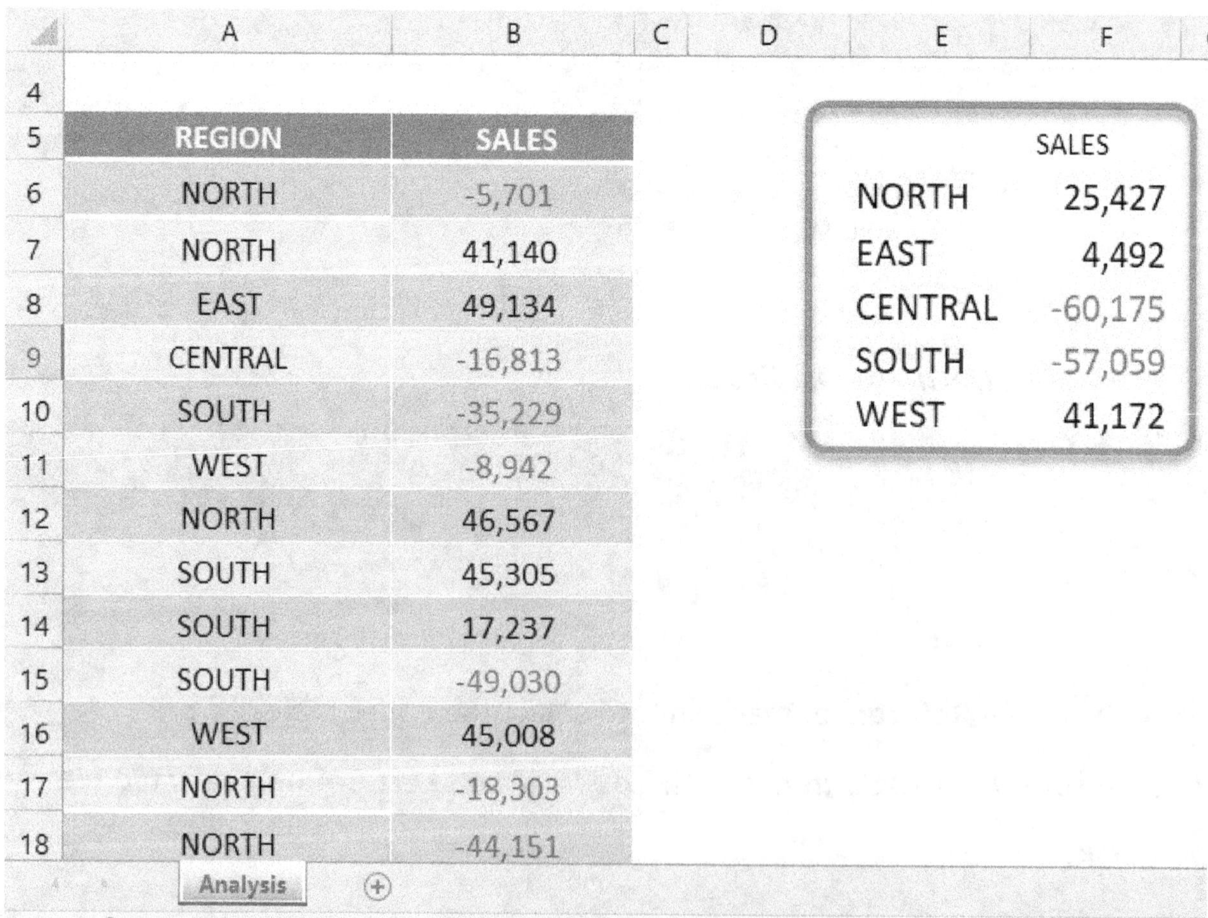

Convert Text to Speech

Did you know that you can convert text to speech in Excel? Yes, Excel has this cool functionality built in so that it can read aloud your text in your Excel worksheet! This is proofreading version 2.0!

STEP 1: Right click anywhere on the Excel ribbon and select **Customize the Ribbon**

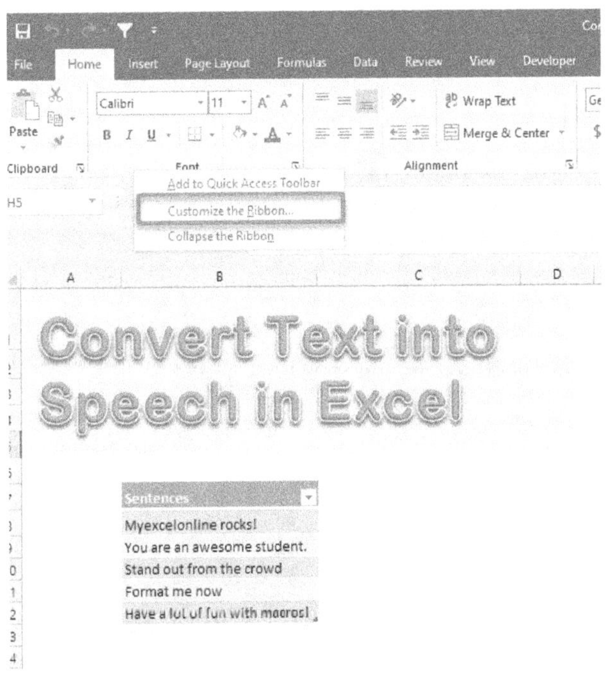

STEP 2: Select **New Group** and we'll create a new group inside our Home Tab

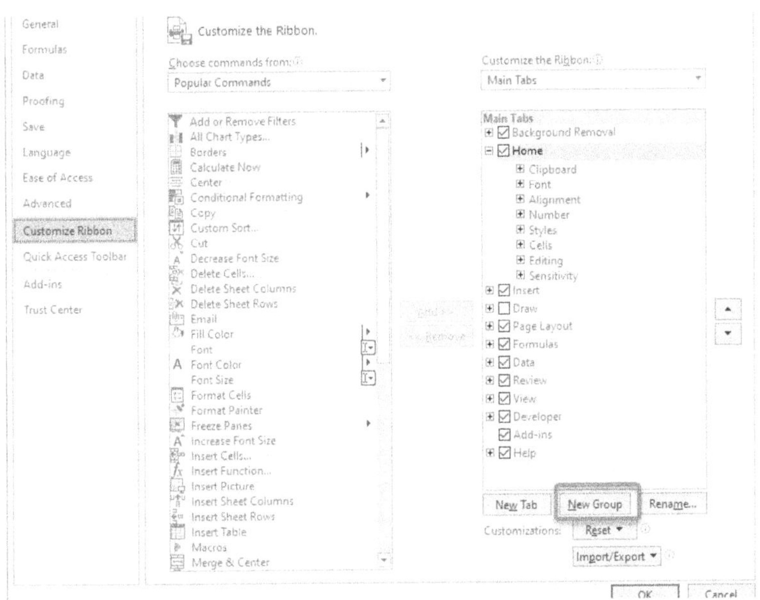

STEP 3: Click **Rename** and select any symbol you like and then name your group: *Text to Speech*

Click **OK**.

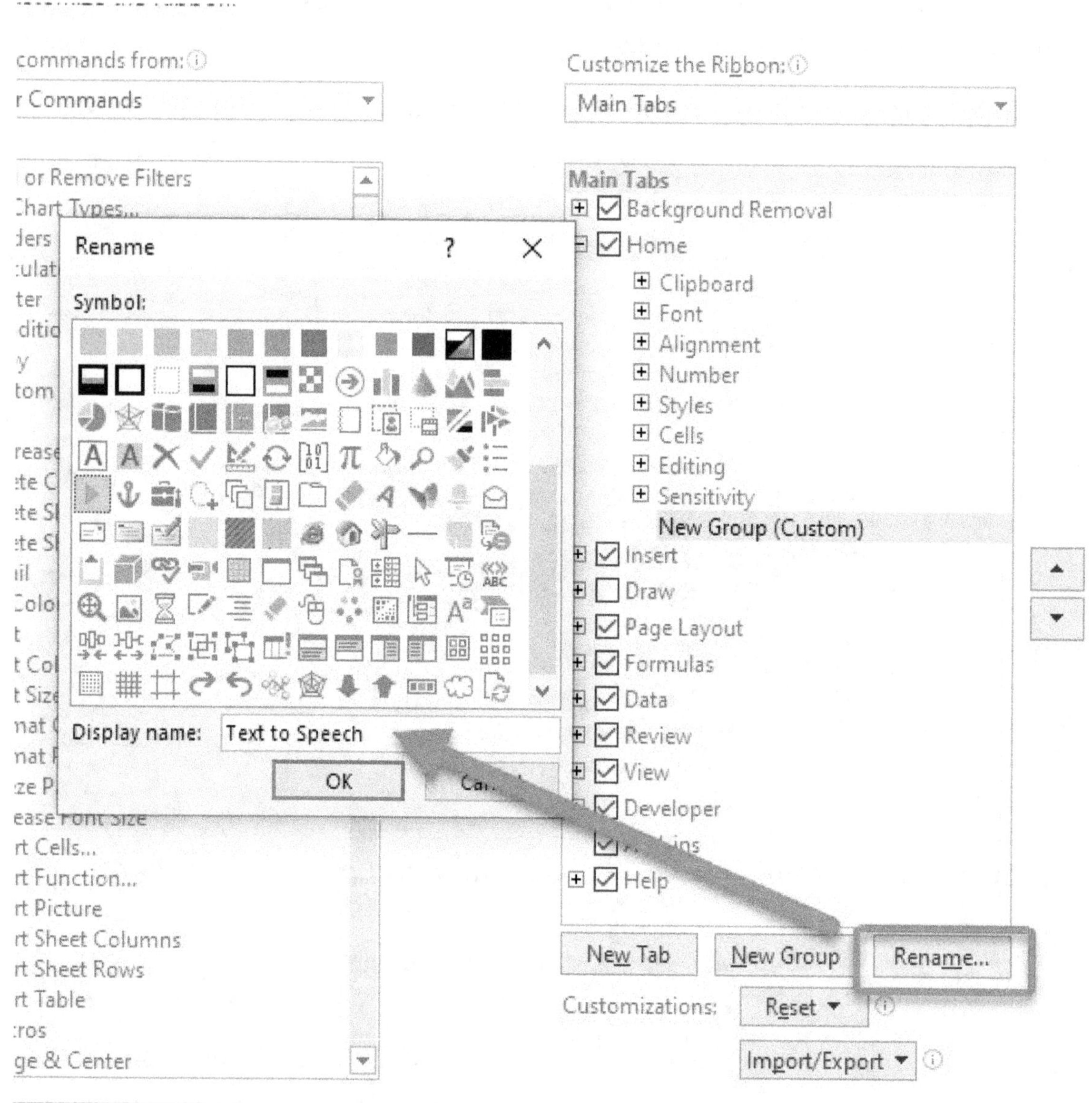

STEP 4: Change the dropdown to **Commands Not in the Ribbon** and you will see all the Excel goodness that are not yet included in your Excel Ribbon!

Scroll down to select the commands that start with **Speak** and click **Add** to add them one by one

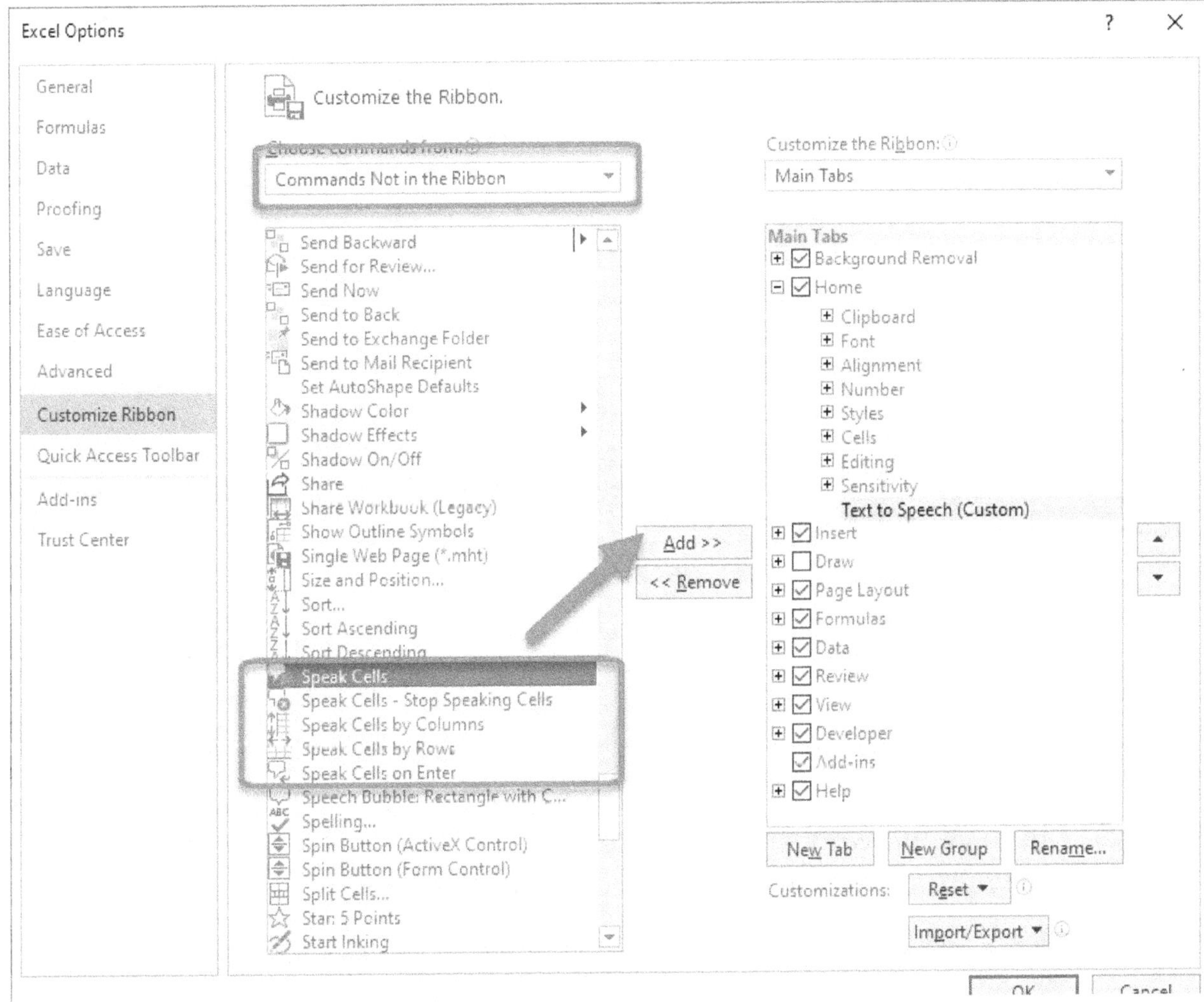

STEP 5: Now the commands are added inside the **Text to Speech** group. Looking good!

Click **OK**

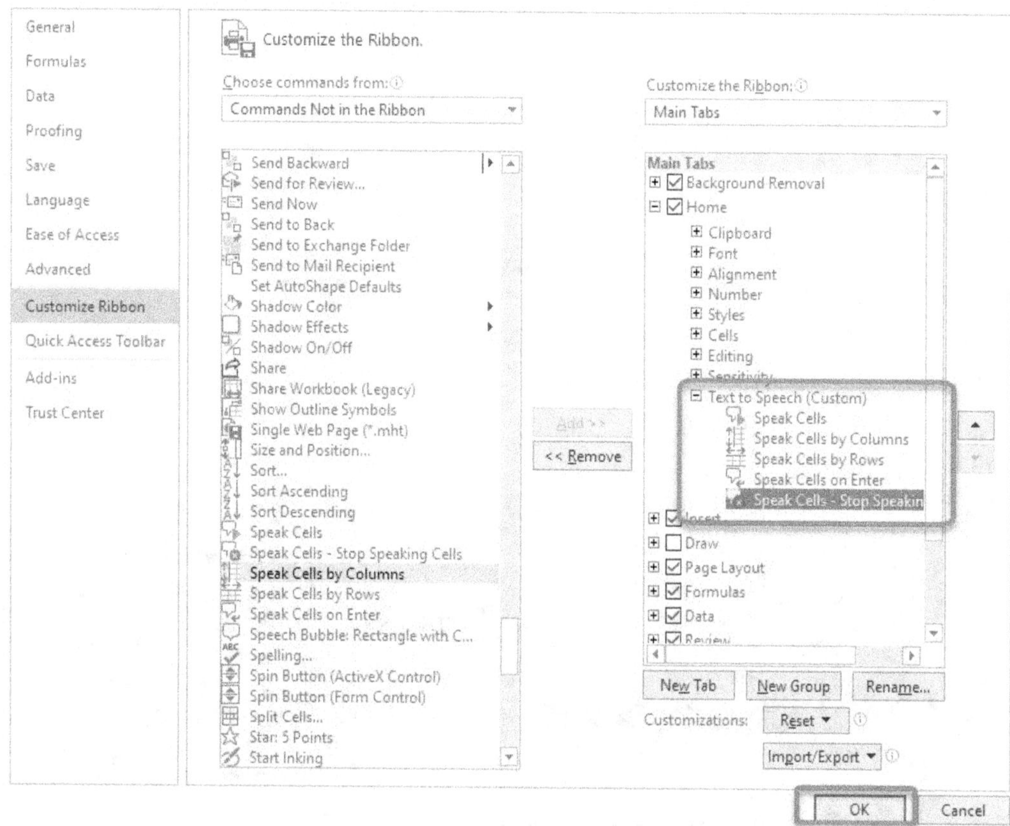

Now you can have fun with the text to speech commands! Try highlighting the text that you want to listen to, then select **Speak Cells!**

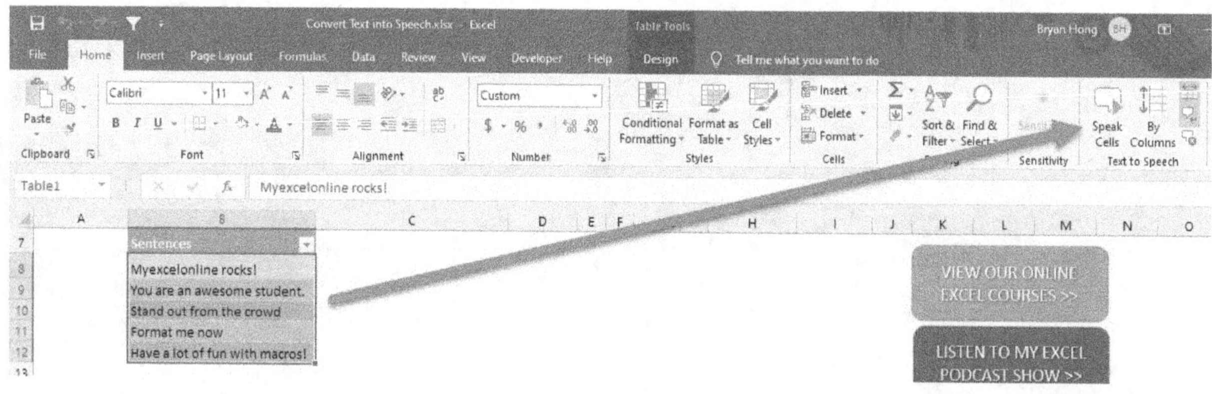

Copy The Cell Above In Excel

Sometimes we get data that is downloaded from an external source and it is not formatted properly.

You may have cells with missing data and cases where you want to copy the cell directly above to fill in your empty cell in Excel.

This can be achieved with the following steps:

STEP 1: Highlight your data set

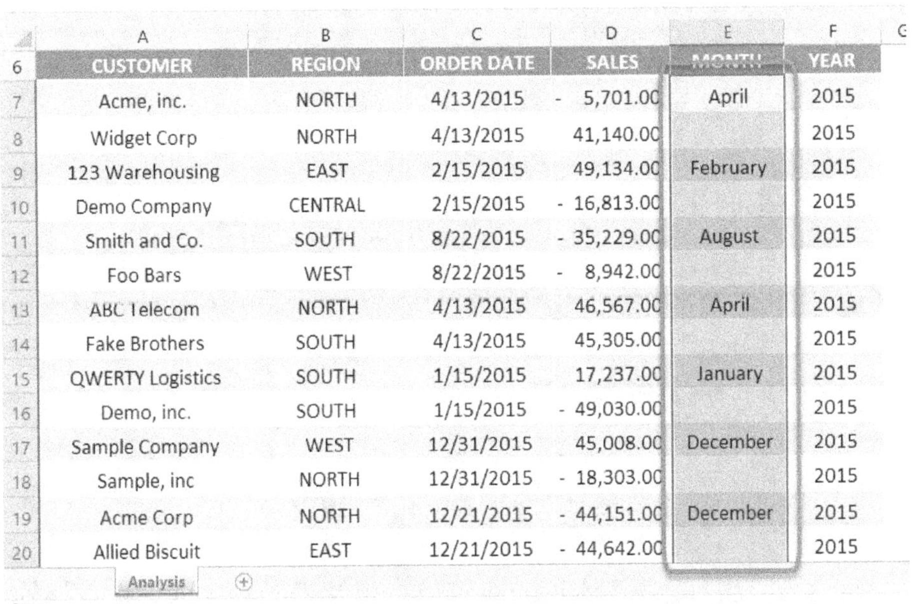

STEP 2: In the ribbon menu select *Home > Find & Select > Go to Special* or just press the keyboard shortcut *CTRL+G*

Click **Special**

 Select the *Blanks* option and press *OK*

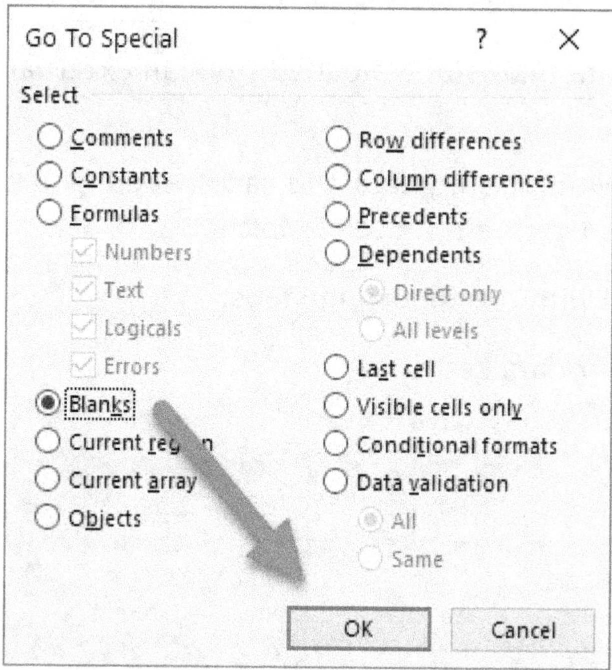

This highlights all your blank cells:

	SALES	MONTH	YEAR	
E	- 5,701.00	April	2015	
	41,140.00		2015	
	49,134.00	February	2015	
	- 16,813.00		2015	
	- 35,229.00	August	2015	
	- 8,942.00		2015	
	46,567.00	April	2015	
	45,305.00		2015	
	17,237.00	January	2015	
	- 49,030.00		2015	
5	45,008.00	December	2015	
5	- 18,303.00		2015	
5	- 44,151.00	December	2015	
5	- 44,642.00		2015	

	A	B	C	D	E	F	G
					E7		
					=E7		

	A	B	C	D	E	F	G
6	CUSTOMER	REGION	ORDER DATE	SALES	MONTH	YEAR	
7	Acme, inc.	NORTH	4/13/2015	- 5,701.00	April	2015	
8	Widget Corp	NORTH	4/13/2015	41,140.00	=E7	2015	
9	123 Warehousing	EAST	2/15/2015	49,134.00	February	2015	
10	Demo Company	CENTRAL	2/15/2015	- 16,813.00		2015	
11	Smith and Co.	SOUTH	8/22/2015	- 35,229.00	August	2015	
12	Foo Bars	WEST	8/22/2015	- 8,942.00		2015	
13	ABC Telecom	NORTH	4/13/2015	46,567.00	April	2015	
14	Fake Brothers	SOUTH	4/13/2015	45,305.00		2015	
15	QWERTY Logistics	SOUTH	1/15/2015	17,237.00	January	2015	
16	Demo, inc.	SOUTH	1/15/2015	- 49,030.00		2015	
17	Sample Company	WEST	12/31/2015	45,008.00	December	2015	
18	Sample, inc	NORTH	12/31/2015	- 18,303.00		2015	
19	Acme Corp	NORTH	12/21/2015	- 44,151.00	December	2015	
20	Allied Biscuit	EAST	12/21/2015	- 44,642.00		2015	
	Analysis	⊕					

STEP 5: Finally, and most importantly, you need to press **CTRL+ENTER** so that the formula can be filled in to all the selected blank cells.

	A	B	C	D	E	F	G
6	CUSTOMER	REGION	ORDER DATE	SALES	MONTH	YEAR	
7	Acme, inc.	NORTH	4/13/2015	- 5,701.00	April	2015	
8	Widget Corp	NORTH	4/13/2015	41,140.00	April	2015	
9	123 Warehousing	EAST	2/15/2015	49,134.00	February	2015	
10	Demo Company	CENTRAL	2/15/2015	- 16,813.00	February	2015	
11	Smith and Co.	SOUTH	8/22/2015	- 35,229.00	August	2015	
12	Foo Bars	WEST	8/22/2015	- 8,942.00	August	2015	
13	ABC Telecom	NORTH	4/13/2015	46,567.00	April	2015	
14	Fake Brothers	SOUTH	4/13/2015	45,305.00	April	2015	
15	QWERTY Logistics	SOUTH	1/15/2015	17,237.00	January	2015	
16	Demo, inc.	SOUTH	1/15/2015	- 49,030.00	January	2015	
17	Sample Company	WEST	12/31/2015	45,008.00	December	2015	
18	Sample, inc	NORTH	12/31/2015	- 18,303.00	December	2015	
19	Acme Corp	NORTH	12/21/2015	- 44,151.00	December	2015	
20	Allied Biscuit	EAST	12/21/2015	- 44,642.00	December	2015	
	Analysis	⊕					

Dependent Dropdown Lists

The INDIRECT function is really cool as it opens up a lot of interesting combinations in Excel.

We will use the power of the INDIRECT function right now on creating **Dependent Dropdown Lists**.

STEP 1: We have our data ordered in the following columns: **Category, Meat, Beverage, Breakfast.**

Notice that the **Category** column has the values **Meat, Beverage and Breakfast**. You will see why in our example below.

Category	Meat	Beverage	Breakfast
Meat	Beef	Water	Hotdog
Beverage	Chicken	Soda	Pancake
Breakfast	Pork	Juice	Eggs
		Shake	Bacon

STEP 2: We are going to assign **Named Ranges** for all four columns.

The **Name Box** is on the far left of the **Formula Bar.**

Highlight the **Category** values, and type in the **Name Box** the name *Category*

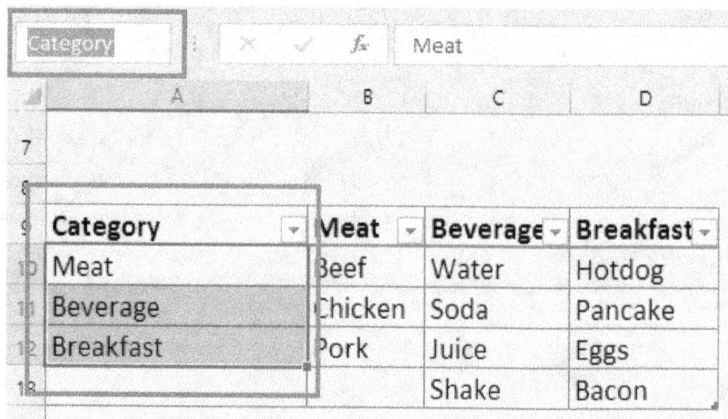

STEP 3: Do the same for the other three columns:

Meat column values - Meat (Named Range)

Beverage column values - Beverage (Named Range)

Breakfast column values - Breakfast (Named Range)

After you created all these **Named Ranges**, click on the **Name Box dropdown** and see our newly created **Named Ranges:**

STEP 4: Let us start creating the dropdown lists, select the cell you want to place the first **dropdown list.**

Go to *Data > Data Validation*

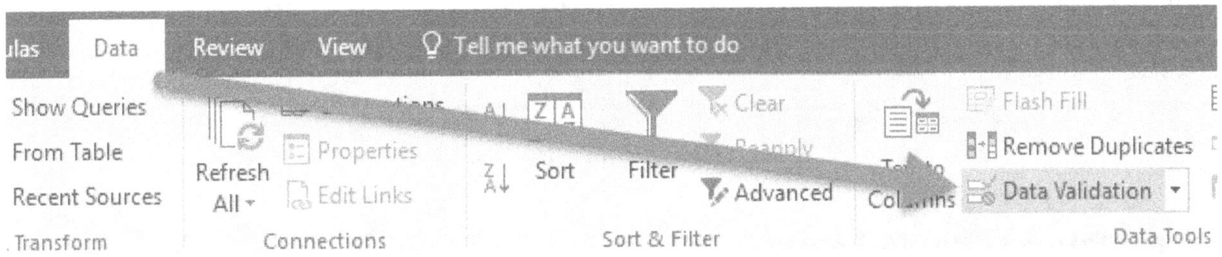

STEP 5: Choose **List** in the **Allow** drop-down, and in the **Source** area, type in *=Category*

The reason we are doing this is to use the *Category* Named Range we defined in **Step 2.**

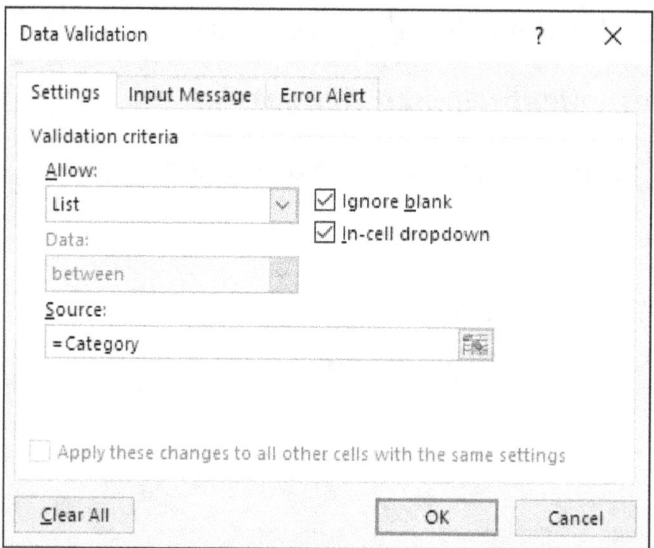

Click **OK.** Try out your drop-down list:

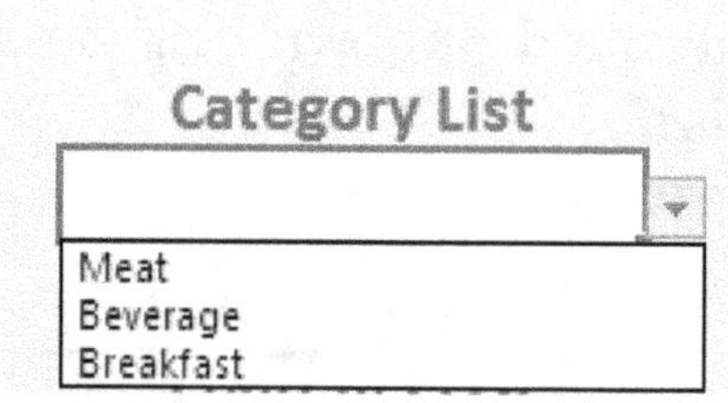

STEP 6: The moment you have been waiting for, it's time to use our **INDIRECT** function!

Select the cell where you want to place the **dependent drop-down list**.

Go to *Data > Data Validation*

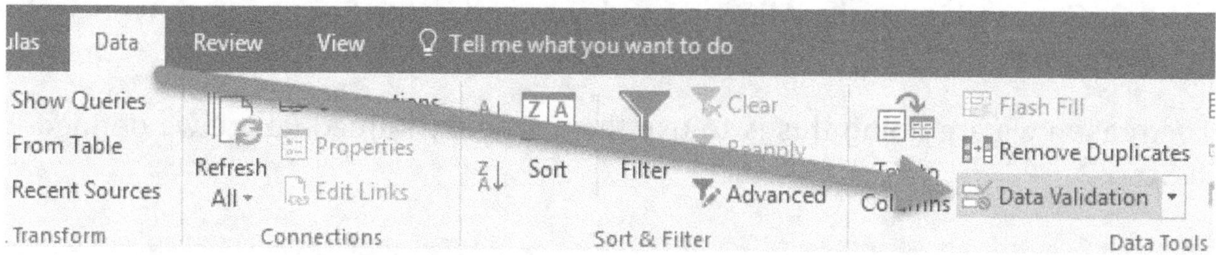

STEP 7: Choose **List** in the **Allow** drop-down, and in the **Source** area, type in *=INDIRECT($H$10)*

This will return the Named Range values from the drop-down list selected in cell H10.

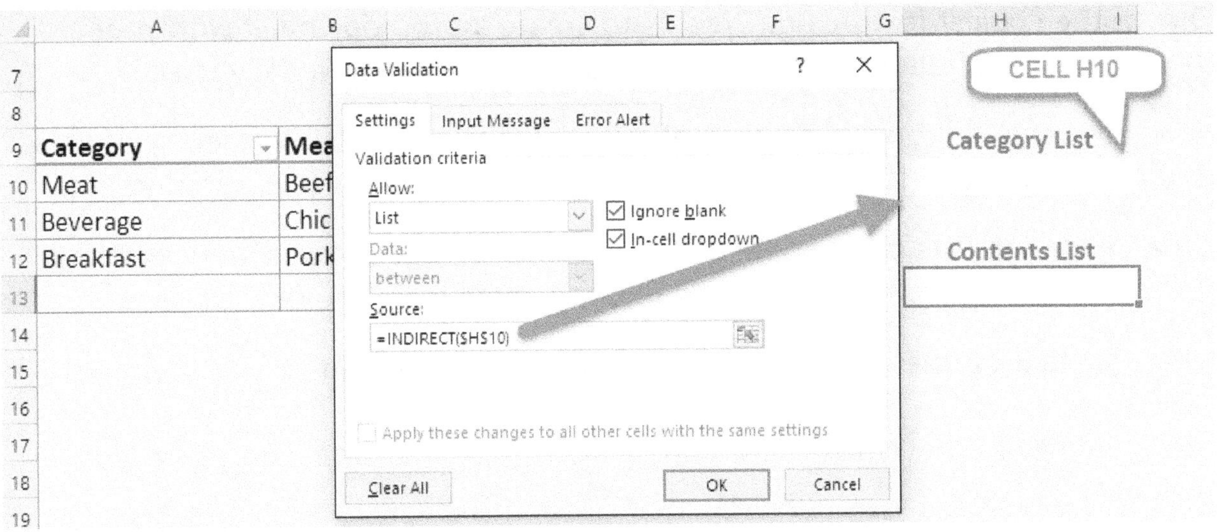

Click **OK.** You will get this error initially, just click **Yes** to continue:

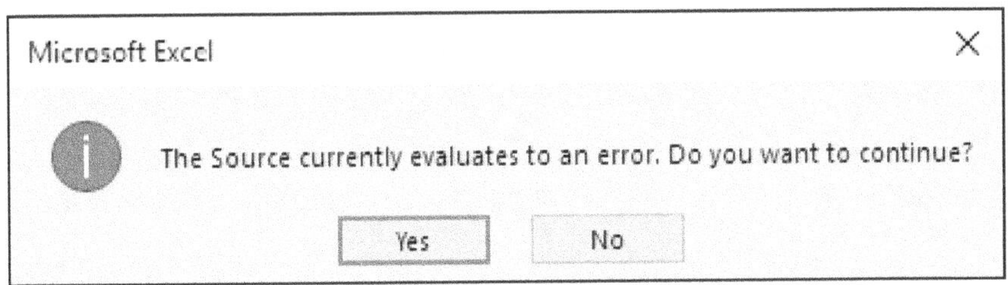

For example, if we pick *Meat* in the **Category List** dropdown, **INDIRECT** will calculate this as the **"Meat" Named Range** we defined earlier and return its values in the **Content List** dropdown.

The *Meat* Named Range would represent the values: *Beef, Chicken, Pork*:

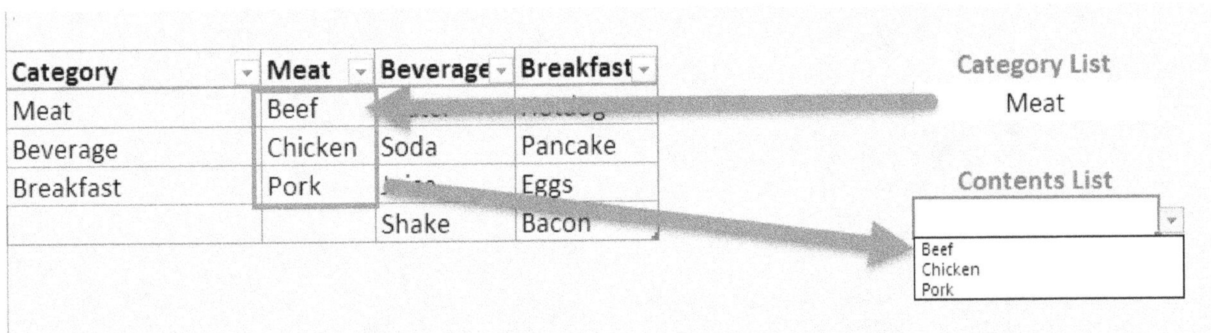

Drop Down List with Data Validation

One of the coolest features of Excel is to create a drop down list with your data. It is one of the first things that I learned and use on a daily basis.

You can create a drop down list to eliminate manual entry and re-entry of data, as well as reduce data entry mistakes if you rely on other users entering data.

Data Validation lists can also be used on a form or a template where external users can choose from the drop down list to enter their choices.

STEP 1: **Click on the cell** that you want to enter your list in

	A	B	C	D	E	F
3	CUSTOMER	REGION	ORDER DATE	SALES	MONTH	YEAR
4	Acme, inc.	NORTH	4/13/2014	$55,815	April	2014
5	Widget Corp	SOUTH	12/21/2014	$94,908	December	2014
6	123 Warehousing	EAST	2/15/2014	$57,088	February	2014
7	Demo Company	WEST	5/14/2014	$56,539	May	2014
8	Smith and Co.	NORTH	6/28/2015	$63,116	June	2015
9	Foo Bars	SOUTH	1/15/2015	$38,281	January	2015
10	ABC Telecom	EAST	8/22/2015	$57,650	August	2015
11	Fake Brothers	WEST	12/31/2015	$90,967	December	2015
12						
13						

STEP 2: Go to the ribbon and choose *Data > Data Validation > List*

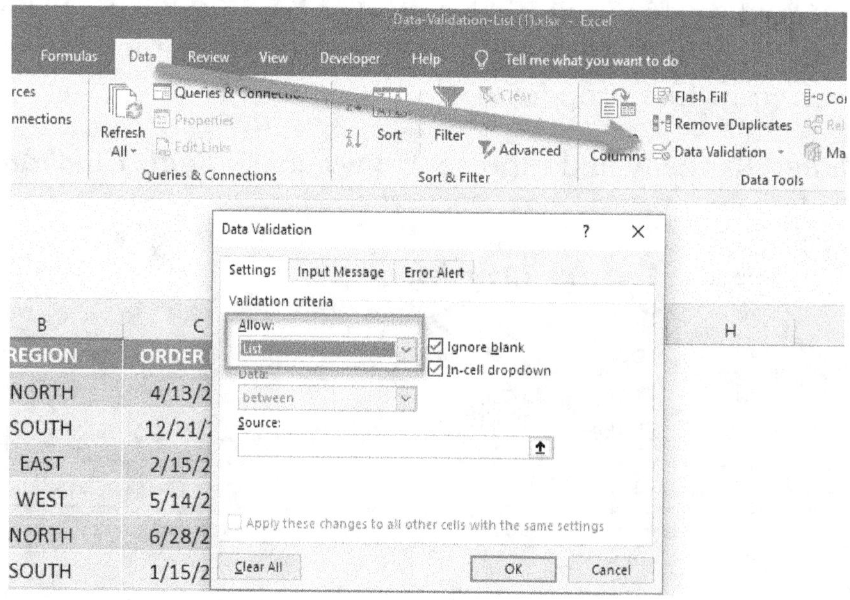

 Click in the Source box and **select the range that includes your list of text/values** and press **OK**

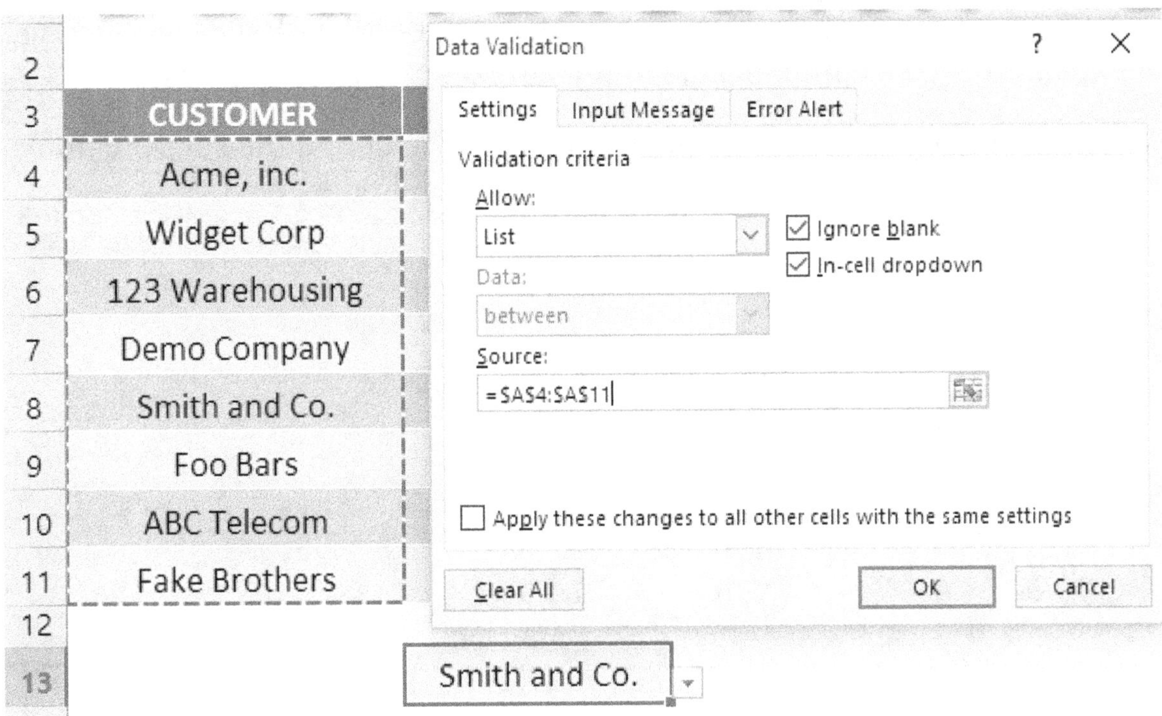

Drop Down Menu

Apart from creating a simple Drop Down Menu/List or Data Validation List, you can expand this concept to include it in your Excel Table or Database.

That way you don't have to do repetitive tasks like entering the same customer over and over again or copying and pasting time and time again.

See how easy it is to implement this in under 1 minute!

STEP 1: Have your list of values ready

	A	B	C	D	E	F
3	CUSTOMER	REGION	ORDER DATE	SALES	MONTH	YEAR
4		NORTH	4/13/2014	$55,815	April	2014
5		SOUTH	12/21/2014	$94,908	December	2014
6		EAST	2/15/2014	$57,088	February	2014
7		WEST	5/14/2014	$56,539	May	2014
8		NORTH	6/28/2015	$63,116	June	2015
9		SOUTH	1/15/2015	$38,281	January	2015
10		EAST	8/22/2015	$57,650	August	2015
11		WEST	12/31/2015	$90,967	December	2015
12						
13		Acme Inc.				
14		Widget Corp				
15		123 Warehousing				
16		Demo Company				
17						

	A	B	C	D	E	F
3	CUSTOMER	REGION	ORDER DATE	SALES	MONTH	YEAR
4		NORTH	4/13/2014	$55,815	April	2014
5		SOUTH	12/21/2014	$94,908	December	2014
6		EAST	2/15/2014	$57,088	February	2014
7		WEST	5/14/2014	$56,539	May	2014
8		NORTH	6/28/2015	$63,116	June	2015
9		SOUTH	1/15/2015	$38,281	January	2015
10		EAST	8/22/2015	$57,650	August	2015
11		WEST	12/31/2015	$90,967	December	2015
12						
13		Acme Inc.				
14		Widget Corp				
15		123 Warehousing				
16		Demo Company				
17						

STEP 3: Go to *Data > Data Validation*

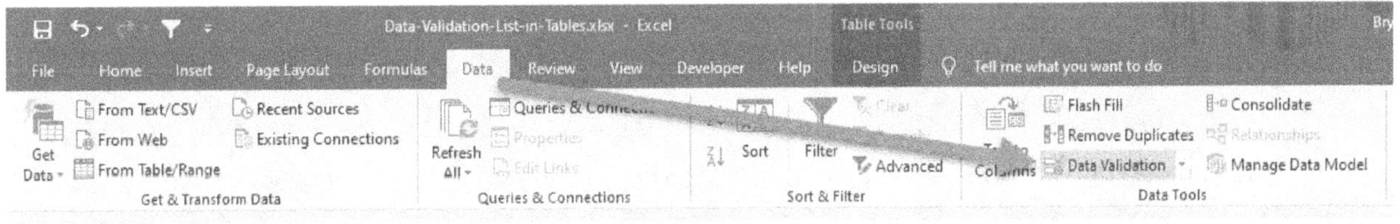

Select **List** and for the **Source**, select the list of values for your **drop down list**. Click **OK**.

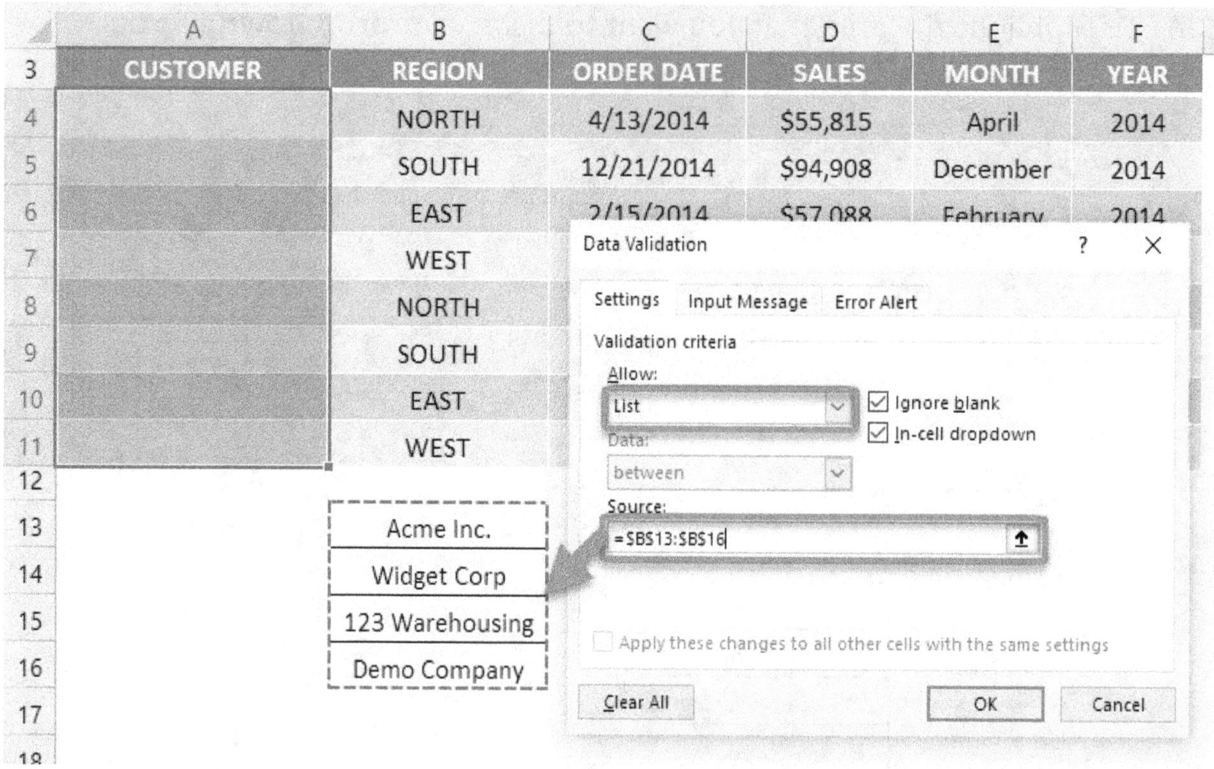

STEP 4: You can test it out now on your table! You can also update the values in your source list and it gets reflected in your drop down list!

	A	B	C	D	E	F
3	CUSTOMER	REGION	ORDER DATE	SALES	MONTH	YEAR
4	123 Warehousing	NORTH	4/13/2014	$55,815	April	2014
5	Demo Company	SOUTH	12/21/2014	$94,908	December	2014
6		EAST	2/15/2014	$57,088	February	2014
7		WEST	5/14/2014	$56,539	May	2014
8		NORTH	6/28/2015	$63,116	June	2015
9		SOUTH	1/15/2015	$38,281	January	2015
10		EAST	8/22/2015	$57,650	August	2015
11		WEST	12/31/2015	$90,967	December	2015
12						
13	Acme Inc.					
14	Widget Corp					
15	123 Warehousing					
16	Demo Company					

Dynamic Data Validation List

What's a dynamic data validation drop down list in Excel, you say?

Well, as you add new data into your Excel Table, your drop down list automatically gets updated.

That is a cool feature and it means that you do not need to update your data validation source reference each time you update your data with a new entry, saving you heaps of time in the long run.

STEP 1: Convert your data to an Excel Table by selecting its range and pressing the keyboard shortcut **Ctrl + T**

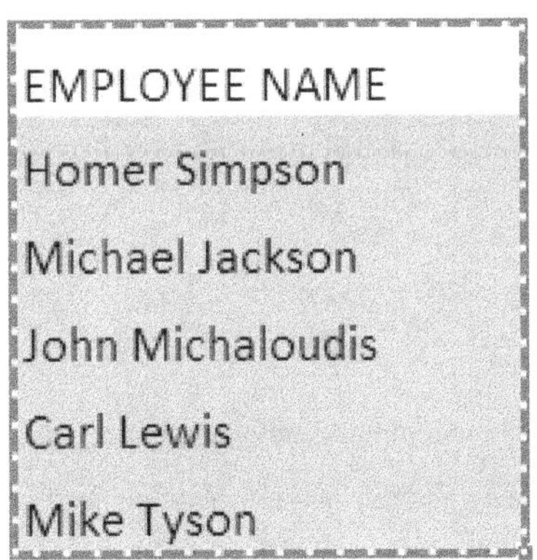

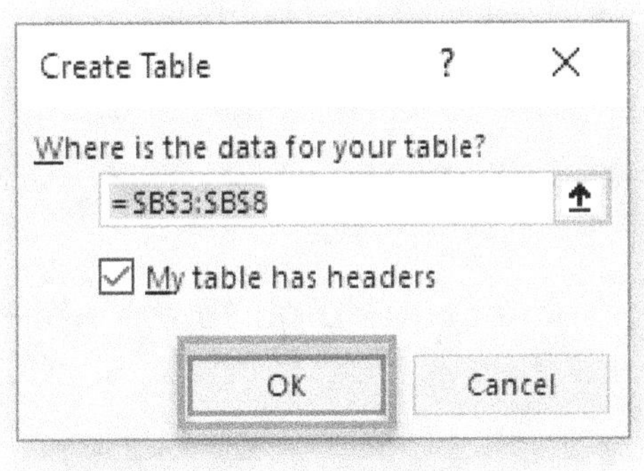

STEP 2: Select your Table's column by hovering over the Excel Table and left clicking when the arrow pointer shows

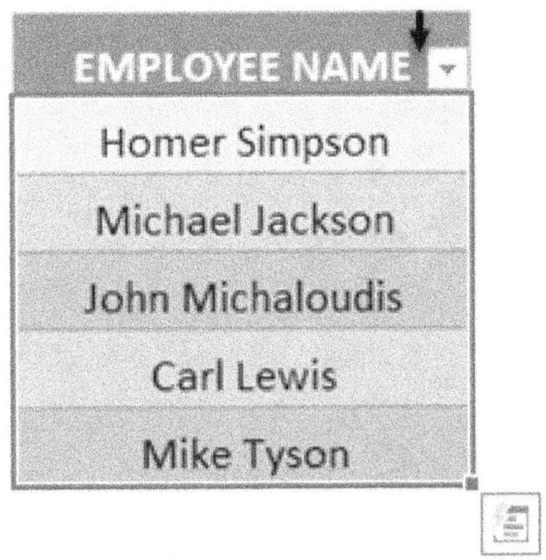

STEP 3: In the ribbon go to ***Formulas > Define Name >*** enter a custom name with no spaces (we will put this name in step 5) and press OK

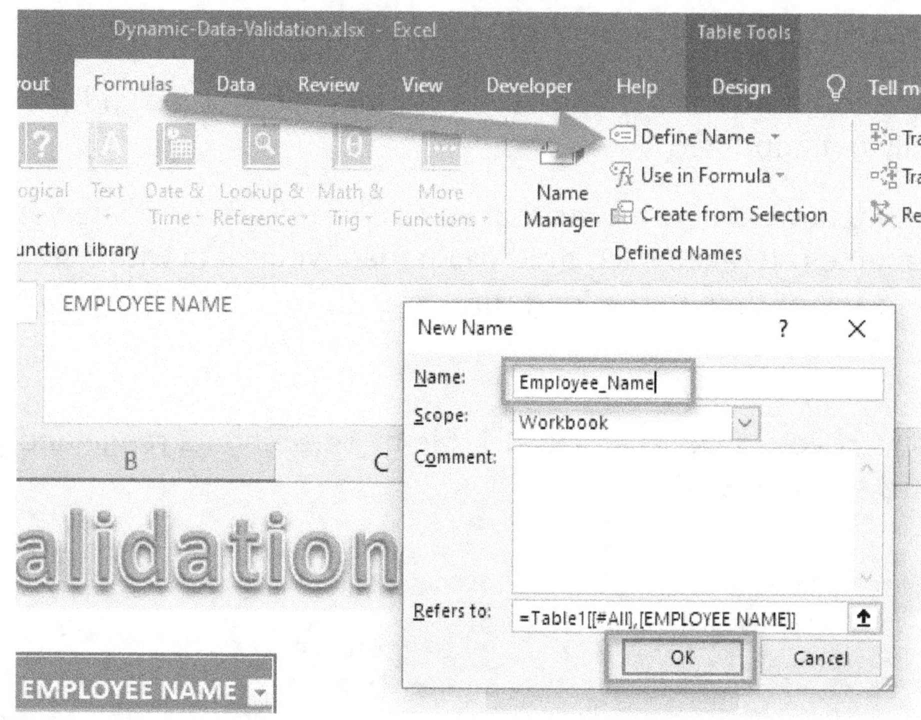

STEP 4: Click in a cell and go to the ribbon and choose ***Data > Data Validation > List***

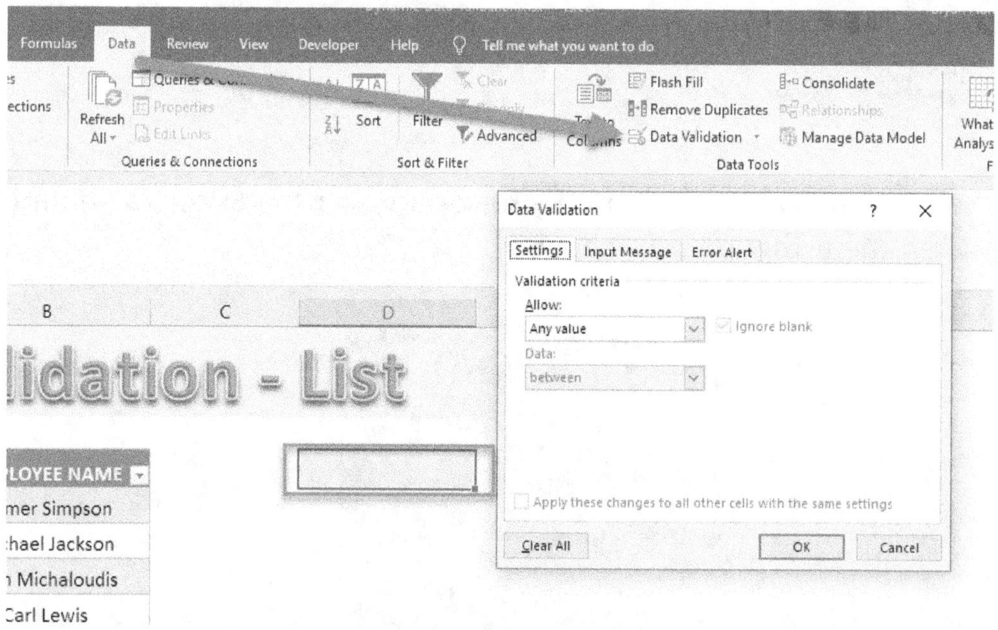

STEP 5: In the Source box enter the name you created in **Step 3** and press OK

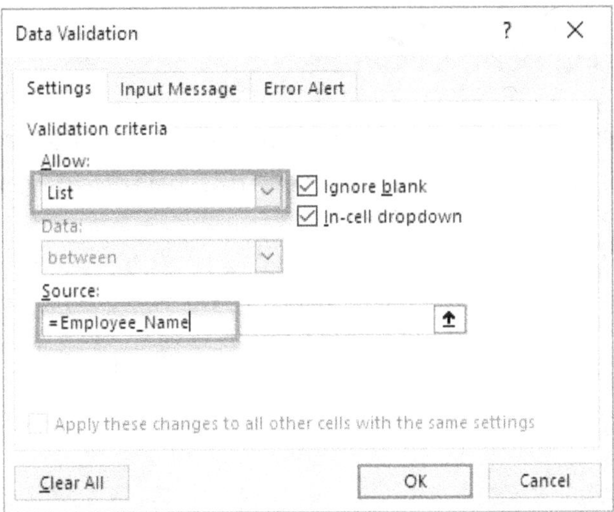

STEP 6: If you want to add extra data into your Excel Table, hover with your mouse in the bottom right-hand corner and when you see a double arrow, drag down.

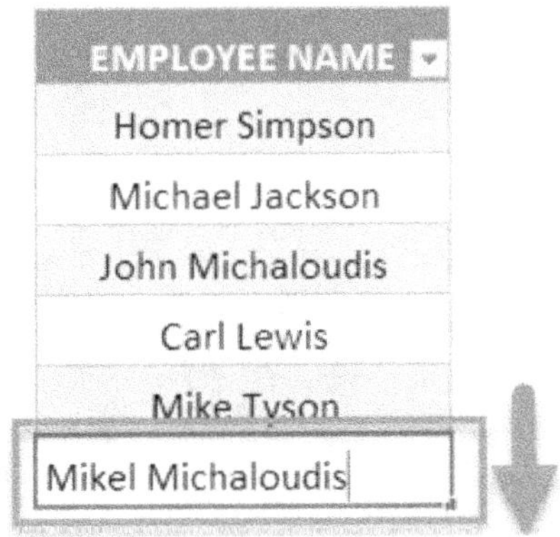

STEP 7: Enter a new entry and this will automatically be updated in your drop down list.

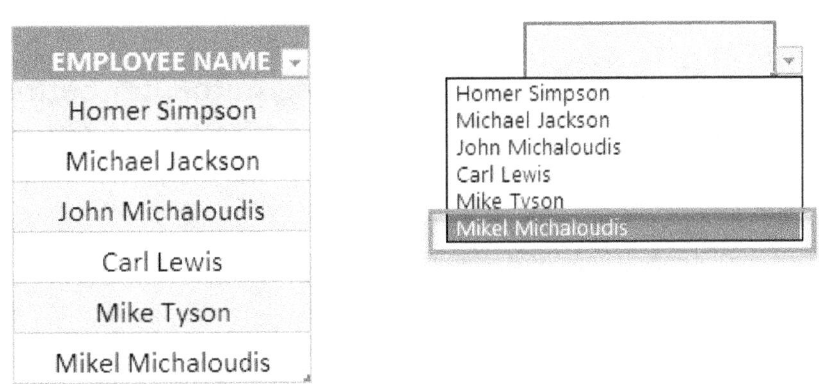

Filter by Selection

When you have an array of data in Excel you can quickly select an item and press the AutoFilter button which will filter that selection in your data.

You can then go over to another column within your data and select another item, apply the same steps above and further filter your data.

This is a quick and easy way to drill down into your data.

This is our data table.

CUSTOMER	REGION	ORDER DATE	SALES (ths)	SALES (mill)
Acme, inc.	NORTH	4/13/2015	27,181 ths	27 mill
Widget Corp	NORTH	12/21/2015	33,902 ths	34 mill
123 Warehousing	EAST	2/15/2015	111,610 ths	112 mill
Acme, inc.	CENTRAL	6/28/2015	139,435 ths	139 mill
Widget Corp	SOUTH	8/22/2015	77,710 ths	78 mill
123 Warehousing	WEST	12/31/2015	118,179 ths	118 mill
Acme, inc.	NORTH	4/13/2015	48,208 ths	48 mill
Widget Corp	SOUTH	6/28/2015	83,359 ths	83 mill

STEP 1: For this trick to work you need to put the **AutoFilter** button in the *Quick Access Toolbar* by going to *File > More > Options > Quick Access Toolbar*

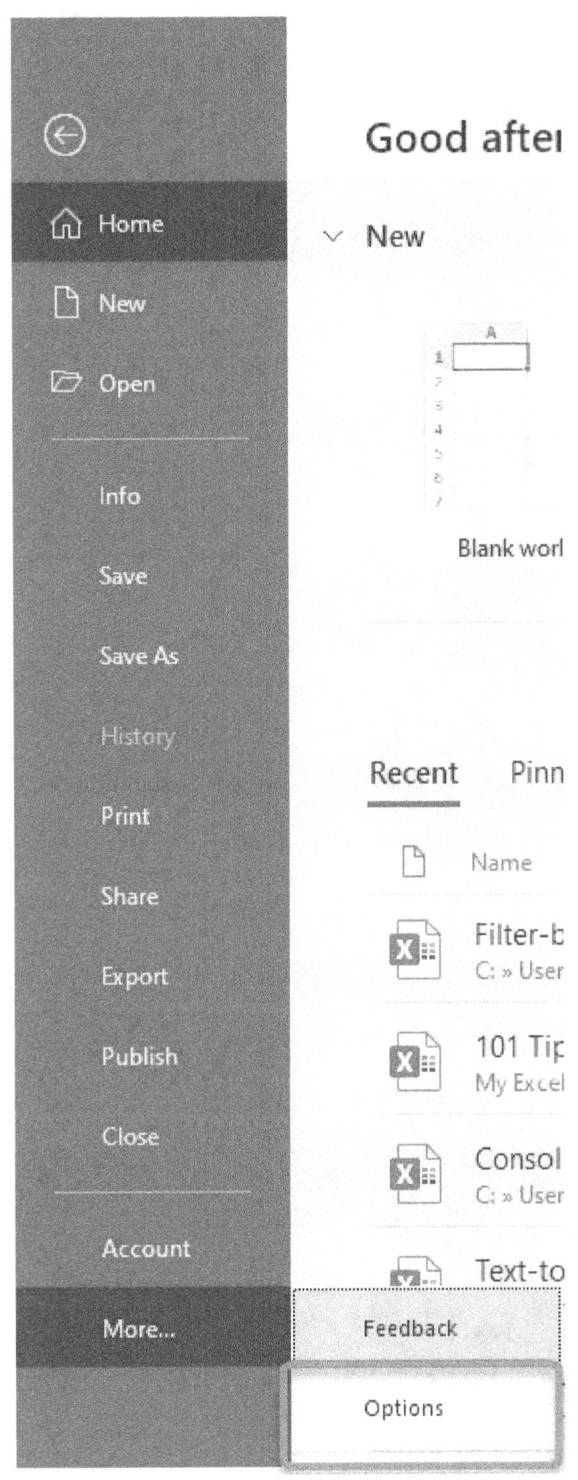

STEP 2: Then you need to go to *Choose commands from > All Commands > AutoFilter > Add > OK*

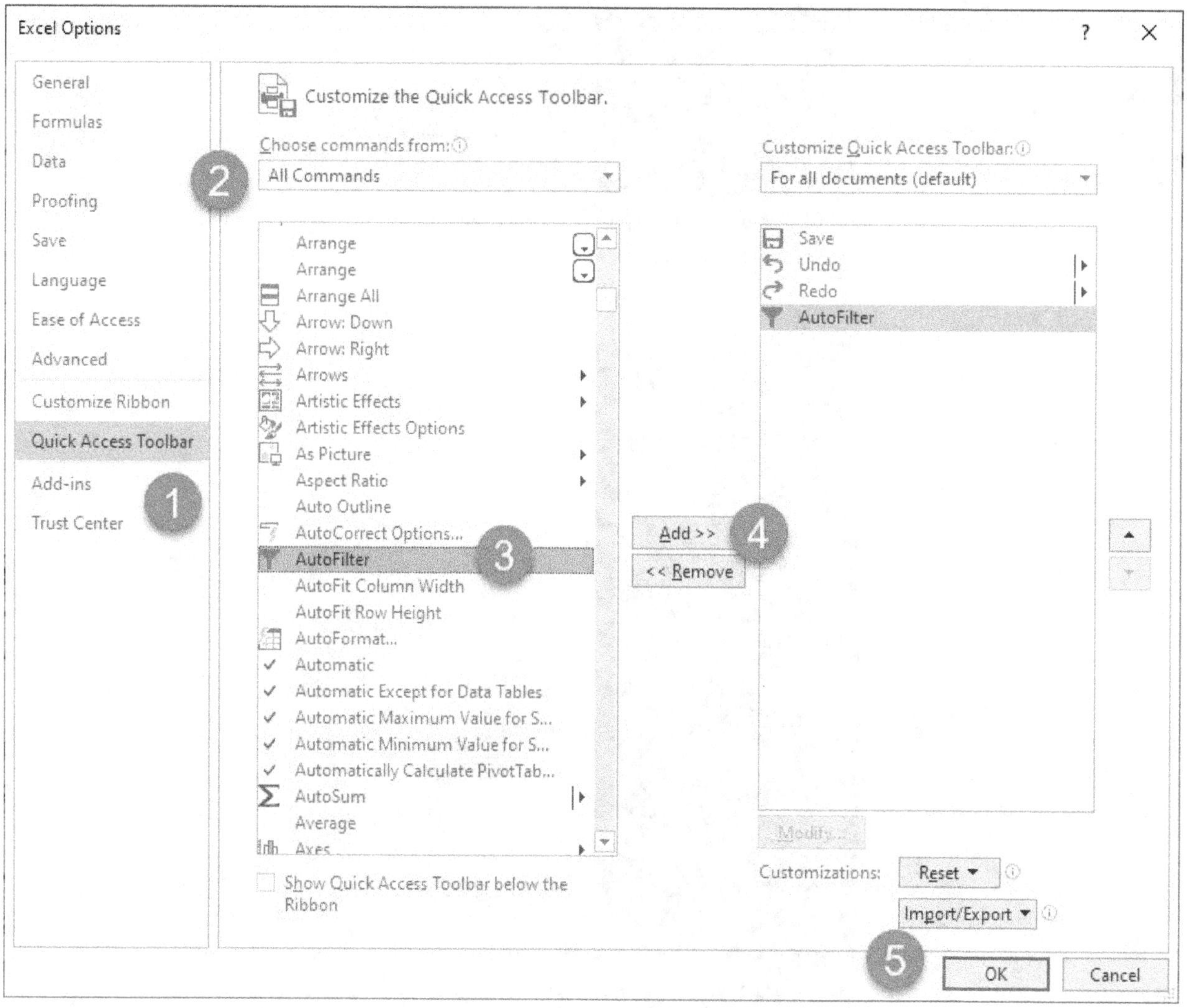

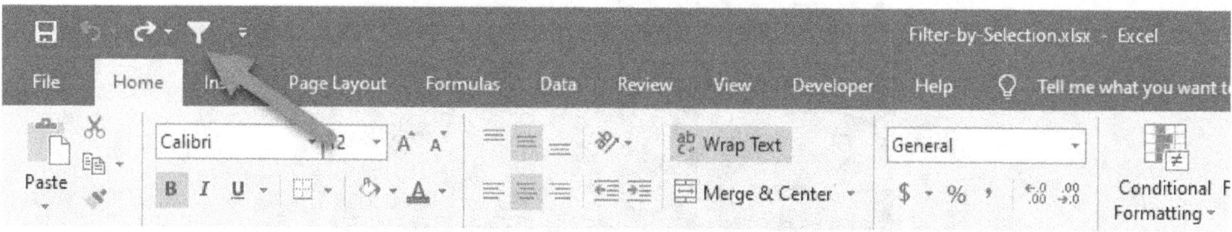

You can now see the **AutoFilter icon** on top.

STEP 3: You can then click anywhere in your data, click the AutoFilter button in your Quick Access Toolbar and see the magic!

Let us say we want to filter the data by **Region - North.** Click on any **NORTH value.**

Afterwards click on the **AutoFilter icon**.

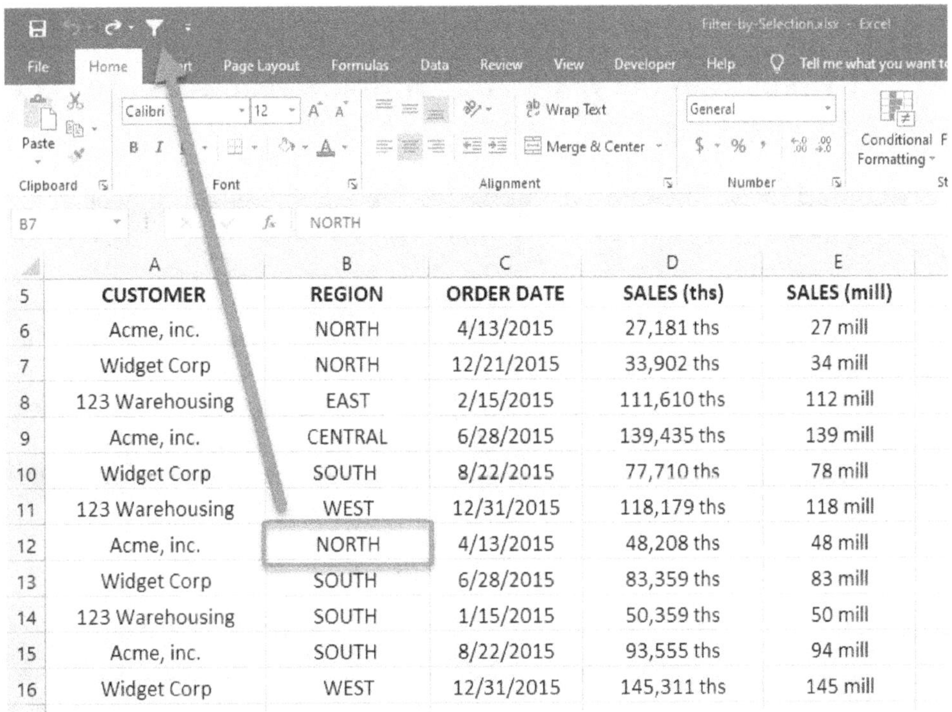

Your table is now filtered by the **NORTH REGION** with a single click!

	A	B	C	D	E
5	CUSTOMER	REGION	ORDER DATE	SALES (ths)	SALES (mill)
6	Acme, inc.	NORTH	4/13/2015	27,181 ths	27 mill
7	Widget Corp	NORTH	12/21/2015	33,902 ths	34 mill
12	Acme, inc.	NORTH	4/13/2015	48,208 ths	48 mill
17	123 Warehousing	NORTH	4/13/2015	58,710 ths	59 mill
18	Acme, inc.	NORTH	12/21/2015	97,078 ths	97 mill
23	123 Warehousing	NORTH	4/13/2015	69,856 ths	70 mill
27	Acme, inc.	NORTH	12/31/2015	21,346 ths	21 mill
28	Widget Corp	NORTH	12/31/2015	6,396 ths	6 mill
33					

Find & Replace

The ***Find & Replace*** feature or CTRL+H shortcut allows you to amend your data in seconds. Imagine you had thousands of rows of data that was downloaded from an external system with the wrong date. A simple CTRL+H will save you heaps of time! See how below.

STEP 1: Let us try replacing the years 2015 with the year 2021. Select all of the **Order Dates**

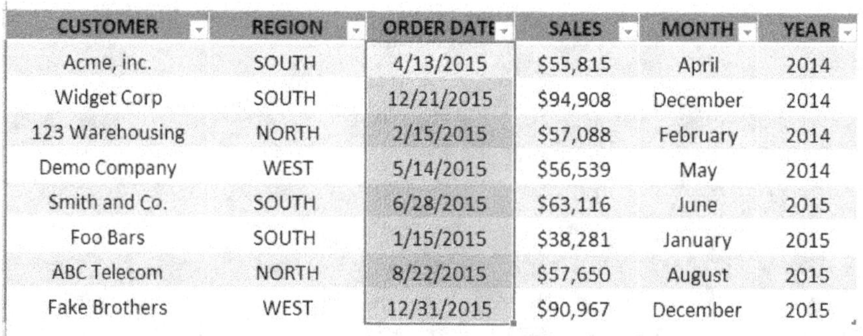

CUSTOMER	REGION	ORDER DATE	SALES	MONTH	YEAR
Acme, inc.	SOUTH	4/13/2015	$55,815	April	2014
Widget Corp	SOUTH	12/21/2015	$94,908	December	2014
123 Warehousing	NORTH	2/15/2015	$57,088	February	2014
Demo Company	WEST	5/14/2015	$56,539	May	2014
Smith and Co.	SOUTH	6/28/2015	$63,116	June	2015
Foo Bars	SOUTH	1/15/2015	$38,281	January	2015
ABC Telecom	NORTH	8/22/2015	$57,650	August	2015
Fake Brothers	WEST	12/31/2015	$90,967	December	2015

STEP 2: Go to ***Home > Find & Select > Replace***

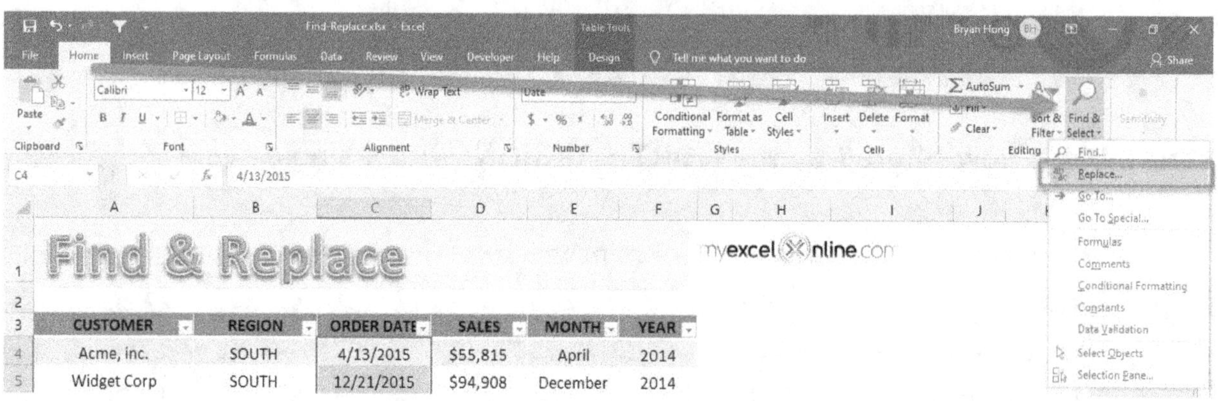

STEP 3: We want to replace 2015 with 2021. Type that in, then click **Replace All**

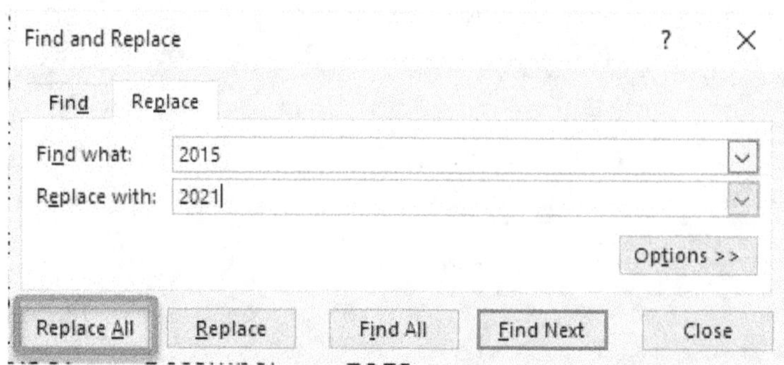

Click **OK**. Your values are now replaced

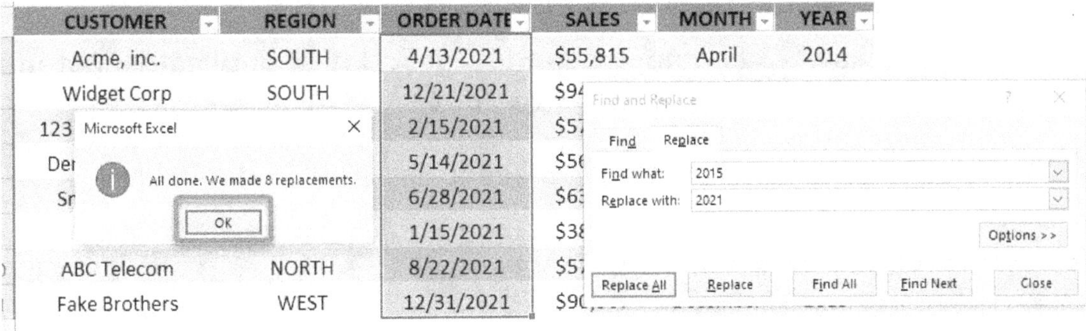

STEP 4: You can also use it to remove values. Let us say we want to remove the **NORTH Region**

Select the values of the **REGION Column**. Go to *Home > Find & Select > Replace*

Type in the values to find the **NORTH** text and replace it with a blank.
Click **Replace All**

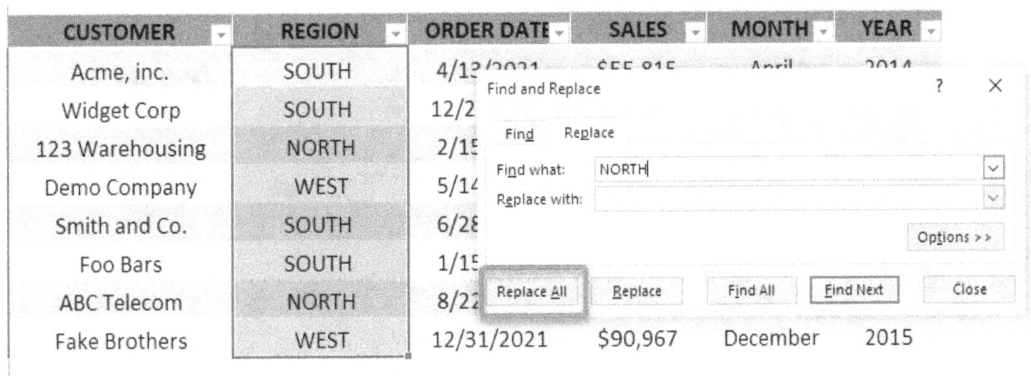

The **NORTH** values are now removed!

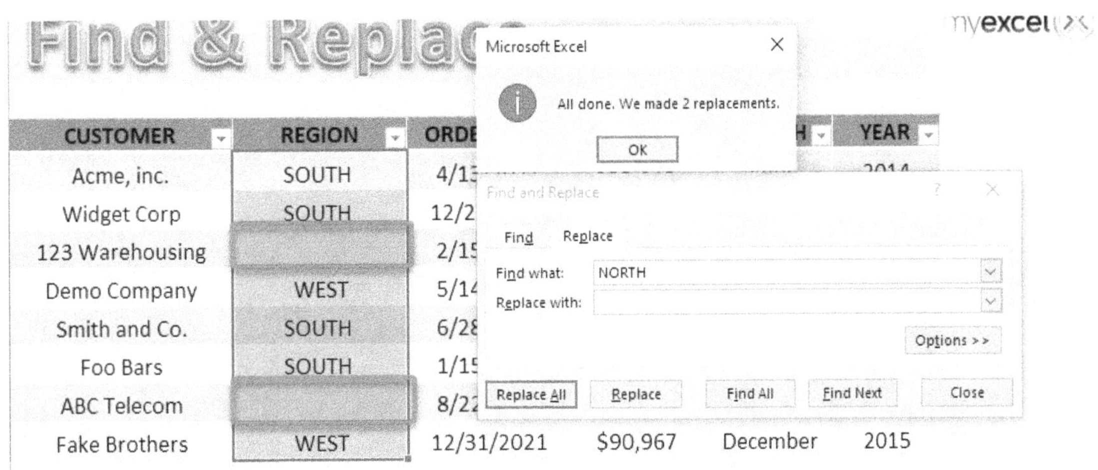

Find & Highlight Duplicates in Excel

Normally when we have dirty data, we tend to get a lot of duplicates. But in Excel it is very easy to **spot the duplicates** for your data cleanup!

Here is our sample list of words, you can see it has a lot of duplicates:

account	person	economic	rush	women
rainstorm	letters	flat	trains	warlike
tight	sick	lucky	destruction	pollution
alive	threatening	mouth	children	mark
ticket	ill	talk	prickly	talk
wistful	relation	collect	cook	unit
regret	minor	gaping	bury	ticket
leather	ticket	mist	torpid	aromatic
mouth	receptive	hose	gaping	protective
rinse	letters	mysterious	trains	mouth

STEP 1: Select your list of words / data:

account	person	economic	rush	women
rainstorm	letters	flat	trains	warlike
tight	sick	lucky	destruction	pollution
alive	threatening	mouth	children	mark
ticket	ill	talk	prickly	talk
wistful	relation	collect	cook	unit
regret	minor	gaping	bury	ticket
leather	ticket	mist	torpid	aromatic
mouth	receptive	hose	gaping	protective
rinse	letters	mysterious	trains	mouth

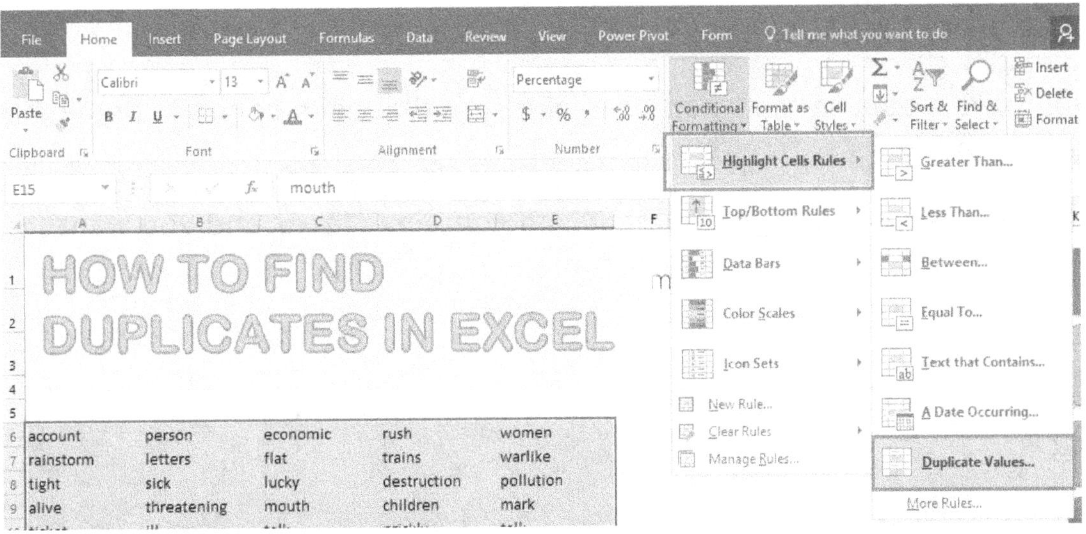

STEP 3: You can select the formatting that you want. For our example, we selected **Green Fill with Dark Green Text.** Click **OK.**

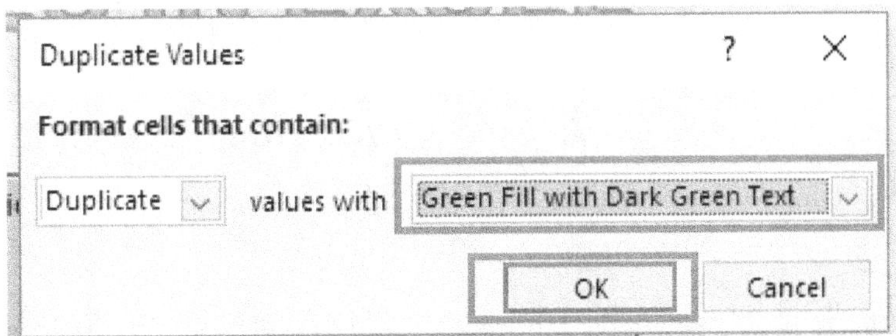

You will now see the magic happen; **all of the duplicate values** are now highlighted in your Excel worksheet!

account	person	economic	rush	women
rainstorm	letters	flat	trains	warlike
tight	sick	lucky	destruction	pollution
alive	threatening	mouth	children	mark
ticket	ill	talk	prickly	talk
wistful	relation	collect	cook	unit
regret	minor	gaping	bury	ticket
leather	ticket	mist	torpid	aromatic
mouth	receptive	hose	gaping	protective
rinse	letters	mysterious	trains	mouth

Find Errors with Go to Special Constants

Say you have a data set and want to make sure that each column contains what it is supposed to.

For example, say we have a column which contains **_Dates_** and you want to check that there are no cells which contain **_Text_**.

This is our source table, we want to get the order dates that are in the text format.

	A	B	C	D	E
3	CUSTOMER	REGION	ORDER DATE	SALES	MONTH
4	Acme, inc.	NORTH	4/13/2015	$55,815	$94,908
5	Widget Corp	NORTH	12/21/2015	$94,908	December
6	123 Warehousing	EAST	2/15/2015	$57,088	February
7	Smith and Co.	#N/A	6/28/2015	$63,116	June
8	ABC Telecom	2015	8/22/2015	$57,650	August
9	Fake Brothers	WEST	August	$56,897	$38,281
10	Acme, inc.	NORTH	4/13/2015	$55,815	April
11	Smith and Co.	SOUTH	6/28/2015	$63,116	June
12	Foo Bars	SOUTH	January	$38,281	January
13	ABC Telecom	#N/A	8/22/2015	$57,650	August
14	Fake Brothers	WEST	12/31/2015	$90,967	December

	A	B	C	D	E
3	**CUSTOMER**	**REGION**	**ORDER DATE**	**SALES**	**MONTH**
4	Acme, inc.	NORTH	4/13/2015	$55,815	$94,908
5	Widget Corp	NORTH	12/21/2015	$94,908	December
6	123 Warehousing	EAST	2/15/2015	$57,088	February
7	Smith and Co.	#N/A	6/28/2015	$63,116	June
8	ABC Telecom	2015	8/22/2015	$57,650	August
9	Fake Brothers	WEST	August	$56,897	$38,281
10	Acme, inc.	NORTH	4/13/2015	$55,815	April
11	Smith and Co.	SOUTH	6/28/2015	$63,116	June
12	Foo Bars	SOUTH	January	$38,281	January
13	ABC Telecom	#N/A	8/22/2015	$57,650	August
14	Fake Brothers	WEST	12/31/2015	$90,967	December

STEP 2: Press **CTRL + G** to open the **Go To** dialog. Select **Special.**

 We want to select the text values in the **Order Date** column.

To do that, select **Constants** and ensure that only **Text** is ticked (Because our invalid values are in the text format).

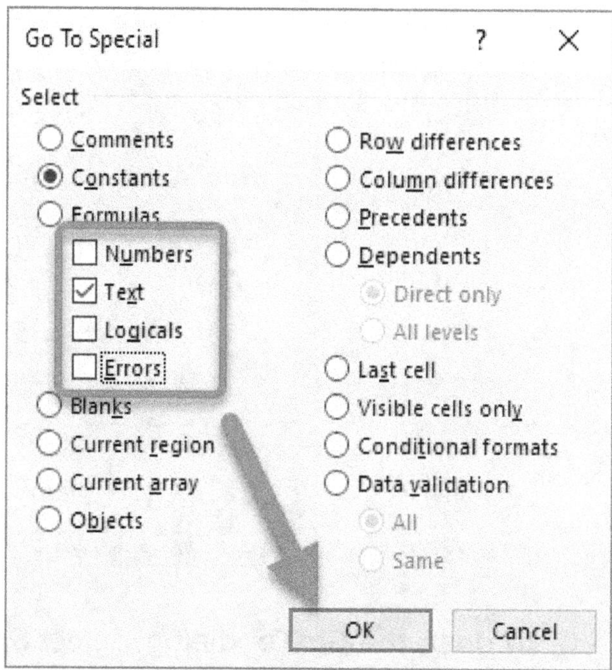

Now Excel has highlighted the text values for you and you can make the necessary changes!

	A	B	C	D	E
3	CUSTOMER	REGION	ORDER DATE	SALES	MONTH
4	Acme, inc.	NORTH	4/13/2015	$55,815	$94,908
5	Widget Corp	NORTH	12/21/2015	$94,908	December
6	123 Warehousing	EAST	2/15/2015	$57,088	February
7	Smith and Co.	#N/A	6/28/2015	$63,116	June
8	ABC Telecom	2015	8/22/2015	$57,650	August
9	Fake Brothers	WEST	August	$56,897	$38,281
10	Acme, inc.	NORTH	4/13/2015	$55,815	April
11	Smith and Co.	SOUTH	6/28/2015	$63,116	June
12	Foo Bars	SOUTH	January	$38,281	January
13	ABC Telecom	#N/A	8/22/2015	$57,650	August
14	Fake Brothers	WEST	12/31/2015	$90,967	December

Flash Fill: How to Use In Excel

Flash Fill in Excel was introduced in Excel 2013.

It is very handy as Excel predicts the rest of your inputs based on the first entry that you have placed. Once its prediction is correct and you confirm it, it will fill the rest of the rows literally **in a flash!**

The cool thing with Excel's **Flash Fill** is there is no need to use formulas and removes manual repetitiveness, saving you heaps of time in the process!

ACTIVATE FLASH FILL:

If the Flash Fill does not work automatically, you need to activate in from Excel's backend by going to:

File > Options > Advanced > Automatically Flash Fill

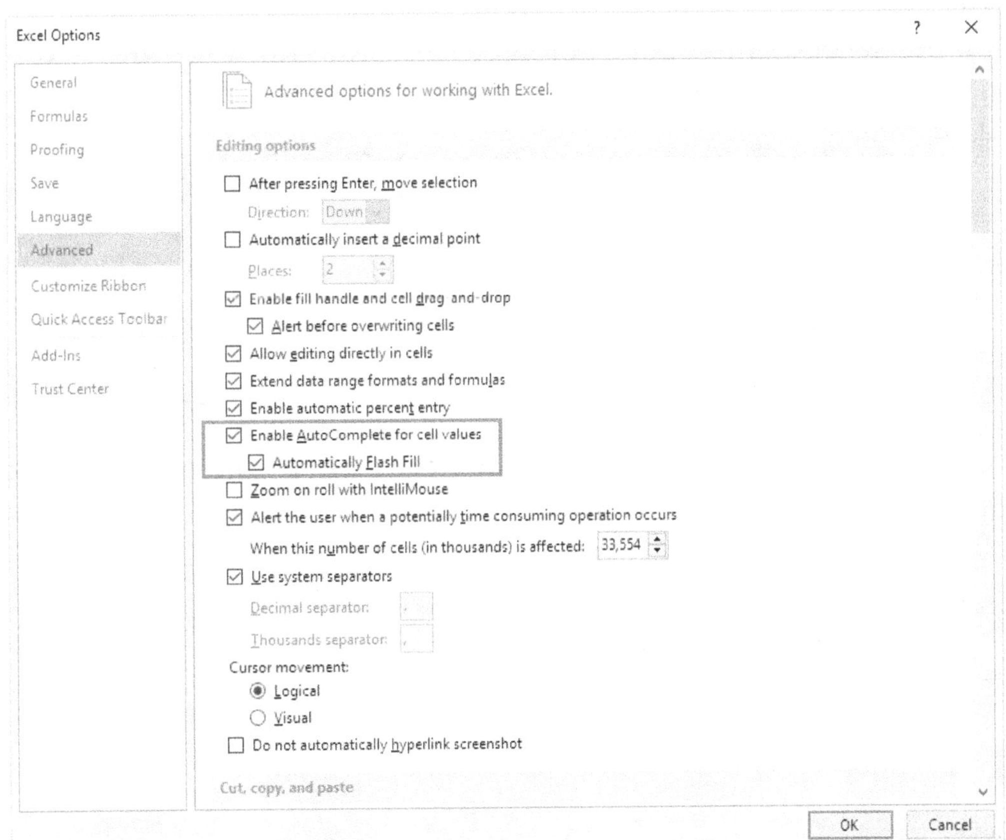

To demonstrate the power of Excel's Flash Fill, we will start off with this table of
data we need to populate:

	First Name	Last Name
Homer Simpson		
Ian Wright		
John Michaloudis		
Michael Jackson		

STEP 1: Type *Homer* as the first entry in the **First Name**

	First Name	Last Name
Homer Simpson	Homer	
Ian Wright		
John Michaloudis		
Michael Jackson		

STEP 2: In the second entry, once you type the first letter **I** for *Ian,* Excel will
auto-suggest to **Flash Fill** the rest of the First Names.

	First Name	Last Name
Homer Simpson	Homer	
Ian Wright	Ian	
John Michaloudis	John	
Michael Jackson	Michael	

Just in case Flash Fill does not start automatically when you are expecting for it
to match your pattern, you can start it manually by clicking **Data > Flash Fill**.
Another alternative is to press **Ctrl+E**.

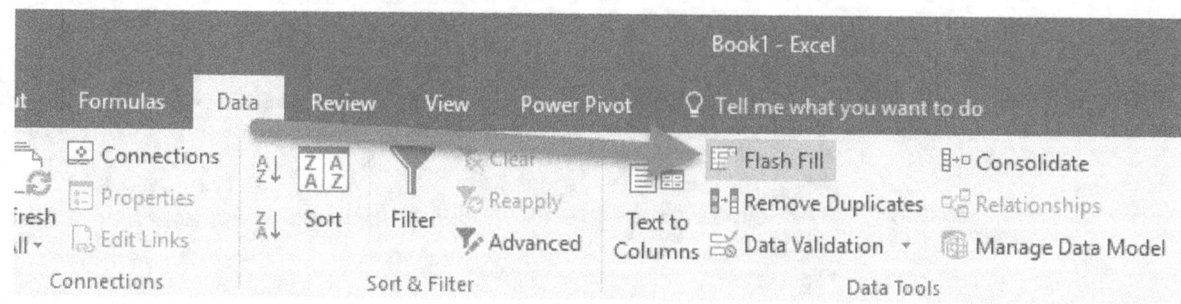

STEP 3: If the flash fill looks good, press **Enter.**

	First Name	Last Name
Homer Simpson	Homer	
Ian Wright	Ian	
John Michaloudis	John	
Michael Jackson	Michael	

STEP 4: Type *Simpson* as the first entry in the **Last Name**

	First Name	Last Name
Homer Simpson	Homer	Simpson
Ian Wright	Ian	
John Michaloudis	John	
Michael Jackson	Michael	

STEP 5: In the second entry, once you type the first letter **W** of *Wright,* Excel will auto-suggest to **Flash Fill** the rest of the Last Names.

	First Name	Last Name
Homer Simpson	Homer	Simpson
Ian Wright	Ian	Wright
John Michaloudis	John	Michaloudis
Michael Jackson	Michael	Jackson

STEP 6: If the flash fill looks good, press **Enter.** Your data is now complete without the use of a single formula!

	First Name	Last Name
Homer Simpson	Homer	Simpson
Ian Wright	Ian	Wright
John Michaloudis	John	Michaloudis
Michael Jackson	Michael	Jackson

Flash Fill: Add Hyphens To Serial Numbers

Flash Fill allows you to combine, extract, move & transform data that belongs in one column, into a new column.

One of the cool uses of **Flash Fill** is formatting numbers. In our example below, we are going to add hyphens within our serial numbers!

To demonstrate the power of Excel's Flash Fill, we will start off with this table of data we need to apply our formatting on:

Unformatted SSN	Formatted SSN
123456789	
478923744	
980412833	
491823821	
239842394	
123981293	

STEP 1: Type *123-45-6789* as the first entry in the **Formatted SSN** column.   We also want the rest of the SSNs to be formatted this way.

Unformatted SSN	Formatted SSN
123456789	123-45-6789
478923744	
980412833	
491823821	
239842394	
123981293	

STEP 2: In the second entry, once you type the first number **4** of **478923744,** Excel will auto-suggest to **Flash Fill** the rest of the **Formatted SSN** column.

Excel is smart enough to infer that you are trying to apply this formatting.

If the Flash Fill looks good, press **Enter.**

Unformatted SSN	Formatted SSN
123456789	123-45-6789
478923744	478-92-3744
980412833	980-41-2833
491823821	491-82-3821
239842394	239-84-2394
123981293	123-98-1293

IMPORTANT: If Flash Fill doesn't start automatically in your selected cell when you type in data that matches a pattern, you will need to **start Flash Fill manually**.

This is done by clicking on **Data > Flash Fill** or by pressing the Flash Fill keyboard shortcut **CTRL+E**

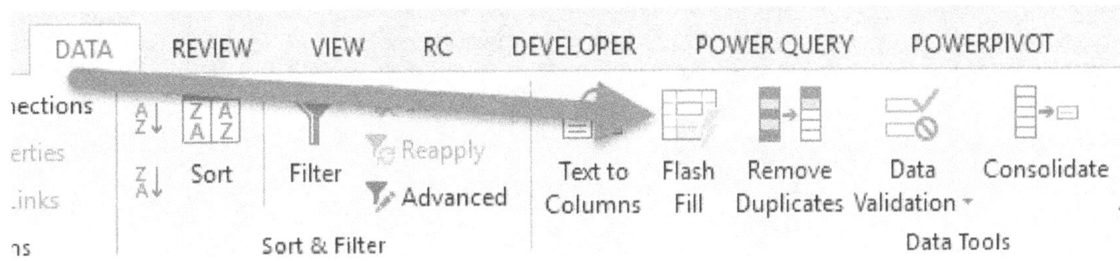

STEP 3: What is very impressive is Excel was able to apply the same formatting to the rest of the table **without the use of a single formula!**

Unformatted SSN	Formatted SSN
123456789	123-45-6789
478923744	478-92-3744
980412833	980-41-2833
491823821	491-82-3821
239842394	239-84-2394
123981293	123-98-1293

Flash Fill: Convert Values to Dates

Flash Fill allows you to combine, extract, move & transform data that belongs in one column, into a new column.

One of the cool uses of **Flash Fill** is to convert your values into Excel dates automatically.

To demonstrate the power of Excel's Flash Fill, we will start off with this table of data where we need to convert to dates:

Text Format	Date Format
20160423	
20151230	
20131211	
20161122	
20150530	
20140322	

STEP 1: Type **04-23-2016** as the first entry in the **Date Format column.**

Text Format	Date Format
20160423	04-23-2016
20151230	
20131211	
20161122	
20150530	
20140322	

STEP 2: We want the rest of the Text to be formatted this way, so in the second entry, type **12-30-2015.**

(It is recommended to even type in a 3rd entry when dealing with dates, as there are many permutations and regional time formats!)

Notice that Excel did not auto-suggest to Flash Fill. There are times that this happens.

Text Format	Date Format
20160423	04-23-2016
20151230	12-30-2015
20131211	
20161122	
20150530	
20140322	

Since Flash Fill did not start automatically when you are expecting for it to match your pattern, you can start it manually by highlighting the entire column you want it to fill.

Then click **Data > Flash Fill** or another alternative is to press **Ctrl+E** keyboard shortcut!

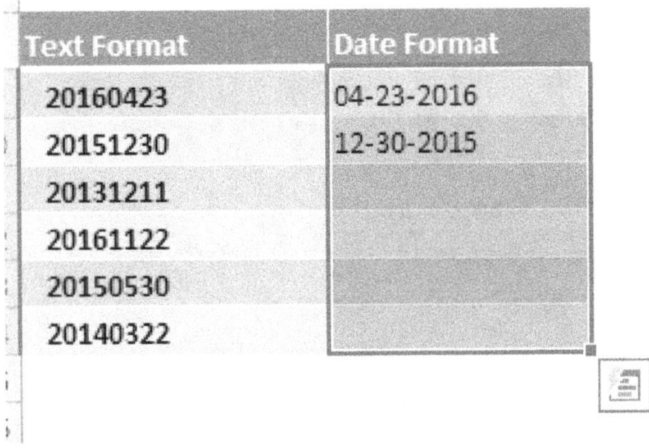

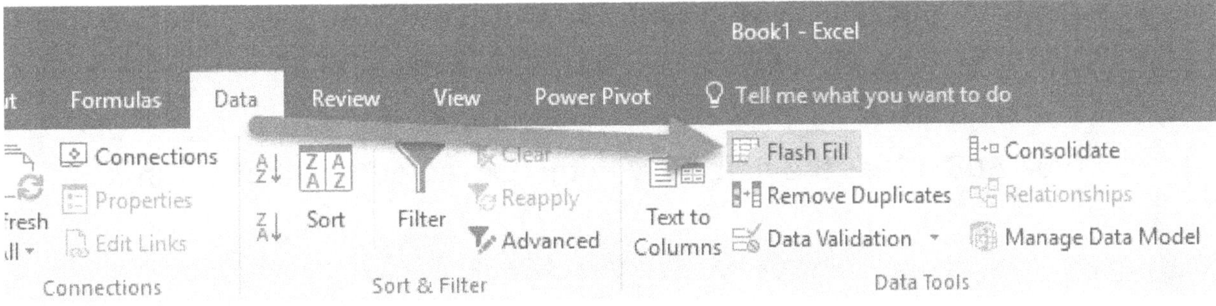

STEP 3: You now have your data auto-populated using **Flash Fill.**

What is very impressive is Excel was able to apply the same date format pattern to the rest of the table **without the use of a single formula!**

Text Format	Date Format
20160423	04-23-2016
20151230	12-30-2015
20131211	12-11-2013
20161122	11-22-2016
20150530	05-30-2015
20140322	03-22-2014

Flash Fill: Extract Numbers

One of the cool uses of **Flash Fill** is extracting the numbers from your text automatically.

To demonstrate the power of Excel's Flash Fill, we will start off with the following table of data:

Text	Extracted Number
This is 803.45 only	
47512 is my number	
Pay me 9924.34	
What is 98212	
90432	
Just 123 Number	

Our mission is to **extract the numbers** from within the text cells. We can use a VBA macro or complex formulas (which will take time to figure out and implement) or simply use Flash Fill...

STEP 1: Type **803.45** as the first entry in the **Extracted Number column:**

Text	Extracted Number
This is 803.45 only	803.45
47512 is my number	
Pay me 9924.34	
What is 98212	
90432	
Just 123 Number	

STEP 2: In the second entry, once you type the first number **4** of **47512,** Excel will auto-suggest to **Flash Fill** the rest of the numbers.

Excel is smart enough to infer that you are trying to extract the numbers in the text.

If the Flash Fill looks good, press **Enter.**

Text	Extracted Number
This is 803.45 only	803.45
47512 is my number	47512
Pay me 9924.34	9924.34
What is 98212	98212
90432	90432
Just 123 Number	123

IMPORTANT: If Flash Fill doesn't start automatically in your selected cell when you type in data that matches a pattern, you will need to **start Flash Fill manually**.

This is done by clicking on **Data > Flash Fill** or by pressing the Flash Fill keyboard shortcut **CTRL+E**

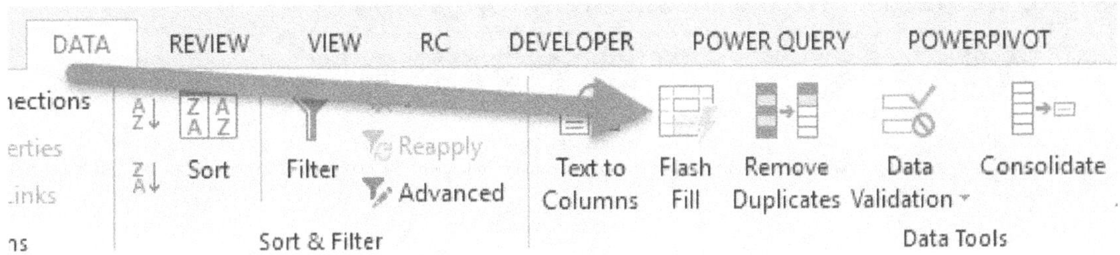

What is very impressive is regardless of the location of the number -**Beginning, middle or the end**, Excel was able to extract this number **without the use of a single formula or VBA!**

Text	Extracted Number
This is 803.45 only	803.45
47512 is my number	47512
Pay me 9924.34	9924.34
What is 98212	98212
90432	90432
Just 123 Number	123

Flash Fill: Fix Incorrect Formatting

Ever had the scenario where your data is formatted differently?

Example: First names starting with lower case, last names all in upper case, middle initials in either cases...This drives me nuts!

Luckily, we have **Flash Fill** which can automatically convert the entire data set into one consistent format.

To demonstrate the power of Excel's Flash Fill, we will start off with this table of data where we need to fix the inconsistent formatting:

First Name	Middle Initial	Last Name	Full Name
Homer	a	Simpson	
iAn	B	wright	
JOHN		MICHALOUDIS	
michael	D	JACKSON	

STEP 1: Type **_Homer A Simpson_** as the first entry in the **Full Name column.**

First Name	Middle Initial	Last Name	Full Name
Homer	a	Simpson	Homer A Simpson
iAn	B	wright	
JOHN		MICHALOUDIS	
michael	D	JACKSON	

STEP 2: We want the rest of the Text to be formatted this way, so in the second entry, type **_Ian B Wright._**

Notice that Excel did not auto-suggest to Flash Fill. There are times that this happens.

First Name	Middle Initial	Last Name	Full Name
Homer	a	Simpson	Homer A Simpson
iAn	B	wright	Ian B Wright
JOHN		MICHALOUDIS	
michael	D	JACKSON	

Since Flash Fill did not start automatically when you are expecting for it to match your pattern, you can start it manually by highlighting the entire column you want it to fill.

Then click **Data > Flash Fill** (Another alternative is to press the **Ctrl+E** keyboard shortcut).

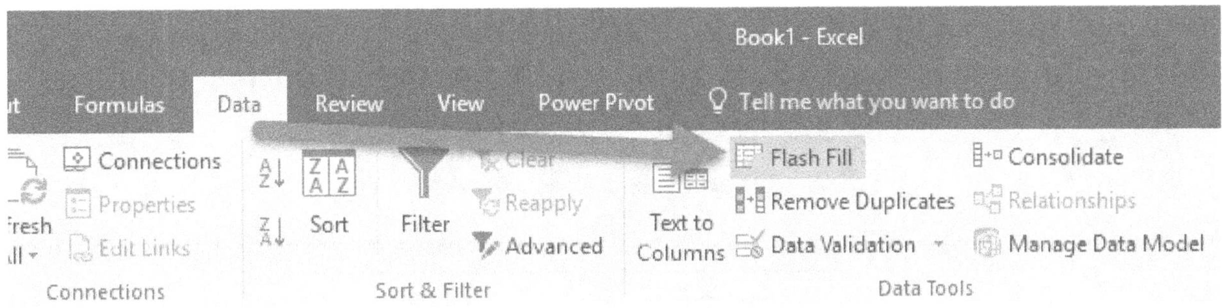

STEP 3: You now have your data auto populated using **Flash Fill.**

What is very impressive is Excel was able to apply the same format pattern to the rest of the table **without the use of a single formula!**

Adios inconsistent formatting :)

First Name	Middle Initial	Last Name	Full Name
Homer	a	Simpson	Homer A Simpson
iAn	B	wright	Ian B Wright
JOHN		MICHALOUDIS	John Michaloudis
michael	D	JACKSON	Michael D Jackson

Goal Seek To Find Formula Result

If you have a formula and want to show a specific result, but you do not know what input values to change within the formula, then Excel's Goal Seek feature is the one for you.

Imagine you are calculating the payment terms on a loan.

Your PMT formula gives you an amount of $1,450 but you can only afford to repay $1,000. You can use Goal Seek to find out what **Principal** you can borrow based on your $1,000 budget.

STEP 1: Enter your 3 input variables that you will need to use for your PMT formula - **Interest Rate of 3.50%, Term of 240 months & Principal of $250,000**

	A	B	C
4			
5		RATE	3.50%
6		TERM	240
7		PRINCIPAL	250,000
8		PAYMENT	-1,450

STEP 2: Enter the PMT function in cell C8 =**PMT(Interest Rate/12, Term, Principal)** which will give you a monthly payment amount of -$1,450

	B	C
5	RATE	3.50%
6	TERM	240
7	PRINCIPAL	250,000
8	PAYMENT	=PMT(C5/12,C6,C7)

STEP 3: Select the cell C8 and go to **Data > What If Analysis > Goal Seek**

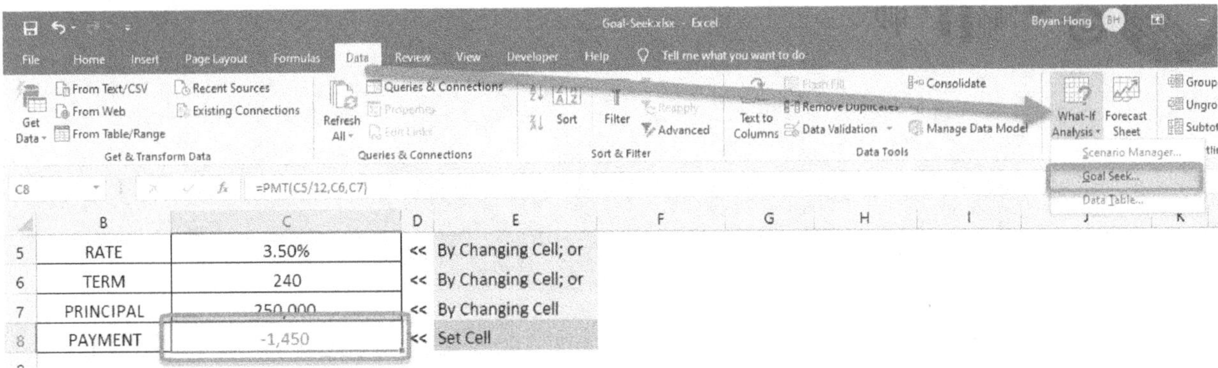

STEP 4: SET CELL: Enter the reference for the cell that contains the formula that you want to resolve. In our example, this reference is cell C8

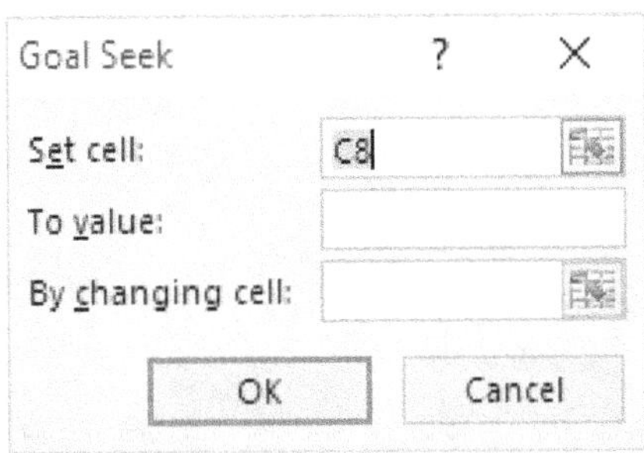

STEP 5: TO VALUE: Type the formula result that you want. In our example, we want the payment to be -$1,000 (Note that this number is negative because it represents a payment)

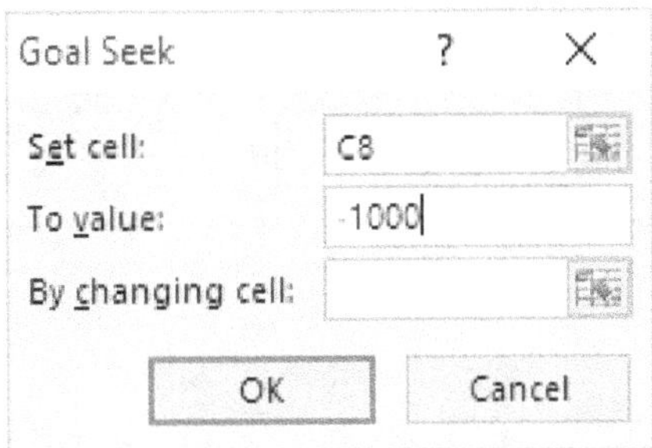

STEP 6: BY CHANGING CELL: Enter the reference for the cell that contains the input value that you want to adjust e.g. One of our 3 variables (Interest Rate, Principal & Term). In our example, this reference is cell C7 for the Principal

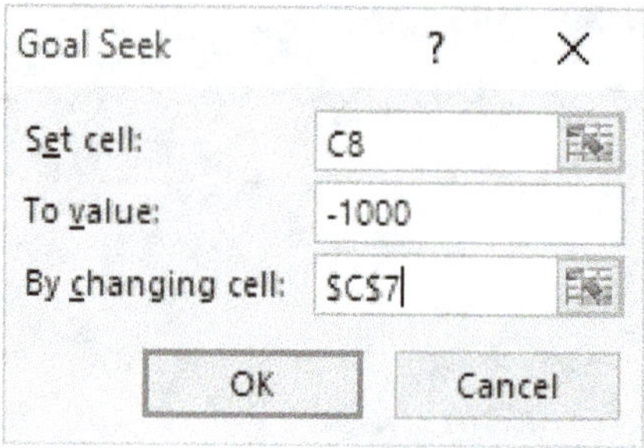

STEP 7: Press OK and Goal Seek will run and produce a result. **Press OK to keep the results or Cancel to discard**

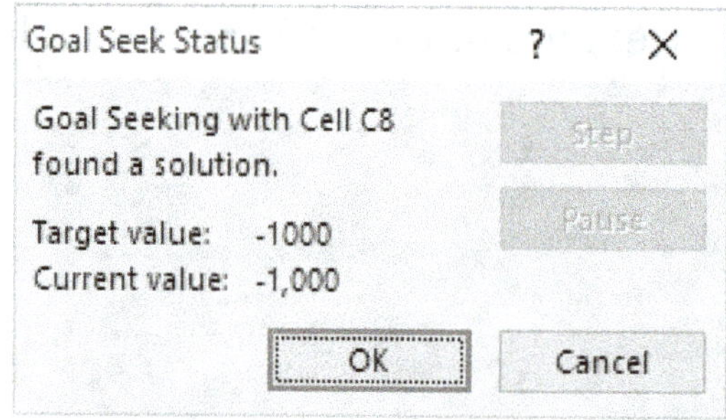

	A	B	C
4			
5		RATE	3.50%
6		TERM	240
7		PRINCIPAL	172,426
8		PAYMENT	-1,000

Goal Seek To Meet Your Profit Goal

Say you have a quarterly Profit Statement and your Sales for Q1 and Q2 have been reasonably well but in Q3 they dropped dramatically. You are left with one quarter to meet your Net Profit goal of $200,000.

You can use Excel's Goal Seek feature (under What If Analysis) to find out what Sales you need to achieve in Q4 in order to meet your Net Profit goal of $200,000.

STEP 1: Select the cell that you want to achieve your goal of $200,000 which is the Total Net Profit in cell **F7,** which is a Sum formula **(Important: This cell must be a formula for the Goal Seek to work)**

	A	B	C	D	E	F
4		Q1	Q2	Q3	Q4	TOTAL
5	REVENUE	256,000	325,600	241,000		822,600
6	PROFIT MARGIN	12%	14%	15%	20%	
7	NET PROFIT	30,720	45,584	36,150	0	112,454
8						

STEP 2: Go to *Data > What If Analysis > Goal Seek*

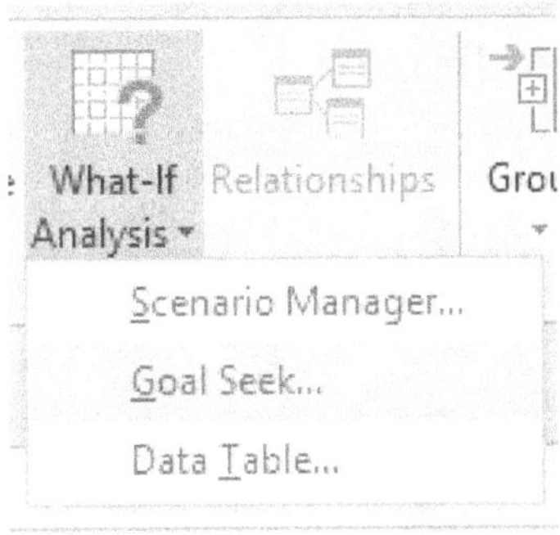

STEP 3: **SET CELL:** This is the cell that contains the goal we want to achieve - **F7**

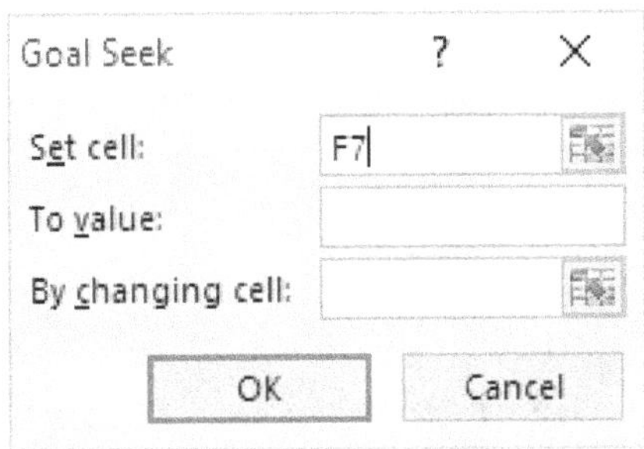

STEP 4: **TO VALUE**: Type the goal value that you want to achieve. In our example, it will be **200,000**

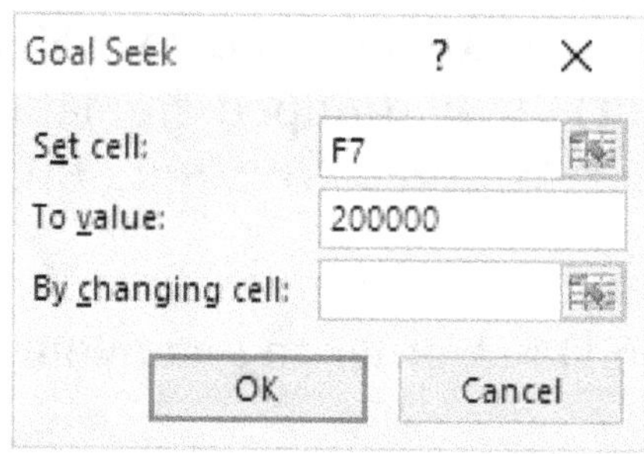

STEP 5: **BY CHANGING CELL:** Enter the reference for the cell that contains the input value that you want to adjust. In our example it is the **Q4 Sales forecast in cell E5**

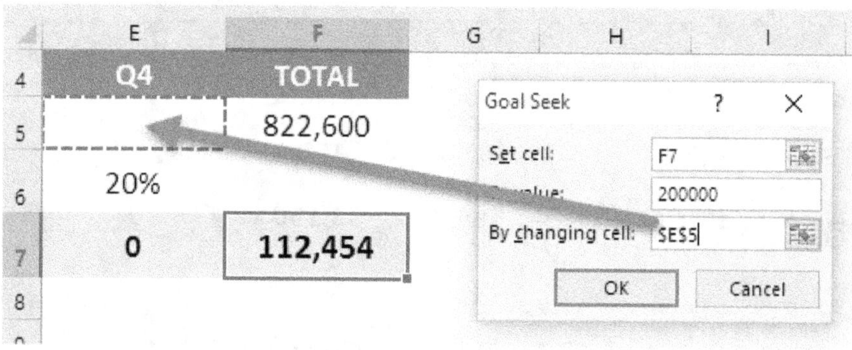

STEP 6: **Press OK** and Goal Seek will run and produce a result. **Press OK to keep the results or Cancel to discard**

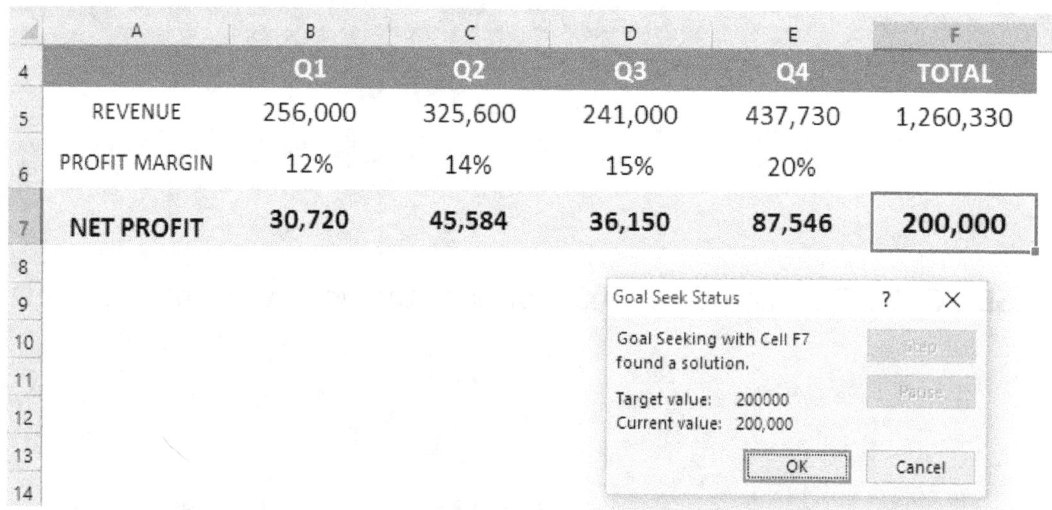

With Goal Seek we need to achieve Q4 Sales of $437,730 in order to achieve our Net Profit goal of $200,000. Over to the Sales team then to make it happen!

Group Worksheets in Excel

Ever had a time when you needed to modify data across multiple worksheets? It is very easy to do this using the Group Worksheets feature in Excel!

Let us say we have this same mistake on multiple worksheets - see the **Dvv** typo in the screenshot below. We want to change this to **Dec**

MONTH	SALES
Jan	47320
Feb	48821
Mar	26257
Apr	34413
May	41662
Jun	23960
Jul	24175
Aug	17553
Sep	33918
Oct	27356
Nov	41469
Dvv	19600

Main | 2016 | 2017 | 2018

The same spelling mistake is also done for the other 2 worksheets (2017 & 2018):

STEP 1: Hold the **CTRL** button and select the worksheets with the left mouse button that need editing.

For our example, we need to select the 2016, 2017, and 2018 worksheets while holding the **CTRL** button (this will turn each selected sheet to a white color).

STEP 2: Edit the cell in any one of the worksheets. Let us change the *Dvv* to *Dec and press ENTER.*

This will change all of the worksheet values to reflect the same change.

MONTH	SALES
Jan	47320
Feb	48821
Mar	26257
Apr	34413
May	41662
Jun	23960
Jul	24175
Aug	17553
Sep	33918
Oct	27356
Nov	41469
Dec	19600

Main | 2016 | 2017 | 2018

MONTH	SALES
Jan	23278
Feb	46850
Mar	22499
Apr	49238
May	10696
Jun	40847
Jul	20903
Aug	17226
Sep	46724
Oct	20530
Nov	14982
Dec	18024

Main | 2016 | 2017 | 2018

MONTH	SALES
Jan	34384
Feb	38874
Mar	31122
Apr	47248
May	31205
Jun	47913
Jul	39525
Aug	36015
Sep	39360
Oct	18480
Nov	42508
Dec	12808

Main | 2016 | 2017 | 2018

STEP 3: To ungroup the worksheets, **right click** on the worksheet tabs and select **Ungroup Sheets** (super important to do this when you finish making your changes).

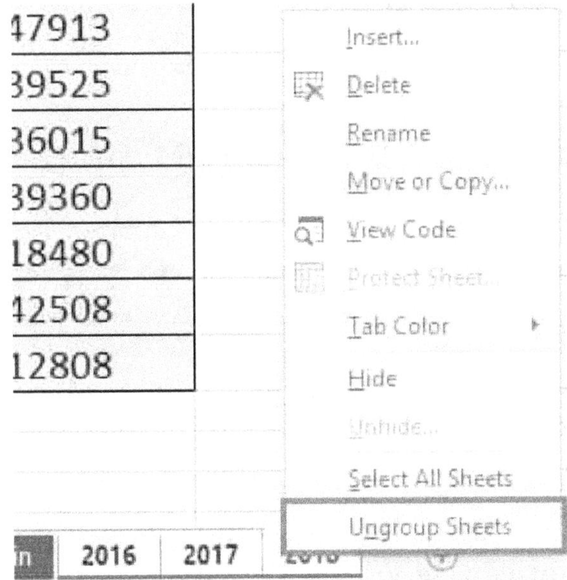

How To Create A Custom List In Excel

A **Custom List** in Excel is very handy to fill a range of cells with your own personal list. It could be a list of your team members at work, countries, regions, phone numbers or customers.

The main goal of a custom list is to remove **repetitive work and manual errors** in inputting.

To demonstrate the power of Excel's Custom Lists, we'll explore what's currently in Excel's memory as a default list:

STEP 1: Type *February* in the first cell

STEP 2: From that first cell, **click the lower right corner and drag** it to the next 5 cells to the right

STEP 3: Release and you will see it get auto-populated up to July (The succeeding months after February)

February		March	April		May	June	July

At first, it might seem like magic on how Excel does this!

Let us go straight into the Options in Excel to view how it's being done, and how you can **create your own Custom List:**

STEP 4: Select the **File** tab

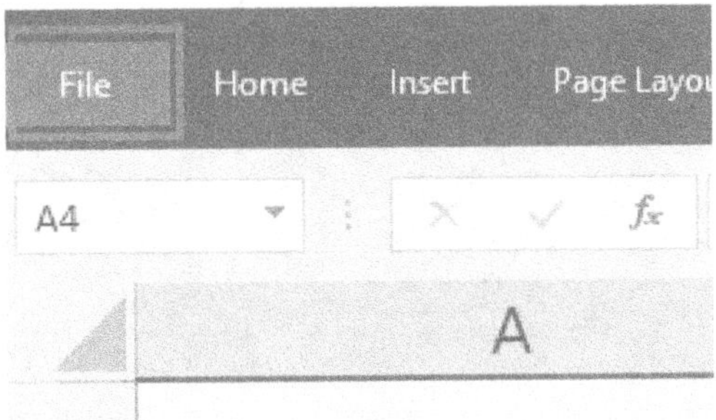

STEP 5: Click **Options**

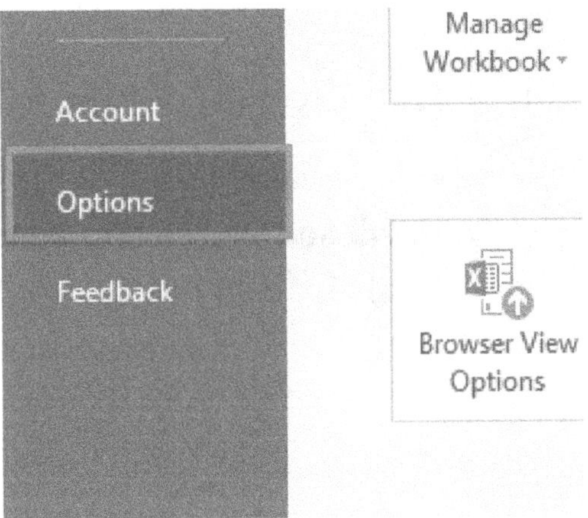

STEP 6: Select the **Advanced** option

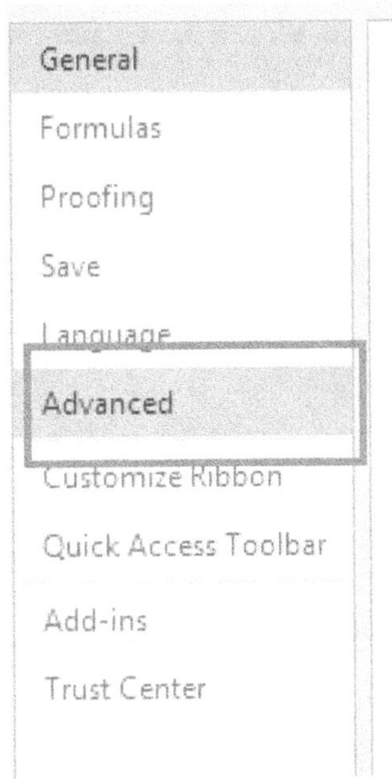

 Scroll all the way down and under the **General** section, click **Edit Custom Lists**

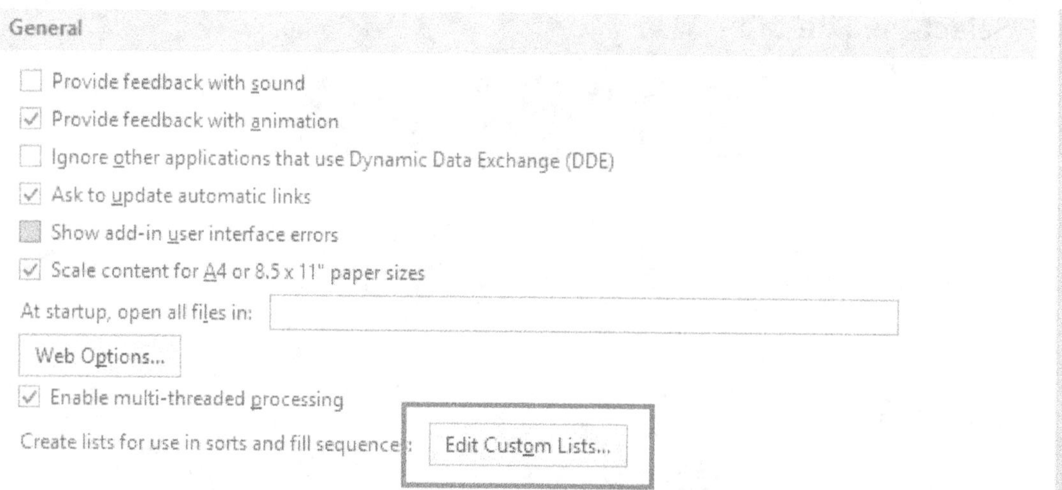

Here you can see the built-in default Excel lists of the calendar months, and the days.

If you click on a Custom List, you will see under **List entries** that it is greyed out and you cannot make any changes. This indicates that it is a default Excel Custom List.

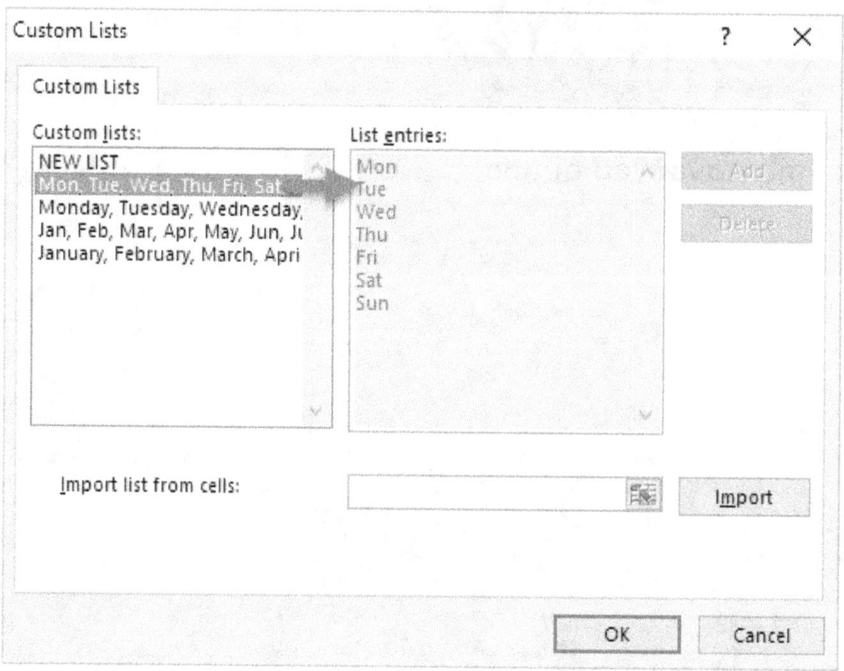

STEP 8: You can **create & add your own Custom List** under the *List entries* section. **Click on NEW LIST** under the Custom Lists area and then **manually enter your list**, entering one entry per line:

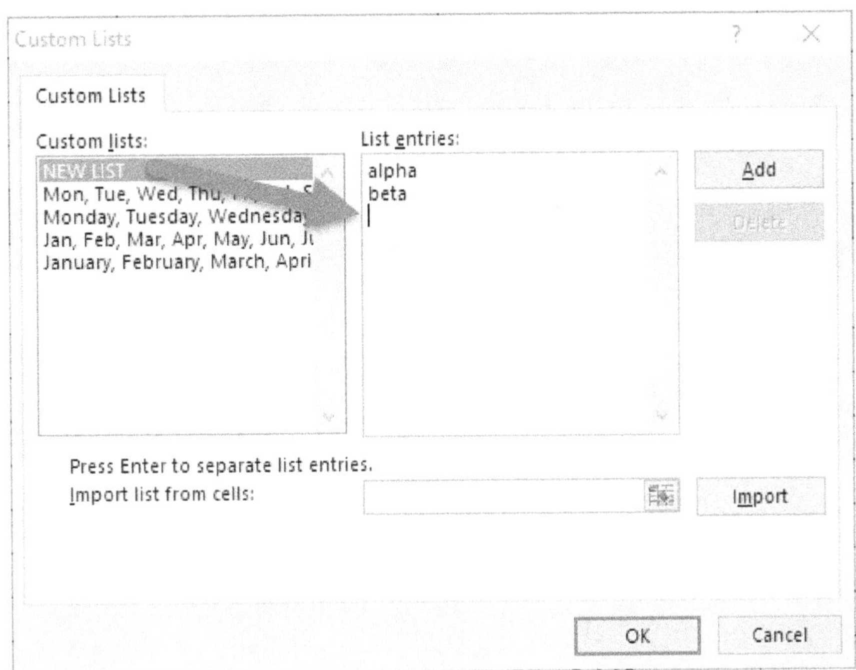

After typing the values, click **Add**.

In our screenshot below, we added the values of the Greek alphabet (alpha, beta, gamma, and so on)

Click **OK** once done.

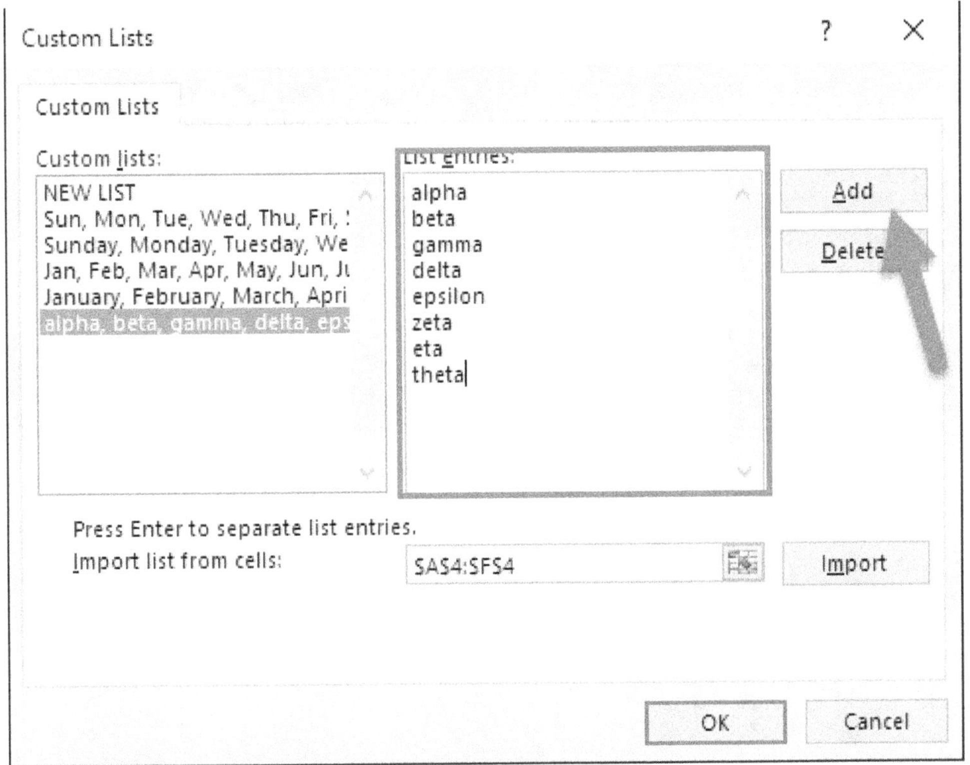

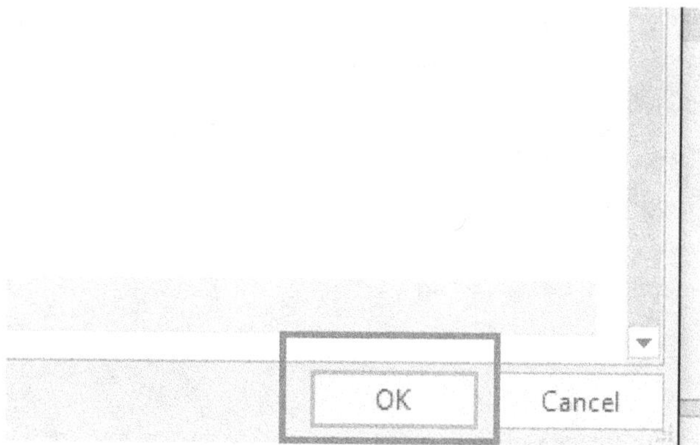

STEP 10: Now let's go back into our Excel workbook to see our new Custom List in action. Type *alpha* on a cell

STEP 11: From that cell, **click the lower right corner and drag it** to the next 5 cells to the right

STEP 12: Release and you will see it get auto-populated to zeta, which is based on our **Custom List created in Step 8**

alpha	beta	gamma	delta	epsilon	zeta

Hyperlinks: Buttons

Excel's hyperlink capability is amazing but many people don't use it as they don't know its full capabilities.

With a hyperlink you can link an object/text to open an existing file on your desktop, go to a website, open up an email to a specific contact or go to a cell within your workbook.

I will show you in the example below how you can create a hyperlink in a shape and then click on the shape to go to a specific section within your workbook without the need to scroll.

To have a better idea, this is how our workbook is setup, we have 3 main sections that we want the buttons to navigate to:

Sales

SALES	NA	EU	APAC	TOTAL
TOTAL	441,177	387,358	347,564	1,176,099
1401	45,761	26,028	30,033	101,822
1402	34,477	13,411	42,902	90,790
1403	49,019	44,454	20,627	114,100
Q1	129,257	83,893	93,562	306,712
1404	41,554	16,481	40,105	98,140
1405	22,795	21,894	41,604	86,293
1406	40,596	49,937	20,186	110,719
Q2	104,945	88,312	101,895	295,152
1407	42,395	41,726	23,948	108,069
1408	22,246	19,246	33,600	75,092

Costs

COSTS	NA	EU	APAC	TOTAL
TOTAL	235,780	192,379	198,846	**627,005**
1401	36,609	20,822	24,026	81,458
1402	24,823	9,656	30,889	65,369
1403	3,922	3,556	1,650	9,128
Q1	65,354	34,035	56,566	155,954
1404	33,243	13,185	32,084	78,512
1405	16,412	15,764	29,955	62,131
1406	3,248	3,995	1,615	8,858
Q2	52,903	32,943	63,654	149,500
1407	33,916	33,381	19,158	86,455
1408	1,602	1,386	2,419	5,407
1409	[illegible]	[illegible]	[illegible]	55,806

Profit

PROFIT	NA	EU	APAC	TOTAL
TOTAL	205,397	194,979	148,718	**549,094**
1401	9,152	5,206	6,007	20,364
1402	9,654	3,755	12,013	25,421
1403	45,097	40,899	18,977	104,972
Q1	63,903	49,858	36,996	150,758
1404	8,311	3,296	8,021	19,628
1405	6,383	6,130	11,649	24,162
1406	37,348	45,942	18,571	101,861
Q2	52,042	55,369	38,241	145,652
1407	8,479	8,345	4,790	21,614
1408	[illegible]	[illegible]	[illegible]	[illegible]

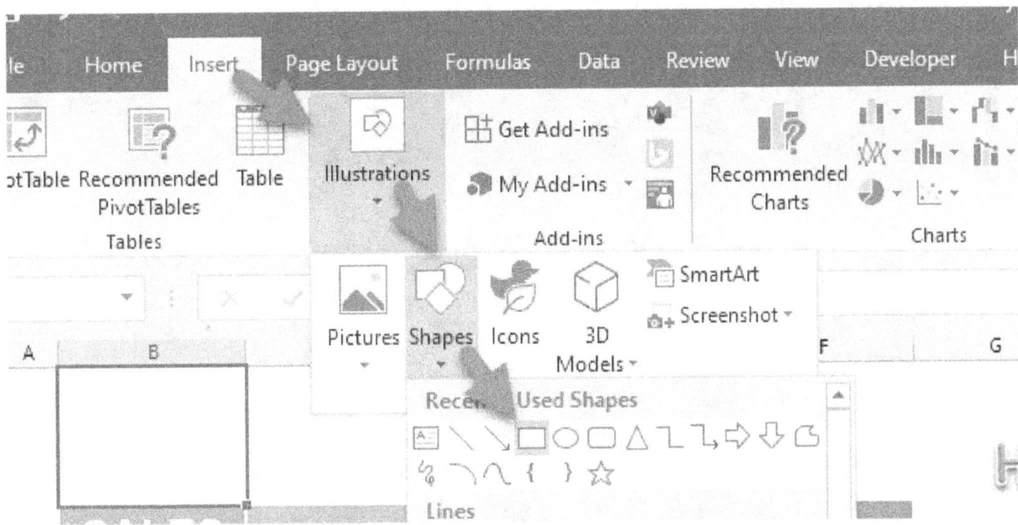

STEP 2:   Create a rectangle and type **SALES**. Update the formatting to make the text look bigger and centered.

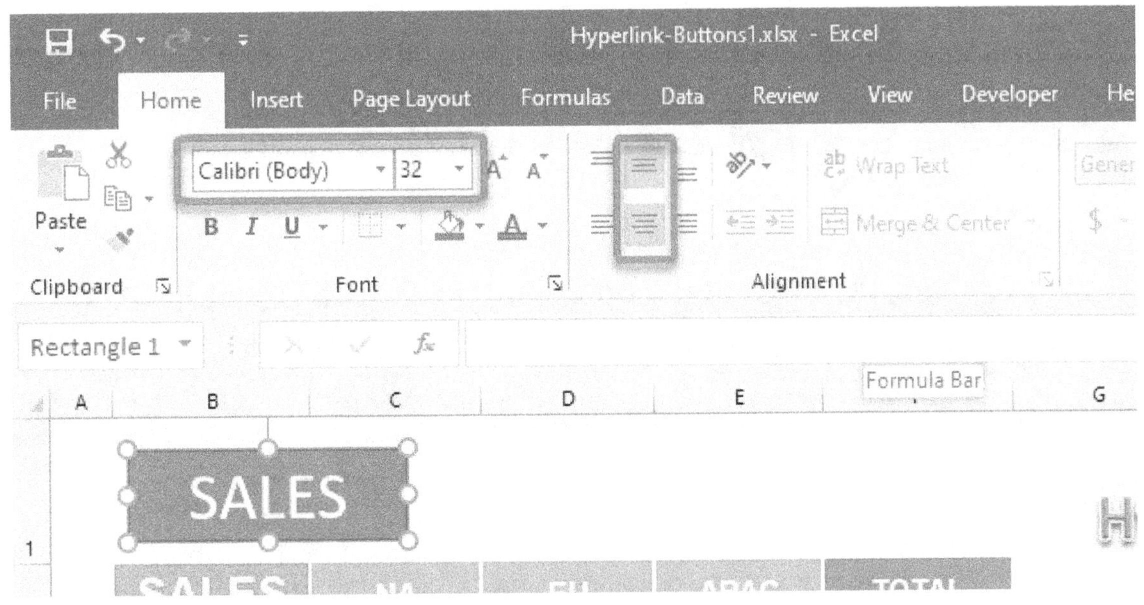

STEP 3:   While holding **CTRL + SHIFT,** drag your first button using left-click to instantly duplicate it. Do it twice.

 Go to *Format > Shape Style* and pick the formatting you want. Do it for all buttons to differentiate them from one another.

Make sure to change the text of the other buttons to **COSTS** and **PROFIT**.

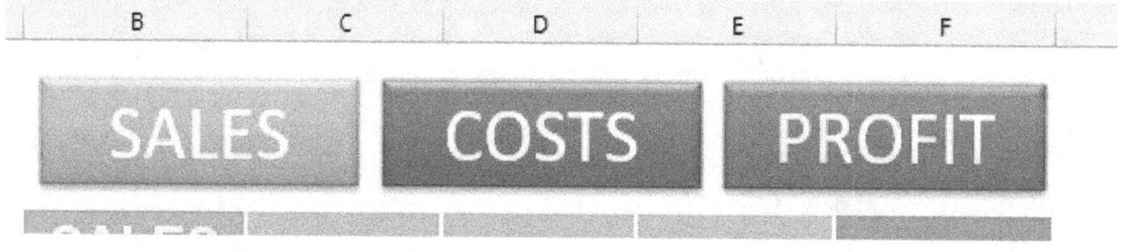

   We will now create the cell that our button will navigate to.

Select the blank cells beside the SALES table. Then select *Home > Merge & Center*

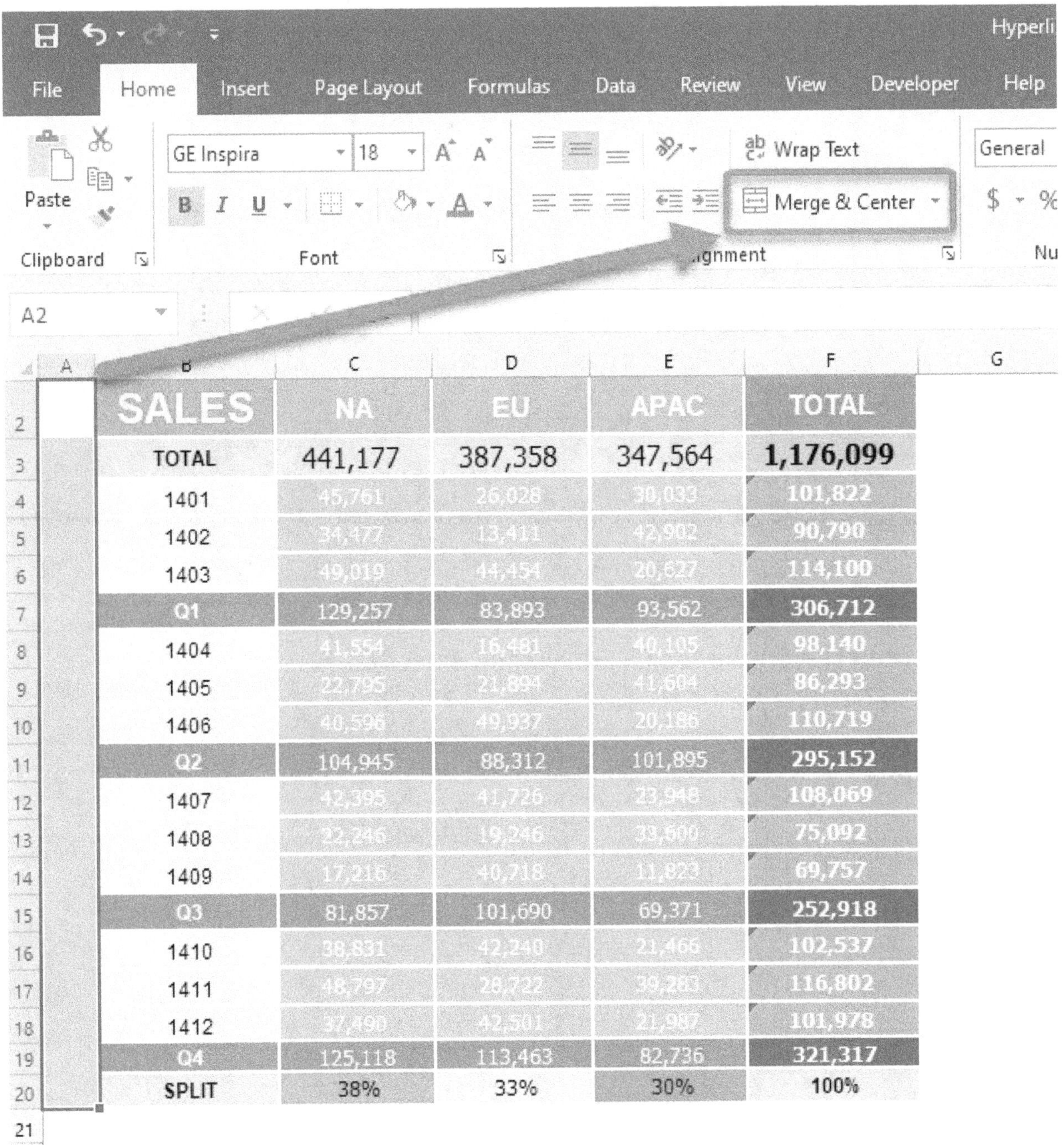

	SALES	NA	EU	APAC	TOTAL	
	TOTAL	441,177	387,358	347,564	1,176,099	
	1401	45,761	26,028	30,033	101,822	
	1402	34,477	13,411	42,902	90,790	
	1403	49,019	44,454	20,627	114,100	
	Q1	129,257	83,893	93,562	306,712	
	1404	41,554	16,481	40,105	98,140	
	1405	22,795	21,894	41,604	86,293	
	1406	40,596	49,937	20,186	110,719	
	Q2	104,945	88,312	101,895	295,152	
	1407	42,395	41,726	23,948	108,069	
	1408	22,246	19,246	33,600	75,092	
	1409	17,216	40,718	11,823	69,757	
	Q3	81,857	101,690	69,371	252,918	
	1410	38,831	42,240	21,466	102,537	
	1411	48,797	28,722	39,283	116,802	
	1412	37,490	42,501	21,987	101,978	
	Q4	125,118	113,463	82,736	321,317	
	SPLIT	38%	33%	30%	100%	

STEP 6:   Copy the cell reference. For SALES this is cell A2.

SALES	NA	EU	APAC	TOTAL
TOTAL	441,177	387,358	347,564	1,176,099
1401	45,761	26,028	30,033	101,822
1402	34,477	13,411	42,902	90,790
1403	49,019	44,454	20,627	114,100
Q1	129,257	83,893	93,562	306,712
1404	41,554	16,481	40,105	98,140
1405	22,795	21,894	41,604	86,293
1406	40,596	49,937	20,186	110,719
Q2	104,945	88,312	101,895	295,152
1407	42,395	41,726	23,948	108,069
1408	22,246	19,246	33,600	75,092
1409	17,216	40,718	11,823	69,757
Q3	81,857	101,690	69,371	252,918
1410	38,831	42,240	21,466	102,537
1411	48,797	28,722	39,283	116,802
1412	37,490	42,501	21,987	101,978
Q4	125,118	113,463	82,736	321,317
SPLIT	38%	33%	30%	100%

STEP 7:   Right click on the SALES Button and select **Link.**

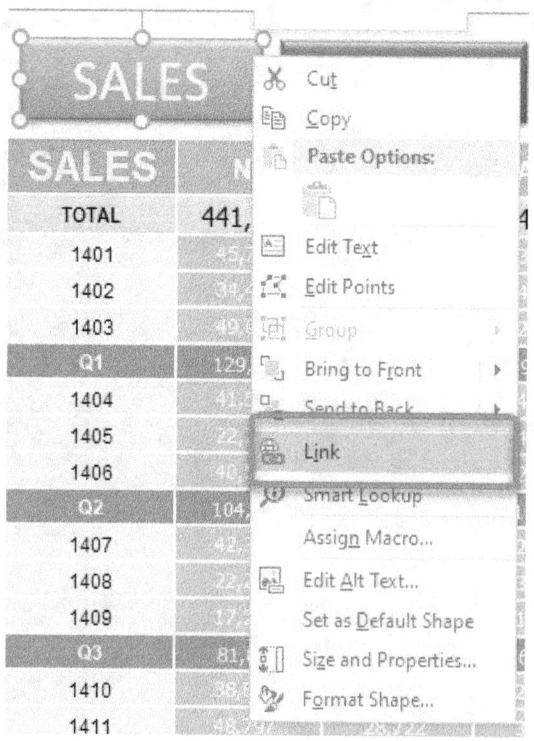

STEP 8:   Make sure **Place in This Document** is selected then place the cell reference **A2.** Press OK.

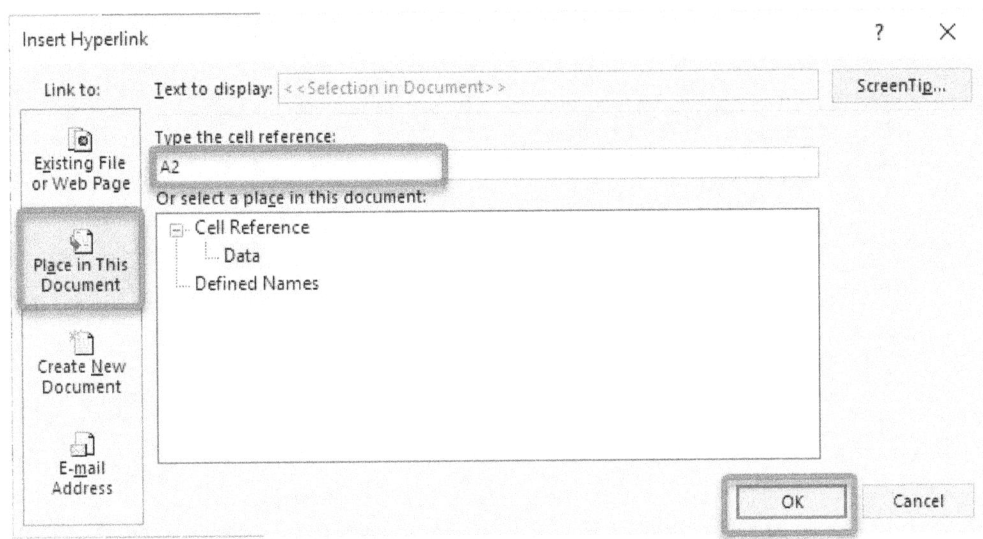

STEP 9:   Do the same for COSTS. Select the blank cells beside the COSTS table. Then select *Home > Merge & Center*. Copy the cell reference. For COSTS this is cell A26.

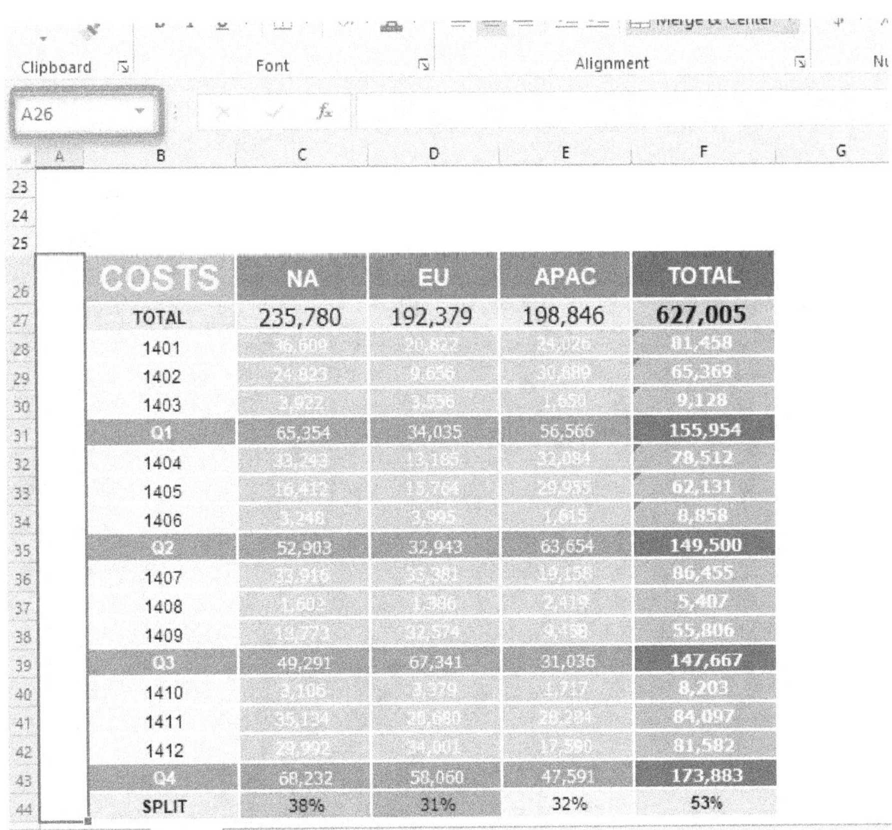

COSTS	NA	EU	APAC	TOTAL
TOTAL	235,780	192,379	198,846	627,005
1401	36,609	20,822	24,026	81,458
1402	24,823	9,656	30,889	65,369
1403	3,922	3,556	1,650	9,128
Q1	65,354	34,035	56,566	155,954
1404	33,243	13,185	32,084	78,512
1405	16,412	15,764	29,955	62,131
1406	3,248	3,995	1,615	8,858
Q2	52,903	32,943	63,654	149,500
1407	33,916	35,381	19,158	86,455
1408	1,602	1,386	2,419	5,407
1409	13,773	32,574	9,458	55,806
Q3	49,291	67,341	31,036	147,667
1410	3,106	3,379	1,717	8,203
1411	35,134	20,680	28,284	84,097
1412	29,992	34,001	17,590	81,582
Q4	68,232	58,060	47,591	173,883
SPLIT	38%	31%	32%	53%

STEP 10: Right click on the COSTS Button and select **Link.** Make sure **Place in This Document** is selected then place the cell reference **A26.** Press OK.

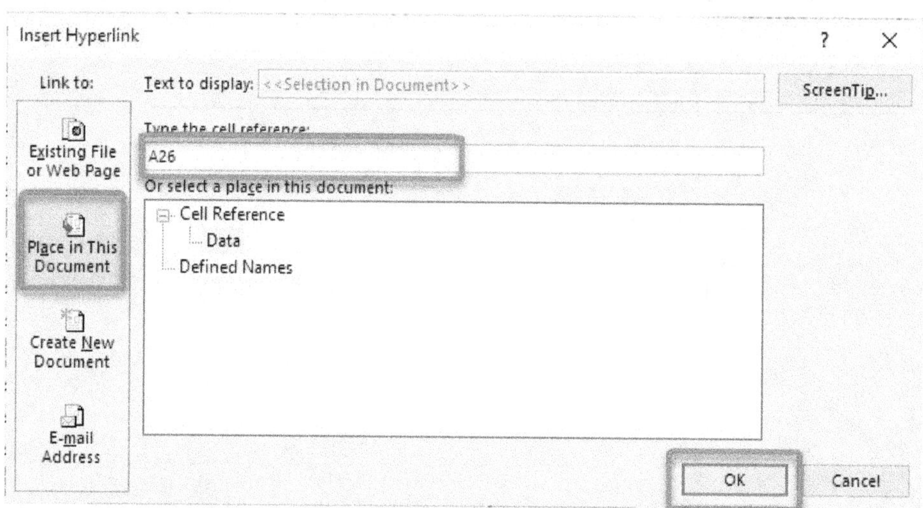

STEP 11: Select the blank cells beside the PROFIT table. Then select *Home > Merge & Center*. Copy the cell reference. For PROFIT this is cell A48.

PROFIT	NA	EU	APAC	TOTAL
TOTAL	205,397	194,979	148,718	549,094
1401	9,152	5,206	6,007	20,364
1402	9,654	3,755	12,013	25,421
1403	45,097	40,896	18,977	104,972
Q1	63,903	49,858	36,996	150,758
1404	8,311	3,296	8,021	19,628
1405	6,383	6,130	11,649	24,162
1406	37,348	45,942	18,571	101,861
Q2	52,042	55,369	38,241	145,652
1407	8,479	8,345	4,790	21,614
1408	20,644	17,860	31,181	69,685
1409	3,443	8,144	2,365	13,951
Q3	32,566	34,349	38,335	105,251
1410	35,725	38,861	19,749	94,334
1411	13,663	8,042	10,999	32,705
1412	7,498	8,500	4,397	20,396
Q4	56,886	55,403	35,145	147,434
SPLIT	37%	36%	27%	47%

STEP 12: Right click on the PROFIT Button and select **Link.**

Make sure **Place in This Document** is selected then place the cell reference **A48.** Press OK.

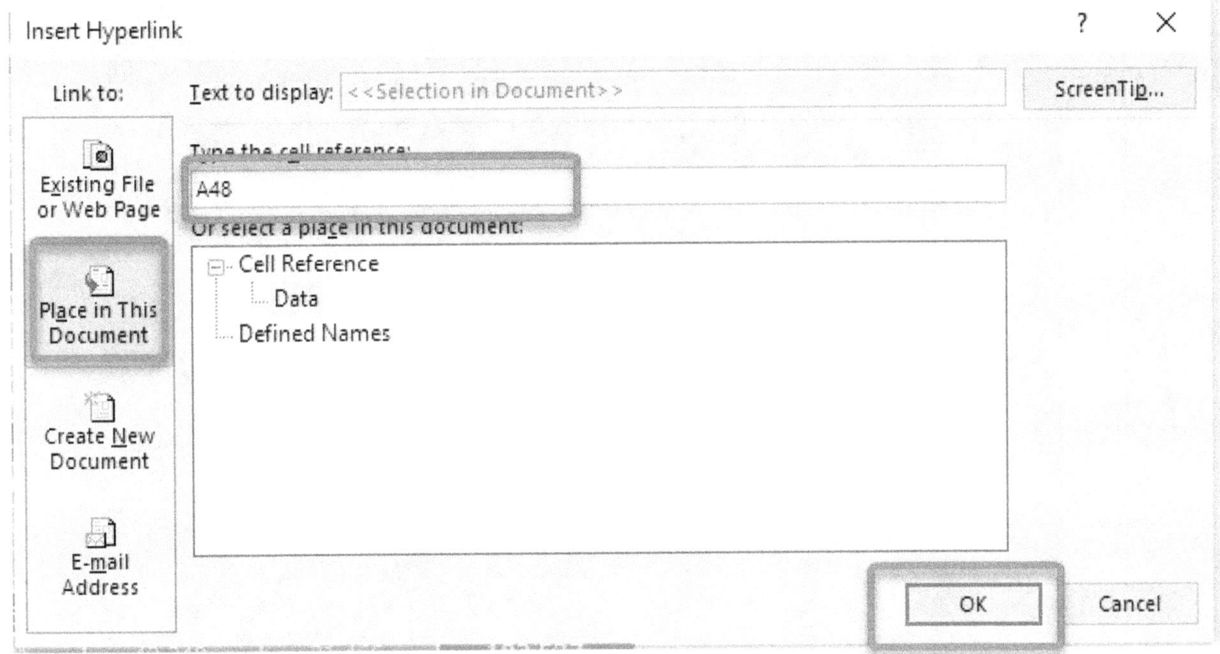

STEP 13:   Let's freeze in place the top row that contains our buttons.

Go to **_View > Freeze Panes > Freeze Top Row_**

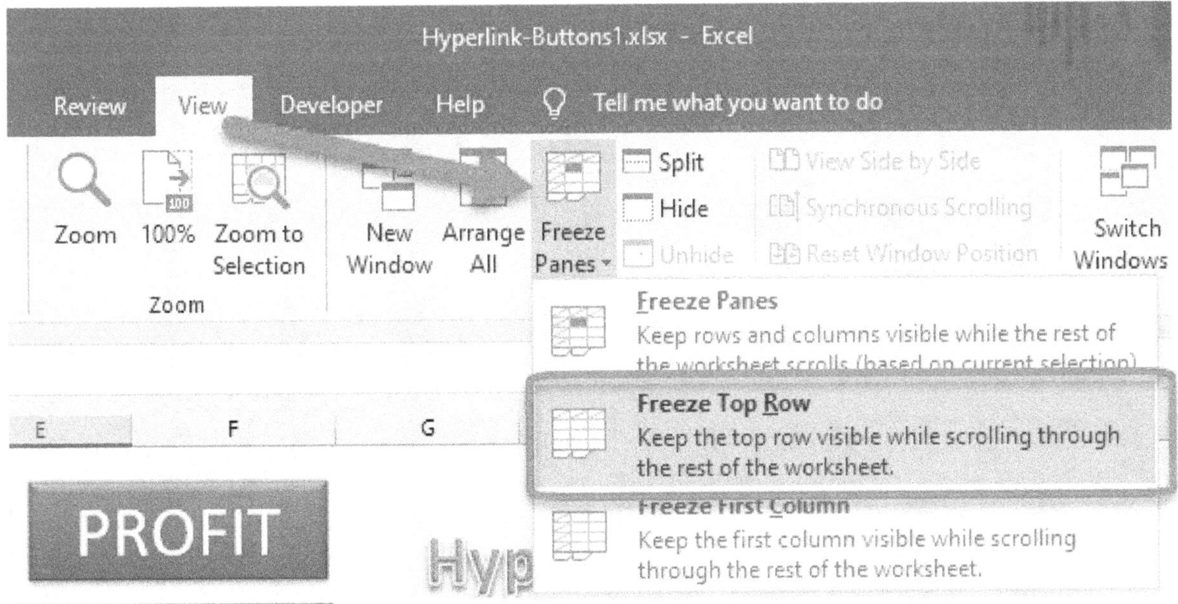

Now try clicking on the buttons and you will be impressed with the instant navigation!

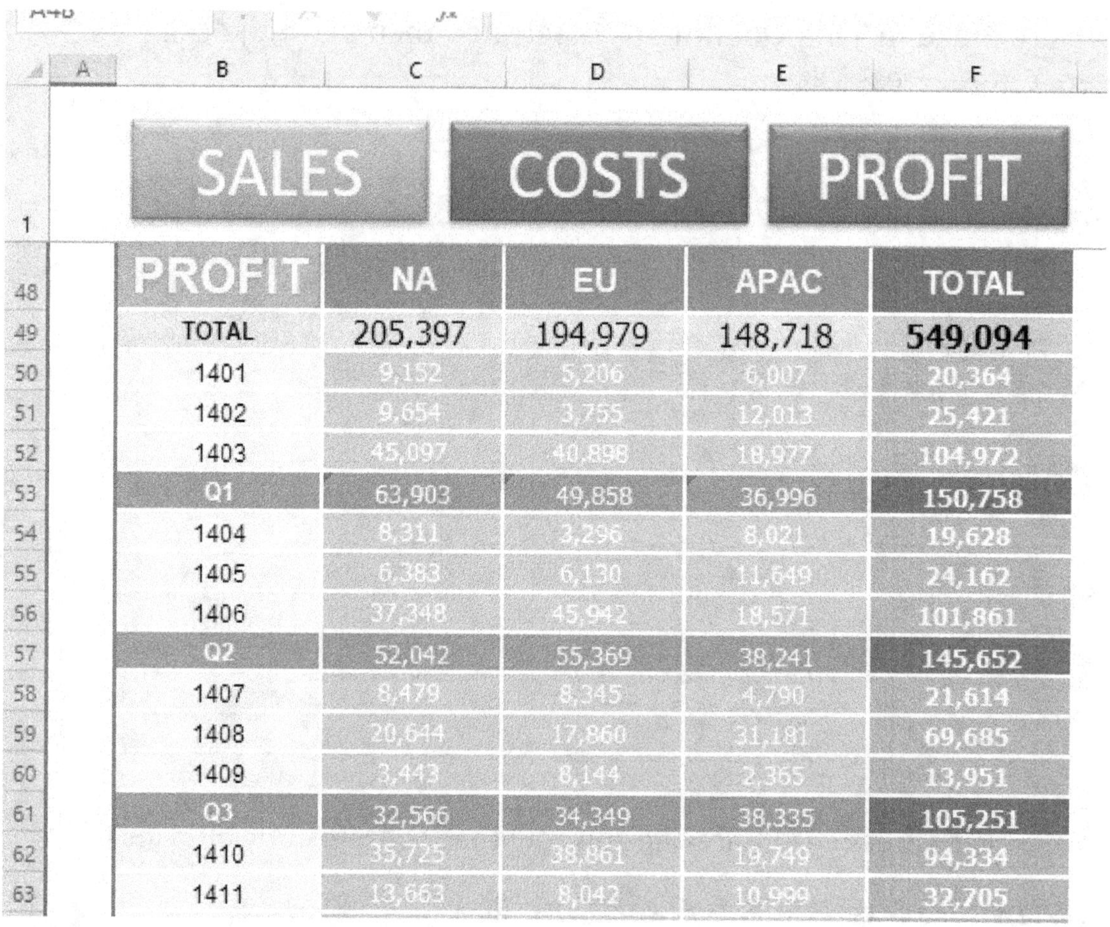

PROFIT	NA	EU	APAC	TOTAL
TOTAL	205,397	194,979	148,718	**549,094**
1401	9,152	5,206	6,007	20,364
1402	9,654	3,755	12,013	25,421
1403	45,097	40,898	18,977	104,972
Q1	63,903	49,858	36,996	150,758
1404	8,311	3,296	8,021	19,628
1405	6,383	6,130	11,649	24,162
1406	37,348	45,942	18,571	101,861
Q2	52,042	55,369	38,241	145,652
1407	8,479	8,345	4,790	21,614
1408	20,644	17,860	31,181	69,685
1409	3,443	8,144	2,365	13,951
Q3	32,566	34,349	38,335	105,251
1410	35,725	38,861	19,749	94,334
1411	13,663	8,042	10,999	32,705

Hyperlinks: Fix Links to a Named Range

Hyperlinks in Excel must be one of the funkiest features that I love playing around with!

They allow you to create interactive buttons within Excel (without the need to create a Macro) and you can make them take you to any cell or range within your Excel worksheet.

One shortfall is that when you set a Hyperlink to go to a cell reference, it will always reference the said cell, regardless of any additions/deletions to your rows/columns.

For example, if you tell it to go to C10, it will always go to C10. Add a new column in Column B, the hyperlink will still end up at C10.

Sometimes this is not the outcome we want to achieve.

I will show you a trick where you can fix the referenced cell/range using a Named Range, so that it does not move as the worksheet changes.

STEP 1: **Highlight the range** or **select the cell** that you want the Hyperlink to refer to:

SALES	NA	EU
TOTAL	441,177	387,358
Jan	45,761	26,028
Feb	34,477	13,411
Mar	49,019	44,454
Q1	129,257	83,893
Apr	41,554	16,481
May	22,795	21,894
Jun	40,596	49,937
Q2	104,945	88,312
Jul	42,395	41,726
Aug	22,246	19,246
Sep	17,216	40,718
Q3	81,857	101,690
Oct	38,831	42,240
Nov	48,797	28,722
Dec	37,490	42,501
Q4	125,118	113,463
SPLIT	38%	33%

 Go to the **Name Box** on the top left-hand corner of the worksheet and enter a name (with no spaces):

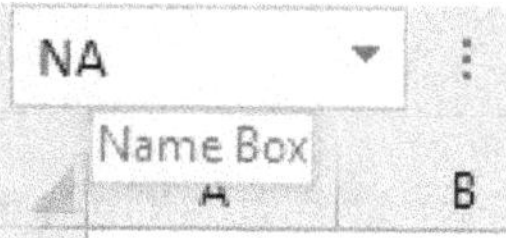

STEP 3: Insert a Shape and **right click on the Shape** and choose **Hyperlink**:

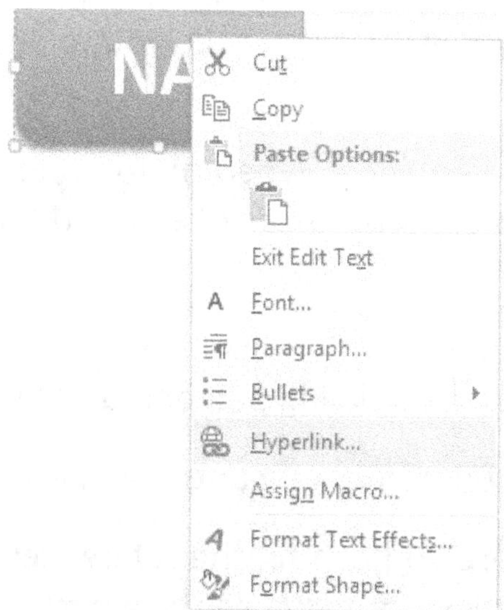

This will open up the **Insert Hyperlink** dialog box. **Select the Defined Name that you set up in Step 2** and press **OK.**

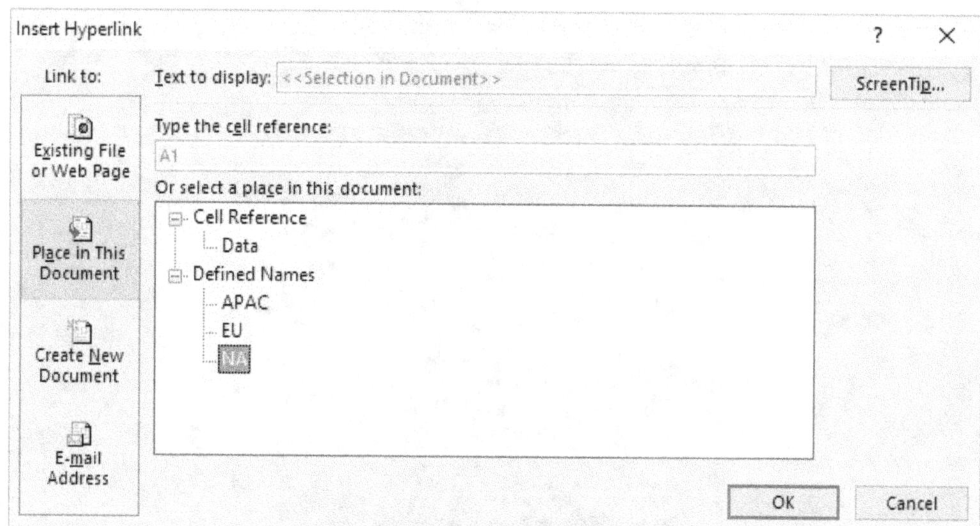

STEP 4: Clicking on the Shape will highlight your referenced range.

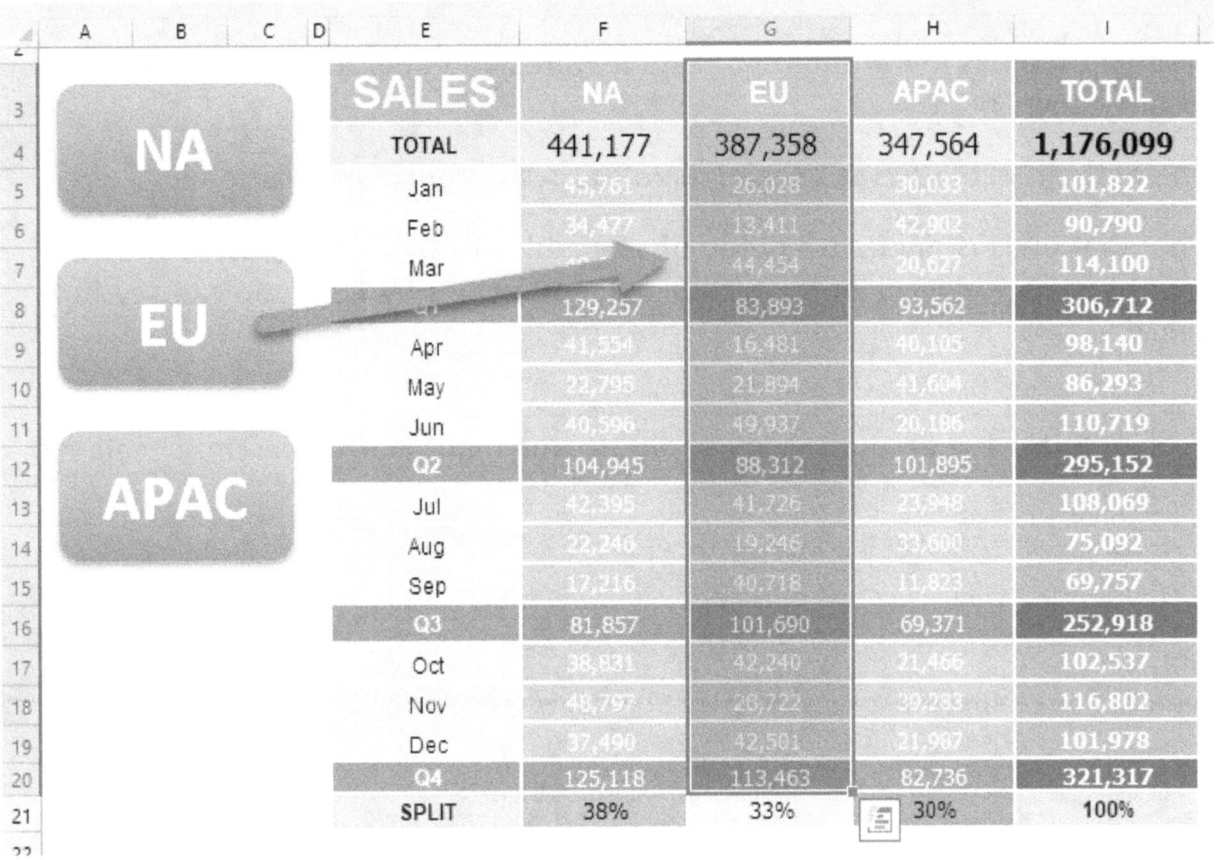
NA
EU
APAC
SALES
NA
EU
APAC
TOTAL
TOTAL 441,177 387,358 347,564 1,176,099
Jan 45,761 26,028 30,033 101,822
Feb 34,477 13,411 42,902 90,790
Mar 44,454 20,627 114,100
129,257 83,893 93,562 306,712
Apr 41,554 16,481 40,105 98,140
May 22,795 21,894 41,604 86,293
Jun 40,596 49,937 20,186 110,719
Q2 104,945 88,312 101,895 295,152
Jul 42,395 41,726 23,948 108,069
Aug 22,246 19,246 33,600 75,092
Sep 17,216 40,718 11,823 69,757
Q3 81,857 101,690 69,371 252,918
Oct 38,831 42,240 21,466 102,537
Nov 48,797 28,722 39,283 116,802
Dec 37,490 42,501 21,987 101,978
Q4 125,118 113,463 82,736 321,317
SPLIT 38% 33% 30% 100%

You can add extra Columns/Rows in your worksheet and clicking on your Hyperlink will follow your referenced range!

Paste Special: A Values Multiplier

Paste Special has a few different Paste features and operations that many users do not know about.

One of them is the **Paste Special > Values > Multiply** combination.

What that does is multiply a range of selected cells by a value, called the multiplier. So if you want to increase all your values by 10%, you can see how below:

STEP 1: **Enter the amount to multiply by** (the multiplier) in an empty cell, e.g. 1.10

YEAR	REGION	SALES $
2014	NORTH	3583
2014	EAST	47713
2014	SOUTH	96331
2014	WEST	55156
2015	NORTH	2701
2015	EAST	42919
2015	SOUTH	96916
2015	WEST	21795

STEP 2: **Copy** that cell

YEAR	REGION	SALES $
2014	NORTH	3583
2014	EAST	47713
2014	SOUTH	96331
2014	WEST	55156
2015	NORTH	2701
2015	EAST	42919
2015	SOUTH	96916
2015	WEST	21795

STEP 3: **Select the data range** you want to multiply, **Right Click and select Paste Special**

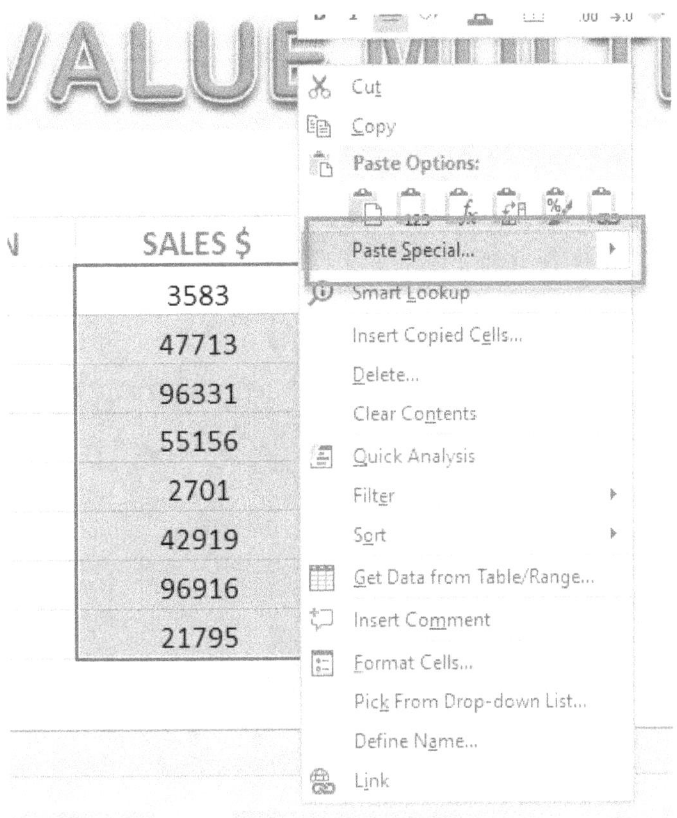

STEP 4: Select **Values & Multiply** and press OK

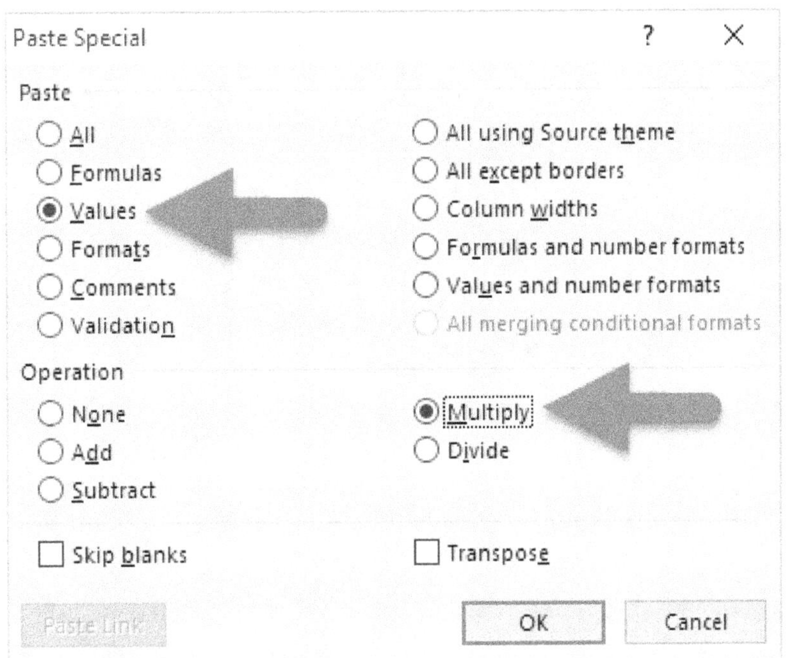

Your values have now been multiplied by the multiplier!

YEAR	REGION	SALES $		1.1
2014	NORTH	3941.3		
2014	EAST	52484.3		
2014	SOUTH	105964.1		
2014	WEST	60671.6		
2015	NORTH	2971.1		
2015	EAST	47210.9		
2015	SOUTH	106607.6		
2015	WEST	23974.5		

(Ctrl) ▼

Paste Special: Add Values To a Range

Paste Special has a few different Paste features and operations that many users do not know about.

One of them is the ***Paste Special > Values > Add*** combination.

What that does is it adds a value to a range of selected cells. Let us say that business is doing so well and we want to increase all of the employee bonuses by $1000 in one go!

STEP 1: **Enter the amount to add to** in an empty cell. In our case, 1000.

	A	B	C	D	E
4	YEAR	EMPLOYEE	BONUS $		1000
5	2021	John	3,000		
6	2021	Jane	1,500		
7	2021	Paul	1,200		
8	2021	Ray	2,500		

STEP 2: **Copy** that cell

	A	B	C	D	E
4	YEAR	EMPLOYEE	BONUS $		1000
5	2021	John	3,000		
6	2021	Jane	1,500		
7	2021	Paul	1,200		
8	2021	Ray	2,500		

STEP 3: **Select the data range** you want to add to, **Right Click and select Paste Special**

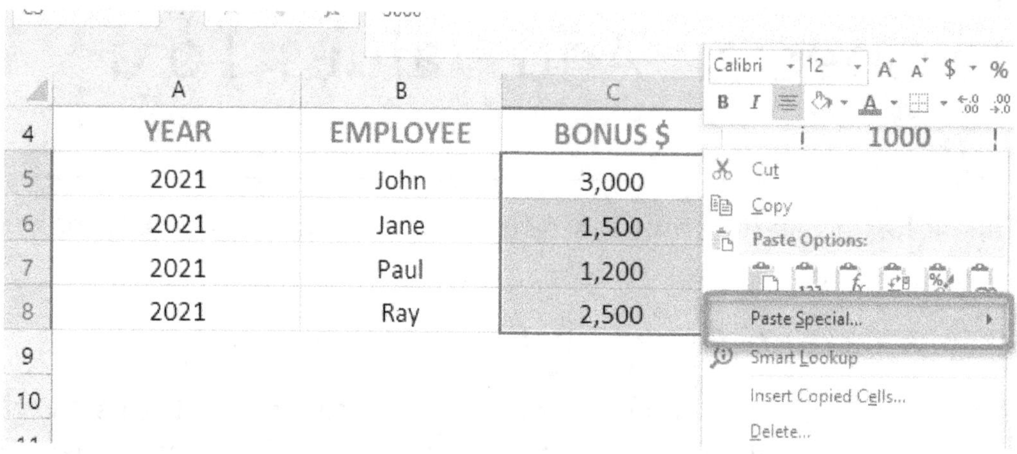

STEP 4: Select **Values & Add** and press **OK**

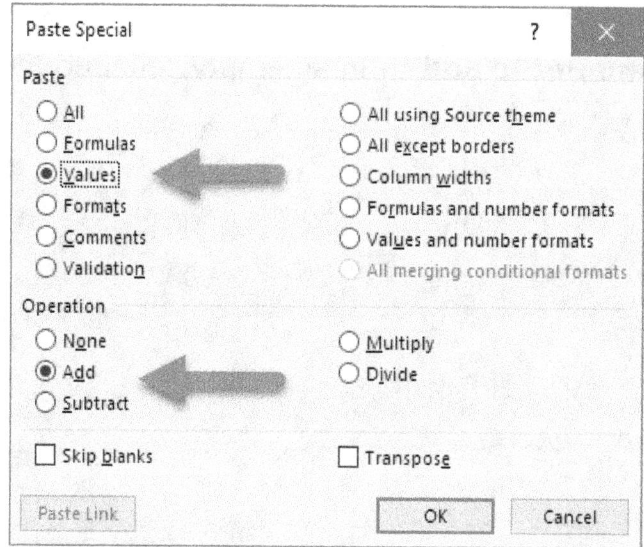

Your values have now been added by $1000!

	A	B	C	D	E
4	YEAR	EMPLOYEE	BONUS $		1000
5	2021	John	4,000		
6	2021	Jane	2,500		
7	2021	Paul	2,200		
8	2021	Ray	3,500		
9					
10					

Power Query: Consolidate Multiple Worksheets

Power Query (Get & Transform) is simply an awesome feature in Excel!

I get lots of queries asking me if there is a way to easily combine Tables from multiple sheets in the same workbook with Power Query

With Power Query, the answer is YES!

If you have multiple Excel worksheets that are in the same format and their underlying differences are their values and dates (e.g. January Sales List, February Sales List, March Sales-List, etc), then we can easily use Power Query to consolidate multiple worksheets..

Here's our 3 multiple worksheets:

STEP 1: Make sure that each worksheet's data is in an **Excel Table** by clicking in the data and pressing **CTRL+T**

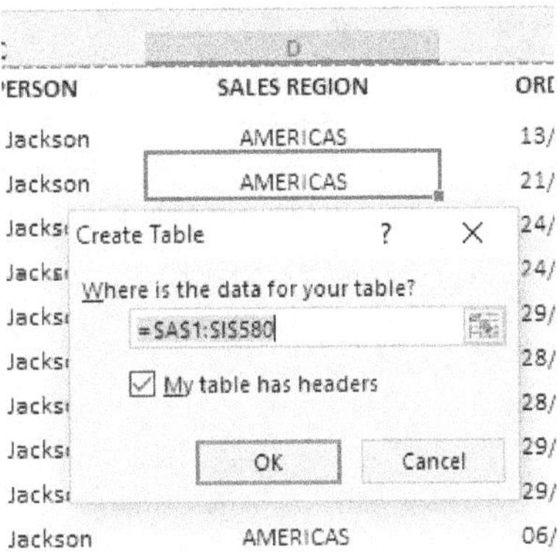

STEP 2: Click in each of the worksheet's data that you want to consolidate and select **Data > Get & Transform Data > From Table/Range**

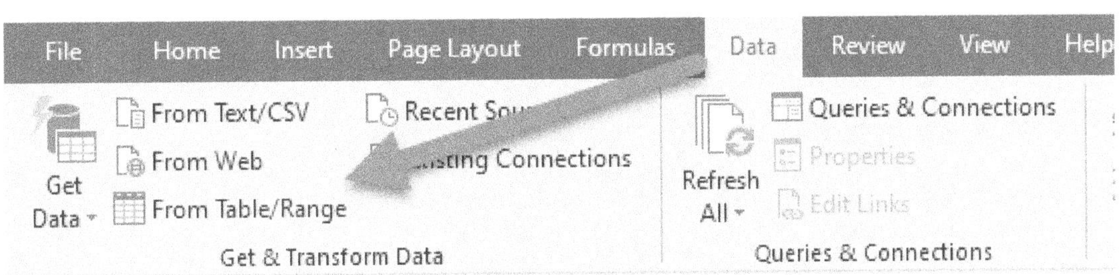

STEP 3: This will open up the **Query Editor** and all you have to do here is press **Close & Load**.

Make sure to do Step 2 & 3 for each worksheet you want to consolidate

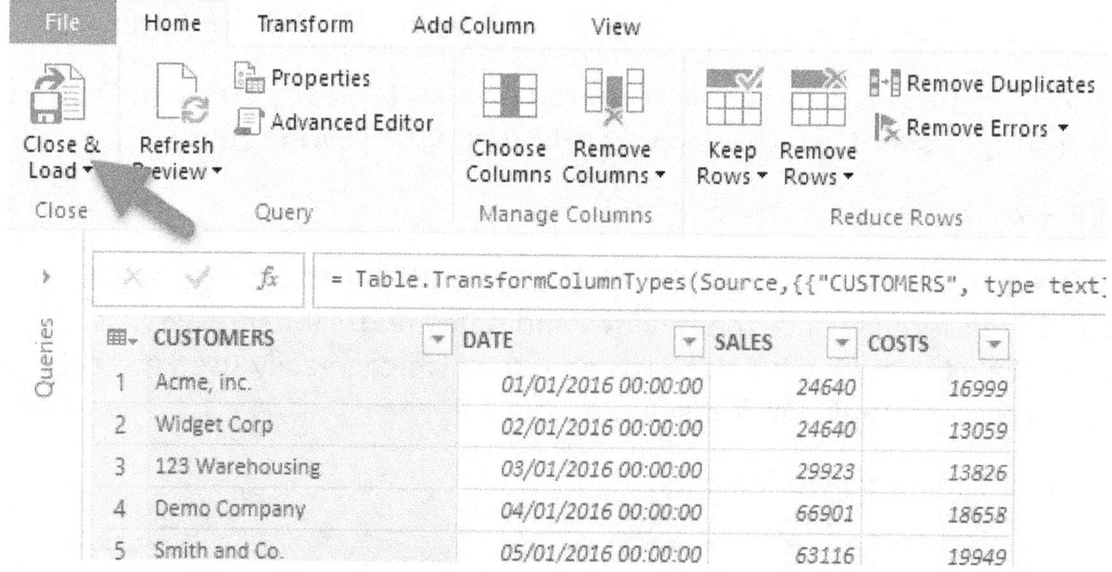

STEP 4: Select **Data > Get Data > Combine Queries > Append**

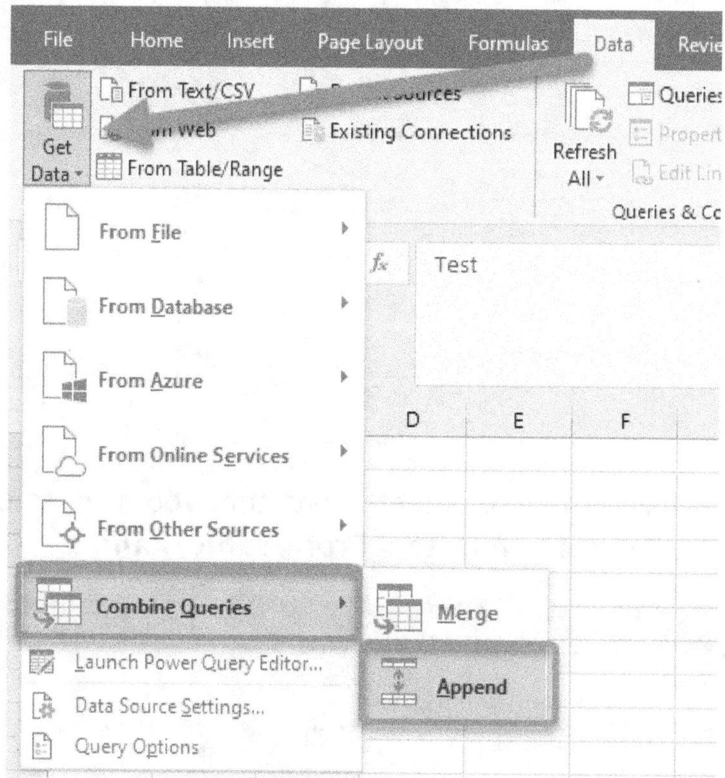

STEP 5: Choose the **Three or more tables** option

STEP 6: Add the tables to append from the **Available Tables** (from the left) to the **Tables to Append** (to the right) by selecting and pressing the **Add** button.

You can also organize the order that you want your consolidated table to appear by moving the Tables up or down

Press the OK button!

STEP 7: This will open up the **Query Editor** once again. Choose **Close & Load**.

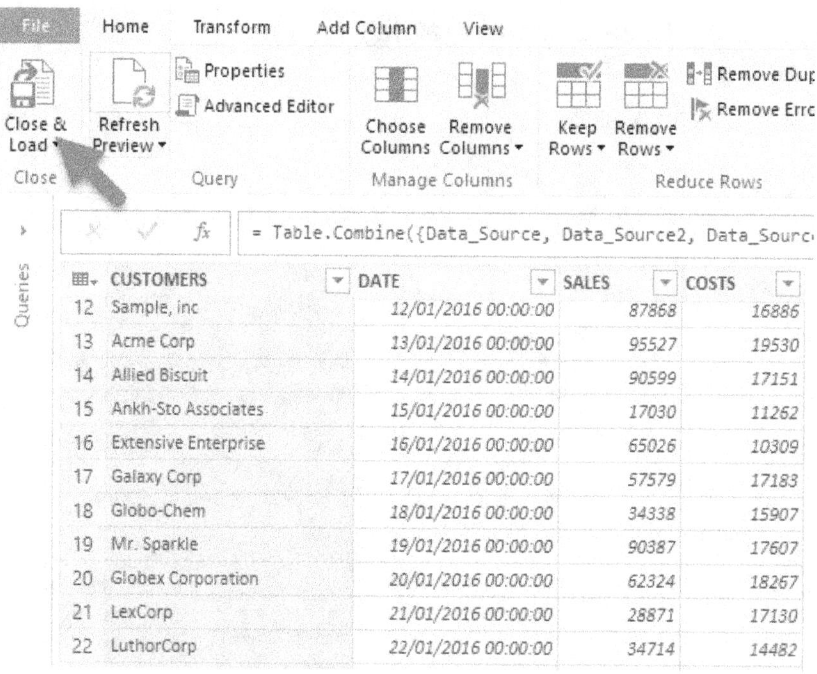

	CUSTOMERS	DATE	SALES	COSTS
12	Sample, inc	12/01/2016 00:00:00	87868	16886
13	Acme Corp	13/01/2016 00:00:00	95527	19530
14	Allied Biscuit	14/01/2016 00:00:00	90599	17151
15	Ankh-Sto Associates	15/01/2016 00:00:00	17030	11262
16	Extensive Enterprise	16/01/2016 00:00:00	65026	10309
17	Galaxy Corp	17/01/2016 00:00:00	57579	17183
18	Globo-Chem	18/01/2016 00:00:00	34338	15907
19	Mr. Sparkle	19/01/2016 00:00:00	90387	17607
20	Globex Corporation	20/01/2016 00:00:00	62324	18267
21	LexCorp	21/01/2016 00:00:00	28871	17130
22	LuthorCorp	22/01/2016 00:00:00	34714	14482

STEP 8: This will open up a brand new worksheet which will consolidate all the worksheets into one big Table:

	CUSTOMERS	DATE	SALES	COSTS
58	Sombra Corporation	2/26/2016 0:00	56847	32996
59	Sto Plains Holdings	2/27/2016 0:00	39034	32836
60	Tessier-Ashpool	2/28/2016 0:00	57749	10244
61	Wayne Enterprises	2/29/2016 0:00	86406	18475
62	Acme, inc.	3/1/2016 0:00	31234	24747
63	Widget Corp	3/2/2016 0:00	25235	26141
64	123 Warehousing	3/3/2016 0:00	44375	39544
65	Demo Company	3/4/2016 0:00	15683	19855
66	Smith and Co.	3/5/2016 0:00	43398	21938
67	Foo Bars	3/6/2016 0:00	62112	33920
68	ABC Telecom	3/7/2016 0:00	17339	14076
69	Fake Brothers	3/8/2016 0:00	21409	36514
70	QWERTY Logistics	3/9/2016 0:00	43555	42535
71	Demo, inc.	3/10/2016 0:00	26633	44501
72	Sample Company	3/11/2016 0:00	45623	37385
73	Sample, inc	3/12/2016 0:00	41068	45830
74	Acme Corp	3/13/2016 0:00	69248	39633
75	Allied Biscuit	3/14/2016 0:00	62127	20617
76	Ankh-Sto Associates	3/15/2016 0:00	55624	30964
77	Extensive Enterprise	3/16/2016 0:00	94286	15181
78	Galaxy Corp	3/17/2016 0:00	11426	40052

 From this consolidate worksheet you can **Insert a Pivot Table** and do your analysis:

Row Labels	Sum of SALES
⊟ Qtr1	
Jan	1,578,651
Feb	1,701,605
Mar	1,369,747
Grand Total	**4,650,003**

This is how you can combine tables and use Power Query consolidate multiple worksheets feature.

Power Query: Consolidate Multiple Workbooks

One of the most sought after a query from the millions of Excel users around the world is:

How do I consolidate multiple Excel workbooks into one?

There are a couple of ways you can do this, using VBA or complex formulas but the learning curve is steep and out of reach for most Excel users.

Luckily with Power Query (Get & Transform), this consolidation task can be done in a couple of minutes! That's right, only a couple of minutes.

STEP 1: **Create a New Folder** on your Desktop or any directory and name it to whatever you like e.g. ***2016 Sales***

Move an Excel Workbook in this Folder that contains your Sales data e.g. ***January 2016.xlsx***

STEP 2: Open a **NEW Excel Workbook** and go to ***Power Query > From File > From Folder***

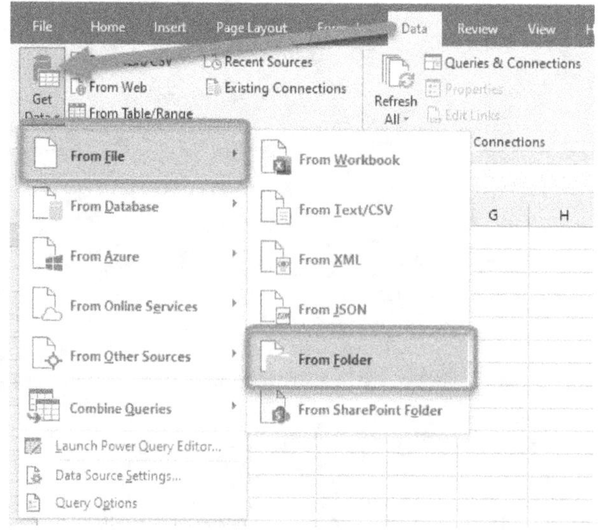

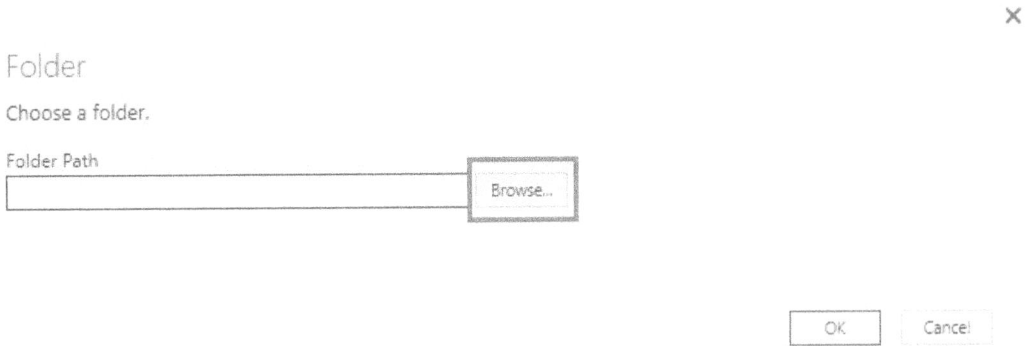

This will bring up the *Browse for Folder* dialogue box and you need to **select the folder you created in Step 1** and press **OK.**

This is how you can use Power Query load multiple files from folder feature.

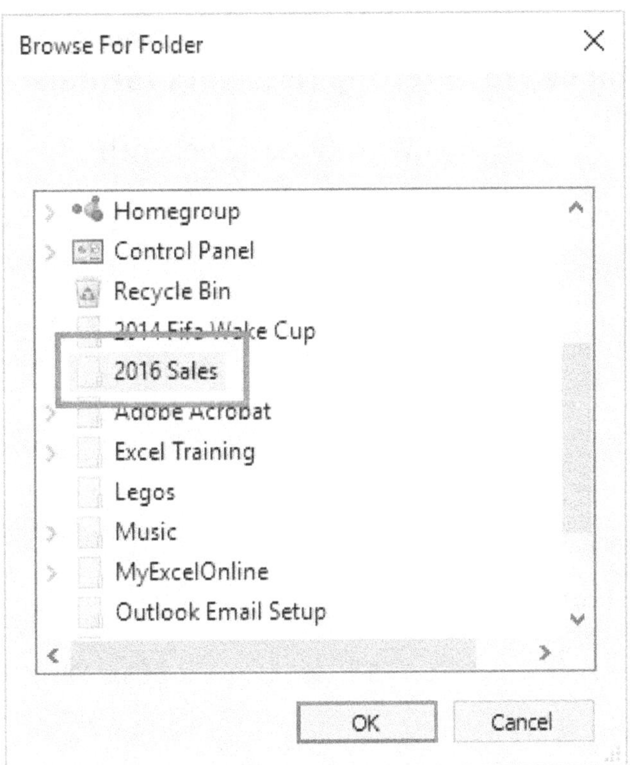

STEP 4: This will open up the **Query Editor.**

From in here you need to **select the first 2 columns** (hold down the CTRL key to select) and **Right Click on the column heading** and choose **Remove Other Columns**

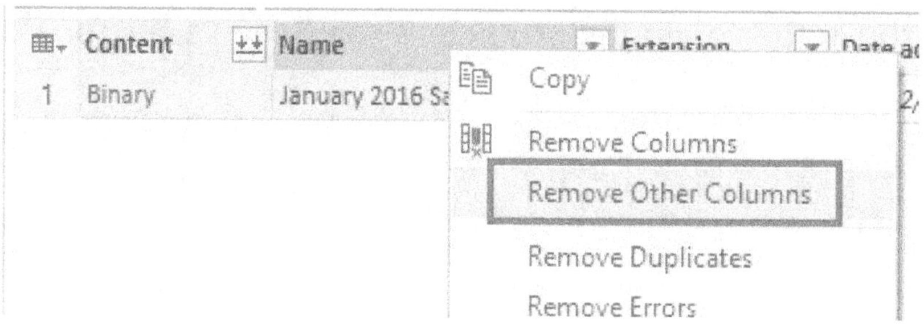

STEP 5: You need to go to ***Add Column > Add Custom Column***

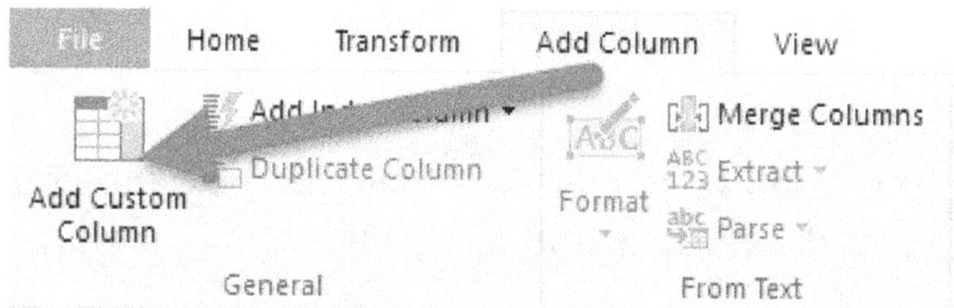

STEP 6: This will bring up the ***Add Custom Column*** dialogue box.

In here you need to **name the new column** e.g. ***Import***, and within the Custom Column Formula you need to **enter the following formula**:

$$= Excel.Workbook([Content])$$

This will import the workbooks from within the Folder that you selected in Step 3

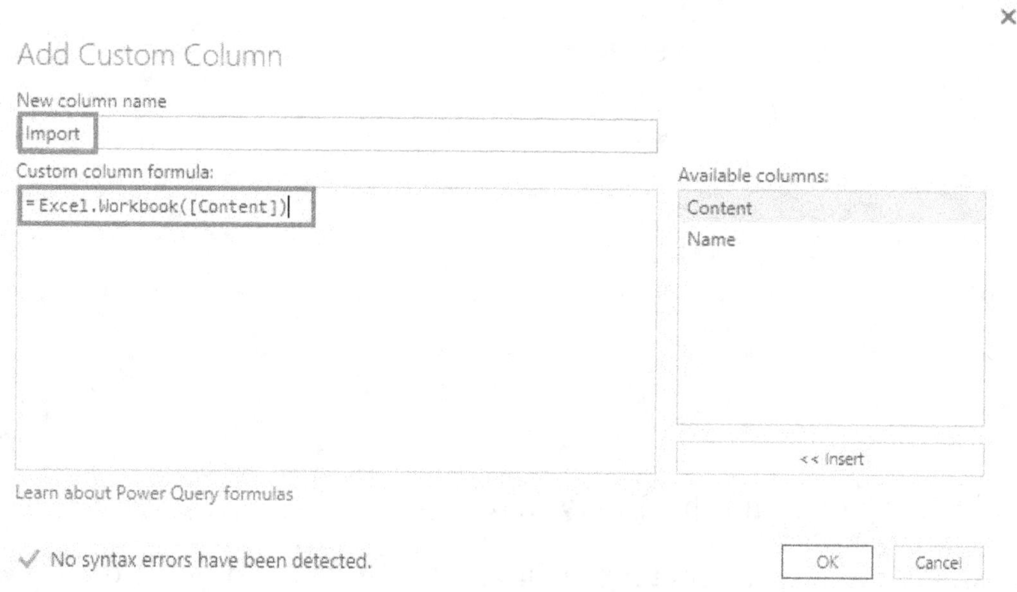

STEP 7: You now have a new column called *Import*.

Click on the Expand Filter and select the **Data** box only and press **OK**. This will import the workbook from the folder

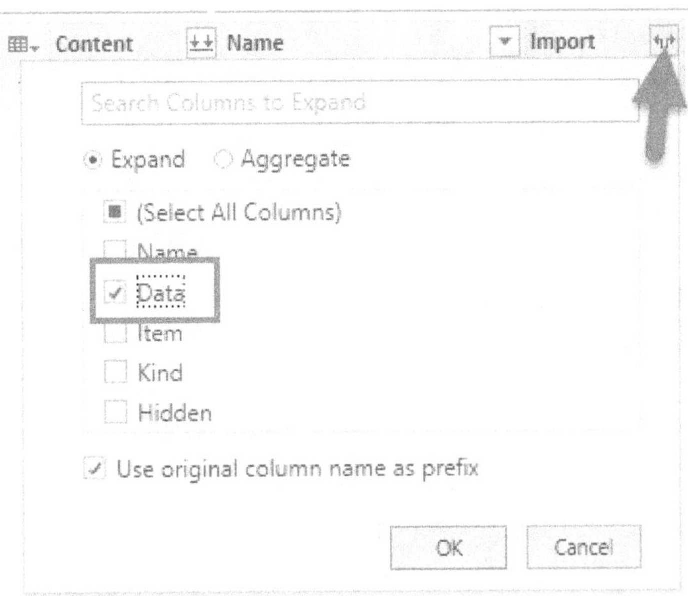

STEP 8: **Click on the Expand Filter** from the *Import Data* column and select **OK**. This imports all the columns' data from within the workbook

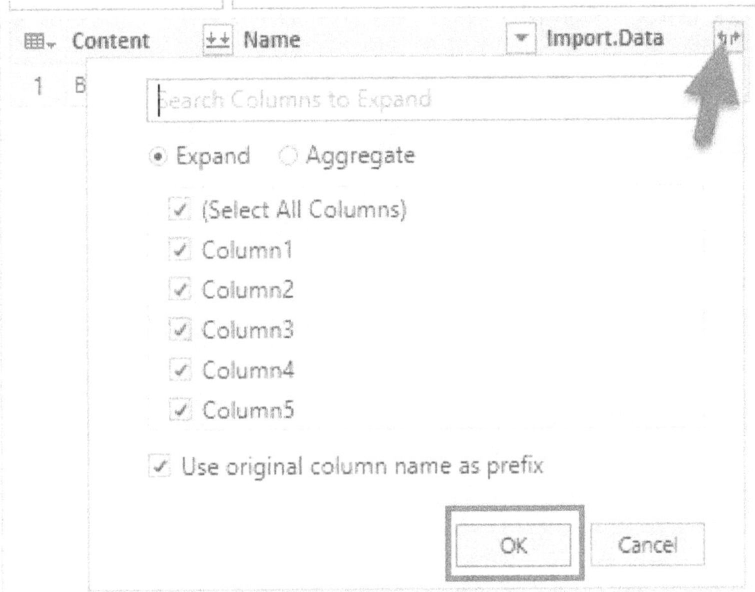

STEP 9: Now it is time to transform the data by making some cosmetic changes!

Remove the Content column by **Right-Clicking** and choosing **Remove**

STEP 10: Select the *Import.Data.Column1* and **filter out the CUSTOMER** heading and press **OK**. This will also remove the other column's headers

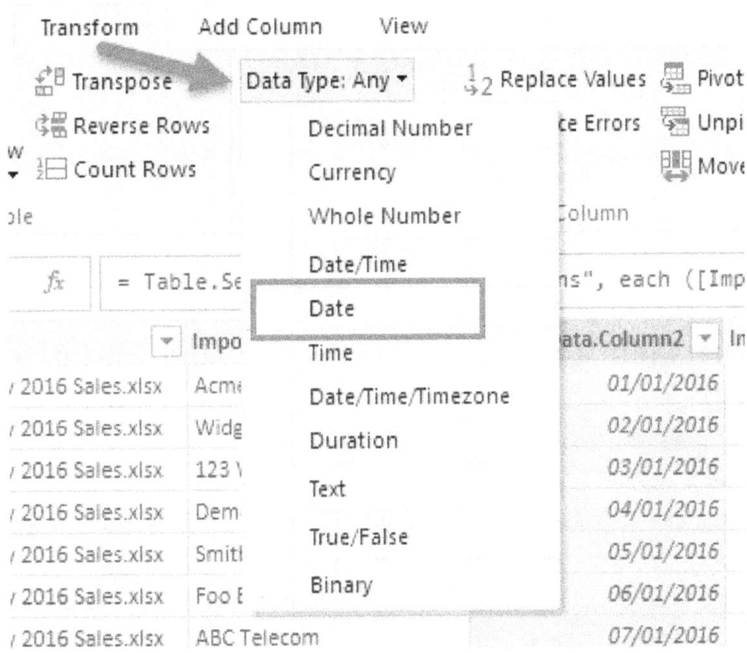

STEP 12: **Select the** *Sales* **column** and go to ***Transform > Data Type > Currency***

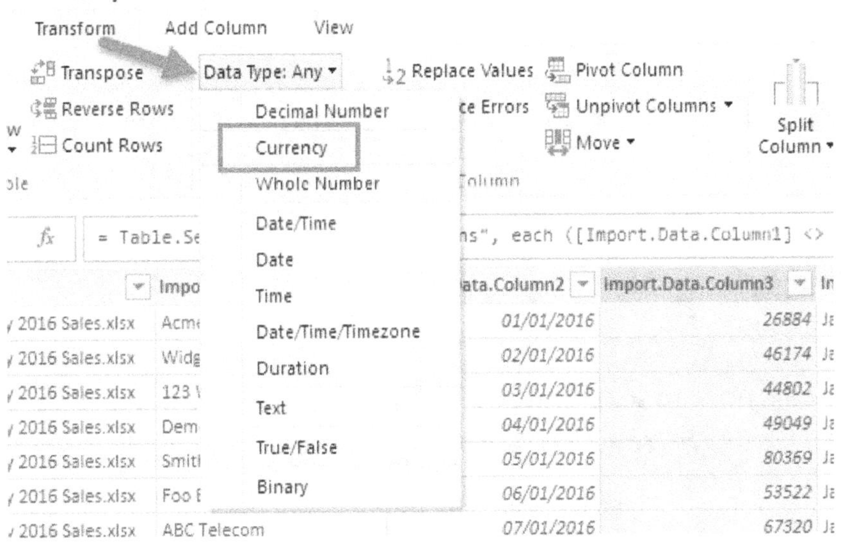

STEP 13: **Rename the column headings** to whatever you like by **double clicking on the column header**, renaming and pressing **OK**

Customers	Date	Sales $	Month	Ye	
Acme, inc.	01/02/2016	77231	February		916
Widget Corp	02/02/2016	42638	February		2016

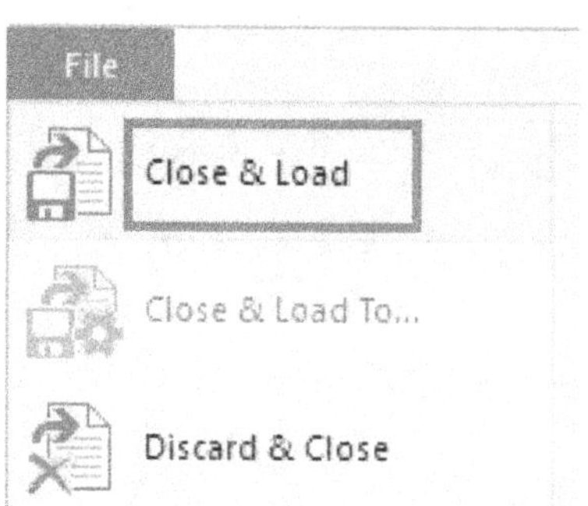

This will put the data into a new worksheet within your workbook

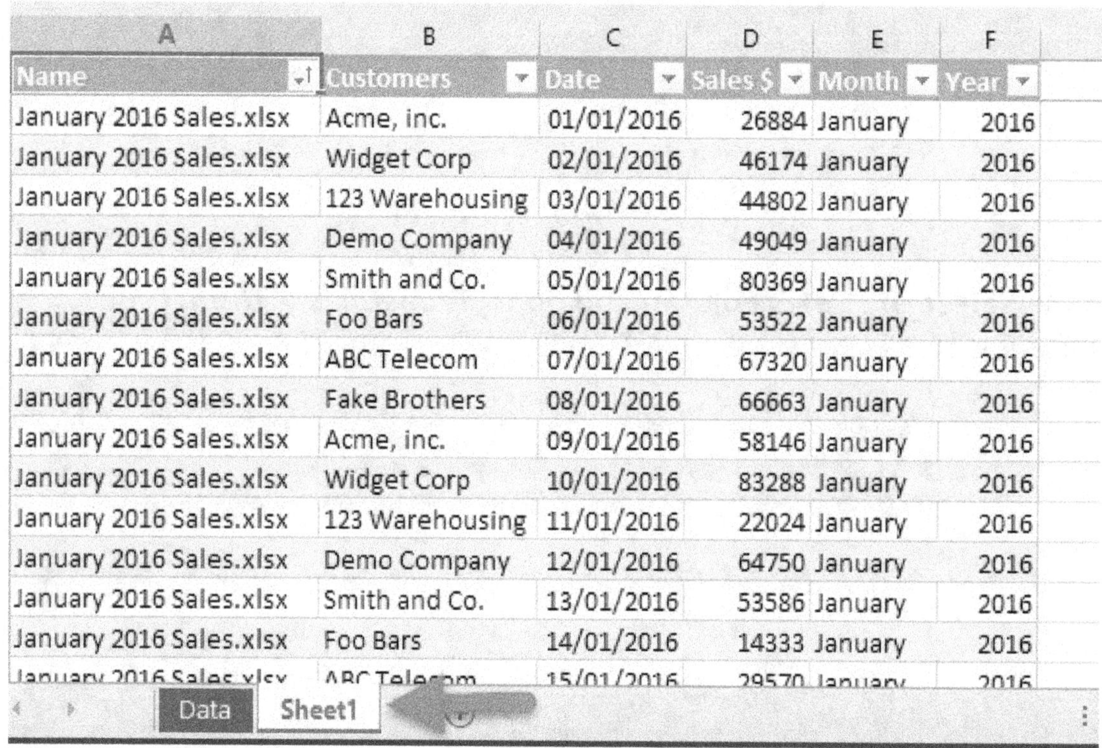

Name	Customers	Date	Sales $	Month	Year
January 2016 Sales.xlsx	Acme, inc.	01/01/2016	26884	January	2016
January 2016 Sales.xlsx	Widget Corp	02/01/2016	46174	January	2016
January 2016 Sales.xlsx	123 Warehousing	03/01/2016	44802	January	2016
January 2016 Sales.xlsx	Demo Company	04/01/2016	49049	January	2016
January 2016 Sales.xlsx	Smith and Co.	05/01/2016	80369	January	2016
January 2016 Sales.xlsx	Foo Bars	06/01/2016	53522	January	2016
January 2016 Sales.xlsx	ABC Telecom	07/01/2016	67320	January	2016
January 2016 Sales.xlsx	Fake Brothers	08/01/2016	66663	January	2016
January 2016 Sales.xlsx	Acme, inc.	09/01/2016	58146	January	2016
January 2016 Sales.xlsx	Widget Corp	10/01/2016	83288	January	2016
January 2016 Sales.xlsx	123 Warehousing	11/01/2016	22024	January	2016
January 2016 Sales.xlsx	Demo Company	12/01/2016	64750	January	2016
January 2016 Sales.xlsx	Smith and Co.	13/01/2016	53586	January	2016
January 2016 Sales.xlsx	Foo Bars	14/01/2016	14333	January	2016
January 2016 Sales.xlsx	ABC Telecom	15/01/2016	29570	January	2016

Data   Sheet1

STEP 15: You can now **Insert a Pivot Table** to do your analysis by going to *Insert > Pivot Table > New/Existing Worksheet*

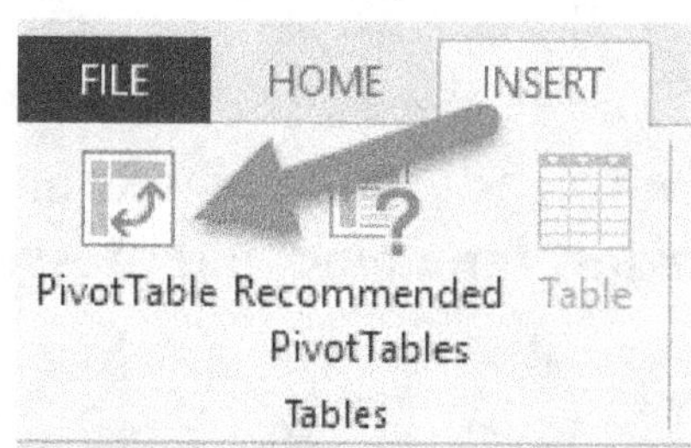

Put the Months in the ROWS and the Sales $ in the VALUES area:

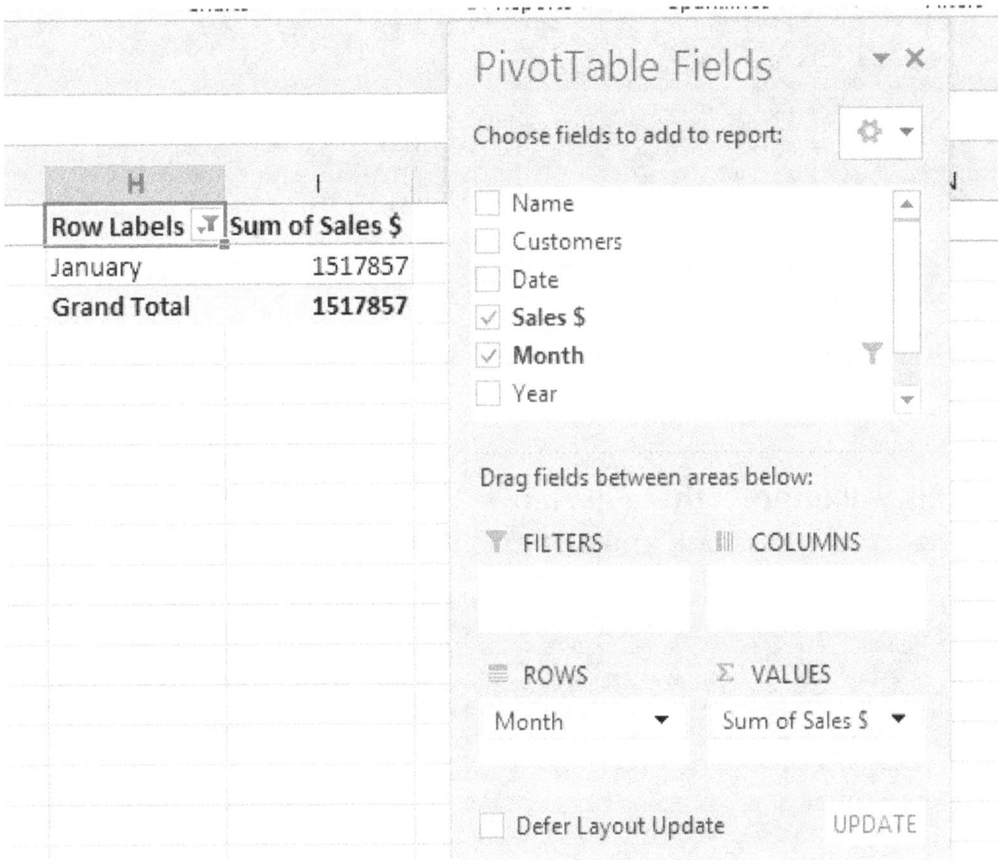

STEP 16: Now for the very cool part!

You can **move similar workbooks into the Folder we created in Step 1,** say for subsequent months e.g. *February 2016.xlsx, March 2016.xlsx etc*

Take Note: The Excel Workbooks have to have the same format and number of columns as in the workbook we imported in Step 1

STEP 17: In your Excel workbook, **click on the imported data** and this will open up the **Workbook Queries pane** (If this does not open, go to *Power Query > Show Pane*)

Click the Refresh button (or you can go to *Table Tools > Query > Refresh*)

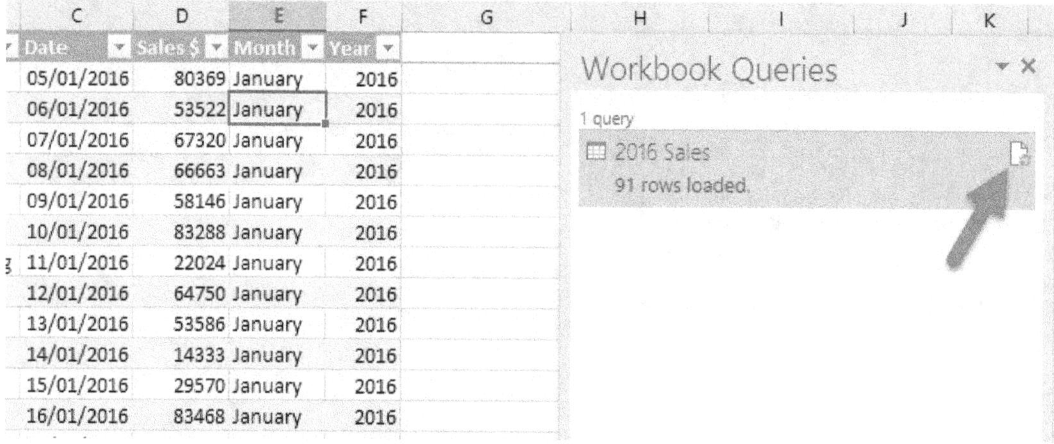

STEP 18: This will **import the** *February 2016.xlsx* **and** *March 2016.xlsx* **data** into the Excel workbook and **append it to January's data**

STEP 19: Now you can **Refresh the Pivot Table** and the new imported data will be reflected

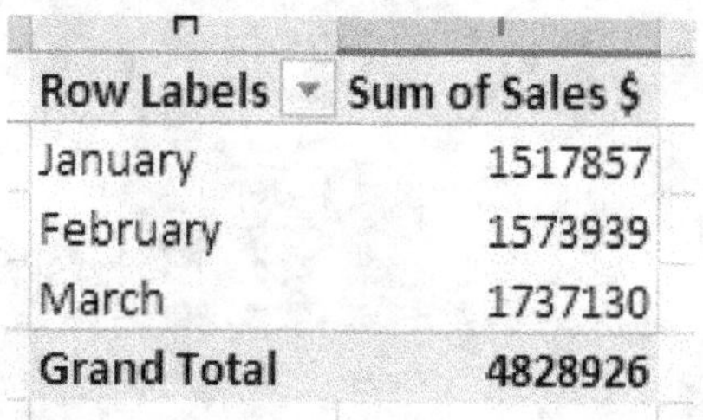

Row Labels	Sum of Sales $
January	1517857
February	1573939
March	1737130
Grand Total	**4828926**

Next month all you have to do is drop in the new month's workbook into the 2016 Sales Folder and Refresh the Query & the Pivot Table to see the results!

Power Query: Unpivot Data

Power Query allows you to extract data from any source, clean and transform the data and then load it to another sheet within Excel, Power Pivot or the Power BI Designer canvas.

One of the best features is to Unpivot Columns.

What that does is transforms columns with similar characteristics (e.g. Jan, Feb, March...) and puts them in a unique column or tabular format (e.g. Month), which then allows you to do further analysis using Pivot Tables which was not possible before unpivoting.

STEP 1: Highlight your data and go to **Data > Get & Transform Data > From Table/Range**

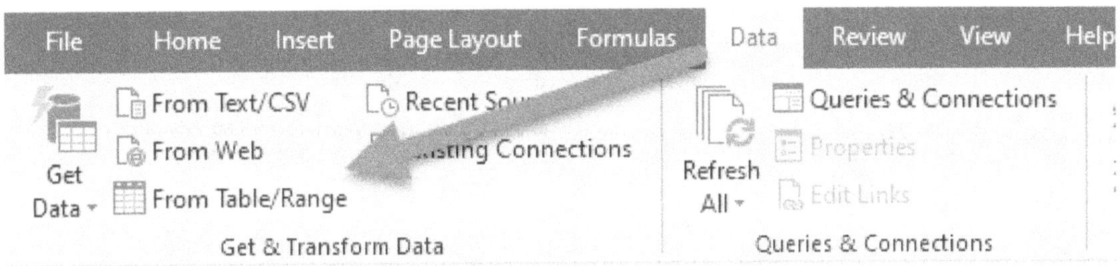

STEP 2: This opens the Power Query editor and from here you need to select the columns that you want to unpivot

CUSTOMER	Jan	Feb	Mar	Apr	May	Jun	Jul	Aug	Sep	Oct	Nov	Dec
1 Acme, inc.	1625	3866	7068	5276	4822	8421	6138	4932	6864	7780	9601	3091
2 Widget Corp	1481	1424	8957	3753	1159	6678	4639	2799	5354	8349	7218	7879
3 123 Warehousing	8704	6881	3161	4636	4011	8291	3595	7724	6106	2402	4304	6439
4 Demo Company	4118	3671	2425	9649	9152	8631	8253	3070	7745	2232	8616	4337
5 Smith and Co.	9273	9492	4711	7431	1223	6151	2442	7277	6641	9998	5727	2771
6 Foo Bars	9640	3024	7757	8310	4151	7381	9517	4715	5928	2734	9207	3528
7 ABC Telecom	8566	8602	3657	3915	4000	8649	7186	7489	4353	3137	6220	8772
8 Arsenal FC	9522	4893	9454	6286	5074	5808	9930	7884	9007	7183	7414	2612
9 Fake Brothers	3325	6938	9708	8632	1425	6944	9987	4418	5076	2439	3164	7128

STEP 3: You then need to go to the **Transform** tab and select **Unpivot Columns**

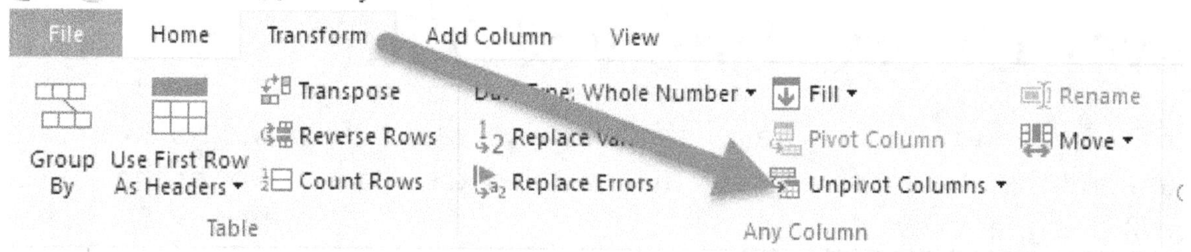

STEP 4: Go to the *File* tab and choose ***Close & Load***

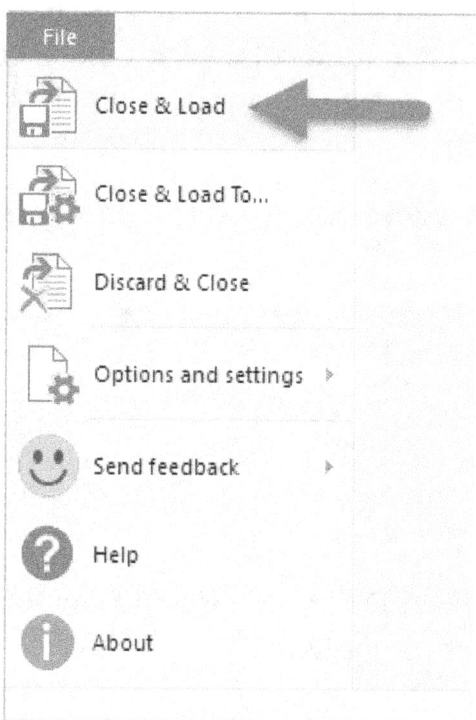

STEP 5: This will load and open the unpivoted data into a new worksheet with your Excel workbook. Now you can go crazy with your super analytical work, using **Pivot Tables** or other tools.

	A	B	C
1	CUSTOMER	Attribute	Value
2	Acme, inc.	Jan	1625
3	Acme, inc.	Feb	3866
4	Acme, inc.	Mar	7068
5	Acme, inc.	Apr	5276
6	Acme, inc.	May	4822
7	Acme, inc.	Jun	8421
8	Acme, inc.	Jul	6138
9	Acme, inc.	Aug	4932
10	Acme, inc.	Sep	6864
11	Acme, inc.	Oct	7780
12	Acme, inc.	Nov	9601
13	Acme, inc.	Dec	3091
14	Widget Corp	Jan	1481
15	Widget Corp	Feb	1424
16	Widget Corp	Mar	8957
17	Widget Corp	Apr	3753
18	Widget Corp	Ma	115

Quick Reports With Excel Custom Views

Whenever I wanted to print my Excel worksheet for a report, I usually had to trim down the data and do changes like hiding the columns so it could fit into one page.

Other common scenarios would be, hiding employee salaries or filtering out sensitive customer data.

It is cumbersome because after printing it out I had to undo the layout changes one by one!

Thankfully Excel has **Custom Views** that lets you revert and save your layout changes in a single click!

STEP 1: You need to set a default view first.

Once you have the layout that you use most of the time, go to *View > Custom Views*:

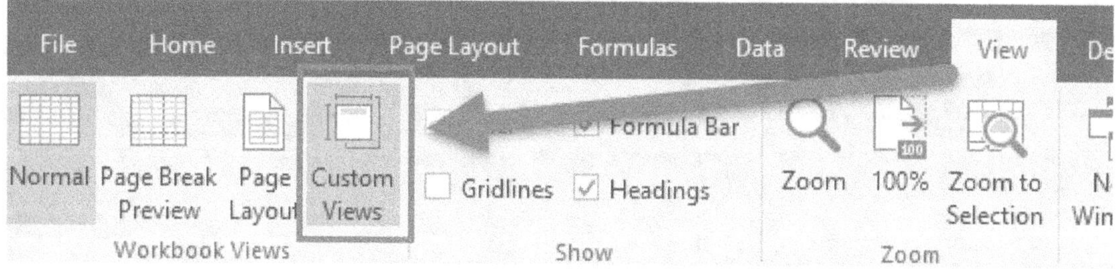

STEP 2: Click **Add** to create a new Custom View.

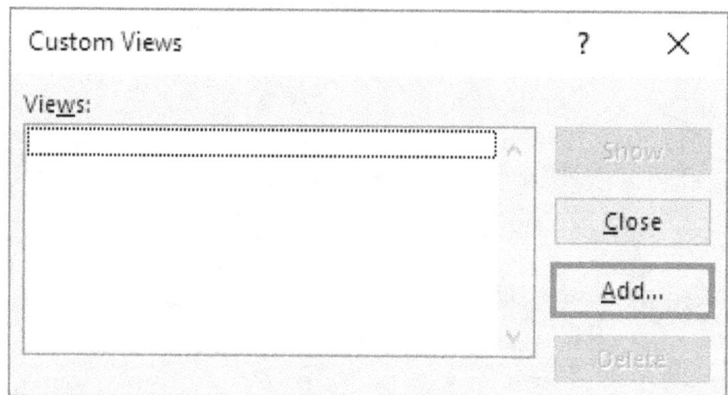

Type in **Normal View** and click **OK.**

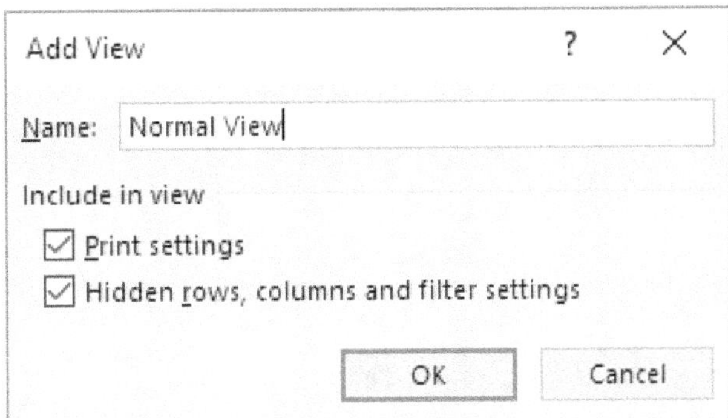

STEP 3: In preparation for the second **Custom View**, select the first 4 columns, right click and select **Hide.**

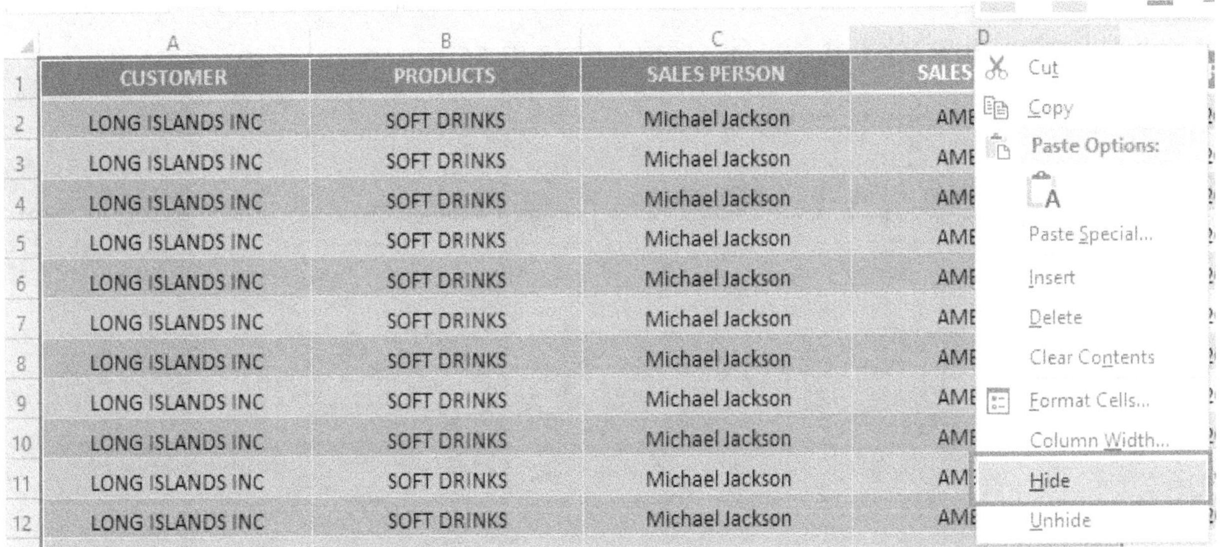

STEP 4: Go to *View> Custom Views*:

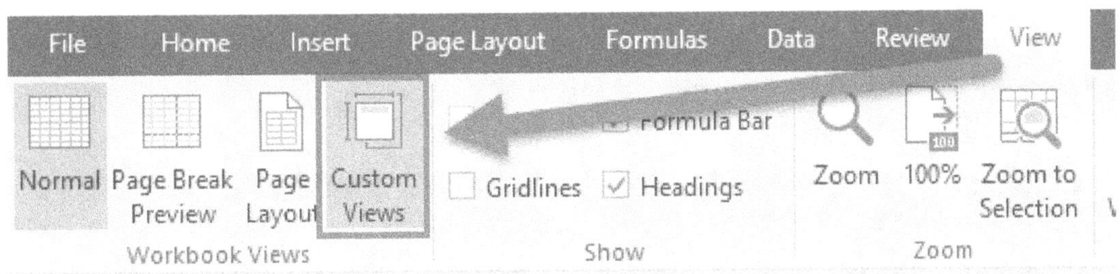

 Click **Add** to create a new Custom View.

Type in **Hidden Columns** and click **OK.**

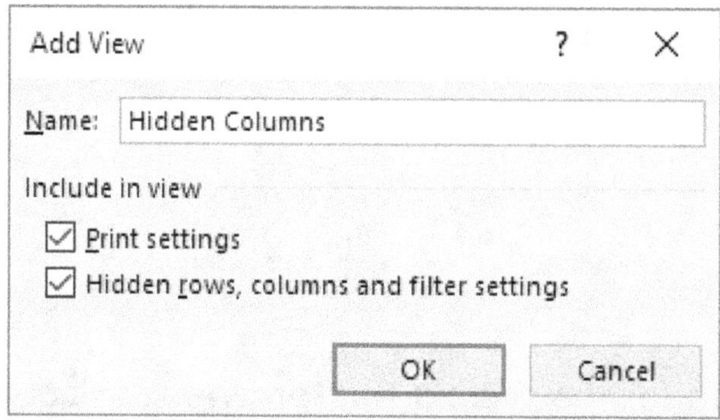

STEP 6: Let us now try out our Custom Views in action.

Go to *View > Custom Views.*

Select **Normal View** and click **Show.**

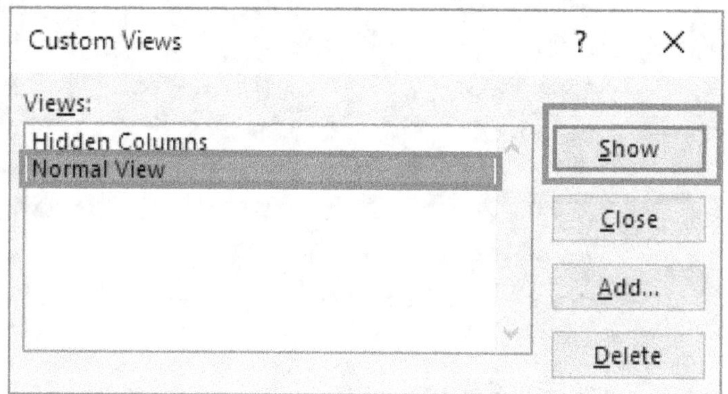

You can see all of the columns displayed.

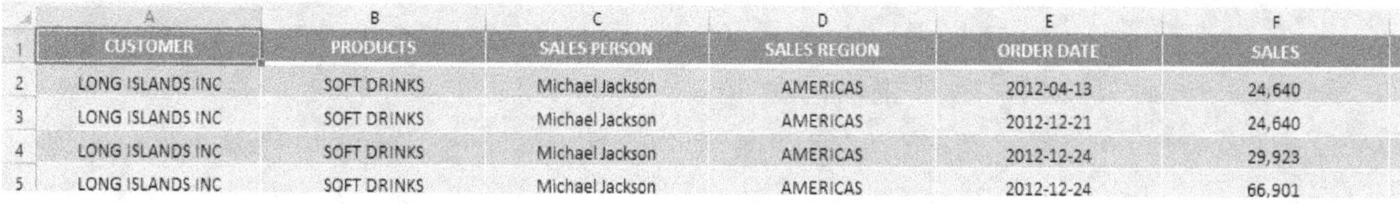

	A	B	C	D	E	F
1	CUSTOMER	PRODUCTS	SALES PERSON	SALES REGION	ORDER DATE	SALES
2	LONG ISLANDS INC	SOFT DRINKS	Michael Jackson	AMERICAS	2012-04-13	24,640
3	LONG ISLANDS INC	SOFT DRINKS	Michael Jackson	AMERICAS	2012-12-21	24,640
4	LONG ISLANDS INC	SOFT DRINKS	Michael Jackson	AMERICAS	2012-12-24	29,923
5	LONG ISLANDS INC	SOFT DRINKS	Michael Jackson	AMERICAS	2012-12-24	66,901

STEP 7: Now let us try the second custom view.

Go to *View > Custom Views.*

Select **Hidden Columns** and click **Show.**

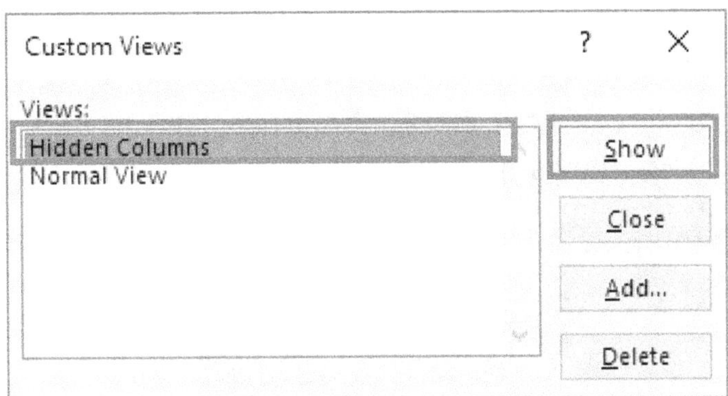

The columns are hidden right away in a click!

	E	F	G	H	I
	ORDER DATE	SALES	FINANCIAL YEAR	SALES MONTH	SALES QTR
1					
2	2012-04-13	24,640	2012	January	Q1
3	2012-12-21	24,640	2012	February	Q1
4	2012-12-24	29,923	2012	March	Q1
5	2012-12-24	66,901	2012	April	Q2
6	2012-12-29	63,116	2012	May	Q2
7	2012-06-28	38,281	2012	June	Q2
8	2012-06-28	57,650	2012	July	Q3

Smart Lookup in Excel

There were times when I was working in a spreadsheet and I had to do a quick internet search to understand some of the words in my cells.

The process was, copy the text, paste on my browser, and click search.

Little did I know that since **Excel 2016**, there is a feature called **Smart Lookup!** Smart Lookup allows me to make word searches inside Excel!

Let us say we want to know more about these names in our spreadsheet:

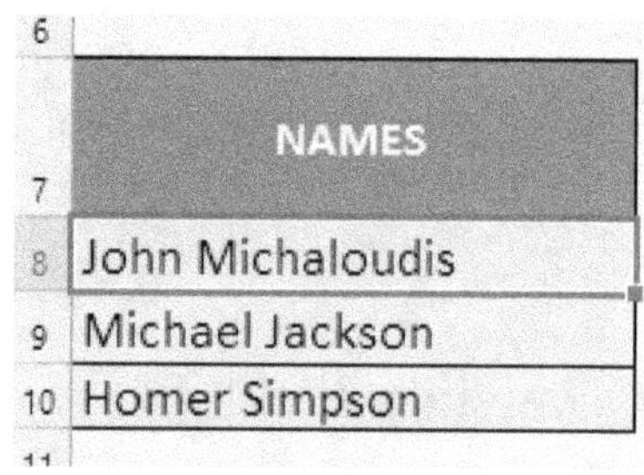

The steps are very straightforward, which are outlined below:

STEP 1: Pick first the name or cell containing the text you want to search:

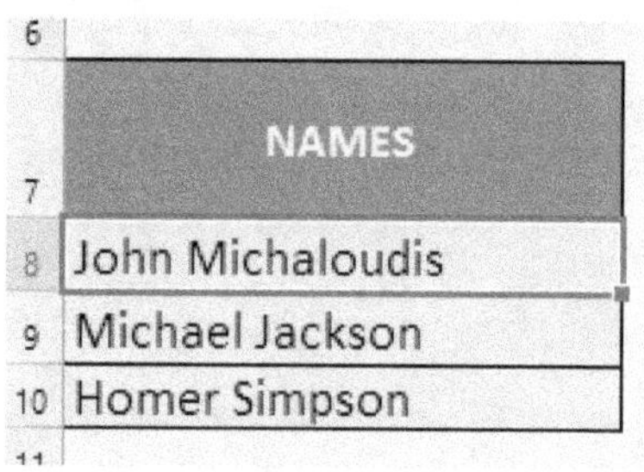

STEP 2: Go to **Review > Smart Lookup:**

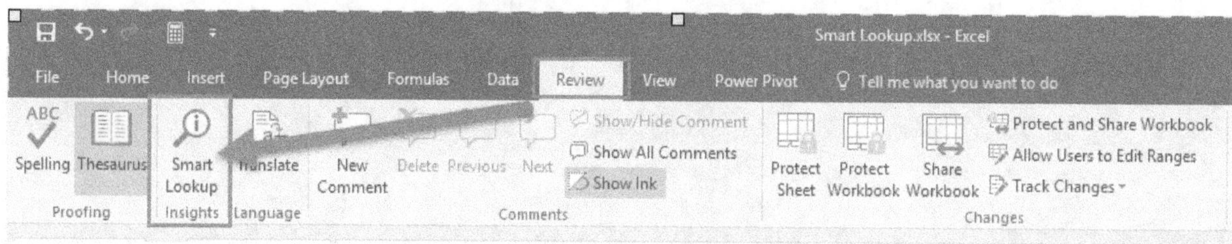

 You can now see my picture and details inside Excel which is using Bing's web search inside the Smart Lookup pane! Thanks **Smart Lookup!**

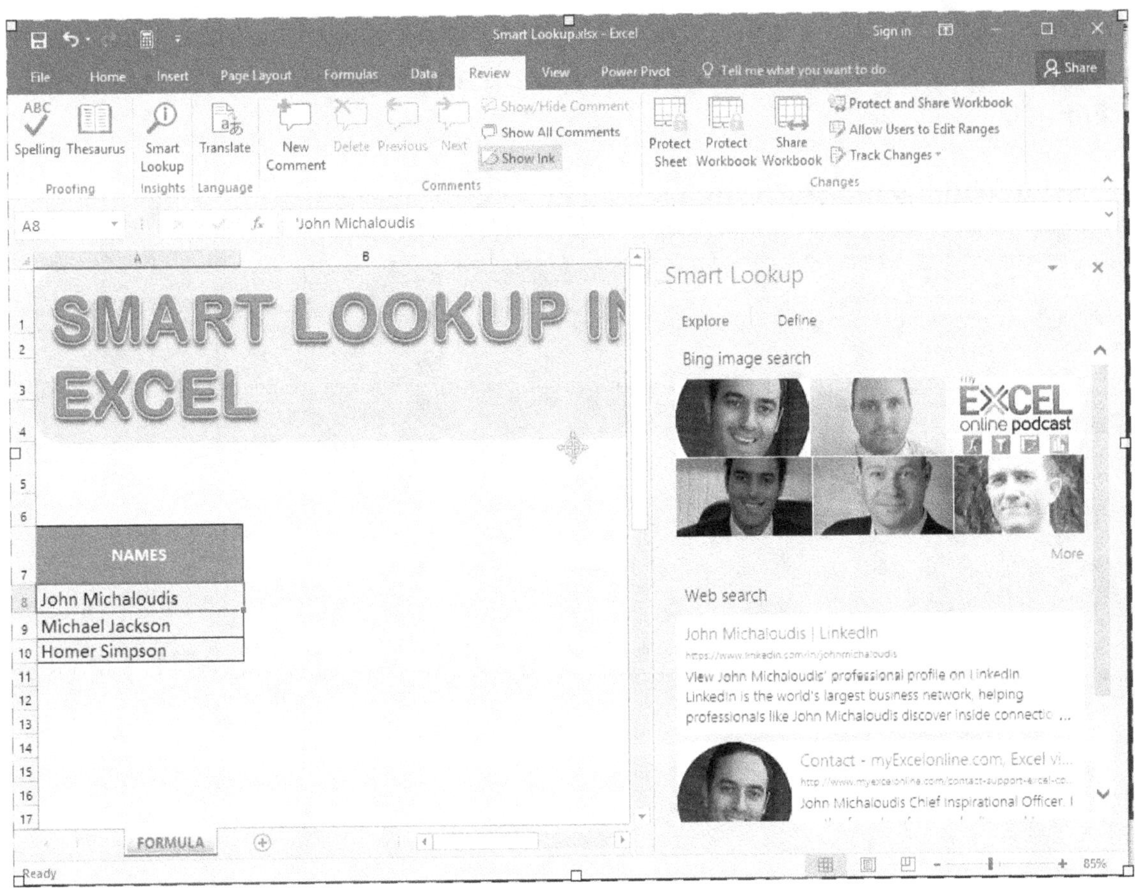

Sparklines: Add Marker Colors

When using Sparklines, did you know that you can customize specific parts to show your color of choice? It's very easy to do and we will do this on 2 types of Sparklines!

Here is our **Win/Loss Sparkline**:

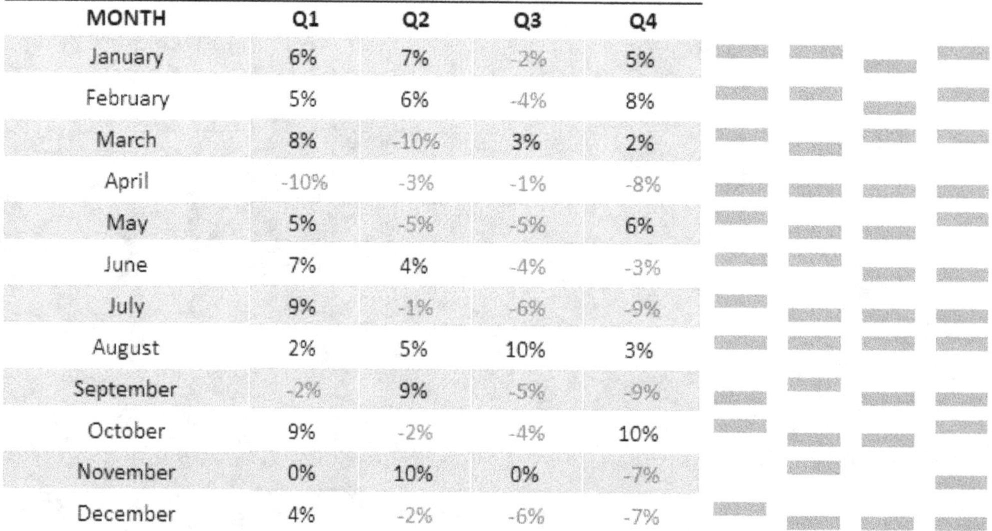

MONTH	Q1	Q2	Q3	Q4
January	6%	7%	-2%	5%
February	5%	6%	-4%	8%
March	8%	-10%	3%	2%
April	-10%	-3%	-1%	-8%
May	5%	-5%	-5%	6%
June	7%	4%	-4%	-3%
July	9%	-1%	-6%	-9%
August	2%	5%	10%	3%
September	-2%	9%	-5%	-9%
October	9%	-2%	-4%	10%
November	0%	10%	0%	-7%
December	4%	-2%	-6%	-7%

And here is our **Column Sparkline**:

REGION	JAN	FEB	MAR	APR	MAY	JUN	JUL	AUG	SEP	OCT	NOV	DEC
NORTH	86	61	67	90	41	35	41	91	67	59	9	88
SOUTH	44	25	28	34	25	76	3	40	1	74	37	92
EAST	19	10	73	90	98	52	74	33	58	17	25	94
WEST	76	90	87	87	46	43	30	90	86	13	9	26
NORTH EAST	13	36	29	20	15	90	72	61	28	17	12	61
SOUTH EAST	89	25	45	10	86	52	90	87	27	8	90	38
NORTH WEST	16	24	61	45	70	5	5	48	100	34	35	72
SOUTH WEST	3	8	15	86	32	45	97	59	12	97	98	18
CENTRAL	54	44	33	90	47	64	14	25	98	18	81	30
HIGHLANDS	36	62	40	75	57	46	22	62	76	63	25	8

STEP 1: To change the negative color of your Win/Loss Sparkline you need to select ***Marker Color > Negative Points > Select Color***

Let us select Red.

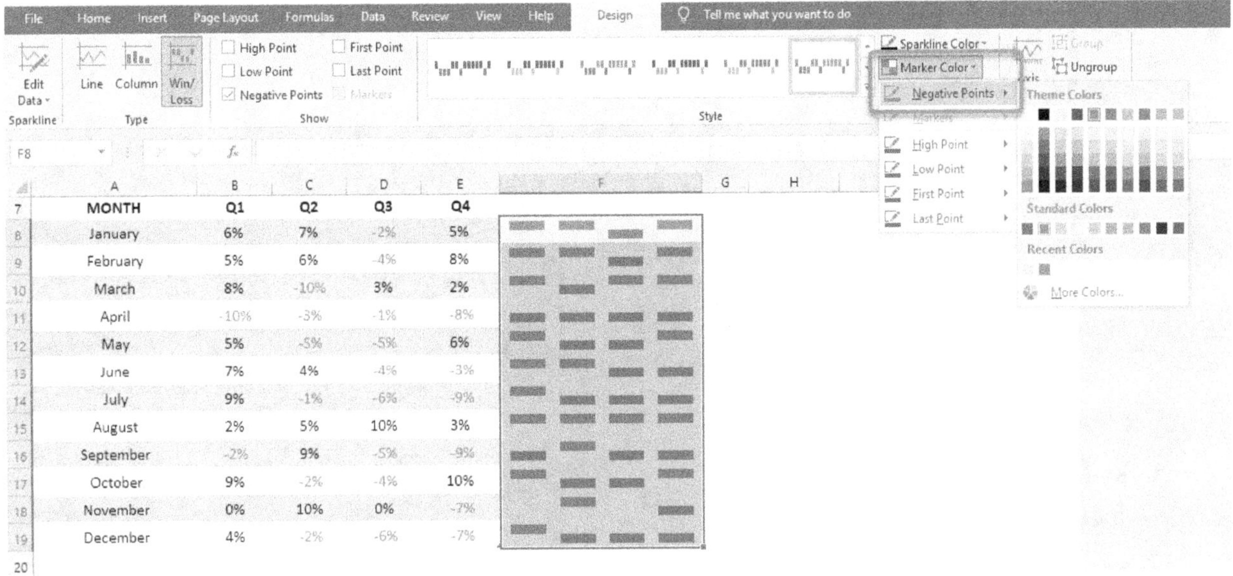

STEP 2: To change the high point color of your Win/Loss Sparkline you need to select *Marker Color > High Point > Select Color*

Let us select Green.

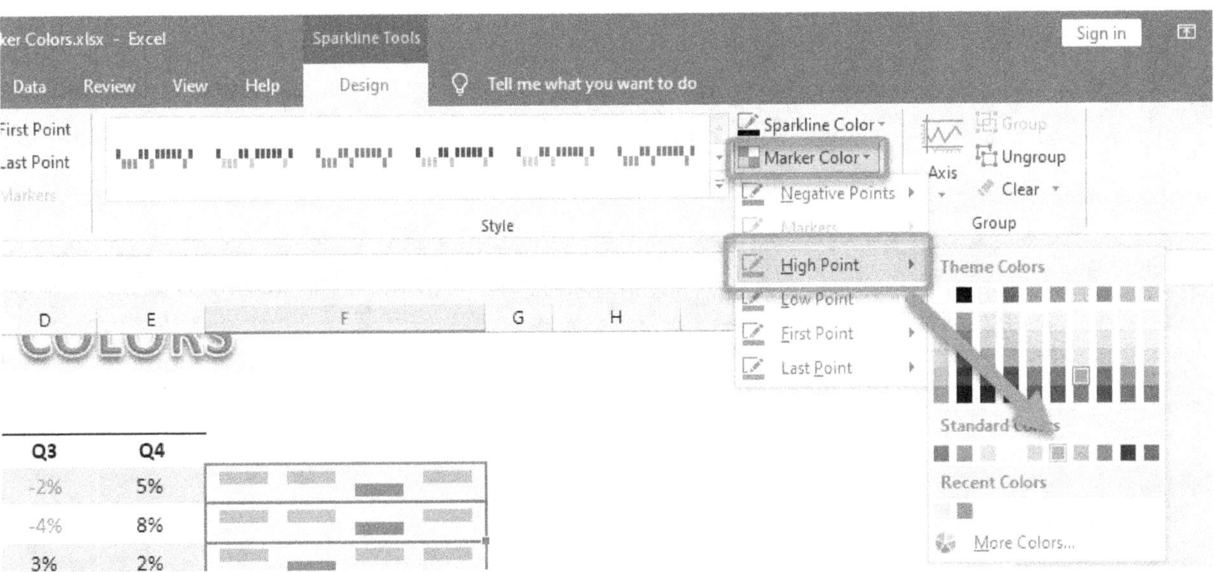

Your Sparkline is now ready!

MONTH	Q1	Q2	Q3	Q4
January	6%	7%	-2%	5%
February	5%	6%	-4%	8%
March	8%	-10%	3%	2%
April	-10%	-3%	-1%	-8%
May	5%	-5%	-5%	6%
June	7%	4%	-4%	-3%
July	9%	-1%	-6%	-9%
August	2%	5%	10%	3%
September	-2%	9%	-5%	-9%
October	9%	-2%	-4%	10%
November	0%	10%	0%	-7%
December	4%	-2%	-6%	-7%

STEP 3: To change the low point color of your Column Sparkline you need to select *Marker Color > Low Point > Select Color*

Let us select Red.

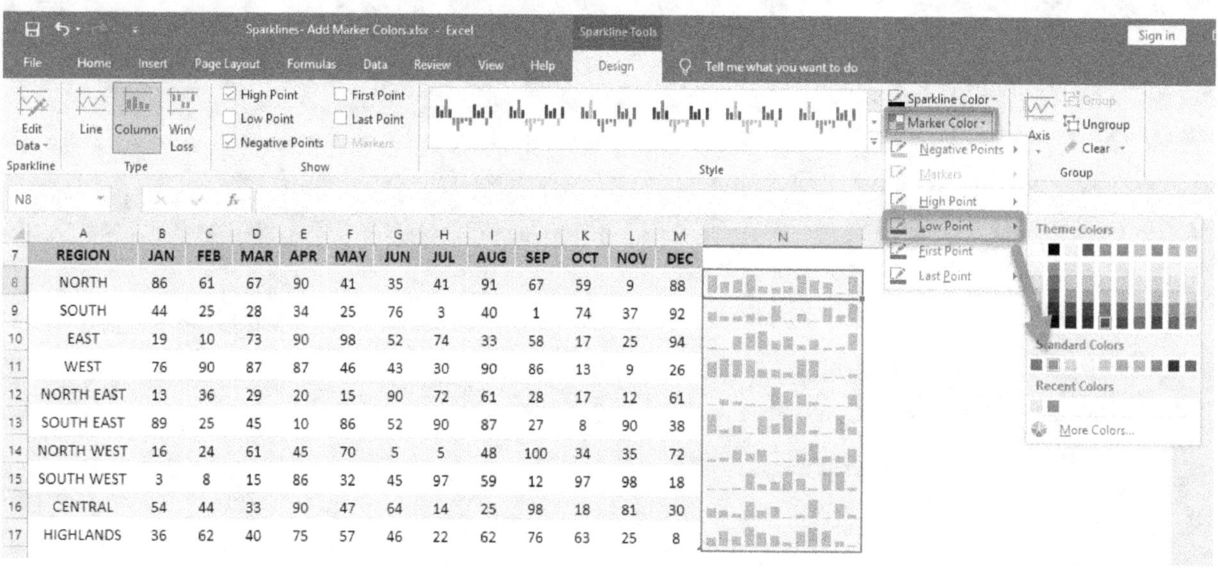

STEP 4: To change the high point color of your Column Sparkline you need to select *Marker Color > High Point > Select Color*

Let us select Green.

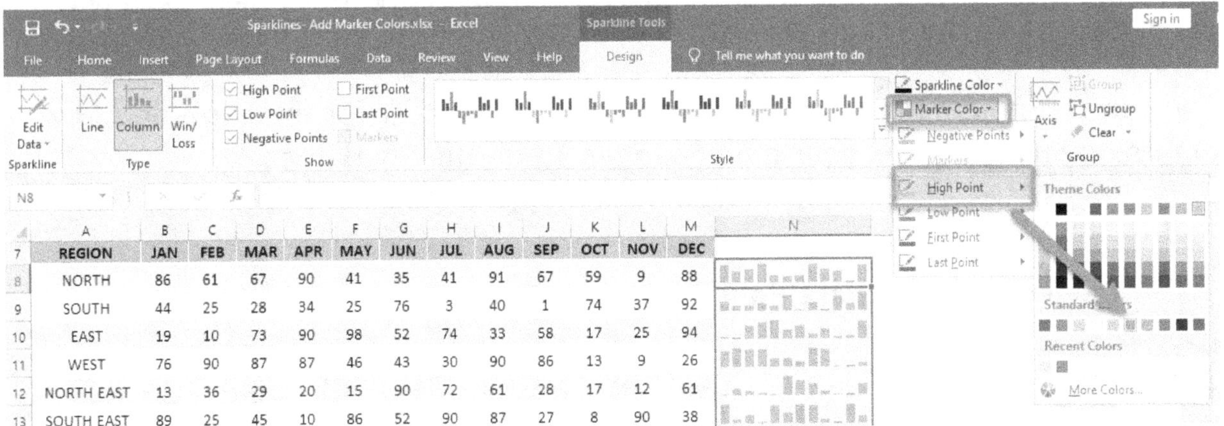

REGION	JAN	FEB	MAR	APR	MAY	JUN	JUL	AUG	SEP	OCT	NOV	DEC
NORTH	86	61	67	90	41	35	41	91	67	59	9	88
SOUTH	44	25	28	34	25	76	3	40	1	74	37	92
EAST	19	10	73	90	98	52	74	33	58	17	25	94
WEST	76	90	87	87	46	43	30	90	86	13	9	26
NORTH EAST	13	36	29	20	15	90	72	61	28	17	12	61
SOUTH EAST	89	25	45	10	86	52	90	87	27	8	90	38

Your Sparkline is now ready!

REGION	JAN	FEB	MAR	APR	MAY	JUN	JUL	AUG	SEP	OCT	NOV	DEC
NORTH	86	61	67	90	41	35	41	91	67	59	9	88
SOUTH	44	25	28	34	25	76	3	40	1	74	37	92
EAST	19	10	73	90	98	52	74	33	58	17	25	94
WEST	76	90	87	87	46	43	30	90	86	13	9	26
NORTH EAST	13	36	29	20	15	90	72	61	28	17	12	61
SOUTH EAST	89	25	45	10	86	52	90	87	27	8	90	38
NORTH WEST	16	24	61	45	70	5	5	48	100	34	35	72
SOUTH WEST	3	8	15	86	32	45	97	59	12	97	98	18
CENTRAL	54	44	33	90	47	64	14	25	98	18	81	30
HIGHLANDS	36	62	40	75	57	46	22	62	76	63	25	8

Sparklines: Column

Sparklines were introduced in Excel 2010 and they show a graphical representation of your data in one cell. A Column Sparkline is best used when you have lots of data points.

You can style them in different colors and add a marker for the **High** and **Low** points of your data. As your data changes so do the Sparklines.

STEP 1: Select the **Numbers Range**

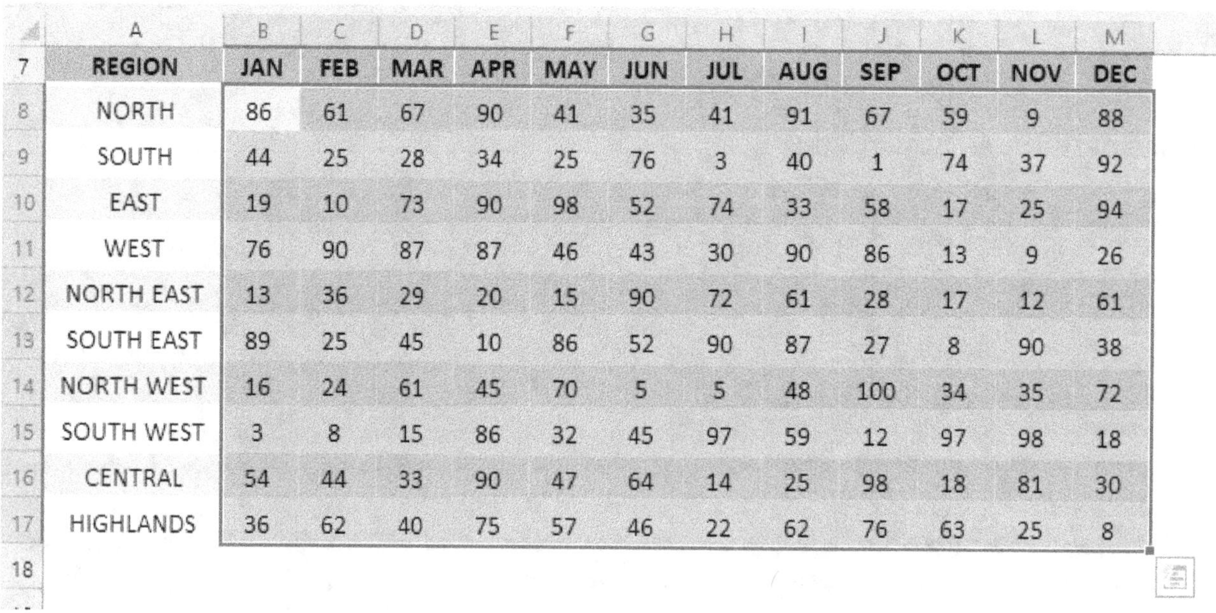

	A	B	C	D	E	F	G	H	I	J	K	L	M
7	REGION	JAN	FEB	MAR	APR	MAY	JUN	JUL	AUG	SEP	OCT	NOV	DEC
8	NORTH	86	61	67	90	41	35	41	91	67	59	9	88
9	SOUTH	44	25	28	34	25	76	3	40	1	74	37	92
10	EAST	19	10	73	90	98	52	74	33	58	17	25	94
11	WEST	76	90	87	87	46	43	30	90	86	13	9	26
12	NORTH EAST	13	36	29	20	15	90	72	61	28	17	12	61
13	SOUTH EAST	89	25	45	10	86	52	90	87	27	8	90	38
14	NORTH WEST	16	24	61	45	70	5	5	48	100	34	35	72
15	SOUTH WEST	3	8	15	86	32	45	97	59	12	97	98	18
16	CENTRAL	54	44	33	90	47	64	14	25	98	18	81	30
17	HIGHLANDS	36	62	40	75	57	46	22	62	76	63	25	8
18													

STEP 2: Go to *Insert > Sparklines > Column*

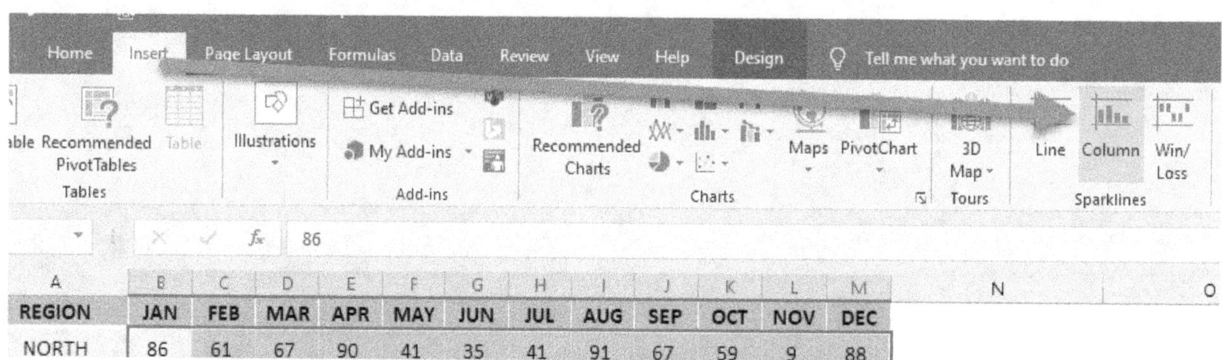

STEP 3: Select the location on where to put your sparklines.

Click **OK**.

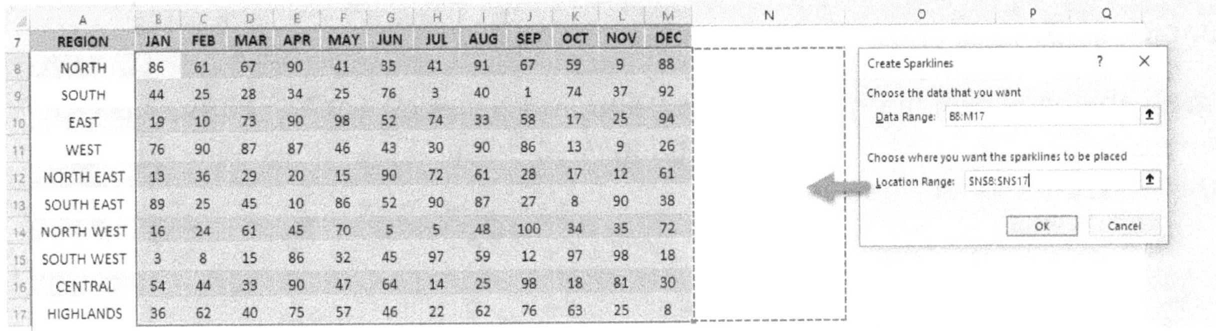

You now have your Sparkline ready!

Sparklines: Lines

Sparklines are a handy way to show a graphical representation of your data in one cell.

You can style them in different colors and add a marker for the **High** and **Low** points of your data. As your data changes so do the Sparklines, which gives them that much more power.

 Select the **Numbers Range**

	A	B	C	D	E
7	**MONTH**	**Q1**	**Q2**	**Q3**	**Q4**
8	January	90,871	94,151	36,305	165,000
9	February	49,859	56,757	75,200	130,000
10	March	70,779	12,600	59,880	23,458
11	April	84,084	10,497	70,886	71,775
12	May	30,464	75,200	34,330	38,129
13	June	78,318	21,615	29,288	67,729
14	July	67,819	86,526	37,856	79,894
15	August	28,506	68,783	18,593	96,922
16	September	71,404	59,187	86,627	40,548
17	October	20,096	46,131	49,298	46,927
18	November	78,951	12,210	91,133	34,003
19	December	71,114	55,421	21,964	56,346
20					

STEP 2: Go to *Insert > Sparklines > Line*

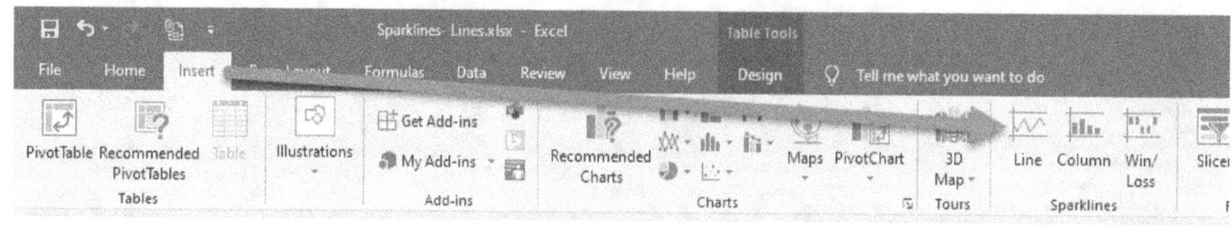

 Select the location on where to put your sparklines.

Click **OK**.

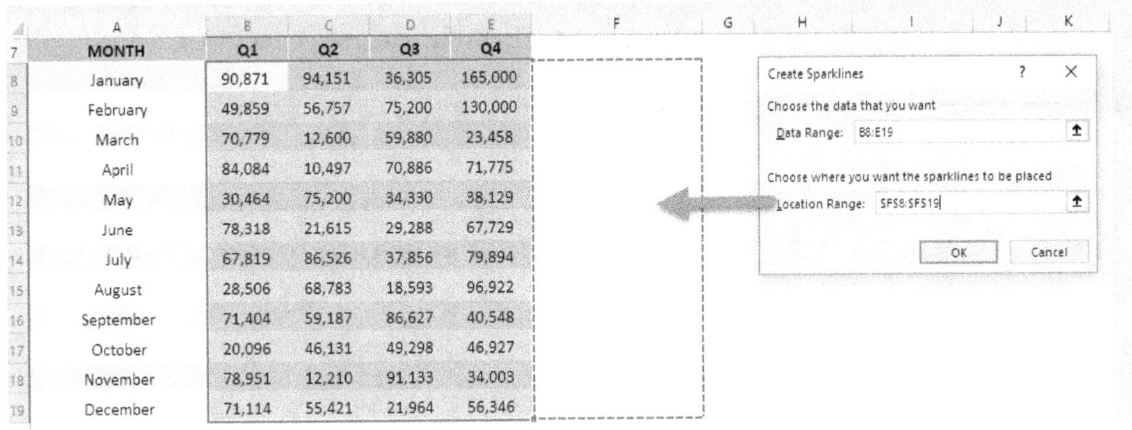

You now have your Sparkline ready!

	A	B	C	D	E	F	G
7	**MONTH**	**Q1**	**Q2**	**Q3**	**Q4**		
8	January	90,871	94,151	36,305	165,000		
9	February	49,859	56,757	75,200	130,000		
10	March	70,779	12,600	59,880	23,458		
11	April	84,084	10,497	70,886	71,775		
12	May	30,464	75,200	34,330	38,129		
13	June	78,318	21,615	29,288	67,729		
14	July	67,819	86,526	37,856	79,894		
15	August	28,506	68,783	18,593	96,922		
16	September	71,404	59,187	86,627	40,548		
17	October	20,096	46,131	49,298	46,927		
18	November	78,951	12,210	91,133	34,003		
19	December	71,114	55,421	21,964	56,346		

Sparklines: Win or Loss

When you have a large data set with positive and negative numbers, a great way to visualize the trend is to add a **Win/Loss Sparkline** next to your data.

That way you or the reader can easily spot the trends and patterns.

To enter a Win/Loss Sparkline in Excel you firstly need to follow these steps:

STEP 1: Select your data

	A	B	C	D	E
7	**MONTH**	**Q1**	**Q2**	**Q3**	**Q4**
8	January	6%	7%	-2%	5%
9	February	5%	6%	-4%	8%
10	March	8%	-10%	3%	2%
11	April	-10%	-3%	-1%	-8%
12	May	5%	-5%	-5%	6%
13	June	7%	4%	-4%	-3%
14	July	9%	-1%	-6%	-9%
15	August	2%	5%	10%	3%
16	September	-2%	9%	-5%	-9%
17	October	9%	-2%	-4%	10%
18	November	0%	10%	0%	-7%
19	December	4%	-2%	-6%	-7%

STEP 2: Go to *Insert > Sparklines > Win/Loss*

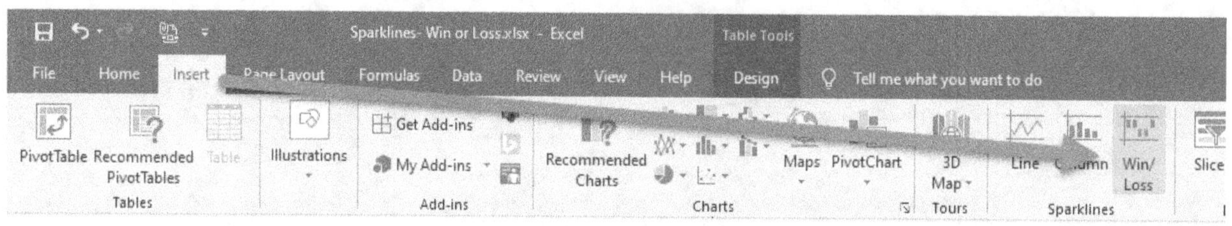

STEP 3: Select the range that you want to insert the Win/Loss Sparklines (this is usually the next column after your data ends) and press **OK**

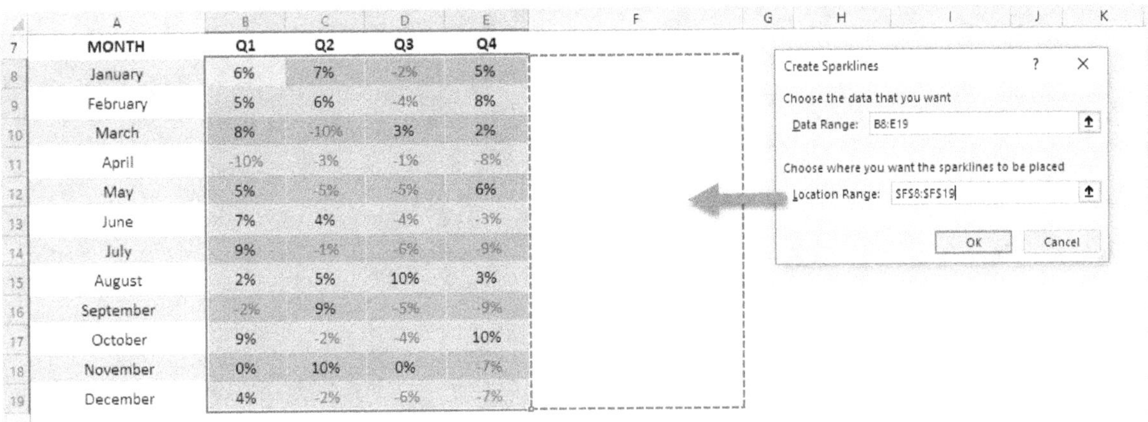

STEP 4: You can change the Style of the Sparkline by clicking in the Sparkline (which activates the **_Sparkline Tools Tab_** in the ribbon) and then choosing the **_Style_** drop down box

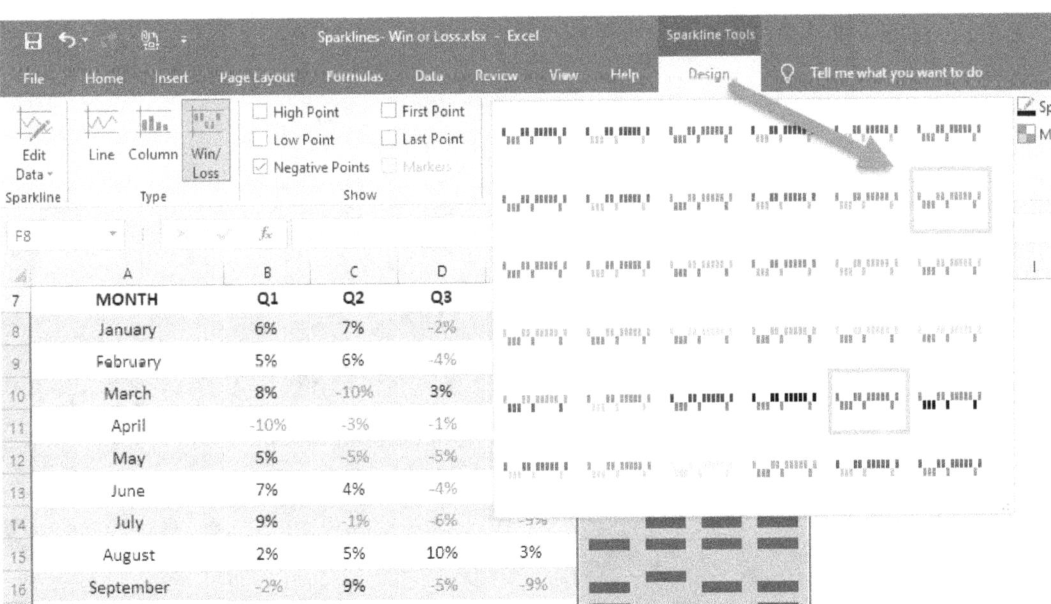

Your Sparkline is now ready!

	A	B	C	D	E	F
7	MONTH	Q1	Q2	Q3	Q4	
8	January	6%	7%	-2%	5%	
9	February	5%	6%	-4%	8%	
10	March	8%	-10%	3%	2%	
11	April	-10%	-3%	-1%	-8%	
12	May	5%	-5%	-5%	6%	
13	June	7%	4%	-4%	-3%	
14	July	9%	-1%	-6%	-9%	
15	August	2%	5%	10%	3%	
16	September	-2%	9%	-5%	-9%	
17	October	9%	-2%	-4%	10%	
18	November	0%	10%	0%	-7%	
19	December	4%	-2%	-6%	-7%	

View Multiple Worksheets in Excel

I usually have a workbook that has a lot of worksheets, and I have to view multiple sheets at the same time. Switching tabs back and forth just to compare the contents drives me nuts!

Did you know that you can **view multiple worksheets** in Excel? Let me show you how!

STEP 1: Go to *View > Window > New Window*

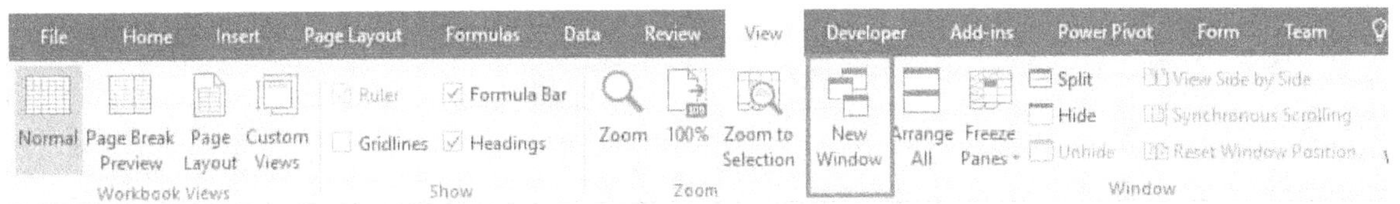

You will notice that there is a new window that is opened. You can notice that there is a number at the end of the filename indicating the window number - **.xlss:2**

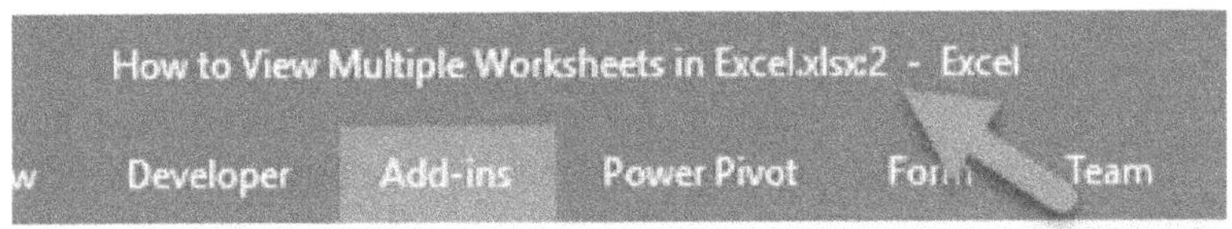

STEP 2: Now let's arrange the windows to view all of them side by side!

Go to *View > Window > Arrange All*

Select **Vertical** and Click **OK**.

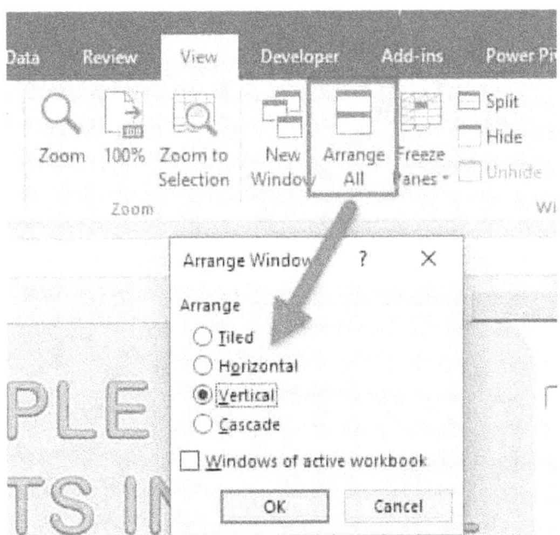

Now you can view multiple worksheets from the same Excel file!

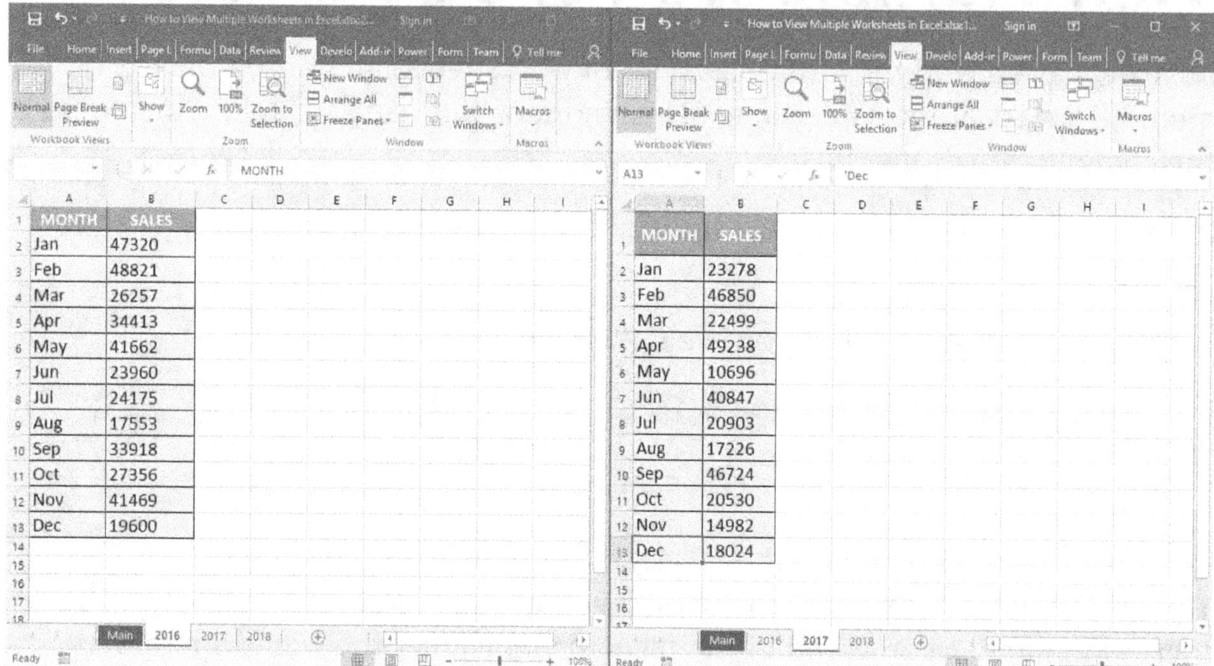

Windings Symbols in Excel

Wingdings is a symbolic font that a lot of us use for fun. I do that a lot too! But what if we wanted those cool symbols to be of good use in Excel?

Whenever I tried typing using the Wingdings font, I was not sure which symbol I would get!

I will show you how easy it is to pick a **cool Wingdings Symbol** and use it in your Excel worksheet!

Here is a sample usage of a Wingdings symbol for stock prices:

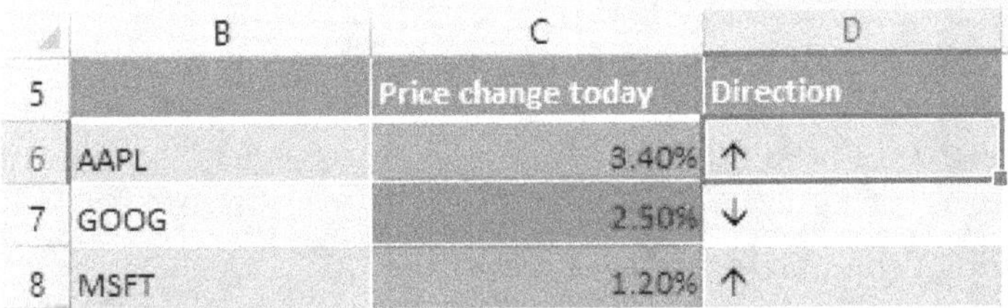

STEP 1: Select the cells that you want to place the symbols in:

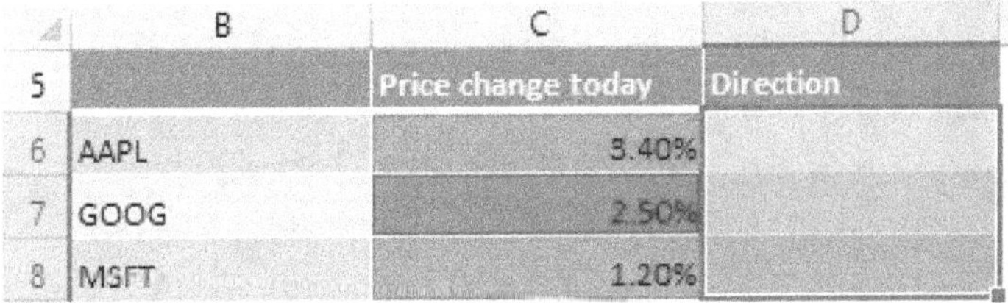

From the **Font dropdown**, select **Wingdings:**

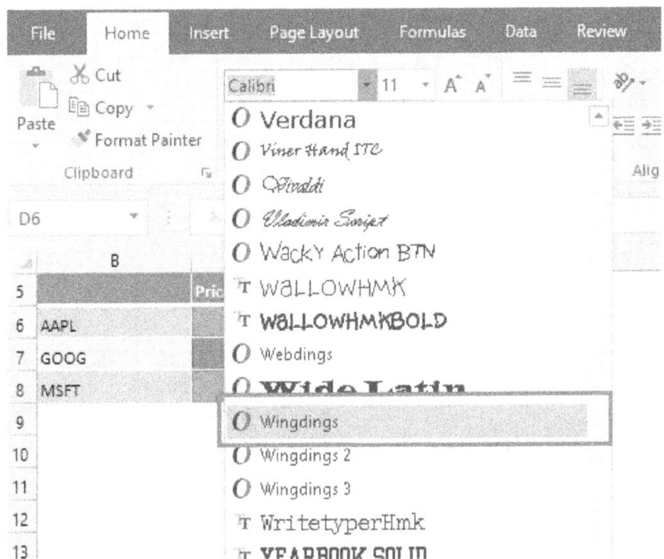

 Now that our cells are able to accept Wingdings symbols, go to
Windows Start (Windows 10) > Search Bar > Character Map

If you have an older version of Windows, go to **Start > All Programs >
Accessories > System Tools > Character Map**

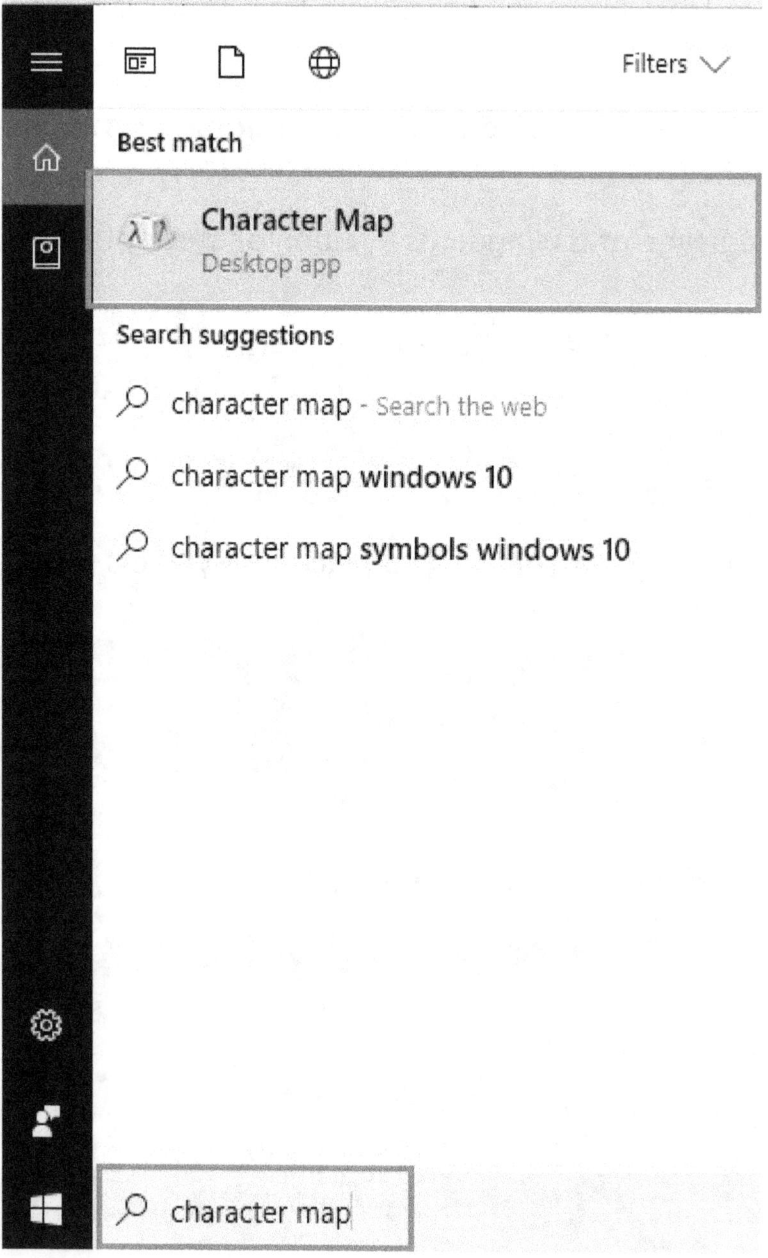

STEP 3: You will now see all the characters! Ensure the **Font is Wingdings.**

Double click on the symbol you want to use. Click **Copy.**

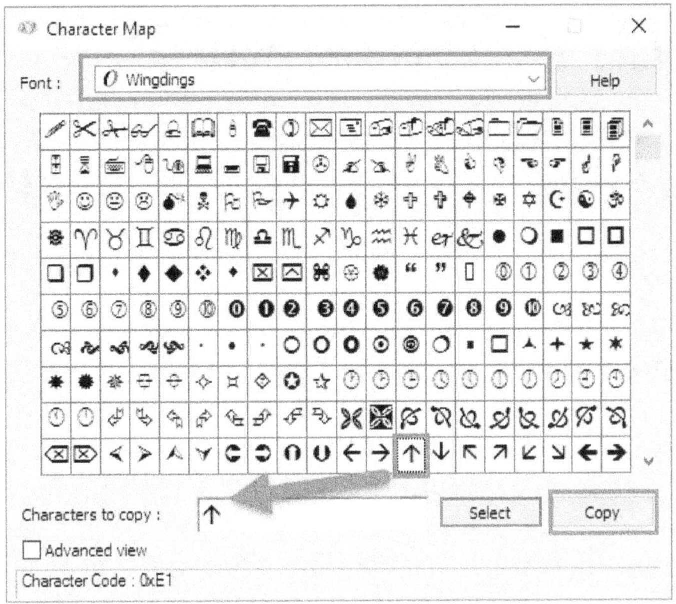

STEP 4: Go to your Excel Spreadsheet and click **Paste**.

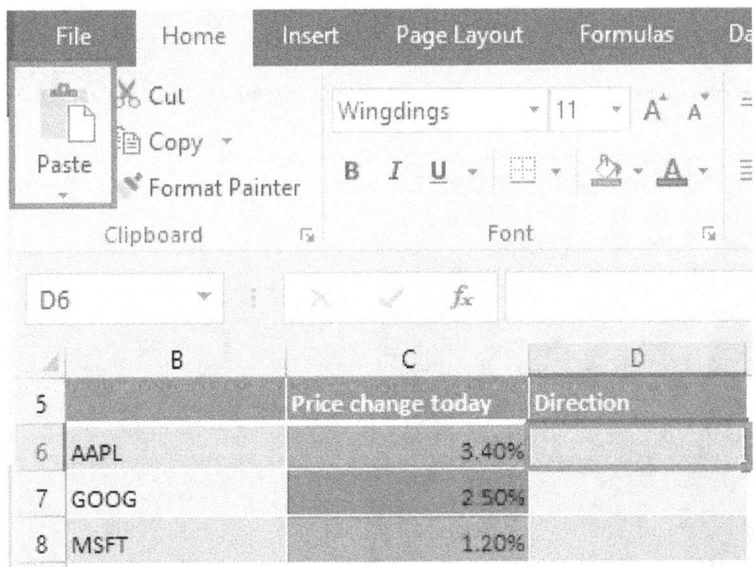

Do the rest for the other cells, and you have used **Wingdings Symbols!**

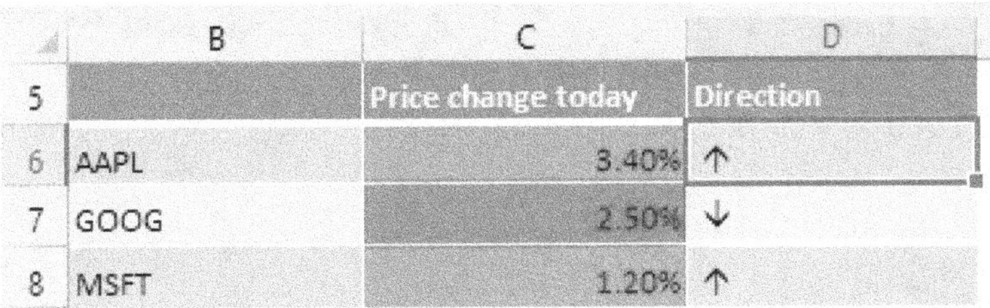

NOTE: Another way is to click in a blank cell and go to **Insert > Symbol > Font: Windings > Insert > Close.**

101 EXCEL BOOK SERIES

Check out our best selling Excel eBooks at discounted prices now! Learn the 101 Most Popular Excel Formulas and 101 Ready To Use Excel Macros!

☞ View All Our Excel eBooks: https://ebooks.myexcelonline.com/

We have also created paperback book versions of our 101 Book Series which you can have delivered to your home via Amazon:

☞ View Our Amazon Paperback: 101 Most Popular Excel Formulas:
https://www.myexcelonline.com/101FormulasPaperback

☞ View Our Amazon Paperback: 101 Ready To Use Excel Macros:
https://www.myexcelonline.com/101MacrosPaperback

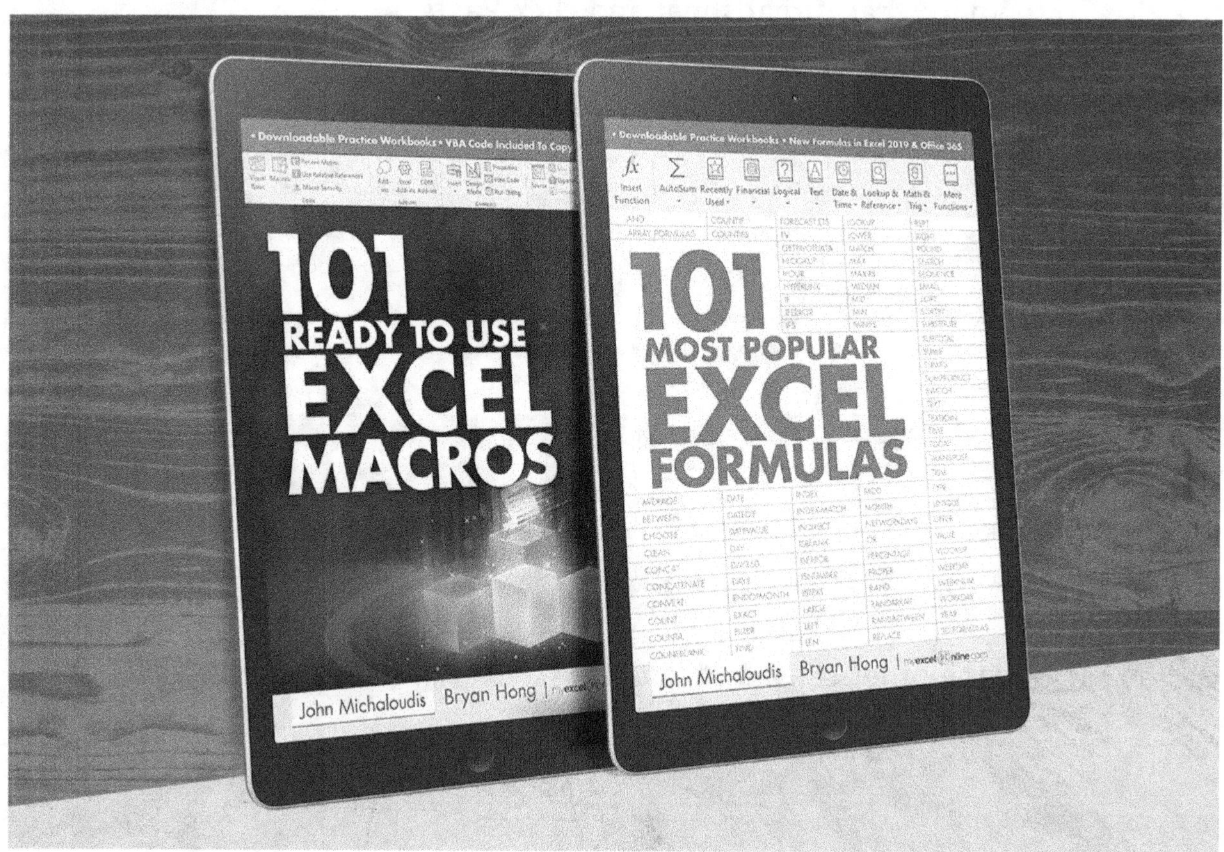

MYEXCELONLINE ACADEMY COURSE

We are offering you access to our online Excel membership course – The MyExcelOnline Academy – **for only $1 for the first 30 days!**

Use this **$1 Trial link** to get access to this special reader offer!

https://www.myexcelonline.com/$1trial

EXCEL EXPERT CONSULTATIONS

Ever have that nagging issue in Excel?

We offer fast, expert consulting help to solve your Excel problems quickly on Formulas, Macros, VBA, Pivot Tables, Charts, Dashboards, Power BI, Power Query, Modifying Templates, Recovering Corrupt Files, Access, Microsoft Office plus More!

☞ Get a Free Consultation Quote

https://www.myexcelonline.com/microsoft-excel-consulting-services

Thank You!

Here is the **download link** that has all the workbooks covered in this book (type this URL to your web browser):

☞ https://www.MyExcelOnline.com/tips-download-paperback

Here is the **link and password** to the Free 20-Hour Microsoft Excel Course (type this URL to your web browser):

☞ https://www.myexcelonline.com/free-excel-course

☞ Password: **101excel**

We would like to thank you again for taking the time to check out our Excel Tips Book! We hope you've found value in it and can use it as a guide to help you gain more Excel knowledge which will make you more productive, give you more confidence and ultimately make you stand out from the crowd!

You can also go directly to other Excel services & products here:

www.MyExcelOnline.com/webinars to get free online Excel training!

www.MyExcelOnline.com/academy/enroll-eg/ to enroll to our Flagship Excel Course and be an Excel Expert in no time!

ebooks.MyExcelOnline.com to get our bestselling Excel Books!

www.MyExcelonline.com/blog to get daily tutorials on Formulas, Pivot Tables, Charts, Analysis, Macros & Power BI!

Feel free to email us regarding anything Excel related, improvements and additions to this book at support@myexcelonline.com

To Your Success!

John Michaloudis & Bryan Hong

MyExcelOnline.com